The Expression of Phasal Polarity in African Languages

Empirical Approaches to Language Typology

Editors
Georg Bossong
Bernard Comrie
Kristine Hildebrandt
Jean-Christophe Verstraete

Volume 63

The Expression of Phasal Polarity in African Languages

Edited by
Raija L. Kramer

DE GRUYTER
MOUTON

ISBN 978-3-11-108790-0
e-ISBN (PDF) 978-3-11-064629-0
e-ISBN (EPUB) 978-3-11-064253-7

Library of Congress Control Number: 2020952339

Bibliographic information published by the Deutsche Nationalbibliothek
The Deutsche Nationalbibliothek lists this publication in the Deutsche Nationalbibliografie;
detailed bibliographic data are available on the Internet at http://dnb.dnb.de.

© 2022 Walter de Gruyter GmbH, Berlin/Boston
This volume is text- and page-identical with the hardback published in 2021.
Typesetting: Integra Software Services Pvt. Ltd.
Printing and binding: CPI books, GmbH, Leck

www.degruyter.com

Acknowledgments

Thanks to Roland Kießling for encouragement, helpful comments, stimulating discussions and pleasant evenings at Roxielloquia.

Thanks to Lennart Fuhse for his formatting and indexing assistance in preparing this publication, for his loyalty and critical remarks, and for repatriating Norbert.

Thanks to Anica Erbstößer for providing technical support during the conference, for establishing and maintaining contacts in the field, and for her friendship.

Thanks to Bernard Comrie for reading carefully through the whole manuscript to offer insightful editorial advice.

Thanks to Birgit Sievert, Kirstin Börgen and Julie Miess from De Gruyter Mouton for their excellent editorial work.

Contents

Acknowledgments —— V

I Introduction

Raija L. Kramer
Introduction: The expression of phasal polarity in African languages —— 3

Johan van der Auwera
Phasal polarity – warnings from earlier research —— 25

II Phasal polarity expressions in African languages

Rasmus Bernander
The phasal polarity marker -(a)kona in Manda and its history —— 41

Zarina Molochieva, Saudah Namyalo and
Alena Witzlack-Makarevich
Phasal Polarity in Ruuli (Bantu, JE.103) —— 73

Nico Nassenstein, Helma Pasch
Phasal polarity in Lingala and Sango —— 93

Bastian Persohn
Phasal polarity in Nyakyusa (Bantu, M31) —— 129

Rozenn Guérois
The expression of phasal polarity in Cuwabo
(Bantu P34, Mozambique) —— 161

Roland Kießling
Phasal polarity in Isu – and beyond —— 199

Solange Mekamgoum
Phasal polarity in Ngômbà —— 215

Raija L. Kramer
Phasal polarity expressions in Fula varieties of northern Cameroon —— 237

Klaudia Dombrowsky-Hahn
Phasal polarity expressions in Bambara (Mande): Pragmatic distinctions and semantics —— 267

Georg Ziegelmeyer
What about phasal polarity expressions in Hausa – Are there any? —— 295

Yvonne Treis
The expression of phasal polarity in Kambaata (Cushitic) —— 311

Axel Fanego
Phasal Polarity in Amazigh varieties —— 335

Bernhard Köhler
Phasal polarity expressions in Ometo languages (Ethiopia) —— 365

Anne-Maria Fehn
Phasal polarity in Khwe and Ts'ixa (Kalahari Khoe) —— 391

Alice Mitchell
Phasal polarity in Barabaiga and Gisamjanga Datooga (Nilotic): Interactions with tense, aspect, and participant expectation —— 419

III Grammaticalization processes and historical developments of phasal polarity expressions in African languages

Ljuba Veselinova, Maud Devos
NOT YET expressions as a lexico-grammatical category in Bantu languages —— 445

Dmitry Idiatov
The historical relation between clause-final negation markers and phasal polarity expressions in Sub-Saharan Africa —— 497

Lijun Li, Peter Siemund
**From phasal polarity expression to aspectual marker:
Grammaticalization of** *already* **in Asian and African varieties
of English** —— 515

Index —— 545

I Introduction

Raija L. Kramer
Introduction: The expression of phasal polarity in African languages

1 Introduction

> Our civilisation is *still* in a middle stage, scarcely beast, in that is *no longer* wholly guided by instinct; scarcely human, in that is *not yet* wholly guided by reason
> (Dreiser [1900] 1981: page)

In this quote, the American novelist Theodore Dreiser provides the picture of our civilization as passing in three phases: a preceding one ("guided by instinct"), an ongoing one ("being in a middle stage"), and a following one ("guided by reason"). His points of reference are two situations: the current state (-guided by instinct, -guided by reason) and the two temporally adjacent states (+guided by instinct, + guided by reason). I.e., he relates the actual state to antecedent and following states with opposite polarity value explicitly expressing that polarity changes of the current state have happened (*no longer*) or (probably) will take place (*still, not yet*). By doubting Dreiser's civilization line and insisting that 'scientific woman is *already* guided by reason', one may add a further perspective on a positive situation ("guided by reason") preceded by a contrary state.

Dreiser's civilization concept can be represented as a time line with three phases, and the perspectives taken can be depicted by arrows pointing from one reference point (the "current state") to the second reference point, a sequential (preceding or following) phase, with different truth value, cf. Figure 1. The experience of alternating and sequentially linked polarity phases of a state-of-affairs seems to be so central to speakers of Standard Average European languages such as English, French, German, or Dutch that in these languages, they are expressed by grammatical means, mostly adverbial operators.

Since the 1970s linguistic studies have started to seriously concentrate on linguistic means to express the notion of temporally sequential positive and negative phases of a state-of-affairs in Standard Average European languages. The research on such expressions has resulted in a bulk of literature and different approaches to their conceptualization. Influential impulses for typological studies of such expression types came especially from Löbner (1989), van der Auwera

---

Raija L. Kramer, University of Hamburg

https://doi.org/10.1515/9783110646290-001

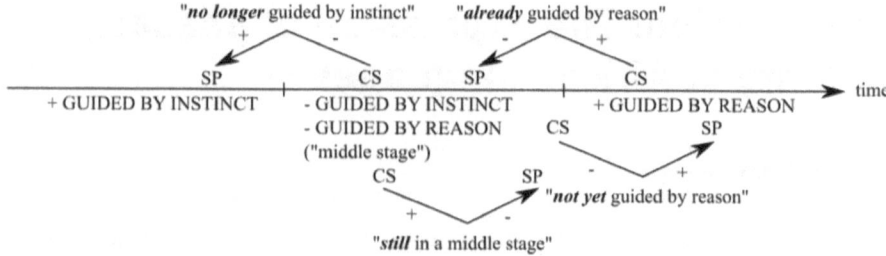

Figure 1: Dreiser's civilization line.

(1993, 1998), and Van Baar (1997). They provide definitions of this domain as well as parameters for describing and comparing expressions of ALREADY, STILL, NOT YET, NO LONGER concepts in individual languages.

Grammatical expressions of the concepts ALREADY, STILL, NOT YET, and NO LONGER are included in a grammatical category that Van Baar terms as phasal polarity and defines as "structured means of expressing polarity in a sequential perspective" (Van Baar 1997: 40). His typological research on phasal polarity expressions was the first that also includes non-European languages. He comparatively analyses phasal polarity expressions in different languages while committing to the consensus found in the literature that the phasal polarity domain consists of the four main categories ALREADY, STILL, NOT YET, NO LONGER. Van Baar does not restrict his research to phasal polarity items of a specific word class, but his restriction criteria are the "specialization" and "generalization" of items in phasal polarity expression, i.e. he considers only grammaticalized elements that properly function as phasal polarity markers ("specialized") and are generally applicable in contexts with different TAM distinctions ("generalized").

A requirement important for typological work in particular, and for linguistic theory in general is cross-linguistic comparability, i.e. one should be able to identify a grammatical phenomenon across different languages. As Croft (2003: 13) states, "[o]ne cannot make generalizations about subjects across languages without some confidence that one has correctly identified the category of subject in each language and compared subjects across languages". Van Baar's inclusion of non-European languages in his cross-linguistic study of phasal polarity expressions was thus an essentially needed first step.

With regard to African languages, it is claimed that phasal polarity expressions are well-attested, at least in the Niger-Congo phylum (Carlson 1994: 345; Comrie 1985: 53). However, available data on African languages suggests that phasal polarity concepts and their encoding strategies differ from what has been found in European languages. I will first address some of the basic conceptual assumptions concerning the Phasal polarity domain that have been identified (for mainly European languages) in the literature. Data from African languages may question some of these assumptions and point to the important contributions of these languages to typological analyses of phasal polarity. Particularly, I concentrate in the following paragraphs on (a) Van Baar's generalization and specialization criteria, (b) the paradigmaticity of phasal polarity systems, and (c) the perspectivity of phasal polarity concepts.

2 The generalization and specialization criteria

One of Van Baar's (1997: 57–61) main criteria to identify a phasal polarity item in an individual language is the possibility of its generalization, i.e. to extend its possible contexts of use (when compared to its original context of use), e.g. its occurrence across different TAM distinctions found in a specific language. Therefore, he decidedly excludes expressions as e.g. *up to present* in English that signal a meaning similar to that marked by *not yet* in negative clauses, cf. (1a)–(1b), but have severe tense restrictions that are not imposed on the latter expressions, cf. (1c)–(1d).

(1) *Up to present* and *not yet* expressions in English (Van Baar 1997: 58)
    a. *Up to the present, there haven't been serious problems.*
    b. *There haven't been serious problems yet.*
    c. *?*Up to the present, he wasn't/isn't/won't be here.*
    d. *He wasn't/isn't/won't be here yet.*

Van Baar does not extend this restriction to all phasal polarity expressions, because, for instance, he includes the Hausa auxiliary *rigaa/rìgaayaa* (which originally meant "to precede") as an ALREADY expression in his sample although he explicitly mentions that it can only be used with the completive aspect (cp. Van Baar 1997: 145). In contrast, the Hausa temporal adverbial *(a) yanzu* "(at) now" that can context-dependently be interpreted as a STILL expression is not classified as a phasal polarity item with respect to the generalization criterion as it can only be used with the present tense (Van Baar 1997: 60).

Van Baar's choice is surely led by the fact that the expression of (retrospective) ALREADY ('have already Ved') can be ascribed as core meaning to the auxiliary *rigaa/rìgaayaa*, while STILL function is just one possible interpretation of the temporal adverbial *(a) yanzu* (similar to "up to present" in the English example above). By considering the non-generalizable auxiliary *rigaa/rìgaayaa* as a phasal polarity item, he already extenuates his own generalization criterion. That repealing this criterion is required becomes obvious in the light of phasal polarity expression strategies in African languages. In many of these languages, items dedicated to the encoding of phasal polarity concepts belong to the verbal system as auxiliaries or as verbal affixes. Their use tends to be less generalizable over TAM distinctions because they are often an integral part of this domain. Although it should be pointed out that cross-linguistically, phasal polarity and TAM domains interact in a very intricate way, this interrelation is even more fundamental with elements that decidedly function as TAM markers. Examples of auxiliaries and verbal flectional morphemes signalling phasal polarity meaning are given in the examples in (2) and (3).

(2) Auxiliaries signalling phasal polarity concepts in Tswana
    a. ALREADY coding in Tswana
        bá-sétsì   *bá-bù:á*
        S.CL2-remain:PRF:CJ   S.CL2-speak:CIRC:PRS
        'They are already speaking.'
    b. STILL coding in Tswana
        kì-ǹtsí   *kí-à-bérê:kà*
        S.1SG-be:PRF:CJ   S.1SG-DJ-work:PRS
        'I am still working.'
        (Creissels 2017: 18–19)

(3) Verbal TAM morphemes signalling phasal polarity concepts in the East Bantu languages Kori and Totela
    a. ALREADY coding in Kori
        ka-áz-'ó-o-síìl-a
        1SG-ALREADY-OBJ-INF-hear-FV
        'I have already heard it (before).'
        (Schadeberg and Mucanheia 2000: 147, cited in Löfgren 2018: 22)
    b. STILL coding in Totela
        ndì-chì-hùpúl-à
        1SG-PERS-think-FV
        'I'm still thinking.'
        (Crane 2011: 325, cited in Löfgren 2018: 20)

Creissels (2000: 239) states that many functions (among others phasal polarity), which in Standard Average European languages are covered by adverbials, are coded by auxiliaries in African languages. In Tswana, for instance, the auxiliaries *sétsì* (> *sálá* 'remain') and *ǹtsé* (> *ǹná* 'be') used in the perfect and followed by the semantically relevant verb in the present tense code ALREADY and STILL meaning with a state-of-affairs in the present, cf. (2a)–(2b). In many other African, especially Bantu languages, phasal polarity concepts are expressed by verbal morphology as it is shown by the examples from Koti and Totela (both East Bantu). In Koti, the verbal prefix *áz-* marks ALREADY in a resultative meaning, i.e. a specific state-of-affairs has come into existence and a past polarity change point is made explicit resulting in a specific state at reference time, cf. (3a). The "persistive" prefix *chi-* in Totela signals STILL meaning in the present, cf. (3b). In these languages, phasal polarity items are thus inextricably linked to their function of expressing TAM distinctions.

However, what should be respected more seriously is Van Baar's specialization criterion, i.e. the question of whether signalling phasal polarity can be indicated as a core function of a particular grammatical element or just as a possible interpretation in a specific context. It is important to differentiate between pragmatically motivated interpretations that can be retrieved from the broader interactional context on the one hand, and the meaning(s) of an item, on the other.

Ameka (2008: 141–142; 2018) makes this point using the example of Ewe, a Kwa language spoken in Ghana and Togo. He shows that in this language, the item *ga* functions as a marker primarily signalling the repetition or the restitution of a state-of-affairs, cf. (4a)–(4b). A STILL interpretation may also be achieved and reinforced by using an intensifier *ko* or its triplicative derivation *ko-koo-ko*, cf. (4c). Ameka (2008: 142) stresses that this reading is not substantial to the *ga* item but derives from its interaction with a factative verb that has present interpretation. However, in constructions marked for the negative (in clauses with different aspectual distinctions, but not with the negative imperative!), *ga* seems to have specialized to express the NO LONGER meaning (Ameka 2008: 142, 153; 2018), cf. (4d)–(4e).

(4) Readings of the repetitive marker *ga* in Ewe
    a. Repetitive reading (+ intensifier *áké* 'again')
        me-ga-vá   *yi*   *áké*
        1SG-REP-come   go   again
        'I have passed again.'
    b. Restitution reading
        ékemá súbɔ́lá-wó ga-kɔ́-nɛ   *yi-a*   *nú.ɖu.xɔ.me*
        then   servant-PL REP-carry-HAB:3SG go-HAB dining.room
        'Then the servants carry him back to the dining room.'

c. STILL ("persistive") reading
   é-ga-le   aha   no-m   ko
   3SG-REP-be.at:PRS   alcohol   drink-PROG only
   'He is still drinking alcohol.'
d. NO LONGER readings
   Mawuli mé-ga-le   sukuu=ɔ   dzí   o
   Mawuli NEG-REP-be.at:PRES   school=DEF   upper.surface   NEG
   'Mawuli is no longer in school.'
e. mé-ga-no-na   aha   o
   3SG:NEG-REP-drink-HAB   alcohol   NEG
   'He no longer drinks alcohol.'
   (Ameka 2008: 142; 2018)

According to these examples, the repetitive element *ga* cannot be analysed as a specialized phasal polarity item – at least not on its own and regardless of the construction in which it appears. Hence, polysemy and various functions of possible phasal polarity items as well as different contexts of their appearance must carefully be considered so that core, peripheral meanings and context-induced interpretations are distinguishable.

3 The paradigmaticity of phasal polarity

The existence of specialized items for phasal polarity meanings is not sufficient for identifying a phasal polarity category in an individual language. Further, an a priori claim of a possible phasal polarity category with a number of up to four subcategories would be an assumption that may indeed be misleading and provoke critiques of the Eurocentric design of the typological approach. Because, if we attempt to trace a (closed) phasal polarity paradigm in an individual language, it hinders us from properly describing the possible polyfunctionality of items expressing phasal polarity concepts and from specifying their more and less central meanings. Grammatical items used in phasal polarity expressions are often part of a wider paradigm and should thus be studied in relation to other elements of the same category, which share the same word class and syntactic status.

In Hausa, for example, Van Baar (1997: 116) states that there are grammaticalized expressions for the four major phasal polarity concepts ALREADY, NO LONGER, STILL, and NOT YET. Ziegelmeyer (this volume) denies this assumption and argues for the ALREADY element *rig-* as the only element dedicated for expressing phasal polarity. However, if we accept Van Baar's notion of the Hausa phasal polarity system for the moment, Hausa would be in line with the "Expressibility Hypotheses" stating that "the majority of languages have all four phasal polarity-types" (Van Baar 1997: 118).

Nonetheless, it would be deceptive to determine phasal polarity as a grammatical *category* in Hausa. The Hausa items that Van Baar lists as occurring in phasal polarity expressions with the respective polarity value are *rigā/rigāyā* (ALREADY), *kuma* (NO LONGER), *har yànzu* (STILL), and *tùkùna* (NOT YET). The ALREADY item *rigā* 'to have already done, to have done before' is a verb, the NO LONGER item *kuma*[1] 'also, and' is a coordinating particle, the STILL item *har yànzu* 'until now' is an adverbial phrase, and the NOT YET item *tùkùna* 'first (of all), before' is a temporal-aspectual adverb. Thus, even if we accepted the occurrence of four specialized phasal polarity items in Hausa, they do not constitute a paradigm but share formal properties with other elements that allow us to group them together and indicate their classification as belonging to different grammatical categories instead.[2]

Let us consider as an example the ALREADY marker *rigā*, which is the only element that is agreed upon to be a specialized phasal polarity item. If we look at the wider paradigm to which this item belongs, for formal as well as functional reasons, we find that it is included in a set of aspectual auxiliaries that

---

1 The item *kuma* is possibly related to the auxiliary *kumà* 'repeat V, do V again' (Newman 2000: 65). Van Baar (1997: 276) also discusses a relation between *kuma* 'also' and the verb *kumà* but states that it is opaque.

2 Also from a semantic point of view, it is questionable whether the assumed Hausa phasal polarity expressions are related by the feature of paradigmatic complementarity, which, according to Van Baar (1997: 61), is the "constant factor" a phasal polarity system is based on. This feature presupposes as governing paradigmatic principle that "a certain type of (positive or negative) expression is asserted, whereas the logical alternative of such an expression is presupposed or expected" (Van Baar 1997: 61). This paradigmatic property leads to the *conceptual* oppositions of ALREADY-NOT YET and STILL-NO LONGER. That *rigā/rigāyā* (ALREADY) is the logical alternative to *tùkùna* (NOT YET) and vice versa, or that *kuma* (NO LONGER) evokes a presupposed/expected *har yànzu* (STILL) scenario could not be confirmed (Zoch p.c.; Umma Aliyu Musa p.c.). As for *rigā* (ALREADY), Jaggar (2009: 66) states that it is the "corresponding assertive, positive-oriented [. . .] notion" to *tùkùna* (NOT YET), though this might be a conclusion drawn from the semantic relation between the adverbials *already* and *not yet* in the metalanguage English.

appear in coordinate structures (cp. Caron 2015:33). In the following table, Table 1, I present some selected elements of this auxiliary class:

Table 1: "Aspectual" auxiliaries in Hausa (Caron 2015: 33; Newman 2000: 64–70).

Aspectual auxiliary	English gloss
ƙāɽā	'repeat, increase V'
ɽiƙā	'continue to V'
dainà	'stop V-ing'
ƙārḕ	'finish V-ing'
fāɽā	'begin to V'
kumà	'V again'
fayḕ	'do too much of V'
ragḕ	'V less than before'
ɽigā	'have already Ved, have Ved before'

These auxiliaries signal the internal temporal structure and highlight phases of the state-of-affairs expressed by the related verb phrase. This may be one reason why *rigā* appears in ALREADY expressions that rather mark "neutral scenarios" of temporally successive phases highlighting the prior occurrence of a state-of-affairs, cf. (5a), while "counterfactual scenarios" are expressed by discourse particles such as *ai* 'indeed, well', cf. (5b).

(5) a. Neutral phasal polarity scenario
　　　nā　　　rigā　　　nā　　　ci　　　àbinci
　　　1SG.CPL　precede　1SG.CPL　eat　　food
　　　'I have already eaten' (no other scenario of following phases is expected);
　　　(Umma Aliyu Musa p.c.)
　b. Counterfactual phasal polarity scenario
　　　Fatima　　　ai　　　　　tanã　　　　Kano
　　　Fatima　　　indeed　　　3SG.CONT　　Kano
　　　'Fatima is already/indeed in Kano' (contrary to the addressee's expectation that she is not there)
　　　(Umma Aliyu Musa p.c.)

Since items used for encoding phasal polarity are normally part of one (or different) larger (but closed, since functional) paradigm(s) in an individual language, it may be worthwhile to discuss them in reference to these paradigms in order to identify meaning components which enable us to identify and explain their central function(s).

4 The perspectivity of phasal polarity

The assumed four main phasal polarity concepts are subcategorized in two to three possible scenarios in Van Baar's study, cf. Figure 2.

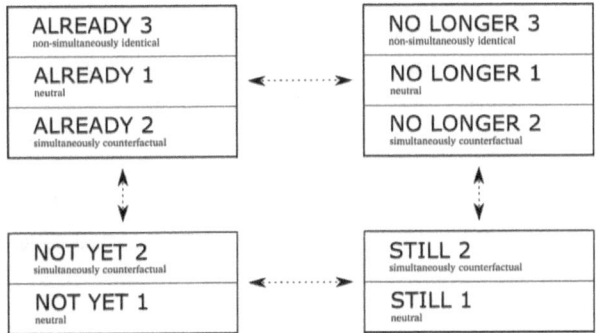

Figure 2: The representation of phasal polarity-systems (Van Baar 1998: 65).

What is schematized here is that phasal polarity items and constructions are not only claimed to encode two sequential phases with opposite polarity values, but that pragmatics may play a major role, too, i.e. possible presuppositions with regard to the existence or non-existence of an alternative polarity switch point. For instance, the possible three scenarios ("neutral", "simultaneously counterfactual", "non-simultaneously identical") of the ALREADY concept, cf. Figures 3–5, differ in the assumption of polarity switch points, but

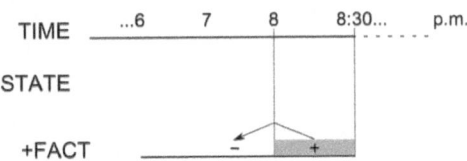

Figure 3: The neutral scenario of ALREADY.

share two central features. The phase at actual time is positive in all cases and the combined sequence of phases with different polarity values in the real (continuous line, +FACT) or presupposed (dotted line, -FACT) scenarios is a negative phase followed by a positive one.

The three ALREADY scenarios in Figures 3–5 illustrated by concrete examples are adapted and slightly modified from Van Baar (1997: 27–29) and van der Auwera (1998: 46–47). The background shared by the presented ALREADY examples should be considered as follows: Fiona is partaking in a talent show and has a solo singing performance from 8:00 to 8:30 p.m. She asks her friend Jane to come before her performance and wish her good luck. Against this background, Jane's utterance *Fiona is already singing* allows for two interpretations depending on the existence of an alternative polarity switch point.

In the "neutral" scenario (Figure 3), Jane just comes too late (between 8:00 and 8:30 p.m.), and her utterance contrasts two phases (the actual positive one and the preceding negative one) that are different in time as well as in polarity value. An alternative polarity switch point is not involved.

In the "simultaneously counterfactual" scenario (Figure 4), Jane comes on time (before 8:00), but finds that Fiona's singing performance has been rescheduled to an earlier point in time. Here, the actual positive phase is contrasted with a phase that is different in polarity value but not in time. There is the presupposition of an alternative polarity switch point relative to which the actual turning point is early.

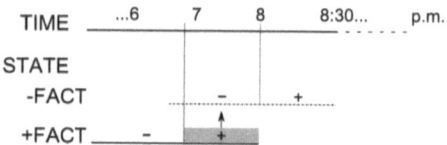

Figure 4: The simultaneously counterfactual scenario of ALREADY.

The third scenario included in the ALREADY concept is "non-simultaneously identical": The current phase is contrasted with a phase that is not different in polarity value but in time: the actual polarity switch point is late with regard to the expected one. In English, the non-simultaneously identical scenario is signalled by the adverbial items *finally, at last*. Jane's utterance *Fiona is finally singing* would refer to this scenario (Figure 5): Fiona's performance has been delayed to a point after 8:30 p.m. and thus, the polarity switch point occurs later than expected.

If we discuss, for instance, constructions in Swahili containing a verb form inflected by the TAM morpheme *-mesha-*, which are commonly translated as 'X has already Ved', we may ask for the status of *-mesha-* as an ALREADY item. The example in (6a) is taken from a Swahili version of the "Story of Sidi-Nouman"

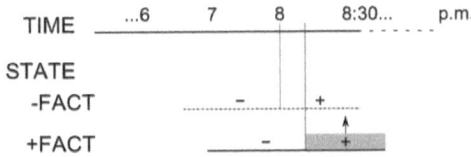

Figure 5: The non-simultaneously identical scenario of ALREADY.

reflecting the husband's explanation for his spouse's lack of appetite during a meal. At reference time, she does not eat and by the utterance *nikafikiri labda ameshakula kifunguakinywa* 'I thought that maybe, she has already eaten breakfast', this phase (-eating) is contrasted with a preceding phase with opposite polarity value (+eating).

In (6b), the *mesha*-construction[3] is shifted to future time by using a future form of the auxiliary *kuwa* 'to be'. Here again, the phase at reference time (here, at a future point in time) is negative (-eating) and relates to a preceding positive phase (+eating).

(6) a. *Mesha* constructions in Swahili
[...] *Ni-ka-fikiri   labda   a-mesha-kula   kifunguakinywa*
[...] 1SG-CONS-think maybe 1-*mesha*-eat   KI:breakfast
na   kwamba   ha-na   njaa
and   COMPL   1.NEG-have N:hunger
'[I was very annoyed about her stubborn behaviour, but I thought that maybe, she is not used yet to eat together with men.] I thought that maybe, she has already eaten breakfast and that she is not hungry, [or maybe, she wants to eat alone].'
(Adam 2006: 198)

b. *u-sipo-kwenda   kwa haraka   wa-ta-kuwa*
2SG-NEG.SITU-go PREP N:hurry   2-FUT-be
wa-me-kwisha   kula kabla   hu-ja-fika
2-PERF-*kwisha*   eat   before *hu-ja-fika*
'If you don't hurry, they will already have eaten before you arrive'
(Polomé 1967: 149)

---

3 The constructions SC-*me-kwisha* V, SC-*me-kwisha ku*-V are commonly interpreted as intermediate steps of a grammaticalization process leading to the expression type SC-*mesha*-V (Marten 1998). Nicolle (1998: 11) states that these intermediate forms fundamentally encode the same grammatical (aspectual) meaning as the *mesha*-construction.

c. *wa-mesha-imba*
2-*mesha*-sing
'(i) They have already sung.'
'(ii) They do not sing anymore.'
(Schadeberg 1990: 11)

In all examples in (6), the phase at reference time is negative, while denoting a preceding positive phase. The actual situation at reference time (-) is referred to from the perspective of the past state (+). This is the reason why Schadeberg (1990:11) notes that the construction in (6c) "neben ihrer Haupt-Lesung (i) auch zum Ausdruck von Lesung (ii) dienen kann [. . . :] (i) 'sie haben schon gesungen' (ii) 'sie singen nicht mehr'" (beside its main interpretation (i), may be used to express (ii) . . . (i) 'they have already sung', (ii) 'they no longer sing', transl. R.K.).

The two translations *schon* 'already' and *nicht mehr* 'no longer', which Schadeberg sees the necessity to provide, may be due to the fact that the semantics of the *mesha*-construction overlap with features of both ALREADY and NO LONGER concepts. The item -*mesha*- is a means to express that sequentially conceptualized polarity but (current) reference time and the perspective taken do not match: the reference time is at the negative phase of the state-of-affairs while the perspective taken is retrospectively from its positive phase. Thus, the -*mesha*- construction shares with NO LONGER the reference time at a negative phase with a preceding positive phase, and with ALREADY the view point (perspective) from a positive phase, cf. Figure 6.

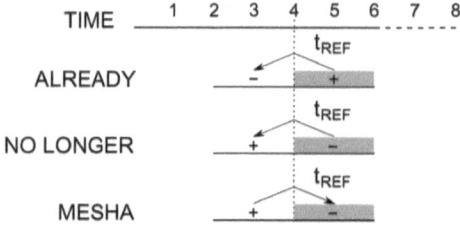

Figure 6: The neutral scenario of ALREADY, NO LONGER, and MESHA.

In languages such as English, French or German, a *mesha* interpretation can be achieved in a construction combining the ALREADY item with a perfect verb form, e.g., in English, *she has already eaten*. Here, the perspective is shifted to a point before reference time where the state is −eating, i.e. the polarity sequence is presented from the viewpoint of the preceding state +eating and its completion (end point). Likewise, in Swahili, an ALREADY interpretation results from the combination of -*mesha*- with a verbal predicate that semantically includes a coming-to-be phase, e.g. *wa-mesha-lala* (2-*mesha*-fall.asleep) 'they already sleep/they are already sleeping' (Schadeberg 1990: 10). In this case, the perspective is shifted to reference time where +sleeping is actual.

What I would like to emphasize here is the importance to include perspectivity in the description of the semantics of a phasal polarity expression and to recognize that the identicalness of reference time and perspective is not necessarily given.[4] Further, aspectuality, grammatical aspect, as well as predicate semantics (i.e. *Aktionsart* properties) play an important role in perspectivizing the sequential polarity phases. The perspectivity parameter extends the four-fold phasal polarity domain and allows for the inclusion of expressions that emphasize different instances (positive/negative state, polarity change point) of the combined phasal sequence.

5 The structure of the book

The book at hand is the outcome of the international conference on "The Expression of Phasal Polarity in sub-Saharan African languages" held in February 2018 at the University of Hamburg. The editor widened the book's perspective to include articles on phasal polarity in languages of the whole African continent as well as authors who did not participate in the Hamburg conference.

The phasal polarity category is mentioned as "well attested at least in Niger-Congo" (Carlson 1994: 345), especially in Bantu languages (Comrie 1985: 53). Nevertheless, the expression of phasal polarity concepts has not received major attention in African languages. In most descriptive works on these languages, phasal polarity expressions are not identified, are inadequately delineated, or are analysed in a rather unsystematic way. Typological approaches to the phasal polarity category are also scarce and mainly based on European languages (van der Auwera 1998), even though Van Baar (1997) also considers non-European languages, among others six African languages, namely Bari, Nama, Ewe, Hausa, Krongo, and Tigrinya. The necessity of this volume thus results from the tremendous research gap on this issue.

---

4 Smessaert (2007: 28) also stresses ACTUAL POLARITY, POLARITY TRANSITION, and PERSPECTIVE as the main parameters for defining the meaning of the Dutch phasal polarity elements *nog niet* (NOT YET), *al* (ALREADY), *nog* (STILL), and *niet meer* (NO LONGER).

To allow for the description of phasal polarity expressions in African languages in a consistent and comparable format, the editor provided a "Position paper on Phasal Polarity expressions" to the authors of the volume (Kramer 2017). This paper was provided as a standardized *grille d'enquête* by taking up former typological descriptive approaches to phasal polarity. By integrating these approaches, it proposes six functional-structural parameters (coverage, pragmaticity, telicity, wordhood, expressibility, paradigmaticity) for describing and analysing phasal polarity expressions.

Alongside the present introduction to this volume, the introductory chapter also contains van der Auwera's concise overview of typological approaches to phasal polarity expressions. In his summary, van der Auwera reminds us to distinguish carefully between the possible "neutral" and "counterexpectational" uses of phasal polarity markers and warns against an oversimplification of languages' phasal polarity systems, which is often displayed in approaches that offer excessively symmetrical accounts. Further, he insists upon the use of subtle methodology and the invention of tools that are required for appropriately describing an intricate matter such as phasal polarity expressions.

The second section of the book comprises descriptions of phasal polarity expressions in individual African languages and language groups from Niger-Congo, Mande, Afro-Asiatic, Khoe-Kwadi (formerly classified as "Central Khoisan"), Nilotic, and Omotic. The authors' focus is on different facets of this subtle subject or they provide general formal and functional delineations of phasal polarity expressions in a certain language (group). The chosen approaches owe much to specific research interests (e.g. language contact, grammaticalization, pragmatics) as well as to the fact that the current papers generally present first approaches to phasal polarity in these languages. In most cases, linguistic data is not or just partly collected with the aim to specifically trigger phasal polarity expressions but is based on larger corpora captured in contexts of natural discourse.

Most, namely five, of the section's papers dedicate themselves to phasal polarity expressions in individual Narrow Bantu languages. This is not surprising because it is a widely recognised fact that in many of these languages, phasal polarity relates to tense and aspect encoded by verbal inflection, tone or the use of multiple verb (i.e. auxiliaries or serial verb) constructions (Nurse 2003: 92). The concepts of STILL, NOT YET, and retrospective ALREADY, are widely expressed by grammatical means and inextricably linked with a certain tense in Narrow Bantu. It is thus not accidental that the first Africanistic paper concentrating on grammatical phasal polarity expressions (cf. Schadeberg 1990) deals with Swahili, the probably most studied and best understood Narrow Bantu language.

Bernander's paper on Manda (Bantu N11) shows that the phasal polarity marker -(a)kona is specialized to express STILL and NOT YET concepts. Although STILL and NOT YET expressions were once related by internal negation, in the modern Manda variety, the negator in the NOT YET expression has been lost and there are just constructional differences left to distinguish the two continuative phasal polarity meanings. Bernander discusses the origin and historical background of -(a)kona in detail and establishes as its plausible source a copulative item borrowed from Old Nguni in a number of N10 Bantu languages. This peculiar development of the STILL/NOT YET marker in Manda may be an explanation for its unusual morpho-syntactic behaviour in this language.

Molochieva, Namyalo and Witzlack-Makarevich discuss the phasal polarity system in Ruuli (Bantu JE10). They show that the verbal prefix *kya-* is involved in STILL, NOT YET, and NO LONGER constructions that express neutral scenarios more frequently than counterfactual meanings. A specialized ALREADY item is not evident in this language. While NO LONGER is encoded as external negation of STILL in Ruuli, NOT YET expressions are not marked by a negative morpheme. Just like in Manda, STILL and NOT YET expressions show constructional differences but are not related by internal negation.

Nassenstein delineates the phasal polarity system of Lingala (C36, reclassified as C30B) with two STILL items *lisúsu* and *nánu* that both are involved in the formation of negative phasal polarity expressions: NOT YET is related to *nánu* (STILL1) by internal negation, NO LONGER is related to *lisúsu* (STILL2) by external negation. The ALREADY concept can be expressed by the French borrowing *déjà* 'already' or, with a retrospective reading, by the auxiliary *–si* whose origin is the finish-verb *kosíla*. Lingala's phasal polarity expressions are discussed in a paper together with another Central African riverine contact language, Sango that belongs to the Ubangian group (Pasch, see below).

Guérois (Cuwabo, Bantu P34) and Persohn (Nyakyusa, Bantu M31) provide in-depth descriptions of phasal polarity expressions. Guérois shows that Cuwabo has no specialized constructions for expressing ALREADY, but that this concept is one context-induced interpretative possibility of perfective constructions or expressed by the Portuguese loan *já* 'already'. In Nyakyusa, a dedicated ALREADY marker is attested only for the non-simultaneously identical ("finally") scenario. In both languages, specialized markers for expressing STILL, NOT YET, and NO LONGER exist. Guérois describes the Cuwabo phasal polarity items as formally different (enclitic, prefix, adverb) and not belonging to the same grammatical paradigm. She shows two strategies for NOT YET expressions that differ in frequency and pragmatic sensitivity: the more often used prefixal *ná-* construction is stated as inherently counterexpectational, the less frequent enclitic *=vi* construction allows for 'neutral' and 'counterfactual' interpretations. For Nyakyusa, Persohn notices the relation of internal negation between STILL and NOT YET expressions in which an auxiliary-like element is involved, whereas NO LONGER constructions with the adverb *kangı* 'again' stand outside this paradigm. He further shows that NOT YET and NO LONGER constructions are suitable context-dependently for expressing both neutral and counterfactual scenarios, and that STILL expressions are more sensitive in terms of pragmaticity because one construction type (STILL + negative present perfective) is clearly preferred in counterfactual scenarios.

Two papers concentrate on phasal polarity in (non-Narrow Bantu) Bantoid Grassfields languages. Kießling gives an overview about strategies for encoding phasal polarity in Isu (West Ring, Grassfields) and shows that just one item can be counted as a specialized phasal polarity marker, i.e. the "hybrid adverbs" *nám(ɔ́)*. The other concepts are expressed by polysemous items, most of which belong to the same category of hybrid adverbs. Looking beyond Isu at related Ring languages, Kießling notices that encoding strategies of phasal polarity concepts vary considerably across the area, though most West-Ring languages have in common that they operate on a system with a single dedicated STILL item, i.e. cognates of Isu *nám(ɔ́)* 'still'. However, phasal polarity items in the considered Ring languages have in common that they involve adverbials for which a verbal origin can be attested. Mekamgoum offers an in-depth description and analysis of encoding strategies of phasal polarity in Ngemba (Ŋgə̂mbà). As an insider of the language community, she delineates very knowledgeably the function of phasal polarity expressions. Like Kießling, she shows that in Ngemba, too, phasal polarity adverbials originate from verbs or still are full-fledged verbs.

Two papers deal with phasal polarity in non-Bantu Niger-Congo languages of the Atlantic and Ubangi branches. Pasch discusses strategies for encoding phasal polarity in Sango (Ubangi) that make use of adverbs for expressing ALREADY (*awe*/*déjà*) and NO LONGER (*mbeni*/*encore* + NEG) and the verb *de* 'continue' for rendering STILL and NOT YET. The encodings of the two latter concepts are formally related in Sango, i.e. NOT YET is expressed as internal negation of *de* 'STILL'. Like in Lingala (cf. Nassenstein) that is discussed in the same paper, Sango's phasal polarity system is influenced by the contact language French from which ALREADY and NO LONGER items *déjà* and *encore* have been borrowed.

Kramer analyses phasal polarity encoding strategies in Fula varieties (Atlantic) of Northern Cameroon and puts an emphasis on differences between them. She states that in the non-standardized, commonly spoken variety (AFC, "Adamawa Ful Communis") paradigmaticity tendencies can be observed that the (more) standardized, mainly written variety (SAF, "Standardized Adamawa Fula") lacks. This tendency, although carefully regarded as just one possible variant of a phasal polarity paradigm variable of the flexible AFC continuum, is interpreted as a factor of grammaticalization whose increase may lead to the reduction of paradigms' sizes.

One paper focuses on a Mande language. Dombrowsky-Hahn shows that the Bambara phasal polarity system is highly sensitive to pragmaticity values distinguishing neutral and counterfactual scenarios by lexical substitution (ALREADY) or co-occurrence of phasal polarity items (STILL, NOT YET). She also reveals different origins of phasal polarity items in Bambara that she subdivides into system-internal, language-internal and system-internal, language-external sources (real language-external sources, i.e. borrowed phasal polarity items are not attested for Bambara). Beside cross-linguistically attested language-internal but system-external origins, e.g. items referring to COMPLETION as sources for ALREADY markers or repetitive morphemes as sources for STILL items, she uncovers a source that seems to be idiosyncratic to Bambara, namely a numeral ONE that has developed into an element signalling an ALREADY expression.

As for the Afro-Asiatic phylum, we find contributions to phasal polarity expressions in languages of the Chadic, Cushitic, and Berber branches. In the Chadic language Hausa, Ziegelmeyer shows that phasal polarity meanings may be achieved via verbal, periphrastic, and adverbial strategies. However, the respective constructions and items involved are not specialized for encoding phasal polarity but allow for phasal interpretations in certain contexts. Ziegelmeyer considers the verb *rig-* 'precede, have already done' as the only possible candidate for a real phasal polarity item in Hausa and notes that in other Chadic languages, 'precede'-verbs have been semantically extended for expressing (retrospective) ALREADY meaning. Ziegelmeyer notes that phasal polarity does not play a crucial role in Hausa and that in a protolanguage, phasal polarity expressions possibly did not exist at all.

As in Hausa, Treis convincingly asserts that the Cushitic language Kambaata entirely lacks dedicated phasal polarity expressions (with the only possible exception of the NOT YET construction). However, there is a range of constructions that may be used to express phasal polarity in Kambaata. These non-specialized means are formally heterogeneous and their phasal interpretation arises from the context only.

Fleisch discusses phasal polarity expressions in the Amazigh varieties of Tashelhiyt and Tarifit (Berber). He provides an overview of their formal encoding strategies which show a great degree of similarity but also significant variation on a micro-level. In Amazigh varieties, ALREADY expressions appear to be neither conceptually nor formally closely related to the other three phasal polarity notions, which show a systematic interplay of their formal exponents. Fleisch notes that the Amazigh phasal polarity expressions should be analysed in terms of a "continuative account" that closely relates to the domains of aspectuality/actionality.

Köhler focuses on a comparative discussion of phasal polarity strategies in Ometo varieties (Omotic, formerly classified as Afro-Asiatic) and states that morphologically complex items are involved in expressions that may be interpreted as signalling STILL, NOT YET and NO LONGER meaning. Constructions rendering the NO LONGER concept are not attested in these varieties.

Fehn provides a first dedicated study on phasal polarity expressions in Khoe languages (formerly classified as "Central Khoisan") focusing on Khwe and Ts'ixa. Although these languages are closely related, they display rather diverse strategies to signal phasal polarity meaning. Despite the variation in phasal polarity expressions, some items exist that allow for a historical discussion and possibly support reconstructions at different proto levels.

Mitchell examines strategies for rendering phasal polarity meanings in varieties of the Southern Nilotic language Datooga. Based on data of natural discourse, she briefly describes possible realizations of phasal polarity concepts in Datooga and concludes that there are no items or constructions for which phasal polarity can be attributed as core meaning. In the main part of the article, she concentrates on the semantics of the verbal prefix údú- that appears with continuative, iterative, immediate past, and avertive-like functions. The prefix údú- intricately interacts with tense and aspect and may context-dependently give rise to STILL and NO LONGER interpretations.

In section three, phasal polarity markers and expressions are described and analysed from a historical perspective. Veselinova & Devos focus on NOT YET expressions in Narrow Bantu languages. They give an overview about formal properties and the distribution of specialized NOT YET markers in 141 languages throughout the Bantu area. Their hypothesis is that these markers are innovations and were absent in Proto-Bantu, and they provide grammaticalization mechanisms (conventionalization and reanalysis) that have led to the development of NOT YET expressions in Bantu.

Idiatov notes that phasal polarity markers tend to occupy the same constructional slot as clause-final negation markers in a very wide range of languages of Sub-Saharan Africa. He discusses semantic and formal links between these elements and shows that in some Mande languages, there are traceable historical relations between negation and phasal polarity markers, namely the grammaticalization of a phasal polarity element into a default negator. He acknowledges that this grammaticalization path is rather rare from a cross-linguistic perspective and concedes that a negation marker evolved from a phasal polarity item usually maintains phasal semantics or is restricted to certain TAM constructions.

The last paper in this volume goes beyond African linguistics and creates a link between phasal polarity expression strategies in African and Asian languages by focusing on English varieties of Asia and Africa. Based on large corpora, Li and Siemund present contact-induced developments of the phasal polarity item *already* into an aspectual marker. They concentrate on the functional change of *already* in Colloquial Singapore English and show that similar processes can be observed in other Asian but also African varieties of English (namely Cameroon English, Nigerian English, Ghanaian Pidgin, Sierra Leone Creole, and Cape Flats English).

The papers of the volume shed new light on a domain whose conceptualization has so far been dominantly shaped by linguistic features of Standard Average European languages. They should be regarded as a starting point for a serious discussion on the appropriateness of imposing (solely) Standard Average European shaped concepts such as ALREADY, NOT YET, STILL and NO LONGER and their linguistic reflexes on non-European languages. They hopefully show the necessity of and give rise to further investigation of other alternative conceptualizations of phasal polarity in non-Standard Average European, here African languages.

Abbreviations

CIRC	circumstantial	NEG	negative
CJ	conjoint	OBJ	object index
CL	noun class	PERS	persistive
CONT	continuative	PL	plural
CPL	completive	PRF	perfect
DEF	definite	PROG	progressive
DJ	disjoint	PRS	present
FV	final vowel	REP	repetitive
HAB	habitual	S	subject index
INF	infinitive	SG	singular

Bibliographic references

Adam, Hassan. 2006. *Masimulizi kamilifu ya alfu lela u lela au siku elfu moja na moja* [The complete tales of 'Alfu lela u lela' or One Thousand and One Nights]. Vol. 3. Dar-Es-Salaam: Mkui na Nyota.

Ameka, Felix K. 2008. Aspect and modality in Ewe: A survey. In Felix K. Ameka & Mary Esther Kropp Dakubu (eds.), *Aspect and modality in Kwa languages*, 135–194. (Studies in Language Companion Series; 100). Amsterdam & Philadelphia: John Benjamins.

Ameka, Felix K. 2018. Phasal polarity in Ewe: Diversity of constructions and dialect differences. Paper presented at the International Conference on The expression of Phasal Polarity in sub-Saharan African languages, University of Hamburg, 3–4 February. Unpublished manuscript.

Bybee, Joan. 1998. "Irrealis" as a Grammatical Category. *Anthropological Linguistics* 40 (2). 257–271.

Carlson, Robert. 1994. *A grammar of Supyire*. (Mouton Grammar Library, 14). Berlin & New York: Mouton de Gruyter.

Caron, Bernard. 2015. Hausa grammatical sketch. Paris: HAL archives-ouvertes.fr. https://halshs.archives-ouvertes.fr/halshs-00647533/document (accessed 16 September 2019).

Comrie, Bernard. 1985. *Tense*. (Cambridge textbooks in linguistics). Cambridge: Cambridge University Press.

Creissels, Denis. 2000. Typology. In Bernd Heine und Derek Nurse (eds.), *African languages: An introduction*, 231–258. Cambridge: Cambridge University Press.

Creissels, Denis. 2017. Grammaticalization in Tswana. http://www.deniscreissels.fr/public/Creissels-gramm.Tswana.pdf (accessed 07 December 2018).

Croft, William. 2003. *Typology and universals*. 2nd ed. (Cambridge textbooks in linguistics). Cambridge: Cambridge University Press.

Dreiser, Theodore. 1981 [1900]. *Sister Carrie*. Philadelphia: University of Philadelphia Press.

Jaggar, Philip J. 2009. Quantification and polarity: Negative adverbial intensifiers ('never ever'. 'not at all', etc.) in Hausa, in Norbert Cyffer, Erwin Ebermann & Georg Ziegelmeyer (eds.): *Negation patterns in West African languages and beyond*, 57–69. Amsterdam & Philadelphia: John Benjamins.

Jakobson, Roman. 1990. Some Questions of Meaning. In Linda Waugh & Monique Monville-Burston (eds.), *On language*, 315–323. Cambridge: Harvard University Press.

Kramer, Raija L. 2017. Position paper on Phasal Polarity expressions. Hamburg: University of Hamburg. https://www.aai.uni-hamburg.de/afrika/php2018/medien/position-paper-on-php.pdf (accessed 04 June 2019).

Löbner, Sebastian. 1989. 'Schon – erst – noch': An integrated analysis, *Linguistics and Philosophy* 12/2: 167–212.

Löfgren, Althea. 2018. Phasal Polarity systems in East Bantu. Stockholm: Stockholms universitet. BA thesis. Available online at https://su.diva-portal.org/smash/get/diva2:1214149/FULLTEXT01.pdf (accessed 06 April 2019).

Marten, Lutz. 1998. Swahili -*kwisha*: Sketching the path of grammaticalization. *SOAS Working Papers in Linguistics and Phonetics* 8. 141–163.

Newman, Paul. 2000. *The Hausa Language: An encyclopedic reference grammar*. (Yale language series). New Haven & London: Yale University Press.

Nicolle, Steve. 1998. A relevance theory perspective on grammaticalization. *Cognitive Linguistics* 9. 1–35.

Nurse, Derek. 2003. Aspect and tense in Bantu languages. In Derek Nurse & Gérard Philippson (eds.), *The Bantu languages*, 90–102. London & New York: Routledge.

Polomé, Edgar. 1967. *Swahili language handbook*. Washington: Center for Applied Linguistics.

Schadeberg, Thilo. 1990. Schon – noch – nicht – mehr: Das Unerwartete als grammatische Kategorie im Kiswahili. *Frankfurter Afrikanistische Blätter* 2. 1–15.

Schadeberg, Thilo C. & Francisco Ussene Mucanheia. 2000. Ekoti: The Maka or Swahili language of Angoche. Cologne: Köppe.

Smessaert, Hans. 2007. The evaluation of aspectual distance, speed and progress. In Louis de Saussure, Jacques Moeschler & Genoveva Puskas (eds.), *Tense, mood and aspect: Theoretical and descriptive issues*, 27–45. Amsterdam & New York: Editions Rodopi.

Van Baar, Theodorus M. 1997. *Phasal polarity*. Dordrecht: Foris Publications.

Van der Auwera, Johan. 1993. 'Already' and 'still': Beyond duality, *Linguistics and philosophy* 16/6: 613–653.

van der Auwera, Johan. 1998. Phasal adverbials in the languages of Europe, in Johan van der Auwera & Dónall P.O. Baoill (eds.): *Adverbial constructions in the languages of Europe*. Berlin/New York: Mouton de Gruyter, pp. 25–145.

Johan van der Auwera
Phasal polarity – warnings from earlier research

For Tim Van Baar (1961–2012)

1 Introduction

"Phasal polarity" is the term devised by Van Baar (1997: 1) for the semantic domain served by the English adverbs *already* and *still* and the adverbial phrases *not yet* and *no longer*.

(1) a. *Paul is in Paris already.*
     b. *Paul was still in Paris.*
     c. *Paul won't be in Paris yet.*
     d. *Paul is no longer in Paris.*

A rough description would say that (1a) and (1d) express the beginning of a phase, a positive one in (1a) and a negative one in (1d), and equally also the end or the completion of a phase, a negative one in (1a) and a positive one in (1d). As for (1b) and (1c) they concern the continuation of a phase, a positive one in (1b) and a negative one in (1c). With paraphrases using the notions of completion and continuation, one can understand that phasal polarity is generally considered to be a dimension of aspect (Hirtle 1977; König 1991: 141; Plungian 1999: 314) or at least to belong "to the periphery of the aspectual domain" (Plungian 1999: 313). Of course, studies of aspect usually focus on verbs and those of phasal polarity have so far mostly focused on particles, adverbs or particle/adverb combinations and phrases, but phasal polarity can be expressed by both (Van Baar 1997: 213–322).

Phasal polarity also relates to tense. Thus Comrie's (1985: 54) NOT YET tense in Luganda does not merely express a NOT YET meaning, it is a NOT YET in the present.

(2) Luganda
    te-tu-nna-genda.
    NEG-1PL-not.yet-go
    'We have not gone yet.'

Johan van der Auwera, University of Antwerp

Such deictic anchoring is not found in English. As the examples in (1a-c) show, the time stretches in which Paul has just arrived in Paris, continues to be in Paris or isn't there yet can be in the present, past or future. This makes *already* etc. different from *up to now* or *henceforth*, even though in sentences like (3a) and (3b) the meanings of the two construals come very close.

(3) a. *I have not been in Paris yet.*
     b. *Up to now I have not been in Paris.*

Both van der Auwera (1993, 1998) and Van Baar (1997: 57–61, 137–142) focused on tense neutral expressions like *not yet* and excluded *up to now not*. By the same token (2) would have to be excluded. With the wisdom of hindsight, however, it is clear that this conclusion is too severe. The Luganda case is not an isolated case and it may well be typical for Bantu languages, in general (see Comrie 1985: 53; Nurse 2008: 194; Löfgren 2018). And in Europe, where phasal polarity tends to be expressed by tense neutral adverbials, there seem to be restrictions, too. Thus, the Irish 'already' word *cheana*, for instance, is claimed to be incompatible with a future tense (Van Baar 1997: 138). The relation between phasal polarity and tense – as well as mood and other aspects of "aspect", for that matter – is thus best considered as a parameter of variation (as in Kramer 2017).

2 Two warnings from European and world-wide typology

The eighties and nineties saw a lot of work on phasal polarity for the languages of Europe, most elaborately for German and English, and there was a consensus that phasal polarity items make up a symmetrical system. Arguably the 'tidiest' systematization was due to Löbner (1989),[1] whose analysis (the "Duality Hypothesis") involved a geometry superficially similar to the Aristotelian Square and called the "Duality Square". The basic idea was widely accepted (e.g. Garrido 1992; König 1991; Vandeweghe 1992; Krifka 2000) and it is still relevant today (see 3 below).

---

[1] The ideas surfaced in Löbner's earlier work. For references see Löbner (1989) and the later Löbner (1990).

It is the Löbner (1989) account that I criticized in (1993) and I will do it again, in a different way, in this paper.

2.1 "Already"

For the Duality Square one only needs two concepts, say ALREADY and NOT, and these can related in three ways. Importantly, ALREADY and NOT are not the English lexemes here. The latter will be represented in italics. But since English serves as the metalanguage, the concepts and the lexemes are related: thus ALREADY is the meaning of *already*. As to the three relations, first ALREADY can be negated, yielding NOT ALREADY: this is the external negation of ALREADY. Second, ALREADY can scope over NOT, yielding ALREADY NOT, yielding the internal negation of ALREADY. Third, ALREADY can be negated internally as well as externally, yielding NOT ALREADY NOT. This was called a "duality" relation. By putting ALREADY in a corner, the combinations with negation in the three other corners and the application of the three negations as arrows, one arrives at the square in Figure 1.

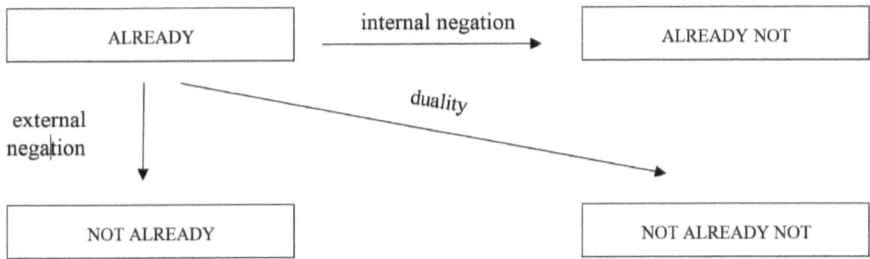

Figure 1: A phasal polarity square.

This constellation can be fleshed out with four additions, all of them already implied in the simple square in Figure 1. First, just like the external negation of ALREADY yields NOT ALREADY, so the external negation of ALREADY NOT yields NOT ALREADY NOT. Second, just like the internal negation of ALREADY gives ALREADY NOT, so the internal negation of NOT ALREADY gives NOT ALREADY NOT. Third, just like the dual of ALREADY is NOT ALREADY NOT, the dual of ALREADY NOT is NOT ALREADY NOT NOT, which, given that adjacent negations cancel each other, is the same as NOT ALREADY. Fourth, duality is a symmetrical relation: when α is the dual of β, then β is the dual of α. With these additions we arrive at Figure 2.

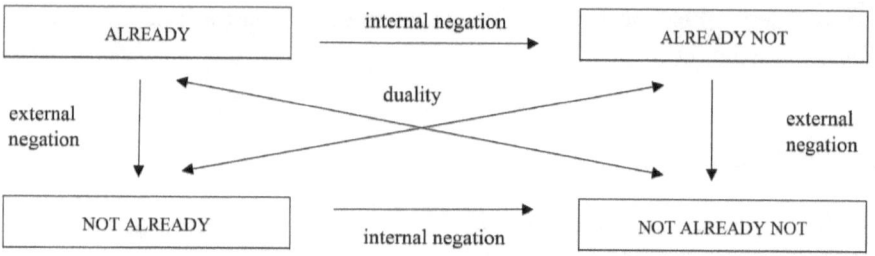

Figure 2: A phasal polarity square.

This representation is not immediately enlightening for a language like English. For ALREADY the insight is minimal: English has a lexeme *already* and the square hypothesis says that *already* means ALREADY, which is a trivial claim. For the ALREADY NOT corner the square says that whatever a language uses there means ALREADY NOT, but English does not normally use *already not*, but instead *no longer*, *no more*, *not any longer* and *not any more*. Mutatis mutandis, the same goes for the NOT ALREADY corner: to express NOT ALREADY, English does not normally use *not already* but *not yet*. It is true that *not already* is not impossible. It is acceptable in an echoic (metalinguistic) context.

(4) You say that he is in Paris already. No, he is not in Paris already. He has not even left Marseille yet.

In questions and conditionals *already not* is fine too.

(5) *If you haven't already, check out our February e-newsletter.*
(https://www.sylviagroup.com/blog/if-you-havent-already-check-out-our-february-e-newsletter/, accessed on 22-8-2018)

(6) *Why hasn't he asked you already?*
(https://www.quibblo.com/quiz/8YzN7pn/Why-hasnt-he-asked-you-already, accessed on 22-8-2018)

But *not already* is not exactly the same as *not yet*, as can be seen when comparing (5) and (6) with (7) and (8).

(7) *If you haven't yet, check out our February e-newsletter.*

(8) *Why hasn't he asked you yet?*

The version with *not already* involve the expectation that the state of affairs already obtains. (9) and (10) paraphrases (5) and (6).

(9) *There is a good chance that you have already checked out our February e-newsletter, but in case you haven't, do it.*

(10) *He should have asked you already, but in case he hasn't, why hasn't he?*

(7) and (8) do not convey this additional meaning.[2]

The important points are that *not already* and *not yet* are not synonymous and that the Duality Hypothesis has nothing to say about this.[3] The latter also does not say anything about the difference between *no longer, no more, not . . . any longer* and *not anymore*. As (11) and (12) illustrate, these four items are subtly different.

(11) a. *He is no longer in Paris.*
 b. *He is not in Paris any longer.*
 c. *?He is no more in Paris.*
 d. *He is not in Paris anymore.*

(12) a. **He will no longer come.*
 b. **He won't come any longer.*
 c. **He will come no more.*[4]
 d. *He won't come anymore.*

A preliminary conclusion is that even just the facts of English show that the validity of the square hypothesis is questionable: (i) it does not explain why English resists expressing ALREADY NOT as *already not* and NOT ALREADY as *not already*, (ii) it does not explain why when *not already* does occur, it does not

---

[2] The difference between *not already* and *not yet* is exactly the same as that between interrogative *already* and *yet*.

(a) *Has she arrived yet?*
(b) *Has he arrived already?*

[3] Note that the very fact that *not already* is possible makes it impossible to maintain that *yet* is "really" *already* too, but just a suppletive form. For if it is "just" a suppletive, why doesn't it supplete for *already* in (4) to (6)? It is interesting to see that Traugott and Waterhouse's (1969), who support the suppletion claim, are forced to claim that whereas *yet* in *not yet* is really *already*, the *already* in *not already* is a different *already*.

[4] The starred examples are grammatical with the sense that he will come on no further occasion.

mean the same as *not yet*, (iii) it does not explain the differences between *no longer, no more, not any longer* and *not anymore*. It remains true, of course, that one can validly investigate to what extent languages employ their ALREADY markers for the expression of NOT YET and NO LONGER or a meaning related to these, though subtly different – this is the parameter of variation that Kramer (2017: 3–6) calls "coverage". In Spanish, for instance, *ya* is 'already' and *ya no*, literally 'already not', is the Spanish rendering of *no longer*.

(13) Spanish
    a. *Ya está aquí*
       already is   here
       'He is here already.'
    b. *Ya no está aquí*
       already is not here
       'He is no longer here.'

In Classical Nahuatl *ye* is 'already', and 'not yet' is the univerbation *aya* of *ye* and the negator *a*.

(14) Classical Nahuatl
    a. *ye   iztaya.*
       already it.is.becoming.white
       'It is becoming white.'
       (Andrews 2003: 174)
    b. *Aya   temo.*
       not.already it.descends
       'It does not yet descend.'
       (Andrews 2003: 76)

So the duality hypothesis offers at least a partial explanation why the Spanish and Classical Nahuatl systems are possible. But note that it remains mysterious why there are many languages like Spanish and why the Classical Nahuatl system is "very rare" (Van Baar 1997: 22).[5]

---

[5] It is indeed always Classical Nahuatl that is referred to ((König 1991: 144; van der Auwera 1993: 631; Van Baar 1997: 22; Kramer 2017: 5). Van der Auwera (1993: 631) hesitantly mentions Fon – without data. The only other language known for which a combination of ALREADY and NOT is said to yield NOT YET is Latin (Schadeberg 1990: 13). However, in Latin *iam* 'already' and *non* 'not' usually yield 'no longer'. The one example in Schadeberg (1990: 13) is a conditional. It may well be that the 'not yet' meaning of *non iam* is of the same nature as that of *not already* illustrated in (5).

2.2 "Still"

As far as we know, no language ever puts the equivalent *not already not* in the NOT ALREADY NOT corner. Instead, they use another primitive. In English this is *still* and the claim is that its meaning, i.e., STILL, is the same as NOT ALREADY NOT. Figure 3 adds STILL, not just in the corner where it occurs as a primitive, but also in the other corners.

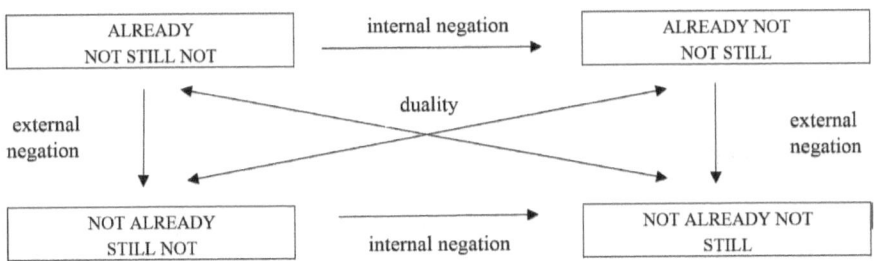

Figure 3: A phasal polarity square.

Enriched this way, some of the worries expressed about the usefulness of the duality hypothesis for English might be alleviated. There is actually no need to expect a language to always express ALREADY NOT as *already not*. It may just as well express it as *not still*. But this is not what happens in English. The corner which is now understood to house not only ALREADY NOT but also NOT STILL is not normally expressed with *not still*. Once again *not still* has echoic uses and fares better in questions and conditionals.

(15) You say that he is still in Paris. No, he is not still in Paris. He left for Marseille 5 days ago.

(16) Why don't' you go have a nice day with Dad? That is, if he isn't still hiding from you.
(https://www.google.be/search?hl=en&tbm=bks&ei=mE-KW7SrA8adkg X404yQDg&q=%22if+he+isn%27t+still%22&oq=%22if+he+isn%27t+still% 22&gs_l=psy-ab.12. . .17187.17549.0.20569.3.3.0.0.0.0.56.151.3.3.0. . ..0. . .1c.1. 64.psy-ab..0.0.0. . ..0.PLmxm3sDPmY, accessed on 1-9-2018)

(17) If we had made love, why isn't he still in bed with me?
(https://books.google.be/books?id=8eBRAAAAQBAJ&pg=PA194&lpg= PA194&dq=%22why+isn%27t+he+still%22&source=bl&ots=EOPZk_

r9gz&sig=C-Ka4_2BMBX_-_uBIacB5_ADrI&hl=en&sa=X&ved=2ahUKEwiLjdD8sZndAhURPFAKHYwUCvEQ6AEwBXoECAUQAQ#v=onepage&q=%22why%20isn't%20he%20still%22&f=false, accessed on 1-9-2018)

The fact of the matter is that a declarative non-echoic sentence does not use *not still*.

The situation is a little different for the NOT ALREADY – STILL NOT corner. Different from *not still* the phrase *still not* is perfectly fine in non-echoic declaratives.

(18) *John is still not in London.*

But *still not* is more emphatic than *not yet*. There is an expectation that John is in London at the time referred in (18). In van der Auwera (1993, 1998) I accounted for the difference with a "Double Alternative Hypothesis". Imagine that John is on the train to London. The speaker thinks that the train is to arrive at 6 PM, it is now 5 PM, there is no expectation that John should be in London at 5 PM. There is an expectation that he will arrive at 6 PM and the use of *not yet* contrasts the negative *not yet* at 5 PM with the later positive stage at 6 PM. This the scenario represented in Figure 4: the horizontal arrow is the timeline and it is divided in a negative and positive phrase. The doubly pointed arrow represents the contrast invoked by *not yet*.

Figure 4: One reading of *not yet*.

But here is a different scenario. The speaker again thinks that the train is to arrive at 6PM, but it is 6.15 PM now and John is still on the train. This is unexpected and the current state of affairs of John being on the train is not contrasted with a later one in which he arrived, but a simultaneous though counterfactual one in which he should have arrived. With respect to this expected arrival the real arrival will be late. This counterexpectational scenario is represented in Figure 5. The dashed line is the expected counterfactual timeline. The negative state of affairs is compared with a simultaneous though unreal positive one.

An important point is that *not yet* also allows the counterexpectational reading, but it does not force it. *not yet* simply allows both readings, and

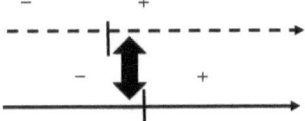

Figure 5: Still not.

the choice is context-dependent. In (19) the context of the *when* clause rules out *still not*.

(19) a. When a child is born, she has not yet experienced anything.
b. ??When a child is born, she still has not experienced anything.

Interestingly, (19) is still called "expectational" by Veselinova (201b),[6] following Plungian (1999: 318). The latter considers the category of "phasal polarity" to be the same as that of "counterexpectation". This is not correct: there really is not any expectation that the child has already experienced something before birth. Plungian's position is itself inspired by the approach of Heine et al (1991: 193), who call *not yet* – as well as *already, still* and *no longer* – "counterexpectation markers". They only look at *not yet* – not at *still not*, nor at similar variations for the other phasal items (see below). And they also do not get alarmed by examples such as (20) (Heine et al 1991: 193).

(20) *As usual, he was not yet up at noon.*

In their view, the counterexpectation only relates to *he was not yet up at noon*. Just how *as usual* undoes the counterexpectation is not made clear and I propose that it is better to claim that the counterexpectational reading of *not yet*, different from that of *still not*, is possible but not necessary.

Counterexpectational phasal markers, I argued in van der Auwera (1993, 1998), can appear in each corner. (21) shows a counterexpectational "already".

(21) *Some infections are already no longer treatable with current drugs.*

---

[6] The example is due to Östen Dahl (personal communication to Ljuba Veselinova) and it is supposed to show that *not yet* need not involve a contrast with two points of time. I propose that was in fact an earlier point of time or, better, a stretch of time, viz., the time stretch of the unborn child, which contrasts with the time stretch of the "born child". Note this is an analysis of a sentence, not a position in the debate about the extent to which unborn children experience anything.

(http://theconversation.com/yes-we-must-prescribe-fewer-antibiotics-but-were-ignoring-the-consequences-89266, accessed on 22-08-2018)

In van der Auwera (1998: 83) I estimated that *already no longer* is not idiomatic, different from what we find in e.g. German. Only a comparative corpus study will show to what extent the idiomaticity and frequency of such constructions differ crosslinguistically.

(22) *Wöber bei Ajax schon nicht mehr zu ersetzen*
Wöber at Ajax already no longer to replace
'It is already the case that Wöber can no longer be replaced in the Ajax.'
(https://peterlinden.live/woeber-bei-ajax-schon-nicht-mehr-zu-ersetzen-kommt-huetter-ins-strauchen/)

The interesting thing here is that this strategy has the negator flanked by two phasal particles.[7] English does not have a counterexpectational STILL marker, but it is not hard to find one in the other languages of Europe, e.g. in Dutch or French.

(23) a. *Hij is nog ziek*
he is still sick
'He is still stick.'
b. *Hij is nog altijd ziek*
he is still always sick
'He is still sick.' (counter to one's expectation)

(24) a. *Il est encore malade*
he is still sick
'He is still sick.'
b. *Il est toujours malade*
he is always sick
'He is still sick.' (counter to one's expectation)[8]

---

[7] Kramer (2017) mentions the *schon nicht mehr* phenomenon as a pragmatic phenomenon not (directly) related to the Double Alternative hypothesis, different from the proposals in van der Auwera (1993, 1998) and van Baar (1997). It is, of course, true that the strategy yielding counterexpectation in the ALREADY corner is different from that in the STILL corner. But even in just the STILL corner there are different strategies (see (23) and (24) below).
[8] The sentence is vague: it can also mean that the subject is always sick.

In fact, for the world at large, Van Baar (1997: 77) claims that "hardly any language [. . .] makes no formal distinction" between the neutral and the counterexpectational STILL use. For ALREADY languages seem to be less disposed to have two such markers.⁹ Van Baar has a 25 language sample, and he only reports a special counterexpectational ALREADY marker, in addition to a neutral marker, for 4 languages, viz. Burmese, Irish, Korean and Classical Nahuatl. Note that this does not mean that one should not attribute the two readings to *already*. This is shown by the "famous" dialogue brought into the literature by Mittwoch (1993: 73–75).

(25) A: *I've applied for American citizenship.*
      B: *Is your husband also applying?*
      A: *He is already American, for he was born the America.*

The relevant reading here is the counterexpectational one: the husband's being American contrasts with the counterfactual scenario in which he is not American yet and still has to be apply for citizenship.¹⁰

Two more comments on the subject of ALREADY. First, in Van Baar's sample languages it would seem that most languages have a neutral ALREADY. It is by no means excluded that there are languages whose only ALREADY marker would be the counterexpectational one (Kramer 2017: 9). Second, if we are going to take expectations seriously, one will have to study more readings and markers than commonly studied in phasal polarity work. It is true that *already* in (26) can be taken to mean that Mary has arrived earlier than expected, but the opposite, an arrival that is later than expected, can be expressed too.

(26) a. *Mary has already arrived.*
      b. *Mary has finally arrived.*

Except for van der Auwera (1993, 1998) and Van Baar (1997) markers such as *finally* have not been included in phasal polarity studies.

The lesson of this section is the same as that of the preceding. The duality hypothesis is too simple. It does not tell us (i) why *still* is not regularly used for

---

9 Languages may well have more than one marker but with a different division of labor. Thus German has two 'already' words, *schon* and *bereits*, both of which are vague between the neutral and the counterexpectational readings.
10 This use is also similar to the one sketched in (19): in the real world the stretch of time in which the husband was not American is one in which he was not born yet.

"not still", (ii) how to account for the counterexpectational uses, and (iii) that there is more to expectation than what can be expressed by markers like *already, still, not yet* and *no longer*.

3 These warnings are relevant for Sub-Saharan Africa

The general warnings about symmetry and counterexpectation, espoused by Van Baar (1997) and myself, are heeded by Van Baar's analyses of Bari, Ewe, Hausa, Nam and Tigrinya. In this section I briefly discuss Plungian (1999); Heine, Claudi and Hünnemeyer (1991), then Schadeberg (1990), Nurse (2008), and Löfgren (2018).

Plungian and Heine are both Africanists-turned-typologists and for phasal polarity their ideas are at least partially formed on the basis of Bantu languages. I have already issued a warning about their notion of counterexpectation. A second warning concerns their embracing symmetry. This is most clearly visible when Plungian (1999: 315) characterizes the four phasal notions as shown in (27).

(27) t_i t_o
     a. already   –   +   'begin'
     b. no longer   +   –   'stop', 'not continue', 'begin not'
     c. still   +   +   'continue', 'not stop', 'not begin not'
     d. not yet   –   –   'not begin'

This set-up is basically equivalent to Löbner (1989).

Heine, Claudi and Hünnemeyer (1991: 193) also offer a symmetry account, but one that brings in counterexpectation as well.

(28) a. already   =   beginning earlier than expected
      b. no longer   =   end earlier than expected
      c. still   =   end later than expected
      d. not yet   =   beginning later than expected

This account is in complete correspondence harmony with Schadeberg (1990), who Heine at al refer to and support. Schadeberg's analysis, prompted by three Bantu languages, German, Greek and Latin – in the format of Heine et al (1991) is shown in (29).

(29) a. already   = unexpectedly early beginning and duration of a situation
     b. no longer   = unexpectedly early end of a situation
     c. still   = unexpectedly delayed end of a situation
     d. not yet   = unexpectedly delayed beginning and duration of a situation

The Heine and Schadeberg accounts are suspicious because they embrace both symmetry and counterexpectation. This is not to say that there couldn't be any languages, to wit African languages, that do have the simple systems sketched in (27)–(29). However, the worldwide observations should put us on our guard. Van Baar (1997: 77), it will be remembered, found that most languages do distinguish between neutral and counterexpectational "still". This includes four of the African languages he studied, i.e., Bari, Ewe, Hausa, Nama – only Tigrinya does not. This contrasts with the findings in Löfgren (2018). She studied 46 East Bantu languages and she didn't find a single language with dedicated markers for the two *still* meanings. The reason for the difference is likely to be the methodology. Though Löfgren (2018) is an excellent exploratory study, it is based on existing grammatical descriptions and there phasal polarity is typically not given a solid account. Van Baar (1997) combines grammatical descriptions and a questionnaire specifically made for phasal polarity. This brings us to what is perhaps the most important warning of all, subsuming the ones geared to being careful about symmetry and expectations. Despite appearances phasal polarity is a semantically subtle subject matter, demanding subtle tools.

Bibliographic references

Andrews, J. Richard. 2003. *Introduction to Classical Nahuatl*. Norman: University of Oklahoma Press.
Comrie, Bernard. 1985. *Tense*. Cambridge: Cambridge University Press.
Garrido, Joaquin. 1992. Expectations in Spanish and German adverbs of change. *Folia Linguistica* (26). 357–402.
Heine, Bernd, Ulrike Claudi & Friederike Hünnemeyer. 1991. *Grammaticalization: a conceptual framework*. Chicago: University of Chicago Press.
Hirtle, W. H. 1977. Already, still and yet. *Archivum Linguisticum* VII N.S. 28–45.
König, Ekkehard. 1991. *The meaning of focus particles. A comparative perspective*. London: Croom Helm.
Kramer, Raija L. 2017. Position paper on Phasal Polarity expressions. Hamburg: University of Hamburg. https://www.aai.uni-hamburg.de/afrika/php2018/medien/position-paper-on-php.pdf (accessed 06 April 2019).

Krifka, Manfred. 2000. Semantics of *still* and *already*. In Andrew K. Simpson (ed.), *Proceedings of the Twenty-Sixth Annual Meeting of the Berkeley Linguistics Society: General session and parasession on Aspect*, 401–412. Berkeley: Berkeley Linguistics Society.

Löbner, Sebastian. 1989. German *schon-erst-noch*: an integrated analysis. *Linguistics and Philosophy* (12). 167–212.

Löbner, Sebastian. 1990. *Wahr neben Falsch. Duale Operatoren als die Quantoren natürlicher Sprache*. Tübingen: Niemeyer.

Löfgren, Althea. 2018. *Phasal polarity systems in East Bantu*. Stockholm: University of Stockholm bachelor thesis.

Mittwoch, Anna. 1993. The relationship between *schon/already* and *noch/still*. *Natural Language Semantics* (2). 71–82.

Nurse, Derek. 2008. *Tense and Aspect in Bantu*. Oxford: Oxford University Press.

Plungian, Vladimir A. 1999. A typology of phasal meanings. In Werner Abraham & Leonid Kulikov (eds.), *Tense-aspect, transitivity and causativity. Essays in honour of Vladimir Nedjalkov*, 311–321. Amsterdam: Benjamins.

Schadeberg, Thilo C. 1990. SCHON – NOCH – NICHT – MEHR: Das Unverwartete als grammatische Kategorie im KiSwahili. *Frankfurter Afrikanistische Blätter* (2). 1–15

Traugott, Elizabeth C. & John Waterhouse. 1969. 'Already' and 'yet': a suppletive set of aspect-markers? *Journal of linguistics* (5). 287–304.

Van Baar, Tim. 1997. *Phasal polarity*. Amsterdam: University of Amsterdam doctoral dissertation.

van der Auwera, Johan. 1993. 'already' and 'still': beyond duality. *Linguistics and philosophy* (16). 613–653.

van der Auwera, Johan. 1998. Phasal adverbials in the languages of Europe, In Johan van der Auwera with Dónall P. Ó Baoill (ed.), *Adverbial constructions in the languages of Europe*, 25–145. Berlin: Mouton de Gruyter.

Vandeweghe, Willy. 1992. *Perspectivische evaluatie in het Nederlands. De partikels van de al/nog/pas-groep*. [Perspectival evaluation in Dutch. The particles of the *al/nog/pas* group]. Gent: Koninklijke Akademie voor Nederlanse Taal-en Letterkunde.

Veselinova, Ljuba. 2016. Expectations shaping grammar: searching for the link between tense-aspect and negation. Manuscript.

II Phasal polarity expressions in African languages

Rasmus Bernander
The phasal polarity marker -(a)kona in Manda and its history

1 Introduction

Manda (iso 639–3: mgs) is a Bantu language – coded as N11 in Guthrie's (1948) referential classification – spoken by approximately 30 000 speakers along the eastern shores of Lake Nyasa (Lake Malawi) in southern Tanzania.[1] In Manda, the marker -(a)kona, inflected for subject indexation, is employed to express the phasal polarity concepts of STILL and NOT YET. This study sets out to describe the formal and functional properties of this marker in Manda. In addition, it will offer an account of its contact-induced origin and current development. It is shown that despite its auxiliary verb-like appearance, -(a)kona does not share the properties of an auxiliary nor does it originate from a lexical verb. Instead, this study argues that it stems from a "copulative", i.e. an element of non-verbal origin which acquired copula-like features through the addition of a subject marker and eventually became specialized as a phasal polarity marker. What is more, this study shows that the phasal polarity marker -(a)kona in Manda is the result of a recent innovation triggered by language contact with a

---

[1] The vast bulk of the data presented in this article has been collected during field work conducted in the Manda speaking area on various occasions throughout the years 2014–2017 for the purposes of my doctoral dissertation (Bernander 2017). The reader is referred to this work for more general information about the Manda language and the Manda speaking community. Some of the results presented in this paper have also been presented there, although many aspects of the analysis have been reinterpreted and strengthened in light of the study by Kramer (2017), as well as by the work of Van Baar (1997) and van der Auwera (1993, 1998). I would like to direct special thanks to my Manda speaking consultants (plus my additional Mpoto and Matengo informants) as well as to Raija Kramer and an anonymous reviewer for their helpful remarks on a previous draft. Thanks are also due to the audience for their comments on presentations about -(a)kona given at SOAS (in October 2016), at the 14th International Conference of Africanists, in Moscow, Russia (in October 2017) and at the 9th World Congress of African Linguistics in Rabat, Morocco (in August 2018). This work has partially been supported by Kone Foundation, here gratefully acknowledged. The usual disclaimer applies.

Rasmus Bernander, University of Helsinki

https://doi.org/10.1515/9783110646290-003

South African Nguni variety, spoken by the invaders and rulers of parts of southern Tanzania in the late 19th century.

This study is organized in the following manner. After this introduction follows section 2, where a general overview of the complete phasal polarity paradigm in Manda is offered, including a brief presentation of the strategies employed in expressing the related concepts of ALREADY and NO LONGER. The remainder of the paper is devoted to the marker -*(a)kona* and its use in the continuative phasal polarity expressions of STILL and NOT YET. In section 3, the formal and functional characteristics of -*(a)kona* are described. Section 4 addresses the fact that -*(a)kona* is a rare marker from a comparative perspective and has an ambiguous categorical status. Section 5 offers an account of the history of -*(a)kona* and the constructions of which it is a part, tracing its peculiar etymology and disentangling the processes behind its recruitment and further development as a phasal polarity marker. Section 6 contains a brief summary and some concluding remarks.

2 Expressions of phasal polarity in Manda: A general introduction

Before embarking on an elaborate presentation and analysis of the specific formal and functional features of -*(a)kona*, this section sets out to offer some background information on the language typology of Manda followed by a more general overview of the entire paradigm of phasal polarity expressions found in the language.

2.1 Some introductory remarks on the language structure of Manda

In order to facilitate the following description and analysis, this section presents background information on some typological traits of the Manda language, particularly its verbal structure and its strategy of negation, which both are notions closely linked to that of phasal polarity. Regarding the verbal structure, Manda adheres to the typical traits of an (Eastern) Bantu language with complex verbal morphology (see e.g. Nurse 2008: 28–78), consisting of several affixes marking concepts related to that of phasal polarity – such as tense, aspect and taxis – directly on the verb stem. The concatenative verb template in Manda, consisting of various morphological slots dedicated to affixes of certain functional categories can be represented in the following manner (where brackets indicate optionality):[2]

(Pre-SM-) (SM-) (-TAM1-) (-OM-) -ROOT (-EXT) -TAM2

Figure 1: The Manda verbal template.

See Bernander (2017: 145) for an inventory of the various TAM constructions found in Manda that results from different combinations of affixes in these various slots. It is important to point out that some of these constructions in Manda fluctuate between a realization with the subject marker only and a realization where the vowel of the subject marker coalesces with an /a/ in the TAM1 slot, without there being any semantic differences. This is still a phenomenon in need of further exploration and explanation. It is attested in other languages of this Bantu speaking area as well (e.g. Mpoto N14; Botne 2019). As will be further described in §3.1, -(a)kona is also affected by this morphophonological fluctuation (hence the <a> in brackets).

Manda is a tonal language, but with a highly restricted and predictable tone system consisting of an obligatory high tone on either the stem-initial position or the antepenult and/or penult. Although the assignment of tone may have a contrastive effect, this is only so to a limited extent. As tone plays no important role with regard to the phasal polarity expressions (or their development) in Manda, this feature is not further discussed here (readers are instead referred to Bernander 2017: 54–56).

Of more importance for this specific study is the formation of periphrastic (or complex) verb constructions in Manda. Periphrastic verb constructions are formed in two ways: either as auxiliary + infinitive verb (~deverbal noun), as in (1), or as a serial construction, as in (2), where both verbs are finite and inflected for the same subject. It should be noticed that in the latter case, the first verb is always a copula in (present day) Manda (in this example the verb -y- 'be(come)').

---

[2] Abbreviations used in this template as well as in the glosses of this article are the following: 1, 2, 3 . . . (nominal or pronominal) noun class prefix / degree of temporal remoteness; 1, 2, 3 sg / pl person; APPL applicative; COMPL completive; CONS consecutive; DEM demonstrative; EXT Extension (= derivational suffix); FUT future; FV final vowel; INF infinitive; LOC locative noun class; NEG negative; NOND nondum (= 'not yet'); OM object marker; PER persistive (= 'still'); PFV perfect(ive); POSS possessive pronoun; PROSP prospective; PST past; SM subject marker; TAM tense, aspect, mood. Notice that Manda marks some TAM functions (like future tense) with morphemes in the Pre-SM slot.

(1) ni-bít-a   ku-kɪláwǒk-a ku-Dár
    SM1SG-PROSP-FV   INF-return-FV LOC17-Dar-es-Salaam
    'I am going to return to Dar-es-Salaam.'

(2) kiláwu   ya-ní-y-i   ni-jéng-íti
    tomorrow FUT-SM1SG-be(come)-FUT   SM1SG-build-PFV
    '(By) tomorrow I will have built (it).'

This section will be closed with a brief note on the negation system in Manda. Unlike the common Bantu strategy (but in accordance with many other languages in the area), negation is never marked directly on the verb in the present-day version of Manda. Standard negation is marked merely with a free-standing postverbal particle, either *he* or *lepa~lepe* (or even *lepi*).

(3) pícha   y-áki   i-ka-wǒk-a   hé
    9.picture SM9-POSS3SG   SM9-CONS-depart-FV NEG
    'Her picture didn't go away,
    i-tám-a   mú-mú-tu   i-ka-wǒk-a   lépa
    SM9-SIT-FV   LOC18-3-HEAD   SM9-CONS-depart-FV NEG
    it is stuck in my head, it didn't go away.'

As illustrated in (3) above, these negative particles may be used more or less interchangeably. However, *lepa~lepe* is used more frequently (see Bernander 2017: 314–315). Other, non-standard, negators in Manda are also unbound. They include the negative auxiliary *-kotok-*, used as a prohibitive and for related functions (see Bernander 2017: 322–333, 2018), and the negative existential *kwawaka* (see Bernander 2017: 334–340).

2.2 The Manda phasal polarity paradigm

Following Van Baar (1997: 2; see also Kramer 2017; Löbner 1989; Krifka 2000; van der Auwera 1993, 1998; Schadeberg 1990; Heine et al. 1991), the concept of phasal polarity is defined in this paper as the combined notions of contrast in polarity, i.e. the existence or non-existence of a situation (in contrast to some other situation), with phasal values, i.e. the relative sequencing of these two contrasting situations. In other words, phasal polarity markers are "structured means of expressing polarity in a sequential perspective" (Van Baar 1997: 40). Additionally, phasal polarity expressions are typically associated with the notion of counter-factuality or counter-expectation – i.e. that the contrasting situation runs counter to some presupposition – a characteristic specifically put forward as a defining factor in studies on Bantu languages as well as African languages more generally (see e.g. Schadeberg 1990; Heine et al. 1991; Nichols 2011: 131; Kramer 2017).

The set of expressions of phasal polarity found in Manda, hence constituting the exhaustive phasal polarity paradigm in the language, is introduced in (4).[3]

(4) (a) n-**ákóna**   ni-lím-a   ng'ǔnda w-ángu
       SM1SG-**PER** SM1SG-cultivate-FV 3.plot   3-POSS1SG
       'I am **still** cultivating my plot.'

   (b) n-**ákóna**   ku-lím-a   ng'ǔnda w-ángu
       SM1SG-**NOND** INF-cultivate-FV 3.plot   3-POSS1SG
       'I have not cultivated my plot yet.'

   (c) ni-**málí'**   ku-lím-a   ng'ǔnda w-ángu
       SM1SG-**COMPL**(<'finish'-PFV) SM1SG-cultivate-FV 3.plot   3-POSS1SG
       'I have **already** cultivated my plot.'

   (d) ni-lím-a   **hé** ng'ǔnda w-ángu **kávílı**
       SM1SG-cultivate-FV NEG   3.plot   3-POSS1SG **anymore** (<'again')
       'I am **no longer** cultivating my plot.'

As seen from these examples (more substantially explained with regard to both form and function in the following sections of this article), -(a)kona functions as the substantive element in the semi-schematic constructions expressing both STILL (4a) and NOT YET (4b). From a comparative-conceptual point of view and with regard to the issue of terminology, these constructions with -(a)kona may be associated with two functional categories and subsequently labelled after them. Firstly, the construction in (4a) will be referred to as a "persistive" – a term used by e.g. Nurse (2008) for markers of STILL or constructions that "affirm that a situation has held continuously since an implicit or explicit point in the past up to the time of speaking" (Nurse 2008: 165).[4] Similarly, the construction in (4b) will be referred to as a "nondum" – a term used by Veselinova (2015; Veselinova & Devos, *this volume*) for

---

[3] Notice that the "underlying" subject marker in example (4a) and (4b) is the standard ni- and that the alternative form of the SM1SG in this case stems from a regular type of coalescence with the initial /a/ of -(a)kona, where ni- + a > na-a > n-a.

[4] Although markers labelled as "persistive" and "completive" (used to refer to the expression of ALREADY in this article), are typically treated as aspectual in the (Bantu) literature (rather than explicitly categorized as markers of phasal polarity), I make use of these terms (also in the interlinearization of examples) as they encompass closely interrelated concepts and are thus useful for comparative reasons.

NOT YET markers or constructions "used for the encoding of non-realized expectations for either actions or states" (Veselinova & Devos, *this volume*: 443).⁵ These two expressions may, in turn, be treated together as forming a sub-paradigm of non-telic or continuative phasal polarity expressions related through internal negation, i.e. STILL [NEG [p]] => NOT YET (cf. Kramer 2017). These continuative phasal polarity expressions are the focus of this study and will be further described and analyzed in the remaining sections of this article. The rest of this section offers a brief presentation of the two remaining (telic) phasal polarity expressions found in Manda. The first one, illustrated in (4c) and discussed in §2.3.1, makes use of the auxiliary verb -*mal*- to expresses the notion of ALREADY. The second one, NO LONGER, illustrated in (4d) and further discussed in §2.3.2, is expressed by the adverbial *kavılı* plus sentence negation.

2.3 Additional phasal polarity expressions in Manda – a brief description

2.3.1 The expression of ALREADY

The concept of ALREADY is expressed in Manda with the auxiliary -*mal*-, referred to (and glossed) as a *completive* marker in Bernander (2017), following Nicolle (2012). The completive in Manda is an auxiliary, transparently derived from the lexical verb -*mal*- meaning 'finish, complete' (originating from the Proto-Bantu root *-*mad*-, with reflexes with a similar meaning attested in all Bantu subgroups; cf. Bastin et al. 2002). When functioning as a completive, the auxiliary -*mal*- is inflected with the perfect(ive) suffix -*ili* ~ -*iti* (often truncated to -*i*' due to the tendency of final syllable deletion in Manda; cf. Bernander 2017: 53), occurring with and operating on a second, infinitive verb which conveys the main situation of the proposition. Example (5) illustrates the use of -*mal*- to express the concept of ALREADY in Manda as a positive, inchoative phasal polarity expression, with a retrospective focus on the completion of a situation which holds at the time of reference, but which is not anticipated to continue to hold (cf. van der Auwera 1998; Nicolle 2012; Kramer 2017).⁶

---

5 See Bernander (2017: 262) and Veselinova & Devos (*this volume*) for several alternative terms used for NOT YET constructions in the literature.
6 These semantic components of retrospective focus and discontinuation overlap with those of NO LONGER (discussed in §2.3.2). Indeed, according to Schadeberg (1990), a similar completive

(5) a-máli' ku-mál-a ku-télék-a gwáli
    SM1-COMPL INF-finish-FV INF-cook-FV 14.ugali
    'She has already finished preparing the ugali.'

Note that -*mal*- co-occurs with its own etymon as the lexical verb in this example, one of several clear indications of its specialized status as phasal polarity marker vis-à-vis its lexical source. Intrinsically, this also illustrates that -*mal*- may still be used as a full (lexical) verb in Manda (see also (27) for another example of this fact). In contrast to the phasal polarity expressions with -*(a)kona*, there are also formal indications of the grammaticalization of -*mal*- into an auxiliary (as further discussed in section 4).

The recruitment of a terminative verb like -*mal*- to express the phasal polarity concept of ALREADY is common both across the Bantu speaking area and also cross-linguistically (see e.g. Heine & Kuteva 2002: 134). It should be further noted that the source construction with an inflected auxiliary verb, and with the main, lexical verb in the form of a deverbal noun (~infinitive), also reflects a typical auxiliary construction in Bantu (see e.g. Heine 1993:64–65; Nurse 2008:61; Anderson 2011).

Similarly to what has been pointed out by Vander Klok and Matthewson (2015; see also Schadeberg 1990; Heine et al. 1991), the auxiliary -*mal*- in Manda may also carry a reading of counter-expectation, in which case it indicates that the situation has held earlier than expected.[7] Example (6) is uttered in a context where the speaker is commenting on a passing police officer; the construction with -*mal*- is used in this instance to express astonishment based on the fact that it is a) only noon and b) the referent is still on duty.

(6) a-máli' kú-nyw-a
    SM1-COMPL INF-drink-FV
    'He has already (been) drinking (~he is already drunk)?!'

---

construction with a "finish"-verb in Swahili (G42) has "no longer" as an available second reading. I did not find any evidence of such a second reading in my Manda data. However, -*mal*- does occur in the language with another conceptually interrelated function, namely that of a resumptive (or tail-head linkage) marker, operating on a second (main/lexical) verb which recapitulates the preceding (and thus no longer holding) event in the discourse (see Bernander 2017: 198).

[7] And not later than expected, i.e. it has a reading more similar to the use of English *already* than to that of Turkish *artık* (cf. van der Auwera 1998).

With this said, however, there are some indications that this pragmatic effect of counter-expectation and earliness might undergo neutralization, which, together with the bleaching of the required component of a succeeding negative phase, makes the auxiliary -*mal*- gain a function more reminiscent of a perfect. This is an issue in need of further research, but it would seem to adhere to a more general tendency where a verb meaning 'finish' develops into a completive ALREADY and then further to a perfect (see e.g. Bybee et al. 1994: 69–81; Heine and Kuteva 2002: 134).

2.3.2 The expression of NO LONGER

The final phasal polarity expression to be briefly described is NO LONGER, contrasting with ALREADY by expressing a negative rather than a positive state where a situation does *not* hold, while simultaneously implying a prior point in time where this situation *did* hold (see e.g. Kramer 2017). This phasal polarity category is arguably articulated in the most deviant manner relative to the other phasal markers in Manda, as it is expressed by a regularly negated predicate and the adverb *kavɪlɪ* 'again' (see Persohn *this volume*, for a corresponding NO LONGER-construction in neighboring Nyakyusa M31). This formal make-up is in contrast with both the *de facto* auxiliary verb -*mal*- used for the expression of ALREADY as well as the auxiliary-like STILL/NOT YET-constructions with -*(a)kona*. The adverb *kavɪlɪ* is derived from the numeral stem -*vɪlɪ* 'two' with the nominal prefix of noun class 12 (used with some productivity for deriving adverbs in Manda). The NO LONGER construction in Manda is illustrated in (7), where the predicate is negated with one of the two standard negators found in the language, namely the post-verbal particle *lepa~lepe*. (Recall that the other standard negator is *he*, also a post-verbal negator).

(7) va-mánda   vá-lǐm-a   lépe   ma-pémba   kávílɪ
    2-Manda   SM2-cultivate-FV   NEG   6-millet   anymore
    'The Manda (community) does no longer cultivate millet.'

Thus, *kavɪlɪ* has arguably gained an additional meaning component under negation (Van Baar 1997:50), comprising not only a "disrepetitive" reading of NOT AGAIN (to borrow the terminology of van der Auwera 1998), but also a phasal reading of (dis-)continuity, i.e. NO LONGER.

2.4 Some remarks about the complete phasal polarity system in Manda

After this general overview of all the phasal polarity expressions found in Manda, some remarks can be made about the paradigm as a whole, based on the criteria provided by Kramer (2017). As seen, there exists a strategy for at least some kind of overt coding of all four variants of phasal polarity in Manda, each node of the phasal polarity paradigm being represented with a specific expression. This further suggests that Manda is a language with a relatively rigid paradigm of phasal polarity markers. The only example of an element occurring in more than one phasal polarity construction is *-(a)kona*, which is used to express both STILL and NOT YET.

However, these expressions consist of a disparate set of markers occurring in different types of constructions, thus indicating a relatively asymmetric internal paradigmaticity. The phasal polarity markers have different categorical status, varying not only in the word classes to which they belong but also in the constructional contexts they occur in. Hence, the phasal polarity markers of Manda cannot be "syntactically parallelized" (Kramer 2017: 16). As will become clearer in the following more detailed account, this fact relates particularly to the continuative phasal polarity expressions with *-(a)kona*, both regarding the ambiguous categorical status of *-(a)kona* but also the complex formal relationship between the positive and negative constructions, the expression of NOT YET not merely being the negating of its positive counterpart.

3 Phasal polarity expressions with *-(a)kona*

After some background information regarding the complete phasal polarity paradigm in Manda, including a brief presentation of the other (telic) phasal polarity markers of the language, this section, as well as the remainder of this article, will focus on the two (non-telic) continuative phasal polarity expressions of STILL and NOT YET. Both concepts are expressed with constructions containing *-(a)kona* as the substantive element. In this section, the formal characteristics of *-(a)kona*, as well as its function(s) as a phasal polarity marker, are described in detail.

3.1 Basic formal characteristics

The element *-(a)kona* most typically occurs in a position directly preceding the main predicative expression on which it operates. It is not an invariable form, as it is obligatorily inflected with a subject marker (SM), a prefix regularly used for nominal indexation on verbs in Manda (cf. Figure 1; §2.1). As touched upon already in §2.1, the vowel of the SM prefix almost always coalesces with an /a/ in present day Manda, regardless of its original quality, when occurring on the stem /kona/. This can be seen in (8), where the SM indexing noun class 9 occurs as /ya/, despite the fact that it "underlyingly" has the form (y)i-, i.e. its basic representation consists of the vowel /i/.

(8) yakona
 yi-a-kona
 SM9-a-kona
 'It is still/not yet. . .'

However, there is much more free variation with regard to the presence or absence of this /a/ in the older Manda sources as well as in the neighboring languages. As far as I have been able to tell, there are no semantic differences in these various allomorphic realizations, which seems to adhere to a more general (morpho-)phonological phenomenon in Manda and its neighbors which, in turn, is still in need of further elucidation.

3.2 The expression of STILL (-(a)kona in persistive constructions)

As already touched upon, -(a)kona is used in Manda to express both the positive continuative STILL as well as the negative continuative NOT YET, hence functioning as both a persistive and as a nondum marker in the language. This section addresses the use of -(a)kona as a persistive, i.e. its use to express the positive continuation of a situation which already started in the past. This concept is expressed in a construction where -(a)kona directly precedes the predicative expression, typically a lexical verb. As illustrated in (9), in these cases, both -(a)kona and this predicative verb are inflected with an identical subject marker with the same referent.

(9) v-ákóna va-yímb-a nyímbʊ mu-kanísa
 SM2-PER SM2-sing-FV 10.songs LOC18-9.church
 'They are still singing songs in church.'

However, the main predicative expression of a persistive construction with -(a)kona might also be a non-verbal word, as is the case in (10) below. In these cases, -(a)kona also contributes a copula-like function to the construction. Notice the co-referentiality between the subject and the predicative adjective.

(10) nkóngo gúla gw-ákóna gu-chóko
     3.tree DEM3 SM3-PER 3-small
     'That tree is still small.'

In all these constructions, -(a)kona is used to express that the situation, which has already held from an earlier point in time, continues to hold at reference time. In addition to this retrospective component, however, the persistive also contains a prospective component indicating that a change might occur at some point in time in the future, where the given situation does not hold anymore (as discussed by van der Auwera 1998: 39–40). Such a prospective element of the termination of the situation is clearly evident in example (11), where the potential time frame is even explicitly expressed. Notice that this is once again an example where the persistive operates on a non-verbal predicate.[8]

(11) n-ákóna   ku-Songéa   kóma   ni-hʊválíl-a
     SM1SG-PER   LOC17-Songea   but   SM1SG-hope-FV
     'I'm still in Songea, but I hope that
     wikéndi   ya-ní-y-i   ni-kiláwíki   ku-Litúhi
     9.weekend FUT-SM1SG-be-FUT SM1SG-return.PFV LOC17-Lituhi
     (for the) weekend, I will have returned to Lituhi.'

3.3 The expression of NOT YET (-(a)kona in nondum constructions)

Besides marking positive continuation, -(a)kona is also used in forming the nondum construction in Manda, i.e. the expression of NOT YET. In this case, the typical verbal collocate is not marked finitely but occurs in the infinitive (~deverbal noun) form.

(12) t-ákóna   ku-lóngél-a   náko
     SM1PL-NOND INF-speak.APPL-FV with.him
     'We have not spoken with him yet.'

---

8 For the discussion in §5, it is also worth pointing out that it is the locative noun prefix and not -(a)kona which provides the locative component of this proposition.

That -*(a)kona* may be used to render the polar meanings of both STILL and NOT YET is not particularly surprising, given the fact that they are semantically "exactly the same", both "retrospectively continuative and prospectively geared towards possible change" (van der Auwera 1998: 40). The only difference between the concept of STILL and that of NOT YET is that the polarity of the situation conveyed in the proposition is negative in the latter case. In Van Baar's (1997: 35) words (see also van der Auwera 1993: 627), the nondum marks a "continuation of absence". In other words, it marks that a given situation which did not hold at an earlier point in time does not hold at reference time either. However, there is once again a prospective component of a likely change in the future, where the given situation will hold. Example (13) is a good illustration of this use of -*(a)kona* in Manda; here it indicates that the bread in question – which has been put in a pot on the fire-place – was not baked at all at an earlier point in time and is not properly baked at the time of reference either, but will (most likely) be well-baked after some additional time in the fire.

(13) *nkáti   gw-ákóna kú-py-a   bwína*
     3.bread SM3-NOND INF-be(come)_baked-FV well
     'The bread is not well-baked yet.'

Formally, this overlap in the expression of the persistive and the nondum in Manda adheres to the more general cross-linguistic tendency which stipulates that an element of a positive phasal polarity expression reappears in its "polarity antagonist" (Van Baar 1997: 82), a tendency which most typically affects STILL and NOT YET (Van Baar 1997: 29). However, this connection is usually characterized by the addition of a negator to the positive phasal polarity marker (Van Baar 1997: 52). It is thus notable that the negative nondum construction with -*(a)kona* is in fact not negatively marked in any way in Manda. Section 5 elaborates on the historical factors at play leading up to this fact. However, it suffices to mention at this point that it is not unusual *per se* for nondum markers to replace or be devoid of any negative marking, either cross-linguistically (Veselinova 2015) or in other Bantu languages (see Güldemann 1998; Nurse 2008: 148; Abe 2015; Veselinova & Devos *this volume*).

This lack of a negator for forming nondums entails that there is only the formal make-up of the entire construction, and in essence the form of the predicate verb, which decides whether the meaning conveyed is to be interpreted with a positive or negative phasal value. This fact, as explicitly illustrated in the minimal pair in (14), emphasizes the importance of treating these phasal polarity expressions in Manda holistically as constructions, rather than exclusively focusing on the substantive element of -(a)kona.

(14) (a) ákóna   a-lémba
          SM1.PER SM1-write-FV
          'She is still writing.'
     (b) ákóna   ku-lémb-a
          SM1.NOND INF-write-FV
          'She hasn't written yet.'

In addition, it is also important to point out that -(a)kona with its negative polar reading may be used in isolation as a negative pro-sentence or an answer particle, referring back to a previous proposition (of which -(a)kona agrees in subject marking with an earlier referent).[9]

(15) (Q:) u-tónd-íti?
          SM2SG-be(come)_tired-PFV
          'Are you tired?'
     (A:) lépa ni-tónd-í'   lépa n-ákóna
          no   SM1SG-be(come)_tired-PFV NEG SM1SG-NOND
          'No, I'm not tired, not yet.'

This kind of patterning was also noted as a salient trait in the cross-linguistic sample of Van Baar (1997: 295), who even posits a universal on this account, namely: "if a STILL-expression is used as an isolated expression, it is invariably used for the expression of NOT YET". This fact has also been explicitly pointed out for Bende (F12; Abe 2015) also a south-western Tanzanian Bantu language spoken not far from Manda. Recall from §3.2 that -(a)kona can operate on a non-verbal predicate, in which case it expresses a positive, persistive meaning. Taken together, this means that the reading of polarity differs both with regard to the form of a verbal predicate (finite verb = positive reading vs. nonfinite verb = negative reading) but also with regard to propositions without a verbal predicate (occurrence of non-verbal predicate = positive reading vs. no occurrence of a predicate = negative reading).

---

[9] Notice that the double use of *lepa* in this example reflects the polysemy of this form as both a negative answer particle 'no' and a sentential negator.

3.4 The marking of counter-expectation with -(a)kona

This section discusses the component of "counter-expectation" in connection to the phasal polarity expressions with -(a)kona in Manda, i.e. that the situation depicted in the proposition in some manner contrasts with some presupposition or assumption expressed, either explicitly or implicitly, in the previous discourse. As pointed out by Heine et al. (1991: 202; see also Van Baar 1997: 61), the notion of counter-expectation (or that of "counter-factual scenarios"; cf. Kramer 2017) corresponds inversely to the general semantic make-up of the respective phasal value of a phasal polarity expression. Thus, the persistive, which marks a situation that continues to hold, can also be used to mark the assumed termination of a situation that has not taken place. Similarly, the nondum, which marks a situation that did not hold and continues not to do so, may be used to indicate that an assumed inception and duration of that situation has not taken place. The reading of counter-expectation is, as far as I have been able to tell, not possible to disentangle from a more neutral reading in Manda, but has to be retrieved from the context. Judging from my collection of Manda data (and as also indicated in the examples in §3.2 and §3.3), a counter-expectational component is far from necessary. In fact, there are virtually no examples in my collection of spontaneous speech (e.g. narratives, expository accounts, conversations etc.) where a positive STILL-construction is used to mark counter-expectation. Thus, the notion of counter-expectation is arguably not central to these phasal polarity-constructions. With that said, both the positive STILL-construction and the negative NOT YET-constructions with -(a)kona are readily available and acceptable for forming propositions with a counter-expectational reading, as illustrated with this pair of elicited sentences, both referring to the same contextual background.

(16)   {'My God, I have waited for Michael for half an hour now'}
   (a)   ákóna   á-v-íli   ku-ndmdǐma
       SM1.PERS   SM1-be(come)-PFV   LOC17-9.toilet
       'He is still (sitting) on the toilet?!'
   (b)   ákóna   ku-pít-a   ku-ndmdǐma
       SM1.NOND   INF-go_out-FV   LOC17-9.toilet
       'He has not yet left the toilet?!'

There are also several instances of counter-expectational nondum expressions in my collection of spontaneous speech in Manda. One example is the proposition in (17), in which the speaker corrects the misinformed presupposition, previously expressed by the addressee, that the referent (the speaker's son) holds the position of a police officer.

(17) lépa, ákóna kú-y-a polísi
   no   SM1.NOND INF-be-FV 1a.police_officer
   'No, he is not a police officer yet.'

In fact, however, the referent is studying to become a police officer. Thus, this construction with -(a)kona also expresses the prospective aspect connected to this pair of phasal polarity markers (as discussed in §3.2 and §3.3), in this case that the situation – although not holding at the moment – most likely will hold in the future.

While on the topic of counter-expectation, it should be added that the positive persistive construction with -(a)kona may be negated through standard negation.[10] In this case the reading is similar to the -(a)kona + infinitive construction – i.e. the nondum – as it portrays the situation as not having taken place either in the past or at reference time. However, this construction puts more focus on the neglect itself. That is, it highlights the pertaining non-implementation of the situation encompassed in the predicative expression, rather than the situation itself. Moreover, it is speaker-oriented. Thus, it behaves in these senses similarly to Van Baar's (1997: 2, 35, 168) characterization of the comparable English expression of *still not*. However, it seems to differ in the sense that it does not necessarily express the speaker's disbelief, but rather runs counter to the hopes or expectations of the addressee (cf. Schadeberg 1990; Nurse 2008: 166). Notice that it continues to stand in relation to the focus on different phases of STILL and NOT YET. Thus, unlike (18), where the implementation of the act is delayed but there is an intention to fulfil it, (19) instead conveys that it is exactly the intention not to fulfil the act which persists.

(18) t-ákóna ku-bít-a ku-sheléhe
   SM1PL-PER INF-go-FV LOC17-9.party
   'We have not gone to the party yet.'
   {'But we intend to go there, we are just late.'}

---

10 In fact, it is acceptable to apply standard negation also to the nondum construction, resulting in a reading similar to a proximative or immediate future. Such a construction has only been elicited, however, and there are no examples in the spontaneous data.

(19) t-ákóna   ti-bít-a   lépa ku-sheléhe
     SM1PL-PER SM1PL-go-FV NEG LOC17-9.party
     'We are still not going to the party.'
     {'We have decided not to go and we are keeping that promise (still).'}

3.5 The interrelation of -*(a)kona* with expressions of TAM

Except for subject marking, -*(a)kona* cannot be inflected for tense, aspect or mood (TAM). However, it is possible to anchor both of the continuative phasal polarity expressions in an utterance time different from the "here and now" of the present by placing them in a periphrastic construction. Positive persistives of this kind are formed by shifting the tense inflection of the following predicate verb from the present tense to the past or the future, the latter temporal reference being illustrated in (20). Negative nondum constructions are formed with a preceding copula verb -*y*- 'be(come)' inflected for tense. This results in highly complex, 3-word predicative constructions, as seen in example (21), which illustrates a past tense construction with a negative polarity reading. Persistive constructions with a non-verbal predicate are also formed with the preceding copula verb -*y*- carrying the proper tense marking, as seen in (22).

(20) n-ákóna   ya-ni-yímb-áyi
     SM1SG-PER FUT-SM1SG-sing-FUT
     'I will still be singing'

(21) ni-ka-y-í'   n-ákóna   kú-ly-a
     SM1SG-PST1-be(come)-PFV SM1SG-NOND INF-eat-FV
     'I hadn't eaten yet.'

(22) ni-ka-y-í'   n-ákóna   mw-ána
     SM1SG-PST1-be(come)-PFV SM1SG-PER 1-child
     'I was still a child.'

With regard to the notion of aspect, it should be noted that -*(a)kona* in its use as a persistive may in fact be compatible with the perfect(ive), as illustrated in (23).

(23) gólo   a-l-íli   sana gwáli,
    yesterday   SM1.PST2-eat-PFV   a_lot 14.ugali
    ákóna   a-túp-íli
    SM1.PERS   SM1-be(come)_full-PFV
    'Yesterday he ate a lot of *ugali* (and) he is still full.'

However, in analogy with what has been pointed out by Persohn (2017: 21, 114, 127, 133, 2019) for Manda's neighbor Nyakyusa (M31), such constructions are only possible when the lexical verb encodes a resultant state (i.e. in this case 'be full'). A persistive construction with *-(a)kona* and a verb in the perfect(ive) without a lexicalized resultant state, like the punctive *-fik-* 'arrive' in (24), is thus considered ungrammatical. As illustrated in (25) and (26), however, such a verb is compatible with *-(a)kona* in a negative persistive construction as well as in the nondum construction.

(24) **t-ákóna   tu-fík-íli
     SM1PL-PER   SM1PL-arrive-PFV

(25) *t-ákóna   tu-fík-íli   lépe*
     SM1PL-PER   SM1PL-arrive-PFV   NEG
     'We have still not arrived.'

(26) *t-ákóna   ku-fík-a*
     SM1PL-NOND INF-arrive-PFV
     'We have not arrived yet.'

It should be stressed that although constructions where *-(a)kona* is used outside the realm of the present imperfective are acceptable, as exemplified in this section, there are strikingly few examples like these in my collection of spontaneous speech.[11] To this it should be added that it seems that *-(a)kona* is blocked altogether from being used with the subjunctive mood, as there are no examples of such constructions in my corpus and speakers also reject such constructions as unacceptable.

---

[11] This tendency may be strengthened by the wide referential range of the present tense in Manda, which may be used in a manner similar to a "historical present" as well as for marking assertive future.

3.6 A note on additional, non-phasal uses of -(a)kona

Adhering to the more general trait of phasal polarity markers as exhibiting a "multiplicity of uses" (van der Auwera 1998: 26), -(a)kona has other, yet interrelated, uses in Manda outside the realm of phasal polarity.

There are two additional functions associated with -(a)kona in Manda. Firstly, -(a)kona may be used as a hypotactic conjunction expressing 'before'. In this case, -(a)kona occurs in a construction formally identical to the nondum construction, i.e. it (directly) precedes a verb which occurs in the infinitive/deverbal noun form, as illustrated in (27).[12]

(27) a-wʊy-íli ku-nyúmba
 SM1.PST2-return(home)-PFV LOC17-9.home
 ákóna ku-mál-a li-héngu
 SM1.before INF-finish-FV 5-work
 'She returned home before finishing the work'

The difference between this construction and the nondum construction is the dependent status of the clause in which -(a)kona occurs itself. Similarly, the main semantic difference relates to the fact that the negative situation encompassed in an adverbial clause with -(a)kona as a conjunction is directly linked to the situation expressed in the main clause predicate, rather than related to a discourse-based presupposition. That a phasal polarity marker additionally functions as a conjunction is common typologically (Van Baar 1997: 275–276, 291) and it appears that a relationship between a nondum and 'before' is an especially common semantic relationship of this kind (Veselinova & Devos, *this volume*).

In addition to its function as a subordinating conjunction, -(a)kona inflected with the subject marker of a locative noun class – typically that of class 16 – in collocation with the adjective -choko(pi) 'small, little', modifying and agreeing with -(a)kona, expresses the meaning 'soon'. This is illustrated in (28).

(28) ya-u-sóv-i p-ákóna pa-chokópi
 FUT-SM14-be.lost-FUT LOC16-PER LOC16-soon
 'It will soon be lost (the flour).'

---

[12] Notice that the infinitive verb in this example happens to be -mal- which in this case is not used as a marker of ALREADY but as a full (lexical) verb (cf. the discussion in §2.3.1).

Notice that this construction with -(a)kona differs from those previously discussed, in that, in this case, it does not agree with a nominal constituent but may only occur with a fixed and more expletive-like locative subject marker, thus producing a more independent and invariable expression. What is more, unlike other constructions with -(a)kona, this adverbial phrase occurs after the predicate verb, in the canonical syntactic position of a prototypical adverb in Manda.

These additional functions are clearly related to those of phasal polarity, although it is not obvious that they are necessarily derived from either of the phasal polarity expressions or if they represent individual pathways of change (adhering to Van Baar's 1997: 342 "plane model"). What is obvious, however, and what once again is important to point out, is the fact that it is the construction as a whole – of which -(a)kona only forms a part – which decides the specific semantic instantiation of this polysemic element and, in extension, the interpretation of the entire proposition.

4 The ambiguous categorical status of -(a)kona

Although -(a)kona can be accounted for quite straightforwardly as a phasal polarity marker, there are also several peculiarities connected to this element. To begin with, it is a rare marker of STILL and NOT YET from a comparative point of view. As far as I know (see also Veselinova & Devos, *this volume*) a persistive and/or nondum construction with (cognate forms of) -(a)kona only appears in Manda and a limited set of its closest affiliates. Furthermore, as already touched upon in §2.1, Bantu languages are renowned for being both agglutinative and verb-centered, resulting in a rich set of verbal morphology. Consequently, it is typically the case across the Bantu family that at least the notion of STILL is expressed with a "persistive" verb prefix (Nurse 2008: 145), which has even been reconstructed for Proto-Bantu (Meeussen 1967) and typically surfaces as -ka- around the area where Manda is spoken (Güldemann 1996: 138–143, 1998; Nurse 2008: 243; Persohn, *this volume*).

It is often the case, however, that this persistive prefix does not attach directly to the lexical verb root but to a copula (or some other light verb), forming part of a complex construction – that is, a construction similar to the one described for -(a)kona, where the main situation of the proposition is expressed in a subsequent second verb, or, alternatively, operates on a non-verbal predicative expression. Example (29) from Zaramo (G33) and example (30) from Chewa (N31b), are cases in point.

(29) tu-**ha**-li   tu-gul-a
    SM1PL-**PER**-be   SM1PL-buy-FV
    'We are still buying.' [Zaramo]

(30) ba-**ka**-li   ku-tali
    SM2-**PER**-be   LOC17-far
    'They are still far away.' [Chewa]
    (Güldemann 1998: 167)

As well as being a rare instantiation of a STILL/NOT-YET-marker in Bantu, -(a)kona also has an ambiguous categorical status. As may be deduced from the presentation of -(a)kona in the previous section, it is "auxiliary"-like, i.e. it appears and behaves similarly to an auxiliary verb when taken at face value. It is used to express notions commonly associated with a verbal marker (as mentioned in the previous paragraph) and it agrees with the subject in a manner characteristic of verbs.[13] In addition, -(a)kona ends with a vowel /a/, reminiscent of the "default" final vowel of Bantu verb stems (cf. Nurse 2008: 261). The constructions with -(a)kona are also syntagmatically similar to the complex verbal constructions expressing continuative phasal polarity found in other Bantu languages (Veselinova & Devos, *this volume*; Nurse 2008: 145–148). Despite these superficial correspondences, however, it is hard to account for -(a)kona as an auxiliary, whether in relation to other auxiliaries in Manda or to the cross-linguistically valid criteria outlined by Van Baar (1997: 221–224; see also Heine 1993; Anderson 2006, 2011).

To begin with, -(a)kona lacks verbal properties, of which at least some would be expected to persist in an auxiliary. Thus, except for subject indexation, -(a)kona cannot carry any other inflectional morphology typical of a verb in Manda. It may not be inflected with other types of nominal indexation such as relative markers or object markers, nor can it be derived with extensions, i.e. suffixes marking various syntactic and/or semantic reconfigurations. Similarly, it may not be (directly) inflected for TAM, as discussed in §3.5 above. Crucially, -(a)kona cannot be traced etymologically to any lexical verb, neither in Manda, nor from a comparative stance. In fact, -(a)kona cannot be linked to any language-internal linguistic material at all.

---

13 Notice furthermore that given Van Baar's (1997: 244–245) criteria of word class categorization in relation to phasal polarity markers, the fact that -(a)kona is regularly and variably inflected disqualifies it as a particle, whereas the fact that it can be used to modify nominal constituents (as non-verbal predicates) also excludes it from being characterized as an adverb.

In addition to its lack of these general verbal characteristics, -(a)kona also lacks the specific morpho-syntactic traits characterizing auxiliary verbs in Manda (cf. Bernander 2017). Consequently, it fails Van Baar's (1997: 220–221) conditions of a "grammaticalized" phasal polarity expression, that is, a construction which has been altered both semantically and formally, resulting in a new form-meaning pair that differs from its source. This lack of formal adaption becomes evident when -(a)kona is compared to the completive -mal- (described in §2.3.1), which is both a phasal polarity marker and a *bona fide* auxiliary. For example, as illustrated in (31) (also in (10), (11), §3.2 above), -(a)kona may occur with and operate on non-verbal constituents. This contrasts with auxiliaries in Manda, which, in their acquired status as grammaticalized function words, exclusively operate on verbs. Consequently, an auxiliary like -mal- may only collocate with a non-verbal constituent when it has its original, lexical meaning, as illustrated in (32).

(31) ákóna   nchúmba w-ángu
     SM1SG-PER 1.fiancé 1-POSS1SG
     'She is still my fiancé.'

(32) u-mál-i'   má-lávi   gh-ángu
     SM2SG-finish(**COMPL)-PFV   6-peanuts 6-POSS1SG
     'You have finished my peanuts.' / **'You have already my peanuts.'

Moreover, there is a general restriction on auxiliaries in Manda – which is, indeed, a formal indication of their decategorialized status relative to their lexical etymon – that they cannot stand alone but must always occur together with the verb they operate on. This diagnostic, which conforms to Van Baar's (1997: 238) isolation tests, is another indication of whether a phasal polarity expression is grammaticalized or not. (See also Bernander 2017 for a more elaborate account of this syntactic phenomenon regarding auxiliaries in Manda). As illustrated in the ellipsis construction in (33), when the auxiliary -mal- is used to convey the phasal polarity concept of ALREADY, it cannot stand alone (A2) but must co-occur together with the verb expressing the main event of the clause (A1). However, as seen in (34), -(a)kona is not affected by this restriction, i.e. both A1 and A2 are acceptable (elided) answers to the question in (34) (see also (15) in §3.3).

(33) (Q:) a-máli'   ku-yás-a   ki-tábu?
          SM1-COMPL INF-lose-FV 7-book
          'Has she already lost the book?'

| | (A:) | eh, | a-mál-í' | | ku-yás-a | /(A2:) | **a-málí(ti) |
| | | yes | SM1-COMPL-PFV | | INF-lose-FV | | SM1-COMPL |

'Yes, she has already lost it.'/ 'She has already (lost it).'

(34) (Q:) w-ákóna   ku-hémél-a ki-tábu ki-nyipa?
           SM2SG-NOND INF-buy-FV 7-book 7-new
   'Haven't you bought a new book yet?'
(A1:) éna, n-ákóna   ku-hémél-a
      yes, SM1SG-NOND   INF-buy-FV
   'No (lit. yes), I have not bought (it yet).'
(A2:) éna, n-ákóna
      yes, SM1SG-NOND
   'No (lit. yes), I have not (bought it yet).'

The remainder of this study sets out to clarify these described synchronic peculiarities of *-(a)kona* by accounting for its origin and historical background.

5 The etymology of *-(a)kona* and its recruitment as a phasal polarity marker

As explained in the presentation of *-(a)kona* so far in this article, it is in many ways an unusual phasal polarity marker, given its rare form, its ambivalent word class membership, as well as the fact that it may be used to express both positive and negative statements without the use of any negator. A proper account of these formal and functional peculiarities of this phasal polarity marker in Manda demands an explanation of its origins and subsequent development, which, in turn, will facilitate an understanding of its idiosyncratic form and behavior. However, the semasiological background of *-(a)kona* is complex, and an extensive account of its reconstruction is, unfortunately, beyond the limited scope of this article. While this section offers a brief account, more socio-historical contextualization, illustrations and discussions can be found in Bernander (2017: 16–17, 19–29, 266–271). Fundamentally, what a historical-comparative approach does is that it identifies two important traits of the element *-(a)kona* (+ subject marking): i) *-(a)kona* ultimately derives from a word and a construction which was borrowed from South African Nguni, and ii) *-(a)kona* is structurally a "copulative", i.e. an element of non-verbal origin used as a copula which became a phasal polarity marker through joint processes of semantic generalization and specialization in Manda and its neighbors.

The borrowing scenario of -(a)kona relies, to begin with, on the sociohistorical fact that a large group, initially of South African origin and speaking a Nguni (S40) variety, arrived in the area of southern Tanzania where Manda is spoken, in the mid-19th century. This arrival occurred at a time when Manda and the neighboring varieties had not consolidated as ethnic communities and subsequently as individual languages (Park 1988). The Nguni invaded and subjugated the previous inhabitants, whose descendants became part of the Nguni (~Ngoni) community but did not shift to the medium of communication of their rulers. Instead, a diglossic situation prevailed between "Old Ngoni" and "New Ngoni". Whereas Old Ngoni indeed was a Nguni (S40) language, albeit altered in relation to its sister languages in South(ern) Africa (cf. Doke 1954: 237), New Ngoni was mainly a blend of various southern Tanzanian tongues spoken by the previous inhabitants and other captives from the area who had been assimilated into the Ngoni community. It is New Ngoni which constitutes Tanzanian Ngoni (N12) as spoken today (see especially the lexico-statistical and phonological evidences for such a conclusion put forward in Nurse 1988; see also Ngonyani 2001, 2003: 1–3; Rosendal & Mapunda 2014; Mous 2019 and further references in these works). New Ngoni is not only Manda's closest neighbor but is also considered its closest affiliate.[14] Old Ngoni has become extinct and is generally understood as having left few linguistic traces in New Ngoni or in neighboring languages like Manda (see e.g. Nurse 1985, 1988; Ngonyani 2001). Nonetheless, linguistic remnants do exist from this Nguni variety, and the comparative data suggests that -(a)kona is one of them.

That -(a)kona in Manda was borrowed from Nguni is indicated in Table 1, which compares the functional and constructional range (i.e. "type" I–IV) of the element °kona[15] in Old Ngoni, as well as in Manda and its closest affiliates of the N10 subgroup, including New Ngoni. As a point of reference and in order to make the differentiation between the southern Tanzanian varieties and the Nguni varieties clearer, I have added Zulu (which Old Ngoni is presumed to have

---

[14] This conclusion is based on both lexico-statistics and phonology (Nurse 1988; Gray and Roth 2016) as well as on speakers' self-perception of mutual intelligibility and cultural similarity (Anderson et al. 2003).

[15] This element, with the same semantic features as in Old Ngoni, surfaces as <khona> with <h> in Zulu and other South African Nguni languages, where it marks aspiration. Aspiration, which is a non-contrastive feature in Manda and New Ngoni, as well as in the other N10 languages, is not marked in Spiss' grammar of Old Ngoni, although it is not clear if this is really due to phonological loss or is merely an orthographic shortcoming (see Doke 1954: 237).

originated from; see Ebner 1939; Doke 1954:237) and Malawian Ngoni (another Nguni offshoot from the 19th century emigration) to this table.[16]

This comparative table indicates the source and the direction of diffusion and semantic shift to which this element has been subject. The types in the first row refer to meaning, word class membership and/or constructional type. Type III is not different in meaning from type II. However, the construction in which it occurs is different, being a more complex construction, i.e. a concatenation with the subject marker resulting in a more complex, copulative, function. A "no" entails that the meaning described above does not exist in a variety and "yes" that it does. Question marks represent less certain cases. It should be stressed that this table only shows whether or not a reflex of °*kona* is attested with a certain meaning in a given language.[17] Similarly, the table does not mark the strategies used instead of °*kona* for expressing continuative phasal polarity.

As suggested by this table, *kona* ultimately stems from a free-standing pronoun (type I), the "absolutive" and "emphatic" pronoun *-ona* inflected in the locative class 17. Notice that neither this pronoun nor the inflectional paradigm it is derived from exist in the N10 languages. As a matter of fact, Ebner (1955: 160) makes explicit reference to this pronoun type when discussing the linguistic differences between Old and New Ngoni. As further seen in the table, this pronoun has an additional function as a non-deictic locational~temporal adverb in the Nguni varieties, including Old Ngoni (type II). Importantly, just as in the other Nguni languages, *kona* was also used as a "copulative" (type III) in Old Ngoni, that is, a non-verbal constituent "conjugated as the verb proper by the employment of subjectival concords" (Doke 1927: 225). Consider example (35):

(35) *kuse   kuwa   u-kona*
     be.good   that   SM2SG-here
     'It is good that you are here.' [Old Ngoni]
     (Spiss 1904: 305)

---

16 I have not added Zambian Ngoni nor Mozambican Ngoni to this list. For Zambian Ngoni, I have no other source than Brelsford (1956: 95) who merely notes that "Linguistically Ngoni was a dialect of Zulu but it has disappeared [. . .] and widely dispersed Ngoni usually use the language of the area they now occupy". Mozambican Ngoni is not included as it a) denotes an originally southern Tanzanian variety spoken by a community who only adapted the name Ngoni as they left southern Tanzania for the northern provinces of Niassa and Cabo Delgado in Mozambique roughly 80 years ago (Kröger 2013) and b) appears to use a different continuative phasal polarity marker than a reflex of *-(a)kona* (cf. Kröger n.d.).

17 As the sources on most of these languages are non-exhaustive, the risk that the non-existence of a certain meaning may be due to a lacuna in the source(s) rather than to its non-existence in the language must of course be taken into consideration.

Table 1: The meaning and use of -kona in Old Ngoni and N10.[18]

Languages		I. EMPHATIC PRONOUN: 17-ona '(the place) itself'	II. ADVERB 'here, there'; 'now, then'	III. COPULATIVE 'S be (here/present)'	IV. STILL – NOT YET	Sources
NGUNI (S40)	Zulu	yes	yes	yes	no	Grout (1859), Doke (1927), Cope (1984)
	Malawian Ngoni	yes	yes	yes	no	Elmslie (1891)
	Old Ngoni	yes	yes	yes	no(?)	Spiss (1904), Doke (1954)
N10	New Ngoni	no	yes(?)	yes	yes	Spiss (1904), Ebner (1939), Ngonyani (2003)
	Matengo	no	no	yes	yes	Häflinger (1909), Zimmer (n.d.), Yoneda (2006), Kayuni (p.c.)
	Mpoto	no	no(?)	no(?)	yes	Makwaya (p.c.), Botne (2019)
	Manda	no	no	no	yes	field notes, NT (1937), *Missa Mbalafu* (n.d.)

The ability to derive copulatives in this manner is described as a distinctive feature of Nguni languages in general (see Doke 1954: 79–80). Compare example (36) taken from present day Zulu.

---

18 Spiss (1904) mostly contains information on Old Ngoni, but also an accompanying word list of New Ngoni (i.e. modern Tanzanian Ngoni; N12). Therefore, this work is cited in both columns.

(36) aba-ntu   ba-khona   bodwa
    2-people   2-be.here   2.alone
    'The people are here alone.' [Zulu]
    (Cope 1984: 85)

However, forming copulatives in this manner is not a productive strategy in the southern Tanzanian languages. Thus, there is neither a pronoun *kona*, nor is there a strategy of turning this pronoun into a copulative in these languages. Recall furthermore that no inherent source for *-(a)kona* could be found in Manda. Still, there is an overlap in meaning between *kona* of Old Ngoni and *kona* of the N10 languages. This strongly suggests that *-(a)kona* was copied into the N10 languages in the form of a locative adverb (II), together with the constructional strategy of forming a copulative by the addition of a subject marker (III).[19] However, only at a later stage (type IV), and exclusively in the N10 languages, did the element get extended in use and specialized into a marker of phasal polarity. Thus, this is a function it never acquired in the donor language Old Ngoni nor in other Nguni languages (which make use of other strategies, mainly verb prefixes, to mark these concepts).[20] However, the fact that Spiss at least on one occasion translates *akona* as *er ist noch da* 'he is still there' suggests that this inference already existed in Old Ngoni (see Spiss 1904: 371). In any case, positing this copulative as the source would adhere to the typologically salient fact that a phasal polarity item initially stems from borrowed material, which does not necessarily have the function of expressing phasal polarity in the donor language (van der Auwera 1993: 628–629, 1997: 67–73; Van Baar 1997: 126–129). Another cross-linguistic generalization which can be made concerns the typical source meaning(s) of the etymon in question. Firstly, the original meaning(s) of *-(a)kona* are largely consistent with the typical source meanings posited for a persistive (Van Baar 1997: 90–95; van der Auwera 1993, 1998; Heine and Kuteva 2002: 218). More generally, it complies with the essential strategy of employing copulas and locative markers for all kinds of grammatical expressions devoted to the notion

---

[19] There are also some possible diachronic factors at play with regard to the N10 languages which the table does not show. Thus, for both Matengo and New (Tanzanian) Ngoni, only the older sources from the early 20th century mention the meaning/usage pattern of type II and III along with type IV, whereas the sources from the early 21st century only mention the phasal polarity meanings.

[20] Various constructions with the verbal prefix *-se-* but also *-ka-* (cp. the *-ka-* discussed in §4) are attested for the expressions of STILL/NOT YET both in Old Ngoni (Spiss 1904: 296) and today's Zulu (Cope: 1984).

of ongoing activity, most typically that of progressive aspect (see e.g. Nurse 2008: 259; Bybee et al. 1994: 129).

Importantly, positing that *-(a)kona* is an element of non-verbal origin would explain many of the formal peculiarities characterizing the persistive/nondum in Manda. As described in §4, *-(a)kona* cannot be linked to any lexical verb source in Manda and, with the exception of verbal subject indexation, it lacks verbal features, whether those of a lexical or an auxiliary verb. This absence of verbal properties may thus be explained by the simple fact that *-(a)kona* does not stem from a verb but an adverb (and ultimately a pronoun) being used as a verb. In addition, the persistent copula-like status of *-(a)kona* explains the fact that *(a)kona* as a phasal polarity marker can collocate with non-verbal constituents as well as occurring in isolation, in contrast with a more dependent auxiliary. Taking these facts together, the development of the copulative *-(a)kona* into a persistive can quite straightforwardly be accounted for as a case of semantic extension.

A trickier question to answer concerns the motivation behind recruiting *-(a)kona* as a phasal polarity marker. A plausible explanation from a functional point of view would be the need in Manda (and its neighbors) for a more expressive (counter-factual?) persistive/nondum, given the ample indications that what appears to be the reflex of the original persistive (a reflex of the *-ka-* described in §4) has become generalized into a marker of simultaneous taxis and/or imperfective aspect (see e.g. Bernander 2017: 199–201). That there exist remnants of an earlier continuative phasal polarity marker would put further weight to the hypothesis that *-(a)kona* was (relatively) recently introduced. From a formal point of view, the recruitment of *-(a)kona* might have been facilitated by the fact that its copulative configuration resonated well in morpho-syntactic terms with the features of the original persistive/nondum construction, which also was complex and which, in addition to having a persistive prefix, contained a copula.

5.1 On the loss of an explicit negator in the nondum construction

As noted in earlier parts of this article, *-(a)kona* is used in Manda to express NOT YET without any overt negator. This phenomenon is not unheard of across the Bantu speaking family (see e.g. Veselinova & Devos, *this volume*, Nurse 2008: 147–148; Güldemann 1998; Abe 2015). It is usually explained as originating from a shift from "affirmative meaning to negative inference" (Nurse 2008: 148), induced by the inceptive status and thus non-factual reading of an infinitive verb. That is, 'S (is) still *to* X' > 'S have not yet X' (where S = the Subject and X = the situation expressed by the infinitive verb). However, although this might be the case for other Bantu languages with an analogous nondum construction, this is most likely not what has happened in Manda. The historical and comparative data instead clearly indicates that in fact there used to exist an overtly expressed negator of the form *na-* ~ *nga-*, but that it has disappeared from present-day Manda. Consider Table 2 below, which compares the present-day nondum construction in Manda (in the very last column) with the formal realization of the same phasal polarity concept in both of Manda's closest affiliates, as well as in the older Manda sources.

Table 2: The nondum construction in Manda in comparison.

Language		Form	Source
Mpoto (N14)		SM-(a)kona # **nga**-INF-B-a	Makwaya (pers. comm)
Matengo (N13)		SM-(a)kona # **ngaa** INF-B-a	Häflinger (1909: 184), Yoneda (2006: 99), Kayuni (pers. comm.)
Ngoni (N12)		SM-(a)kona # **na**-INF-B-a	Ngonyani (2003:87), Ebner (1939:33–34)
Manda (N11)	-Historical data	SM-(a)kona # **n(g)a**-INF-B-a	NT (1937), *Missa Mbalafu* (n.d.)
	-Present data	SM-(a)kona # **(Ø-)**INF-B-a	field notes

The bolded element in this table is the negative prefix, which – as can clearly be seen – is present in all the other languages. The only exception to this tendency to have a pre-verbal nasal-initial negator – and thus the only variety which lacks a negative prefix in the construction of the nondum – is Manda as spoken today, where the negator is absent (symbolized in the table with a zero morph). Thus, compare the Manda nondum construction with that of its closest affiliate Ngoni.

(37) w-akona **na**-ku-geg-a chi-dengu
 SM2SG-NOND **NEG**-INF-carry-FV 7-basket
 'You have not yet carried the basket.' [Ngoni]
 (Ngonyani 2003: 87)

Importantly, the table shows that a negative prefix of a similar shape and position to that of its affiliates also existed even in earlier varieties of Manda. Example (38), from the translation of the New Testament (1937), illustrates this fact.

(38) saa   y-ake   y-akona   **na**-ku-hich-a
     9.hour 9-POSS3SG SM9-NOND   NEG-INF-come-FV
     'His hour had not yet come'
     (NT 1937; John 7:30)

Taking these comparative and diachronic facts into account strongly suggests that the constructional make-up of the nondum in Manda is partly the result of the omission of a previously occurring negative prefix. It should be pointed out that this reconstructed construction with a negator more readily adheres to the dual conceptualization of phasal polarity markers (Löbner 1989; Krifka 2000) and to a typologically more salient formal realization (Van Baar 1997: 98), where the concept of NOT YET is expressed by internal negation of STILL. This suggests that there used to be a more coherent systematization of the continuative phasal polarity expressions in Manda, based on a compositional relationship of internal negation.

So why has this negator been lost in Manda? The answer to that question is related to the obsolete status of this negator in general in Manda.[21] Unlike the other N10 languages, which still make use of this negative prefix also in other contexts other than nondum constructions, *n(g)a-* has been completely levelled out as part of a Jespersen's Cycle scenario and in present-day Manda is replaced by post-verbal particles (see Bernander 2017: 318–320 for further details about this omission).[22]

6 Summary and conclusions

This article has described expressions of phasal polarity in Manda, with the focus on the phasal polarity expressions STILL (the persistive) and NOT YET (the nondum), both concepts being expressed with the marker *-(a)kona*. It has described the (extensive) functional and formal range of this phasal marker and, in addition, the etymology of *-(a)kona*, the mechanics behind its recruitment into a phasal polarity marker and its further development and reconfigurations within

---

[21] In present day Manda, this negator only surfaces as a petrified part of the negative copula *núkúya* < °*na-kuya* 'NEG.to be' (and probably also in the negative relative *-anga*).
[22] A plausible additional driving force for the omission of the negative prefix in the specific nondum construction is the fact that the final syllable of *-(a)kona* and the negative prefix are tautophonic. Hence, the omission of the negator might have been triggered by a more general preference in Manda for haplology, i.e. the deletion of one of two identical adjacently occurring syllables.

this paradigm. As argued, -*(a)kona* originates from borrowed material which can be traced to a Nguni copula-like construction ("copulative"), construed by the application of a verbal subject marking to a locative/temporal adverb (ultimately a locative pronoun), which, as a local innovation in Manda (and other N10 languages), became extended in meaning into a phasal polarity marker.

This scenario of both context-induced change and further semantic development within the recipient language(s) further explains why Manda (and other N10 languages) has this comparatively unusual phasal polarity marker, with an idiosyncratic form and unusual morpho-syntactic behavior.

Interestingly, these findings would seem to contradict the general understanding that the Nguni variety ("Old Ngoni") spoken in Tanzania had a limited impact on the speech communities of southern Tanzania – including on Manda – and calls for the reassessment and further scrutiny of this contact situation and its linguistic effects.

Bibliographic references

Abe, Yuko. 2015. Persistive in Bende – On the grammaticalization path. *Asian and African Languages and Linguistics* (9). 23–44.
Anderson, Gregory. 2006. *Auxiliary verb constructions*. Oxford: Oxford University Press.
Anderson, Gregory. 2011. Auxiliary verb constructions in the languages of Africa. *Studies in African Linguistics* 40 (1&2). 1–409.
Anderson, Heidi, Susanne Krüger & Louise Nagler. 2003. *A sociolinguistic survey of the Manda language community*. Ms, SIL Tanzania.
Bastin, Yvonne, André Coupez, Évariste Mumba & Thilo Schadeberg. (eds.). 2002. *Bantu lexical reconstructions 3 / Reconstructions lexicales bantoues 3*. Tervuren: Royal Museum for Central Africa. http://www.africamuseum.be/collections/browsecollections/human sciences/blr
Bernander, Rasmus. 2017. *Grammar and grammaticalization in Manda: An analysis of the wider TAM domain in a Tanzanian Bantu language*. Gothenburg: University of Gothenburg PhD thesis.
Bernander, Rasmus. 2018. The grammaticalization of -kotok- into a negative marker in Manda (Bantu N.11). *Linguistics* 56 (3). 653–679.
Botne, Robert. 2019. Chimpoto N14. In Mark Van de Velde, Koen Bostoen, Derek Nurse, Gérard Philippson (eds.), *The Bantu Languages*, 692–732. London: Routledge.
Brelsford, William Vernon. 1965. *The tribes of Zambia*. Lusaka: Printed by the Govt. Printer.
Bybee, Joan, Revere Perkins & William Pagliuca. 1994. *Evolution of grammar: tense, aspect, and modality in the languages of the world*. Chicago: University of Chicago Press.
Cope, Anthony T. 1984. An outline of Zulu grammar. *African Studies* 43 (2). 83–102.
Doke, Clement. 1927. *Textbook of Zulu grammar*. Cape Town: Masker Miller Longman.
Doke, Clement. 1954. *The Southern Bantu languages*. London/New York: Published for the International African Institute by Oxford University Press.

Ebner, Elzear. 1939. *Kisutu Grammatik*. Mission Magagura, Tanganyika. Peramiho: St. Benedictine Mission. Ms.
Ebner, Elzear. 1955. *The history of the Wangoni*. Peramiho. Ndanda: Benedictine Publications.
Elmslie, Walter Angus. 1891. *Introductory grammar of the Ngoni (Zulu) language: as spoken in Mombera's country*. Aberdeen: G. & W. Fraser.
Gray, Hazel & Tim Roth. 2016. New perspectives on the genetic classification of Manda (Bantu N.11). *SIL Electronic Working Papers 2016–001*. Dallas: SIL International.
Grout, Lewis. 1859. *The Isizulu: A Grammar Of The Zulu Languages*. Whitefish: Kessinger Publishing.
Guthrie, Malcolm. 1948. *The classification of the Bantu languages*. London: Oxford University Press.
Güldemann, Tom. 1996. *Verbalmorphologie und Nebenprädikationen im Bantu: Eine Studie zur funktional motivierten Genese eines konjugationalen Subsystems*. Bochum: Brockmeyer.
Güldemann, Tom. 1998. The relation between imperfective and simultaneous taxis in Bantu: late stages of grammaticalization. In Catherine Griefenow-Mewis, Ines Fiedler & Brigitte Reineke (eds.), *Afrikanische Sprachen im Brennpunkt der Forschung: Linguistische Beiträge zum 12. Afrikanistentag Berlin, 3.-6. Oktober 1996*, 157–177. Köln: Rüdiger Köppe.
Heine, Bernd. 1993. *Auxiliaries: Cognitive forces and grammaticalization*. New York: Oxford University Press.
Heine, Bernd, Ulrike Claudi & Friederike Hünnemeyer. 1991. *Grammaticalization: A conceptual framework*. Chicago: University of Chicago Press.
Heine, Bernd & Tania Kuteva. 2002. *World lexicon of grammaticalization*. Cambridge: Cambridge University Press.
Häflinger, Johannes. 1909. Kimatengo Wörterbuch. *Mitteilungen des Seminars für Orientalische Sprachen zu Berlin* 12. 31–214.
Johnson, William P. & Thomas H. Hicks. 1937. *Kilagano kya hino kya Bambo witu nu njokosi witu Yesu Kristo* [New Testament in Manda]. London: British and Foreign Bible Society.
Kramer, Raija. 2017. *Position paper on phasal polarity expressions*. Hamburg: University of Hamburg. https://www.aai.uni-hamburg.de/afrika/php2018/medien/position-paper-on-php.pdf
Krifka, Manfred. 2000. Alternatives for Aspectual Particles: Semantics of still and already. In Lisa J. Conathan, Jeff Good, Darya Kavitskaya, Alyssa B. Wulf & Alan C.L. Yu (eds.), *Proceedings of the Twenty-Sixth Annual Meeting of the Berkeley Linguistics Society: General Session and Parasession on Aspect*, 401–412. Berkeley: Berkeley Linguistics Society.
Kröger, Heidrun. 2013. Demonstratives in Mozambican Ngoni. Paper presented at the 5th International Conference on Bantu languages, Paris, 12–15 June.
Kröger, Heidrun. n.d. *Notes on Ngoni*. Ms, SIL Mozambique.
Löbner, Sebastian. 1989. 'Schon – erst – noch': An integrated analysis. *Linguistics and Philosophy* 12 (2). 167–212.
Meeussen, Achiel E. 1967. Bantu grammatical reconstructions. *Africana linguistica* 3. 79–121.
Missa Mbalafu. [The gospel in Kimanda]. n.d. Likoma: UMCA press.
Mous, Maarten. 2019. Language contact. In Mark Van de Velde, Koen Bostoen, Derek Nurse, Gérard Philippson (eds.), *The Bantu Languages*, 355–380. London: Routledge.

Ngonyani, Deogratias. 2001. The Evolution of Tanzanian Ngoni. In Derek Nurse (ed.), *Historical language contact*, 321–353. Köln: Rüdiger Köppe.

Ngonyani, Deogratias. 2003. *A Grammar of Chingoni*. München: Lincom Europa.

Nichols, Peter. 2011. *A morpho-semantic analysis of the persistive, alterative and inceptive aspects in siSwati*. London: School of Oriental and African Studies PhD thesis.

Nicolle, Steve. 2012. Diachrony and grammaticalization. In Robert Binnik (ed.), *The Oxford Handbook of Tense and Aspect*, 370–397. Oxford: Oxford University Press.

Nurse, Derek. 1985. Review of Moser, R, Aspekte der Kulturgeschichte der Ngoni in der Mkoa wa Ruvuma, Tansania. *Journal of African Languages and Linguistics* 7 (1). 207–11.

Nurse, Derek. 1988. The diachronic background to the language communities of southwestern Tanzania. *Sprache und Geschichte in Afrika* 9. 15–115.

Nurse, Derek. 2008. *Tense and aspect in Bantu*. Oxford: Oxford University Press.

Park, George. 1988. Evolution of a regional culture in East Africa. *Sprache und Geschichte in Afrika* 9. 117–204.

Persohn, Bastian. 2017. *The verb in Nyakyusa: A focus on tense, aspect and modality (Contemporary African Linguistics 2)*. Berlin: Language Science Press.

Persohn, Bastian. 2019. Aspectuality in Bantu: On the limits of Vendler's categories. *Linguistic Discovery* 16 (2). 1–19.

Rosendal, Tove & Gastor Mapunda. 2014. Is the Tanzanian Ngoni Language threatened? A Survey of Lexical Borrowing from Swahili. *Journal of Multilingual and Multicultural Development*. 35 (3). 271–288.

Schadeberg, Thilo. 1990. Schon – noch – nicht – mehr: Das Unerwartete als grammatische Kategorie im Kiswahili. *Frankfurter Afrikanistische Blätter* 2. 1–15.

Spiss, Cassian. 1904. Kingoni und Kisutu. *Mitteilungen des Seminars für Orientalische Sprachen zu Berlin, 3. Abteilung: Afrikanische Studien* VII. 270–414.

Van Baar, Tim. 1997. *Phasal polarity*. Dordrecht: Foris Publications.

van der Auwera, Johan. 1993. 'Already' and 'still': Beyond duality. *Linguistics and philosophy* 16 (6). 613–653.

van der Auwera, Johan. 1998. Phasal adverbials in the languages of Europe. In Johan van der Auwera & Dónall P.O. Baoill (eds.): *Adverbial constructions in the languages of Europe*, 25–145. Berlin/New York: Mouton de Gruyter.

Vander Klok, Jozina & Lisa Matthewson. 2015. Distinguishing *already* from perfect aspect: A case study of Javenese *wis*, *Oceanic Linguistics* 54 (1). 172–205.

Veselinova, Ljuba. 2015. Not-yet expressions in the languages of the world: a special negator or a separate cross-linguistic category? Paper presented at Diversity Linguistics: Retrospect and Prospect, Max Planck Institute for Evolutionary Anthropology, Leipzig, 1–3 May.

Yoneda, Nobuko. 2006. *Vocabulary of the Matengo language*. Tokyo: Research Institute for Languages and Cultures of Asia and Africa (ILCAA), Tokyo University of Foreign Studies.

Zimmer, Franz. n.d. [Matengo grammar sketch and dictionary]. Ms.

Zarina Molochieva, Saudah Namyalo and
Alena Witzlack-Makarevich
Phasal Polarity in Ruuli (Bantu, JE.103)

1 Introduction

This paper deals with the expression of phasal polarity in Ruuli (also known as Ruruuli/Lunyala, ISO 639–3: ruc), a previously undescribed Great Lakes Bantu language (Niger-Congo). Within Great Lakes Bantu, Ruuli belongs to the Rutara group of the West Nyanza branch (Schoenbrun 1997). Apart from Ruuli, the Rutara group includes such better-described languages as Nkore-Kiga (ISO 639–3: cgg and nun) and Haya (ISO 639–3: hay). Ruuli is spoken mainly in the Nakasongola and Kayunga districts of the central region of Uganda. The speakers primarily reside in the districts of Kayunga, Nakasongola, Kiryandongo, Amolator, Buyende, Masindi, Hoima, and Luweero. The number of ethnic members of the community is over 230,000 (190,122 indicated to be Baruli, 47,699 indicated to be Banyara, Uganda Bureau of Statistics 2016). However, the actual number of Ruuli speakers is difficult to determine. Ruuli is not an official language and the orthography has been only recently introduced. Most speakers are multilingual: They are often fluent in Ganda, the language of the majority in the area, as well as English, the institutional language of Uganda. In addition, many speakers also speak languages of the neighboring ethnic communities, these are mostly closely related Bantu languages, such as Sogo and Nyoro.

Ruuli is a typical Bantu language: The dominant constituent order is SVO. Each noun in singular and plural belongs to one of the 20 noun classes. The noun classes are numbered from 1 to 23 corresponding to the reconstructed Proto-Bantu noun classes (see e.g. Van de Velde 2019: 237–239). The nominal prefixes on the nouns are not segmented in the examples, the gloss indicates the class in round brackets after the respective nouns, as e.g. in *abaweesi* 'blacksmith(2)' in (1c). Ruuli nouns regularly carry an augment, also known as pre-prefix or initial vowel (see e.g. Van de Velde 2019: 247–255). The augment appears before the noun class prefix and has the forms *a-*, *o-*, or *e-*. The augment is neither segmented nor glossed in the examples in this paper, as e.g. in *abaweesi* 'blacksmith(2)' in (1c).

Zarina Molochieva, University of Kiel, Germany
Saudah Namyalo, Makerere University, Uganda
Alena Witzlack-Makarevich, The Hebrew University of Jerusalem

https://doi.org/10.1515/9783110646290-004

The verbal inflectional morphology is primarily prefixing. Prefixes express such inflectional categories as negation, argument indexing, tense and aspect. Most derivational categories, such as the causative and applicative, as well some other inflectional categories, such as tense, aspect, and mood, are marked by the suffixes. In the examples, we neither segment nor gloss the final vowel on the verb. The glosses of the argument indexing on the verb follow the following conventions: the first and second person arguments are lossed with a combination of person and number indication, as in *n-a-som-ere* (1sgS-PST-study-PFV) 'I studied' in (1b), whereas the indexing of the third person arguments which trigger different prefixes depending on the noun class are glossed for the respective class only, as in *oKato a-kya-li* (Kato(1) 1S-PERS-be) 'Kato is', as in (1a). That is, if the numeral 1 or 2 in the glosses is used in combination with the indication of number, it refers to the person, and when it is used without the indication of number, it indicates the noun class.

Ruuli is a tone language. As at present its tone system is still being analyzed by the team, tone is not indicated in the examples, however, we are certain that no aspects of the analysis presented below depend on it.

The data used in the present study come from a corpus of naturalistic speech comprising over 200,000 words, as well as from elicitations. The corpus was collected in 2017 and 2018 in various locations in Uganda by the team of the project 'A comprehensive bilingual talking Luruuli/Lunyara-English dictionary with a descriptive basic grammar for language revitalisation and enhancement of mother-tongue based education' (PI Saudah Namyalo, funded by Volkswagen Foundation).

The paper is structured as follows: In Section 2 we give a survey of expressions to encode phasal polarity in Ruuli. Section 3 addresses the issue of pragmaticity. Section 4 treats telicity. Section 5 covers expressibility. Section 6 discusses the paradigmaticity of the phasal polarity paradigm. Finally, Section 7 offers some concluding remarks.

2 Phasal polarity in Ruuli

In this section we provide an overview of Ruuli expressions to encode phasal polarity. The major item involved in the expression of phasal polarity is the so-called persistive prefix *kya-* 'PERS', which forms part of the verbal paradigm. Constructions with this prefix express three of the concepts of phasal polarity, viz. STILL, NOT YET, and NO LONGER. They are discussed and illustrated in Section 2.1. Section 2.2 discusses the expression of phasal polarity by other means.

2.1 Expression of phasal polarity with the persistive prefix *kya-*

The expression of the three concepts of STILL, NOT YET and NO LONGER all involve the persistive prefix *kya-*. A grammatical persistive marker is uncommon cross-linguistically, but common in Bantu. In many Bantu languages it surfaces as a reflex of the Proto-Bantu postinitial *kí (Nurse 2008: 145). The reflexes of this prefix are found in all the closely related Rutara languages (see Muzale 1998). In E10–20 languages (as well as in F10, S30–40, and K20) the prefix has reflexes of the shape *kí+a (Nurse 2008: 147). This is also the case for the Ruuli persistive prefix *kya-*. The persistive in the Bantu languages is often described as belonging to the aspect system of the respective languages (Nurse 2008: 145–147). Löfgren (2018) provides an overview of the distribution of this marker in a range of East Bantu languages.

The construction encoding STILL is the most basic one in Ruuli: the main verb carries the persistive prefix *kya-*, as in (1a–c).

(1) a. *Abantu ba-ingi ba-**kya**-kolesya emole oku-omboka*
 people(2) 2-many 2s-PERS-use reed(10) INF-build
 ennyumba z-aabwe
 house(10) 10-2POSS
 'Many people **still** use reeds to construct their houses.' (elicited)
 b. *N-a-som-ere nga n-**kya**-li mu-to.*
 1sgS-PST-study-PFV while 1sgS-PERS-be 1-young
 'I studied, while I was **still** young.' (LL-M-KIBBALE-170221-FS-4B)
 (LL-M-KIBBALE-170221-FS-4B)
 c. *Abaweesi ga-**kya**-li=yo*
 blacksmith(2) 6s-PERS-be=23.LOC
 'Do the blacksmiths **still** have them (i.e. spears)?'(lit. 'As for the blacksmiths, are they (i.e. the spears) still with them?')
 (LL-M-KIBBALE-170221-FS-4B)

The expression of NO LONGER is coded on the basis of external negation of STILL: the negative prefix attaches to a verb which already carries the persistive prefix *kya-*, as in (2a–b).

(2) a. *Abantu ba-ingi **ti-ba-kya**-kolesya emole*
 people(2) 2-many NEG-2s-PERS-use reed(10)
 okw-omboka ennyumba z-aabwe.
 INF-build house(10) 10-2.POSS
 'Many people **no longer** use reeds to construct their houses.' (elicited)

b. *Naye enaku zi-ni abaana **ti**-ba-**kya**-zi-maite*
but day(10) 10-PROX child(2) NEG-2S-PERS-10O-know.PFV
'But these days children **no longer** know them.'
(LL-M-KIBBALE-170221-FS-4B)

The expression NOT YET is coded by a positive form with the persistive prefix *kya-* attached to the auxiliary *li* 'be' followed by the infinitive of the lexical verb, as in (3a–b). As *kya-* on the main verb on its own is used to express STILL, one can say that NOT YET is coded on the basis of external negation of STILL, though no negative element is involved.

(3) a. *Abantu ba-ingi ba-**kya**-li ku-kolesya emole*
people(2) 2-many 2S-PERS-be INF-use reed(10)
okw-omboka ennyumba z-aabwe.
INF-build house(10) 10-2.POSS
'Many people do **not yet** use reeds to construct their houses.' (elicited)
b. *Abasigazi ba-ni ba-**kya**-li ku-eteja kusai kintu ki-ni.*
boy(2) 2-PROX 2S-PERS-be INF-understand well thing(7) 7-PROX
'These boys do **not yet** understand well this thing.'
(LL-N-BBALE-170220-FS-2)

The same construction (i.e. the persistive prefix *kya-* on the auxiliary *li* followed by the infinitive of the lexical verb) is also used in adverbial clauses of time and is frequently translated with 'before' (this meaning of the persistive morpheme is labeled *precedence* in Güldemann 1998 following Dammann 1956), as in (4), also see (13).

(4) *Naye eirai ni tu-**kya**-li abaana ti-tu-a-ba-bala-nga.*
but in.the.past CONJ 1pls-PERS-be child(2) NEG-1pls-PST-2O-count-HAB
'But in the past, before we became born again Christians we used not to count children.' (lit. 'But in the past, when we were **not yet** born-again Christians, we used not to count children.')
(LL-R-NAKASONGOLA-170225-FS-1A)

2.2 Expression of phasal polarity by other means

Whereas the three expressions of STILL, NOT YET and NO LONGER employ the dedicated persistive prefix *kya-*, ALREADY is expressed in a number of ways in Ruuli (see also Section 5). The most common way is to use a periphrastic construction with a complement-taking predicate *mala* 'to finish' in the perfective form followed by the infinitive of the main verb, as in (5a–b).

(5) a. *Kubanga   egavumenti   a-a-**maare**   oku-tu-eeiteja.*
       because   government(9)   1S-PST-finish.PFV   INF-1plO-recognize
       'Because the government has **already** recognized us.'
       (LL-N-BBALE-170220-FS-2)
    b. *O-**maare**   oku-sumba.*
       2sgS-finish.PFV   INF-cook
       'You have cooked **already**.' (elicited)

A non-PhP reading of the complement-taking predicate *mala* 'to finish' is illustrated in (6).

(6) *Naye   aba-ndi   ba-aba   omu   maka*
    but   2-other   2S-go   18.LOC   home(6)
    *ga-bafumbo   mu-**maare**   oku-kola   emirimo*
    6.GEN-married.person(2)   2plS-finish.PFV   INF-do   work(4)
    ka-n-ab-e   owa   munywani   w-ange   tu-nyumy-e=mu.
    LET-1sgS-go-SBJV   16.LOC   friend(1)   1-1sgPOSS   1plS-converse-SBJV=18.LOC
    'But others go to the homes of the married people, (they tell themselves that) you have finished doing the work, so let me go to my friend and we'll converse.'
    (LL-R-NAKASONGOLA-170224-FS-2)

In many Bantu languages, the verb 'finish' figures in the tense-aspect-mood categories with an anterior or completive meaning (Nurse 2008: 305). For instance, in Swahili the verb *kwisha* 'to finish' has developed into a grammaticalized tense-aspect marker *-sha* with the meaning of 'present perfective-completive' (Marten 1998: 143–144). In Ruuli, it seems that this process is also under way and on many occasions the construction with *mala* 'to finish' followed by an infinitive is translated with the perfective of the verb in the infinitive (see Section 5).

It should be noted that the construction with the verb *mala* 'to finish' in Ruuli can have other interpretations. In the subordinate clause the verb *mala* 'to finish' can have posterior meaning 'after', as in (7).

(7) Ni-a-a-maare   oku-ba-eta   n-a-koba   n-a-ba-et-ere.
    NAR-1S-PST-finish.PFV INF-1O-call NAR-1S-say 1S-PST1O-call-PFV
    'After calling them, he said, "I called them".'
    (LL-R-NAKASONGOLA-170224-FS-2)

The second strategy to express ALREADY is by using the adverb *irai*, as in (8). Its primary meaning is 'in the past, long time ago' and is illustrated in (9).

(8) a. *OKato*   *a-a-ik-ire*   ***irai***   *e*   *Kampala.*
       Kato   1S-PST-reach-PFV   **in.the.past** 23.LOC   Kampala
       'Kato is already in Kampala' or 'Kato has already reached Kampala.'
       (elicited)
    b. *Oisenga*   *wa-amu*   *n-a-ku-koba*   *nti*
       aunt(1)   1-2sgPOSS   NAR-1S-2sgO-say   QUOT
       nje   *n-a-ku-komeirye*   ***irai***   *musigazi.*
       1sg   1sgS-PST-2sgO-choose.APPL.PFV **in.the.past**   boy(1)
       'Your aunt would tell you "I have already selected for you a boy".'
       (LL-N-BBALE-170220-FS-2)
    c. *Ba-a-fun-ire*   ***irai***   *obugaiga.*
       2S-PST-acquire-PFV **in.the.past**   wealth(12)
       'They have already acquired wealth.'
       (LL-R-WSKAYUNGA-170217-FS-1A)

(9) *Era* ***eirai***   *ba-a-tu-emba-nga*   *nti* ...
    and   **in.the.past**   1S-PST-1plO-sing-HAB   QUOT
    'And in the past they used to sing about us ... '
    (LL-N-BBALE-170220-FS-2)

Third, a plain perfective form is occasionally translated into English by the speakers of Ruuli with 'already', as in (10).

(10) *O-a-sanga*   *nga*   *a-gu-tund-**ire**.*
     2sgS-PST-encounter CONJ   1S-3O-sell-**PFV**
     'You would encounter (him), when he has **already** sold it.'
     (LL-X-KIBBALE-170221-FS-2)

2.3 Summary

In what follows we summarize our observations of the expressions of phasal polarity following Kramer's (2017) six parameters, which in turn are based on the synthesis of Löbner's *Duality Hypothesis* (Löbner 1989), van der Auwera's *Double Alternative Hypothesis* and *Continuative Paradigm* (van der Auwera 1993, 1998), as well as Van Baar's (1997) *Phasal polarity typology*. The six parameters are coverage, telicity, wordhood, paradigmaticity, expressibility, and pragmaticity. The first three parameters deal with the semantic properties of the phasal polarity, whereas the other three cover their structural properties. Table 1 summarizes the individual constructions presented in Sections 2.1 and 2.2.

Table 1: The expression of phasal polarity concepts in Ruuli.

ALREADY no dedicated expression, a complement taking verb *mala* 'to finish', the adverb *irai* 'in the past, long time ago', as well as the perfective are used		NO LONGER NEG + *kya-* 'PERS' on the main verb
		external negation
NOT YET *kya-* 'PERS' on *li* 'be' + INF of the main verb	internal negation	STILL *kya-* 'PERS' on the main verb

As was indicated in Section 2.1, though the three constructions used to encode the phasal polarity expressions of STILL, NOT YET and NO LONGER are different, they all employ the persistive prefix *kya-*. There is no dedicated expression for ALREADY and several encoding techniques are employed: These are the periphrastic construction with the verb *mala* 'to finish', the adverb *irai* 'in the past', as well as the form with the regular perfective suffix *-ire* and its allomorphs. Thus, Ruuli can be characterized as a language with a flexible phasal polarity coverage system. Furthermore, with respect to the parameter of expressibility, Ruuli has one structural gap, namely for the expression of ALREADY, which is not overtly marked by a dedicated item. Finally, with respect to the parameter of wordhood, Ruuli employs a bound prefix (the persistive *kya-*) to express STILL, NOT YET and NO LONGER.

The remaining four parameters of pragmaticity, telicity, expressibility and paradigmaticity deserve some elaboration and are discussed in Sections 3 to 6 respectively.

3 Pragmaticity

In this section we discuss the pragmatic properties of the phasal polarity in Ruuli. Kramer's (2017) pragmaticity parameter is based on van der Auwera's (1993) *Double Alternative Hypothesis*, i.e. a phasal polarity expression may signal two different scenarios depending on a language and context, viz. differentiate between pragmatically neutral phasal polarity expressions involving temporal-sequentially related phases and counterfactual phasal polarity expressions where a positive situation is contrasted to a simultaneously expected negative situation.

Many examples from the corpus, as well as elicited examples suggest that both the neutral and counterfactual interpretations are possible with this expression. Examples (11)–(12) illustrate the concept STILL encoded with the persistive prefix *kya-*. (11) is uttered in a situation where one speaker mentioned that his parents died long ago. Another speaker reacts to it with the utterances in (11). As the speakers know each other, only the pragmatically neutral interpretation is possible, whereas the counterfactual reading is very unlikely. In a different context, however, e.g. when the speakers do not know each other, these two utterances are open to the counterfactual reading.

(11) Naye   nje   n-**kya**-li   mwana.
     but   1sg   1sgS-PERS-be   child(1)
     Oite   w-ange   n'   omange ba-**kya**-li   ba-omi.
     father(1)   1-1sgPOSS   COM   my.mother(1)-2S-PERS-be   2-alive
     'But as for me, I am **still** a child. My father and mother are **still** alive.'
     (LL-N-KYERIMA-170220-FS-8)

(12) provides a counterfactual example of STILL: The speaker was asked about the ongoing drought and the famine it was expected to cause. The speaker's answer ('we still have sweet potatoes') contradicts the expectation of the interlocutor, as in reality the speaker's family still has enough food and is not experiencing any famine.

(12) Onzala   a-li=wo   naye onzala   ti-ya-maani muno.
    famine(9)   1S-be=16.LOC   but   famine(9) NEG-9-big   much
    Abantu   ba-lina   emmere,
    man(2)   2S-have   food(9)
    ebiyaata   bi-baire   bi-**kya**-li=wo.
    sweet.potato(8) 8-AUX.PFV   8S-**PERS**-be=16.LOC

    Tu-**kya**-li   ku-ika   ku   nzala   ya   maani.
    1plS-**PERS**-be INF-reach   17.LOC   famine(9)   9. GEN strength(9)
    'There is famine, but it is not too bad. People have food, we still have sweet potatoes. We have **not yet** reached the terrible famine.'
    (LL-N-KYERIMA-170218-NA-3)

Also the two other phasal polarity expression built with the persistive *kya-* (NOT YET and NO LONGER) allow both the neutral and the counterfactual reading without any encoding difference.

The counterfactual scenario for NOT YET is illustrated with the last utterance in (12) ('We have not yet reached the terrible famine') produced in the same context discussed above. The neutral reading of NOT YET is illustrated in (13). It is quite common in temporal adverbial clauses:

(13) Nga ebidima bi-kya-li   kw-iza   tu-a-lum-isya-nga   busika
    CONJ hoe(8)   8S-PERS-be INF-come   1plS-PST-dig-CAUS-HAB small.hoe(10)
    bu-ni.
    10-PROX
    'Before the hoes arrive (lit. when hoes did not yet arrive), we dug with these small hoes.'
    (LL-N-KIDERA-170221-FS-5A)

The encoding of the concept NO LONGER with the persistive *kya-* can also have both readings. The last utterance in (14) illustrates the neutral reading. This utterance is part of the discussion of the traditional practices and all the interlocutors are well aware that there are no more prayers to the traditional gods (i.e. that there is a consensus negative situation) and no expectations of the positive situations are available in this scenario.

(14) Oku   isana   ni-ba-aba   ni   ba-ramya.
     17.LOC   drought(5)   NAR-2S-go   CONJ 2S-pray
     Obundi   oKanca   ni-a-ba-juna   oikendi   ni-a-toony.
     sometimes   God(1)   NAR-1S-2O-help rain(1)   NAR-1S-rain

     Olundi   ni-a-gaana.
     sometimes   NAR-1S-fail
     Naye   lwaki   ti-tu-**kya**-bi-kola   enaku   zi-ni   bairange?
     but   why   NEG-1plS-PERS-7O-do   day(10) 10-PROX   my.friend(2)
     'During the drought, they would go and pray. Sometimes God would help them, and it would rain. Sometimes it would not (rain). But why are we **no longer** doing them (i.e. the prayers to the traditional gods) nowadays, my friends?'
     (LL-N-WSKAYUNGA-170218-FS-1A)

An example of the counterfactual scenario of the use of NO LONGER is given in (15). The first speaker (not part of the example) explains in details how one used to collect water from various sources. The second speaker exclaims in surprise the utterance in (15), following which the first speaker lists various reasons (deforestation, etc.) as to why water stopped coming from the ground counter to the second speaker's expectations.

(15) Amaizi   ag-o   **ti-ga-kya-liga**   mu   itakali   oba?
     water(6) 6-MED   NEG-6S-PERS-come   18.LOC   ground(5)   INTER
     'That water no longer comes from the ground?'
     (LL-R-WSKAYUNGA-170218-FS-4)

With all the three phasal polarity expressions build with the persistive prefix *kya-* the neutral reading is much more common in the data from the corpus. On the other hand, during the elicitation sessions the speakers more readily provided examples or contexts for examples with the phasal polarity items with the counterfactual reading. We explain this observation not by its centrality to the phasal polarity items presented above but rather by its pragmatic 'extremity' in Van Baar's (1997) terms and thus easier interpretability to the speakers, who can fall back on such notions as surprise.

As with other means of expression of phasal polarity in Ruulu, also the non-specialized expressions of the phasal polarity concept ALREADY (see Section 2.2 for some examples) allow for a counterfactual reading: In (16) both the context of the story, as well as the interjection *haa!* signal a surprise:

(16) *Haa! Ba-ku-aba oku-iza owakame nga a-a-ab-ire*
INTERJ 2S-PROG-go INF-come rabbit(1) CONJ 1S-PST-go.PFV
irai.
in.the.past
'Ha! By the time they got there, Mr. Rabbit had already left. (And then they started chasing him.)'
(LL-N-KITATYA-170220-FS-6)

The majority of examples of ALREADY are often ambiguous between the phasal polarity and non-phasal polarity reading. Among the tokens interpreted as expressing ALREADY by the speakers the majority has the neutral reading.

4 Telicity

In the section we discuss the telicity parameter of the phasal polarity and give a description of the turning points of the telic expressions ALREADY and NO LONGER. The telicity parameter in Kramer's position paper is based on van der Auwera's (1998: 50) classification of the ALREADY concept in three groups depending on the points of polarity change. The point of polarity change can be relatively early, late or general in comparison to the background assumption.

As we discussed in Section 2.2, the Ruuli adverb *irai* can be interpreted as ALREADY in certain contexts. It can also be used in the counterfactual situation with an "early" evaluation of the point of change, as in (17): In (17a) the girl is not expected to be at school at this age, in (17b) Mr. Rabbit escaped too early, before his captors came back.

(17) a. *Omwara w-ange owa myaka eibiri naye a-a-ab-ire*
daughter(1) 1-1sgPOSS 1.GEN year(4) two but 1S-PST-go-PFV
irai *omu isomero.*
in.the.past 18.LOC school(5)
'My daughter is 2 years old, but she is already going to school.' (elicited)

b. *Haa! Ba-ku-aba oku-iza owakame nga a-a-ab-ire*
   INTERJ 2S-PROG-go INF-come rabbit(1) CONJ 1S-PST-go.PFV
   irai.
   in.the.past
   'Ha! By the time they got there, Mr. Rabbit had already left. (And then they started chasing him.)'
   (LL-N-KITATYA-170220-FS-6)

Also, the construction with the verb *mala* 'to finish' seems to only express the EARLY point of change with counterfactual readings, as in (18).

(18) Context: The hunters installed the nets and then started to flash the animals with some noise. When the animals hear the noise, they run to escape from this noise.)
   *Kaisite **ba-maare** oku-bi-tayiiza.*
   yet   **2S-finish.PFV**   INF-8O-surround
   'And yet they have **already** surrounded them. (And these animals fell into the nets.)'
   (LL-R-NAKASONGOLA-170224-FS-1B)

The other telic phasal polarity expression which can have different turning points is NO LONGER. The turning points of the NO LONGER expression, i.e. late, early, and general, are all marked with the same item, as in (19).

(19) *Bantu ti-ba-kya-endya ku-kola bbe.*
   person(2) NEG-2S-PERS-want INF-work no
   'People no longer want to work, no.'
   (LL-N-BBALE-170220-FS-2)

An example of the counterfactual scenario with NO LONGER is given in (20). The first speaker explains in detail how one used to collect water from various sources. The second speaker exclaims in surprise the utterance in (20), following which the first speaker lists various reasons (deforestation, etc.) as to why water stopped coming from the ground counter to the second speaker's expectations. Example (15) repeated as (20a) shows that the turning point (water stopping from coming) is earlier than expected. The elicited example in (20b) provides an additional illustration.

(20) a. *Amaizi   ag-o   **ti-ga-kya**-liga   mu   itakali   oba?*
 water(6) 6-MED NEG-6S-PERS-come 18.LOC ground(5) INTER
 'That water no longer comes from the ground?'
 (LL-R-WSKAYUNGA-170218-FS-4)
 b. *N-a-taka-nga   oku-bona Edwardi e   Kampala naye*
 1sgS-PST-want-HAB INF-see Edward 23.LOC Kampala but
 t-a-kya-li   *mu   Kampala.*
 NEG-1S-PERS-be 18.LOC Kampala
 'I wanted to meet Edward in Kampala, but he is **no longer** in Kampala.'
 (elicited)

5 Expressibility

Expressibility concerns the possibility of formal coding of phasal polarity expressions (Kramer 2017). As mentioned in Section 2.2, Ruuli lacks a specialized expression for the concept ALREADY, whereas the other three concepts STILL, NO LONGER, NOT YET are marked with a dedicated construction. This gap is in line with Van Baar's (1997: 118) prediction that in languages with one gap in the phasal polarity-system, either NO LONGER or ALREADY would be missing.

The phasal polarity meaning of ALREADY can be provided by the functionally vague construction with the adverb *irai* 'in the past, earlier', illustrated in (5), one of the examples is repeated in (21) for convenience.

(21) *Ba-a-fun-ire   **irai**   obugaigai.*
 2S-PST-acquire-PFV **in.the.past** wealth(12)
 'They have already acquired wealth.'
 (LL-R-WSKAYUNGA-170217-FS-1A)

In line with Kramer's (2017) reasoning, one can argue that though expressions such as the one in (21) come close to the meaning of ALREADY, *irai* 'in the past' on its own only makes reference to the timing of the (positive) state of affairs and by itself does not presuppose an earlier negative state.

Section 2.2 also discussed another way of the expression of ALREADY via the construction with the predicate *mala* 'to finish'. A naturalistic example illustrating the phasal polarity reading is given in (4a). An elicited example is provided in (22): it can be interpreted as a simple perfective (22a), as a construction with the phasal polarity reading of ALREADY (22b), as well as a complementation construction in (22c) which links two separate states-of-affairs, viz. 'to finish' and 'to cook'.

(22) **O-maare**   oku-sumba.
  2sgS-finish.PFV INF-cook
  a. 'You have cooked.'
  b. 'You have already cooked.'
  c. 'You have finished cooking.' (elicited)

In elicitations speakers also accept a combination of the complement-taking predicate *mala* 'to finish' with the adverb *irai* 'in the past', as in (23). Speakers invariably translate such examples with 'already'. This combination, however, never occurs in our corpus.

(23) *N-a-***maare**   ***irai***   oku-bona ente   itaanu.
  1sgS-PST-**finish.PFV** **in.the.past** INF-see cow(10) five
  'I have already seen five cows.' (elicited)

6 Paradigmaticity

This section discusses the parameter "paradigmaticity". Not much needs to be added about internal paradigmaticity. As Table 1 shows, in terms of internal paradigmaticity Ruuli has an asymmetric phasal polarity paradigm.

From an external viewpoint, the paradigmaticity parameter describes the relation between members of the phasal polarity paradigms and members of the corresponding non-phasal polarity paradigms, restricted to paradigms of the domains of Tense, Mood and Aspect. Before we discuss the properties of interaction of the phasal polarity with the tense-aspect system, we will give a short introduction into the tense-aspect system of Ruuli. Ruuli has an elaborate tense-aspect system similar to other Bantu languages (see, for example, Botne & Kershner 2008 and Nurse 2008). The tense markers are prefixes, whereas the aspect markers can be both prefixes, as well as suffixes. Ruuli overtly marks the past and the future. The present is an unmarked form. As other Bantu languages (Nurse 2008: 22), Ruuli makes a distinction between remote and recent past, as well as between remote and recent future. The distance between remote and recent past and likewise the future is measured as follows: for the recent past starting from 'just a few minutes ago' (immediate past) until today earlier time (might also include events from yesterday); concerning the remote past the cut-off point is starting from yesterday and earlier. The remote and recent past and future are differentiated by tone. In the present, only three tense-aspect forms can be used: the unmarked present, the progressive (marked by the prefix *ku-*) and the persistive form with the prefix *kya-*, which either expresses STILL (with a positive verb form) or NOT YET (with a negative verb form) (see Section 2.1).

The regular persistive is used without any tense-aspect-marker. However, the prefix *kya-* can appear with the perfective suffix *-ire*. The perfective suffix *-ire* on its own "indicates the view of a situation as a single whole, without distinction of the various separate phases that make up that situation" (Comrie 1976: 16). The semantics of the construction with the prefix *kya-* and the perfective suffix *-ire* is slightly different due to the aspectual properties of the perfective suffix. Examples taking persistive *kya-* and perfective *-ire* no longer express the phasal polarity meaning STILL, instead they express the meaning often translated with 'so far', as in (24), i.e. it describes an event or state which happened in the past and was ongoing, it might but does not have to end at some later phase, thus there is no contrast of situations with different polarity values. A similar situation in Hausa is discussed in Van Baar (1997: 153).

(24) a. *N-**kya**-li-**ire**   matooke   go-nkai.*
    1sgS-PERS-eat-PFV matoke(6) 6-only
    'So far, I have eaten only matoke (and nothing else).' (elicited)
  b. *Yee n-**kya**-byal-**ire**   baala ba-ereere.*
    yes 1sgS-PERS-give.birth.to-PFV girl(2) 2-only
    'Yes, I have so far given birth **only** to girls.'
    (LL-R-NAKASONGOLA-170225-FS-1A)

According to the examples (24), we conclude that Ruuli has an asymmetric paradigm which has a non-corresponding relationship between the phasal polarity item and the specific tense-aspect markers.

7 Concluding remarks

In this paper we discussed the phasal polarity in Ruuli in terms of Kramer's (2017) six parameters: coverage, wordhood, pragmaticity, telicity, expressibility, and paradigmaticity.

To conclude, we can say that Ruuli has a flexible phasal polarity system involving one item, i.e. prefix *kya-* to express the three concepts of STILL, NOT YET and NO LONGER. The concept of ALREADY is expressed either by a complement-taking verb, or by an adverb, or occasionally by the plain perfective, therefore there is a gap in terms of expressibility. Furthermore, there is no difference in the encoding of counterfactual and neutral scenarios in terms of paradigmaticity, as well as in the point of the polarity changes in terms of telicity, since these concepts use the same item, the interpretation of which depends on the context. The paradigmaticity parameter is analyzed as asymmetric due to the non-corresponding relationship of the phasal polarity item and semantics of the tense-aspect markers.

Abbreviations

1, 2, 3, etc.	noun class	PERS	persistive
APPL	applicative	PFV	perfective
CONJ	conjunction	POSS	possessive
HAB	habitual	PST	past
INF	infinitive	pl	plural
INTER	interjection	S	subject
LOC	locative	sg	singular
NAR	narrative	O	object
NEG	negation	QUOT	quotative

Appendix 1: Tense and aspect forms in Ruuli

Tense-aspect	Pattern	AUX	sumb 'cook'
Present	S[1]-PRS-Σ-PFV		s-Ø-súmb-à
Present Progressive	S-PROG-Σ-FV		s-ku-súmb-à
Persistive I	S-PERS-Σ-FV		s-kya-súmb-à
Past	S-PST-Σ-FV		s-á-súmb-à
Near Future I	S-FUT-Σ-FV		s-à-sùmb-á
Remote Future	S-FUT-Σ-FV		s-lí-súmb-à
Immediate Perfective	S-Σ-FFV		s-sùmb-írè
Recent Perfective	S-PST-Σ-PFV		s-á-súmb-írè
Remote Perfective	S-PST-Σ-RPFV		s-á-sùmb-ìré
Recent Habitual Past	S-PST-Σ-FV-HAB		s-á-sumb-a-ngà
Remote Habitual Past	S-PST-Σ-FV-RHAB		s-á-sùmb-à-ngá
Near Habitual Future	S-FUT-Σ-FV-HAB		s-à-sumb-a-ngà
Remote Habitual Future	S-FUT-Σ-FV-RHAB		s-à-sùmb-à-ngá
Remote Habitual Future with auxiliary	S-PROG-*iz*-FV INF-Σ-FV-RHAB	*iz* 'come'	s-ku-ìz-á ku-súmb-á-ngà
Persistive 'not yet'	S-PERS-*li* INF-Σ-FV	*li* 'be'	s-kya-li INF-súmb-à
Immediat Past Progressive	S-*bba*-PFV S-PROG-Σ-FV	*bba* 'be'	s-bbá-íré S-PROG-súmb-à
Recent Past Progressive	S-PST-*bba*-PFV S-PST-Σ-FV	*bba* 'be'	s-á-bbá-íré S-PROG-súmb-à
Remote Past Progressive	S-PST-*bba*-PFV S-PROG-Σ-FV	*bba* 'be'	s-á-bbà-ìré S-PROG-súmb-à
Recent Perfective with auxiliary	S-PST-*li* S-Σ-RPFV	*li* 'be'	s-a-li s-sùmb-írè
Remote Perfective with auxiliary	S-PST-*li* S-Σ-RPFV	*li* 'be'	s-á-li s-sumb-iré
Immediate Perfective with auxiliary	S-*bba*-PFV S-Σ-PFV	*bba* 'be'	s-bbá-íré s-sùmb-írè

---

[1] Subject marker.

(continued)

Tense-aspect	Pattern	AUX	sumb 'cook'
Recent Perfective with auxiliary	S-PST-*bba*-PFV S-Σ-PFV	*bba* 'be'	s-*á-bbà-ìrè* s-*sùmb-ìrè*
Remote Perfective with auxiliary	S-PST-*bba*-PFV S-Σ-RPFV	*bba* 'be'	s-*á-bbá-íré* s-*sumb-iré*
Near Future II	S-PROG-*yab*-FV INF-Σ-FV	*yab* 'go'	S-PROG-*yàb-á* INF-*súmb-à*
Future Indefinite	S-PROG-*iz*-FV INF-Σ-FV	*iz* 'come'	S-PROG-*ìz-á* INF-*súmb-à*

Bibliographic references

Botne, Robert & Tiffany L. Kershner. 2008. Tense and cognitive space: On the organization of tense/aspect systems in Bantu languages and beyond. *Cognitive Linguistics* 19 (2): 145–218.

Bybee, Joann, Revere Perkins & William Pagliuca. 1994. *The Evolution of Grammar. Tense, Aspect, and Modality in the Languages of the World*. Chicago: University of Chicago Press.

Comrie, Bernard. 1976. *Aspect*. Cambridge: Cambridge University Press.

Comrie, Bernard. 1985. *Tense*. Cambridge: Cambridge University Press.

Dammann, Ernst. 1956. Das situative Formans *ki* in einigen Bantusprachen. *Mitteilungen des Instituts für Orientforschung* 4.2: 424–434.

Güldemann, Tom. 1998. The relation between imperfective and simultaneous taxis in Bantu: late stages of grammaticalization. In Ines Fiedler, Catherine Griefenow-Mewis & Brigitte Reineke (eds.), *Afrikanische Sprachen im Brennpunkt der Forschung: Linguistische Beiträge zum 12. Afrikanistentag Berlin, 3–6 Oktober 1996*, 157–177. Cologne: Rüdiger Köppe.

Hewson, John, Derek Nurse & Henry Muzale. 2000. Chronogenetic staging of tense in Ruhaya. *Studies in African Linguistics*. 29 (2): 33–58.

Katamba, Francis. 2003. Bantu nominal morphology. In Derek Nurse & Gérard Philippson (eds.), *The Bantu languages*, 103–120. London: Routledge.

Kramer, Raija. 2017. *Position paper on Phasal Polarity expressions*. Unpublished manuscript. University of Hamburg. https://www.aai.uni-hamburg.de/afrika/php2018/medien/position-paper-on-php.pdf

Löbner, Sebastian. 1989. Schon - erst - noch: An integrated analysis. Linguistics and Philosophy 12 (2): 167–212.

Löfgren, Althea. 2018. *Phasal Polarity Systems in East Bantu*. Stockholm: Stockholm University bachelor thesis.

Marten, Lutz. 1998. Swahili -*kwisha*: sketching the path of grammaticalization. *SOAS Working Papers in Linguistics and Phonetics* 8: 141–163
Muzale, Henry. 1998. *A reconstruction of the Proto-Rutara Tense/Aspect System*. St. John's: University of Newfoundland dissertation.
Nurse, Derek. 2003. Aspect and tense in Bantu languages. In Derek Nurse & Gérard Philippson (eds.), *The Bantu Languages*, 90–102. London: Routledge.
Nurse, Derek & Gérard Philippson (eds.). 2003. *The Bantu languages*. London: Routledge.
Nurse, Derek. 2008. *Tense and Aspect in Bantu*. Oxford: Oxford University Press.
Schoenbrun, David L. 1997. *The historical reconstruction of Great Lakes Bantu: Etymologies and distributions*. Cologne: Rüdiger Köppe.
Sørensen, Marie-Louise & Alena Witzlack-Makarevich. 2020. Clausal Complementation in Ruuli. Studies in African Linguistics 49 (1): 84–110.
Uganda Bureau of Statistics. 2016. *The National Population and Housing Census 2014 – Main Report*. Kampala, Uganda.
Van Baar, Theodorus M. 1997. *Phasal polarity*. Dordrecht: Foris Publications.
Van de Velde, Mark. 2019. Nominal morphology and syntax. In Mark Van de Velde, Koen Bostoen, Derek Nurse & Gérard Philippson, *The Bantu Languages*, 2nd Edition, 237–269. London: Routledge.
van der Auwera, Johan. 1993. 'Already' and 'still': Beyond duality. *Linguistics and philosophy* 16 (6): 613–653.
van der Auwera, Johan. 1998. Phasal Adverbials in the languages of Europe. In Johan van der Auwera & Dónall P.O. Baoill (eds.), *Adverbial constructions in the languages of Europe*, 25–145. Berlin: Mouton de Gruyter.

Nico Nassenstein, Helma Pasch
Phasal polarity in Lingala and Sango

1 Introduction

The present article investigates expressions of phasal polarity or sequential polarity in the two most important vehicular languages of the north-western half of the Congo-Ubangi basin, Sango and Lingala (see Map 1). As is true for many other African languages (Kramer 2017: 1), phasal polarity has not yet been a topic of investigation in the two languages.

The two languages are dealt with in this article because they emerged in their present forms as a result of the conquest of the territories along the Congo and Ubangi rivers during colonization of the Congo basin and Ubangi-Shari by the Belgians and the French. While from the very beginning Lingala had influence on Sango (Pasch in print), the reverse was not the case. A linguistic feature motivating the discussion of the two languages in one article is that some of the phasal polarity items are derived from verbs and they still have verbal features.

Expressions of phasal polarity describe bi-phase situations in which the two phases are related sequentially. They are, furthermore, contrasted to each other by opposite polarities which are indicated by phasal polarity items, usually adverbs. The transition of polarity takes place at the points where the first phase ends and the second phase begins. Phasal polarity is discussed on the basis of four phases, which are often named after the respective English phasal polarity items: NOT YET, ALREADY, STILL and NO LONGER. Van Baar (1997: 1) illustrates the four phases in examples (1a–d).

(1) a. Peter is *not yet* in London
     b. Peter is *already* in London
     c. Peter is *still* in London
     d. Peter is *no longer* in London

On a timeline, the phases are arranged as illustrated in Figure 1.

Van Baar claims that these expressions not only describe situations, followed or preceded by another situation of opposite polarity, but also indicate the speaker's attitude towards the situation described. In his example (b), *already*

Nico Nassenstein, Johannes Gutenberg-Universität Mainz
Helma Pasch, Universität zu Köln

https://doi.org/10.1515/9783110646290-005

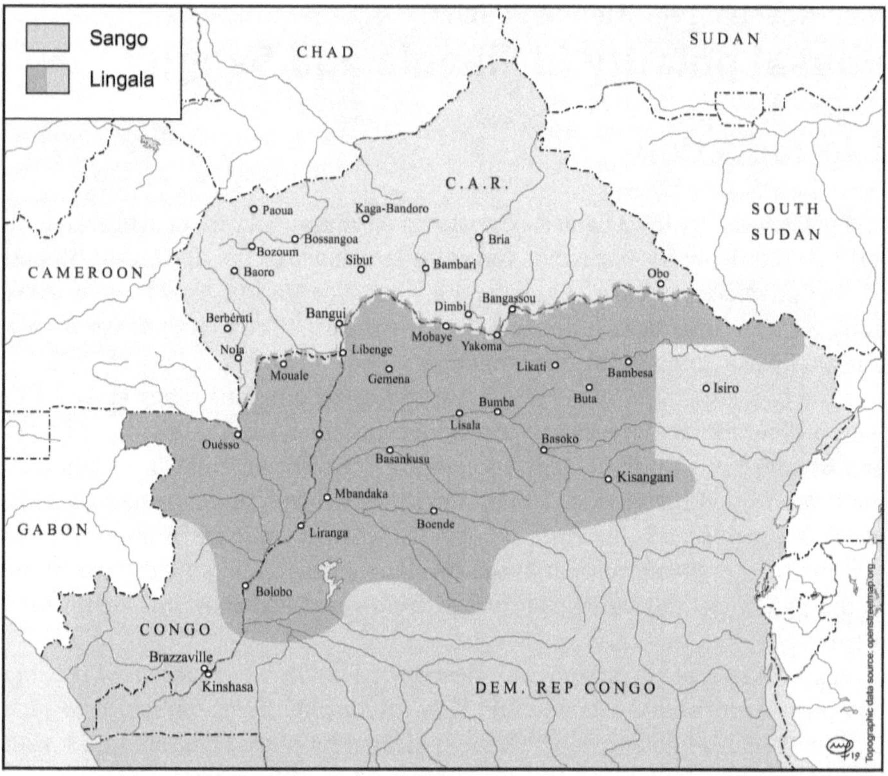

Map 1: Geographical distribution of Lingala and Sango.

indicates either that the situation described has begun at a preceding point, or that the speaker assumes that it has begun earlier than actually expected. The concept *still* expresses the continuation of a state, while *not yet* conveys

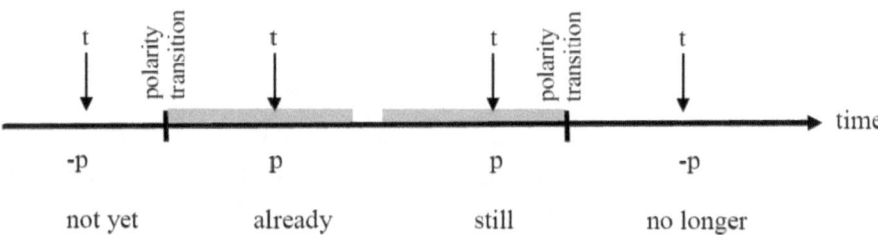

Figure 1: Organization of the four polarity phases on a timeline (adapted from Van der Auwera 1989: 43).

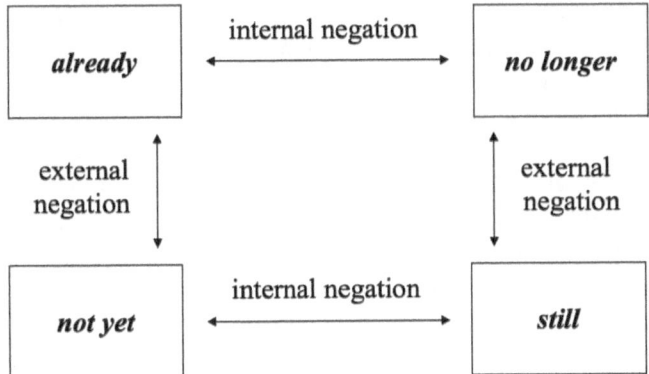

Figure 2: Semantic relations between phasal polarity concepts (Löbner 1989: 172).

the negation of such continuation and *no longer* expresses the discontinuity of a situation. Continuation is apparently irrelevant with regard to *already*. To the binary features of positive (p) and negative polarity (–p), Smessaert (2009) adds the attributes "beginning" and "ending", as well as "prospective" and "retrospective". The NOT YET phase has a prospective view on the beginning of a coming situation while the ALREADY phase has a retrospective view on the beginning of an ongoing situation. The STILL phase is prospective with regard to the ending of an ongoing situation and the NO LONGER phase is retrospective with regard to the end of a past situation.

According to Löbner (1989), expressions of phasal polarity are related in a system of external and internal negation. In his *Duality Hypothesis*, he claims that they are the negatives of one another by external or internal negation. External negation is here understood as the negation of the entire clause, and internal negation as that of one or more constituents.

In the languages investigated in this article – both contact languages that have undergone a considerable degree of change throughout the course of their history (see Meeuwis 2006, Pasch 1997) – the marking of phasal polarity is less frequent than in the European languages investigated by Van Baar (1997) and Van der Auwera (1998). In many cases, it is not obligatory, nor unequivocally used and understood; but is instead dependent on context, culture and world knowledge. The analysis is not always easy, because the items used for indications of phasal polarity are also used with other meanings. In texts, expressions of phasal polarity are fairly rare, and, when eliciting examples from language consultants, the frequency of such expressions increases with the acquaintance and understanding of the types of constructions that the researcher is looking for.

Our aim is to outline indications of phasal polarity in Lingala and Sango in order to determine the semantic differences and commonalities of the indicating items. Furthermore, it is to explore whether similar forms and constructions could be the result of contact between the languages or from contact with French. Our hypothesis is that phasal polarity concepts in Sango and Lingala reveal a structural similarity greater than Lingala shares with other Bantu languages (see Schadeberg 1990, Löfgren 2018). In both languages, a considerable degree of variation and competing strategies are found (see Sections 2.1 for the ALREADY phase in Lingala and 3.2 for the expression of STILL and NOT YET in Sango) with slight contextual differences.

The paper is organized as follows: Section (2) deals with phasal polarity in Lingala, Section (3) describes phasal polarity in Sango. Preliminary conclusions are drawn in Section (4), with a specific focus on borrowed and shared strategies; including the discussion of phasal polarity in the context of interaction and contact between languages. The data presented is mainly drawn from elicited examples with speakers of both languages unless otherwise noted.

2 Lingala

Lingala[1] is a Bantu language spoken in the Congo basin by at least 25 million speakers as an L1 or L2 language, (re-)classified as C30B by Maho (2009) with the ISO code [lin]. Lingala emerged out of a contact situation and developed from the 1880s to the turn of the 20th century (Samarin 1986, 1991) out of pidginized Bobangi with Bobangi as its main lexifier (with a high degree of lexical similarity), first labeled *"langue commerciale"*, then "Bangala" (1890s) and later (around 1901) "Lingala" (see Meeuwis 2010, 2013). Contact with different languages such as French, Kiswahili, Kikongo-Kituba and West African languages

---

[1] All Lingala examples were – if not marked differently – kindly provided by Bobo Kitenge, a mother-tongue speaker of Lingala, and thereafter cross-checked and discussed with Carter Omende, who also added helpful explanations on the competing concepts of ALREADY. Some others were taken from a larger Lingala corpus kindly provided by the African Music Archive (AMA), JGU Mainz. We are indebted to the speakers of both languages (especially to our colleague Germain Landi), who helped us to understand the complex concept of phasal categories, and we warmly thank Axel Fleisch for sharing cross-linguistic ideas on the topic. We acknowledge Michael Meeuwis' useful comments and very valuable ideas on an earlier draft of this paper. Warm thanks go to the anonymous reviewers and the volume editor for all support. We are indebted to Kieran Taylor for proofreading the manuscript and improving our English. All common disclaimers apply.

have contributed to radical changes in its structure. From its emergence as a commercial medium it spread upstream via today's Kisangani into the Uele basin and was implemented as a primary medium of the Belgian colonial army (*Force Publique*). A new variety of Lingala was created, standardized and adapted by Catholic (De Boeck 1904) and Protestant missionaries (Stapleton 1903).[2] Today Lingala is one of several national languages in DR Congo and Republic of the Congo, but is not used for official purposes. Along with its prominent use by the police and military in the DR Congo, Lingala is the primary medium of Congolese music, and, as such, has further given rise to several sociolects primarily spoken in the large cities (Nassenstein 2015b). There are some morphological and phonological differences between the Lingala of the capital cities Kinshasa and Brazzaville, rural varieties spoken along the Congo River, and the distinct, yet closely related language Bangala, spoken mainly in the Haut-Uele and Bas-Uele Provinces (classified as C30A).

Structurally, Lingala follows SVO word order and reveals a reduced morphology; especially in terms of plural-marking on the noun (with a tendency to develop a general plural marker of noun class prefix 2 *ba-*), and agreement on the verb (a threefold distinction between +ANIMATE singular and plural, and number neutral −ANIMATE). While subject-marking only reveals the above-mentioned differences in agreement, which stand in contrast to Bobangi which had a full-fledged and class-dependent system,[3] object-marking on the verb and its functions have been taken over by emphatic personal pronouns. Lingala has a complex tense-aspect distinction (Brisard and Meeuwis 2009) which exhibits more intricate differences than that of the neighboring contact language Kikongo-Kituba. Negation functions similarly to Sango (see Section 3) and is marked only by the invariable, clause-final marker *té*. Lexical and grammatical borrowings from French are common. In terms of lexicon, Lingala has further extensively borrowed from English, different varieties of Kikongo, Kiswahili and Portuguese.

Studies that focus on phasal polarity concepts in Bantu languages (see Bernander, Molochieva et al., Guérois, Persohn in this volume) are scarce; yet, numerous Bantu languages make use of morphological STILL markers (e.g., the prefix *-c(y)a-* in some Interlacustrine Bantu languages), sometimes labeled persistive or perstitive (Nurse 2008: 24). Many languages also make use of experiental perfect markers that intrinsically contain a notion of ALREADY, see for

---

[2] In the past decades, these efforts of linguistic engineering have been the topic of criticism in their historical contextualizations and with regard to their inherent language ideologies (Meeuwis 2009).
[3] We are grateful to numerous enlightening discussions with Michael Meeuwis.

instance Kiswahili varieties of the DR Congo with a prefixed aspectual marker *-lishaka-* (Nassenstein 2015a). Schadeberg (1990) analyzes phasal polarity in Kiswahili from the point of view of expectation and counter-expectation. Nurse (2008: 166) also observes "a formal and functional connection between these negative 'not yet/counter-expectional' forms and the persistive" in Bantu. Löfgren (2018) presents the only comparative study on the topic, an overview[4] of data from 46 Bantu languages. She comes to the conclusion that NOT YET is expressed in most of the languages in her sample, while the three other categories are less salient (see Figure 3).

Crosslinguistic frequency of PhP expressions

PhP	NOT YET	ALREADY	STILL	NO LONGER
Distribution	36 (0.78)	16 (0.35)	27 (0.59)	12 (0.26)

Figure 3: Phasal polarity in 46 Bantu languages (Löfgren 2018: 15).

The hierarchy for her set of analyzed Bantu languages (Löfgren 2018: 16) as an overall sample shows considerable differences to that put forward by Van der Auwera (1998).

Lingala is a Bantu language, but language contact and change have contributed to it having a very different system in comparison to other languages from the Bantu area. Phasal polarity in Lingala is marked by the adverb *nánu* when indicating the STILL phase, the negated forms *lisúsu té* for the NO LONGER phase, and *nánu té* for the NOT YET phase. The expression of ALREADY, however, follows another pattern. It may be indicated either by *déjà*, borrowed from French (as is also the case in Sango, see Section 3), or by the auxiliary *sí*, a result of morphological erosion and grammaticalization (Meeuwis 2010). While some speakers regard the two forms as free variants, they are actually used in complementary distribution, depending upon the intended semantics. As can be seen in Figures (4) and (5), the internal negation between NOT YET and STILL along with the external negation between NO LONGER and STILL can be recognized as corresponding phasal markers. The ALREADY phase, however, is not connected to the others and constitutes the most weakly established category (based on our interactions with speakers). Interestingly, there is no borrowed element *encore* ('still') from French, while it is incorporated in Sango (cf. Section 3.3).

---

[4] It is worth mentioning that Löfgren's study is actually a BA thesis.

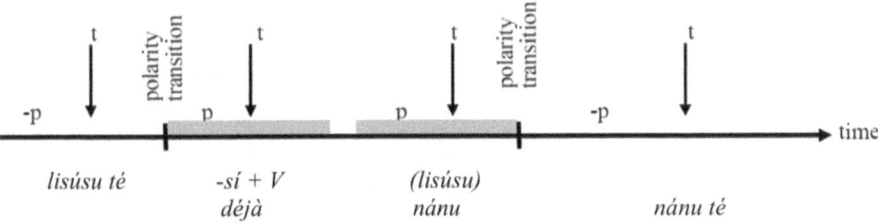

Figure 4: Organization of the four polarity phases of Lingala on a timeline.

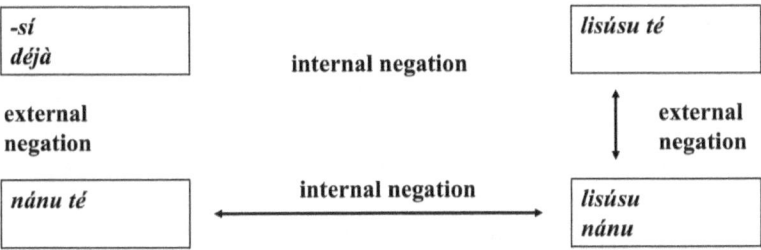

Figure 5: Internal and external negation in the overview of phasal polarity categories in Lingala.

In the following sections, first the expressions of the positive polarity phases will be discussed (2.1–2.2), and then those of the negative polarity phases (2.3–2.4), with a general overview presented in the concluding Section (2.5).

2.1 ALREADY

The ALREADY phase in Lingala can either be expressed with the adverbial *déjà* borrowed from French (2), or with the auxiliary *sí*, a defective verb derived through a process of grammaticalization from the full verb *kosíla* 'finish, end'. *Sí* is only inflected for person and number, not for tense and aspect, e.g., *nasí* 'I already did', *osí* 'you already did', *así* '(s)he already did', etc. and it subordinates the fully inflected main verb (ex. 3). This construction resembles the grammaticalized *-(kw)isha;* a perfect marker across several Bantu languages such as Kiswahili (Ashton 1944), which also has the inherent notion of ALREADY. In contrast, *déjà* is invariable and commonly follows the inflected verb. Both strategies were given by speakers as possible ALREADY items.

(2) na-món-á yó **déjà** na wenze
SM1SG-see-PRS2 2SGO already LOC [NP9]market
'I have already seen you (at an unspecified moment) at the market'[5]

(3) **a-sí** a-pasól-í lí-ki yangó
SM3SG-already SM3SG-break-PRS1 NP5-egg DEM
'She has already broken the egg [and now only eggshells remain; implying that they were intact before].'
(Orchestre Comet Mambo, 1970s)

A more detailed analysis of both constructions reveals a clear semantic difference between them. The *sí* construction is inherently completive and can be explained as a perfect of result (cf. Comrie 1976). With regard to example (4), speakers stressed the fact that, after the women have finished cooking, the food would still be on the table (and hot; thus retrospective and prospective, as it is ready to be eaten), while in (ex. 5), the fact of having eaten results in being full, which marks it as retrospective and completive. In example (6), the speakers explained the completive reading with the argument that an encounter with a leopard has a strong resultative effect on the present moment: the statement that someone has already seen a leopard (in the wilderness) implies that (s)he has survived the encounter, which is both retrospective and resultative.[6] Meeuwis (2010: 141) characterizes this as "already-perfect", and illustrates it with example (7), which implies that the house is now owned by the addressee.

(4) ba-mamá **ba-sí** ba-lámb-í
NP2-woman SM3PL-already SM3PL-cook-PRS1
'The women have already cooked.'

(5) ba-sodá **ba-sí** ba-lí-á
NP2-soldier SM3PL-already SM3PL-eat-PRS2
'The soldiers have already eaten [and are full now].'

---

5 The distinction of present, perfect and past tense in this paper is in agreement with Meeuwis (2010). It has to be noted that there is an extensive discussion on the (debated) tense-aspect system in Lingala, cf. Nurse (2008: 130) and Brisard & Meeuwis (2009), for instance. Meeuwis' model of -í (PRS1), -á (PRS2), -ákí (PST1) and -áká (PST2) is a practical and reader-friendly solution. The co-occurrence of TA markers -í (PRS1) and -á (PRS2) with phasal items in regard to their semantics is not explicitly dealt with here.
6 In most cases an encounter with a leopard is fatal.

(6) **O-sí**   o-món-á   léopard?
    SM2SG-already SM2SG-see-PRS2 leopard
    'Have you already seen a leopard? [If so, you apparently survived.]'

(7) **bo-sí**   bo-sómb-í   ndáko
    SM2PL-already SM2PL-buy-PRS1 [NP9]house
    'You have already bought a house.'
    (adapted from Meeuwis 2010: 141)

Unlike the grammaticalized *sí*, the French *déjà* may also be employed in cases where no completive reading is intended. Furthermore, it can also be used when the retrospective point of view either refers back to an unspecified (ex. 8) or a specific ongoing situation (ex. 9) that causes results or after-effects (of a situation that had been caused long before). In other cases, *déjà* indicates past tense in collocation with verbs borrowed from French that do not license TA markers (ex. 10); however, such constructions are rare.

(8) na-kend-á   **déjà**   Brazzaville
    SM1SG-go-PRS2 already B.
    'I already went to Brazzaville [at some point; implying I already know Brazzaville].'

(9) e-band-ákí   ko-béba **déjà**   na 1969
    SM3SG:INAN-begin-PST1 INF-rot   already LOC 1969
    'It already started to worsen in 1969.'
    (http://www.mbokamosika.com)

(10) Fally a-gagné   **déjà**   fara-fara   du siècle
     F.   SM3SG-win already   "phare-à-phare"-concert of.the.century
     '[The] musician Fally [Ipupa] already won the competitive show of the century.'
     (http://www.mbokamosika.com)

In example (11) both markers of the ALREADY phase are found, with very different meanings. This sentence was elicited when trying to collect better examples to illustrate the completive reading of *sí*. The language consultant eventually found an example that makes evident the contrasting uses and meanings of *déjà* and *si*. The two items can describe two simultaneous but different situations, or one situation from two perspectives. The completed action, the cooking being completed (the food being ready to eat) is indicated by *sí*. In the new situation where the same food is "already boiling" (waiting to be eaten), ALREADY is expressed with *déjà* which has no sense of completion but is clearly inchoative and prospective. We may conclude that, out of the two ALREADY items in example (11), the one related to the completed cooking event is retrospective and the other, related to the steaming food ready to be eaten, is prospective.[7]

(11) ba-mamá **ba-sí** ba-lámb-í, bi-lóko
 NP2-woman SM3PL-already SM3PL-cook-PRS1 NP8-thing
 e-bél-í **déjà**
 SM3SGINAN-boil-PRS1 already
 'The women have already cooked [added all ingredients and heated the saucepan] and the things are now already boiled/ready.'

Actual inchoative aspects may also be expressed with the verb *koyá* 'to come' (ex. 12), which often is not in harmony with the ALREADY meaning of *sí* (completive) or *déjà* (non-completive), but rather has the meaning 'finally'. It appears to indicate counter-expectation, i.e. a situation materialized only after the addressee had expected it to do so.

(12) to-yá-ákí ko-yóka yangó malámu
 SM1PL-come-PST1 INF-hear O3SG:INAN good
 'We came to understand it well/we finally understood it correctly.'
 (adapted from Meeuwis 2010: 140)

The marker *-á* is a third implicit strategy that indicates the ALREADY phase. Translations of verbs with this suffix contain often the adverb 'already'; as can also be seen in example (13). In the grammars of Lingala, the suffix *-á* is usually analyzed as a perfective marker, indicating a resulting state (with stative verbs) or the endpoint of an action (with dynamic verbs) (Meeuwis 2010: 130). However, Nurse (2008: 52) characterizes it as the 'far past' and adds in a footnote that the

---

7 A more general discussion (to be conducted elsewhere) could also critically address the question whether the strategies employed in Lingala and other Bantu languages actually correspond to the sense of ALREADY expressed with phasal items in European languages. Alternatively, the strategies in Lingala could potentially be subsumed under the label ALTERATIVE, changing a state or alternating an event (also including counter-expectations). We are grateful to Axel Fleisch for profound discussions on this matter.

distinction of the suffixed markers -í vs. -á may sometimes be encoded as "perfective vs. anterior" (ibid.) in analogy with corresponding forms in the lexifier language Bobangi.

(13) mo-lakisi   a-kaból-á   ba-cahier   epái   ya   ba-ána
SM1-teacher SM3SG-distribute-PRS2 NP2-workbook among CON NP2-child
'The teacher already distributed the workbooks among the children.'

2.2 STILL

The item *nánu*, an invariable adverb sometimes spelt *naino* according to old missionary grammars, is the equivalent of 'still' and can stand in various positions in the Lingala sentence. Most often it is in the clause-initial position or follows the verb. It indicates that, at a point of reference in the STILL phase, a situation is given that will no longer be given at another reference point in the next phase (as in 14). A second item indicating STILL is the adverb *lisúsu* 'again, further, more', which is derived from *mosúsu* (PL *misúsu*) 'other'.

Examples (14–15) show, furthermore, that *nánu* may also indicate that an ongoing situation began in the preceding phase. In the subsequent phase, the action has already been accomplished and the necessity for it to be done is therefore no longer given. The phasal items *nánu* and *lisúsu* are the only STILL items found in Lingala as there is no persistive affix as in other Bantu languages. In contrast to the ALREADY phase, which may be marked by an item borrowed from French, Lingala has not borrowed the French adverb *encore* to express the STILL phase.

(14) a-zó-ték-a   **nánu** na zándo
SM3SG-PRG-sell-FV still LOC [NP9]market
'(S)he is still selling at the market.'

(15) óyo e-seng-él-ákí   **nánu** ko-sál-ama
DEM SM3SG:INAN-beg-APPL-PST1 still INF-do-PASS
'This (one) that still had to be done.'

(16) e-zal-í   **nánu** mwá pási
SM3SG:INAN-be-PRS1 still a.bit difficult
'It is still a bit difficult.'

There is a semantic overlap between the phasal items for STILL, *nánu* and *lisúsu* ('more, again, further'). It can be observed in particular when speakers talk about remaining amounts of inherently diminishing liquids or masses (countable and uncountable), such as "three beers" (ex. 17) or "5,000 francs" (ex. 18), i.e. they may have been larger at a point of reference in the preceding phase. Here, phasal polarity is not restricted to a measurement of time, as such, but to time in correlation with an expectable decrease of the respective amounts. For example, the fact that there are still three beers (left), means that at some point of reference in the next phase some of the beer will no longer remain. Some speakers, however, do not recognize any difference between *nánu* and *lisúsu*, but use them as free variants despite their divergent semantic readings; as in (17) and (18). These speakers confirmed that either item could be used in the two sentences.

(17) ma-sanga   e-zal-í   **nánu** misáto na frigo
 NP6-alcohol SM3SG:INAN-be-PRS1 still three LOC [NP9]fridge
 'There are still three beers in the fridge/ . . . left.'

(18) mw-ána mo-báli a-zal-í   **lisúsu** na 5,000 francs
 NP1-child NP3-man SM3SG-be-PRS1 more COM NUM francs
 'The boy still has 5,000 francs/ . . . left/also . . . has (apart from other things).'

The semantically close iterative meaning of *nánu* has been mentioned by De Boeck (1904: 22) in his prescriptive study. For '*répète (dis encore)*' [repeat (say again)] he gives the Lingala expressions *loba lisusu* and *loba naïnu*. In current use, this function has been taken over by *lisúsu* – at least when talking about upholding the intention to do something. This meaning is close to that of *nánu* in (19); where the attitude of the speaker plays a role. In some elicited examples where one would expect *nánu*, speakers opted for *lisúsu* when the same iterative meaning ('again') was intended.

(19) O-ling-í   **lisúsu** ko-kende ville?
 SM2SG-like-PRS1 still   INF-go   city
 'Do you still want to go to town?/Do you want to go to town again?/Do you also want to go to town (in addition to other things)?'

The semantic complexity of *nánu* is increased further through its use as modal particle, as in *Toséka nánu moké!* ('So, let's first laugh a bit!'/'Let's then laugh for a bit!'). In most contexts, when serving as modal particle, it can be translated as 'first'.

Nánu and *lisúsu*, along with being synonymous STILL items, are also used in negative polarity, but not for the same phases. While *nánu té* marks the NOT YET phase, *lisúsu té* marks the NO LONGER phase. This means that the negation of *lisúsu* by *lisúsu té* is an internal one, while that of *nánu* is external, according to Löbner's (1989) model. The depiction of the semantic relations of polarity items in Lingala therefore requires a more complex design (Figure 5).

2.3 NOT YET

The NOT YET phase is expressed with the negated item of the STILL phase, *nánu té*, and thus constitutes the negation of the STILL phase (see Figure 4). It describes ongoing situations which are not yet evident at a reference point in this phase, but which will be given at a reference point in the following phase.

(20) to-zó-lál-a   **nánu té**   malgré tángo
     SM1PL-PRG-be.asleep-FV yet   NEG despite [NP9]time
     'We are not yet (falling) asleep despite the late hour (time).'

Interestingly, the two elements of *nánu té* may stand next to each other, but they may also be split by verbs or adjuncts (ex. 21–22). It has not yet been investigated whether a different position of the negated phases also contributes to a deviating semantic reading; this may still be discussed elsewhere.

(21) mw-ána **nánu** a-kóm-í   na Kikwit **té**
     NP1-child yet   SM3SG-arrive-PRS1 LOC K.   NEG
     'The child has not yet arrived in Kikwit.'

(22) ba-zw-í   **nánu** li-fúti   na bangó **té**
     SM3PL-receive-PRS1 yet   NP5-salary CON 3PL   NEG
     'They have not yet received their salary.'

The same construction is already documented in De Boeck's (1904: 23) Lingala grammar (see ex. 23) and therefore most likely does not constitute a recent innovation. This, however, does not necessarily imply that speakers used it like this at De Boeck's time as his work is throughout prescriptive (and meant to be prescriptive).

(23) ba-sukol-i   bi-koto   bi-angai   **nainu te**
SM3PL-clean-PRS1 NP8-shoe PP8-POSS1SG yet   NEG
'On n'a pas encore nettoyé mes souliers
[they have not yet cleaned my shoes].'
(adapted from De Boeck 1904: 23)

Nánu is not possible as a fragment answer to a simple question in Lingala, only *nánu té* or *té* can be used in this case (modified from ex. 21: *Mwána akómí na Kikwit?* 'Has the child arrived in Kikwit?' – *(Nánu) té*).

2.4 NO LONGER

The NO LONGER phase, indicated with *lisúsu té*, reveals only slight semantic relationships of phasal polarity with the STILL phase (in specific contexts when quantities are addressed, see above) and none with the ALREADY phase. This means that the relation *lisúsu* <> *nánu te* is semantically weaker than the corresponding relation of *nánu* <> *nánu té*. Apart from meaning NO LONGER, it therefore also translates as 'no more' or 'not any further', in quantitative terms of material items. Its use is regular and there are no free variants of any kind.

(24) O-béng-is-í   ngái **lisúsu** epái na yó **té?**
SM2SG-call-CAUS-PRS1 O1SG longer at   CON 2SG NEG
'Why have you no longer invited me to your place?'
'Why do you no longer invite me to your place?'

(25) ba-ngúná   ba-bét-í   **lisúsu** ma-sási   **té**
NP2-enemy SM3PL-beat-PRS1 longer NP6-bullet NEG
'The enemies/rebels no longer shoot; the enemies/rebels have no longer fired a shot; the enemies/rebels have not fired one more shot.'

(26) to-zá   **lisúsu** na   besoin ya   mbóngo   **té**
SM1PL-be longer COM need   CON [NP9]money NEG
'We no longer (urgently) need money.'

See also the early mentioning of *lisúsu té* in De Boeck's prescriptive grammar (ex. 27).

(27) *e-meseni moko bw-atu a-ko-banga* **lisusu te**
SM3SG:INAN-be.used one NP14-canoe SM3SG-FUT-fear-FV longer NEG
'Quand on est habitué à la pirogue, on n'a plus peur
[when one is used to the canoe, one no longer fears]'
(adapted from De Boeck 1904: 30)

2.5 Summary of phasal polarity in Lingala

The phasal items for all four categories constitute adverbs, *déjà*, *lisúsu (té)* and *nánu*, while the ALREADY phase can, in addition, be marked by the auxiliary *sí*. The different behavior of *nánu té* and *lisúsu té*, which negate different positive phases, make it difficult to fully apply Löbner's (1989) model to Lingala. The graphic presentation is summarized in one figure containing *nánu té* and *lisúsu té* (see Figure 5).

It becomes evident in the analysis that the ALREADY phase represents a special case: Not only are two semantically distinctive strategies employed (plus a TA marker with an inherent and implicit ALREADY sense), but it is also interesting that neither is found in early Lingala (cf. De Boeck 1904). The borrowing of the French adverb *déjà* with some probability occurred after the grammaticalization and erosion of *kosíla* ('to finish') and may therefore constitute a more recent phenomenon (yet, *déjà* was already documented in the 1940s and 1950s, but many earlier sources do not mention it). The adverb items of the STILL, NOT YET and NO LONGER phases, *nánu* and *lisúsu*, are all mentioned in the early stages of Lingala in the course of missionary interventions and its standardization (De Boeck 1904).[8] Altogether, in regard to the use of phasal items, Lingala with its more simplified morphology significantly deviates from other Bantu languages (as shown by Löfgren 2018).

---

[8] This, again, does not mean that people actually spoke like this. It simply shows that missionaries were aware of these items and included them in their studies.

3 Sango

Sango[9] is an Ubangian language spoken by the total population of about three million people in Central African Republic; beyond the borders it plays a role only in the communities of emigrants. It emerged by the turn of the 20th century from a riverine second language variant of Ngbandi, which constitutes its lexifier language, as a result of intensive language contact along the Congo and Ubangi rivers during precolonial and colonial times. A number of interferences from different Bantu languages serve as proofs of this development (Pasch 1996, in print). It is the national language of the country and besides French the second official language. Despite its status and great efforts by Christian missions and different NGOs, it has not yet become a generally used medium of written communication and it constitutes primarily an oral medium.

The word order is rigid S-V-O-X, syntactic relations being indicated by word order or by prepositional phrases. Sango has retained only little morphology from Ngbandi. The plural prefix *a-*, the agent-marker *wa-* and the nominalizing suffix *-ngo* are the only bound morphemes in the noun phrase, and in the verb phrase there is only the subject marker *a-* prefixed to verbs in case of nominal subjects. Anaphoric pronouns as subjects occupy the same position as the sole indication of conjugation. Like in Lingala plural is normally marked only on +HUMAN nouns while –HUMAN nouns are number-neutral. The morphological and tonal marking of tense and aspect of Ngbandi has been lost, and only the progressive and near future are morphologically marked by a construction with the copula *yeke,* possibly borrowed from Kikongo, and a nominalized verb. Depending on the vernacular languages of speakers, Sango is spoken with two, three or four tones (Bouquiaux 1978: 34–38), but since the functional load of tones is minimal they need not be marked in written texts.[10] Negation is marked by the negating particle *ape* or *pepe* which is in clause-final position and a rela-

---

[9] Examples in this section are taken from different texts, among others from Samarin (1967) and from personal conversations in Central African Republic. They have all been discussed with Germain Landi without whose help exact good understanding of many expressions would have been difficult. He provided comparative examples in order to clarify ambiguities and discrepancies, which otherwise would have remained unnoticed.

[10] Cf., however, Diki-Kidiri (1977: 51) who stresses the function of tones in Sango, and who claims that it is necessary to mark tones in written texts in order to make them understandable.

tive clause which has positive polarity may follow.[11] The former is the more frequent form in spoken language, while the latter, more in conformity to standard Sango, is primarily used in written texts.

As mentioned above, phasal polarity in Sango is normally understood from context. Nevertheless, explicit indication is possible. Some of the items indicating phasal polarity are retained from Ngbandi; others are borrowed from French. The major phasal polarity items of Ngbandi origin are *de, ade,* or *de . . . pepe* indicating the NOT YET phase, *awe* the ALREADY phase, *de* the STILL phase and *mbeni*[12] *pepe* the NO LONGER phase. Note that two of the NOT YET items also have positive polarity.

The phasal polarity items of French origin are *déjà* 'already' and *encore* 'still', both adverbs. *Encore* in collocation with the negation parker *pepe* may also be used as NO LONGER item. The first two have retained their semantics from French while the third has modified it. This modification allows the expression of NO LONGER, which before the arrival of the Europeans may not have been a grammatical category in the language. The impression of speakers that *mbeni pepe* is typically used in the Protestant Bible but not in the Catholic Bible might indicate that this construction was created as a solution to overcome problems of translating the Bible into Sango without using French words.[13] It follows that there is no set of four phase-marking particles which correspond to those we know from Dutch, German, French and English. On a timeline, the items which express the different phases are arranged as shown in Figure 6.

---

[11] The negation marker of the verb in the main clause may follow the inserted relative clause.

le   a-mu   ye   so   mo yeke ba   pepe
eye SM-take thing DEM 2SG COP   see NEG
'The eyes do not take the thing that you are looking at.'

[12] In positive polarity, *mbeni* has a number of functions. As an adverb in positive clauses it indicates repetition of an action, *mbu gwe na kodoro mbeni* (1SG go PREP again) 'I went again to the village'. In prenominal position, it is used as an indefinite marker, e.g. *mbeni zo oko ayeke* (INDEF person one he.is) 'there is somebody'. In combination with postnominal *ndé* 'different' it indicates 'another (thing)', e.g. *mbeni ye nde* 'a different thing'.

[13] The Catholic and Protestant Sango religiolects are discussed in Pasch (1994).

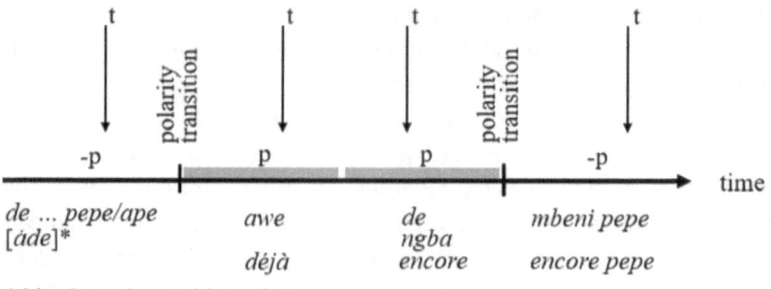

Figure 6: Organization of the four polarity phases of Sango on a timeline.

The graphic representation of the semantic relations between the phasal polarity concepts will be given at the end of this section. In the following text the different phases will be discussed separately, first those of positive polarity ALREADY (3.1.) and STILL (3.2.), then those of negative polarity, NOT YET (3.3.) and NO LONGER (3.4.). The relations between these phases are discussed in 3.5.

3.1 The ALREADY phase

In the ALREADY phase, ongoing states or activities are located which were not yet given at any point of reference in the preceding phase, but only from the point of polarity transition. It is normally marked by *awe*, which is often conceived of as an adverb and translated as 'already'. It may also be analyzed as an impersonal verb form meaning 'it is finished/achieved, has ended', retained from Ngbandi where it developed in a grammaticalization process from the conjugated verb form *a-we* (SM-end) 'it is done/finished/completed, it has come to an end' before the emergence of Sango. Note that in Sango the verb *we* 'be done' is not used. The situation marked by *awe* is illustrated in Figure 7 which is based on Löbner's (1999: 53) illustration of the meaning of German *noch nicht* and *schon*.

In several European languages, the verbs which describe the ongoing situation in the ALREADY phase allow an inchoative interpretation, so that this phase is called inchoative or ingressive (Van der Auwera 1998: 35). The semantics of *awe*, which is inherently completive, makes an inchoative reading difficult. We claim that from the point of view of aspect the situations marked by *awe* in example (28) are those of results of some prior situations. With regard to these examples, one may speak of a perfect of result, and with regard to examples which are in the past (ex. 29–30) of a perfect-of result-in-the-past (cf. Comrie 1976: 56).

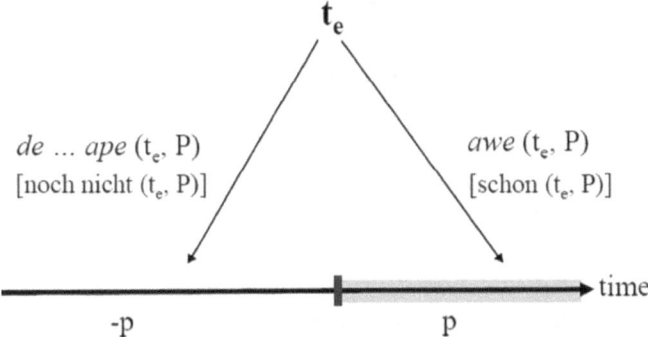

Figure 7: The *de . . . ape* phase and the *awe* phase.

(28) *mbi ga   mbi si   **awe***
     1SG come 1SG arrive already
     'I am already here [I have arrived].'

(29) *mbi gwe ti   pika lo, andaa lo kwi **awe***
     1SG go SUB   beat 3SG but   3SG die already
     'I went to shoot him, but he was already dead [he had already died].'

The completive meaning of *awe* is particularly evident in an expression which many Europeans used in the last decades of the last century as a refusal to requests from beggars by whom they felt bothered and to whom they did not want to give anything (ex. 30). The situation described shows again a perfect of result, but it also alludes inchoatively to a world without beggars.

(30) *mu   na   mbi a-kwi   **awe***
     give PREP 1SG SM-die already
     '*Give-me* has already died.'

Quite often impolite refusal of any kind is expressed by the one-word-answer *awe!* which means simply 'No! It's over.'

This sense of completion is also illustrated in the reproachful reaction by a young woman after Helma Pasch had thanked her in an inconvenient way for some assistance, a story which happened in 1990. As soon as the woman, who did not know French, heard *singila*,[14] she burst out with her corrective reply (ex. 31). It turned that even though *singila* is a genuine Sango word, its use was neither considered more correct nor more polite than that of *merci*.

(31) Singila awe!   Merci!
     singila already
     'Singila is over! [Say] Merci!'

In case the verb or copula predicate describe situations which have an impact on what follows many speakers use *déjà* instead of *awe* (ex. 32) or they combine the two (ex. 33). *Déjà* obviously has retained the inchoative meaning from French, and it appears that *awe* is adopting that meaning.

(32) mbi yeke na   Bangui **déjà**
     1SG COP PREP B.   already
     'I am already in Bangui.'

(33) mbi gwe ti si   na   boulangerie, kandaa mapa
     1SG go SUB arrive PREP bakery   but   bread
     a-hunzi **(déjà) awe**
     SM-end already
     'I went to the bakery, but the bread was already sold out.'

On the bilingual website Sängö tî Bêafrîka, which presents the standard variant of Sango, practically devoid of loanwords from European languages, *awe* is treated in the Sango text as equivalent of *déjà* (ex. 34) and the two are not combined. This example documents the transfer of the inchoative meaning onto *awe* quite clearly.

(34) Mo yeke nyibaba **awe**?
     2SG COP member already
     'Are you already a member [of the Club]?'

Awe is, of course, also used in combination with the inchoative verbs *tonda* and *commencé*, 'begin'. In and of themselves *tonda* or *commencé* do not indicate phasal polarity, they do so only when accompanied by the phasal polarity

---

14 *Singila* forms part of the Catholic religiolect. In daily speech *merci* is used instead.

item *awe*. Note that in example (35) *awe* marks only the beginning of the action described by the main verb as completed, not the entire action.

(35) e   tonda/commencé ti   lu   ye   da   **(awe)**
     1PL begin   SUB plant thing there already
     'We have already begun to plant things there'
     [answer to the question: how far have you proceeded in you work]

In a few examples, the particle *awe* has an impact on the reading of a verb. This is the case with regard to *ma*, the equivalent of 'to hear' and 'to understand'. When used without *awe* it means 'hear, listen' (ex. 36a) while in combination with *awe* it is rather used in the sense 'agree, have understood' (ex. 36a), a meaning which confirms the achievement marking function of *awe* (ex. 36b). A phasal polarity reading, however, is not given by either of the two examples.

(36) a. *mbi ma* 'I heard.' b. *mbi ma* **awe** 'I have understood, I agree.'

Some utterances express quite clearly phasal polarity even though they contain neither a phasal verb nor a phasal polarity item. A well-known example is *Bangui a-hinga mbi* (Bangui SM-know 1SG) 'Bangui knows me', a common way of saying 'I have already been to Bangui' implying some degree of familiarity with the town.

3.2 STILL

The STILL item signals that a situation is ongoing at the reference phase but will not be given at a reference point in a subsequent phase. In Sango, it is regularly expressed with the copula verb *de* in its meaning 'continue to have some quality until quality changes'. The specific quality of the situation may be described by a nominal predicate (ex. 37), a prepositional phrase giving an attribute (ex. 38) or a location (ex. 39a–b). Occasionally, the temporal meaning may be related to geographical and temporal distance (ex. 40). The ongoingness may optionally be underlined by *encore* (ex. 39b). In combination with a nominal subject *de* has the subject marker *a-* which has low tone (37, 40). It is important to note that in this meaning *de* cannot occur without a complement.

(37) kotara   ti   mbi a-**de**   fi
     grandfather SUB   1SG SM-continue   living.person
     'my grandfather is still alive'

(38) lo   **de**   na   gangu   ti   lo
     3SG continue   PREP strength SUB   3SG
     '(s)he is still at the peak of her/his strength'

(39) a. lo   **de**   na   lege
        3SG continue   PREP way
        '(s)he is still on the way'
     b. lo   **de**   **(encore)** na   Bangui
        3SG continue   still   PREP B.
        '(s)he is still in Bangui'

(40) Baba,   kodoro   **a-de**   yongoro mingi!
     father village SM-continue   far   very
     'Father, the village is still far away!'

De has the synonym *ngba* 'to remain, stay, continue to be', an aspectual verb which does, however, not indicate in and of itself phasal polarity. Unlike *de* which has a clear prospective sense, *ngba* is purely continuative. The qualities of ongoing states are described by subordinate nominalized verbs (ex. 41) or by nominal predicates (ex. 42a). Both situations may be expected to end at some point in the future, a fact which is, however, not expressed by *ngba*, but rather by context and world knowledge. Suffering, e.g., normally does not last forever (ex. 41), and the desire of unmarried people who want to get married in example (42a) is understood by speakers in whose society marriage is a normal step in everyone's reproductive age. With reference to societies where it is normal for young people to remain unmarried for the rest of their lives this is expressed in the same way (ex. 42b) since phasal polarity does not play a role.

(41) mbi **ngba**   ti   hu-ngo   pino
     1SG remain   SUB see-NOM   suffering
     'I am still suffering.'

(42) a. *tongana koli na wali* **a-ngba** *kumbamba*
    when man PREP woman SM-stay unmarried.person
    ala yeke toto lakwe ti sala mariage.
    3PL COP cry always SUB make marriage
    'When man and woman are still unmarried, they cry all the time in order to get married.'

(42) b. *koli na wali* **a-ngba** *kumbamba*
    man PREP woman SM-stay unmarried.person
    'Men and women remain unmarried.'

When used without a complement *de* has the meaning 'continue to be undone, to be in a specific situation/condition which is expected to change'. It indicates the STILL phase, but with regard to a situation which is not given but expected, hence translations in other languages indicate the NOT YET phase. The cassava plantation in example (43) is still in need of cultivation, a need which will end at a point of reference in the following NO LONGER phase, when cultivation work will start or be finished. The expectation that the given situation is going to change alludes to the NOT YET phase. The reference to a specific cassava plantation in collocation with *de* is enough information for everybody acquainted with agriculture in Central African Republic to know which type of work has to be done. It must be noted that the expression is ambiguous. The plantation may be waiting for the beginning of the work or the termination of it, in case it has already started. Similar ambiguity is given in example (44).

(43) *yaka ti gozo* **a-de**
    plantation SUB cassava SM-continue
    'The [work on the] cassava plantation will/must be continued/finished.'
    [the cassava field is still undone]

(44) *(ngoyi ti) ngu* **a-de**
    season SUB water SM-continue
    'The rainy season is awaiting, has not yet begun.'
    'The rainy season is awaiting, has not yet ended.'

In serial verb constructions where *de* constitutes the first and *hunzi* 'end, finish' the second verb the NOT YET phase is not only alluded to by *de* (ex. 45), but it is directly indicated by the subordinate verb (cf. Figure 8).

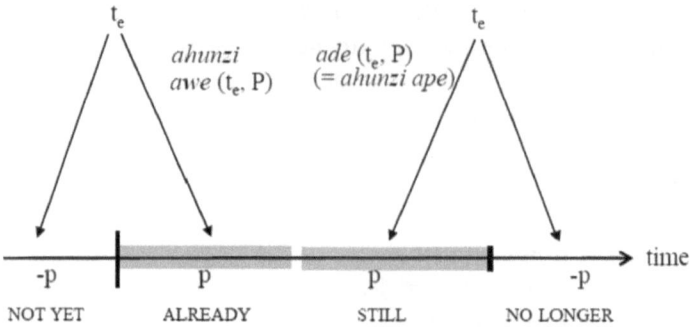

Figure 8: *Áde* indicating the STILL phase and *ahunzi* indicating the NOT YET phase.

(45) lo   de   lo   hunzi kwa   ti   lo   ape
     3SG continue 3SG finish work SUB 3SG NEG
     'S/he did not yet finish his/her work.'

The lexicalized impersonal form of *de* 'continue to be undone', *áde* 'it remains undone/unfinished' has a high tone on the first syllable. It may also be used as a one-word answer to the question whether something has already been done or not and it is normally translated as 'not yet'. It may, however, be complemented by a clausal explanation which is in the negative polarity (ex. 46).

(46) Ballon   ni   a-hunzi   awe?
     football.match DEF SM-finish already
     'Is the football match over?'
     Áde,   (a-hunzi   ape)
     it.remains.undone SM-finish NEG
     'Not yet [it stays undone], (it is not over)'

Áde, which does not allow a complement, describes an action or a situation as – depending on the context – not yet started or not yet finished. Note that *áde* has positive polarity. A verbally close expression in German is *(das) dauert noch* ('it still takes time'). It has retained the high tone of Ngbandi which is now carried by the subject marker.[15]

---

15 In the lexifier language Ngbandi the high tone marking the near future precedes the verb. In this language *de* is a copula verb which also has the meaning 'to continue to do s.th.'. Lekens (1958: 104) gives 'être encore' and 'nog zijn' as equivalents of *dɛ* in French and Dutch respectively, and he adds that it "drukt de ongedaanheid van iets uit" (expresses that something has

As shown in the preceding section (3.2.) the lexicalized verb form *áde*, albeit normally translated as 'not yet', is not a term indicating one specific phase with some implication concerning the situation in the following one (ex. 47). *Áde* additionally implies the expectancy not only of the end of the given situation, but even more of a change, i.e. it alludes to the NOT YET phase which according to Van der Auwera is not related to the STILL phase.

(47) **áde,**   *(lo gwe ape)*
    it.is.undone 3SG go NEG
    'Not yet, ((s)he has not yet gone).' [it continues, (s)he did not go, but she will go]

In positive polarity *áde,* like *de,* indicates the STILL phase, where a situation is given which will no longer be given at a point of reference in the following phase, but which is expected to change. That situation is characterized by the absence of a specific condition which the expected change will provide. Positive polarity of the NOT YET item has not been discussed in any study on phasal polarity, and it makes the application of Löbner's duality hypothesis with regard to *áde* difficult.

Furthermore, *áde* also alludes to the NOT YET phase, which is not sequentially related to the STILL phase. In example (45) that specific situation is described by the negated subordinate phasal verb *hunzi* 'end, finish' which in the given context indicates the NOT YET phase (Figure 9). It explains what the undoneness of the football match means in particular, i.e. that it has not yet ended.

If the answer to the question about the end of the football match is expressed with *ngba,* there is no phasal polarity reading. The verb form is not impersonal, but *ballon* 'football-match' is the understood subject, referred to anaphorically by the subject-marker *a-*.

(48) **A-ngba** *(ti gwe).*
    SM-STAY SUB go
    'It continues (to go on).'

---

not yet been done). This sense is, however, only given when *dɛ* is used without a complement and has a preceding high tone making the imperfective (Tucker & Bryan 1966: 94), e.g. *zongo ́dɛ̀* 'the rainy season has not yet begun/has not yet ended'. In combination with a subordinate verb, *dɛ* expresses 'continue to do s.th., continue to be somehow/somewhere', *ló dɛ ká ta-légɛ* (3SG continue there mother-way) 's/he is still on the way' (Lekens 1958: 104).

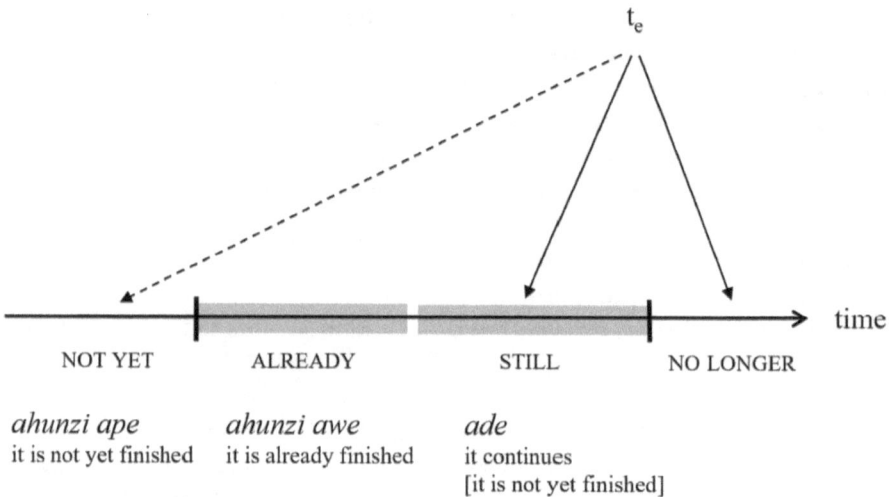

Figure 9: *Áde* indicating the STILL phase and alluding to the NOT YET phase.

The examples (37, 38, 39a, b, 43, 44, 45a) show that *de* indicates phasal polarity in and of itself, while *ngba* (ex. 41, 42a, b, 45b) can do so only if supported by context.

3.3 NOT YET

While *de* in combination with a predicative expression or a subordinate verb marks the STILL phase, *de . . . pepe* marks the NOT YET phase. This makes the phasal polarity system a flexible one (Kramer 2017: 1-2). It expresses that a situation is not given at the reference time, but that it will be given or is expected to be given at a reference point in the subsequent phase. *De* may constitute the first verb in a serial verbal construction[16] (ex. 49, 50a), the verb in a main clause which introduces a subordinate clause (ex. 50b) or a copula verb with a locative complement (51a, b).

(49) depuis   mama   ti   mbi   a-du   mbi   so,
     since   mother SUB   1SG   SM-bear   1SG   DEM
     mbi **de**   mbi ba   nyama ti   sese   a-gbo   kamba na
     2SG continue   1SG see   animal SUB   earth SM-trap   cord   PREP

---

16 Serial verb constructions of Sango are discussed in Pasch (1996: 234–237).

nduzu **pepe**
sky NEG
'Since the time my mother bore me, I haven't seen a terrestrial animal trapped in the sky.'

The construction in example (50b) which some speakers consider close to Ngbandi is not frequently used. Example (50c), the normal way to describe the given situation, shows that the situation described in examples (50a) and (50b) may be described without explicit indication of phasal polarity. The transformational verb *ga* 'become',[17] the age of the person concerned and the knowledge that children in the course of time become adults is sufficient information to make it understood.

(50) a. mbi **de**   mbi ga   wali   **ape**
       1SG continue 1SG come woman NEG
       'I have not yet become a woman.'
    b. mbi **de**   titene   mbi ga   wali   **ape**
       1SG continue in.order.to 1SG come woman NEG
       'I have not yet become a woman.'
    c. mbi ga   wali   **ape**
       1SG come woman NEG
       'I have not become a woman.'

The application of Löbner's model is a bit complicated since the verb *de* constitutes the STILL item and it forms part of the NOT-YET item. In example (51a) the negator *ape* has scope only over the verb *de* and optionally the adverb *encore*, i.e. *de . . . ape* may be qualified as internal negation of *de* (ex. 50b). The external negation, requires, however, another verb, as shown in example (51c.) It negates the entire proposition in example (50c), hence is qualified as external negation.

(51) a. lo **de**   na Bangui **(encore)** **ape**
       3SG continue PREP B.   still   NEG
       '(S)he is not yet in Bangui.'
       [internal: s/he is (NOT) still in Bangui]
       [external: (NOT) s/he is already in Bangui]

---

[17] The basic meaning of *ga* is 'come'.

b. lo **de**   (*encore*) na   Bangui
   3SG continue   still   PREP B.
   '(S)he is still in Bangui.'

c. lo yeke na   Bangui **déjà/awe**
   3SG COP PREP B.   already
   '(S)he is already in Bangui.'

Note that examples (51a) and (51b) are both prospective, while example (51c) is prospective with *déjà*, and retrospective with completive *awe*.

3.4 NO LONGER

The NO LONGER phase is indicated by the indefinite marker *mbeni* 'some, other' in combination with the negation particle (ex. 52). The French adverb *encore* 'still, again' in the position of *mbeni* fulfills the same function (ex. 53). Neither of the two constructions is frequent and they are mostly found in texts translated from French or English.

(52) na   ngu   tí e   susu a-yeke **mbeni pepe**
     PREP water SUB 1PL fish SM-COP again NEG
     'In our rivers [waters] there are no more fish.'

(53) mbi ye   ti nyõ   eregi   **encore pepe**
     1SG love SUB drink strong.alcohol again   NEG
     'I don't drink alcohol anymore.'

The fact that for speakers of Sango *mbeni pepe* sounds like Protestant biblical Sango suggests that this form actually emerged and became diffused as a result of the translation of the Bible and other religious texts by Protestant missionaries. Since in daily speech *encore pepe* is more frequent than *mbeni pepe*, we may assume that use of the latter was encouraged in order to avoid French loanwords. While *mbeni pepe* is always clause-final, *encore pepe/ape* may be in clause-final position (ex. 52, 53) or discontinuous, *encore* following the verb and *pepe/ape* being at the end of the clause (ex. 54). In complex sentences *ape* may be opposed to *awe*, the first in declarations that certain things cannot be done anymore, the second in the explanation why this is so (ex. 54 and 55). The order of declaration and explanation is free.

(54) mbi yeke gwe **encore** na   klasse **ape**: seminaire
    1SG COP   go   again PREP class   NEG   lesson
    a-commencé **awe**
    SM-begin   already
    'I will not enter class anymore: the lesson has already started.'

(55) ya   ti   mbi a-si   **awe**,   mbi ye   ti   te
    stomach POSS 1SG SM-full already 1SG want SUB eat
    ye   **encore ape**
    thing   no longer
    'I am already full and do not want to eat anything more.'

On the Website Sängö tî Bêafrîka (n.d.), which is known for its use of standard Sango,[18] *mbeni pepe* is used with the meaning 'none', without temporal or aspectual meaning.

(56) a-buku   nde-nde   mingi a-yeke sigigi   na
    PL-book different-RED   many   SM-COP come.out   PREP
    su-ngo   sango[19] so   sego ni   a-yeke da   **mbeni pepe**
    écrire-NOM S.   DEM tone DEF SM-COP present INDEF   NEG
    'Many different books have appeared in some Sango orthography where there are no tones indicated.'

It appears that internal negation of *mbeni pepe* or *encore pepe* providing a phasal polarity expression is not possible, but STILL and ALREADY are both negated externally. Example (52) is the negation of the entire proposition in example (57) and not of one or more components. Likewise, example (58a) negates the entire propositions in examples (58b) and (58c).

(57) susu **a-de**   na   ngu   tî   e
    fish SM-continue PREP water SUB 1PL
    'In our rivers [waters] there are still fish.'

---

18 Standard Sango is the variant used by the presenters in television and radio. It is also used for publications at the Institut de Linguistique Appliquée de l'Université de Bangui (Pasch, in print).
19 *Su-ngo Sango* (write-NOM S.) is the term for 'Sango orthography'.

(58) a. lo   a-mu na   e   nginza **mbeni pepe**
       3SG take PREP 1PL money again   NEG
       'He doesn't give us money anymore.'
   b. lo   **de**   ti   mu   na   e   nginza
       3SG remain SUB give PREP 1PL money
       'He is still giving us money.' [the money giving process is not finished]
   c. lo   **ngba** ti   mu   na   e   nginza
       3SG remain   SUB give PREP 1PL money
       'He still gives us money.' [now and in the future]

Mbeni without the negator means 'again' (59a), which is not negated by *mbeni pepe* (ex. 57), nor is the ALREADY item *awe* (ex. 59b), which may be explained by the completive meaning of *awe*. Here again external negation is given.

(59) a. **Mbeni** mbi gwe na   kodoro
       again   1SG go   PREP village
       'I went again to the village.'
   b. *Mbi   gwe na   klasse **awe**.*
       1SG go   PREP class   already
       'I went already to class.'

3.5 Summary of phasal polarity in Sango

The phasal polarity items of Sango show some significant differences to those of the languages investigated until now. The same verb *de* is the polarity item for the STILL phase and part of the polarity item for the NOT YET phase. In both phases, it has prospective meaning, but in combination with complements, it indicates that a given situation is ongoing, while without complement it indicates the undoneness of an action or the non-givenness of a situation. It is understood that the respective situation is expected to change. Striking is the fact that the lexicalized form *áde* 'it is undone', which also indicates the NOT YET phase, has positive polarity. It expresses that the given, unspecified situation of the subject is ongoing, a situation where an expected change has not yet started or not been finished.

Only one polarity phase, NO LONGER, is clearly expressed by an adverb, *mbeni pepe*. This makes comparison with the adverbial equivalents in other languages easy. Unfortunately, this item is not very frequent. ALREADY is also expressed by an adverb, *awe* 'it is finished', but this item has retained the completive meaning of its verbal origin. While in most languages ALREADY has a prospective sense, in Sango it is retrospective which makes comparison difficult. The French loanword *déjà*, which does not have a retrospective sense, is preferred in copula constructions which describe states and not events.

Although it is possible to indicate phasal polarity in Sango, speakers do not make much use of it. In particular, expressions in the NO LONGER phase are rare and the items given to mark it indicate they are recent developments. The ALREADY and the NOT YET concepts are the ones most firmly established and most frequently used. NOT YET is most frequently heard as the one-word answer *áde*. STILL is less frequent and NO LONGER is rare. On a continuum the frequency can be outlined as follows. This order is close to the one that Löfgren (2018: 15) established for a sample of Bantu languages. It differs from the languages investigated by Van der Auwera (1998: 44-45) where it is the ALREADY concept which is not overtly marked by an adverb and for which the items have been borrowed. It appears to be more in harmony with the non-European languages investigated by Van Baar (1997: 117), who observes that here the sole lexical gap is given with NO LONGER. The frequency of use can be seen in the following hierarchy (Figure 10).

Figure 10: Frequency hierarchy of phasal polarity items in Sango.

The semantic relations between the four concepts are depicted in Figure 11.

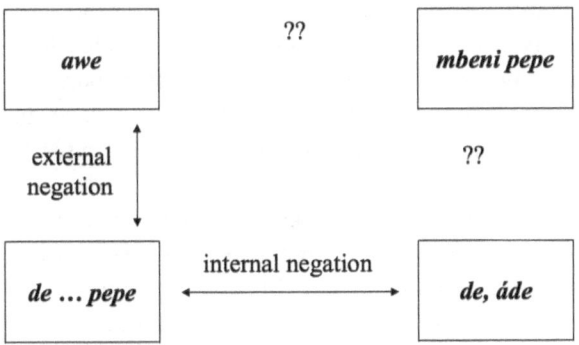

Figure 11: Semantic relations between the phasal polarity concepts of Sango.

4 Conclusions

Despite the different typological profiles of Lingala and Sango and their different genetic affiliation, the two languages share certain commonalities in terms of phasal polarity, which correlate, however, also with different uses of given items and structures. The first conclusion is that both languages share the semantic relations between the phasal polarity concepts. The distribution of external and internal negation within the phasal polarity system is, however, not identical, with a clear internal negation only occurring between STILL and NOT YET. Second, in both languages NO LONGER is the least frequently expressed phasal polarity, which is also in agreement with what Löfgren (2018) observes for East African Bantu languages. Third, the ALREADY phase can hardly be characterized as inchoative or ingressive since the respective items inherently indicate completion or perfect of the state or event described by the verb, in Lingala by the already-perfect *sí* and in Sango by the adverb *awe*. This state or event is, however, the direct cause of the situation given in the ALREADY phase. Fourth, both languages have borrowed adverbial phasal polarity items from French: While *déjà* is frequently used in Lingala for all non-completive events whenever *sí* is not used, it is not frequent in Sango, where it co-occurs mostly with the synonym *awe*. The item *encore*, however, is not used in Lingala, but – negated – in Sango. *Encore pepe* and *mbeni pepe* reveal a low frequency, but of the two, *encore pepe* or *encore ape* is more often heard in spoken Sango. The low frequency of the two indicates that the concept did not exist at all before the arrival of Europeans, and that only the translation of religious and other texts made it necessary to find a way of verbalizing it. It must be noted that Europeans tend to feel uneasy when NO LONGER cannot be expressed, while speakers of Sango feel uneasy when urged to verbalize this or other phasal polarities, when they see no need to do so (as explained above).

The similarities in the semantic relations and the weak expression/markedness of the NO LONGER phase may be features of Bantu languages which have been adopted by Sango. They may also potentially be areal features shared by Bantu and Ubangian languages. Since most of the latter have not yet been investigated with regard to phasal polarity, the answer to this question must be left open at this (early) point.

Both languages share polarity items derived from verbs. Moreover, one of the commonalities is that items borrowed from French (*encore; déjà*) reveal slight semantic differences in both Sango and Lingala in contrast to their donor language French. Also, in both languages the phasal polarity items are far less frequently used than in European languages, and require a careful (semantic) analysis. Another feature shared by both languages is the completive reading of the ALREADY markers.

The differences with regard to the items borrowed from French may be classified as quite common differences due to contact of individual languages with the same model language. Due to the analogy of absent morphological phasal polarity markers (apart from the grammaticalized equivalent of ALREADY in Lingala), the question of mutual contact and/or parallel developments of the phasal polarity systems may be raised.

Abbreviations

COM	comitative	NP1	noun class prefix 1
CON	connective	O	object marker
COP	copula	PL	plural
DEF	definite marker	PREP	preposition
FV	final vowel	PRG	progressive aspect
IMP	imperfective	PRS1	"present tense 1"
INAN	inanimate	PRS2	"present tense 2"
INF	infinitive	PST1	"past tense 1"
LOC	locative marker	SG	singular
NEG	negation	SM	subject marker
NOM	nominalization suffix		

Bibliographic references

Aikhenvald, Alexandra Y. 2006. Serial verb constructions in typological perspective. In Alexandra Y. Aikhenvald & Robert M. W. Dixon, *Serial Verb Constructions: A Crosslinguistic Typology*, 1–68. Oxford: Oxford University Press.

Ashton, Ethel O. 1944. *Swahili Grammar (Including Intonation)*. London: Longmans, Green & Company.

Bouquiaux, Luc, Marcel Diki-Kidiri & Jean-Marie-Kobozo. 1978. *Dictionnaire Sango-Français*. Paris: SELAF.

Brisard, Frank & Michael Meeuwis. 2009. Present and perfect in Bantu: The case of Lingala. *Journal of African Languages and Linguistics* 30. 21–43.

Comrie, Bernard. 1976. *Aspect*. Cambridge: Cambridge University Press.

De Boeck, Egide. 1904. *Notions du Lingala ou langue du haut-fleuve*. Nouvelle-Anvers: Imprimerie Mission du S. Coeur.

Diki-Kidiri, Marcel. 1977. *Le Sango s'écrit aussi . . . Esquisse linguistique du sango, langue nationale de l'Empire Centrafricain*. Paris: SELAF.

Kramer, Raija L. 2017. Position paper on Phasal Polarity expressions. Hamburg: University of Hamburg. https://www.aai.uni-hamburg.de/afrika/php2018/medien/position-paper-on-php.pdf (accessed 10 October 2018).

Krifka, Manfred. 2000. Alternatives for aspectual particles: semantics of 'still' and 'already'. Paper presented at the Twenty-Sixth Annual Meeting of the Berkeley Linguistics Society, University of Berkeley. 401–412. https://amor.cms.hu-berlin.de/~h2816i3x/Publications/schon.pdf (accessed 10 October 2018).
Lekens, Benjamins. 1958. *Ngbandi Idioticon II. Ngbandi en Frans-Nederlands.* Tervuren: RMCA.
Löbner, Sebastian. 1989. 'Schon – erst – noch': An integrated analysis, *Linguistics and Philosophy* 12(2): 167–212.
Löbner, Sebastian. 1999. Why German schon and noch are still duals: a reply to van der Auwera. *Linguistics and Philosophy* 22. 45–107.
Löfgren. Althea. 2018. Phasal Polarity Systems in East Bantu. Stockholm: University of Stockholm BA thesis. http://www.diva-portal.org/smash/get/diva2:1214149/FULLTEXT01.pdf (accessed 15 October 2018).
Maho, Jouni Filip. 2009. NUGL Online: The online version of the New Updated Guthrie List – A referential classification of the Bantu languages. https://brill.com/fileasset/downloads_products/35125_Bantu-New-updated-Guthrie-List.pdf (accessed 15 October 2018).
Meeuwis, Michael. 2006. The Lingála-Kiswahili border in north-eastern Congo. Its origins in Belgian colonial state formation of the late nineteenth and early twentieth centuries. *Africana Linguistica* 12(1): 113–135.
Meeuwis, Michael. 2009. Involvement in language: The role of the Congregatio Immaculati Cordis Mariae in the history of Lingala. *The Catholic Historical Review* 95 (2). 240–246.
Meeuwis, Michael. 2010. *A Grammatical Overview of Lingála.* LINCOM Studies in African Linguistics 81. Munich: LINCOM.
Meeuwis, Michael. 2013. Lingala. In Susanna Maria Michaelis, Philippe Maurer, Martin Haspelmath & Magnus Huber (eds.), *The Survey of Pidgin and Creole Languages*, 25–33. Oxford: Oxford University Press.
Nassenstein, Nico. 2015a. *Kisangani Swahili. Choices and Variation in a Multilingual Urban Space.* Munich: LINCOM.
Nassenstein, Nico. 2015b. The emergence of Langila in Kinshasa (DR Congo). In Nico Nassenstein & Andrea Hollington (eds.), *Youth Language Practices in Africa and Beyond*, 81–98. Berlin: Mouton de Gruyter.
Nurse, Derek. 2008. *Tense and Aspect in Bantu.* Oxford: Oxford University Press.
Pasch, Helma. 1994. Religiolekte des Sango. In Thomas Bearth, Wilhelm J. G. Möhlig, Beat Sottas & Edgar Suter (eds.), *Perspektiven afrikanistischer Forschung: Beiträge zur Linguistik, Ethnologie, Geschichte, Philosophie und Literatur, X. Afrikanistentag, Zürich, 23.-25. Sept. 1993*, 271–288. Cologne: Köppe.
Pasch, Helma. 1996. Sango. In Sarah Thomason (ed.), *Contact Languages. A Wider Perspective*, 209–270. Amsterdam: John Benjamins.
Pasch, Helma. 1997. The choice of a common medium of communication in language contact situations. In Martin Pütz (ed.), *Language Contact: Conditions, Conflicts and Constraints*, 45–54. Amsterdam: John Benjamins.
Pasch, Helma. in print. Variations of Sango. In Susanne Mohr & Helene Steigertahl (eds.), *Urbanized African Sociolinguistics.* Special issue of *Sociolinguistic Studies* 14 (3).
Samarin, William J. 1967. *A Grammar of Sango.* (Janua Linguarum, Series Practica, XXXVIII.) The Hague, Paris: Mouton & Co.
Samarin, William J. 1986. Protestant missions and the history of Lingala. *Journal of Religion in Africa* 16 (2). 138–163.

Samarin, William J. 1990/1991. The origins of Kituba and Lingala. *Journal of African Languages and Linguistics* 12. 47–77.
Schadeberg, Thilo. 1990. Schon – noch – nicht mehr: Das Unerwartete als grammatische Kategorie im Kiswahili. *Frankfurter Afrikanistische Blätter* 2. 1–15.
Smessaert, Hans. 2009. The evaluation of aspectual distance, speed and progress. In Louis de Saussure, Jacques Moeschler, Genoveva Puskas, Genoveva Puskás (eds.), *Tense, Mood and Aspect: Theoretical and Descriptive Issues. Cahiers Chronos* 17, 27–45. Amsterdam and New York: Rodopi.
Stapleton, Walter Henry. 1903. *Suggestions for a Grammar of "Bangala": The "Lingua Franca" of the Upper Congo, with Dictionary*. Yakusu: Baptist Missionary Society.
Tucker, Archibald N. and Margaret A. Bryan. 1966. *Linguistic Analyses: The Non-Bantu Languages of North-Eastern Africa. (Handbook of African Languages)* Oxford: Oxford University Press.
Van Baar, Tim. 1997. *Phasal Polarity*. Amsterdam: IFOTT.
Van der Auwera, Johan. 1998. Phasal adverbials in the languages of Europe. In Johan van der Auwera, in collaboration with Dónall P. Ó. Baoill (eds.), *Adverbial Constructions in the Languages of Europe*, 25–145. Berlin: Mouton de Gruyter.

Bastian Persohn
Phasal polarity in Nyakyusa (Bantu, M31)

1 Introduction

This chapter gives a descriptive analysis of phasal polarity expressions in Nyakyusa (ISO 693-3: nyy), a Bantu language of Tanzania.[1]

In the following, first some geographic and demographic background information on Nyakyusa is given (Section 1.1), then the language's structural profile is addressed (Section 1.2). This is followed by a brief outline of Nyakyusa's tense-aspect system (Section 1.3), remarks on previous descriptions and mentions of Nyakyusa's phasal polarity expressions (Section 1.4), and a note on data collection (Section 1.5).

1.1 Geographic and demographic background

Nyakyusa is spoken in the Mbeya Region of Tanzania, on the shores of Lake Nyasa and in the hills extending to the north of it. Estimates of Nyakyusa speaker numbers range between 730,000 and 1,080,000 (Muzale & Rugemalira 2008; Simons & Fenning 2018). In Maho's (2009) updated version of Guthrie's (1971) referential system, Nyakyusa receives the code M31. Its closest relatives are Ndali (M301; ndh), which borders Nyakyusa to the west, and Ngonde (M31d) to the south, across the Malawian border.

1.2 Structural profile

In its overall morphological and syntactic profile, Nyakyusa is a typical Narrow Bantu language with a basic SVO constituent order, a highly agglutinative

---

[1] The author wishes to thank all his Nyakyusa language assistants for their time and patience, Amani Lusekelo, Daniel King, Helen Eaton, Maud Devos, and Rasmus Bernander (in alphabetical order) for insightful discussions, and Mary Chambers for proofreading. The usual disclaimer applies.

Research on Nyakyusa was made possible by a PhD scholarship from the a.r.t.e.s. Graduate School for the Humanities Cologne (2013–2016) and by the Deutsche Forschungsgemeinschaft (DFG, German Research Foundation) project #389792965 (since April 2018).

Bastian Persohn, University of Hamburg

morphology, and a full-fledged noun class system. In terms of phonological structure, Nyakyusa possesses sixteen phonemic consonants (counting prenasalized plosives as biphonemic), seven phonemic vowels (transcribed as *i, ɪ, e, a, o, ʊ, u*) and distinctive vowel length. Unlike many other Bantu languages, Nyakyusa is not a tonal language. See Persohn (2017a: chapter 2) for a grammatical sketch of Nyakyusa and the contributions in Van de Velde et al. (2019) on Bantu morphosyntax in general.

1.3 Introduction to the Nyakyusa tense-aspect system

Phasal polarity is intimately linked to the expression of tense and aspect. Therefore, a brief overview of Nyakyusa's tense-aspect system, focussing on the present and past tense, is provided. For a more comprehensive description, see Persohn (2017a: chapters 6–8).

In the present (or non-past) as well as in the past tense, Nyakyusa makes a basic distinction between imperfective and perfective aspect. The imperfective member of the opposition has, with most verbs, both a progressive and a habitual/generic reading. The imperfective simple present additionally has a futurate reading. Examples in (1a, b) illustrate the imperfective present and past, respectively.

(1) a. *i-kʊ-mog-a*
 SP$_1$-PRS-dance-FV
 'S/he is dancing / dances / will dance.'
 b. *a-a-mog-aga*
 SP$_1$-PST-dance-IPFV
 'S/he was dancing / used to dance.'

In addition to the general imperfective, Nyakyusa possesses a periphrastic progressive consisting of the copula *lɪ* plus an infinitive additionally marked for locative class 16, as illustrated for the present tense in (2).

(2) *a-lɪ   pa-kʊ-mog-a*
 SP$_1$-COP 16(LOC)-15(INF)-dance-FV
 'S/he is dancing.'

The reading of the perfective paradigms is highly dependent on the actional class (a.k.a. aktionsart, lexical aspect, etc.) of the lexical verb and its complements. The Bantu languages are known to express many states and "adjectival concepts" (Dixon 1982) through a class of verbs commonly referred to as "inchoative" (e.g. Nurse 2008: 97; see Crane & Persohn 2019 for discussion), and Nyakyusa is no exception to this. With inchoative verbs the default reading of the perfective aspect is a stative one, as illustrated for the present tense in (3a). With other classes of verbs the perfective denotes an eventuality that has passed (3b).

(3)   a. *a-kaleele*
         SP_1-be(come)_angry.PFV
         'S/he is angry.' (default reading)
   b. *a-mog-ile*
         SP_1-dance-PFV
         'S/he (has) danced.'

Lastly, Nyakyusa features two dedicated inflectional paradigms restricted to use in past narratives. The more frequent of these markers is illustrated in the matrix clause of (4) below. For an introduction to narrative morphology in Bantu, see Nurse (2008: 120–123).

In contrast with the sequence-of-tense rules common in European languages, Nyakyusa employs the present tense paradigms in temporal clauses and several other types of subordinate clauses. In these cases, the temporal orientation of the subordinate clause is provided by the matrix clause and context (Persohn 2017a: 195–201). This is illustrated in (4), where the present perfective in the temporal clause introduced by *bo* constrains the eventuality described in the matrix clause to a time after the subject's arrival.

(4)   **bo   *a-fik-ile***   *kʊ-ka-aja*
       as SP_1-arrive-PFV   17(LOC)-12-homestead
       a-lɪnkʊ-m̩-bʊʊl-a   *ʊ-n-kasi*   *a-lɪnkʊ-tɪ*
       SP_1-NARR-OP_1-tell-FV   AUG-1-wife SP_1-NARR-say
       'When he arrived home he told his wife.' (Saliki and Hare)

1.4 Previous treatments of phasal polarity in Nyakyusa

Previous remarks on phasal polarity in Nyakyusa can be found in Persohn (2017a: 113–140, 186–190, 196), which contains some information on the persistive marker. This marker is also mentioned in passing in Nurse's (1979: 125) short grammatical sketch, as well as in two longer sketch grammars from the turn of the 20th century (Schumann 1899: 38; Endemann 1914: 83). The contribution of the present chapter goes beyond these previous works by describing the expression of all four phasal polarity concepts (ALREADY, STILL, NO LONGER, NOT YET). It also incorporates the six parameters that Kramer, based on the works of Löbner (1989), van der Auwera (1993, 1998), and Van Baar (1997), synthesizes in her (2017) position paper on phasal polarity: coverage, pragmaticity, telicity, wordhood, expressibility, and paradigmicity.

1.5 Data collection

The data for this chapter come from a number of sources. The first source is a corpus of 42 texts, most of which are folk narratives. Some of these texts stem from the author's original fieldwork, while others are the product of literacy workshops by SIL International and were kindly made available by Helen Eaton. The written texts have been checked for phonemic spelling in collaboration with language assistants. An additional oral rendition of a folk narrative was made available by Knut Felberg. Further textual data was taken from earlier Nyakyusa text collections (Berger 1933; Busse 1942, 1949). The textual data has been augmented by extensive elicitation during four field trips to Tanzania between 2013 and 2019, as well as with two Nyakyusa speakers living in Germany. More data come from participant observation in the field.

Lastly, a translation of the New Testament into Nyakyusa by SIL International – kindly made available by Daniel King in April 2019 – was consulted. The New Testament was used to search for tokens of phasal polarity expressions that had already been identified. It was also employed for a parallel text search, as this text offers itself for this use due to its availability in multiple languages and its readily segmentable structure (Dahl & Wälchli 2016, among others), as well as to the fact that the process of translating it into Nyakyusa was informed by previous translations into English and the national language Swahili (Helen Eaton, p.c.). As parallel texts, the English *New International Version* (NIV)[2] and the Swahili *Neno* (SNT) translation, both of which were available to the Nyakyusa translators, were used. The parallel text comparison was utilized to find possible Nyakyusa expressions of phasal polarity based on the use of such expressions in the parallel verses of the English and Swahili translations; see Section 3.

---

2 Scripture quotations taken from *The Holy Bible, New International Version*® NIV®, Copyright © 1973, 1978, 1984, 2011, by Biblica, Inc.™ Used by permission. All rights reserved worldwide.

The transcriptions of all examples in this chapter have been adapted to the practical orthography used in Persohn (2017a).

The remainder of this chapter is structured as follows. In Section 2, the Nyakyusa persistive and its role in the expression of STILL and NOT YET is examined. This is followed by an overview of expressions for ALREADY in Section 3 and NO LONGER in Section 4. In Section 5, the parameter of expressibility is addressed, and Section 6 is a note on the parameter of paradigmaticitiy. The chapter concludes in Section 7.

2 The persistive: 'still' and 'not yet'

A key element in the Nyakyusa phasal polarity system is the so-called *persistive*, a common grammatical category in Bantu languages (Nurse 2008: 45). The Nyakyusa persistive consists of a bound root *kaalɪ*, which requires a subject prefix, hence SP-*kaalɪ* and which can also take a past tense prefix, yielding SP-*a-kaalɪ*. In terms of Kramer's (2017) parameter of wordhood, the Nyakyusa persistive therefore constitutes a highly grammaticalized element with verbal characteristics.

The present persistive is identical in shape to the negative past copula (see Persohn 2017a: 303).[3] These two constructions can, however, clearly be distinguished through their distribution and meaning. While the exact diachronic source of the persistive is unknown, it is likely that it involved a construction featuring the copula *lɪ*. Some indications for this interpretation are discussed in Section 2.4.

The Nyakyusa persistive can be used on its own, as is briefly discussed in Section 2.1. More commonly, however, it occurs together with a complement, which can be any of the following:
– an inflected verb (including the defective copula *lɪ*)
– an infinitive (with the augment or a locative prefix)
– a predictive nominal
– a locative nominal

An example of the persistive is given in (5).

(5) tʊ-kaalɪ   tʊ-kʊ-bop-a.
     SP₁ₚₗ-PERS SP₁ₚₗ-PRS-run-FV
     'We are still running / still run.' (elicited)

---

3 The morphological makeup of the negative past copula is SP-*ka-a-lɪ* (SP-NEG-PST-COP).

As can be gathered from (5), one of the functions of the Nyakyusa persistive is to express the phasal polarity notion of STILL. The persistive is also involved in the expression of NOT YET. Given this dual function, Nyakyusa has to be classified as a flexible language concerning Kramer's (2017) parameter of coverage.

In the following, first the bare persistive is discussed (Section 2.1). This is followed by a description of the persistive in expressions of STILL, distinguishing between its use with complements inflected for the imperfective or progressive aspect (Section 2.2), the perfective aspect (Section 2.3), and with the copula (including existentials and the expression of predicative possession), predicative nominals and locative nominals (Section 2.4). Following this discussion of expressions of STILL, the employment of the persistive in the expression of NOT YET is examined, first with infinitival complements (Section 2.5), then with complements in the negative counterpart to the present perfective (Section 2.6).

2.1 The bare persistive

When the persistive is used without an overt complement, the default interpretation is that of 'not yet', as illustrated in (6, 7). In this respect, Nyakyusa follows Van Baar's (1997: 295) proposed universal that "a still-expression used as an isolated expression [. . .] is invariably used for the expression of not yet". See Bernander (this volume) and Abe (2015) on similar cases in the Bantu languages Manda (Tanzania, mgs) and Bende (Tanzania, bdp), respectively.

(6) *ɪ-li-sikʊ   ly-a   kw-and-a   a-a-bʊʊk-ile*
AUG-5-day 5-ASSOC 15(INF)-begin-FV SP$_1$-PST-go-PFV
kʊ-kʊ-keet-a   ɪ-fi-lombe   muno
17(LOC)-15(INF)-watch-FV AUG-8-maize   whether
*fi-j-ɪɪl-iile   ʊkʊtɪ kalɪ fi-bɪfiifwe   pamo   **fi-kaalɪ***
SP$_8$-be(come)-APPL-PFV COMP   Q   SP$_8$-ripen.PFV or   SP$_8$-PERS
'On the first day he went to look at how the maize was looking to see if it had ripened yet or not.' (Thieving monkeys)

(7) *bo mu-kʊ-pɪlɪk-a   ɪ-sy-a   bw-ite*
as SP$_{2PL}$-PRS-hear-FV AUG-10-ASSOC 14-war
m̩bʊjo~m̩-bʊ-jo,   mu-lɪng-iis-a   kʊ-tiil-aga.
REDUPL~18(LOC)-14-place SP$_{2PL}$-NEG.SUBJ-come-FV 15(INF)-fear-IPFV
ɪ-syo   mpaka   si-bonek-e,   looli ʊ-bʊ-malɪɪkɪsyo
AUG-DEM$_{10}$ no_matter_what SP$_{10}$-happen-SUBJ but   AUG-14-end

bo   bʋ-kaalɪ
DEM₁₄   SP₁₄-PERS
'When you hear of wars and rumours of wars, do not be alarmed. Such things must happen, but the end is still to come (lit: but the end, not yet).' (Mark 7: 13)

However, in an answer to a polar question containing the persistive plus a non-infinitival complement, a bare persistive in Nyakyusa is understood as elliptic. This is illustrated in (8).

(8)   bʋle,   ʋ-kaalɪ   kʋ-manyil-a?   ee,   n-gaalɪ
    Q   SP₂SG-PERS   SP₂SG.PRS-learn-FV   yes   SP₁SG-PERS
    'Are you still studying? – Yes, I still am.' (overheard)

2.2 'Still': Persistive plus imperfective or progressive aspect

In this section, the use of the persistive plus a verb inflected for imperfective aspect, i.e. the simple present and past imperfective, and the periphrastic progressive, are discussed.

Examples (9, 10) illustrate the phasal polarity notion of STILL contributed by the persistive together with the progressive readings of the imperfective simple present and the past imperfective, respectively. (11) is an example of the periphrastic present progressive.

(9)   Context: Yesterday Elephant helped to fix Hare's hoe with his tusk.
    gwe   kanya   kalʋlʋ   kaabʋno   ɪ-li-ino   ly-a
    PRON₂SG   pal   hare(1a)   because   AUG-5-tooth   5-ASSOC
    mmajolo   **lɪ-kaalɪ**   **li-kʋ-m-bab-a**   na=lɪlmo
    yesterday   SP₅-PERS   SP₅-PRS-OP₁SG-hurt-FV   COM=now/today
    'Hare, my friend, yesterday's tooth still hurts.'
    (Busse 1942: 221)

(10)   Context: Yesterday there was a wedding celebration in our neighbourhood.
    pa-kɪ-lo   pa-ka-tɪ   **ba-a-kaalɪ**   **ba-a-mog-aga**
    16(LOC)-7-night   16(LOC)-12-middle   SP₂-PST-PERS   SP₂-PST-dance-IPFV
    n=ʋ-kw-ɪmb-a
    COM=AUG-15(INF)-sing-FV
    'Late at night they were still dancing and singing.' (elicited)

(11) Context: I get a phone call during lunch.
n-gaalı   n-dı   pa-kʊ-ly-a.
SP₁SG-PERS SP₁SG-COP 16(LOC)-15(INF)-eat-FV
a=n-gʊ-kʊ-kom-el-a   piitaasi
FUT=SP₁SG-PRS-OP₂SG-beat-APPL-FV later
'I'm still eating. I'll call you back later.' (elicited)

Examples (9–11) feature activity verbs in the sense of Vendler (1957), i.e. verbal lexemes that express a process that is extended in time and not inherently oriented towards a point of culmination. An important class of verbs in Nyakyusa, as well as in other Bantu languages, are those that express the coming-to-be of a change of state in the imperfective paradigms; see Crane & Persohn (2019) for extensive discussion. Not all such verbs, however, can have the progressive reading in collocation with the persistive. In slightly simplified terms, the current understanding of aspectuality in Nyakyusa has it that the lexical verb (plus arguments) needs to express a processual change (vis-à-vis a mere preparatory phase to a change); see Persohn (2017a: chapter 5, 2018). (12) illustrates a verb that cannot have a reading of a persistent ongoing change of state in the simple present.

(12) a-kaalı   i-kʊ-kalal-a
SP₁-PERS SP₁-PRS-be(come)_angry-FV
'S/he still gets angry.'
not: 'S/he is still getting angry.' (elicited)

As indicated in Section 1.3 and hinted at in example (12), both the imperfective simple present and the past imperfective also have habitual/generic readings. (13, 14) illustrate these together with the persistive.

(13) mu-n-jini   a-ba-ndʊ   b-ingi   bi-kʊ-job-a
18(LOC)-9-city(<SWA) AUG-2-person 2-many SP₂-PRS-speak-FV
ky-ene   ɪ-kɪ-Swahılı. looli n-ka-aja   a-ba-ana
7-only AUG-7-S.   but 18(LOC)-12-homestead AUG-2-child
ba-kaalı bi-kʊ-manyil-a ɪ-kɪ-Nyakyʊsa
SP₂-PERS SP₂-PRS-learn-FV AUG-7-Ny.
'In the city many people only speak Swahili. But in the village the children still learn Nyakyusa.' (elicited)

(14) bo n-dɪ   n-keke   bo ʊ-gwe   **n-aa-kaalɪ**
     as SP₁SG-COP 1-young as AUG-PRON₂SG SP₁SG-PST-PERS
     n-aa-kwes-aga   ɪ-n-gambo.   n-jɪ-lek-ile   ɪ-fy-ɪnja
     SP₁SG-PST-smoke-IPFV AUG-9-tobacco SP₁SG-OP₉-stop-PFV AUG-8-year
     fy-a   lʊlʊʊ~lʊ
     8-ASSOC REDUPL~PROX₁₁
     'When I was your age I still used to smoke. But I stopped a few years ago.'
     (elicited)

The imperfective simple present additionally has a futurate reading (Persohn 2017a: 154–155). This reading is also available in collocation with the persistive, as illustrated in (15).

(15) Context: We planned to go to Tukuyu tomorrow. I want to know if that plan is still on.
     bʊle, **tʊ-kaalɪ   tʊ-kʊ-bʊʊk-a** kʊ-Tʊkʊjʊ kɪlaabo?
     Q   SP₁PL-PERS SP₁PL-PRS-go-FV 17(LOC)-T. tomorrow
     'Are we still going to Tukuyu tomorrow?' (elicited)

In Nyakyusa, all those verbal paradigms that allow for a future-oriented reading, such as the imperfective simple present in (15), can be augmented by a proclitic aa=.[4] This proclitic serves as a "shifter" (Nurse 2008: 316), setting the eventuality described by its host verb in a "dissociated" (Botne & Kershner 2008: 152) future reference frame (Persohn 2017a: 250–255). As illustrated in (16), the employment of this clitic is compatible with the host verb being the complement of the persistive.

(16) na=a-ma-jolo   **ba-kaalɪ   aa=bi-kʊ-mog-a**
     COM=AUG-6-evening SP₂-PERS FUT=SP₂-PRS-dance-FV
     'In the evening they will still be dancing.' (elicited)

As Kramer (2017) points out, phasal polarity expressions differ with regard to their pragmatic sensitivity, that is, with regard to their compatibility with pragmatically neutral scenarios (in the case of STILL, the mere continuation of a state-of-affairs) and counterfactual ones (in the case of STILL, the continuation of a state-of-affairs counter to expectations).

---

4 Diachronically speaking, proclitic aa= goes back to a verb of motion (j)a 'go' (Persohn 2017a: 250).

While the preceding examples can be understood to involve neutral scenarios, (17, 18) illustrate that the collocation of the persistive plus imperfective aspect can equally well be used in counterfactual scenarios. Thus in (17), where the simple present is employed in its habitual/generic reading, the sibling's unchanged fashion choices contradict what is generally assumed for their age group. In (18) the continuation of studying, expressed through the simple present in its progressive reading, runs counter to the expectation that at the time of utterance the addressee should be sleeping.

(17) ʊ-n-kʊlʊ gw-angʊ a-lɪ n=ɪ-fy-mja ma-longo,
AUG-1-older_sibling 1-POSS$_{1SG}$ SP$_1$-COP COM=AUG-8-year 6-ten
ma-na leelo **a-kaalɪ i-kʊ-fwal-a** ngatɪ mw-ana
6-four now/but SP$_1$-PERS SP$_1$-PRS-dress/wear-FV like 1-child
n-niini
1-small
'My older sibling is forty years old, but he still dresses like a small child.' (elicited)

(18) It's late in the evening. Your younger sibling is still studying for an exam.
fiki **ʊ-kaalɪ kw-ɪmb-a?** ka-lambalal-e!
why SP$_{2SG}$-PERS SP$_{2SG}$.PRS-study-FV ITV-lie_down/sleep-SUBJ
'Why are you still studying? You should go to bed!' (elicited)

2.3 'Still': Persistive plus perfective aspect

Many Nyakyusa verbs that denote a change of state can be used in the perfective aspect as the complement of the persistive, expressing the continuation of the resultant state. (19) illustrates this for the present perfective, and the elicited example in (20) for its past tense counterpart.

(19) n-gʊ-ba-pyelesy-a mu-job-e pa-bw-elu ʊkʊtɪ
SP$_{1SG}$-PRS-OP$_{2PL}$-beseech-FV SP$_{2PL}$-speak-SUBJ 16(LOC)-14-white COMP
mu-kaalɪ mu-ŋ-gan-ile
SP$_{2PL}$-PERS SP$_{2PL}$-OP$_1$-love-PFV
'I urge you, therefore, to reaffirm your love for him (lit: that you say clearly that you still love him).' (2 Corinthians 2: 8)

(20)   mmajolo   n-aa-lond-igw-aga   n=ʊ-lʊ-bʊnjʊ   fiijo
       yesterday   SP₁SG-PST-want-PASS-IPFV   COM=AUG-11-morning   INTENS
       kʊ-m-bombo.   bo   n-gʊ-sook-a=po   ʊ-n-kasi   gw-angʊ
       17(LOC)-9-work as SP₁SG-PRS-leave-FV=16(LOC) AUG-1-wife 1-POSS₁SG
       a-a-kaalɪ   a-a-lambaleele
       SP₁-PST-PERS SP₁-PST-lie_down/sleep.PFV
       'Yesterday I had to be at work very early. When I left home my wife was still asleep.' (elicited)

In current studies of actionality in Bantu languages, the possibility of a verb (plus arguments) occurring in the frame of persistive plus perfective aspect is commonly taken as an indication that the resultant state forms part of the lexicalized actional potential; see Crane & Persohn (2019) for discussion. (21) is an example of a verb that cannot occur in this frame, although it expresses a change in a property of the subject.

(21)   *a-m-ıısi   **ga-kaalɪ ga-talaliile**
        AUG-6-water   SP₆-PERS   SP₆-cool.PFV
        (intended: 'The water is still cool.')

While the previous examples feature neutral scenarios, (22, 23) illustrate that the collocation of the persistive with the perfective aspect is also available in counterfactual scenarios. In (22) the persistent tiredness contrasts with the expectation that a long nap will eliminate fatigue. In (23) the continuation of the state of sleep is contrasted with the expectation that the subject should be awake at noon.

(22)   Context: You have been tired the whole day. So you had a nap.
       n-dambaleele   a-ma-sala   ma-bılı. leelo   **n-gaalɪ**
       SP₁SG-lie_down/sleep.PFV AUG-6-hour   6-two   now/but   SP₁SG-PERS
       n-gateele
       SP₁SG-be(come)_tired.PFV
       'I slept for two hours, but I am still tired.' (elicited)

(23)   Context: It is nearly midday. You are at home and somebody comes to
       visit your brother. You tell them that he is still sleeping.
       keet-a   bʊ-k-iile   fiijo.   fiki   **a-kaalɪ**
       watch-IMP   SP₁₄-be_daylight-PFV   INTENS   why   SP₁-PERS
       a-lambaleele?
       SP₁-lie_down/sleep.PFV
       'It's very late. Why is he still sleeping?' (elicited)

2.4 'Still': Persistive plus other predicates

As well as the predicates inflected for the imperfective or perfective aspect illustrated in the preceding two subsections, the Nyakyusa persistive can take a range of other predicates, with or without an overt copula, as its complement.

Examples (24–26) illustrate the persistive with a predicative nominal, a past copula plus adjective, and a present copula plus ideophone, respectively; concerning the defective copula *lɪ*, see Persohn (2017a: 303–305).

(24) *piitaasi a-ɪnkʊ-ba-setʊk-ɪl-a   a-b-iitɪki*
later   SP₁-NARR-OP₂-emerge-APPL-FV AUG-2-believer
ɪɪ-mia   i-haano a-ba   ba-a-lɪ   pamopeene.
AUG-hundred.10(<SWA) 10-five   AUG-PROX₂ SP₂-PST-COP together
*b-ingi   ṉdɪ   a-bo   na   ʊlʊ   **ba-kaalɪ b-ʊʊmi,***
2-many   18(LOC) AUG-DEM₂ COM now   SP₂-PERS   2-alive
ba-mo   ba-fw-ile
2-one   SP₂-die-PFV
'After that, he appeared to more than five hundred of the brothers and sisters at the same time, most of whom are still living, though some have fallen asleep (lit: have died).' (1 Corinthians 15: 6)

(25) *ɪ-ky-ɪnja   ky-a   mmajolo   ɪ-m-bwa   j-ɪɪtʊ   **j-aa-kaalɪ***
AUG-7-year   7-ASSOC yesterday AUG-9-dog 9-POSS₁ₚₗ   SP₉-PST-PERS
j-aa-lɪ   niini.   lmo   jɪ-kʊl-ile
SP₉-PST-COP small.9   now   SP₉-grow-PFV
'Last year our dog was still tiny. Now he has grown up.' (elicited)

(26) Context: Mwakyoma has been very quiet during the last days, and also today.
*Mwakyoma **a-kaalɪ**   a-lɪ   mwe*
Mwakyoma SP₁-PERS   SP₁-COP IDEOPH.silent
'Mwakyoma is still silent.' (elicited)

Examples (27, 28) illustrate the persistive plus locative complement in the present tense and in the past tense, respectively. The double marking of locative class 17 in (28) is a common device in Nyakyusa and adds an emphatic or exclusive meaning; see Persohn (2017a: 44).

(27) Context: Hare is bragging about his running skills.
 m-bagiile   *ʊkʊtɪ*   *n-ga-fik-e*   *kʊ-bʊ-malɪɪkɪsyo*
 SP$_{1SG}$-be_able.PFV   COMP   SP$_{1SG}$-ITV-arrive-SUBJ   17(LOC)-14-end
 n=ʊ-kʊ-gomok-a   *bo*   *ʊ-kaalɪ*   *ʊ-lɪ*   *pala~pa-la*
 COM=AUG-15(INF)-return-FV   as   SP$_{2SG}$-PERS   SP$_{2SG}$-COP   REDUPL~16(LOC)-DIST
 n-gʊ-lek-ile
 SP$_{1SG}$-OP$_{2SG}$-let-PFV
 'I can (go) reach the end and return while you are still there where I left you.' (Hare and Chameleon)

(28) *na=a-ma-jolo,*   *ɪ-lii-booti*   *ly-a-lɪ*   *pa-ka-tɪ*
 COM=AUG-6-evening   AUG-5-boat   SP$_5$-PST-COP   16(LOC)-12-middle
 pa-a   *sʊmbɪ*   *Jesu*   *a-a-kaalɪ*
 16(LOC)-ASSOC   big_body_of_water(1a)   J.   SP$_1$-PST-PERS
 kʊ-kw-i-sɪɪlya   *mw-ene*
 17(LOC)-17(LOC)-5-shore   1-alone
 'And when even was come, the ship was in the midst of the sea, and he (Jesus) (still) alone on the land.' (Mark 6: 47)

The fact that in (24) and (28) no overt copula is used in contexts that in the absence of the persistive strictly require such a linking element (Persohn 2017a: 305–307) can be taken as an indication that the /lɪ/ portion of the persistive diachronically goes back to the copula *lɪ* and has preserved this function to a certain extent. The exact morphosyntactic and semantic factors that govern copula use with nominal and locative predicates within the scope of the persistive require further investigation.

Predicative possession is expressed in Nyakyusa by the combination of a copula and the comitative *na* (Persohn 2017a: 310–311). (29) illustrates this construction in the present tense as the complement of the persistive.

(29) *namanga* **mu-kaalɪ mu-lɪ**   *na=a-ka-jɪɪlo*   *a-ka-a*
 because   SP$_{2PL}$-PERS   SP$_{2PL}$-COP   COM=AUG-12-custom   AUG-12-ASSOC
 pa-k-iisʊ
 16(LOC)-7-land
 'That is because you are still worldly (lit: . . . still have the custom of [on] earth).' (1 Corinthians 3: 3)

Lastly, existentials in Nyakyusa consist of a copula verb plus an enclitic locative demonstrative. In the case of the copula *lɪ*, the enclitic triggers raising of the vowel segment to first degree /i/ (Persohn 2017a: 322–324). (30) illustrates the persistive together with a present tense existential.

(30) po   ʊ-lʊ-fingo   lw-a   Kyala **lʊ-kaalɪ lʊ-li=po**
     then   AUG-11-promise   11-ASSOC   God   SP₁₁-PERS   SP₁₁-COP=16(LOC)
     kʊ-ba-ndʊ,   ʊ-kw-ingɪl-a   m̩-bʊ-jo   bw-ake
     17(LOC)-2-person   AUG-15(INF)-enter-FV   18(LOC)-14-place   14-POSS₃SG
     ʊ-bw-a   kʊ-tʊʊsy-a
     AUG-14-ASSOC   15(INF)-rest-FV
     'The promise of entering his rest still stands (lit: . . . is still there for people . . .).' (Hebrews 4: 1)

Concerning the parameter of pragmaticity, examples (24–30) feature scenarios best understood as neutral. Examples (31–34) illustrate counterfactual scenarios, i.e. scenarios in which the continuation of the relevant state-of-affairs runs counter to expectation. In (31) the clothes' cleanliness, expressed by the copula *lɪ* plus the ideophone *swe*, runs counter to the expected results of an outdoor football match, whereas in (32) the status of certain followers runs counter to their self-conception. In (33) the continuing possession of a car is at odds with the expectation that a senior citizen not capable of driving anymore would give away or sell their car. Lastly, in the context of (34), it would be expected that the town's many unfortunate people occupy the entire space of the dining hall, the opposite of which is expressed by the combination of the present persistive plus the existential construction.

(31) Context: Your child has played football outside.
     a-kin-ile   ʊ-m-pɪla,   looli   ɪ-my-enda   gy-ake   **gɪ-kaalɪ**
     SP₁-play-PFV   AUG-3-ball   but   AUG-4-clothe   4-POSS₃SG   SP₄-PERS
     gɪ-lɪ   **swe**
     SP₄-COP   IDEOPH.bright_white/clean
     'S/he played football, yet his/her clothes are still clean.' (elicited)

(32) gw-esa ʊ-jʊ   i-kʊ-tɪ,   "n-dɪ   n̩-dʊ-muli,"   kʊ-no
     1-all   AUG-PROX₁   SP₁-PRS-say   SP₁SG-COP   18(LOC)-11-light   17(LOC)-PROX
     a-m̩-beng-ile   ʊ-mw-itɪki   n-nine,   **a-kaalɪ   a-lɪ**
     SP₁-OP₁-hate-PFV   AUG-1-believer   1-companion   SP₁-PERS   SP₁-COP

mu-n-giisi
18(LOC)-9-darkness
'Anyone who claims to be in the light but hates a brother or sister is still in the darkness.' (1 John 2: 9)

(33) ʊ-mw-isʊkʊlʊ   gw-angʊ a-ka-bagɪl-a   kangɪ
     AUG-1-grandparent 1-POSS$_{1SG}$ SP$_{1SG}$-NEG-be_able-FV again
     ʊ-kʊ-pot-a,   looli **a-kaalɪ a-lɪ**   **n=ii-galɪ**
     AUG-15(INF)-steer-FV but SP$_1$-PERS SP$_1$-COP COM=5-car
     'My grandfather can't drive anymore, but he still has a car.' (elicited)

(34) Context: A servant was sent to gather all the poor, crippled and blind of the town and to invite them to a banquet.
     n-twa, m-bomb-ile ɪ-si   gʊ-n-dagiile,   leelo
     1-lord SP$_{1SG}$-do-PFV AUG-PROX$_{10}$ SP$_{2SG}$-OP$_{1SG}$-order.PFV now/but
     ʊ-bʊ-jo   bʊ-kaalɪ bʊ-li=po.
     AUG-14-place SP$_{14}$-PERS SP$_{14}$-COP=16(LOC)
     'Sir [. . .] what you ordered has been done, but there is still room.' (Luke 14: 22)

2.5 'Not yet': Persistive plus infinitive

The most common way of expressing the phasal polarity notion of NOT YET in Nyakyusa consists of the persistive plus infinitive. (35, 36) illustrate this for the present tense and past tense, respectively.

(35) nsyɪsyɪ   a-ɪnkʊ-m̩-bʊʊl-a   kalʊlʊ   a-ɪnkʊ-tɪ   "ɪɪ-nyama
     skunk(1a)   SP$_1$-NARR-OP$_1$-tell-FV hare(1a) SP$_1$-NARR-say AUG-meat(9)
     jɪ-p-iile   is-aga   tʊ-ly-ege!"   po   kalʊlʊ
     SP$_9$-be(come)_burnt-FV come-IPFV SP$_{1PL}$-eat-IPFV.SUBJ then hare(1a)
     a-ɪnkʊ-tɪ   "taasi. **jɪ-kaalɪ ʊ-kʊ-py-a.**"
     SP$_1$-NARR-say yet   SP$_9$-PERS AUG-15(INF)-be(come)_burnt-PFV
     'Skunk told Hare "The meat is done, come let's eat!" Hare said "Later. It's not yet done."' (Hare and Skunk)

(36) *namanga* *m̩-bepo* *mw-ikemo* ***a-a-kaalɪ***
because 1-spirit 1-holy SP₁-PST-PERS
ʊ-kʊ-n-sololok-el-a *na=jʊ-mo* *m̩-ba-ndʊ* *a-bo*
AUG-15(INF)-OP₁-descend-APPL-FV COM=1-one 18(LOC)-2-person AUG-DEM₂
'Because the Holy Spirit had not yet come on any of them'
(Acts 8: 16)

As Veselinova and Devos (this volume) show, the use of the persistive plus infinitive to denote the concept of NOT YET is also found in a number of other Eastern Bantu languages.

The collocation of persistive plus infinitive is also commonly used in temporal adverbial clauses to express temporal precedence, that is, in these contexts 'when NOT YET' yields 'before'. Veselinova and Devos (this volume) point out that the use of NOT YET expressions to signify temporal precedence is recurrent across the Bantu language family. (37) is an illustration with a matrix clause featuring the past imperfective in its habitual/generic reading. (38) illustrates an adverbial clause of precedence with a subjunctive in directive function, hence oriented towards future time. Recall from Section 1.3 that in Nyakyusa temporal clauses, the present (or non-past) paradigms are used, receiving their temporal interpretation from the matrix clause.

(37) ***bo ba-kaalɪ*** *ʊ-kw-and-a* *ʊ-kʊ-mog-a*
as SP₂-PERS AUG-15(INF)-begin-FV AUG-15(INF)-dance-FV
ba-a-fwal-aga *ɪ-my-enda* *ɪ-my-elu,* *pamo*
SP₂-PST-dress/wear-IPFV AUG-4-cloth AUG-4-white or
a-ma-golole a-m-eelu.
AUG-6-sheet AUG-6-white
'Before starting to dance, they would put on white clothes, or white sheets' (The custom of dancing)

(38) *gw-ikasy-e* *ʊ-kw-is-a* *m̩bɪbɪ~m̩bɪbɪ* ***bo***
SP2SG-try_one's_best-SUBJ AUG-15(INF)-come-FV REDUPL~fast as
ka-kaalɪ *ʊ-kʊ-fik-a* *a-ka-balɪlo* *a-ka-a* *m-ma-pepo.*
SP₁₂-PERS AUG-15(INF)-arrive-FV AUG-12-time AUG-12-ASSOC 18(LOC)-6-cold
'Do your best to get here before winter (lit: . . . when winter has not yet arrived).' (2 Timothy 4: 21)

Examples (35–38) all feature a "bare" infinitive. Alternatively, an infinitive marked for locative noun class 16 (and hence without the augment) can also be used.[5] Similar variation in the marking of the infinitival complement is found with phasal verbs (such as 'continue' or 'stop'), as well as with modal and manipulation verbs, but cannot be said to be a feature of infinitives in Nyakyusa beyond these cases; see Persohn (2017a: 323–331). It is noteworthy that the younger language assistants used class-16-marked infinitives more frequently than the older ones, and that locative-marked forms are not attested in the written sources. In one instance, an infinitive marked for locative class 18 is attested (40).

(39) *i-kʊ-j-a   pa-kʊ-kwel-a   kangɪ, paapo*
SP₁-PRS-be(come)-FV 16(LOC)-15(INF)-climb-FV again because
*ɪ-kɪ-kapʊ   kɪ-mo   **kɪ-kaalɪ pa-kw-isʊl-a***
AUG-7-basket 7-one SP₇-PERS 16(LOC)-15(INF)-be(come)_full-FV
'He is about to climb up again, because one basket is still empty.'
(Elisha Pear Story)

(40) *ga-kaalɪ   n-kʊ-kom-a*
SP₆-PERS   18(LOC)-15(INF)-ripen-FV
'They (the bananas) are not yet ripe.' (overheard)

2.6 'Not yet': Persistive plus negative present perfective

In the present tense, an alternative expression for the concept of NOT YET consists of the persistive plus the negative counterpart to the present perfective, formed by a prefix *ka-* and the default final vowel *-a*. All attested tokens of this expression in the textual data, including in the New Testament, feature counterfactual scenarios (the delayed inception of a state-of-affairs being counter to expectation). The following two examples illustrate this. In (41), the lack of success in finding an explanation runs counter to the expectation that the narrator would have found one after thinking about it for his entire life. In (42), astonishment is expressed that the disciples, even after being reminded of a miracle, still have not understood that worrying about food is unnecessary.

---

5 Variation between PERS AUG-INF and PERS 16(LOC)-INF is also attested in neighbouring Ndali (Botne 2008: 118).

(41) Context: Speaking about a wondrous event that the narrator witnessed as a child.
na=kʊ-lɪlɪno   kʊ-no   n-ikw-inogon-a
COM=17(LOC)-now/today   17(LOC)-PROX   SP$_{1SG}$-PRS-consider-FV
m̩bʊsikʊ~m̩-bʊ-sikʊ   ɪnga   n-gʊmbwike.   looli
REDUPL~18(LOC)-14-time   if/when   SP$_{1SG}$-remember.PFV   but
ɪ-n-dɪgaanio   syo   **n-gaalɪ**   **n-ga-si-many-a**
AUG-10-explanation   DEM$_{10}$ SP$_{1SG}$-PERS   SP$_{1SG}$-NEG-OP$_{10}$-know-FV
'Even today I think about it whenever I remember it. But an explanation I have not found yet.' (Busse 1949: 208–209)

(42) Context: The disciples have just been reminded of the miracle of feeding 4,000 people with just a few loaves of bread and a handful of fish. Yet they still worry about food.
a-ɪnkʊ-ba-laalʊʊsy-a   a-ɪnkʊ-tɪ   "po   leelo   **mu-kaalɪ**
SP$_1$-NARR-OP$_2$-ask-FV SP$_1$-NARR-say   then now/but SP$_2$-PERS
mu-ka-syagani-a?"
SP$_{2PL}$-NEG-understand-FV
'He said to them: Do you still not understand?' (Mark 8: 21)

The observation from the textual sources is corroborated by data from elicitation, where the collocation of persistive plus the negative counterpart to the present perfective was strongly preferred in counterfactual scenarios. (43) illustrates such a case.

(43) Context: We are in a restaurant and have eaten. Now we are about to leave. The waiter calls.
   a. *taasi.*   **mu-kaalɪ**   **mu-ka-homb-a**
      yet   SP$_{2PL}$-PERS   SP$_{2PL}$-NEG-pay-FV
   b. 'Wait, you have not paid yet.' (elicited)
     #*taasi.*   **mu-kaalɪ**   **ʊ-kʊ-homb-a**
      yet   SP$_{2PL}$-PERS   AUG-15(INF)-pay-FV

It is conceivable that the better compatibility of this collocation with counterfactual scenarios is linked to its "literal" meaning of a persistent non-happening ('still have not'). Thus, Van Baar (1997) considers English *still not* a counterfactual NOT YET expression, with "which the speaker indicates that the absence of a certain situation, which is expressed by means of a negative sentence, extends beyond his/her hopes or expectations" (Van Baar 1997: 25).

3 The expression of 'already'

The phasal polarity concept of ALREADY deserves a short explanation. Despite the meaning of its English namesake, this concept encompasses markers that denote a change from negative to positive polarity, independent of whether the turning point is construed as early (e.g. English *already*), late (e.g. English *finally*, Turkish *artık*), or not evaluated for its temporal location at all (e.g. Spanish *ya*); see Kramer (2017: 11–12).

As for marking early (or neutral) changes in polarity, which van der Auwera (1998: 50) labels "already inchoatives", Nyakyusa does not have a fully integrated dedicated expression. A first indication of this "gap" comes from the absence of such a marker in the text corpus. What is more, when trying to elicit ALREADY expressions in contexts such as those in (44) and (65) below, the language assistants would use the relevant tense-aspect paradigms without any additional device indicating the transgression in polarity.

(44) Context: Your parents live in a different city, far away. They are coming to visit you and their arrival was expected for late afternoon. It is midday and your brother calls you over the phone.
ba-fik-ile,   ba-lɪ   pa-ka-aja
SP$_2$-arrive-PFV SP$_2$-COP   16(LOC)-12-homestead
'They have arrived [already], they are at (our) home.' (elicited)

Further evidence for the absence of an already inchoative comes from a parallel text search of the New Testament. The assumption was that if Nyakyusa had a dedicated expression for early or neutral changes from negative to positive polarity, it would be expected to be found in at least some of the verses that contain a comparable expression in one of the two parallel texts. Thus the English *New International Version* was searched for the word *already*, while the Swahili *Neno* translation was searched for the adverb *tayari* 'already',[6] as well as for forms of the grammaticalized markers *me-kwisha~me-sha* 'PFCT-already' and *li-kwisha~li-sha* 'PST-already' (see Ashton 1947: 271–272; Mpiranya 2014: 45).

---

6 Swahili *tayari* has another meaning 'ready (in the sense of being prepared)' (TUKI 2014). Tokens featuring this meaning were not considered.

The findings from the parallel text comparison corroborate the initial picture. As (45–47) illustrate, typically the transgression in polarity is not made explicit at all, even in verses where both the English and the Swahili translations feature ALREADY expressions. As these examples also show, the absence of such a dedicated expression cannot be traced back to the parameter of paradigmaticity: while (44, 45) and (65) below feature counterfactual scenarios, the scenarios in (46, 47) are best understood as neutral.

(45) ʊ-mʊ-ndʊ   gw-esa   ʊ-jʊ   i-kʊ-n-keet-a   ʊ-n-kiikʊlʊ
     AUG-1-person 1-all   AUG-PROX₁   SP₁-PRS-OP₁-watch-FV   AUG-1-woman
     n=ʊ-kʊ-n-nyonyw-a,   bo   **a-logilwe**   nagwe
     COM=AUG-15(INF)-OP₁-long_for-FV   by_then   SP₁-copulate.PFV   COM.DEM₁
     mu-n-dumbula   j-aake
     18(LOC)-9-heart 9-POSS₃ₛ𝒢
     'Anyone who looks at a woman lustfully has already committed adultery with her in his heart.'
     (SWA: *amekwisha kuzini* 'SP₁-PFCT-already 15(INF)-commit_adultery')
     (Matthew 5: 28)

(46) ʊ-ne   **m-ba-bʊʊl-ile**   ɪɪ-nongwa   ɪ-syo,   looli
     AUG-PRON₁ₛ𝒢 SP₁ₛ𝒢-OP₂ₚ𝒧-tell-PFV   AUG-issue.10   AUG-DEM₁₀   but
     mu-ka-a-pɪlɪkiisye.   po   fiki   mu-kʊ-lond-a
     SP₂ₚ𝒧-NEG-PST-listen.PFV then   why   SP₂ₚ𝒧-PRS-want-FV
     m-ba-bʊʊl-e   kangɪ?
     SP₁ₛ𝒢-OP₂ₚ𝒧-tell-SUBJ   again
     'I have already told you and you did not listen. Why do you want to hear it again? (lit: . . . want me to tell you again)'
     (SWA: *nimekwisha waambia* 'SP₁ₛ𝒢-PFCT-already OP₂ₚ𝒧-say-APPL-FV')
     (John 9: 27)

(47) Context: Money is taken from one servant and given to one that already has plenty.
     n-twa, keet-a   **a-lɪ**   **na=syo**   ɪ-n-dalama   ɪ-fi-jabo
     1-lord look-IMP SP₁-COP   COM=DEM₁₀   AUG-10-money   AUG-8-piece
     kalongo!
     ten
     'Sir [. . .], he already has ten!'
     (SWA: *tayari anayo* 'already SP₁-be_with-DEM₆')
     (Luke 19: 25)

Several strategies were encountered to achieve a similar effect to that of an already inchoative. The common denominator of all these is the signalling of temporal precedence ('(have) verbed before'). Thus, in several instances, an adverbial *kılıngaani* was found, as in (48). This element has a wider meaning, along the lines of 'before, beforehand', as illustrated in (49). In one instance, an etymologically and semantically related adverb *ngaani* was used; see (50). As illustrated in (51), this element also has a more general meaning of temporal precedence. Both *kılıngaani* and *ngaani* can, therefore, not be considered specialized expressions of phasal polarity.

(48) *namanga   m-ba-bʊʊl-ile   kılıngaani   ʊkʊtı   a-ba-juuta*
      because   SP$_{1SG}$-OP$_{2PL}$-tell-PFV before   COMP   AUG-2-jew
      na   a-ba   ba-ka-j-a   ba-juuta ba-fwene
      COM AUG-PROX$_2$ SP$_2$-NEG-be(come)-FV 2-jew   SP$_2$-be_equal.PFV
      itolo   b-oosa   bi-kʊ-longosi-gw-a   n=ʊ-bʊ-tʊla   nongwa
      just   2-all   SP$_2$-PRS-lead.CAUS-PASS-FV COM=AUG-14-err   issue.10
      'For we have already made the charge (lit: I told you beforehand) that Jews and Gentiles alike are all under the power of sin.' (Romans 3: 9)

(49) *kangı   a-a-lond-aga   ʊ-kʊ-bʊ-setʊl-a   ʊ-bʊ-sisya*
      again   SP$_1$-PST-want-IPFV   AUG-15(INF)-OP$_{14}$-reveal-FV   AUG-14-glory
      bw-ake   ʊ-bʊ-kʊlʊmba, kʊlı   a-ba   a-a-lond-aga
      14-POSS$_{3SG}$ AUG-14-big   17(LOC)   AUG-PROX$_2$ SP$_1$-PST-want-IPFV
      ʊ-kʊ-ba-pel-el-a   ı-kı-sa,   a-ba
      AUG-15(INF)-OP$_2$-make-APPL-FV AUG-7-sympathy   AUG-PROX$_2$
      a-a-ba-tendekiisye   kılıngaani   ʊ-kʊ-ba-p-a=po
      SP$_1$-PST-OP$_2$-prepare.PFV before   AUG-15(INF)-OP$_2$-give-FV=16(LOC)
      ʊ-bʊ-sisya   bw-ake
      AUG-14-glory 14-POSS$_{3SG}$
      'What if he did this to make the riches of his glory known to the objects of his mercy (lit: to those that he wanted to make mercy for), whom he prepared in advance for glory.' (Romans 9: 23)

(50) po   n-si-tumul-iile   **ngaani** ıı-nongwa   ı-sy-a
    then SP1SG-OP10-judge-APPL.PFV before   AUG-issue.10 AUG-10-ASSOC
    mu-ndʋ   ʋ-jo,   ʋ-jʋ   a-bomb-ile   sisii~syo
    1-person AUG-DEM1   AUG-PROX1   SP1-do-PFV   REDUPL~DEM10
    'I have already passed judgement in the name of our Lord Jesus on the one who has been doing this.' (1 Corinthians 5: 3)

(51) Ndaabıti bo   a-si-bon-iile   **ngaani** ı-sy-a
    David   as   SP1-OP10-see-APPL.PFV   before   AUG-10-ASSOC
    n-ky-eni,   a-a-si-job-ile   ı-sy-a
    18(LOC)-7-forehead SP1-PST-OP10-speak-PFV AUG-10-ASSOC
    kʋ-syʋk-a   Meesija
    15(INF)-be_resurrected-FV   Messiah
    'Seeing what was to come (lit . . .those things of ahead), he spoke of the resurrection of the Messiah.' (Acts 2: 31)

In one instance *litaasi*, one of the variant forms of a multifunctional word 'yet, first; wait a bit' (see also examples (35, 43)) was encountered (52). While the strategies so far feature adverbials, the last strategy to be mentioned features a verbal element. In (53), the verb *tala* 'go ahead' is used.[7] Like the adverbial examples so far, this seems to signal the temporal precedence of the initial act of giving grace.

(52) Pilati bo   i-kʋ-pılık-a   ʋkʋtı Jesu a-fw-ile   **litaasi**
    P.   as   SP1-PRS-hear-FV   COMP   J.   SP1-die-PFV yet
    a-ımkʋ-swig-a   po   a-ımkʋ-n-koolel-a   ʋ-n-dongosi gw-a
    SP1-NARR-wonder-FV   then   SP1-NARR-OP1-call-FV AUG-1-leader 1-ASSOC
    ba-sikali a-ımkʋ-ŋ-daalʋʋsy-a   ınga   Jesu a-fw-ile   nalooli
    2-soldier SP1-NARR-OP1-ask-FV   if/when   J.   SP1-die-PFV really
    litaasi.
    yet
    'Pilate was surprised to hear that he (Jesus) was already dead. Summoning the centurion, he asked him if Jesus had already died.' (Mark 15: 44)

---

7 Concerning the locative enclitic =*po*, see Persohn (2017b).

(53) ʊ-kʊ-kong-an-a   n=ʊ-kʊ-sit-a
     AUG-15(INF)-follow-RECP-FV COM=AUG-15(INF)-AUX.NEG-FV
     kw-agɪlw-a   kw-ake   Kyala   a-tʊ-p-eele
     15(INF)-diminish-FV   15(INF)-POSS₃SG God(1a) SP₁-OP₁PL-give-PFV
     tw-esa ii-pyana ongiile=po   p-ii-pyana   ɪ-lɪ
     1PL-all 5-grace SP₁.add.PFV=16(LOC) 16(LOC)-5-grace AUG-PROX₅
     ly-a-tal-ile=po
     SP₅-PST-go_ahead-PFV=16(LOC)
     'Out of his fullness we have all received grace in place of grace already
     given. (lit: . . . he has given us grace, he has added it to the grace that had
     gone ahead)' (John 1: 16)

As the preceding discussion has shown, Nyakyusa does not possess a native and specialized already inchoative. However, it seems that the Swahili expression *tayari* – itself a loan from Omani Arabic – is increasingly being borrowed into the language in the shape of *tajalɪ*. (54) is an example. Concerning the parameter of telicity (the compatibility with early or late evaluations in counterfactual scenarios), (55) shows that *tajalɪ* is infelicitous with a late change.

(54) Context: Your brother is late for dinner.
     bo a-fik-ile   ɪ-fi-ndʊ   **tajalɪ**   **fi-taliile**
     as SP₁-arrive-PFV AUG-8-food already(<SWA) SP₈-cool.PFV
     'When he arrives, the food will already be cold.' (elicited)

(55) Context: Your sister is on her way to Dodoma. Her bus was scheduled to
     arrive in the afternoon. Late at night she calls you.
     #tajalɪ   n-gʊ-fik-a
     already(<SWA) SP₁SG-PRS-arrive-FV
     (intended: 'Finally I am arriving.')

The language assistants consulted all perceived *tajalɪ* as a Swahili intrusion and were hesitant to use it in elicitation. Given this hesitance, as well as the non-occurrence of *tajalɪ* in the text corpus, including the New Testament, one may consider it a not (yet) fully integrated part of the Nyakyusa phasal polarity system. See Guérois (this volume) for a similar case in the Mozambican Bantu language Cuwabo (chw).

Returning to expressions of a late transgression in polarity, several different strategies were observed. The first strategy consists in the use of general 'now'-expressions. This is illustrated in (56) with *ʊlʊ* 'now', formally a class 11 proximal demonstrative. The addition of the augment-less class 11 referential demonstrative *lo* seems to provide focus on *ʊlʊ* (see Persohn 2017a: 305). In a similar vein, in (64) below, *ɪmo* 'now' is employed for a late evaluation of the relevant change in polarity.

(56) Context: Your sister is on her way to Dodoma. Her bus was scheduled to arrive in the afternoon. Late at night she calls you.
 lo   ʊlʊ   n-gʊ-fik-a
 DEM$_{11}$ now(PROX$_{11}$) SP$_{1SG}$-PRS-arrive-FV
 'Now [finally] I am arriving.' (elicited)

The second strategy consists of the use of a semantically and compositionally transparent adverbial *kʊmmalɪkɪsyo* 'at the end', as illustrated in (57).

(57) *n-gʊ-sekel-a   fiijo   mu-n-twa,   paapo   kʊ-m-malɪkɪsyo*
 SP$_{1SG}$-PRS-rejoice-FV INTENS 18(LOC)-1-lord because 17(LOC)-3-end
 mw-andiisye   kangɪ   ʊ-kʊ-m-baasy-a.   mw-andiisye
 SP$_{2PL}$-repeat.PFV again AUG-15(INF)-OP$_{1SG}$-worry-FV SP$_{2PL}$-repeat.PFV
 mw-a-m-baasy-aga   bwila, looli mu-ka-a-kag-ile   itolo
 SP$_{2PL}$-PST-OP$_{1SG}$-worry-IPFV always but SP$_{2PL}$-NEG-PST-expel-PFV just
 looli a-ka-balɪlo a-ka-a   kʊ-bomb-a   bo ʊ-lo
 but AUG-12-time AUG-12-ASSOC 15(INF)-do-FV as AUG-DEM$_{11}$
 'I rejoiced greatly in the Lord that at last you renewed your concern for me. Indeed, you were concerned, but you had no opportunity to show it.' (Philippians 4: 10)

The third and last strategy consists of the use of an expression *kʊbʊʊbo*, as illustrated in (58).[8] The language assistants paraphrased the meaning of this element as 'at last; after a long effort or prolonged waiting'. As far as can be extrapolated from the data, *kʊbʊʊbo* seems like the best candidate for a specialized expression of a late change to positive polarity, or an "artık inchoative" in van der Auwera's (1998: 50) terms. It is, however, only attested twice in the translation of the New Testament, and in elicitation it was not offered spontaneously.

---

8 The etymology of this expression remains unclear. Its shape indicates a nominal plus the locative class 17 prefix *kʊ-*. However, no corresponding nominal could be identified.

(58) a-ka-balɪlo ka-a   k-ingi   ʊ-n̩-dongi   a-a-kaan-aga,
AUG-12-time 12-ASSOC 12-many AUG-1-judge SP₁-PST-refuse-IPFV
looli **kʊbuʊbo** *a-lɪnkw-inogon-a   mu-n-dumbula a-lɪnkʊ-tɪ*
but at_last   SP₁-NARR-consider-FV 18(LOC)-9-heart SP₁-NARR-say
'For some time he (the judge) refused. But finally he said to himself . . .'
(Luke 18: 4)

To summarize, Nyakyusa does not have a specialized expression for an early (or general) change in positive polarity (van der Auwera's "already inchoative"). While Swahili *tayari* is being borrowed into the language, it cannot (yet) be considered an integrated part of the Nyakyusa phasal polarity system. As for denoting a late transgression in polarity (van der Auwera's "artɪk inchoative"), *kʊbuʊbo* 'at last' seems like a good candidate, although the limited attestations do not allow for a conclusive judgement.

4 'No longer': Negation plus *kangɪ* 'again'

The phasal polarity concept of NO LONGER is expressed in Nyakyusa by the combination of a negated verb form plus the adverb *kangɪ* 'again'. This collocation has thus undergone a shift in meaning from the negation of an iteration to a NO LONGER expression. The same development has been observed by Van Baar (1997: 49–50) for the Papuan languages Abun (Western New Guinea; kgr) and Usan (Papua New Guinea; wnu). Bernander (this volume) reports the same for Nyakyusa's neighbour Manda.

(59) illustrates the expression of NO LONGER with the negative counterpart (marked by *ti-*) to the simple present in its habitual/generic reading. (60) illustrates the discontinuation of a state denoted by the inchoative verb *bagɪla* 'be able, can', employing the negative counterpart to the present perfective (see Section 2.6). (61) is an example with a negated past tense existential construction. Lastly, in (62), *kangɪ* is used together with the negative counterpart to the subjunctive mood plus the imperfective suffix (see Persohn 2017a: 284–288), expressing the obligation to discontinue a habit.

(59) Context: Your friend lives in Europe.
*iis-aga   kʊkʊtɪ ky-mja. leelo   **a-ti-kw-is-a   kangɪ***
SP₁.PST.come-IPFV every 7-year now/but SP₁-NEG-PRS-come-FV again
'S/he used to come every year. But now s/he does not come anymore.'
(elicited)

(60) *m-bal-ıl-a*   *ı-ky-ʊma*   *ky-angʊ*   *ı-kı*
     OP$_{1SG}$-count-APPL-IMP   AUG-7-rich   7-POSS$_{1SG}$ AUG-PROX$_7$
     kw-ɪmɪlɪl-a!   **ʊ-ka-bagɪl-a**   *ʊ-kʊ-j-a*
     SP$_{2SG}$.PRS-supervise-FV   SP$_{2SG}$-NEG-be_able-FV   AUG-15(INF)-be(come)-FV
     kangɪ   *mw-ɪmɪlɪli!*
     again   1-supervisor
     'Give an account of your management, (lit: count for me the wealth that you supervise) because you cannot be manager any longer.'
     (Luke 16: 2)

(61) *ʊ-m-paalanga*   *ʊ-gw-a*   *kw-and-a*   *gʊ-la*   *n=ɪ-k-iisʊ*
     AUG-3-heaven   AUG-3-ASSOC   15(INF)-begin-FV   3-DIST   COM=AUG-7-land
     ɪ-ky-a   *kw-and-a*   *kɪ-la*   *fy-a-sook-ile=po*
     AUG-7-ASSOC   15(INF)-begin-FV   7-DIST   7-PST-leave-PFV= 16(LOC)
     ɪɪ-nyanja   *j-oope*   **jɪ-ka-a-li=po**   **kangɪ.**
     AUG-sea.9   9-also   SP$_9$-NEG-PST-COP=16(LOC)   again
     'The first heaven and the first earth had passed away, and there was no longer any sea.' (Revelations 21: 1)

(62) *tʊ-ba-kem-el-e,*   **ba-lɪnga-job-aga**   **kangɪ**
     SP$_{1PL}$-OP$_2$-bark-APPL-SUBJ   SP$_2$-NEG.SUBJ-speak-IPFV   again
     n=ʊ-mu-ndʊ   *gw-esa*   *jʊ-la*   *mu-n-gamu*   *j-aa*   Jesu
     COM=AUG-1-person   1-all   1-DIST   18(LOC)-9-name   9-ASSOC   J.
     'We must warn them to speak no longer to anyone in his (Jesus') name.'
     (Acts 4: 17)

Concerning the parameter of pragmaticity, the preceding examples illustrate the expression of NO LONGER in neutral scenarios. Example (63) illustrates a counterfactual scenario, in that the discontinuation of giving milk runs counter to the expectation of a healthy cow's behaviour. See also (64, 65) below for two further cases of counterfactual scenarios.

(63) Context: I am worried about one of my cows. I ask somebody for help.
     kalɪ   *fi-ki*   *fi-j-aag-ile*   *ɪɪ-ng'ombe*   *j-angʊ?*
     Q   8-what   SP$_8$-OP$_9$-find-PFV   AUG-cow.9   9-POSS$_{1SG}$
     jɪ-ti-kʊ-soosy-a   **kangɪ**   *ʊ-lʊ-kama.*
     SP$_9$-NEG-PRS-leave.CAUS-FV   again   AUG-11-milk
     'What is wrong with (lit: what has found) my cow? She doesn't give milk anymore.' (elicited)

Concerning the parameter of telicity, that is, the compatibility of the expression with early or late evaluations of the relevant change in polarity with respect to the counterfactual background assumption, the available data suggests that the negation-plus-'again' construction does not rule out early or late changes. That is, following Kramer (2017), it constitutes a neutral NO LONGER expression. Thus, in (64), the change from walking with crutches to walking without them is embedded in a late context, while in (65) the same polarity change is embedded in an early scenario.

(64) Context: I injured my leg and had to use crutches. The doctor said it would take a month for me to be able to walk without them. In the end, it took three months.
lıno   ***n-di-kw-end-el-a***   ***kangı*** *a-ma-gongo*
now   SP$_{1SG}$-NEG-PRS-walk/travel-APPL-FV   again AUG-6-crutch(<SWA)
'Finally (lit: now) I don't (need to) walk with crutches anymore.' (elicited)

(65) Context: I injured my leg and had to use crutches. The doctor said it would take a month for me to be able to walk without them. In the end, it only took two weeks.
n-di-kw-end-el-a   ***kangı*** *a-ma-gongo*
SP$_{1SG}$-NEG-PRS-walk/travel-APPL-FV again   AUG-6-crutch (<SWA)
'I [already] don't (need to) walk with crutches anymore.' (elicited)

5 Expressibility

The parameter of expressibility "concerns the possibility of formal coding of phasal polarity expressions" (Kramer 2017: 14). Considering the Swahili loan *tajalı* as a not (yet) fully integrated element in Nyakyusa (Section 3), Nyakyusa has one structural "gap" in its phasal polarity system, namely in the expression of ALREADY – at least as far as general and early transgressions into positive polarity are concerned. As for the denotation of a late change, several strategies are attested, of which the adverbial *kʊbʊʊbo* 'at last' seems like the best candidate for a dedicated phasal polarity expression. Its low frequency, however, impedes a decisive judgement.

Nyakyusa thus follows the strong global tendency observed by Van Baar (1997: 117), namely that in languages lacking a dedicated expression for only one of the four phasal polarity concepts, it is either ALREADY or NO LONGER that is missing. Nyakyusa further corroborates Van Baar's (1997: 126–129) observation that of all four phasal polarity expressions, it is ALREADY that is most likely to be borrowed.

6 Paradigmaticity

Kramer's (2017) parameter of paradigmaticity refers to the symmetry of a language's phasal polarity system. Following Kramer, this parameter can be approached from an internal or external point of view.

As Kramer (2017: 16) puts it, in internally symmetrical phasal polarity paradigms, "the paradigm contains elements that express logically alternative phasal polarity concepts and can be ascribed the same status of grammatical category", where "logically alternative" refers to the pairs ALREADY–NOT YET and STILL–NO LONGER (see Van Baar 1997: 61).

In Nyakyusa, internal paradigmaticity is marginal at best. As discussed in Section 2.6, in the present tense the phasal polarity concept of NO LONGER can be expressed through the combination of the persistive plus the negative counterpart to the present perfective. If, for the sake of the argument, the persistive is considered a genuine STILL expression, this can be considered a case of internal paradigmaticity through negation. The alternative NOT YET expression, consisting of persistive plus infinitive (see Section 2.5), however, does not constitute the negative counterpart to the expression of STILL. Likewise, the expression(s) of ALREADY through an adverbial – with the limitations summarized in Section 5 – constitutes a syntactic configuration entirely different from that of the expression of NO LONGER through affixal verbal negation plus 'again' (see Sections 3 and 4). For a very similar situation in the Bantu language Manda, spoken in the immediate vicinity of Nyakyusa, see Bernander (this volume).

As for external paradigmaticity, it "is a matter of the relation between members of the phasal polarity paradigms and members of the corresponding non-phasal polarity paradigms [. . .] in the domains of Tense, Mood, and Aspect" (Kramer 2017: 17). As Kramer goes on to point out, external paradigmatic symmetry is rare, and at best partial. To point out just one case of external paradigmatic asymmetry in the Nyakyusa paradigms, the expression of NOT YET through the persistive plus infinitive (see Section 2.5) leads to the loss of the aspectual distinction found in the absence of this phasal polarity expression. Likewise, there is no one-to-one counterpart to the subjunctive mood under the scope of STILL.

7 Conclusion

The present chapter has given a descriptive account of phasal polarity expressions in Nyakyusa. It has thereby provided one of the first in-depth examinations of phasal polarity expressions in a specific Bantu language. In the following, the findings are summarized, based on Kramer's (2017) parameters.

With regard to expressibility, Nyakyusa has one structural "gap" in its phasal polarity system, namely in the expression of ALREADY. As shown in Section 3, Nyakyusa has no "already inchoative" (van der Auwera 1998: 50), i.e. no expression for early (or general) changes to positive polarity, with *tajalı* < SWA *tayari* not (yet) constituting an integrated part of the system. For the evaluation of a late change, several different strategies were encountered, with *kʊbʊʊbo* 'at last' being the most likely candidate for a dedicated phasal polarity expression.

Concerning the parameter of coverage, the Nyakyusa phasal polarity system is to be considered as flexible, given that one element, the persistive, is involved in expressions of both STILL and NOT YET (see Section 2).

As for the parameter of wordhood, the Nyakyusa persistive, which is involved in the expression of the phasal polarity concepts STILL and NOT YET, is an auxiliary-like grammatical element with clearly verbal characteristics and which hosts a subject marker as well as a past tense marker. The situation is mixed for the concept of NO LONGER, which is expressed by the combination of a verbal affix expressing negative polarity with the phonologically and morphologically independent adverb *kangı* 'again'.

With regard to the parameter of telicity, the expression of NO LONGER through a negated verb plus *kangı* 'again' is to be considered a general marker in that it rules out neither late nor early changes.

Concerning pragmaticity, Nyakyusas's expressions for STILL and NO LONGER are equally suitable in neutral and in counterfactual scenarios (see Sections 2.2–2.4 and 4). As for NOT YET, in the present tense the collocation of the persistive plus the negative counterpart to the present perfective is preferred in counterfactual scenarios over the combination of persistive plus infinitive (see Sections 2.5 and 2.6).

Lastly, in terms of paradigmaticity, the Nyakyusa phasal polarity system is best understood as highly internally asymmetrical. Internal symmetry can at best be said to be found with the expression of NO LONGER in the present tense. The Nyakyusa phasal polarity system is also to be considered asymmetrical from an external point of view (see Section 6).

Abbreviations

#	infelicitous	INTENS	intensifier
1...18	noun classes 1–18	IPFV	imperfective aspect
1a	subsidiary noun class 1a	ITV	itive/distal
1SG	first person singular	LOC	locative
1PL	first person plural	NARR	narrative tense
2SG	second person singular	NEG	negation
2PL	second person plural	OP	object prefix
APPL	applicative	PASS	passive
ASSOC	associative ('genitive')	PERS	persistive
AUG	augment ('pre-prefix')	PFCT	perfect
AUX	auxiliary	PFV	perfective aspect
CAUS	causative	POSS	possessive
COM	comitative ('and', 'with')	PRON	pronoun
COMP	complementiser	PROX	proximal demonstrative
COP	copula	PRS	simple present
DEM	demonstrative	PST	past tense
DIST	distal demonstrative	RECP	reciprocal
FUT	future tense	REDUPL	reduplication
FV	final vowel	Q	question marker
IDEOPH	ideophone	SP	subject prefix
IMP	imperative	SUBJ	subjunctive mood
INF	infinitive	SWA	Swahili

Bibliographic references

Abe, Yuko. 2015. Persistive in Bende – on the grammaticalization path. *Asian and African Languages and Linguistics* 9. 23–44.
Ashton, Ethel O. 1947. *Swahili grammar (including intonation)*. London: Longmans, Green and Co.
Berger, Paul. 1933. Konde-Texte. *Zeitschrift für Eingeborenen-Sprachen* 23. 110–154.
Botne, Robert D. 2008. *A grammatical sketch of Chindali (Malawian variety)*. Philadelphia: American Philosophical Society.
Botne, Robert D. & Tiffany L. Kershner. 2008. Tense and cognitive space: on the organization of tense/aspect systems in Bantu languages and beyond. *Cognitive Linguistics* 19 (2). 145–218.
Busse, Joseph. 1942. Konde-Texte. *Zeitschrift für Eingeborenen-Sprachen* 32. 201–224.
Busse, Joseph. 1949. Aus dem Leben von Asyukile Malongo (Nyakyusa-Texte). *Zeitschrift für Eingeborenen-Sprachen* 35. 191–227.
Crane, Thera Marie & Bastian Persohn. 2019. What's in a Bantu verb? Actionality in Bantu languages. *Linguistic Typology* 23 (2). 303–345.
Dahl, Östen & Bernhard Wälchli. 2016. Perfects and iamatives: two gram types in one grammatical space. *Letras de hoje* 51 (3). 325–348.
Dixon, Robert M. W. 1982. *Where have all the adjectives gone?* Berlin: Mouton de Gruyter.

Endemann, Karl. 1914. Erste Übungen in Nyakyusa. *Mitteilungen veröffentlicht vom Seminar für Kolonialsprachen in Hamburg* 31 (Beiheft 10). 1–92
Guthrie, Malcolm. 1971. *Comparative Bantu: an introduction to the comparative linguistics and prehistory of the Bantu languages*. Vol. 2: Bantu prehistory, inventory and indexes. London: Gregg International.
Kramer, Raija. 2017. Position paper on Phasal Polarity expressions. Hamburg: University of Hamburg. https://www.aai.uni-hamburg.de/afrika/php2018/medien/position-paper-on-php.pdf (accessed 20 January 2019)
Löbner, Sebastian. 1989. 'Schon – erst – noch': An integrated analysis, *Linguistics and Philosophy* 12 (2). 167–212.
Maho, Jouni Filip. 2009. NUGL Online. The online version of the new updated Guthrie list, a referential classification of the Bantu languages. https://brill.com/fileasset/downloads_products/35125_Bantu-New-updated-Guthrie-List.pdf (accessed 12 March 2019)
Mpiranya, Fidèle. 2014. *Swahili grammar and workbook*. London: Routledge.
Muzale, Henry R.T. & Josephat M. Rugemalira. 2008. Researching and documenting the languages of Tanzania. *Language Documentation & Conservation* 2 (1). 68–108.
Nurse, Derek. 1979. Description of sample Bantu languages of Tanzania. *African Languages* 5. 1–150.
Nurse, Derek. 2008. *Tense and aspect in Bantu*. Oxford: Oxford University Press.
Persohn, Bastian. 2017a. *The verb in Nyakyusa: a focus on tense, aspect, and modality*. Berlin: Language Science Press.
Persohn, Bastian. 2017b. Locative and extra-locative clitics in Nyakyusa. *Africana Linguistica* 23. 151–165.
Persohn, Bastian. 2018. Aspectuality in Bantu: on the limits of Vendler's categories. *Linguistic Discovery* 16 (2). 1–19.
Schumann, K. 1899. Grundriss einer Grammatik der Kondesprache. *Mittheilungen des Seminars für orientalische Sprachen* 2 (3). 1–86.
Simons, Gary F. & Charles D. Fenning (eds.). 2017. *Ethnologue: languages of the world*. 22nd edition. Dallas: SIL International.
Simons Garry F & Charles D. Fenning (eds). 2018. *Ethnologue: Languages of the World*, 21st edn. Dallas: SIL.
TUKI. 2014. *Kamusi ya kiswahili-kiingereza / Swahili-English dictionary*. 2nd edn. Dar es Salaam: Taasisi ya Uchunguzi ya Kiswahili (TUKI) / Institute of Swahili studies, University of Dar es Salaam.
Van Baar, Tim. 1997. *Phasal polarity*. Amsterdam: IFOTT.
Van de Velde, Mark, Koen Bostoen, Derek Nurse & Gérard Phillippson (eds.). 2019. *The Bantu languages*. 2nd edn. London: Routledge.
van der Auwera, Johan. 1993. 'Already' and 'still': beyond duality. *Linguistics and Philosophy* 16 (6). 613–653.
van der Auwera, Johan. 1998. Phasal Adverbials in the languages of Europe. In Johan van der Auwera & Dónall P. O. Baoill (eds.), *Adverbial constructions in the languages of Europe*, 25–145. Berlin: Mouton de Gruyter.
Vendler, Zeno. 1957. Verbs and times. *The Philosophical Review* 66. 143–160.

Rozenn Guérois
The expression of phasal polarity in Cuwabo (Bantu P34, Mozambique)

1 Introduction

Phasal polarity is used to refer to four time-related expressions denoting opposite phasal values and polarity, i.e. NOT YET, ALREADY, STILL, and NO LONGER. These four concepts form a system where the combination of temporal phases with a given polarity (positive or negative) is coded either lexically or grammatically by specialized markers. Three temporal phasal properties are identified by Plungian (1999), i.e. inchoative (start of an event), continuative (continuation of an event), and terminative (end of an event). Adapting to Plungian's (1999) phasal values, ALREADY is perceived as inchoative, STILL and NOT YET are continuative, and NO LONGER is terminative. These four concepts are thus interrelated on the timeline, in that they encode distinct but sequential phases of an event, starting with NOT YET, followed by ALREADY and STILL, and ending with NO LONGER. In addition to temporal phases, phasal polarity expressions are distinguished in terms of polarity, which opposes two pairs whose respective items are interrelated through negation: NOT YET and ALREADY on the one hand, and NO LONGER and STILL on the other. With the two negative concepts NOT YET and NO LONGER, the situation described by the verb does not hold, whereas with their positive counterparts ALREADY and STILL, the situation does. A third characteristic of phasal polarity expressions is that they lie on the simultaneous duality between expectation (based on background information) and state of affairs, i.e. the real situation.

Phasal expressions in European languages received some attention in the late 1990s (Van der Auwera 1998; Van Baar 1997), but this area of investigation

Acknowledgments: I wish to thank Sérgio Fernando Artur, my main Cuwabo consultant, for his assistance with my questions. This research has been supported by the BOF research funds of Ghent University. For fieldwork investigation, the author has further benefited from a 'Travel grant for a long stay abroad', provided by the Flanders Research Foundation (FWO). I am grateful to these bodies for their generous support. My thanks also go to the reviewers for their insightful comments on an earlier version of this chapter. Any remaining inadequacies are mine.

Rozenn Guérois, CNRS-LLACAN

https://doi.org/10.1515/9783110646290-007

remains fairly unexplored when it comes to African languages, including Bantu. Expressing the four concepts behind the notion of phasal polarity in Bantu languages involves a variety of strategies. Based on the parameters developed by Kramer in her 2017 position paper, this chapter aims to provide a detailed description of the way phasal polarity expressions are coded in Cuwabo, an Eastern Bantu language classified as P34 (Guthrie 1967–71, Maho 2009), spoken by more than 1,000,000 speakers (Mozambican National Institute of Statistics 2017) mostly located in the south-eastern part of Zambézia province in Mozambique. The different ways of categorizing the four phasal polarity concepts are examined, both in terms of formal properties and semantic/functional properties. Whenever possible and relevant, typological and historical issues are discussed.

This chapter is structured as follows: Section 2 presents some background information on Cuwabo. Sections 3 to 6 examine the four phasal polarity concepts in Cuwabo: NOT YET (section 3), ALREADY (section 4), STILL (section 5) and NO LONGER (section 6). These concepts are then discussed in light of Kramer's parameters in section 7. Conclusions are summarized in section 8.

The data provided in this chapter are from the central Cuwabo variety, spoken in Quelimane and its direct vicinity. Most data were collected in Quelimane, Namwinho, Maquival and Macuze between 2011 and 2013 (as part of the author's PhD fieldwork). Elicitation work more directly related to phasal polarity expressions was then carried out during the summer of 2018 in Quelimane. Occasionally, a few examples extracted from Festi and Valler (1994) are provided. Finally, the frequency of phasal polarity items in the languages is assessed. The number of occurrences is established on the basis of three Cuwabo corpora: the author's field data comprising tales, conversations, image descriptions and elicited sentences (17,414 tokens), Festi and Valler's (1994) Cuwabo-Portuguese dictionary, which contains numerous examples (58,080 tokens), and the 2004 Cuwabo Catholic Bible (552,825 tokens).

The metalanguage used for elicitation was Portuguese. Since Portuguese and English have different possibilities for expressing phasal polarity (and many other aspectual properties), each example illustrating phasal polarity includes both Portuguese and English translations. Portuguese translations originate from direct elicitation with Cuwabo speakers. English translations are then based on Portuguese ones. Further note that most Cuwabo data used in this chapter date back from the author's doctoral fieldwork (2011–2013) as part of a grammar writing project (Guérois 2015). Thus, the detection of phasal polarity concepts mostly relies on the Portuguese translations provided by my consultants back then. Only certain examples (explicitly indicated in this chapter) were more recently elicited from original data with the help of my main consultant, and for the purpose of this study.

2 Cuwabo verbal morphology

Cuwabo is a typical Bantu language[1] in its SVO word order, its predominantly head-marking morphology and its extensive system of noun classes and noun class agreement. As in most Bantu languages, Cuwabo has agglutinative verbal morphology, consisting of affixes with different grammatical functions, attached to the verb root, as can be seen in the verbal template in Figure 1. Note that the pre-initial and post-initial positions are referred to in relation to the initial position, itself reserved for subject prefixes. Morphemes which occur at pre-initial and post-initial positions are thus verbal prefixes.

Slots	Function/morphology
Pre-initial	Negation, TAM
Initial	Subject prefix
Post-initial	Negation, TA, AM
Pre-radical	Reflexive or object prefix
Radical	Verb root
Pre-final	Derivation, aspect
Final	TAM, negation
Post-final	Plural imperative suffix, locative, comitative/instrumental, restrictive, intensive, subject pronouns in relatives

Figure 1: The morphological structure of the Cuwabo verb (based on Güldemann's (1999) terminology).

The example in (1) illustrates the range of information that may appear in the verbal template, with temporal and aspectual information, subject agreement, negative polarity and object agreement all appearing as prefixes, while the verb root *ttamag* 'run' hosts the causative suffix and a second person plural subject pronoun in the post-final position.

---

[1] The reader is referred to works such as Williamson and Blench (2000: 11–42), Nurse and Philippson (2003) and Van de Velde and Bostoen (2019).

(1) ohinímúttamagíhéenyú:[2,3]
 o-hi-ní-mu-ttamag-íh-a=inyu
 PP1-NEG-IPFV-OP1-run-CAUS-FV.REL=PRO2PL
 'the one you are making run' (Ddingí)

Within the verbal template in Figure 1, the three bolded slots, i.e. pre-initial (prefix), post-initial (prefix) and post-final (clitic), are of particular relevance for the study of phasal polarity in Cuwabo. The pre-initial and post-initial slots are used to encode negative polarity with, respectively, the markers *ka-* in independent or main clauses, and *hi-* in subordinate clauses. Both these markers serve in the expression of NOT YET (section 4) and NO LONGER (section 6), i.e. the two phasal polarity concepts combining phasal values with negative polarity. Unlike the pre-initial and the initial positions, each reserved for a single prefix,[4] the post-initial slot is multifunctional and may host up to two morphemes dedicated to TAM and polarity. This is illustrated in (2) where the post-initial slot is occupied by two morphemes: in (2a) the perfective aspectual prefix *hí-* follows the past temporal prefix *a-*; in (2b) the negation prefix *hi-* follows the situative marker *a-*.

(2) a. waáfíya   ṇsáká: n'   oótélíwá:
 o-**a**-**hí**-fi-y-a   ní-saká ni-a ó-tel-íw-a
 SP1-PST-PFV.DJ-arrive-FV 5-time 5-CON 15-marry-PASS-FV
 'She had reached the age to get married.' (Mute)

---

2 Each Cuwabo example in this chapter presents on the first tier the sentence as it is heard, i.e. including every surface morpho-phonological process. Underlying representations are then provided on the second tier. Sources are indicated in parentheses at the end of the free translation line of each example. Narratives are indicated by a single word which refers to the story title (e.g. "Ddingí"). Direct elicitation involving translation from Portuguese is indicated as (Elic.). Semi-elicited examples (indicated as (Semi-elic.)) were created by the speaker as a result of different kinds of stimuli.
3 The orthographic system used in this chapter mostly follows IPA symbols, except for the following graphemes: tt and dd stand for the retroflex stops /ʈ/ and /ɖ/; h stands for the glottal stop /ʔ/ often realized on the surface as a glide; dh stands for the voiced dental fricative /ð/; ñg stands for the velar nasal /ŋ/; and lr stands for the retroflex liquid /ɽ/.
4 The pre-initial position, when filled, may be marked either by negative *ka-*, sequential *ba-*, counterfactual *ka-* or resumptive *na-*. The initial position, obligatory filled (except in the 'bare' imperative, unusual in Cuwabo), is reserved for subject prefixes. See Guérois (2019) for more details on Cuwabo verbal morphology.

b. *ddaahíríǹtigí   kabálayá:,   bwenddéná*
   ddi-**a**-**hí**-ríǹt-ig-í   kabála=ya   bwenddé=na
   SP1SG-SIT-NEG-weave-HAB-NEG 9.rope=DEF 5a.mat=5.DEF
   kaṇnáálíbe
   ka-ni-náa-lib-e
   NEG-SP5-FUT-be.strong-FV
   'If I do not weave this rope, this mat will not be strong.' (Semi-elic.)

The possible hosting of two morphemes in the post-initial slot is of importance for the phasal polarity expression NOT YET, which may combine the negation prefix *hí-* and the phasal prefix *na-*, as will be shown in section 4.

The post-final slot, by hosting a range of different grammatical markers (see Guérois 2019), plays an essential role in Cuwabo grammar. It is of interest for the study of phasal polarity in the language, since the concept STILL is expressed by means of the restrictive enclitic =*vi* (section 3).

Cuwabo is a tone language, with both lexical and grammatical high tones. This means that, in addition to verbal inflection, tone melodies play an important role in the encoding of TAM values. See Kisseberth and Guérois (2014) for a detailed analysis.

3 Still

STILL is an atelic concept (Van Baar 1997) with positive polarity: it describes a persistive situation, referring to an event which has previously been going on and still continues at the time of speech. Such an ongoing situation is encoded in Cuwabo through the verbal enclitic =*vi*. In the three examples in (3), the presence of =*vi* indicates that the event expressed by the verb started at some point in the past and is still occurring at the time of utterance, hence the possible translation 'keep Ving'. Since a continuous reading is expressed, the imperfective TA marker *ní-* is often involved, in synthetic constructions (3a–c), as well as analytic constructions (3d) where the auxiliary verb stem *kála* 'be' is followed by an infinitival complement. Depending on the context, two scenarios can be interpreted: i) A surprise scenario (interpretation 1 in (3a)) where the speaker expected the event to stop or be completed sooner. In this case, =*vi* should be interpreted as 'still'; and ii) A neutral scenario (interpretation 2 in (3a)) where the speaker had no previous expectations, but where focus is marked on the event described by the verb. =*vi* is then best interpreted as 'just' or 'only'.

(3) a. *Ddóólríndd'   óónówííbávi.*
Ddóolrínddo ó-ni-ó-ib-á=**vi**
Ddoolrinddo SP1-IPFV.DJ-15-sing-FV=RESTR
Interpretation 1:
Ptg. 'Ddoolrinddo está a cantar ainda.'
Eng. 'Ddoolrinddo is still singing (keeps singing).' (Ddoo)
Interpretation 2:
Ptg. 'Ddoolrinddo está a cantar só.'
Eng. 'Ddoolrinddo is just/only singing (and nothing else).'

b. *Nikúrábedh'   oonáángánávi   wénéwal' oókúl'   oodhúlu*
N.   o-ní-angán-a=**vi**   wénewale ókule   odhúlu
D.   SP1-IPFV.CJ-look=RESTR 17.EDEM.III 17.DEM.III 17.top
Ptg. 'Nikurabedha ainda repara lá em cima.'
Eng. 'Mr.Dugong is still/only looking (= keeps looking) right above.' (Maria)

c. *Mwaapélíiyé:,   kurúmáanj' oónósógóra*
mu-ap-él-e=iye   kurúmaanje ó-ni-ó-sogólr-a
PP18-pluck-APPL-PFV.REL=PRO3SG 1a.bee.sp SP1-IPFV.DJ-15-go.on-FV
ónódhówávi.   íyééné   ónóm̩fwarávi.
ó-ni-ó-dhow-á=**vi**   íyeéné   ó-ni-ó-mu-fwar-á=**vi**
SP1-IPFV.DJ-15-go-FV=RESTR PRO3SG   SP1-IPFV.DJ-15-OP1-follow-FV=RESTR
Ptg. 'Quando tirou, a maribunda segue em frente, vai andando sempre, ela a seguí-la (sempre).'
Eng. 'Now she plucked it, the bee is going forward, going on, she is following it.' (Maria)

d. *Ddiinyákúwá   ddiŋkál'   óobulélávi.*
ddi-hi-nyákuw-á   ddi-ni-kál-a   o-bulél-a=**vi**
SP1SG-PFV.DJ-be.dirty-FV SP1SG-IPFV.CJ-be-FV 15-suffer-FV.H1D=RESTR
Ptg. 'Sou suja e sempre adoeço.'
Eng. 'I am dirty/ugly and I keep falling ill.' (Maria)

It is plausible to assume that the ONLY interpretation arose at a later stage, after the original interpretation STILL first evolved to ALWAYS. Each step of the evolutionary process as shown in Figure 2 would imply some interpretative augmentation of the original meaning of the phasal polarity concept. The interpretative augmentation of the event 'I am still walking' may be equivalent to saying 'I am always walking'. In turn, the interpretative augmentation of 'I am always walking' could be 'I am only walking', i.e. 'the only thing I do is walk'.

```
STILL      'I am still walking.'  ⎫
  ⇓                                 ⎪
ALWAYS    'I am always walking.'   ⎬  Interpretative augmentation
  ⇓                                 ⎪
ONLY      'I am only walking.'    ⎭
```

Figure 2: Interpretative augmentation from STILL to ONLY.

The enclitic =*vi* is not restricted to verbal morphology. It is also found on nouns (4a), adjectives (4b) and adverbs (4c), where it is used to restrict the referential scope of a category and focus exclusively on what is designated. It is translated as 'only', thus matching the later interpretation in the semantic evolution of =*vi* as proposed in Figure 2. In order to cover these different meanings found on different grammatical categories, and following Guérois (2015, 2019), =*vi* is consistently glossed 'RESTR' for 'restrictive'. A possible origin for the enclitic =*vi* is discussed in section 7.4.

(4) a. *Nikúrábedha   ofíy'   óofíyilééye*
       Nikúrabedha   o-fíy-a   o-fiy-ilé=iye
       Dugong   15-arrive-FV PP15-arrive-PFV.REL=PRO3SG
       om̯fwanyilé   baáŕkuvi.
       o-mu-fwany-ilé baárku=**vi**
       SP1-OP1-meet-PFV.CJ 1a.boat=RESTR
       Ptg. 'Nikurabedha, mal que chegou, encontrou o barco só.'
       Eng. 'Mr.Dugong, hardly had he arrived, found only the boat.' (Maria)

   b. *Malábó   mañgónóovî   amosambikánó*
       ma-lábo   ma-ñgóono=**vi**   a-mosambikáno
       6-day   NP6-small=RESTR 2-Mozambican
       awúúbúwéla   wááttamagîha   ázúgu.
       a-hî-ubuwél-a   ó-a-ttamag-îh-a á-zugu
       SP2-PFV.DJ-think-FV 15-OP2-run-CAUS-FV 2-European
       Ptg. 'Depois de só alguns dias, os Moçambicanos pensaram em dar corrida aos brancos.'
       Eng. 'After only a few days, the Mozambicans thought of making the whites run.' (Ima.01g-13.1)

   c. *Ddim̯fúná   dditagîhé   vañgónóvi*
       ddi-ní-fun-á   ddi-tagîh-e   vañgóono=**vi**
       SP1SG-IPFV.CJ-want-FV SP1SG-repeat-SBJV 16.little=RESTR

> ésíle dhĩiwilĩimi.
> ésile dhi-îw-ile=imi
> 8/10.DEM.III PP8/10-hear-PFV.REL=PRO1SG
> Ptg. 'Quero falar só um pouco sobre aquilo que ouvi.'
> Eng. 'I want to talk just a little bit about what I heard.' (Casamento)

Alternatively, STILL can be expressed by the adverbial phrase *na váno*, meaning literally 'until now'. The sentence in (5a) is extracted from Festi and Valler's (1994) Cuwabo-Portuguese dictionary. In their book, the two authors analyze *na váno* as a single morphological unit, i.e. *naváno*. This is categorically refused by my main consultant, who distinguishes the preposition *na* 'and, with, by', used in temporal expressions such as *na maámbéesi* 'in the morning', and *váno* which seems to be a truncated form of *ováno* 'now'. In this environment, the restrictive enclitic *=vi* could be used as in (5b), with or without the adverb *na váno*.

(5) a. *Vátí vaarîbá, na vánó munólába?*
     váti va-hi-rîb-a **na ováno** mu-nî-o-lab-a
     16.ground SP16-PFV.DJ-be.dark-FV until now SP2SG-IPFV.DJ-15-work-FV
     Ptg. 'A noite chegou e estás a trabalhar ainda?'
     Eng. 'The night has come and you are still working?'
     (adapted from Festi and Valler 1994: 205)[5]

   b. *Vátí vaarîbá, (na vánó)*
      váti va-hi-rîb-a **(na ováno)**
      16.ground SP16-PFV.DJ-be.dark-FV until now
      munólábavi?
      mu-nî-o-lab-a=**vi**
      SP2SG-IPFV.DJ-15-work-FV=RESTR
      Ptg. 'A noite chegou e estás a trabalhar ainda?'
      Eng. 'The night has come and you are still working?' (Elic. from (5a))

Importantly, *na váno* 'until now' is restricted to temporal contexts involving the time of utterance, hence it is found in association with imperfective verbs in the present tense (the latter being unmarked in Cuwabo). On the other hand, *=vi* can be used with different TA markers attached to the verb stem, as is shown in section 7.6 about external paradigmaticity.

---

[5] Note that tones and long vowels are not indicated in the original source (Festi and Valler 1994). For better linguistic accuracy, I added them in this chapter.

The restrictive enclitic =*vi* is attested in the three Cuwabo corpora considered in this study, with approximatly similar percentages of occurrences, as shown in Table 1. Its recurrent use in spontaneous discourse suggests that it is still very much productive.

Table 1: Number of occurrences of still phasal polarity item in three Cuwabo corpora.

	Field data	Dictionary	Bible
Number of tokens	17,414	58,080	552,825
=*vi*	31 (= 0.178%)	43 (= 0.074%)	919 (= 0.166%)

4 Not yet

The phasal polarity concept NOT YET indicates that an event described by the verb has not come about at the reference time (usually the utterance time), regardless of any past situation. The non-existence of a situation at a specific reference time reflects negative polarity, and the lack of a clear finishing point or inherent lateness characterizes NOT YET as both continuative and atelic (Van Baar 1997). Another property of NOT YET verb forms is that they usually go against the expectation of the speaker, in that the event occurs later than expected.

NOT YET is commonly rendered through verbal morphology in Bantu languages. Meeussen (1967) tentatively reconstructed the inceptive proto-form *ka- 'already; not yet'. Schadeberg (1990) refers to such verbal forms as 'das Unerwartete', often translated as 'counterexpectational' in English. In Cuwabo, NOT YET is most frequently expressed through the counterexpectational prefix *ná-* combined with standard negation, in synthetic or periphrastic constructions. The restrictive enclitic =*vi*, used to express STILL (see section 3), may optionally be added. More rarely, it can be used as the only phasal polarity marker. All these strategies are analyzed and exemplified in the following subsections.

4.1 Negation + Counterexpectational prefix *ná-*

The prefixation of the counterexpectational marker *ná-* (in the post-initial slot) used together with standard negation constitutes the most common strategy to express NOT YET expressions in Cuwabo. In (6), the speaker is expecting his friend's return. His friend should have arrived by this time, but has not, hence the question *kunámála* . . . 'have you not finished . . . '. In (7), the character

Ddoolrinddo has fallen into the well and is expected to be found dead, but the verb form *kanákwa* indicates she is not.

(6) *Ogákóodd'*   *oódha*   *kunámál'*   *oōsíńtínááŕi?*
    o-gá-koodd-a   ó-dh-a   ku-**ná**-mal-a   ó-sintinaári
    SP2SG-FUT.IPFV.CJ-refuse-FV   15-come-FV   NEG.SP2SG-CE-finish-FV   15-defecate
    Ptg. 'Não vens, ainda não terminaste as tuas necessidades?'
    Eng. 'Are you not coming, have you not done your business yet?' (Páaká)

(7) *Oṃmála*   *wóódda.*   *Só*   *kanákwa.*
    o-hi-mál-a   ó-odd-a   só   ka-**ná**-kw-a
    SP1-PFV.DJ-finish-FV   15-be.thin-FV   but   NEG.SP1-CE-die-FV
    Ptg. 'Já emagreceu, mas não está morta ainda / não morreu ainda.'
    Eng. 'She has turned thin, but she has not died yet.' (Ddoo.)

Although NOT YET expressions in *ná-* using the pre-initial negative marker *ka-* are by far the most common in my corpus, the post-initial negative marker *hi-* may also be used. In fact, the choice between the two negative markers depends on the type of clause: *ka-* is used in independent or main clauses (8a), while *hi-* is restricted to subordinate clauses and tends to be translated in Portuguese as the temporal clause 'antes de V', i.e. in English 'before Ving' (8b).

(8) a. *Kaddinágúliha*   *nígágádda.*
       ka-ddi-**ná**-gul-ih-a   ní-gagádda
       NEG-SP1SG-CE-buy-CAUS-FV   5-dry.cassava
       Ptg. 'Ainda não vendi mandioca seca.'
       Eng. 'I have not sold dry cassava yet.'

    b. *Ddihinágúliha*   *nígágádda, . . .*
       ddi-**hi**-**ná**-gul-ih-a   ní-gagádda
       SP1SG-NEG-CE-buy-CAUS-FV   5-dry.cassava
       Ptg. 'Antes de eu vender mandioca seca, . . .'
       Eng. 'Before I sell dry cassava, . . .'

Morphologically, the *hi-* NOT YET as illustrated in (8b) represents another instance in the language whereby the post-initial slot is occupied by two morphemes (also see (2) above), namely the negation prefix *hí-* and the phasal prefix *na-*. The morphological formulae of each NOT YET expression are compared in Figure 3.

Slots:	Pre-initial	Initial	Post-initial	Radical
ka-NOT YET:	*ka-*	SP-	*ná-*	Verb root
hi-NOT YET:		SP-	*hi-+ná-*	Verb root

Figure 3: Morphological structures available for NOT YET expression.

In the four sentences above, *ná-* appears as a prefix, i.e. synthetically, on the verb stem. However, it may also be part of a periphrastic construction with an auxiliary, *tti*, invariably inflected with both a subject and a negation marker. The lexical verb follows in its infinitival form. This is shown in (9b), as compared to the semantically equivalent synthetic construction in (9a).

(9) a. *Esó   dhiṅddívuúzéewé,   kaddinásúṅza*
      éso   dhi-ní-ddi-vuúz-a=iwe   ka-ddi-**ná**-suṅz-a
      8/10.DEM.II PP8/10-IPFV-OP1SG-ask-FV.REL=PRO2SG   NEG-SP1SG-CE-learn-FV
      Ptg. 'Isso que me perguntaste, ainda não estudei.'
      Eng. 'I have not studied what you are asking me yet.' (Semi-elic.)

   b. *Esó   dhiṅddívuúzéewé,   kaddinátti*
      éso   dhi-ní-ddi-vuúz-a=iwe   ka-ddi-**ná-tti**
      8/10.DEM.II PP8/10-IPFV-OP1SG-ask-FV.REL=PRO2SG   NEG-SP1SG-CE-AUX
      ósúṅzá.
      ó-suṅz-a
      15-study-FV
      Ptg. 'Isso que me perguntaste, ainda não estudei.'
      Eng. 'I have not studied what you are asking me yet.' (Elic. from (9a))

The auxiliary stem *tti* seems to be a grammaticalized form of the verb stem *ttiy* 'leave'. The resulting construction may literally be interpreted as 'I have not left to study yet', meaning that I am still in a state of not having studied.

Typically, the time reference of 'not yet' verb forms entails the utterance time, hence the possible addition of the adverbial NP *na váno* 'until now', as shown in (10). However, depending on the sentence context, future and past temporalities are also available. The interaction of NOT YET with the Cuwabo TAM system is developed in section 7.6.2.

(10) *Múréddáya   na vánó   kanávúlumuwa.*
     mú-reddá=ya   **na váno**   ka-**ná**-vulumuw-a
     1-patient=DEF until now   NEG.SP1-CE-recover-FV
     Ptg. 'O paciente não curou ainda.'
     Eng. 'The patient has not recovered yet.' (Elic.)

4.2 Negation + Restrictive =vi

A second strategy to express NOT YET clauses consists in employing the restrictive enclitic =vi used to express STILL as developed in section 3, in addition to a negative verbal prefix. Thus, the sentence in (11) conveys the exact same message as the one in (7) above.

(11) *Waawóoddá,   kaakwílevi.*
o-á-odd-á   **ka**-a-kw-íle=**vi**
SP1-PST-be.thin-FV   NEG.SP1-PST-die-PFV=RESTR
Ptg. 'Estava magra, mas não estava morta ainda / não tinha morrido ainda.'
Eng. 'She was thin, she was not dead yet / she had not died yet.'
(Elic. from (7))

The association of =vi with a negation marker infers a negative persistive interpretation to the sentence. The sentence in (11) thus functions as the negative counterpart of the affirmative use of STILL as presented in section 3. As will be shown in section 4.4, the occurrences of =vi in NOT YET expressions are overall rare. No example could be found in Festi and Valler's (1994) Cuwabo-Portuguese Dictionary, and only 13 occurrences were retrieved from the Cuwabo Bible.

The fact that the phasal polarity item =vi is involved in the expression of more than one phasal polarity concept, namely STILL and NOT YET, suggests a flexible phasal polarity coverage system (see section 7.1).

4.3 Combination of NOT YET markers

Since the two NOT YET markers *ná-* and *=vi* occupy different verbal slots, they have the possibility to combine. The three sentences in (12), semantically equivalent to the sentence in (7) above, show that *=vi* may attach to either the first auxiliary *li* 'be' which combines both subject and temporal information (12a), the second auxiliary *tti* specialized for the expression of NOT YET (12b), or even the infinitival complement (12c). The position of *=vi* does not affect the meaning in any way.

(12) a. *Waawóoddá,   waálívi   ahinátti   ókwa.*
o-á-odd-á   o-á-li=**vi**   a-hi-**ná**-tti   ó-kw-a
SP1-PST-be.thin-FV   SP1-PST-be=RESTR   SP1-NEG-CE-AUX   15-die-FV
Ptg. 'Já emagreceu, mas não está morta / não morreu ainda.'

Eng. 'She was thin, she was not dead yet / she had not died yet.'
(Elic. from (7))

b. *Waawóoddá,   waálí   ahináttívi   ókwa.*
o-á-odd-á   o-á-li   a-hi-**ná**-tti=**vi**   ó-kw-a
SP1-PST-be.thin-FV   SP1-PST-be   SP1-NEG-CE-AUX=RESTR   15-die-FV
Ptg. 'Já emagreceu, mas não está morta / não morreu ainda.'
Eng. 'She was thin, she was not dead yet / she had not died yet.'
(Elic. from (7))

c. *Waawóoddá,   waálí   ahinátti   ókwavi.*
o-á-odd-á   o-á-li   a-hi-**ná**-tti   ó-kw-a=**vi**
SP1-PST-be.thin-FV   SP1-PST-be   SP1-NEG-CE-AUX   15-die-FV=RESTR
Ptg. 'Já emagreceu, mas não está morta / não morreu ainda.'
Eng. 'She was thin, she was not dead yet / she had not died yet.'
(Elic. from (7))

The unique example of the co-occurrence of *ná-* and *=vi* found in Festi and Valler's (1994) Cuwabo-Portuguese Dictionary is provided in (13).

(13) *Pereira   múndda   wááye   kunámálávi,*
Pereira   mú-ndda   ó-aye   ku-**ná**-mal-a=**vi**
Pereira   3-field   PP3-POSS3SG   NEG.SP3-CE-finish-FV=RESTR
îyééné   maangónya
îyeéne   maangónya
PRO3SG   1a.lazy.person.H1D
Ptg. 'A machamba do Pereira nunca (ainda não) está pronta por ele ser preguiçoso.'
Eng. 'Pereira's field is not ready yet because he is a lazy man.'
(Adapted from Festi & Valler 1994: 139)

4.4 Occurrences in corpora

In both field data and dictionary corpora, the counterexpectational prefix *ná-* occurs more often in synthetic constructions (39 and 25 times respectively) than in analytical constructions involving the auxiliary *tti* (6 and 18 times respectively). This is however not true for the Bible, which counts more examples of NEG + *ná-tti* + INF constructions (with 396 occurrences) than NEG + *ná-*V constructions (with 280 occurrences). These numbers still point to the fact that the counterexpectational prefix *ná-* is productively used as a NOT YET item in the language. On the other hand, NOT YET expressions involving =*vi* are few. Thirteen examples were found in the Bible translation, one in the dictionary, which also includes the counterexpectational prefix *ná-*, and two were elicited as part of the author's field data, with and without *ná-*. The figures are summarized in Table 2.

Table 2: Number of occurrences of NOT YET phasal polarity items in three Cuwabo corpora.

	Field data	Dictionary	Bible
Total number of tokens	17,414	58,080	552,825
NEG + *ná*-V	39	25	280
NEG + *ná-tti* + INF	6	18	396
NEG + =*vi*	1	0	13
NEG + *ná-* + =*vi*	1	1	0

5 Already

ALREADY is a telic concept with positive polarity: it mirrors the changing point from a negative state to a positive one, when an event starts to occur. It expresses the existence of a situation at a given time of reference, usually the utterance time. For instance, the English sentence *our guests have already left* marks the point where the guests effectively left, as compared to the previous period when they were still here, i.e. they had not left yet. The current situation of absence starts at this point, and not before. In addition, ALREADY may also have a counterexpectational connotation. Thus the sentence *our guests have already left* tends to implicate that the guests left earlier than expected (see Krifka 2000 for more details).

Unlike the two phasal polarity concepts STILL and NOT YET previously analyzed, ALREADY has no one-to-one equivalent in Cuwabo and is rather expressed by means of perfective constructions, without further specification. Perfective constructions can be conjoint or disjoint in Cuwabo. The conjoint/disjoint distinction is an alternation in verb inflection: whereas 'disjoint' forms (marked by the prefix *hi-*) may occur in clause-final position and often imply predicate focus, 'conjoint' forms (marked by the suffix *-ile*) cannot occur clause-finally and often imply term focus on the following phrase.[6] Although conjoint and disjoint perfective verb forms in Cuwabo have a distinct morphology and

---

[6] Such a distinction exists in other Eastern and Southern Bantu languages, such as Bemba, Kinyarwanda, Kirundi, Makhuwa, Tswana, and Zulu (cf. Van der Wal and Hyman 2017).

appear in different pragmatic contexts, they are semantically equivalent: both can be used to express the phasal polarity concept ALREADY as seen in (14) with disjoint verb forms and (15) with conjoint verb forms.

(14) a. *Oddivahilé   míkátté   míinddi   baáhi, ddíítákuna.*
       o-ddi-vah-ilé   mí-katté   mí-inddi baáhi   **ddi-hî-takun-a**
       SP1-OP1SG-give-PFV.CJ 4-rice.cake 4-two   only   SP1SG-PFV.DJ-chew-FV
       Ptg. 'Deu-me dois bolos de arroz só, já comi.'
       Eng. 'He gave me two rice cakes only and I have already eaten them.'
       (Semi-elic.)

   b. *Ora   y'   aárímoós'   éefíyá,*
      ora   ya   árimoóso   e-hi-fíy-a
      9.hour 7/9.CON   1a.lunch   SP7/9-PFV.DJ-arrive-FV
      árímoós'   óopíyíwá
      árimoóso   **o-hi-píy-iw-á**
      1a.lunch   SP1-PFV.DJ-cook-PASS-FV
      Ptg. 'A hora do almoço chegou, o almoço já está pronto.'
      Eng. 'Lunch time came, the lunch has already been cooked.' (Ddoo.)

(15) a. *Ddirurumuwilé   báddiruddilé   vâkúgúlúní.*
       ddi-rurumuw-ilé   **ba-ddi-rudd-ilé**   va-kúgulú=ni
       SP1SG-wake.up-PFV.CJ SEQ-SP1SG-urinate-PFV.CJ 16-9.bed=LOC
       Ptg. 'Acordei enquanto já tinha mijado na cama.'
       Eng. 'When I woke up, I had urinated in bed.' (lit. 'I woke up while I was in a state of having urinated') (Semi-elic.)

   b. *Kuulogíwága   ddaahíkáana   mááre*
      ka-o-log-íw-ag-a   ddi-a-hí-kaana   má-are
      CF-15-tell-PASS-HAB-FV SP1SG-PST-PFV.DJ-have 6-idea
      baddisasanyedhé   makáttámiyo   ába.
      ba-ddi-sasany-edh-é ma-káttamiyo   ába
      SEQ-SP1SG-fix-APPL-PFV.CJ 6-problem   6.DEM.I
      Ptg. 'Se (eu) tivesse uma ideia, já teria resolvido o problema.'
      Eng. 'If I had an idea, I would already have fixed the problem.' (Semi-elic.)

All these sentences, except (14b), were obtained as the result of what I call in this chapter 'semi-elicitation'. More specifically, I asked my main consultant to create Cuwabo sentences using particular TAM categories: the sentence in (14a) satisfies the TAM category of Present Perfective in *hí-*, whereas sentences in (15a–b) belong to the Sequential Perfective category, combining the pre-initial sequential prefix *ba-* and the perfective suffix *-ile*. The Portuguese translations as indicated here faithfully follow those provided spontaneously by my consultants. However, in none of these examples is the presence of *já* 'already' mandatory, and its possible omission does not trigger any change in interpretation. Thus, if the perfective aspectual category has the potential to semantically reflect the phasal polarity concept ALREADY, nevertheless, it should not be considered as a specialized marker. The perfective verb forms *oddivahilé* 'he gave me' (14a), *ehifíya* 'it arrived' (14b) and *ddururumuwilé* 'I woke up' (15a), where *já* 'already' was not provided in the Portuguese translation, confirm that no systematic link should be established between perfective aspectuality and ALREADY phasal polarity. The lack of a dedicated expression for the concept ALREADY reflects an incomplete phasal polarity system in Cuwabo.

Note, however, the possible use of the adverb *já* 'already', borrowed from Portuguese. This temporal adverb is usually associated with perfective verb forms (16a) but is also found in present temporal reference (16b). Surprisingly, the use of *já* in Cuwabo does not necessarily imply its presence in the Portuguese translation, as can be seen in (16a). This may reflect the fact that ALREADY is not a core phasal polarity concept in the language.

(16) a. *Já   oódhówá   owaábála   já*
já   o-hí-dhow-á   o-hi-ábal-a   **já**
already SP1-PFV.DJ-go-FV SP1-PFV.DJ-dress-FV already
sáyoóta,   oódhówa   va   kakávêne.
sáyoóta   o-hí-dhów-a   va   kaká=vêne
9.underskirt SP1-PFV.DJ-go-FV 16.CON same=16.INT
Ptg. 'Foi, vestiu a saiota, voltou para o mesmo sítio.'
Eng. 'She went, put on the underskirt, and came back to the same place.' (Mbílri)

b. *Rapáríga ddabunó kayíy'   óokálá dhiidho.*
rapáriga ddabuno kahíyo   o-kála dhiidho
1a.girl   then   NEG.COP 15-be   naked
Ddabunó já   olí   dhiidhó.
ddabuno **já**   o-lí   dhiidho
then   already   SP1-be naked
Ptg. 'Aí, a senhora ficou nua. Agora já é de ficar nua.'
Eng. 'Then the girl remained naked. Now she is completely naked.' (Mbílri)

The use of the Portuguese adverb *já* 'already' in Cuwabo confirms Van der Auwera (1993: 628–629; 1997: 67–73) and Van Baar's (1997: 126–129) findings that the expression of ALREADY is more prone to borrowing than the other phasal polarity concepts. However, the occurrences of *já* in the three Cuwabo corpora are either extremely rare or simply non-existent, as shown in Table 3. Among the three occurrences found in the author's field data corpus, two (provided in (16)) were uttered by the same speaker from Macuze. My main consultant, also native of Macuze, does not approve of this loan in Cuwabo. Furthermore, it is not attested in Festi and Valler's dictionary, nor is it in the Bible translation. Faced with this near absence of occurrences, I prefer not to include the loan *já* 'already' as part of the Cuwabo phasal polarity system.

Table 3: Number of occurrences of the Portuguese loan *já* 'already' in three Cuwabo corpora.

	Field data	Dictionary	Bible
Total number of words (tokens)	17,414	58,080	552,825
já 'already'	3	0	0

Finally, note that Cuwabo has a dedicated verbal construction to express counterexpectational, built upon the marker *-lá* (< *wíilá* 'say, do') followed by an infinitive complement. The counterexpectational is commonly attested in narrative texts. It is used to express unplanned or unexpected information. It is aspectually similar to the perfective, since the event is seen as a whole, but in addition it encodes mirativity (De Lancey 1997) in the sense that some element of surprise is involved. However, such constructions cannot be associated with the counterexpectational conversational implicature associated with the phasal polarity concept ALREADY, as they do not convey any temporal connotation. The unexpectedness of the event is not expressed in terms of pace or speed of development, but rather in terms of its mere occurrence. For instance, in (17), the change of the protagonist's skin from black to white, expressed through the counterexpectational verb form *olóósáddúwa*, is unexpected as a whole event, and does not implicate that Maria changed earlier than expected.

(17) *"Supeéyó   supeéyo,   míyó   ddimfúná*
    supeéyó   supeéyó   míyo   ddi-ní-fún-á
    9.mirror.H1D 9.mirror.H1D PRO1SG   SP1SG-IPFV.CJ-want-FV
    ddikálé   w'   oocéna."
    ddi-kál-é   wa   o-cén-a
    SP1SG-be-SBJV   1.CON   15-be.white-FV
    Maríy'   óolóósáddúwa,   ddabun'   óókala
    Maríya   o-lá-o-saddúw-a   ddabunó   o-kala
    Maria   SP1-CE-INF-change-FV   now   NAR-be
    muzugu,   okala   w'   oocéna.
    mu-zugu   o-kala   wa   o-cén-a
    1-European.H1D   NAR-be   1.CON   15-be.white-FV
    "Mirror, mirror, I want to be white." Maria changed, she now was a white person, she was white.' (Maria)

6 No longer

The fourth phasal polarity concept, NO LONGER, implies telicity and negative polarity. Like ALREADY, it marks a point of change, but with an opposite polarity balance, i.e. from positive to negative. NO LONGER is thus terminative, in that it marks the end of a situation, which used to hold before the changing point. For instance, NO LONGER in the English sentence *this star no longer shines* marks the point when a given star stops shining. Another feature of NO LONGER is that the new situation involving negative polarity still holds at the utterance time.

In Cuwabo, the expression NO LONGER consists of the adverb *viina* 'too, as well' used together with standard negation, as exemplified in (18). The sentence in (18a) is particularly interesting, since it shows both positive and negative uses of the adverb *viina*, with the clauses 'then I want to annoy you *too*' and 'I *no longer* carry you', respectively. At this stage, it is difficult to estabish the semantic relationship between *viina* used in affirmative contexts with the meaning 'too, as well' and *viina* found in negative contexts meaning 'no longer'.

(18) a. *Agórá akala amfúná   awúpúttule,   míyo*
       agóra akala a-ní-fun-á   a-ú-puttul-e   míyo
       then if   SP1-IPFV.CJ-want-FV SP1-OP2SG-despise-SBJV PRO1SG
       viíná ddabunó ddimfúná   dduúpúttuleni
       viina ddabunó ddi-ní-fun-á   ddi-ú-puttul-e=ni
       too   today   SP1SG-IPFV.CJ-want-FV SP1SG-OP2SG-despise-SBJV=PLA
       mwéetéêne. Míyó kannuúttébani   viina!
       mú-eté=ene míyo **ka**-ni-ni-ú-tteba=ni   **viina**
       PP2PL-all=INT PRO1SG NEG-SP1PL-IPFV-OP2SG-carry-FV=PLA too
       Ptg. 'Agora se (ele) quiser te prejudicar, eu *também* vou lhes prejudicar todos, eu *não* vós carrego *mais*!'
       Eng. 'Then if he wants to annoy you, I want to annoy you *too*, all of you. I will *no longer* carry you!' (Body)

   b. *Attú   ddabunó kamfúná   víina*
       á-ttu   ddabunó **ka**-ní-fun-á   **viina**
       2-person today   NEG.SP2-IPFV-want-FV   too
       biya   dh'   oólôgo.
       biya   dhi-a   ó-logo
       10.stove PP8/10-CON 11-clay
       Ptg. 'As pessoas agora já não querem panelas de barro.'
       Eng. 'Today, people no longer want clay stoves.' (Semi-elic.)

Note that the Portuguese loan *já* 'already' may also be used to express NO LONGER when used with standard negation, as illustrated in (19). However, and similar to the affirmative phasal polarity counterpart ALREADY as already observed in section 5, *já* + negation seems very marginal in the daily use of the language and not acknowledged by all speakers: rather than *já káája* in (19), my main consultant strongly prefers *kaája víina*.

(19) *Já   káája.*
     já   **ka**-á-j-a
     no.longer   NEG.SP1-PST.IPFV-eat-FV
     Ptg. 'Já não comia.'
     Eng. 'He was no longer eating.' (Body)

já + negation also does not occur in the dictionary and in the Bible translation. The figures in Table 4 confirm the scarcity of the adverb *já* in the expression NO LONGER. The use of the adverb *viina* along with standard negation thus constitutes the default strategy to express NO LONGER in Cuwabo.

Table 4: Number of occurrences of no longer phasal polarity items in three Cuwabo corpora.

	Field data	Dictionary	Bible
Total number of tokens	17,414	58,080	552,825
NEG + *viina*	7 (= 0,04%)	8 (= 0,014%)	413 (= 0,075%)
NEG + *já*	1	0	0

7 Kramer's parametric approach

On the basis of Van Baar's (1997) and Van der Auwera's (1998) works, Kramer (2017) has developed six parameters under which phasal polarity items can be analyzed. The first three parameters are concerned with the following semantic criteria: coverage, pragmaticity, and telicity. The last three parameters - wordhood, expressibility and paradigmaticity - pertain to the structural properties of phasal polarity items. Each parameter is discussed in turn below.

7.1 Parameter 1: Coverage

In addition to temporal phases, phasal polarity expressions are distinguished in terms of polarity, which opposes pairs whose respective items are interrelated through negation; it may be that NOT YET and NO LONGER are coded as the negative counterparts of ALREADY and STILL. Internal negation occurs when NOT YET and NO LONGER are derived from STILL and ALREADY respectively. External negation occurs when NOT YET and NO LONGER are derived from ALREADY and STILL respectively. Löbner (1989) refers to this relationship as the Duality Hypothesis. The coverage parameter seeks to establish semantic relations between phasal polarity items in a language in terms of both internal and external negations. Figure 4 provides such a relationship network for Cuwabo.

As can be seen from Figure 4, the Cuwabo phasal polarity system of semantic relations between phasal polarity concepts is not coded overall on the basis of internal and external negation. An obvious first impediment to a parallel system of semantic relations comes from the absence of ALREADY as a specialized phasal polarity concept in the language. A second factor to take into account is the existence of two phasal polarity items for the expression of the phasal polarity concept NOT YET, i.e. the counterexpectational prefix *ná-* and the restrictive enclitic *=vi*, both in addition to a negation marker. The prefix *ná-* is restricted to NOT YET contexts and functions alone. However, the enclitic *=vi* used in NOT YET expressions functions as the counterpart of *=vi* found in STILL

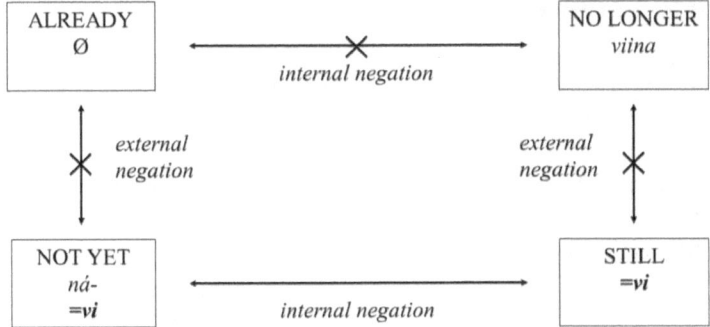

Figure 4: The system of semantic relations between phasal polarity concepts in Cuwabo (after Löbner 1989).

expressions. This constitutes a case of internal negation in the language: the STILL item =*vi* operates in the NOT YET expression as internal negation, in that it is part of the NOT YET expression involving a verbal marker of negation + the verbal enclitic =*vi*, thus corresponding to the relational formula (= still (not V)). Such constructions are illustrated in section 4.2. However, internal negation does not hold between the STILL item =*vi* and the prefix *ná-* which is the most frequent strategy for the expression of NOT YET.

Figure 4 makes it clear that no external negation system is used in Cuwabo to signal NOT YET and NO LONGER expressions. In the case of NOT YET, no phasal polarity item is available for ALREADY to establish a possible connection between the two concepts. As for the STILL item =*vi*, it does not enter into an external negation relation with the NO LONGER concept, expressed by the adverb *viina*.

Kramer, in her position paper, postulates that a language with distinct specialized items, each used for the expression of a different phasal polarity, has a rigid phasal polarity coverage system. Reversely, a language where a given phasal polarity item is involved in the expression of more than one phasal polarity concept, has a flexible phasal polarity coverage system. Following Kramer's reasoning, Cuwabo could be considered as having a semi-flexible phasal polarity coverage system, where only the negative phasal polarity concept NOT YET shares an item with the positive phasal polarity concept STILL. More specifically, NOT YET is realized as internal negation of the STILL expression: both concepts are expressed with the verbal enclitic =*vi*, which, in the case of NOT YET, is negated using standard negation. The continuative STILL is thus used to derive the continuative NOT YET. On the other hand, the NO LONGER expression is not formally linked to a positive phasal polarity item.

7.2 Parameter 2: Pragmaticity

Kramer's pragmaticity parameter is based on two scenarios: one neutral and one counterfactual. In the neutral (or factual) scenario, phasal polarity expressions manifest inherent phases and polarity as part of a pragmatically indifferent temporality of events. It does not rely on expectations. The counterfactual (or counterexpectational) scenario is, on the other hand, pragmatically motivated. It relies on the simultaneous duality of expectation based on background information on the one hand, and state of affairs, i.e. the real situation, on the other.

Cuwabo phasal polarity expressions differ in regard to their degree of pragmatic sensitivity, as shown in Figure 5. Relevant examples already presented at the beginning of the chapter are referred to in the fourth column.

Phasal polarity concept	Form	Pragmaticity	See example(s)
STILL	=vi	NEUTRAL/COUNTERFACTUAL	(3)
NOT YET	ná- (+ NEG)	COUNTERFACTUAL	(6)-(7)
NOT YET	=vi (+ NEG)	NEUTRAL/COUNTERFACTUAL	(11)
NO LONGER	viína (+ NEG)	NEUTRAL/COUNTERFACTUAL	(18)

Figure 5: Link between phasal polarity and pragmaticity.

With the phasal polarity items =vi for STILL/NOT YET and viína for NO LONGER, both neutral and counterfactual interpretations are available and the distinction seems to be context-sensitive. On the basis of my corpus, the neutral interpretation for these two phasal polarity items prevails, confirming Van Baar's (1997: 65) suggestions. However, the NOT YET phasal polarity item ná- is in turn inherently counterfactual, in that it presents an unexpected state of affairs as its core meaning, as shown in section 4.1. This semantic/pragmatic specialization of the NOT YET item ná- is not specific to Cuwabo. Other Eastern Bantu languages have the same (or similar) grammatical prefix, which Schadeberg (1990) labelled *das Unerwartete*, i.e. 'unexpected', and glossed as counterexpectational.

7.3 Parameter 3: Telicity

Unlike the two continuative and atelic phasal polarity concepts STILL and NOT YET, ALREADY and NO LONGER imply a point of change between two sequential situations: the current situation, which is the new point of reference, and the preceding situation which came to an end. Both these sequential situations have opposite polarity values: from a negative to a positive situation in the case of ALREADY, and from a positive to a negative situation in the case of NO LONGER. The point of polarity change may be early or late in relation to the expected background scenario. Alternatively, it may be insensitive to the earliness/lateness distinction, and have a general atemporal interpretation in the case of a neutral background scenario (see Van der Auwera 1993 and Van Baar 1997 for more detailed explanations).

In Cuwabo, earliness and lateness do not seem to be very relevant when it comes to the sole telic phasal polarity expression present in the language, i.e. NO LONGER. The general interpretation rather seems to prevail. Thus, in NO LONGER expressions provided in (20), repeated from (18), the turning point from 'carry' to 'no longer carry' and from 'want' to 'no longer want' appears to occur without any previous temporal expectations.

(20) a. *Agórá akala amfúná   awúpúttule,   míyó*
       agóra akala a-ní-fun-á   a-ú-puttul-e   míyo
       then if   SP1-IPFV.CJ-want-FV SP1-OP2SG-despise-SBJV PRO1SG
       viíná ddabunó ddimfúná   dduúpúttuleni
       viina ddabunó ddi-ní-fun-á   ddi-ú-puttul-e=ni
       too   today   SP1SG-IPFV.CJ-want-FV SP1SG-OP2SG-despise-SBJV=PLA
       mwéetéêne. Míyó kannuúttébani   viina!
       mú-eté=ene míyó **ka**-ni-ni-ú-tteba=ni   **viina**
       PP2PL-all=INT PRO1SG NEG-SP1PL-IPFV-OP2SG-carry-FV=PLA too
       Ptg. 'Agora se (ele) quiser te prejudicar, eu *também* vou lhes prejudicar todos, eu *não* vós carrego *mais*!'
       Eng. 'Then if he wants to annoy you, I want to annoy you *too*, all of you. I will *no longer* carry you!' (Body)

   b. *Attú   ddabunó kamfúná   viína*
      á-ttu   ddabunó **ka**-ní-fun-á **viina**
      2-person today   NEG.SP2-IPFV-want-FV too
      biya   dh'   oólôgo.
      biya   dhi-a   ó-logo
      10.stove PP8/10-CON 11-clay
      Ptg. 'As pessoas agora já não querem panelas de barro.'
      Eng. 'Today people no longer want clay stoves.' (Semi-elic.)

7.4 Parameter 4: Wordhood

Phasal polarity items are formally and structurally diverse, ranging from adverbs to verbal affixes or auxiliaries. Kramer's wordhood parameter deals with the independence, or whenever relevant, the degree of grammaticalization of phasal polarity expressions in a given language. In Cuwabo, phasal polarity items do not form a formal paradigm with a unified categorial status. However, verbal morphology, by hosting markers for NOT YET and STILL, plays an essential role. Table 5 illustrates the morphological status of Cuwabo phasal polarity items.

Table 5: Morphological status of Cuwabo phasal polarity items.

	NOT YET	STILL	NO LONGER
Adverb			viina
Auxiliary	ná-tti		
Prefix	ná-		
Enclitic	=vi	=vi	

As evidenced in Table 5, Cuwabo phasal polarity items belong to different grammatical categories, and while the adverb *viina* for NO LONGER is the only independent phasal polarity item, *ná-* for NOT YET and *=vi* for both STILL and NOT YET, phasal polarity items are bound morphemes which depend on verb forms. NOT YET is the only phasal polarity concept possibly expressed through several strategies, i.e. a periphrastic auxiliary construction, prefixation or encliticization. Among these strategies, the synthetic use of the counterexpectational prefix *ná-* seems overall slightly more frequent, as shown in section 4.

It is likely that the two bound morphemes *=vi* and *ná-* underwent a process of grammaticalization, although the exact pathway is not entirely clear at this stage. Assuming that boundedness is an indicator of the degree of grammaticalization (Heine et al. 1991), the NOT YET prefix *ná-* appears as the most grammaticalized phasal polarity marker. Occupying the postinitial slot, typically used for TA marking (Güldemann 1999), it is fully incorporated into the TA system of the language. In this position, it cannot occur together with other TA markers. The same NOT YET marker is found in several Northern Mozambican languages, such as Makhuwa (van der Wal 2009: 106), Koti (Schadeberg and Mucanheia 2000: 122), and Matuumbi (Odden 1996: 66). A possible source for *na-* may be found in the NOT YET auxiliary *naamba* attested in other languages of the same region, i.e. Makonde (Kraal 2005: 242), Makwe (Devos 2008: 341) and Mwani (Floor 2010: 15). In these languages, the auxiliary *naamba* takes a negation marker and is followed by an infinitive verbal complement. The NOT YET prefix *ná-* found in Cuwabo, Makhuwa, Koti and Matuumbi, would be a further step in the grammaticalization process, whereby the auxiliary *naamba* and the verbal complement merged into a synthetic construction, causing the form *naamba* to be truncated and the infinitive prefix deleted. This grammaticalization pathway is summarized in Figure 6.

NOT YET constructions	Languages
SP-NEG-*naamba* + INF	Makonde, Makwe, Mwani
⇓	
SP-NEG-*na*-Inflected.Verb	Cuwabo, Makhuwa, Koti, Matuumbi

Figure 6: From NOT YET auxiliary *naamba* to prefix *na*-.

The geographic distribution of the NOT YET markers *naamba* and *na-* in Northern Mozambican languages tends to point to a common origin, reconstructable to a certain level in Eastern Bantu as the verb stem *naamba*, whose original meaning cannot be determined with certainty at this stage.

The restrictive enclitic =*vi*, used to express both STILL and NOT YET phasal polarity concepts, occurs in the postfinal slot, i.e. at the extreme right edge of the verb form, also used in Cuwabo for marking plural imperative, locative, comitative/instrumental, and subject pronouns in relatives. The encliticization of =*vi* seems to be an innovation internal to Cuwabo. It is not attested in its sister language Lomwe-Makhuwa (P31/32), nor in Sena (N44), spoken on both western and southern fringes. At this stage, postulating a pathway of grammaticalization for the development of *vi* as an enclitic seems difficult. Since Cuwabo has SVO word order, it is expected that verbal enclitics originate from nouns. However, no corresponding nominal form seems to exist synchronically, and from a diachronic perspective, no proto-form could be found as a possible match. Furthermore, and as seen in section 3, =*vi* may also be attached to other grammatical categories, such as nouns, adjectives and adverbs, in which case it is translated as 'only'. Assuming that =*vi* as a verbal enclitic meaning 'still' is the same as =*vi* found with other word categories with the meaning 'only', it seems more likely that its lexical origin is found in adverbs or any other adjunct word, typically occupying the right edge of the clause. A possible source for =*vi* could then be the adverb *viina* 'too, as well', used in the expression of NO LONGER (alongside negative polarity). This would presuppose a grammaticalization pathway as proposed in Figure 7, whereby the focus-sensitive clausal particle *viina* 'too, as well' would have: i) formally shrunk to the enclitic =*vi*; ii) semantically evolved into a scalar particle ('still'), then into another focussing particle ('only'); iii) pragmatically reduced its effect on a single element in the clause, either verbs (for 'still'), or verbs, nouns, adjectives and adverbs (for 'only'). The semantic relationship and the grammaticalization path between the two functions of =*vi*, 'still' and 'only' is discussed in section 3.

Form	Meaning	Action scope
viina	'too, as well'	Clause
⇓		
=*vi*	'still'	Verbs
⇓		
=*vi*	'only'	Verbs, Nouns, Adjectives, Adverbs

Figure 7: Grammaticalization pathway from *viina* to =*vi*.

7.5 Parameter 5: Expressibility

Kramer's parameter of expressibility is concerned with the existence of specific coding strategies in the expression of phasal polarity items. It may happen that a given phasal polarity system does not exhibit specialized items for each of the four phasal polarity concepts.

In Cuwabo, all phasal polarity concepts have a one-to-one equivalent, except ALREADY. As already seen in section 5, ALREADY sentences are not formally differentiated from perfective constructions. This is illustrated in (21) where two translations (with or without *já* 'already') are possible, without any change of interpretation or context of use. More examples are provided in Section 5 above.

(21) Perfective/ALREADY expression in Cuwabo
Máfúgi   aávúdda   musákûní:,   ddiíráyíla.
má-fugi   a-á-vudd-a   mu-sáku-ni   **ddi-hí-rayíl-a**
6-banana   SP6-PST-be.rotten-FV 18-basket-LOC SP1SG-PFV.DJ-throw.away-FV
Ptg. 'As bananas que estavam podres no cesto, *(já)* deitei.'
Eng. 'The bananas that were rotten in the basket, I have *(already)* thrown them away.' (Semi-elic.)

Such an ALREADY gap in the Cuwabo phasal polarity system follows the pattern of European languages which have the possibility to formally express three phasal polarity concepts out of four. In this case, Van der Auwera (1997: 36–37) observes that the missing phasal polarity concept is consistently ALREADY.

7.6 Parameter 6: Paradigmaticity

The paradigmaticity parameter investigates the symmetrical properties of the phasal polarity system. Kramer makes a further distinction between internal and external paradigmaticity. From an internal perspective, paradigmaticity assesses the possibility of pairing phasal polarity concepts on the basis of opposite polarity. External paradigmaticity, in turn, investigates how phasal polarity paradigms interact with TAM categories. Both internal paradigmaticity and external paradigmaticity are described below.

7.6.1 Internal paradigmaticity

In Cuwabo, no internal symmetry exists among phasal polarity paradigms displaying polarity opposition, i.e. ALREADY versus NOT YET, and STILL versus NO LONGER. In the first case, illustrated in (22), the phasal polarity paradigm ALREADY versus NOT YET is asymmetrical because the counterexpectational prefix *ná-* used to express NOT YET simply lacks a formal expression for the alternative scenario, i.e. the expected phasal polarity expression ALREADY. In the case of the phasal polarity paradigm STILL versus NO LONGER, the dedicated phasal polarity items coding these two logically opposite scenarios are syntactically not parallelized in that they do not belong to the same word class category: STILL is coded by means of the restrictive enclitic *=vi* whereas NO LONGER is expressed via the adverb *viina*, as shown in (23).

(22) Internal asymmetric phasal polarity paradigm ALREADY-NOT YET
    a. *Niígúlá*   *máfûgi.*
        ni-hí-gul-á   má-fugi
        SP1PL-PFV.DJ-buy-FV   6-banana
        Ptg. 'Já compramos bananas.'
        Eng. 'We have already bought bananas'

    b. *Kaninátt'*   *úúgulá*   *máfûgi.*
        ka-ni-ná-tti   ó-gul-á   má-fugi
        NEG-SP1PL-CE-AUX   15-buy-FV   6-banana
        Ptg. 'Ainda não compramos bananas.'
        Eng. 'We haven't bought bananas yet.' (Q2_B13)

(23) Internal asymmetric phasal polarity paradigm STILL-NO LONGER
    a. *Ninógúlávi*   *máfûgi.*
        ni-ni-ó-gul-á=vi   má-fugi
        SP1PL-IPFV.DJ-15-buy-FV=RESTR   6-banana
        Ptg. 'Ainda estamos a comprar bananas.'
        Eng. 'We are still buying bananas.' (Q2_B14)

b. *Kaniŋgula   mafugi   viina.*
   ka-ni-nî-gul-á   ma-fugi   viina
   NEG-SP1PL-IPFV-buy-FV 6-banana.H1D too
   Ptg. 'Já não estamos a comprar bananas.'
   Eng. 'We are no longer buying bananas.' (Q2_B14)

7.6.2 External paradigmaticity

In terms of external paradigmaticity, the three phasal polarity concepts formally coded in Cuwabo, i.e. STILL, NOT YET and NO LONGER, show variation. Whereas STILL and NO LONGER are fully symmetric, i.e. they may combine with any TA category, NOT YET is integrated in the Cuwabo TAM system in such a way that interactions with other TA categories are blocked. Each of these phasal polarity concepts is discussed below.

STILL

In section 3, all the examples provided show the use of the restrictive enclitic =*vi* in imperfective verb forms, whose temporality is anchored in the present, i.e. the time of utterance. However, =*vi* is very pervasive in Cuwabo and by no means limited to a specific TA category, when attached to a verb. It can thus be used with different TA markers attached to the verb stem. Most often, and because STILL implies a continuative reading, =*vi* is attached to constructions marked for imperfective. In (24), the auxiliary *ila* (grammaticalized from the verb stem *ilá* 'say; do') hosts the imperfective past marker *á-*. =*vi* is encliticized to the infinitival verbal complement. Continuous future events, illustrated in (25), are expressed synthetically by means of two imperfective prefixes *gá-* (also future-marked) and *ni-*. =*vi* is then added as an enclitic.

(24) *Ddóólrínddo wéél'   owííbávi.*
     D.   o-á-ila   ó-ib-á=**vi**
     D.   SP1-PST.IPFV-AUX 15-sing-FV=RESTR
     Ptg. 'Ddoolrinddo ainda estava a cantar / estava a cantar sempre.'
     Eng. 'Ddoolrinddo was still singing (kept singing).' (Elic. from (3a))

(25) a. *Ddóólrínddó agániibávi.*
    D.   a-gá-ni-ib-á=**vi**
    D.   SP1-FUT.IPFV-IPFV.DJ-sing-FV=RESTR
    Ptg. 'Ddoolrinddo ainda estará a cantar / estará a cantar sempre.'
    Eng. 'Ddoolrinddo will still be singing (will keep singing)' (Elic. from (3a))
  b. *Másíkini ddireélé,   ddigáṁpiyavi.*
    másikini   ddi-reél-e   ddi-gá-ni-piy-a=**vi**
    even if   SP1SG-be.rich-SBJV SP1SG-FUT.IPFV-IPFV.DJ-cook-FV=RESTR
    Ptg. 'Mesmo que me torne rico, continuarei a cozinhar / sempre cozinharei.'
    Eng. 'Even if I become rich, I will keep cooking.' (Elic.)

A continuative interpretation of =*vi* also seems to prevail in (26), with the verb form *ddilóbáálúwavi* 'since I was born', marked by the (highly grammaticalized) counterexpectational auxiliary *lá-*.

(26) *Ddilóbáálúwavi   kaddinájá   mukaje.*
    ddi-lá-ó-baal-úw-a=**vi**   ka-ddi-ná-j-a   mu-kaje
    SP1SG-CE.AUX-15-give.birth-PASS-FV=RESTR NEG-SP1SG-CE-eat-FV 3-fish.sp.H1D
    Ptg. 'Desde que nasci, nunca comi *mukaje*.'
    Eng. 'Since I was born (lit. 'I was given birth'), I have never eaten *mukaje* fish.' (Semi-elic.)

More unexpectedly, =*vi* may co-occur with perfective verb forms, as in (27). Such co-occurrence is unexpected since STILL implies non-completion and continuity, most commonly indicated by the imperfective aspectuality. The event described in (27) must be interpreted as a progressive sequence of the same action, namely singing a song more and more intensely. The event described by the verb is thus punctual, but the presence of =*vi* suggests a repetition of the action, which gives a continuative reading to the whole event.

(27) *Múlóbwana oówáráárihávi.*
    mú-lobwana   o-hí-waraar-íh-a=**vi**
    1-man   SP1-PFV.DJ-be.strong-CAUS-FV=RESTR
    Ptg. 'O homem ficou intensificando-a (i.e. cantou a canção com cada vez mais intensidade).'
    Eng. 'The man kept strengthening / intensifying (it, i.e. the song).' (Mbílri)

Punctual future events, expressed through the auxiliary *ilá* inflected in person and tense and followed by an infinitival complement, may also host the enclitic =*vi*, as shown in (28). In this example, the event expressed by the telic verb *ókwa* 'to die' cannot possibly be repeated, unlike *ówáráárîha* 'to make strong' in (27). In (28), =*vi* rather seems to insist on the certainty of death. More particularly, it implies the unrelated co-occurrence or co-existence of two facts, by asserting that fact 1 – the presence of the interlocutor – does not prevent or affect fact 2 – the coming death of a third character. Such concessive sense of =*vi* could be translated in English as 'no matter what', 'nevertheless' or even 'still', but in its concessive interpretation. Note that the process whereby temporal markers grammaticalize to markers of logical grammatical relations such as concessive is cross-linguistically widespread (Heine and Kuteva 2002).

(28) *Ookálá   vénévá,   kukáḷlévo,*
      o-hi-kál-a   véneva   ku-kál-ile=vo
      SP2SG-PFV.DJ-be-FV 16.DEM.III   NEG.SP2SG-be-PFV=LOC16
      íyéén'   óoneel'   óókwavi.
      íyeéne   o-naa-ilá   o-kw-a=**vi**
      PRO2SG   SP1-FUT.DJ-AUX   15-die-FV=RESTR
      Ptg. 'Que estejas cá ou não, mesmo assim há-de-morrer.'
      Eng. 'Whether or not you are here, he is still going to die.' (Semi-elic.)

Interestingly, the absence versus presence of the restrictive =*vi* in future forms may lead to temporality distinctions. The action expressed by a future verb such as *ddineelóógulá* 'I will buy' in (29a) may be realized as soon as today or in an imminent future. Adding the restrictive enclitic =*vi* as in (29b) indicates a later action, such as a week after the utterance time. This is all the more interesting since Cuwabo does not distinguish its future markers on the basis of temporal subdivisions (e.g. hodiernal versus post-hodiernal). The use of =*vi* to express a non-imminent future suggests a further grammaticalization path of the enclitic.

(29) a. *Ddineelóógulá   máfúgi   ddabuno / mángwáána.*
          ddi-naa-ilá-o-gul-á   má-fugi   ddabuno / mángwaána
          SP1SG-FUT.DJ-AUX-buy-FV 6-banana today   tomorrow
          Ptg. 'Comprarei bananas hoje/amanhã.'
          Eng. 'I will buy bananas today/tomorrow.' (Elic.Q2.B5)

b. *Ddineelóógulávi   máfúgi   sumaán'*
   ddi-naa-ilá-o-gul-á=**vi**   má-fugi   sumaána
   SP1SG-FUT.DJ-AUX-buy-FV=RESTR   6-banana 9.week.H1D
   ééjw'   ééṅdawo.
   éjo   e-ní-dh-a=wo
   7/9.DEM.II PP7/9-IPFV-come-FV.REL=LOC17
   Ptg. 'Comprarei bananas na semana que vem.'
   Eng. 'I will buy bananas next week.' (Elic.Q2.B6)

NOT YET

Just like STILL, the time reference of NOT YET expressions entails the time of utterance. However, in specific contexts, NOT YET-marked verbs may also appear in past and future temporalities. In this case, NOT YET verb forms are formally unmodified, but are embedded in an analytical construction involving an auxiliary verb as first constituent. Since NOT YET-marked verbs cannot be further marked for TA, the presence of the auxiliary serves to host temporal markers.

Two past situations are depicted in (30). Relative verb forms such as *m̥fiyédhîiwé* 'when you arrived' in (30a), marked by the class 18 pronominal prefix *mu-* and the present perfective TA are very common in Cuwabo, especially in narratives where series of events are reported. They are used to establish a temporal connection between two events: when the event in the relative clause occurs in a past time reference, the event in the main clause is holding. The event of the first person singular speaker not having studied was still holding when the second person interlocutor arrived, against expectation. In (30b), the stative verb *wóoddá* 'be thin' acquires a past reading by means of the past prefix *a-*. Against this past stative reading, the verb *ókwa* 'to die' in the NOT YET clause may have a stative reading 'was not dead yet' or anterior past reading 'had not died yet'. In both (30a) and (30b), NOT YET expressions are made past via the auxiliary *li* 'be' which hosts the past prefix *a-*. In this context, it is even possible for the auxiliary *li* to be followed by the analytical NOT YET form, consisting of the auxiliary *tti* and the infinitival complement, as seen in (30b).

(30) a. *M̥fiyédhîiwé,   ddaáli*
        mu-fiy-édh-ile=iwe   **ddi-á-li**
        PP18-arrive-APPL-PFV.REL=PRO2SG SP1SG-PST-be
        ddihinásúṅzá(vi).
        ddi-hi-**ná**-suṅz-a=vi
        SP1SG-NEG-CE-study-FV=RESTR
        Ptg. 'Quando chegaste, não tinha estudado ainda.'
        Eng. 'When you arrived, I had not studied yet.'

b. *Waawóoddá,   waálí   ahinátti   ókwa.*
   o-á-odd-á   o-á-li   a-hi-**ná**-tti   ó-kw-a
   SP1-PST-be.thin-FV SP1-PST-be SP1-NEG-CE-AUX 15-die-FV
   Ptg. 'Estava magra, não estava morta ainda / não tinha morrida ainda.'
   Eng. 'She was thin, she was not dead yet / she had not died yet.' (Elic. from (7))

In (31), the situative verb *ogaafiyá* 'when you arrive' in the subordinate clause, albeit not formally marked for tense, still implies a future temporal interpretation.[7] More specifically, this TA category underlays the prospect of an upcoming event in a next or remote future. In this future temporal context, NOT YET-marked verb forms are necessarily preceded by the auxiliary verb stem *kála* 'be' inflected for present imperfective.

(31) *Ogaafiyá,   míyó   ddiṇkála*
     o-gaa-fiy-á   míyo   **ddi-ni-kál-a**
     SP2SG-SIT-arrive-FV PRO1SG SP1SG-IPFV.CJ-be-FV
     ddihinásúnzávi.
     ddi-hi-**ná**-suńz-a=vi
     SP1SG-NEG-CE-study-FV=RESTR
     Ptg. 'Quando chegares, não terei estudado ainda.'
     Eng. 'When you arrive, I will not have studied yet (lit. 'I am I have not studied yet').'

On the other hand, translating a sentence like 'She has turned thin, but she has not died yet.' (see example (7) treated in section 4) in the future tense would result in the sentence in (32), where simple future markers are used. In this sentence, NOT YET is not formally coded and therefore not explicitly expressed.

(32) *Oneel'   óóoddá   mbonye kanáákwe.*
     o-naa-ilá   ó-odd-á   mbonye ka-náa-kw-e
     SP1-FUT.DJ-AUX 15-be.thin-FV but NEG.SP1-FUT-die-FV
     Ptg. 'Estará magra, mas não estará morta (ainda) / não morrerá (ainda).'
     Eng. 'She will be thin, but she will not die (yet).' (Elic. from (7))

---

[7] Although the translations in the examples only provide a temporal interpretation ('when'), a conditional interpretation ('if') is also possible. From a cross-linguistic viewpoint, this close association between temporal and conditional clause linking has commonly been reported (Dixon 2009: 14). This is possible since a clear temporal connection is established between the two clauses. See Guérois (2017) for more details on Cuwabo situatives and conditionality in general.

As can be expected, in the three sentences in (30) and (31), the adverbial NP *na váno* 'until now' cannot possibly be added, as opposed to NOT YET-marked verbs embedded in present time reference.

NO LONGER

As already explained in section 6, the phasal polarity concept NO LONGER relates to an event which underwent a turning point in terms of polarity, i.e. from positive to negative. Since the new situation involving negative polarity still holds at the utterance time, the NO LONGER phasal polarity item *viina* more frequently associates with imperfective verb forms, as seen in (18) above. Depending on the context, present imperfective verb forms may have a future time reference. Thus in (33), the situative form *ddigaareelá* 'when I am rich' presents an idealized future projection upon which another event (here *kaddiṃpíyá vîina* 'I will no longer cook', in the main clause) will ensue.

(33) *Ddigaareelá,   kaddiṃpíyá   vîina.*
     ddi-gaa-reel-á   **ka**-ddi-ni-píy-a **viina**
     SP1SG-SIT-be.rich-FV NEG-SP1SG-IPFV-cook-FV too
     Ptg. 'Quando estiver rico, não hei-de-conzinhar mais.'
     Eng. 'When I am rich, I will no longer cook.' (Semi-elic.)

However, NO LONGER is not restricted to imperfective aspectuality. In (34), *viina* associates with *kaneéddíle* '(the body) did not walk', marked for present perfective.

(34) *Ṇníngó   neetéêne   kaneéddíle   vîina,   ṇlógúnáṅtí.*
     ni-níngo ni-eté=ene **ka**-ni-édd-ile **viina** ni-lé-o-gúnaṅti
     5-body   PP5-all=INT NEG-SP5-walk-PFV too   SP5-CE-15-lie.down
     Ptg. 'O corpo todo não andou mais, dormiu.'
     Eng. 'The whole body no longer worked (lit. walked), it kept on sleeping.'
     (Body)

8 Conclusion

Table 6 provides a summary of the results of the parametric approach presented in section 7 for the three phasal polarity concepts available in Cuwabo, i.e. STILL, NOT YET and NO LONGER. Parameter 5 on expressibility is not listed, since the notion ALREADY does not have a dedicated marker. It is instead obtained by the TA verbal affixes *hi-* and *-ile*, whose semantic core is perfective. On the

Table 6: Semantic and formal characteristics of Cuwabo phasal polarity items (based on Kramer's parameters).

Phasal polarity concept / Parameter	STILL =vi	NOT YET ná-	NOT YET =vi	NO LONGER viina
P1: External negation	×	×	×	×
P1: Internal negation	yes, with NOT YET =vi	×	yes, with STILL =vi	×
P2: Pragmaticity	neutral/CF	CF	neutral/CF	neutral/CF
P3: Telicity	–	–	–	–
P4: Wordhood	enclitic	prefix	enclitic	adverb
P6a: Internal paradigmaticity	asymmetric (=vi vs viina)	asymmetric (Ø vs ná-)	asymmetric (Ø vs =vi)	asymmetric (=vi vs viina)
P6b: External paradigmaticity	no TA restriction	TA restriction	no TA restriction	no TA restriction

basis of the three Cuwabo corpora analysed in this study, the addition of the borrowed adverb *já* (< Portuguese *já* 'already') does not constitute a productive strategy to fill the phasal polarity gap. ALREADY is thus considered as a missing dedicated phasal polarity concept in Cuwabo.

In terms of coverage (parameter 1), while no external negation is observed, NOT YET constructions in *=vi* are based on the internally negated STILL construction. In other words, the continuative STILL is used to derive the continuative NOT YET. However, NOT YET constructions in *=vi* are not commonly attested as compared to NOT YET constructions in *ná-*. This poor system of semantic relations involving STILL and NOT YET reflects a rather inflexible phasal polarity system.

Phasal polarity items vary in their degree of pragmatic sensitivity (parameter 2): while NOT YET *ná-* is inherently counterexpectational, NOT YET *=vi*, STILL and NO LONGER concepts are more flexible and also accept a neutral scenario depending on the context.

Earliness and lateness are not very relevant when it comes to the telic phasal polarity expression NO LONGER (parameter 3). This means that the turning point from 'V' to 'no longer V' occurs without any previous temporal expectation.

The morphological status of Cuwabo's three phasal polarity markers is diverse (parameter 4). They are either enclitic, prefix or adverb. NOT YET is by default expressed by a prefix (*ná-*) attached either on the main verb or on the auxiliary *tti*, but it may also be conveyed by the verbal enclitic (*=vi*). The boundedness of the markers *ná-* and *=vi* suggest that NOT YET and STILL result each from a grammaticalization process. The prefix *ná-* is largely incorporated in the TA system of the language: it occupies the post-initial verbal position, otherwise used for TA, and it does not co-occur with any other TA markers (parameter 6b). This degree of incorporation is an indicator that NOT YET is a stable category in Cuwabo. NO LONGER is the only Cuwabo phasal polarity item occurring as an adverb.

NOT YET and NO LONGER expressions necessarily involve the marking of standard negation on the verb. NO LONGER is opposed to STILL in terms of polarity, however, the two phasal polarity concepts do not display internal symmetry (parameter 6a). Interactions between phasal polarity and TAM is another source of variation: the NOT YET marker *ná-* is incorporated in the Cuwabo TA system in such a way that it cannot co-occur with other TA markers. On the other hand, phasal polarity markers for STILL and NO LONGER are less restricted and may combine with different TAM categories. Cuwabo thus has partially symmetric external paradigmaticity.

The corpus investigation was proposed to illustrate which phasal polarity expressions have most occurrences in Cuwabo. The most frequent expression are STILL and NOT YET, with NO LONGER being far less common.

Abbreviations

Glossing follows the Leipzig Glossing Rules. The following additional abbreviations are used throughout:

AM	associated motion	LOC	locative
APPL	applicative	NEG	negative
AUX	auxiliary	NP	nominal prefix
CAUS	causative	OP	object prefix
CE	counterexpectational	PASS	passive
CF	counterfactual	PFV	perfective
CJ	conjoint	PL	plural
CON	connective	PLA	plural addressee
COP	copula	POSS	possessive
DEF	definite	PP	pronominal prefix
DEM	demonstrative	PRO	pronoun
DJ	disjoint	REL	relative
EDEM	emphatic demonstrative	RESTR	restrictive
FUT	future	SBJV	subjunctive
FV	final vowel	SEQ	sequential
H1D	First high tone deletion	SG	singular
HAB	habitual	SIT	situative
INT	intensive	SP	subject prefix
IPFV	imperfective	TA(M)	tense aspect (mood)

Numbers in glosses refer to noun classes; high tones are represented with an acute accent, whereas low tones are unmarked. The diacritic ^ indicates a falling pitch, which comes as a result of the tonal process known as 'High-Tone doubling' (Guérois 2015: 121–125), when the mora receiving the doubled H is in phrase-penultimate position. The diacritic ¯ is used on the phonetic level to signal a mid-tone, i.e. as an intermediary tone between H and Ø, more specifically in the process described as 'phonetic upsweep' (Guérois 2015: 92), where phrase-initial primary H tone tends to be less high than doubled H.

Bibliographic references

Anonymous. 2004. *Bíblia-Malebo Okoddela: A Bíblia em língua Etxuwabo* [Bíblia-Malebo Okoddela: The Bible in the Etxuwabo language] (translated by the diocesan team and the Frades Menores Capuchinhos). Quelimane: Dom Bernardo Filipe Governo.

DeLancey, Scott. 1997. Mirativity: The grammatical marking of unexpected information. *Linguistic Typology* 1. 33–52.

Devos, Maud. 2008. *A grammar of Makwe (Palma; Mozambique)*. LINCOM studies in African linguistics. Munich: Lincom Europa.

Dixon, Robert M.W. 2009. The Semantics of Clause Linking in Typological Perspective. In Robert M.W. Dixon and Alexandra Y. Aikhenvald (eds.), *The semantics of clause linking: a cross-linguistic typology*, 1–55. Oxford: Oxford University Press.

Festi, Ludovico & Vito Valler. 1994. *Dicionário Etxuwabo-Português*. Quelimane: Padres Capuchinhos de Trento.

Floor, Sebastian. 2010. *Mwani grammatical sketch*. Maputo: SIL Moçambique.

Guérois, Rozenn. 2015. *A grammar of Cuwabo (Mozambique, Bantu P34)*. Lyon: University of Lyon 2 dissertation.

Guérois, Rozenn. 2017. Conditional constructions in Cuwabo. *Studies in African Linguistics* 46 (2): 193–212.

Guérois, Rozenn. 2019. Cuwabo (P34). In Mark van de Velde & Koen Bostoen (eds.), *The Bantu Languages* (2nd edition), 733–775. Oxford: Routledge.

Güldemann, Tom. 1999. The genesis of verbal negation in Bantu and its dependency on functional features of clause types. In Jean-Marie Hombert & Larry M. Hyman (eds.), *Bantu Historical Linguistics*, 545–587. Stanford: Centre for the Study of Language and Information.

Guthrie, Malcolm. 1967–71. *Comparative Bantu: An Introduction to the Comparative Linguistics and Prehistory of the Bantu Lanuages. 4 Vols*. Farnborough: Gregg International Publishers.

Heine, Bernd, Ulrike Claudi & Friederike Hünnemeyer. 1991. Grammaticalization: A conceptual framework. Chicago: University of Chicago Press.

Heine, Bernd & Tania Kuteva. 2002. World lexicon of grammaticalization. Cambridge: Cambridge University Press.

Kissberth, Charles & Rozenn Guérois. 2014. Melodic H Tones in Makhuwa and Cuwabo. *Africana Linguistica* 20. 181–205.

Kraal, Pieter J. 2005. *A Grammar of Makonde (Chinnima, Tanzania)*. Leiden: Leiden University dissertation.
Kramer, Raija. 2017. Position paper on Phasal Polarity expressions. Hamburg: University of Hamburg. https://www.aai.unihamburg.de/afrika/php2018/medien/position-paper-on-php.pdf (accessed 04 June 2019).
Krifka, Manfred. 2000. Alternatives for aspectual particles: semantics of 'still' and 'already'. Paper presented at the Twenty-Sixth Annual Meeting of the Berkeley Linguistics Society, University of Berkeley, 401–412.
Löbner, Sebastian. 1989. 'Schon – erst – noch': An integrated analysis. *Linguistics and Philosophy* 12 (2). 167–212.
Maho, Jouni Filip. 2009. NUGL Online: The online version of the New Updated Guthrie List – A referential classification of the Bantu languages. http://goto.glocalnet.net/mahopapers/nuglonline.pdf
Meeussen, Achille E. 1967. Bantu Grammatical Reconstructions. *Africana Linguistica* 3. 79–121.
Nurse, Derek & Gérard Philippson (eds.). 2003. *The Bantu languages*. London: Routledge.
Odden, David A. 1996. *The Phonology and Morphology of Kimatuumbi*. Phonology of the world's languages. Oxford: Oxford University Press.
Plungian, Vladimir A. 1999. A typology of phasal meanings. In Werner Abraham & Leonid Kulikov (eds.), *Tense-aspect, transitivity and causativity: Essays in honour of Vladimir Nedjalkov* (Vol. 50), 311–321. Amsterdam: John Benjamins Publishing.
Schadeberg, Thilo. 1990. Schon – noch – nicht mehr: Das Unerwartete als grammatische Kategorie im Kiswahili. *Frankfurter Afrikanistische Blätter* 2. 1–15.
Schadeberg, Thilo & Fransisco U. Mucanheia. 2000. *Ekoti: The Maka or Swahili Language of Angoche*. Cologne: Rüdiger Köppe.
Van Baar, Theodorus M. 1997. *Phasal Polarity*. Amsterdam: IFOTT.
Van de Velde, Mark & Koen Bostoen (eds.). 2019. *The Bantu languages* (2nd Edition). London: Routledge.
Van der Auwera, Johan. 1993. 'Already' and 'still': beyond duality. Linguistics and philosophy 16(6). 613–653.
Van der Auwera, Johan. 1998. *Phasal Adverbials in the Languages of Europe*. Berlin: Mouton de Gruyter.
Van der Wal, Jenneke. 2009. *Word Order and Information Structure in Makhuwa-Enahara*. Utrecht: LOT.
Van der Wal, Jenneke & Larry Hyman (eds). 2017. *The conjoint/disjoint alternation in Bantu*. Trends in Linguistics series. Berlin: Mouton de Gruyter.
Williamson, Kay, & Roger Blench. 2000. Niger-Congo. In Bernd Heine & Derek Nurse (eds), *African languages: An introduction*, 1–42. Cambridge: Cambridge University Press.

Roland Kießling
Phasal polarity in Isu – and beyond

1 Introduction

Isu [isu], also referred to as Esu, is a Grassfields Bantu language of the Ring subgroup (Watters 2003), spoken by approximately 15,400 L1 speakers (Eberhard et al. 2019) in the North West Region of Cameroon. Within Ring, Isu belongs to the West Ring group which also includes Aghem [agq], Bu[1] [lmx], Weh [weh], and Zoa[2] [zhw] and which is parallel to three other branches, i.e. East, South and Central. All in all, the Ring subgroup has a total of some 17 varieties. Section 2 presents a discussion of markers used to express phasal polarity concepts in Isu. Their grammatical aspects are discussed in section 3, before the focus is widened to explore the areal perspective of the expression of phasal polarity across West and Central Ring languages in section 4.

2 The expression of phasal polarity concepts in Isu

Table (1) presents an overview of the morphemes which have been found to express phasal polarity notions in Isu.[3]

(1)   Isu phasal pority items[4]

---

[1] The term Laimbue used in Eberhard et al. 2019 is actually an obscure rendering of the Bu phrase *láim bù è* 'the tongue/language of Bu'.
[2] Also referred to as Zhoa.
[3] The contribution gives an overview of phasal polarity in Isu generally, but will have its limitations concerning semantic detail due to the fact that it mainly relies on mining a limited corpus of some thirty texts of different lengths representing various genres, without being supported by dedicated elicitations geared towards clarifying phasal polarity concepts.
[4] Transcription follows IPA conventions, except for y [j]. Conventions of tone transcription: the acute [´] marks high tones, the grave accent [`] marks low tones, the downward arrow [↓] marks downstep. Contour tones are marked by combining the symbols for high and low, respectively, except for word final contour tones which drop from the low level to extra-low.

Roland Kießling, University of Hamburg

https://doi.org/10.1515/9783110646290-008

STILL	ALREADY	NOT YET	NO LONGER
ná(a)m(ɔ́)	[mɔ̂, mâa, má[↓]á] [tîŋ(ɔ́)]	[kàm(ɔ̀) + NEG]	
	[ɔ̀lrédĩ]	[nám(ɔ́) + NEG]	

At the present stage of knowledge, STILL is the only phasal polarity concept which is expressed by a semantically dedicated item in Isu. The other items in (1) cover a wider range of semantic notions while they come to also express phasal polarity concepts in certain contexts. This type of semantic inclusion by vagueness or polysemy is indicated by square brackets in (1).

2.1 STILL

The concept STILL is expressed by the hybrid adverbial[5] *nám* (imperfective: *náamɔ́*) (Kießling 2011: 253–254). In the examples given in (2a–d), it indicates the sustained duration of the action expressed in the verb *fàʔ* 'work' with reference to a prior point in time.

(2) a. Preverbal hybrid adverbial *nám* 'still' (imperfective: *ná(a)mɔ́*)
  mɔ́ kɔ́ [↓]náam-ɔ́ fàʔ-à   áwɔ̀ dɔ̀ŋ   kĩ̀
  1sg P3 still-IPF work-IPF for 7.chief 7.OF
  'I was still working for the chief.'
 b. mɔ́ náam-ɔ́ fàʔ-à   ŋwɔ̀
  1sg still-IPF work-IPF CF
  'I am still working.'
 c. mɔ́ kĩ̂ [↓]náam-ɔ́ fàʔ-à   áwɔ̀ wè
  1sg F1 still-IPF work-IPF for 3sg
  'I will still work for him.'
 d. mɔ́ mɔ́   [↓]nám fàʔ   áwɔ̀ wè
  1sg P1.FOC still work for 3sg
  'I HAVE (indeed) STILL worked for him.'

These are marked by double grave accent [ˮ]. Desegmentalised floating tones in the glossing are marked by a preceding asterisk *, e.g. *L.

5 The term "hybrid adverbial" denotes a word class in Isu which straddles the borderline between full-fledged verbs on the one hand and invariable adverbs on the other hand in that the items take part in verbal inflection by hosting aspect and subordinative markers without qualifying as full-fledged verbs, since they cannot establish a verbal predication on their own, as detailed and exemplified in section 3.

e. ù má↓á nám téb
   3sg P2.FOC still become.small
   'He STILL (indeed) remainED small.'

f. ŋwǔ↓nî ↓f-ə́ nám dzàŋ   fyî wɔ̀ á↓nə́ ntwà
   19.bird 19-D1 still make.noise exit CPT at 9.pot
   'The bird still made noise from out of the pot.'

g. bə́↓ wù-bǔm ù tsĭy á↓-tə́ŋə́ kà? fə̀ mɔ́ʔɔ̀
   if 1.hunter 1 pass at-under 19.tree 19 SO.same
   f-ĭy sɔ̀ŋ îm-bè̌ nə̀ ù ná(a)m-ə́ ↓bǔm-ə́ ŋwɔ̀
   19-OF 6a.time 6a-two while S3sg still-IPF hunt-IPF CF
   kə́ĩ ↓tsə́ nə̀ ù mɔ̀ŋ-ɔ̀ ŋwɔ̌
   know IMM that S3sg be.lost-IPF CF
   'If a hunter passes under the same tree twice while STILL hunting, know that he IS indeed lost.'
   (Kießling 2011: 151)

The adverbial *nám* 'still' is not restricted at all with respect to crucial tense-aspect categories of Isu. It freely combines with both aspectual categories, i.e. the imperfective aspect in (2a–c) and the perfective aspect in (2d), and with any tense marker, e.g. with the remote past (P3) in (2a), the present tense in (2b), the immediate future (F1) in (2c), the focalised immediate past tense (P1.FOC) in (2d) and the focalised distant past tense (P2) in (2e).

The combined effect of the adverbial *nám* 'still' and the focalised past tense markers *mə́* in (2d) and *má↓á* in (2e) signalizes a counterexpectual validity of the state of affairs. Thus in (2e) the narrator disappoints the audience's expectation about the success of the protagonist's untiring efforts to grow bigger which had previously been elaborated in some detail. A similar situation holds in (2g) where the imperfective form *ná(a)mə́* 'still' combines with the clause focus marker *ŋwɔ̀*, adding up to express the counterexpectual continuation of the action encoded in the verb *bǔm* 'hunt'.

The adverbial *nám* 'still' itself is morphologically marked for aspect, i.e. the perfective form *nám* (2d) alternates with its imperfective counterpart *náamə́* (2a-c), just as the perfective form of the main verb *fà?* 'work' alternates with its imperfective form *fà?à*. This reveals that the adverbial *nám* 'still' actually originates in an erstwhile verb retaining verbal properties, but incapable of establishing a verbal predication single-handedly, as will be elaborated in section 3 below.[6]

---

[6] As correctly observed by an anonymous reviewer, there is the alternative possibility of a non-verb particle developing into an adverbial by acquisition of verbal properties via

2.2 ALREADY

The situation for the expression of the concept ALREADY is not so clear, since Isu lacks a dedicated marker to encode the premature inchoation of an event or action prior to some other reference point or expectation. It is rather the case that this notion could be expressed by a variety of items all of which cover a range of different meanings in themselves, i.e. the hybrid adverbial *fiŋ(ə)* 'readily, promptly' (5), the invariable adverbial *kʰú* 'earlier' (6) and a series of focus markers for various degrees of past tense: *mɔ̂*, *mâa* and *má˅á* (3–4). Thus, example (3a) is a statement which is neutral with respect to focalisation and negative polarity, situated in the immediate past by the marker *mɔ̀* (P1). The examples in (3b) and (3c) differ with respect to information structure, since they involve a different tense marker, *mɔ̂* (P1.FOC), which belongs to the set of focalised past tense markers (Kießling 2017), i.e. it assigns focus to the notion of completion of an action or event against the background of a counterexpectation or contrasting presupposition (see also Watters 1979 for the Aghem situation). In (3b), it is used in combination with the adverbial STILL, resulting in a counterexpectual insistence on the *continuation* of the action *dzùmǐ* 'follow'. As soon as the adverbial 'still' is absent (3c), however, the same marker for the focalised immediate past *mɔ̂* (P1.FOC) could be seen to cover the function of ALREADY, i.e. it asserts the earlier or premature *completion* of an action or event, contrary to expectation.

(3) Expression of ALREADY via focalised past marker *mɔ̂*
    a. *ù   mɔ̀ mîɔ́ dzúmì*
       3sg P1 O1sg follow
       'He followed me.'
    b. *ù   mɔ́ ˅mîɔ́ nám dzúmì*
       3sg P1.FOC O1sg still follow
       'He HAS (indeed) STILL followed me.'
    c. *ù   mɔ́ ˅mîɔ́ dzúmì*
       3sg P1.FOC O1sg follow
       'He HAS (indeed / already) followed me.'

---

analogical transfer from the "degenerate" verbs. However, while there is plenty of evidence for the scenario of loss of verbal properties, the imperfective form only being one of them, there is no evidence whatsoever for an acquisition of verbal properties by a prior non-verb.

The examples in (4) illustrate the semantic effect to assert an earlier completion of an action or event, contrasting with a negative presupposition, for all focalised past tense markers, *mɔ̂*, *mâa* and *má˅á*.

(4) Expression of ALREADY via focalised past markers *mɔ̂*, *mâa* and *má˅á*
    a. *ù*   *mɔ́*   *˅tɛ́b*
       3sg P1.FOC become.small
       'He HAS (indeed / already) become small (today).'
    b. *ù*   *mâa*   *tɛ́b*
       3sg P2.FOC become.small
       'He HAD (indeed / already) become small (yesterday).'
    c. *ù*   *má˅á*   *tɛ́b*
       3sg P3.FOC become.small
       'He HAD (indeed / already) become small (at some point in the past beyond yesterday).'

The hybrid adverbial *tiŋ(ə́)*, positioned after the core verb, primarily denotes the readiness or eagerness of an agent to carry out an action (5a) or, in the case of non-controlled processes, the promptness and extraordinarily speedy course of events coming down on some patient, not restricted or delayed by any impediment or obstacle, as in the case with (5b) ('grow'), which blends over into the domain of phasal polarity, i.e. denoting the realisation / completion of an action or event, premature to some expectation, as is clear in (5b).

(5) Expression of ALREADY included in usage of hybrid adverbial *tiŋ(ə)* 'readily, promptly'
    a. *ábə́˅* *ŋgà* *lá* *kə̀* *tsʷû* *tiŋ*
       if   1pl.incl lack NEG instruct promptly
       áwá   *ŋgàŋ*   *ɲiə́˅*,
       2.children 1pl.incl.POSS now
       'If we do not already instruct our children now . . . (and send them to schools, when shall we ever catch up in development?)'
       (Neumann 2019)
    b. *yú* *sî*   *kwɔ́ʔɔ́*   *tiŋə́*   *wɔ́˅*
       3pl should ascend.IPF promptly.IPF CPT
       á˅nə́ *îmʊɔ̀* *î-˅té*   *y-î*
       in   5.life   5-DEF   5-OF

'(Let's start to train them little by little,) they should already be growing up in that life (= in the activity you want them to be able to carry out).'
(Neumann 2019)

The hybrid adverbial *tíŋ(ə)* is most probably derived from the full-fledged verb *tíŋ* 'push', which seems a semantically plausible source of a marker for the notion of promptness. Accepting this semantic link, *tíŋ(ə)* might even synchronically be viewed as a verb with generalised semantics in asymmetrical serial verb constructions which are highly frequent in Isu (Kießling 2011), attesting to a common path of grammaticalisation from full verb to hybrid adverbial as outlined in section 3 below.

The invariable adverb *kʰú* 'earlier, before' might also be used to achieve an expression of the ALREADY concept (6).[7]

(6) Expression of ALREADY included in usage of adverbial *kʰú* 'earlier, before'
    ù   mâa   àyîə   á   yèe
    3sg P2.FOC 6.issues 6   DEF
    yə̀   kʰú   kɔ́ʔ   á↓nə́ úsìy
    6.OF earlier see   at   3.spiritism
    'He HAD (indeed) already seen the things in his spiritism . . .'
    (Kießling 2011: 56)

In other contexts, the phasal polarity concept ALREADY is expressed by the Pidgin English loan *ɔ̀lrédì* (7), which might be taken as another hint confirming the observation that Isu indeed lacks a dedicated item for the expression of the polarity concept ALREADY.

(7) Expression of ALREADY by English loan *ɔ̀lrédì*
    mə́   mə́   ɔ̀lrédì   dzài nə̀ [á kʰwîy fɛ́↓ ná úʃìə́ á↓nə́ támbà].
    1sg P1.FOC already say that [. . .]
    '(. . .) I HAVE ALREADY said that [we keep things (i.e. domesticated animals) locked in in fences].
    (Neumann 2019)

---

[7] Adverbials, both hybrid as well as non-hybrid, can be grouped in two classes according to their syntax, i.e. those which precede vs. those which follow the core verb.

2.3 NO LONGER

The expression of the notion of NO LONGER could be achieved via external negation of *ná(a)m(ɔ́)* 'still' (8b) or by external negation of another hybrid adverbial *kàm(ɔ̀)* 'again' (9a–c). Since all examples present imperfective contexts, negation is achieved by the imperfective negator *wài*. It is not clear whether constructions with both markers could be used interchangeably, or if there is a more subtle semantic or pragmatic difference.

(8) External negation of *ná(a)m(ɔ́)* 'still' for expression of NO LONGER
  a. ú ŋwɔ̀ fyî ù <u>ná(a)m-ɔ́</u> ↓*téb-ɔ́* ŋwɔ̀̃
     3sg leave exit 3sg still-IPF be.small-IPF CF
     'He left (went out and away) while he was still small.'
  b. ù <u>ná(a)m-ɔ́</u> ↓*téb-ɔ́* dzɨ̌ <u>wài</u>
     3sg still-IPF be.small-IPF evidently NEG.IPF
     'He is (evidently) not small any more / any longer.'

(9) External negation of *kàm(ɔ̀)* 'again' for expression of NO LONGER
  a. yɔ́↓ ù lá <u>wǎi</u> á↓n-î-kàm nǔ,
     since 3sg lack NEG.IPF to-VN-again hide
     ú nǐ fyî bɔ̀ Dì.
     3sg.P3 take go.out CPT Di
     'Since he could no longer hide, he brought out Diy.'
     (Kießling 2011: 73, 246)
  b. ù kî lá <u>kàmɔ̀</u> zîŋɔ́ ↓<u>wái</u>
     3sg F1 lack again.IPF do.IPF NEG.IPF
     '(. . .) he will no longer do it.'
     (Neumann 2019)
  c. ú <u>kâm</u> <u>wài</u> sɔ́ʔɔ́
     8 again be.absent also
     'They (compounds) are no longer there . . .'
     (Neumann 2019)

2.4 NOT YET

There are various ways to express the notion of NOT YET by way of external negation of either the adverbial *ná(a)m(ɔ́)* 'still' (10) or the adverbial *kàm(ɔ̀)* 'again' (11) – which are precisely the ones that have already been found to express the concept NO LONGER above. At the present stage of knowledge it is not clear, whether this is an instance of semantic vagueness or whether syntactic differences, e.g. in the combination with aspect-sensitive negators (imperfective *wài* vs. perfective *kə̀*) might be responsible for the semantic difference.

(10) External negation of *nám(ə́)* 'still' for expression of NOT YET
 mə́ fûk tsə́ ↓ndáw î dzɨ̃m kə̀ nám kɔ̂ʔ
 1sg search IMM 9.house 9 whole NEG.PF still see
 'I searched the whole house and could not find it yet.'

(11) External negation of *kàm(ə̀)* 'again' for expression of NOT YET
 a. *mə́ kə̀ kâm ɲî dzɨ̃*
  1sg NEG.PF again eat evidently
  'I have not yet eaten.'
 b. *mbám mé↓ î mbáa kɔ̂ʔ dzɨ̃ wù*
  9.cobra QUOT 3log really see evidently 1.person
  ù ɣàa w-ɔ̀ zîy↓,
  1 DEF 1-D1 today
  î kúɲî ↓kám wài dzɨ̃ á↓n-î-bɔ̀ʔɔ̀
  3log instead again NEG evidently to-VN-carry
  túw kə̀ dʌ́lə́ k-îy
  7.head 7 become.heavy-IPF 7-OF
  'The cobra said that it has really found its master today, however, it is not yet ready to carry a heavy head and accept shame.'
  (Kießling 2011: 250)

Apart from these strategies, there is an invariable adverbial *ká↓ŋə́* 'never ever' (Kießling 2011: 289) which could be used to express the notion NOT YET in (12a–d).

(12) Expression of NOT YET with *ká↓ŋə́* '(n)ever'
 a. *tám kə́ ká↓ŋə́ bàŋ*
  7.fruit 7 never become.red
  'The fruit has not yet become red / ripe.'
 b. *ú káŋ↓ə́ bɔ̂ʔ maî*
  8 never even finish
  'It (food) has not even (been) finished (yet) (. . .)'
 c. *mə́ ká↓ŋə́ kə̀ ɲî dzɨ̃*
  1sg never NEG.PF eat evidently
  'I have not (yet) eaten.'

d. ù ká˅ŋɔ́ kə̀   ŋwɔ̂ fyî dẑɨ
   3sg never NEG.PF leave exit evidently
   'He has not yet left.'

The puzzle here is that there are contexts such as the ones in (12c–d) where the marker ká˅ŋɔ́ is accompanied by a separate negative marker, i.e. kə̀ for negation[8] in the perfective aspect, whereas in other contexts such as the ones in (12a–b) ká˅ŋɔ́ stands on its own, obviously conflating the semantic notions of premature realisation and negation.

It is not clear whether the morphosyntactic contrast of the constructions ká˅ŋɔ́ kə̀ + Verb (12c) vs. kə̀ kâm + Verb (11a) results in any semantic difference with respect to phasal polarity issues.

3 Aspects of wordhood and grammaticalisation

Regarding aspects of wordhood, the prominent phasal polarity items discussed so far, i.e. ná(a)m(ə́) 'still' and kà(a)m(-ə̀) 'again', are classified taxonomically as hybrid adverbials which serves as a cover term for a word class in a zone of transition between full-fledged verbs and full-fledged adverbs (Kießling 2011: 241–84). This word class owes its existence to the fact that Isu, along with all the rest of the Ring subgroup, is a heavily serialising language with both symmetrical and asymmetrical serialisation. In asymmetrical serialisation, a semantically non-restricted major verb forms the core of the serial construction and might accommodate an entourage of up to four minor verbs which express various more specialised notions in the domains of deictic orientation, path, manner, aspectuality and valency. Some verbal inflectional categories are marked in a concordant way in asymmetrical serial verb constructions, i.e. they are expressed by recurrent markers on every single verb of the series, e.g. imperfective aspect. Thus in (13a) all serialised verbs, i.e. təmî 'stand', kɔ̂ʔ 'see', ɲî 'enter' and diáɲî 'move through', plus the hybrid adverbial màŋ 'just', are in the perfective aspect, whereas in (13b) they are replaced by their imperfective counterparts throughout, i.e. tyîmə́, kɔ̂ʔɔ̀, ɲîə, diáŋə́ and màŋà, respectively.

---

8 Negation is a complex issue in Isu, involving at least three markers which are in complementary distribution with respect to aspect and mood, viz. kə́ (negation of subjunctive) vs. kə̀˘ (negation of imperative and perfective aspect), wài (negation of imperfective aspect).

(13) Concordant marking for aspect: perfective (a) vs. imperfective (b)
 a. *mbám   ɔ́   màŋ   támî   kɔ́ʔ*
   9.cobra 9:DO:P3 just:PF stand:PF see:PF
   ɲî   diáɲî   yɔ̀   wè
   enter:PF   move.through:PF   thither O3sg
   'The cobra just stood and saw him inside immediately.'
 b. *ù   mé˅   mbám   y-ɔ̀   kĭ   màŋ-à   tyîm-ɔ́*
   S3sg QUOT   9.cobra 9-DO   F1   just-IPF[:*L] stand-IPF[:*L]
   kɔ́ʔ-ɔ́   ɲî-ə   ˅diáŋɔ́   wɔ̀   îγé
   see-IPF[:*L]   enter-IPF[:*L] move.through.IPF[:*L]   hither O3log
   'He found that the cobra would just stand and see him inside immediately.'

The point here is that there is a sizable group of items such as *màŋ(-à)* 'just' which visibly take part in verbal inflectional morphology by their participation in aspect marking, but do not qualify as full-fledged verbs, since they cannot establish a verbal predication on their own. This group is called hybrid adverbials and *ná(a)m(-ɔ́)* 'still' and *kà(a)m(-ɔ́)* 'again' are among them.

The asymmetrical serial verb construction in Isu and in other West Ring languages forms a crucial breeding zone for various types of hybrid adverbials, depending on the extent to which they retain verbal properties. The important point here is that the phasal polarity marker for STILL and the adverbial AGAIN are most probably derived from erstwhile verbs.

4 Areal perspective in the Cameroonian Grassfields

4.1 West Ring

Within West Ring (Aghem, Bu, Isu, Weh, Zoa) the system of phasal polarity marking as sketched for Isu seems to be fairly stable, as far as could be judged from the limited data at hand. At least the West Ring varieties for which data are available, Aghem and Weh, both have items for the expression of STILL which are cognate to the Isu adverbial *ná(a)m(ɔ́)*, i.e. Aghem *naam* (14) and Weh *nám* (15).[9]

---

9 All Isu, Weh and Zoa data in this section are taken from the author's fieldwork notes.

(14) Aghem *naam* 'still'
    a. *n   naam sughuun tîmbî*
       1sg   still   nurse.IPF 13.offspring
       'I am still nursing my children.' (ALDEC)
    b. *Kwè naam bighaa tɔ   u*
       Kwɛ still build   3.knowledge 3
       gwɨ̵ɨ̵n   wɨ esum   wo
       cultivating 3 5.farm 3
       'Kwe is still developing the knowledge of farming.' (ALDEC)

(15) Weh *nám* 'still'
    a. *tə̂   năm   ↓kʰə́ nîi↓fú mî↓   ŋkʰə́   ú*
       3sg still must VN-give O1sg 3.money 3.OF
       'He still has to give me money.'
    b. *ń   nám   ↓kúumə́   nù*
       1sg still.IPF gather.IPF CF
       I am still gathering a lot.'

As we turn to Zoa, things become diverse, since the concept STILL is expressed by an adverbial *zàm* 'still' (imperfective: *zèàm*) (16) which is not cognate to the common WR adverbial **nám(ə́)*.

(16) Zoa *zàm* 'still' (imperfective: *zèàm*)
    ḿ   zêam   yɔ̀:mə̀   ŋwə̏
    1sg still.IPF talk.IPF CF
    'I am still talking.'

In spite of the formal divergence there are clear structural parallels to WR **nám(ə́)* with respect to (a) the existence of a dedicated marker for the concept STILL and (b) with respect to its taxonomic status as hybrid adverbial which clearly reveals its source in a prior verb.

Due to data limitations and the absence of a reliable elaboration of sound correspondences across West Ring and beyond, the identification of verbal origins in potential Ring cognates of Zoa *zàm* 'still' and WR **ná(a)m(ə́)* 'still' remains tentative and speculative. However, verbs from other Central Ring languages such as Kuk *nám* (imperfective: *nâ*) 'stay; live' and Kung *ná* 'keep' look like quite convincing candidates which support the assumption that the WR 'still' phasal polarity marker **ná(a)m(ə́)* ultimately derives from a verb meaning 'stay'. The Isu parallel *zèm* 'wake up' though seems less convincing as lexical source of Zoa *zàm* 'still' semantically.

4.2 Central Ring

Beyond West Ring and across the rest of Ring in general, divergencies add up. Even the nearby Central Ring language Men comes up with a phasal polarity system (17) which looks fundamentally different from WR in that it provides dedicated adverbials for the concepts ALREADY and NOT YET, plus another distinct dedicated adverbial for the concept STILL which is not cognate to WR *ná(a)m(ə́) nor to Zoa zàm. Both NOT YET and NO LONGER include external negation.[10]

(17) Men phasal polarity items
STILL   ALREADY   NOT YET   NO LONGER
pá   kàinè   ɲə̀m + NEG   késə́ 'do again'+ NEG

Examples for pá 'still' (17), kàinè 'already' (18), nyə̀m (19) and késə́ 'again' (20) show that all of these adverbials – or "auxiliaries", as Möller (2012: 41–42) calls them – are incorporated into the verbal complex in that they precede the verb while following tense and aspect markers.

(18) Men pá 'still' ((im)perfective)[11]
   a. m̀   fə̀   pá   kìŋə́   ndò   ndē
      1sg P2   still close.IPF PROG   house
      'I was still closing the house.'
      (Möller 2012: 31–32)
   b. è   vá́   ↓fə́ pá   ʒí
      3sg PF   P2   still eat
      'He was still to eat.'
   c. è   pá   ʒíə́   ndò
      3sg still eat.IPF PROG
      'He is still eating.'

(19) Men kàinè 'already' (imperfective: káinə́)[12]
   a. mʌ́   kàinè   ndá?
      1sg.P1 already pay
      'I have already paid.'

---

[10] All Men data in this section are taken from the author's fieldnotes, unless indicated otherwise.
[11] "The auxiliary pá 'still' precedes the head verb and can follow any of the different tenses and together with both the perfective and imperfective aspect." (Möller 2012: 31–32).
[12] The tone contrast of the low tone perfective form kàinè vs. the high tone imperfective form káinə́ noted by Möller (2012: 31-2) remains a morphotonological puzzle so far.

b. è   vɘ↓ fɔ́ <u>kàinè</u> pɔ́in
   3sg PF P2 already come
   'He has already come.'
   (Möller 2012)
c. è   <u>káinɔ́</u>   pɔ̀   ndò
   3sg already.IPF come.IPF PROG
   'He is already coming.'
   (Möller 2012)
d. è   nɘ̀ <u>káinɔ́</u>   pɔ̀
   3sg F1 already.IPF come.IPF
   'He will come already.'
   (Möller 2012)

(20) Men *ɲɘ̀m* ((im)perfective) + *NEG* 'not yet'
   a. m̀ fɔ́ pá'à <u>ɲɘ̀m</u> kìŋ   ndē
      1sg P2 NEG yet   close house
      'I have not closed the house yet.'
      (Möller 2012: 41)
   b. è fɘ̀ pá'à <u>ɲɘ̀m</u> ʒí
      3sg P2 NEG yet   eat
      'He did not eat yet.'
      (Möller 2012: 41)

(21) Men *kɛ́sɛ́* 'do again; return, turn around' (imperfective: *kɛ́sɔ́*) + *NEG* 'no longer'
   a. ʌ́   kɛ́sɛ́ vá   tʃí   vâ   véin   vêi nîŋ
      IS again NEG NEG.COP 1.child 1.POSS.3sg 1? alone
      'It is no longer his child alone.'

There do not seem to be any restrictions regarding the compatibility of these phasal polarity markers with tense and aspect categories. While *kàinè* 'already' and *kɛ́sɛ́* 'again' alternate with distinct imperfective stems *káinɔ́* and *kɛ́sɔ́*, respectively, *pá* and *nyɘ̀m* do not. So in spite of all differences, there is a clear typological parallel which links the West Ring systems presented above and the Central Ring system presented in this section, i.e. all dedicated phasal polarity items are adverbials most of which visibly betray a verbal origin without having the potential to establish a verbal predication on their own.

5 Conclusion

The evidence unfolded above allows for the following four – preliminary – generalisations: (I) In spite of their close genetic relationship, the Ring languages display a remarkable internal diversity with respect to the expression of phasal polarity concepts. While Isu, along with most other West Ring languages, operates a system with a single dedicated item for phasal polarity, i.e. the hybrid adverbial *nám(-ə́)* 'still', which could be reconstructed for a subgroup within West Ring, the nearby Central Ring language Men operates a threefold system of dedicated phasal polarity markers for STILL, ALREADY and NOT YET. (II) The concept NO LONGER is preferably expressed by external negation of a construction with 'again' in various Ring languages. (III) The majority of phasal polarity markers identified in West Ring and Central Ring above pattern with hybrid adverbials attesting to their ultimate verbal origin. (IV) The *absence* of dedicated markers for the expression of the concept of ALREADY in West Ring seems to correlate with the *presence* of a system of focalised past tense markers which include the notion of realisation of an action or event premature to some expectation. This suggests that the degree of elaboration of systems for the dedicated expression of phasal polarity concepts might depend on parameters such as the existence of morphological tense-/aspect-focus systems.

Abbreviations

CF	clause focus	NEG	negative
CFG	centrifugal	O	object
COP	copula	OF	out-of-focus marker
CPT	centripetal	P1	immediate past
D	demonstrative	P2	hodiernal past
DEF	definite	P3	distant past
FOC	focus	PF	perfective
F1	hodiernal (near) future	POSS	possessive
F2	definite (distant) future	PROG	progressive
IMM	immediacy marker	QUOT	quotative
IPF	imperfective	S	subject
L	low tone	VN	verbal noun marker

Numbers refer to person when followed by sg (singular), pl (plural), incl (inclusive), excl (exclusive) or log (logophoric). Otherwise, they refer to noun classes.

Bibliographic references

ALDEC (Aghem Language Development Community). (n.d.). Aghem English dictionary. (Ms.).
Eberhard, David M., Gary F. Simons, and Charles D. Fennig (eds.). 2019. *Ethnologue: Languages of the World*. Twenty-second edition. Dallas, Texas: SIL International. http://www.ethnologue.com.
Hyman, Larry. 1979. *Aghem grammatical structure*. Los Angeles: Department of Linguistics UCLA.
Kießling, Roland. 2011. *Verbal Serialisation in Isu (West Ring) – a Grassfields Language of Cameroon*. Cologne: Rüdiger Köppe.
Kießling, Roland. 2017. A (morpho-(tonological and)) semantic perspective on the tense system of Isu (Grassfields Bantu, Cameroon). In Arne Krause, Gesa Lehmann, Winfried Thielmann & Caroline Trautmann, (eds.), *Form und Funktion. Festschrift für Angelika Redder zum 65. Geburtstag*, 243–258. Tübingen: Stauffenburg.
Möller, Mirjam. 2012. *The noun and verb in Mmen a Center Ring Grassfields Bantu language*. Yaoundé: SIL.
Neumann, Britta. 2019. Attitude and rhetoric in the inauguration speeches of the Fon of Isu. Hamburg: Hamburg University dissertation.
Watters, John R. 1979. Focus in Aghem: a study of its formal correlates and typology. In Larry Hyman (ed.), *Aghem grammatical structure*, 137–189. Los Angeles: Department of Linguistics UCLA.
Watters, John R. 2003. Grassfields Bantu. In Derek Nurse & Gérard Philippson (eds.), *The Bantu languages*, 225–256. London: Routledge.

Solange Mekamgoum
Phasal polarity in Ŋgɜ̂mbà

1 Introduction

Van Baar (1997: 40) defines phasal polarity expressions as "structured means of expressing polarity in a sequential perspective". These refer to expressions such as *already*, *still*, *not yet* and *no longer* in English. They are said to be phasal because "they involve reference points at two related phases implying situations which are contrasted as opposites with different polarity values" (Kramer 2017: 1) and also encode the semantic domain of speaker expectation. The phasal polarity system in Ŋgɜ̂mbà[1] revolves around three items: *ndɜ̌ʔ*, *wwɔ́* and *wǐ* which conceptualize the notions of ALREADY and STILL. Their semantics depends on morphosyntactic constructions and their interaction with tense and aspect. *Wǐ* can be negated externally or internally to express NO LONGER and NOT YET.

This paper gives an overview of phasal polarity concepts in Ŋgɜ̂mbà and starts from a structural and semantic analysis of such items in context to determine the interplay between tense and aspect on the one hand and pragmaticity on the other hand. As such, it seeks to answer the following questions: (a) How does Ŋgɜ̂mbà express phasal polarity? (b) What grammatical properties do phasal polarity expressions in Ŋgɜ̂mbà have? (c) Are there any restrictions to the use of phasal polarity items? (d) Are there semantic relations between those phasal polarity items? (e) How does speaker expectation influence selection of

---

[1] Ŋgɜ̂mbà is a Niger–Congo language of the Bantu Grassfields Bamileke subgroup spoken in five villages of Western Cameroon, namely, Bamendjou and Bameka in the Upper-Plateaux, Bamougoum in the Mifi, Bansoa in the Menoua and Bafunda in the Bamboutos. Its speakers are at about 500,000 according to the census carried out in Cameroon in 1986, the statistics of which were published in 2006 (see Mensah & Mekamgoum 2017: 398). A lot of efforts are now being made to develop the language (e.g. Soh, 2017; Mensah & Mekamgoum 2017; Fossi 2015; Biloa, E., Fossi, A., & Nchare, A. L. 2014; Fossi & Lambo, 2012; Kuitche Fonkou, 1998), though it still needs thorough description.

The data used in this study comes from a corpus of spontaneous interactions and interviews collected in Bamendjou, Bamougoum and Bameka between 2014 and 2016. It is supplemented by the data obtained from interviews with three language consultants and my own data as native speaker of the language. I did all the transcription, glossing and translation of the examples and consulted the language consultants whenever need arose. All the tones are marked as heard in the spoken discourse.

Solange Mekamgoum, University of Hamburg

https://doi.org/10.1515/9783110646290-009

phasal polarity items? These questions will be answered based on the six-parameter framework developed by Kramer (2017) in her position paper. The first three parameters, coverage, pragmaticity and telicity, are concerned with the semantic aspect of phasal polarity expressions; whereas wordhood, expressibility and paradigmaticity deal with their morphosyntactic aspects.

Ŋgə̂mbà is a tone language with strict SVO (1a) word order in affirmative constructions.

(1) SVO word order in affirmative constructions
    a. à   kə̀   péè   ŋkáp
       3sg P1 take.IPF money
       'S/he took the money.'

In a negative sentence, the focus of the negation can either be on the verb (1b) or on the object (1c) yielding and SVO or SOV word order respectively.

    b. à   kà   tʃə̀   <u>pé</u>   ˇŋkáp ˇβɔ́
       3sg P2.IPF NEG take money NEG
       'S/he has not *taken* the money.'
    c. à   kà   tʃə̃   <u>ŋkáp</u> ˇpéé
       3sg P2.IPF NEG money take.IPF
       'S/he has not taken the *money*.'

The semantic difference between these two sentences is that in (1b) where it is the verb that is negated, the action of *pé* 'take' has not occurred at all, in contrast to (1c) in which it is the object that is negated, entailing that the action of *pé* 'take' has really taken place, but not in relation to the money. Negation is marked by the discontinuous adverbials *tʃə̀* . . . *βɔ́* (general) and *kà* . . . *βɔ́* in P0/P1.PF in SVO constructions (1b). The final-sentence negation item is omitted in SOV constructions.

2 General note on tense and aspect

Ŋgə̂mbà presents actions, events or states from a perspective of completion and incompletion so that tense categories are organized around a perfective vs imperfective contrast. The latter motivates morpho-tonological inflections leading to verbs occurring in three[2]forms: (a) a naked form in the infinitive and

---

[2] It can also be considered that Ngemba verbs alternate between two forms: prenasalized vs non-prenasalized if account is taken only of the verb-initial consonant. But considering the whole word requires that the three forms are considered.

imperative (vvɔ̀/vvɔ́[3]); (b) an inflectional prenasalized form (mbvvɔ̀) and (c) an inflectional form ((mb)vvɔ̀-ɔ̀) with a final echo vowel that marks the imperfective aspect. The immediate past (P0) is marked by a floating high tone (PF) usually hosted by the SM/preverbal item, and high tone (IPF) usually hosted by the verb. Today's past (P1) is marked bý nɔ̀ (PF) and̛ kè (IPF). Yesterday's past (P2) is marked by kwў (PF) and kɔ̀ (IPF). Remote past (P3) is marked by lў (PF) and lɔ̀ (IPF). Perfective P2 and P3 are fixed morphemes while their imperfective counterparts have two predictable allomorphic morphemes: kɔ̀/à and lɔ̀/à. The variant with a final -[a] occurs when the marker is followed by the adverb of negation or any other aspectual morpheme that adds the semantic specification of durability (eg. continuative and frequentative) in the occurrence of an event/action. Kɔ̀ is homophonous with the P0/P1 PF adverb of negation. The future is primarily marked by yɔ́ (F0) plus a time-related adverb (pì/F1; tʃwɔ́ʔ/F2; fɔ́/F3). All these future markers have clear verb origins because of their participation in inflectional morphology. There is also an unmarked present tense (T0) which indicates an uncompleted event/action. One important point to be made here is that F0 and P1.PF commonly keep only their suprasegmental features by virtue of morpheme erosion in day-to-day speech.

3 Phasal polarity concepts in Ŋgə̂mbà

Table (1) provides an overview of the items that could be used to express notions of phasal polarity.

Table 1: Phasal polarity items in Ŋgə̂mbà.

ALREADY	STILL	NOT YET	NO LONGER
ndáʔ	wí	wí tʃə̀	tʃə̀ wí
wwɔ́		NEG+wwɔ́/wwɔ́+NEG	
ʒàŋə̀			
déjà			

However, none of these markers is dedicated solely to code phasal polarity. Ndáʔ, wwɔ́, ʒàŋə̀ and wí are polysemous depending on their context of occurrence. Wí is

---

[3] Ngemba marks imperative mood with a high tone docking on the basic verb form from the right.

negated internally and externally to conceptualize NOT YET and NO LONGER, respectively. *Wwɔ́* can either be negated externally or internally to express NOT YET. These items are comprehensively discussed below.

3.1 ALREADY

ALREADY is a positive phasal polarity expression that encodes a reference point when an event or action starts, either prior or later to a given point of reference. The language expresses this notion by two primary polysemous items *ndáʔ* and *wwɔ́* that acquire a phasal polarity meaning 'already' when the context is taken into consideration. These two items are restricted to occur with the perfective aspect markers; whereas *ʒàŋà* and *dèʒá* seem to secondarily be recruited to fill in gaps in imperfective constructions.

Ndáʔ: Ŋgə̂mbà primarily expresses the concept of 'already' via *ndáʔ*. *Ndáʔ* derives from the full-fledged verb *nə̀ láʔ* 'to pin', 'to nail', 'to hammer', 'to hit once and tightly' and can consequently undergo inflections that are inherent to the grammar of the language. As mentioned in Section 2, the use of the perfective aspect in Ŋgə̂mbà also triggers the prenasalization of the verb it applies to. *Láʔ* thus becomes *ndáʔ* in perfective constructions. However, in conveying the idea of 'already' through *ndáʔ*, Ŋgə̂mbà uses PF+*ndáʔ*+full-fledged vrb. In other words, this already inflected item should occur after the PF aspect marker and lacks the ability to singlehandedly establish verb predication. Moreover, *ndáʔ* remains invariable and cannot refer to a future event/action. Otherwise, *ndáʔ* may, in addition to its lexical meaning, convey the grammatical concept of 'punctuality' rather than 'already' as shown later in (15a) and (15b). As indicated in (2b), the grammatical and lexical functions of this item are distinct so that they can be used in collocation (2a–b).

(2) Interpretation of *ndáʔ* 'already' vs. *ndaʔ* 'pin, nail'
 a. â ndáʔ
  3sg.P1.PF pin
  'S/he pinned.'
 b. à lў ˅*ndáʔ* ndáʔ ˅*pàʔà*
  3sg P3.PF **already** nail building
  'S/he roofed the building **already**.'

Ndáʔ 'already' normally occupies the position between the tense+perfective aspect marker and the verb; but can also be followed directly by (a) the particle *tə̀* 'until' which changes its pragmatic perspective or (b) the continuative aspect marker in the immediate past. (3a) illustrates an unexpected early completion of an event/action through the combination of *ndá?* and *tà*. The concept *ndá?* in (3b) marks the inchoative point of change of a sustained duration of a state, that is, the presence of the guests at a location (3b), rather than the eating activity.

(3) Position of *ndá?* in syntactic construction
    a. mà yў   nà [↓]<u>ndá?</u> tà   nttsɔ́ [↓]ʒwó
       PL guests.P1 PF **already** until eat thing
       'The guests have eaten **already** (unexpectedly early).'
    b. mà yŷ   [↓]<u>ndá?</u> mbə́ [↓]ssí nttsɔ́ [↓]ʒwó
       PL guests.P0.PF **already** be LOC eat thing
       PL guests.P0.PF **already** CONT eat thing
       'The guests are **already** (there) eating.'

Wwɔ́: The concept ALREADY can also be expressed by *wwɔ́*, a variable item that takes two forms: simple and derived; whereby the consonant alternates between the approximant *w-* and the homorganic prenasalized voiced velar plosive *g-*. *Wwɔ́* lexically means 'to remain, to be blocked' and functions in that case as full-fledged verb (4a). Its grammatical meaning emerges in contexts where it can no longer establish verb predication on its own. It is in such environments that *wwɔ́* is interpreted as 'already' (4d–e) or 'right at that time' (4b–c). The puzzle remains why the use of *wwɔ́* as cover term for ALREADY is restricted to interrogative sentence types (4d–e).

(4) Expression of 'already' via *wwɔ́*
    a. ì   kwў   [↓]ŋgwɔ́   [↓]ndɑ́ɛ́   nánə́
       3sg P2.PF remain house sit
       'S/he remained seated in the house (yesterday).'
    (b) ì   kə̀   wwɔ́ɔ́   sỳ?   [↓]mə́ yò
       3sg P2.IPF remain.IPF come 1sg.P0 go
       'I left as soon as s/he came.'
    (c) á   kè   ŋgwɔ́ɔ́   ŋwǎk ndʒì?   [↓]nə́ ttsɔ̀ ʒwó
       3sg.P1 IPF remain.IPF arrive moment INF eat thing
       'S/he arrived right at the eating time.'
    (d) ɔ́   [↓]<u>wwɔ́</u>   ndʒó á
       2sg.P0 remain see Q
       'What have you **already** seen?'

(e) (↑tà)   wóp   ↓wwɔ́   ŋwák   ↓á
    (EMPH) 3sg.P0 remain   arrive Q
    'Have they (even) **already** arrived?'

3.2 STILL

Ŋgə̂mbà expresses the notion of STILL with *wí(t)*. Throughout this work, only the form *wí* without the final *-t* will be used because the difference is only idiolectal so that its omission does not create any semantic or grammatical gap. *Wí* is not semantically dedicated to phasal polarity as it originally conceptualizes the notion of 'just' or 'venir juste de' in French; it refers to a non-continuative event that takes place a short time prior to the reference time (5f). Its phasal value interpretation is achieved in three ways. First, *wí* internally modifies the temporal structure and either precedes the tense marker (5a) or follows the locative (5b). In cases illustrated by (5a) and (5b), the events should not be seen as whole. Rather, they should be understood as that there is an underlying complete event, that of (still) being there, and an obvious ongoing activity, that of taking the money. Second, *wí* occurs restrictively with the continuative + imperfective markers altogether if the event or action indicated is viewed as a whole uncompleted activity (5c–e, h). Third, *wí* establishes verbal predication and does not require the continuative aspect (5g–h). The continuative aspect is primarily marked by the combination of three items (5_o); but this aspect can be freely marked by one (5c), fusion of two (5d) or none of these morphemes as result of segmental erosion, leaving floating tones that may dock on the morpheme *wí* (5e). The combination of the continuative aspect and *wí* encodes a continuative period of time when an event/action takes place (5). *Wí* can undergo morphotonological variations depending on its environment of occurrence with the initial consonant *w-* alternating with *ŋg-*. The previous low tone can also spread and docks on it on the left (5a, f, g).

(5) Interaction of *wí* with continuative aspect occurring in free combinations
    ↓*ssí*   *mbə́*   *hó*
    LOC   be   EXIST
    Continuative aspect marker
    a. *A*   *wĭ*   ↓*ssí mbə́ hó mbéé*   ↓*ŋkáp*
       3sg just   CONT   take.IPF money
       'S/he is **still** (there) taking the money.'

b. á ˅ssí ŋgwí hó mbéé ˅ŋkáp
   3sg.P0 LOC just CONT take.IPF money
   'S/he is (there) **still** taking the money.'
c. á ŋgwíí ˅ssí mbéé ˅ŋkáp
   3sg.P0 just.IPF CONT take.IPF money
   'S/he was **still** taking the money (some few minutes ago).'
d. á kĕ ŋgwí ˅ssí mbóó mbéé ˅ŋkáp
   3sg P1.IPF just CONT take.IPF money
   'S/he was **still** taking the money (some few hours ago).'
e. à kǎ ŋgwíí: mbéé ˅ŋkáp
   3sg P2.IPF just.CONT take.IPF money
   'S/he was **still** taking the money (yesterday).'
f. à wĭ ˅mbéé ˅ŋkáp
   3sg just take.IPF money
   'S/he just took the money.'
g. à wĭ fəndœ
   3sg just take
   'S/he is **still** at home.'
h. wóp yŏ pĭ wíí ˅ssí
   3PL F0 F1.IPF just.IPF LOC
   'They will **still** be there.'

Wí can, first, combine with the adverb tə́ 'yet' without the continuative marker (6b–c) to bring in the idea of immediacy in past or future actions/events. It can equally precede the verb yò[4] 'go' and then the main verb in the infinitive mood (6d) to conceptualize the notion of STILL in the immediate future. The use of the immediate future tense marker (F0) brings in the semantic notion of possibility rather than that of futurity (6a).

(6) Expression of wí with immediate future
   a. à yŏ wíí ˅ssí
      3sg F0 just.IPF LOC
      'S/he may **still** be there.'
   b. A wĭ ˅tə́ péé ˅ŋkáp
      3sg just yet take.IPF money
      'S/he is **still** about to take the money.'

---

[4] yò also has the grammatical function of F0. /o/ and /ɔ/ freely alternates in environments other than the infinitve.

c. á   ŋgwíí   tɔ́   ˇpéé   ˇŋkáp
   3sg.P0 just.IPF yet take.IPF money
   'S/he was **still** about to take the money.'

d. à   kǎ   ŋgwí hó   ŋgɔ̀ nà   pé
   3sg P2.IPF just CONT go   INF take
   'S/he was **still** going to take the money.'

'Still' *wí* is used for conceptualizing NOT YET and NO LONGER by way of internal and external negation strategies respectively as does the Turkana language (Dimmendaal 1983: 138, 458–459) which uses the same strategy in deriving these notions from STILL.

3.3 NO LONGER

The concept of NO LONGER, encoded by NEG+*wí*, expresses a negative terminative expression that indicates the end point of change of a sustained event/action within a frame of time. This phasal polarity item keeps all the features of STILL presented in the previous section. It selects the general discontinuous negative adverbial *tʃə̀... βɔ́* in past tense categories, present (7a–c), as well as *lè... βɔ́* in encoding phasal value in a continuative action/event that ends prior to the start of a future event/action (7d). The focus can be shifted by using *tʃə̀... βɔ́* provided the syntactic structure is reorganized (7e). The semantic difference between the two constructions in (7d–e) is that the focus in (7d) is on the sleeping process of the child whereas it is on the waking up action in (7e).

(7) External negation of *wí* for expressing 'no longer'

a. mɛ́   tʃə̀   wǐ   hó   ˇnddíí   βɔ́
   child NEG   just CONT   sleep.IPF NEG
   'The child is (there) **no longer** sleeping.'

b. mɛ́   tʃə̀   hó   ŋgwíí   nddíí   βɔ́
   child NEG   EXIST   just.CONT sleep.IPF NEG
   'The child is **no longer** (there) sleeping.'

c. mɛ́   tʃə̀   ŋgwí   hó   nddíí   βɔ́
   child NEG.P0   just   CONT   sleep.IPF NEG
   'The child was NO LONGER sleeping (some few minutes ago).'

d. mə̀ə̌   pǐ   lìʔí   ↑ʒè   ˇmɛ́ ↑là   wí   ˇssí ˇmbóó
   1sg.F0 F1   moment wake up child NEG just CONT
   nddíí   βɔ́
   sleep.IPF NEG

'The child will **no longer** be sleeping at the moment I will wake up.'
   e. mà   tʃə̌ə̌   pǐ   lí?í   ꜛʒè   ꜜmɛ́ wí   ꜜssí ꜜmbóó
      1sg   NEG.F0 F1 moment wake up child just CONT
      nddíí   βɔ́
      sleep.IPF NEG
      'The moment I will wake up, the child will **no longer** be sleeping.'

Expressing NO LONGER in the immediate future requires that *wí* is combined with either the adverb *tə́* 'yet' (8b) or the verb *yò* 'go' (8c). The use of F0 that normally marks the immediate future rather brings in the semantic notion of possibility (8a).

(8)   *Tʃə̀. . . wǐ* and immediate future
   a. mɛ́   tʃə̀   γɔ̌   <u>wí:</u>   ꜜllí   βɔ́
      child NEG F0 just.CONT sleep NEG
      'The child may **no longer** be sleeping.'
   b. mɛ́   tʃə̀   <u>wǐ</u>   ꜜtə́ fítnə́ βɔ́
      child NEG just yet play NEG
      'The child will **no longer** play.'
   c. mɛ́   tʃə̀   <u>wǐ</u>   ꜜssí   ŋgɔ̀ ꜜnə̀ fítnə̀ βɔ́
      child NEG just CONT go INF play NEG
      'The child is **no longer** going to play.'

Verbal predication can be established solely with the combination of this phasal polarity expression with the continuative aspect (9).

(9)   *NEG+wí* establishing a verbal predication
   a. *Amá*   ꜛtʃə̀ <u>wǐ</u>   sē   βɔ́
      Grandma NEG just market NEG
      'Grandma is **no longer** at the market.'
   b. kə̀dɔ̀ŋ   tʃə̌ə̌   fɔ́ɔ́   wíí hó   βɔ́
      Plantain NEG.F0 F3.IPF just EXIST NEG
      'Plantain will **no longer** exist.'

3.4 NOT YET

Ŋgə̂mbà encodes the concept of NOT YET in two ways: by internally negating *wí* 'still' and via negation of *wwɔ́* 'already'.

Wí tʃə́: The notion of NOT YET via *wí* is achieved in all tense categories by the postposition of the negator *tʃə́* alone (10a) without the sentence-final negation particle *βɔ́* (10) and (B) without the continuative aspect (11).

(10) Expression of NOT YET via internal negation of *wí* in different tenses
    a. ŋgwǐi   tʃə́   Pé
       1sg.P0.IPF.just NEG take
       'I have **not** taken **yet** (now).'
    b. ↓*mɔ́*   ŋgwí   ↓*tʃə́*   ↓*pé*
       1sg.P0. PF just   NEG   take
       'I have **not yet** taken (a few minutes ago).'
    c. ŋkǎ   ↓*ŋgwí* tʃə́ ↓*llí*
       1sg.P2.IPF just   NEG sleep
       'I had **not** slept **yet** (yesterday).'
    d. ŋgɔ́   tʃwɔ́ɔ́   ↓*wí* tʃə́   ↓*llí*
       1sg.F0 F2.IPF just NEG sleep
       'I will **not** have slept **yet** (tomorrow).'

(11) *wí tʃə́* 'not yet' not compatible with the continuative marker
    a. mə̀ yỳ   kǎ   ŋgwí tʃə́ ↓*bhóó* nttsɔ́ɔ́ ʒwó
       PL guests P2.IPF just NEG CONT eat.IPF thing
       '*The guests were **not yet** eating (yesterday).'
    (b) mə̀ yỳ   kǎ   ŋgwí tʃə́ ↓*ttsɔ́* ʒwó
       PL guests P2.IPF just NEG eat thing
       'The guests had **not yet** eaten (yesterday).'

(NEG) wwɔ́ (NEG): The notion of NOT YET can also be expressed by both the external and internal negation of *wwɔ́* (12). This item can alternate between *wwɔ́* (12b, d, e) and *ŋgwɔ́* (12a, c). By negating *wwɔ́* internally in (12a), the focus is put on the eating activity whereas in (12b–d) with its external negation, the focus is shifted to the reference time. The morphosyntactic organization in (12e) makes it clear that the activity of the verb is planned to be anterior to an implied future event/action.

(12) Expression of NOT YET via negation of *wwɔ́*
    a. mə̀ yỳ   kě   ŋgwɔ́   tʃə́ ttsɔ́ ↓*ʒwó*
       PL guests P1.IPF remain NEG eat thing
       'The guests had **not** eaten **yet** (a few hours ago).'

b. mà yỳ kĕ tʃə́ <u>wwɔ́</u> nttsɔ́ ˅ʒwó
   PL guests P1.IPF NEG remain eat thing
   'The guests had **not yet** eaten (a few hours ago).'
c. mà yỳ kà <u>ŋgwɔ́</u> nttsɔ́ ˅ʒwó ˅βhɔ́
   PL guests NEGP0 remain eat thing NEG
   'The guests have **not yet** eaten (some few minutes ago).'
d. mà yỳ tʃə̀ə̆ tʃwɔ́ʔɔ́ <u>wwɔ́</u> ttsɔ́ɔ́ ˅ʒwó
   PL guests NEG.F0 F2.IPF remain eat.IPF thing
   'The guests will **not yet** eat (tomorrow).'
e. mà yỳy̆ tʃwɔ́ʔɔ́ <u>wwɔ́</u> tʃə́ ttsɔ́ ˅ʒwó
   PL guests.F0 F2.IPF remain NEG eat Thing
   'The guests will **not** have eaten **yet** (tomorrow).'

Wwɔ́ can unlike *wí* express NOT YET in combination with the continuative aspect (13).

(13) Expression of NOT YET via *wwɔ́* and continuative aspect
   (a) mà yỳ tʃə̀ <u>wwɔ́</u> mbóó nttsɔ́ɔ́ ˅ʒwó ˅βhɔ́
       PL guests NEG remain CONT eat.IPF thing NEG
       'The guests are **not yet** eating.'
   (b) mà yỳ tʃə̀ <u>ŋgwɔ́</u> mbóó nttsɔ́ɔ́ ˅ʒwó ˅βhɔ́
       PL guests NEG.P0 remain CONT eat.IPF thing NEG
       'The guests were **not yet** eating (some few minutes ago).'
   (c) mà yỳ kĕ ŋgwɔ́ tʃə́ ˅βóó nttsɔ́ɔ́ ˅ʒwó
       PL guests P1.IPF remain NEG CONT eat.IPF thing
       'The guests were **not** eating **yet**.'
   (d) mà yỳ tʃə̀ə̆ fɔ́ <u>wwɔ́</u> βóó ttsɔ́ɔ́ ˅ʒwó ˅βɔ́
       PL guests NEG .F0 F3 remain CONT eat.IPF thing NEG
       'The guests will **not yet** be eating.'

4 Issues of morphosyntactic and semantic interactions of phasal polarity items with tense and aspect

The continuative+imperfective aspect markers interact with (*tʃə/là*)*wí* to attribute them the semantic encoding of STILL and NO LONGER. These items can be followed either by the adverb *tə́* 'yet' (6b–c; 8b) or the derived form of the verb *yò* 'go' +infinitive to express immediacy in a future action/event (6d–e; 8c), rather than the immediate future marker (F0) itself. These two phasal polarity items, STILL and NO LONGER, come before the verb and can also establish verbal predication independently (5g–h; 9a–b). In expressing NO LONGER, the tense marker occupies the position between the main negator 'tʃə̀/lə̀' and wí 'still'. This position can also be occupied by a whole clause so that the focus is shifted to the action/event indicated in the subordinate clause (7d). NOT YET as realized via wí tʃə̀ occurs with the imperfective aspect (marked by a final echo vowel that suffixes on the verbal base) (10a–d), but without the continuative marker (ssí mbé hó or either of its free combinations) (11a–b). The item can neither establish verbal predication singlehandedly nor express the reference time of an immediate future event/action. It selects only the main negator without the second particle. This negation adverb is post-posed to wí. Nevertheless, a locative (14a–b) or βə́ 'be' (emphatic) can be inserted in between (14c). It is this postposition of the main negator in relation to wí that attributes it a phasal polarity meaning.

(14) wí+locative/βə́+NEG
    a. *Lilly*   *wǐ*   *tɔ̃ʔndœ́*   *↑tʃə̀*   *sɔ̃k*   *nét*
       Lilly   just   room   NEG   wash   body
       'Lilly is in the room, **not** having taken a bath **yet**.'
    b. *mɛ́*   *wí*   *kwȳndœ́*   *↑tʃə̀*   *↓lí*
       child   Just   bed   NEG   sleep
       'The child is on the bed, **not** sleeping **yet**.'
    c. *Lilly*   *wǐ*   *↓βə́*   *↑tʃə̀*   *sɔ̃k*   *nét*
       Lilly   just   be   NEG   wash   body
       'Lilly has **not** taken a bath **yet**/Lilly has **still not** taken a bath.'

The expression of NOT YET through wwɔ́ seems to be more flexible with regards to the syntactic arrangement and selection of the negation. It selects both tʃə̀ and kà . . . βɔ́ and occurs without the continuative aspect marker. The Ŋgə̂mbà language can negate wwɔ́ externally if focus is intended to be put on the reference point of change of the action/event (12b–d). Wwɔ́ can be negated internally if focus is meant to be on the action/event indicated by the verb (12a) or to semantically specify the anteriority of an event/action with regards to a future reference time. In other words, it refers to a past event/action in the future (12e). When negated internally, it occurs as fixed expression whereby no lexical or grammatical item can be inserted in between. Contrarily, the use of the external negation strategy may call for the insertion of the tense and aspect markers, as well as a whole clause between the main negation adverb and the phasal polarity expression.

The notion of ALREADY via *wwɔ́* is semantically achieved through perfective constructions in the interrogative sentence type only (cf. 4d–e). The conditions for *ndá?* to express phasal polarity are that it should be preceded by the perfective aspect marker and should additionally lack the ability of establishing verbal predication independently and must not apply to a future event/action (15a). If one of these three conditions is not observed, *ndá?* will then refer to the semantic idea of punctuality as shown in (15b) or 'pin' (15c).

(15) Development from pin through punctuality to ALREADY
    a. mə̀   ɣy̌   kè   ndì?í   ˇsý?ý mbò mə̂   **ndá?**   ˇndá ˇʒwó
       PL   guests. IPF moment come. CONJ 1sg. **already** cook thing
       P1   IPF   P1.PF
       'I had **already** cooked at the moment the guests arrived.'
    b. á   lǎ   ndá?á   né↑tʃə́   mə̀   ˇntsʰœ́
       3sg   P3.IPF.FREQ PUNCTUALITY.IPF arrange PL   dress
       'S/he arranged dresses (frequently) at a given precise period of time.'
    c. à   lў   ˇndá? mbín   ˇnétʃə́
       3sg   P3.PF pin   again   arrange
       'S/he pinned and arranged.'

Ŋgə̂mbà has a way to encode the notion of ALREADY in imperfective continuative constructions (16). This is effected either by borrowing the French adverb '*déjà*' /*dèʒá*/ sentence-finally (16a–b) or by using the preverbal adverbial *(nd)ʒáŋə̀* (16c–d) which would express the idea of 'previously' elsewhere.

    (16) The notion of ALREADY in imperfective continuative constructions

(16) a. mə̀   yỳ   kě   mbóó nttsɔ́ɔ́ ˇʒwó **dèʒá**
       PL   guests P1.IPF CONT   eat.IPF thing **already**
       'The guests were **already** eating (some hours ago).'
    b. mə̀   yỳ   ɣɔ̌ pǐ   βóó   nttsɔ́ ˇʒwó **dèʒá**
       PL   guests FO F1.IPF CONT   eat   thing **already**
       'The guests will be eating **already** (tomorrow).'
    c. mə̀   yỳ   kě   **ndʒá↑ŋə̀** mbóó nttsɔ́ɔ́ ˇʒwó
       PL   guests P1.IPF **already**   CONT   eat.IPF thing
       'The guests were **already** eating (some hours ago).'
    d. mə̀   yỳ   ɣɔ̌ pǐ   **ʒàŋə̌** βóó   nttsɔ́ ˇʒwó
       PL   guests FO F1.IPF **already** CONT   eat   thing
       'The guests will be eating **already** (tomorrow).'

5 Interactions of assertive interrogative sentences with phasal polarity items of opposite polarity

Ŋgômbà has another strategy of encoding phasal polarity expressions by using the interrogative sentence type. These are actually types of rhetorical questions with the pragmatic force of assertions that should be considered as declarative sentences and whose meanings should be deduced by considering the opposite polarity. Examples are provided in pairs in (17) of which the dependent sentence (e.g. a'), i.e. the non-interrogative counterpart to (a), conveys the intended meaning of the main sentence (e.g. a). It appears on the one hand that ALREADY and NOT YET are semantically linked, NOT YET being the external negation of ALREADY via *wwɔ́* and its internal negation via *wǐ* (though this seems not to have a surface realisation) (17a–c). On the other hand, (17d–e) illustrate that there is a semantic relation between STILL and NO LONGER with NO LONGER being the external negation of STILL by means of *wǐ*.

(17) Semantic relations and interpretation of phasal polarity concepts via interrogative sentence of opposite polarity
    a. *mbò   mə̀   kwy̌   tʃə̀   wwɔ́   nttsɔ́   á*
       CONJ 1sg P2.PF NEG remain eat Q
       'Had I **not yet** eaten (yesterday)!'
    a' *mə̀   kwy̌   ndá?   tə̀   nttsɔ́*
       1sg P2.PF **already** till eat
       'I had eaten **already** (earlier than you have expected).'
    b. *mbò   mə̀   kə̌   wwɔ̌   ntstsɔ́   ↓ʒwó   ↓á*
       CONJ 1sg P2.IPF remain eat thing Q
       'Had I **already** eaten!'
    b' *mə̀   kə̌   ŋgwɔ́   tʃə̀   ↓nttsɔ́   ↓ʒwó*
       1sg P2.IPF remain NEG eat thing
       'I had **not yet** eaten (later than you have expected).'
    c. *mbò   mə̀   kə̌   ŋgwí   tʃə̀   ↓ttsɔ́   ↓á*
       CONJ 1sg P2.IPF just NEG eat Q
       'Had I **not yet** eaten (yesterday)!'
    c' *à   kà   ↓mbò   mə̂   ↓ndá?   ↓nttsɔ́*
       3INDF P2.IPF CONJ 1sg.P1.PF NEG eat
       'I had **already** eaten.'

d. wóp ˅tʃə̀ wí hó nttsɔ́ ˅ʒwó βɛ̂˅ɛ́
   3PL NEG just CONT eat thing FOC.Q
   'So, are they **no longer** eating!'

d' wóp wí hó nttsɔ́ ˅ʒwó
   3PL just CONT eat thing
   'They are **still** eating.'

e. ˅á wì hó nttsɔ́ ˅ʒwó ˅á
   3PL.PO just CONT eat thing Q
   'Is s/he **still** eating!'

e' à tʃə̀ wǐ hó nttsɔ́ ˅ʒwó ˅βɔ́
   3PL NEG just CONT eat thing NEG
   'S/he is **no longer** eating.'

6 Coverage

With regards to the aspect of coverage, the notions of ALREADY, STILL, NOT YET, NO LONGER are expressed in Ŋgə̂mbà by polysemous concepts of which *wí* 'still' forms the basis for encoding NOT YET and NO LONGER via internal and external negation strategies. ALREADY readily co-occurs with the perfective aspect and is expressed by *ndáʔ*, and by *wwɔ́* in interrogative constructions. The external and internal negation of *wwɔ́* expresses the notion of NOT YET, leaving a vacuum in imperfective aspect categories, a vacuum that Ŋgə̂mbà fills in by borrowing the French adverb *dèʒá* or by attributing phasal polarity meaning to the preverbal adverbial *ʒáŋə̀*. The ability of Ŋgə̂mbà to recruit these five different aforementioned phasal polarity items confers on it the status of *flexible* phasal polarity system language.

7 Wordhood, and aspects of grammaticalization

One important point to be made concerning aspects of wordhood and grammaticalization of the phasal polarity concepts discussed in this work is that they derive from erstwhile verbs as they all participate in inflectional morphology.

Concerning the grammaticalization processes, (*nd*)*ʒáŋə̀* had developed from the verb *ʒáŋə̀* 'to be light' to acquire the meaning of 'previously'. The latter must have further developed to express the notion of 'already' in a dedicated environment. *Ngwɔ́/wwɔ́* originated from the verb *wwɔ́* 'remain (at a location), to be blocked'. It had acquired the meaning 'right at the time' when functioning as modifier of the verb or negation adverb. This meaning had extended to cover the notion of 'already (not)'. *Ndá?* has probably originated from the verb *lá?* 'pin, button, nail, hammer, hit something once or right on point against another'. It has evolved to aspectual markers that express punctuality of an action/event/process, exactitude, precision and then 'already'. *Lá?* interacts with the imperfective aspect in P3, F0 and F3, to convey the semantic notion of 'preciseness, punctuality and determination in the remoteness of the time of action/event (18). Given that verbs equally take a prenasalized form when preceded by a perfective marker, this seems to be the meaning acquired by *lá?* in expressing 'already' in combination with the perfective aspect marker.

(18) Grammatical meaning of *lá?*+imperfective
    (a) à   là   lă?   ndá?
        3sg P3.IPF once hammer
        'S/he once hammered.'
    (b) àǎ   lă?   kwýlý   pà?à   tɔ́   pfý
        3sg.F0 once tie.IPF house yet die
        'S/he will one day build surely build a house before dying.'

With regard to wordhood, *ndá?*, *wwɔ́* and *ʒáŋə̀* occupy a preverbal position and serve as verb and adverb modifiers, to bring semantic information about the internal temporal structure of an event or action. *Ndá?* is already a derived form from *lá?* and does not inflect further by virtue of the fact that it has already participated in perfective aspect morphology; whereas *(nd)ʒáŋə̀* and *ŋgwɔ́/wwɔ́* alternate between the basic (imperfective) and prenasalized (perfective) forms. Yet, they are all disqualified from being considered full-fledged verbs due to their incapability of establishing a verbal predication on their own. In this regard, they are better candidates for the grammatical class of adverbials. *(Ng)wĭ* can also host aspectual morphology and occurs before the verb in two forms. This item can modify the verb or another adverb. It has two distinct functions. First, as cover term for NOT YET, it expresses time of events/actions in all tense categories, contrary to *ndá?*, *wwɔ́* and *ʒáŋə̀*. Therefore, the function of this concept overlaps between that of an adverbial and a verb. Second, as cover term for STILL and NO LONGER, *wĭ* can, beyond the features mentioned above for NOT YET, singlehandedly establish verbal predication. It functions in this case as a full-fledged verb.

8 The pragmatics of phasal polarity concepts

Ŋgɘ̂mbà successfully plays with interrogative sentence types to achieve meaning of opposite polarity in declarative sentence types. These kinds of questions have dedicated syntactic organizations as illustrated in (17), each sentence-final polar question particle (17d–e) has been chosen deliberately for pragmatic reasons, as well as the use of sentence-initial conjunctive elements which function as emphatic items (17a–c) and the tones pattern on the SM *á* and the phasal polarity item *wì* in (17e). The sentence would be a real interrogative type if the tone pattern is as presented in (19), in contrast with (17e).

(19) à   wǐ   hó   nttsɔ́   ↓ʒwó   ↓á
     3PL just CONT eat   thing   Q
     'Is s/he **still** eating?'
     (Actual and intended meaning).

(17e) ↓á   wì   hó   nttsɔ́   ↓ʒwó   ↓á
      3sg   just CONT eat   thing   Q
      'S/he is **no longer** eating.'
      (Intended meaning).

Wwɔ́ is a very interesting concept with regards to its embodied pragmatic characteristics and needs to be given additional attention in the next paragraph. Its semantic idea of ALREADY is operated restrictively thanks to its interaction with the sentence type of questions (see 4d–e). Its use in this type of interrogative sentences signals *lateness* of expectation of the speaker. The presupposed scenario in (4d) for example is that, the speaker would have expected the hearer to have already seen something at the time of the utterance, but it is likely that the hearer has not yet done so. This same late scenario expression can be achieved by *ndá? ... ndì?ǎ* 'already ... now' in all sentence types (20). A *neutral scenario* of ALREADY is expressed through *ndá?* (see 2b and 3a) and the adverbial phrase *ndá? tɘ̀* signals *earliness* (cf. 3a and 17a').
(20) Late counterexpectational scenario of ALREADY

(20) mɘ̀   kɘ̀   ʒǒ   ntɘ̀   mɔ́   mbǎ   ndá?   ndándœ́   ndì?-ǎ
     1sg   P2. see   friend   2POSS   CONJ.3sg **already** get   moment-
           IPF   married   PROX.DEM
     'I saw your friend. She is finally married now (late scenario).'

The above utterance should be understood within the following background: there were two friends of whom one got married and had children. The other one was still single and other society members considered her a hardened bachelor since time was no longer in her favor. But she ended up getting married in her fifties and the speaker had to report the good news to the hearer in (20).

The external negation of *wwɔ́* to express NOT YET indicates an EARLY turning point of an actual scenario in contrast with a simultaneous presupposed scenario expected to occur later than the actual one (see 12b,c,d; 13a,b,d and 17a). Conversely, its internal negation to express NOT YET signals a *late point of change* within the event/action time axis (cf. 12a,e; 13c and 17b'). The use of the internal negation of *wí* is meant to encode a *neutral scenario* whereby the actual and the expected action or event occur on the same time reference point (see 10, 11 and 17c).

Wwɔ́ becomes more interesting thanks to its potential of shifting the reference point of change. This phasal polarity item can function as pre-modifier of *wí tʃə* to change a *neutral scenario* into a *late* one (21b) or as post-modifier for a *counterexpectational early scenario* (21c).

(21) Pragmatic shift in NOT YET via *wwɔ́* as phasal polarity concept modifier
 a. ŋkáp wí tʃə ˅kùʔ
  money.PO just NEG be enough
  'Money is NOT YET enough (NEUTRAL scenario).'
 b. ŋkáp **wwɔ́** ˅**ŋgwí** tʃə ˅kùʔ
  money.PO remain just NEG be enough
  'Money is NOT YET enough (LATE counterexpectational scenario).'
 c. ŋkáp wí tʃə **wwɔ́** ˅kùʔ
  money.PO just NEG remain be enough
  'Money is NOT YET enough (EARLY counterexpectational scenario).'

Wí interacts with other items in conceptualizing a *late counterfactual scenario* with STILL in which an activity continues to be ongoing whereas it was expected to have terminated before the time of reference. It can either be with the habitual marker *kìʔí* (22b), with the verb to be *βə́* (22c) or with the combination of the two (22d). In the latter case, *βə́* plays an emphatic role.

(22) Expression of *late counterexpectational scenario* of STILL via *wí* +other aspects
 a. pə̀ŋkhý wí ˅ssí mbóó nttsɔ́ ˅ʒwó
  children just CONT eat thing
  'The children are **still** eating (*neutral scenario*).'

b. *pàŋkhý*   *kíʔí*   *wí*   ˅*ssí mbóó*   *nttsɔ́*   ˅*ʒwó*
children   HAB   just   CONT   eat   thing
'The children are **still** eating (*late counterexpectational scenario*).'

c. *pàŋkhý*   *wí*   *βə́*   ˅*ssí mbóó*   *nttsɔ́*   ˅*ʒwó*
children   just   be   CONT   eat   thing
'The children are **still** (forever) eating (*late counterexpectational scenario*).'

d. *pàŋkhý*   *kíʔí*   *wí*   *βə́*   ˅*ssí mbóó*   *nttsɔ́*   ˅*ʒwó*
children   HAB   just   be   CONT   eat   thing
'The children are **still** (forever unexpectedly) eating (*late scenario*).'

The two grammatical items *βə́* and *kíʔí* can also interact with *wí tʃə* to conceptualize a *late counterexpectational scenario* of NOT YET (e.g. 23a). *Kíʔí* also co-occurs as modifier of *wí*, but pre-modified by *tʃə* to rather convey the notion of earliness in a no longer scenario (23b).

(23) Interaction of *kíʔí* and *βə́* to express late NOT YET and early NO LONGER

(23) a. *mɛ́*   *kíʔí*   ˅*wí*   *βə́*   *tʃə*   *llí*
child   HAB   just   be   NEG   sleep
'The child has (still) **not yet** slept (*late counterexpectational scenario*).'

b. *mɛ́*   *tʃə*   *kíʔí*   *wí*   ˅*nddí*   *βɔ́*
child   NEG   HAB   just   sleep   NEG
'The child is **no longer** sleeping (*early counterexpectational scenario*).'

9 Conclusion

At this point, some generalisations can be made about Ŋgə̂mbà regarding its phasal polarity system. First, all the items used by the language to express phasal polarity concepts are either full-fledged verbs or adverbials betraying their origin from erstwhile verbs. Second, Ŋgə̂mbà does not have any item dedicated to the expression of phasal value as it is the environment of occurrence that suggests this meaning. Third, ALREADY is most flexibly conceptualized in Ŋgə̂mbà with four different expressions. Two (*ndáʔ* and *wwɔ́*) occur in scenarios where the event or action expressed by the phasal polarity item is seen as complete and two (*ʒáŋə* and *déʒà*) are used in scenarios where the event or action is seen as incomplete from an outward perspective. STILL and NO LONGER are more rigidly expressed in the sense that they can be encoded by only one item, *wí* and its external negation. This *wí* is also the cover term for the *neutral* scenario of NOT YET by way of an internal negation strategy. The latter concept can be encoded by both the internal and external negation of *wwɔ́*. This evidence makes Ŋgâmbà a highly flexible language with regard to its polarity system. Fourth, Ŋgâmbà can play with the locative clitic in order to put the focus on the aspectual modality of the phasal polarity item or on the temporal structure. Likewise, the language plays with sentence types by using interrogatives to target meaning of the opposite polarity. Fifth, the use of the concept *wwɔ́* in itself is highly pragmatically motivated. It expresses *lateness* in a scenario of ALREADY and NOT YET when internally negated or used as pre-modifier of the main phasal polarity item. It encodes *earliness* in a scenario of NOT YET when externally negated or used as post-modifier of the primary phasal polarity expression. Sixth, Ŋgâmbà recruit the habitual marker and the verb 'be' to conceptualize a *late scenario* of STILL and NOT YET, as well as an *early scenario* of NO LONGER. From a conceptual perspective, Ŋgâmbà presents a symmetric semantic system bringing out a dual relation between ALREADY and NOT YET on the one hand and STILL and NO LONGER on the other hand, with ALREADY and NO LONGER being telic as they obviously imply a point of polarity change; contrary to STILL and NOT YET that are atelic due to their "future status of the moment of polarity change" (Kramer 2017: 2).

Abbreviations

COMP	comparative	LOC	Locative
CONJ	Conjunction	O	Object
CONT	Continuative	P0-P3	Past 0-Past 3 (general to remotest past)
D	Demonstrative		
EMPH	Emphasis	PF	Perfective
EXCL	Exclusive	PL	Plural
EXIST	Existential	POSS	Possessive
F0-F3	Future 0-Future 3 (general to most distant future)	PROX	Proximal
		PRP	Preposition
FOC	Focus	Q	Question marker
FREQ	Frequentative	Sg	Singular
INDEF	Indefinite	SM	Subject marker
INF	Infinitive	T0	Present
IPF	Imperfective		

Bibliographic references

Biloa, Edmond, Achille Fossi, & Abdoylayer L. Nchare. 2004. *Grammaire générative: la théorie minimaliste de Noam Chomsky*. Yaoundé: Cameroon University Press.
Dimmendaal, Gerrit. 1983. *The Turkana language*. Dordrecht: Foris.
Fossi, Achille. 2015. The Determiner Phrase Internal Structure in Ngêmbà. *International Journal of Linguistics*, 7 (1). 42–55.
Fossi, Achille, & Adrienne O. Lambo. 2012. Cultural and Linguistic Hybridizations in Cameroon: English Loanwords in Ngâmbà. *International Journal of Linguistics*, 4 (1). 267–286.
Kramer, Raija 2017. Position paper on Phasal Polarity expressions. Hamburg: University of Hamburg. https://www.aai.uni-hamburg.de/afrika/php2018/medien/position-paper-on-php.pdf. (accessed 5 February 2018)
Kuitche Fonkou, Gabriel. 1988. *Creation et circulation des discours codes en milieu ŋgâmbà mungum*. Lille: University Lille 3 dissertation.
Kuitche Fonkou, Gabriel. 1998. Les évocations de l'espace dans les chants narratifs et les devinettes ngembà. *Ethiopiques: revue socialiste de culture négro-africaine*, (60), 49–55.
Mensah, Eyo, & Solange Mekamgoum. 2017. The communicative significance of Ngâmbà personal names. *African Identities*, 15 (4), 398–413.
Soh, Jean-Philippe. 2017. *Dictionnaire ŋgâmbá-Anglais-Français*. Riga: Editions Universitaires Européennes.
Van Baar, Tim. 1997. *Phasal polarity*. Amsterdam: IFOTT.

Raija L. Kramer
Phasal polarity expressions in Fula varieties of northern Cameroon

1 Introduction

In Fula varieties of northern Cameroon, different phasal polarity systems seem to exist that are paradigmatic to varying degrees. In this paper, I investigate phasal polarity expressions in the written, partly standardized Adamawa variety described in grammars and used for Bible translation, and in the oral variety used for daily interactions, which is described here as a dialect continuum with coexisting and competing linguistic variants. Even though dedicated phasal polarity constructions may be assumed for the standardized variety, the various phasal polarity expression strategies are subject to several aspectual and pragmatic constraints and do not form an entire paradigm. In the oral variety, there is a widely accepted paradigmatic variant of the phasal polarity system, which contains clause-final, invariable items termed 'adverbs' in this paper (but which could also be specified as 'particles' according to other conventions).

In section 1, I will justify the distinction between the two Fula varieties of northern Cameroon and delineate their linguistic characteristics. I will show that the oral variety is not defined by categorical features but rather coexisting variants in a fluid continuum, whereas the standardized variety is rather stable and can be located at one of the outer edges of the continuum. In section 2, I discuss strategies for expressing phasal polarity in the Fula varieties (2.1 ALREADY and STILL; 2.2 NOT YET and NO LONGER) addressing the phasal polarity parameters that I introduced in a position paper on phasal polarity (Kramer 2018; this volume) and briefly repeat at the beginning of the analytical paragraphs. In section 3, I give a concise overview of the different phasal polarity expression strategy systems and briefly discuss their main differences regarding paradigmaticity.

2 Fula varieties in northern Cameroon

Fula is a dialect continuum classified as belonging to the Niger-Congo phylum and clustered with Sereer as a subgroup of the North branch of Atlantic (cf. Pozdniakov/Segerer forth.). It stretches across a vast geographical area along the

Raija L. Kramer, University of Hamburg

https://doi.org/10.1515/9783110646290-010

sub-Saharan belt and is the geographically widest spread macro-language in Africa, with speech communities from southern Mauritania and Senegal in the west as far as Sudan in the east. In spite of its vast geographical spread, Fula is a language of wider communication (*lingua franca*) in northern Cameroon only. The reason for this is that Fulani groups are established as local authorities in the northern parts of what is now Cameroon (dating back to the military expansion of the Sokoto empire in the first half of the 19th century), and the Fula language is not in significant competition with other languages of wider communication in this area.

The Fula of northern Cameroon (and Nigeria) is usually classified as the "Adamawa dialect" of the eastern branch of Fula. The "Adamawa" labelled variety is rather well described (e.g. Taylor 1953; Klingenheben 1963; Stennes 1967; Arnott 1970; Mohamadou 1985; Theil 2008) and is used in projects of broadcasting and bible translation (e.g. Kassühlke 1995 [1983]). However, as already stated by Gottschligg (2006), there is no single Fula dialect in northern Cameroon but several varieties (A1, A2, A3) have to be distinguished, which cannot clearly be assigned to particular social groups or geographical areas. Nevertheless, Gottschligg (2006: 154) claims that in Cameroon, the A1 variety is mostly associated with ethnic Fulani in the Far North region, the A2 variety is used by ethnic Fulani in the North region, and A3 is a contact variety of speakers in the Adamawa region.

I argue in line with Mufwene (2001: 15) that a language must be conceived as an "ensemble of idiolects" with internal diversity and osmotic boundaries rather than an ensemble of (monolithic) lectal groups. Fula is widely used in northern Cameroon and the dynamics of interaction between speakers with diverse linguistic repertoires contributes to the spread of coexisting and competing features within the community. Fula speakers are aware of linguistic variables and often make use of competing variants in their own linguistic behaviour, i.e. the language use of even a single speaker does not have to be consistent (cf. also Boutché, forth.). The linguistic features used to distinguish A1, A2, and A3 varieties can hence not be clearly allocated to locally or socially defined Fula speaker groups of northern Cameroon as classificatory models might suggest.

In this paper, I will differentiate between two Fula varieties in northern Cameroon: the rather stable Standardized Adamawa Fula variety, and the flexible, non-standardized Adamawa Fula Communis. Standardized Adamawa Fula is a relatively invariable (primarily written) variety standardized in descriptive works (see above), used as literary (bible translations, see above) and broadcast language and in prescriptive teaching materials (e.g. Noye 1974; Pelletier/Skinner 1979; Jungraithmayr/Abu-Manga 1989). This variety most closely corresponds to Glottschligg's A1 variety and is often considered as the conservative or 'pure' (*laamnde*) Fula dialect by the speakers themselves (cf. Boutché, forth.).

As Adamawa Fula Communis, I define the spoken Fula variety of northern Cameroon that develops in contexts of heavy language contact. It is characterized by ongoing negotiation and adaption processes and cannot be defined in terms of a bundle of specific linguistic properties because variants of linguistic variables coexist. Subgroups of the Cameroonian Fula-speaking population may show preferences with regard to the selection of linguistic features, and hence specific feature distributions are detectable. Nonetheless, these distribution patterns are not unequivocally assignable to groups defined by social attributes, nor do they relate to specific geographic areas (cf. e.g., the distribution of linguistic features among Fula speakers in working networks of Ngaoundéré, cf. Kramer 2017 [2012], Kramer 2018). Instead, the Adamawa Fula Communis represents a fluid continuum between the conservative Standardized Adamawa Fula and a variety with maximally reduced morphosyntax that corresponds most closely with Gottschligg's A3 variety.

Structurally, the main differences between the two edges of the Fula A1/SAF-A3 continuum concern (a) the nominal declension system (in the sense of Güldemann/Fiedler, to appear), (b) verbal inflection paradigms, and (c) nominal agreement.

In terms of (a)–(c), the A1/Standardized Adamawa Fula variety can be described as follows: (a) More than 20 noun form classes are established by nominal word forms with identical suffixes which reflect number, and a declension system is instantiated by particular pairings of singular-plural and transnumeral nouns. (b) The intricate system of inflectional suffixes that combine functions of aspect, voice, polarity, mood, and information structure leads to more than 20 verbal paradigms. (c) Agreement occurring on target items such as definite modifiers or pronouns reflects the number and gender of the trigger noun.

In a prototypically simplified variety of Cameroonian Fula (=A3), (a) number is not reflected by pairings of noun form classes but a general plural marker (*-ji*) is used or nominal plurality is signalled by modifiers (numerals and quantifiers). (b) Inflectional suffixes primarily reflect aspect (perfective-imperfective) and polarity (affirmative-negative) dichotomies and accordingly, the system of verbal paradigms is reduced. (c) The agreement system is sensitive to number (and partly to animacy) only.

Distinguishing a standardized and mainly written "conservative" variety from an oral variety used by speakers in their daily interactions, I investigate phasal polarity expressions in Cameroonian Fula based on a corpus of written texts (Standardized Adamawa Fula) and a corpus of spontaneous and elicited fieldwork data (Adamawa Fula Communis). Although elicitation does not represent natural discourse, it provides useful clues about the practices of natural speakers' language use when conducted as a "guided conversation about language data" (Mous 2007: 2).

The Standardized Adamawa Fula corpus comprises translations of bible texts (editions from 1995 [1983], 2013, and 2017). The Adamawa Fula Communis data presented in this paper come from eleven speakers in Ngaoundéré, the capital city of the Adamawa region. These Fula L1 and L2 speakers have various ethnic affiliations and linguistic repertoires (besides Fula, mainly Adamawa and Biu-Mandara languages, Hausa, and Kanuri play significant roles). The speakers stem from all three regions of northern Cameroon (5 Adamawa, 2 North, 4 Far North) although none of the sample speakers is an ethnic Fulani from the Maroua (Diamaré) region whose Fula use is usually expected to come close to the Standardized Adamawa Fula variety. The data are hence complemented with two phasal polarity questionnaires that were filled out by my linguist colleague Jean Pierre Boutché who is himself a Fula L1 speaker from the Maroua region (though he is not an "ethnic" Fulani).[1]

3 The expression of phasal polarity in Fula varieties of northern Cameroon

In this section, I discuss strategies for expressing phasal polarity in the Fula varieties of northern Cameroon. Phasal polarity is thought of as concepts of sequential polarity and comprises at least two possible scenario interpretations (cf. Van Baar 1997: 40–49): (1) A state of affairs is related to a temporally preceding/succeeding state of affairs with opposite polarity value ("neutral scenario"); (2) an actual instance (positive/negative state of affairs) of the sequential polarity oppositions contrasts with the presumed occurrence of the polarity sequences evoked in the discourse, i.e. the polarity switch point occurs earlier or later than expected ("counterfactual scenario").

Further, I follow van der Auwera (1993: 627, 1998: 35) who states that central meaning components of phasal polarity expressions are aspectual notions such as continuation (for STILL, NOT YET, NO LONGER) and inchoation (for ALREADY). As these meanings overlap with the functions of verbal aspect morphemes, it is not surprising that in Fula varieties that have grammatical aspect the relationship

---

[1] I am indebted to the Fula speakers who allowed me to use their linguistic data; I am particularly grateful to Jean Pierre Boutché whose help was indispensable for understanding phasal expressions in Fula and for analysing the data presented in this paper.

between phasal polarity and aspect is very intricate. The aspectual phasal polarity meaning components are already comprised in the Fula aspect system, and hence, the expression of phasal polarity is affected (and sometimes even blocked) by aspect marking (cf. also Van Baar 1997: 137).

In the following sections, I discuss the formal and functional properties of phasal polarity expressions in the Fula varieties by addressing questions that concern the central values of the phasal polarity parameters as proposed by Kramer (2017):

a) COVERAGE: Is an item involved in the expression of more than one phasal polarity concept, or are phasal polarity concepts encoded by constructions that each have separate items?
b) PRAGMATICITY: Are there formal differences between the expression of neutral and counterfactual phasal polarity scenarios? Which interpretation occurs more frequently in the respective Fula variety?
c) WORDHOOD: What is the wordhood status (free vs. bound morphemes) of the phasal polarity items? Are adverbial phrases or verbal constructions involved in signalling phasal polarity meanings?
d) EXPRESSIBILITY: Are there specialized items/constructions for the expression of phasal polarity concepts ALREADY, STILL, NOT YET, NO LONGER? What is the functional spectrum of the items/constructions? Are phasal polarity meanings salient or central to their function, or are they rather context-induced interpretations?
e) PARADIGMATICITY: Is it possible to state paradigmatic complementarity with corresponding expression pairs for ALREADY-NOT YET and STILL-NO LONGER? What is the categorical status of the phasal polarity items? To what extent are phasal polarity items combinable with paradigms of the domains of Tense, Aspect and Mood (TAM)?

I answer these questions as far as it is possible (concerning the data available) and reasonable (concerning language specific peculiarities). First, I focus on properties and distribution patterns of affirmative phasal polarity expressions (ALREADY, STILL) and then I turn to the description of encoding strategies and functional properties of negative phasal polarity concepts (NOT YET, NO LONGER) in Fula varieties.

3.1 Formal and functional properties of positive phasal polarity expressions

I start by discussing strategies for expressing the positive phasal polarity concepts STILL and ALREADY. The meaning components of continuation for STILL and inchoation for ALREADY (cf. van der Auwera 1998: 35–37) overlap with aspectual functions: continuative meaning concerns the situational instance of a state of affairs, whereas inchoative meaning concerns one of its boundaries (namely its beginning) (Sasse 1991: 11–14). Fula verbal inflection indicates the basic aspectual distinction between perfective and imperfective, i.e. an aspectual dichotomy focusing on event boundaries and situations respectively. We can thus expect intricate interactions between aspect and phasal polarity expressions or a certain degree of incorporation of phasal polarity meanings into the grammatical domain of aspect for Fula varieties.

3.1.1 ALREADY expressions

In Standardized Adamawa Fula, ALREADY expressions found in the bible texts (in English *already*, in French *déjà*) to signal *neutral* scenarios are rendered by constructions with a perfective verb form and without further marking, cf. (1a)–(1c). The positive phase is related to a preceding negative phase and not to a simultaneous phase contrasting in polarity value. An expectation of an earlier or later polarity switch point is not involved in the scenarios expressed in (1). For instance in (1a), Moses sends Aaron to the Jewish community for a sacrificial offering telling him that God has started a plague. When Aaron arrives at the community's place he is aware of the beginning of the plague and hence, he ascertains that the plague has ALREADY started in the sense that it wasn't there before.

(1) Neutral ALREADY scenario interpretation of perfective expressions in Standardized Adamawa Fula
   a. *nde o yi'i   masiibo **fudɗ-i**   caka   yimɓe.*
      CNJ 1 see:PFV accident begin-PFV among person:ʼBE
      '[So Aaron took it as Moses said and ran into the midst of the assembly.] Then he beheld, the plague has **already** begun among the people.' (Num 17,12)
   b. *koo moy to laari   debbo   bee   suuno*
      IDEF who if look:PFV woman:O with greed:NGO
      wad-i   *Njeenu   bee   muuɗum nder   ɓernde   muuɗum.*
      make-PFV adultery:NGU with POS.1 inside heart:NDE POS.1
      'Everyone who looks at a woman with lustful intent has **already** committed adultery with her in his heart.' (Mt 5,28)

c. *Jemma* **jeŋng-i**
   night   fall-PFV
   'It was **already** night, [and Jesus had not yet come to them.]' (Jn 6,17)

The fact that neutral ALREADY function may be subsumed under the aspect category perfective is not surprising. The perfective binds the designated state of affairs to its boundaries, i.e. the transition points into or out of a situation. In the same way, the neutral ALREADY scenario is interpreted as binding sequentially related phases to a boundary, namely to the polarity switch point dividing the negative phase from its succeeding (actual) positive phase.

For expressing a counterfactual ALREADY scenario implying an unexpected early switch point of polarity values, two strategies are used. The notion of counterfactual ALREADY, i.e. a change of polarity value occurs earlier than expected, may be expressed periphrastically by employing adverbials (e.g. *law bana nii* 'quick like that') and temporal verbs (e.g. *neeɓi* 'it has taken/is a long time'), as in example (2).

(2) Periphrastic constructions to render counterfactual ALREADY meaning in Standardized Adamawa Fula
Pilaatu haydini   nanugo Yeesu maayi **law   bana   nii**
P.   be.astonished:PFV hear:INF Y.   die:PFV quick   like   that
o ewni   mawdo   sooje'en   go, o yami   mo:
1 call:PFV big.one:DO soldier:EN   DEM 1 ask:PFV OBJ.1
"**Neeɓi**   *O maayi   na?*"
take.long:PFV   1 die:PFV   Q
'Pilate was surprised to hear that Jesus has already died (*lit.* has died quickly like that). Summoning to the centurion, he asked him whether he was already dead (*lit.* Is it a long time ago that he has died?).' (Mk 15,44)

Another construction type to express counterfactual ALREADY meaning in Stan-dardized Adamawa Fula involves the concatenation of two perfective verb forms: a first verb providing the predicate frame + a second, clause-final coverb *timmi* 'it is finished'. This construction does not occur frequently in the bible texts but is restricted to contexts where it signals that the polarity switch point of a state-of-affairs occurs earlier than expected. This construction focuses on the state-of-affairs from a retrospective perspective, namely its completion. The phase holding at reference time is affected by the completion of the state-of-affairs and hence, by its discontinuation.

In (3a), the speaker refers to the behaviour of people torturing and killing John the Baptist (i.e. the reborn prophet Elijah), while they did not recognize

Elijah's return at a preceding point in time. Against the people's expectation that the prophet Elijah is still to arrive, the speaker contrasts this state-of-affairs as completed and not occurring any longer. In (3b), the speaker (Saint Paul) warns the addressee (Timothy) of the "heretics" Hymenaeus and Philetus who utter (against the speaker's expectation) that the resurrection (of the dead) is completed, implying that this event will not occur after the polarity switch point.

(3) Counterfactual, retrospective ALREADY expressions with V_{PFV} + *timmi* in Standardized Adamawa Fula
    a. *Ammaa mi ɗon wi'a On Eliya **war-i timmi**,*
       but   1SG LOC say:IFV FOC E.   come-PFV be.finished:PFV
       yimɓe annditaay mo,
       person:ɓE recognize:PFV.NEG OBJ.1
       ɓe mbaɗi mo ko ɓe ngiɗi,
       2   do.PL:PFV OBJ.1 IDEF 2   love.PL:PFV
       ɓe torran Bii.neɗɗo boo bana non.
       2   torture:IFV Son.of.Man too like   in.this.manner
       'But I tell you that Elijah has already come, and they did not recognize him, but did to him whatever they pleased, they will torture the Son of Man like this.' (Mt 17,12)
    b. *Kamɓe ɓe celi laawol gooŋga,*
       2.EMPH 2   swerve.PL:PFV road:NGOL truth:NGA
       ɓe ɗon mbonna nuɗɗinki woɗɓe
       2   LOC   foil.PL:IFV faith:KI certain:ɓE
       *Bee wi'go ummitineeki maayɓe **waɗ-i, timmi**.*
       With say:INF resurrection:KI dead.person:ɓe do-PFV be.finished:PFV
       'They, they have swerved from the road of truth, saying that the resurrection has already happened. They are upsetting the faith of some.' (2 Tim 2,18)

In Adamawa Fula Communis (just like in Standardized Adamawa Fula), neutral ALREADY readings are context-dependent interpretations of constructions with perfective verb forms. Counterfactual ALREADY may be expressed by periphrastic constructions that often involve temporal adverbs or phasal verbs like *fuɗɗ-* 'start' and *timmin-* 'finish'. In (4a), a phasal verb *fuɗɗi* 'X has/is started' is combined with a temporal adverb *ɓoima* 'a long time ago' to signal a polarity switch occurring earlier than expected; in (4b), the phasal verb *timmin-* 'finish' refers to this unexpected early polarity switch point from a retrospective angle.

(4) Periphrastic ALREADY constructions with adverbs and phasal verbs in Adamawa Fula Communis
   a. *Aliyu* ***fuɗɗi*** *kuugal* ***ɓoima***
      A. start:PFV work:NGAL long.time.ago
      'Aliyum is already working' (lit. Aliyum has started work a long time ago) (Mb 2-04a)
   b. *mi* ***timmini*** *nyaamgo*
      1SG finish:PFV eat:INF
      'I have already eaten.' (lit. I have finished eating) (Boutché, traductions 10b)

The specialized counterfactual ALREADY construction (predicate + clause-final perfective co-verb) occurs quite frequently in Adamawa Fula Communis. The perfective coverbs *timmi* or *jinni* appearing in this construction type both render phasal meanings 'be finished' when used as main verbs. In contrast to [perfective main verb + *timmi*] constructions in Standardized Adamawa Fula, this construction type is semantically not limited to the expression of retrospective ALREADY (MESHA) scenarios focusing on the completion of a state-of-affairs and implying its negative phase at reference time (cf. Kramer, this volume). These constructions may also express counterfactual ALREADY in the sense of a positive state at reference time (possibly preceded by a negative phase) contrasting with an expected negative state. It should be noted that a preceding negative state is not necessarily involved in the actual occurring state-of-affairs, e.g. in (5f), sequentiality is just implied in the presupposition (i.e. non-American turning into American citizenship) but not in the actual fact.[2]

Accordingly, the clause-final ALREADY items *timmi* and *jinni* are not restricted to combinations with perfective main verbs, cf. (5a)–(5b), but also appear in constructions with progressive and imperfective verb forms, cf. (5c)–(5d), as well as with non-verbal predications, cf. (5e)–(5g).

---

[2] The example is taken from Mittwoch (1993: 74) and, with reference to Mittwoch (as p.c. or n.d.), is also cited in studies on phasal polarity of Löbner (1989: 183), Garrido (1992: 372), van der Auwera (1993: 622), Van Baar (1997: 42). According to J.P. Boutché (p.c.), the ALREADY meaning of this example may be rendered by a 'predicate + *timmi*' construction although clause-final elements such as the particle *kadi* 'indeed' or the temporal adverb *jonta* 'now' may bear similar interpretations.

(5) Counterfactual ALREADY expressions with predicate + *timmi/jinni* in Adamawa Fula Communis

a. *Mi nyaami* **timmi**
   1SG eat:PFV ALREADY
   'I have already eaten.' (Boutché, traductions 10a)

b. *Aliyu Huuwi* **jinni**
   A. work:PFV ALREADY
   'Aliyu has already worked.' (Ng 2-04b)

c. *Aliyum ɗo huuwa* **jinni**
   A. LOC work:IFV ALREADY
   'Aliyum is already working.' (Ma 2-04a)

d. *O yahan kuugal* **jinni**
   1 go:IFV work:NGAL ALREADY
   '[Aliyum won't be here tomorrow] he will already work.' (lit. he will already go to work) (Mb1 2-04c)

e. *o ɗon haa Garua* **timmi** *naa?*
   1 LOC PREP G. ALREADY Q
   'Is he already in Garoua?' (sita 04_19_0:29)

f. *o Amirkaajo le* **timmi** *nde nii o danyaama e Lesdi Amirka*
   1 American: DO TOP ALREADY when like.this 1 born:PFV.PAS PREP land:NDI A.
   'He is already American, for he was born in America.'

g. *a yi'aay mi ɗo mari wakkude daneejum naa?*
   2SG see:NEG.PFV 1SG LOC possess:PFV beard:NDE white Q
   Mi ndottiijo **jinni**
   1SG old.man:DO ALREADY
   "Haven't you seen (that) I have a white beard? I am an old man already!"

In (5), the clause-final elements *timmi* and *jinni* are glossed as ALREADY elements since they are obviously specialized as well as generalized phasal polarity items. The concatenative constructions with clause-final *timmi* in Standardized Adamawa Fula are dedicated to signalling counterfactual, retrospective ALREADY (or MESHA) scenarios and do not possess other possible readings. Nonetheless, they show restrictions on TAM values: the main verb can only be marked as perfective, pointing to the source construction, i.e. two coordinated perfective verb phrases (that lack an overt linking device). In Adamawa Fula Communis, I assume that the initial structure of two coordinated verb phrases has been reanalysed as a verb phrase with a final *timmi/jinni* adverb or particle respectively and hence, the items were able to generalize across TAM distinctions, cf. Figure 1.

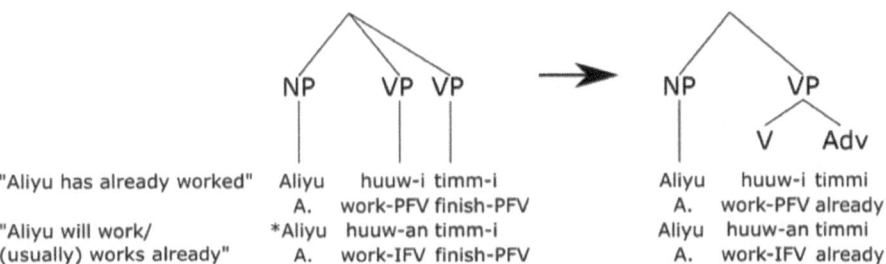

Figure 1: Syntactic reanalysis from coordinated verbal phrases to clause-final particle/adverb.

To sum up, neutral ALREADY scenarios are possible interpretations of expressions with perfective verb forms in certain contexts in the Fula varieties. In Standardized Adamawa Fula, a construction with two concatenated perfective verb forms (a main verb + a coverb *timmi*) is a specialized means to signal counterfactual MESHA scenarios, i.e. scenarios implying an actual negative phase referred to from a retrospective view point, namely the completion of the preceding positive phase. While this construction type is restricted to perfective main verbs in Standardized Adamawa Fula, it has been generalized in Adamawa Fula Communis: In Adamawa Fula Communis, the clause-final elements *timmi* and *jinni*, which are both derived from verbs of finishing, can combine with verbs across different TAM distinctions as well as with non-verbal predicates to express counterfactual ALREADY and MESHA scenarios. Members of the counterfactual ALREADY paradigm in Adamawa Fula Communis have one-to-one correspondences with the members used in affirmative non-phasal polarity expressions and can thus be described as externally paradigmatic.

3.1.2 Still expressions

In the bible texts, the passages rendering STILL scenarios (expressed in the English bible version with *still*, in the French bible version with *encore*) are expressed by a large variety of constructions. The distribution of these constructions is obviously not conditioned by pragmatic factors (such as neutral vs. counterfactual STILL scenarios).

In non-verbal predications denoting states (mainly locatives and existentials) that are inherently continuous and thus not conceived as having boundaries, STILL is often left unmarked, as in (6a)–(6b). In (6a), Joseph addresses his brothers with the question whether their father is still alive, implying that the father's death is a probable alternative scenario (at least in the English bible passage). The assertion in (6b) does not account for a presumed alternative scenario at all: there was a time when Paul stayed with the Christian community in Thessalonica (and could teach them), followed by a phase when he was not with them.

(6) Unmarked continuous scenarios ('still'/'encore') in Standardized Adamawa Fula
    a. *o wi'i:*   *Baaba moodon don bee yoŋki na?*
       1 say:PFV Father POS.2PL LOC with life:KI Q
       'He said: Is your father still alive?'(Gen 43,7b)
    b. *Saa'i*   *mi don no wondi bee moodon,*
       moment:KI 1SG LOG ANT be.with with POS.1PL
       Mi wi'i   On dum
       1SG say:PFV FOC 23
       'When I was still with you I told you this.' (2 Tes 2,5)

Other STILL contexts in expressions with a verbal predicate that focus rather on the continuation of a state of affairs than on a counter-expectational or succeeding negative phase are mostly signalled by periphrastic constructions with the aspectual verb *tokk-* 'continue', cf. (7a)–(7b). In (7a), the continuation of a certain behaviour (*wad- halleende* 'do evil') and its result are addressed, and in (7b), the author rebukes the people of Judah for the continuation of their pagan activities. Further periphrases that express STILL scenarios (counterfactual as well as neutral) include temporal adverbials such as *haa joonta* 'until now', *koo jonta boo* 'even now', *koo hannde boo* 'even today' etc., cf. (7c)–(7d).

(7) Periphrastic STILL constructions with phasal verbs and adverbials
    a. *Ammaa to on* **tokkake**   *wadugo halleende,*
       But   if 2PL continue:PFV.MID make.INF bad.thing:NDE
       nden kam, on kalkan
       then TOP   2PL be.lost.PL:IFV
       'But if you still do wickedly, you shall be lost.' (1 Sam 12,25)

b. *yimɓe* **tokki** *hirsugo*
   person:BE continue.PFV slaughter:INF
   E wulugo uurle haa nokkuuje man
   and burn:INF perfume:NDE PREP place:DE DEM
   'The people still sacrificed and made offerings (*lit.* burned perfume) on the places.' (1 Kings 22,44b)
c. *To goddo wi'i o don nder annoora,*
   if person:DO say.PFV 1 LOC in light
   ammaa o don wanya deerdiiko, nden kam
   but 1 LOC hate:IFV brother:DO:POS.1 then TOP
   haa jonta *o don nder nyiɓre.*
   PREP now 1 LOC in darkness:NDE
   'If someone says he is in the light, but he hates his brother, then he is still (lit.: until now) in darkness.'
d. *Ammaa* **koo hannde boo** *mi cemmbiddo*
   but IND today too 1SG strong.person:DO
   bana nder nyalaade nde Muusa nela yam.
   like in day:NDE DEM.9 M. send:IFV OBJ.1SG
   'But I am still (lit.: even today) as strong today as I was in the day that Moses sent me.' (Josh 14,11)

The clause-final adverb *tawon*,[3] which clearly functions as a specialized phasal polarity item in NOT YET expressions, is often used to express STILL concepts in the bible texts, (8a)–(8c). It is questionable, though, whether *tawon* does really qualify as a dedicated phasal polarity item. *Tawon* also expresses ordinal meaning, namely that a state-of-affairs occurs prior or first in a sequence of events. In (8d), Jacob wants Esau to sell him his birth right before he cedes his meal to him, i.e. sequential precedence is signalled: sell.birthright (1st) – give.meal (2nd). The interpretation of *tawon* as a STILL item or ordinal adverb in affirmative clauses depends on the context. Nonetheless, the STILL reading of *tawon* occurs more frequently than its sequentially ordering interpretation in the bible texts.[4]

---

[3] Like the Hausa adverb *tùkùna* 'first; (not) yet', *tawon* is most probably related to the adverb *dùwô/dùwonyì* 'first, before, though, although, (not) yet' in the neighboring language Kanuri (cf. Ziegelmeyer, this volume).
[4] In the bible texts, the expression of an event's sequential priority is more often signalled by a construction with the verb *aart-* ('to V first, to precede') + infinitive main verb.

(8) Constructions with clause-final *tawon* in the bible texts
    a. *O huli   ngam   o derkeejo   **tawon**.*
       1 fear:PFV because 1 young.man:DO YET
       'He was afraid, because he was still a young man.' (Judg 8,20)
    b. *Yaake o ɗon wolida   bee maɓɓe **tawon**, [. . .]*
       CNJ 1 LOC speak.with:IFV with POS.2 YET
       'While he was still speaking with them, [. . .].' (Gen 29,9a)
    c. *Min   mbiiɓe   ma   yaake en   ɗonno*
       1PL.EXCL tell.PL:BE OBJ.2SG CNJ 1PL.INCL LOC:ANT
      *haa Misra **tawon***
      PREP Egypt YET
      'We told you (this), when we were still in Egypt.' (Ex 14,12a)
    d. *soorranam   daraja   afaaku   ma*
       sell:DAT:OBJ.1SG privilege firstborness POS.2SG
      *hannde   Nden **tawon***
      today:NDE DEM.9 first
      '(Jacob answers:) Sell me your birthright today first!' (Gen 25,31)

In Adamawa Fula Communis, clause-final *tawon* appears as a phasal polarity item only to explicitly express a counterfactual STILL scenario. These constructions are pragmatically very marked: E.g. in (9a), the state of having reached school-age is contrasted to the actual state of before having reached school-age. We can assume the same contrast in (9b): I asked a young man who was serving in a restaurant whether he is the owner of the place and got a negative answer with the explanation that he is still a young man, i.e. he has not yet reached the age to be a responsible shop owner.

(9) Constructions with clause-final *tawon* in Adamawa Fula Communis
    a. *o yidi   Yahgo booko, ammaa o peeto   **tawon***
       1 want:PFV go:INF school but 1 small:DO YET
       'He wants to go to school, but he is still (too) small.' (traductions 17)
    b. *Kay mi derkeejo   **tawon***
       No 1SG young.man:DO YET
       'No, I am still a young man' (21a_03.2018)

That *tawon* possibly specializes into a more grammatical item to express (counterfactual) STILL meaning may be demonstrated further by the phonological process of erosion that *tawon* undergoes in the Adamawa Fula Communis variety and that is commonly associated with grammaticalization processes

(Heine/Reh 1984: 21–24). At least in the elicited data, the phonological substance of *tawon* (with STILL meaning) is often reduced to *taw*, (10a)–(10c).

The occurrence of the clause-final adverb *fahin* 'again' as STILL item in the elicited Adamawa Fula Communis data, (10a)–(10c), should be considered with caution. The use of *fahin* is most likely biased by the meta-language French where the item *encore* occurs that does not only express STILL concepts but also signals the repetitive meaning 'again'.

(10) Constructions with clause-final *taw(on)/fahin* in Adamawa Fula Communis
   a. *Aliyu ɗon Haa Garua ?fahin/**taw(on)***
      A.   LOC PREP G.   again/YET
      'Aliyu is still in Garua.' (1-03a)
   b. *Aliyu ɗon No Haa Garua ?fahin/**taw(on)***
      A.   LOC PREP ANT G.   again/YET
      'Aliyu was still in Garua.' (1-03b)
   c. *Aliyu wonan haa Garua ?fahin/**taw(on)***
      A.   be:IFV PREP G.   again/YET
      'Aliyu will still be in Garua.' (1-03c)

In the dictionaries, the temporal phrase *haa jonta*, which literally means 'until now', occurs as a STILL entry for the Adamawa Fula variety. *Haa jonta* also appears in the elicited Adamawa Fula Communis data, and speakers indicate it as an alternative strategy for STILL coding, cf. (11a)–(11b). Sometimes, *haa jonta* is combined with the adverb *fahin* 'again' or the quantifier *fuu* 'all' to reinforce the STILL meaning, cf. (11c)–(11d). However, the use of the adverbial *haa jonta* is restricted to progressive or unmarked copula constructions (in the bible corpus as well as in the elicited data). Since *haa jonta* primarily expresses the continuation of a state-of-affairs up to the moment of speaking or another internal reference point, it will not be considered here as a dedicated phasal polarity item.

(11) Constructions with the temporal adverbial *haa jonta* 'until now' in Adamawa Fula Communis
   a. *Yiite ɗon huɓɓi* **haa jonta**
      light:NGE LOC turn.on:PFV until now
      'The light is still on.' (Boutché, traductions 2)
   b. *Aliyu ɗon huuwa* **Haa jonta**
      A.   LOC work:IFV Until now
      'Aliyum is still working.' (Ma 2-03a)

c. **haa jonta** o ɗon haa Garua **fahin**
   until now 1 LOC PREP G. again
   'Until now he is still in Garua.' (Mb 1-03a/b)
d. **haa jonta fuu** Piyer ɗon London
   until now all P. LOC L.
   '?*Peter is still always in London.' (Boutché APCC 12)

In summary, the only item that possibly can be claimed to be a dedicated STILL item is the clause-final adverb *tawon* occurring in Standardized Adamawa Fula as well in Adamawa Fula Communis – in the latter variety, however, clause-final *tawon* especially marks counterfactual scenarios. In both varieties, constructions with *tawon* have no TAM restrictions but one-to-one correspondences with constructions of the affirmative non-phasal polarity paradigm and are hence externally paradigmatic. Like many phasal polarity expressions that are often claimed to be borrowings, the STILL item's *tawon* source is (highly possibly) the Kanuri adverb *dùwô/dùwonyì* 'first, before, though, although, (not) yet' that is widely spread in the languages of the area (cf. Ziegelmeyer, this volume).

3.2 Formal and functional properties of negative phasal polarity expressions

In the following paragraphs, I discuss formal and functional properties of negative phasal polarity expressions found in the data corpus. In contrast to the inchoative and continuative phasal polarity concepts, the relevant negative notions NOT YET and NO LONGER are clearly coded by specialized constructions in both Fula varieties.

3.2.1 NOT YET expressions

In the Standardized Adamawa Fula bible texts, two construction types signal NOT YET concepts. The distribution of these types does not depend on pragmatic values (i.e. neutral vs. counterfactual scenarios) but is partly sensitive to the aspect value of the construction. In non-perfective contexts, the auxiliary *siwa(a)* 'to have not yet Ved' is used and appears in the slot between the subject and the infinitive verb form, cf. (12a)–(12b). In such constructions, *siwa(a)* obviously functions as a specialized NOT YET item. Since *siwa(a)* is invariably inflected by the suffix -*a(a)*, a general negative marker that does not reflect values of the categories TAM and voice or polarity value, it does not display typical properties of Fula verbs anymore.

(12) NOT YET constructions *siwa(a)* + INF in Standardized Adamawa Fula
    a. *Njehe   haa juulde   onon kam,*
       go.IMP.PL PREP feast:NDE 2.PL TOP
       *min   mi **siwaa** yahugo*
       1SG.EMPH 1SG NOT.YET go.INF
       'You, go to the feast. Me, I am not going yet.' (Joh 7,8)
    b. *Saa'i   man ɓe keɓ-aay   no   Ruuhu tawon,*
       moment DEM 2   get-PFV.NEG PAST spirit   YET
       *ngam   Yeesu **siwaa** nastugo teddungal. ngam   Yeesu*
       because Y.   NOT.YET enter.INF glory:NGAL because Y.
       'At that moment, they haven't got the Spirit yet, because Jesus is not glorified yet.' (John 7,8)

In aspectually marked constructions, the use of an auxiliary *siwa(a)* is inappropriate in Standardized Adamawa Fula, but the clause-final adverb *tawon* can be used. As can be seen in (13), there are no aspectual restrictions on the use of the item *tawon*: it can appear in constructions with perfective, (13a)–(13b), as well as imperfective verb forms, (13c)–(13d).

(13) NOT YET expressions with *tawon* in Standardized Adamawa Fula
    a. *berniwol Mawni   yaaji*
       city:NGOL get.great:PFV get.large:PFV
       ammaa joodiiɓe   ton duudaay.
       but   inhabitant:BE DIST get.numerous:PFV.NEG
       *ɓe nyiɓt-aay   cuudi **tawon***
       2   build:REV-PFV.NEG hut:DI YET
       'The city was large and great, but the people were few there, and they have not yet rebuilt the houses.' (Neh 7,4)
    b. *moy Jubi   ngesa   inabooje*
       who plant:PFV field:KA grape:DE
       *heɓ-aay   ittugo   ɓiɓɓe   maaje **tawon**?*
       obtain-PFV.NEG remove.INF descendant:BE POS:24 YET
       'Who has planted a vineyard and has not obtained to reap its fruit yet?' (Deut 20,6)

c. *ammaa Mi anndi an e saraaki'en ma,*
   but 1SG know:PFV 2SG and dignitary POS.2SG
   on kul-ataa Jawmiraawo Allah **tawon**
   2PL fear.PL-IFV.NEG Lord God YET
   'But I know that, as for you and your dignitaries, you do not yet fear the Lord God.' (Ex 9,30)

d. *ammaa mi hooc-ataa laamu*
   but 1SG take.away-IFV.NEG kingdom:NGU
   haa Juŋngo maako **tawon**
   PREP hand:NGO POS.1 YET
   '... but I will not yet take the whole kingdom out of his hand.' (1 Kings 11,34)

In positive contexts, as seen in 2.1.2 above, *tawon* signals sequential meaning '(at) first' or (more frequently) functions as a STILL marker. In accordance with Löbner's (1989) notions of semantic relationships between phasal polarity concepts, the *taw (on)* marked STILL and NOT YET expressions formally display the relation of internal negation, i.e. STILL (p) STILL ← internal negation → (not p) ≜ p *tawon* ↔ (not p) *tawon*.

In the Adamawa Fula Communis data, the negative phasal polarity concept NOT YET is mostly expressed by clause-final *taw(on)*. As shown in (14a)–(14e), most speakers accept NOT YET expressions showing one-to-one correspondences to equivalent expressions of the (standard) negation paradigm. Thus, the NOT YET and negative paradigms are symmetric.

(14) NOT YET expressions with *taw(on)* in Adamawa Fula Communis (Quest 1-06a-c; 2-06a-c):

   a. *Aliyu Walaa haa Garua* **taw(on)**
      A. COP.NEG PREP G. YET
      'Aliyu isn't in Garua yet.'

   b. *Aliyu Wonaay (no) Haa Garua* **taw(on)**
      A. be:NEG.PFV (ANT) PREP G. YET
      'Aliyu wasn't in Garua yet.'

   c. *Aliyu Wonataa haa Garua* **taw(on)**
      A. be:NEG.IFV PREP G. YET
      'Aliyu won't be in Garua yet.'

   d. *Aliyu Huuwataa (kuugal)* **taw(on)**
      A. work:NEG.IFV (work:NGAL) YET
      'Aliyu doesn't work/is not working/won't work yet.'

e. *Aliyu huuwaay   (kuugal)   **taw(on)***
   A.   work:NEG.PFV (work:NGAL) YET
   'Aliyu hasn't worked yet.'

Expressions with clause-final *tawon* are often used as answers to positive questions signalling that the state of affairs is not taking place but its occurrence is still a possible future scenario. In (15), we see an example of a regular dialogue between motorcycle mechanics working close to a cookshop. The mechanics regularly come to work very early in the morning and ask the cookshop's employees about the arrival of their female boss (*'has Diija arrived?'*) who normally starts to work a bit later in the morning (*'no, she hasn't arrived yet'*).

(15) *tawon* marked NOT YET answer in Adamawa Fula Communis
   Q: *Diija wari?*
       D.   come:PFV
   A: *Kay o Waraay   **tawon.***
       No   1 come:NEG.PFV NOT.YET
       'Has Diija arrived (already)?' – 'No, she hasn't arrived yet.'

In dictionaries of Eastern Fula varieties, the entry for 'not yet' or 'ne ... pas encore' is often *siwa(a)*. Whereas in the bible texts constructions with *siwaa* + INF frequently express NOT YET scenarios, *siwa(a)* hardly occurs in the data collected in Ngaoundéré. In the Adamawa Fula Communis corpus, if at all, the marker *siwa(a)* rather appears alone or in combination with *tawon* as a negative item fragment in reaction to a positive question, cf. (16a)–(16b).

(16) Answers with single NOT YET items *siwa(a) (tawon)*
   a. *Daada: Fakat A   waawi,   Umar am.*
      mother: Really 2SG be.able:PFV U.   POS.1SG
      *Baaba: **Siwa**! Umar, toy   gaasa ma?*
      father: NOT.YET U.   where hair:KA POS.2SG
      (Context: The father asks his son Umar to indicate Fula body part terms. The son performs the task very well so that his mother assumes that he has successfully finished.) 'Mother: Really, you've got it, my Umar. – Father: (No,) not yet! Umar, where is your hair?' (Boutché Dialogues D6: Hoore Umar)

b. Q: *o ɗon haa Garua timmi naa?*
   1 LOC PREP G. ALREADY Q
   A: **siwa   tawon**
      NOT.YET YET
   'Is he already in Garoua? – (No,) not yet.' (AnEr siwa-tawon 00:08_15)

However, in a questionnaire conducted with my colleague from Maroua, NOT YET meaning is also rendered by using *siwa(a)* constructions, cf. (17a)–(17c). Unlike in the bible texts, here *siwa(a)* is not necessarily followed by an infinitive verb form nor is its occurrence excluded in perfective constructions. To express NOT YET in perfective constructions, a clause with a negative-perfective verb form is combined with a subsequent *siwa(a)* phrase, cf. (17b)–(17c). Similarly to the syntactic reanalysis of *timmi* in ALREADY expressions as a clause-final adverb, and on the basis of analogy with the clause-final phasal polarity adverbs *fahin* and *tawon*, this structure hence possibly leads to the interpretation of the unchangeable *siwa(a)* item as an adverb in clause-final position.

(17) NOT YET constructions with *siwa(a)* in Adamawa Fula Communis
   a. *Zeynabu Kam nyaami **timmi**,*
      Z.   TOP   eat:PFV ALREADY
      *Maryamu On **siwa** nyaamugo.*
      M.   FOC NOT.YET eat:INF
      'Zeynabu has already eaten, Mayramu hasn't eaten yet' (Boutché, traductions 15)
   b. *yiite huɓɓ-aama **timmi** na?*
      light:NGE light-PFV.PAS ALREADY Q
      *a'aa, Yiite huɓɓ-aaki **siwa***
      no   light:NGE light-PFV.NEG.PAS NOT.YET
      'Is the light already switched on? – No, the light isn't switched on yet' (Boutché, traductions 3-4)
   c. *Mi nyaam-aay **siwaa***
      1SG eat-PFV.NEG NOT.YET
      'I haven't eaten yet.' (Boutché, traductions 12)

In elicitation settings, speakers translate and accept questions with clause-final *timmi/jinni* (ALREADY) that trigger NOT YET expressions (*tawon/siwa(a)*), cf. (16b), (17b). Therefore, the paradigmatic complementarity predicted by Van Baar (1997: 63) seems to be appropriate in Fula (at least in Adamawa Fula Communis), i.e. an ALREADY expression (e.g. *o ɗon haa Garua timmi naa?* 'Is he in Garoua already?') invokes the presence of a complementary NOT YET expression (e.g. *siwa tawon* '(no,) not yet'). However, in the Adamawa Fula Communis corpus of *natural* discourse settings, questions that trigger NOT YET expressions usually do not occur marked ALREADY. Hence, it is questionable whether ALREADY-NOT YET is a natural pairing in Adamawa Fula Communis discourse.

In summary, NOT YET is signalled by specialized expressions in both Standardized Adamawa Fula and Adamawa Fula Communis. NOT YET constructions involve either the adverb *tawon* that appears clause-finally or *siwa(a)* that is an auxiliary marked by the general negation morpheme *–a(a)*. Whereas in Standardized Adamawa Fula, the distribution of the two different construction types, i.e. *siw(a)* + INF and clause-final *tawon*, is sensitive to aspectual markedness, Adamawa Fula Communis speakers tend to use clause-final NOT YET markers, *tawon* or *siwa(a)*, in any clause type.

3.2.2 NO LONGER expressions

Two construction types code NO LONGER concepts in the bible corpus: Either (1) a negative construction with the clause-final adverb *fahin* 'again' codes NO LONGER concepts, or (2) an AUX + INF construction with the negated auxiliary *meet-* [*meeɗ-*] 'to have done sth. once before' or the phrasal verb *acc-* 'to leave' signal NO LONGER meaning. The distribution of these NO LONGER constructions in the bible texts suggests that their use is sensitive to different types of states-of-affairs denoted by the predicate. For signalling NO LONGER meaning, *fahin* appears with predicates denoting a situation (state or position), cf. (18a)–(18c), while *meetugo* and *accugo* are used in constructions designating an action, event or experience. Further, to signal NO LONGER concepts, the imperfective is restricted to *meet-*, cf. (19a)–(19c), while perfective marking appears with *acc-*, cf. (20a)–(20c).

(18) NO LONGER expressions with *fahin* in Standardized Adamawa Fula (Situation)
    a. *Mi   jooɗ-ataako   nder duniyaaru **fahin***
       1SG sit-NEG.IFV.MID PREP world   again
       ammaa kamɓe ɓe ɗon njoodi   nder maaru
       But   2.EMPH 2   COP sit.PL:PFV PREP POS.11
       'I am no longer in the world, but they, they are in it.' (John 17,11a)
    b. *ngam   Maajum jonta kam onon   yimɓe   ummaatooje*
       because POS.23   now   TOP 2PL.EMPH person:BE nation:DE
       *naa on   jananɓe   malla hoɗɓe   **fahin***
       NEG 2PL stranger:BE or   alien:BE   again
       'Therefore, now, you people of the nations, you are no longer strangers or aliens [. . .].' (Eph 2,19)

c. *O yami   Yaakubu: "noy innde   ma?"*
   1 ask:PFV Y.   how name:NDE POS.2SG
   o jaabi: "Yaakubu."
   1 answer:PFV Y.
   o wi'i:
   1 say:PFV
   *"a   ewn-ataake   Yaakubu **fahin** ammaa Isra'iila."*
   2SG call-NEG.IFV.PAS Y.   again but   I.
   'He asked him, 'What is your name?' He answered, 'Jacob.' He said, 'Your name shall no longer be called Jacob, but Israel.'" (Gen 32,28-29)

(19) NO LONGER expressions with *meet-* in Standardized Adamawa Fula (imperfective, Action/Event/Experience)
   a. *ngam   taa   ɓe **meet-an**   hulugo*
      because NEG 2   have.done.once.before-IFV fear:INF
      koo hultorgo   koo majjugo
      or   be.afraid:INF or   be.lost:INF
      '[I will set leaders over them for paying attention to them,] for they shall fear no more, nor be afraid, neither be lost." (Jer 23,4)
   b. *ɓe **meet-ataa**   maatugo   dolo*
      2   have.done.once.before-IFV.NEG perceive:INF hunger:NGO
      malla ɗomka
      or   thirst:KA
      *naange malla guldum **meet-ataa**   torrugo   ɓe*
      sun:NGE or heat:DUM have.done.once.before-IFV.NEG torture:INF OBJ.2
      'They will hunger no more, neither thirst anymore, neither the sun nor heat will torture them anymore.' (Rev 7,16)
   c. *saa'i   Man ɓe **meet-ataa**   wi'ugo:*
      moment DEM 2   have.done.once.before-IFV.NEG say:INF
      baabiraaɓe muri   lammuɗum
      father:BE   suck:PFV   sour:DUM
      ammaa ɗum nyii'e   ɓikkoy   mbaati
      but   23 tooth:DE   child:KOY burst.PL:PFV
      'At this time, they will no longer say: 'The fathers have sucked something sour, but it is the children's teeth (that) are set on edge.'' (Jer 31,29)

(20) NO LONGER expressions with *acc-* in Standardized Adamawa Fula (perfective, Action/Event/Experience)
 a. *diga saa'i man*
  since Moment DEM
  *duudɓe Caka pukara'en maako **acc-i***
  many:BE among student:EN POS.1 leave-PFV
  yahdugo bee maako
  walk:PLA:INF with POS.1
  From this moment on, many of his disciples no longer walked with him.' (Joh 6,66)
 b. *diggaali E mallimallooje njinni*
  thunder:DI And hail:DE finish.PL:PFV
  *iyeende **acc-i** toɓugo*
  rain:NDE leave-PFV fall:INF
  'The thunder and the hail ceased, and the rain no longer poured.' (Ex 9,33c)
 c. *nden o Fuufi luwal konu*
  then 1 blow:PFV horn:NGAL battle:NGU
  *yimɓe maako **acc-i** taasnugo Isra'iila'en*
  person:BE POS.1 leave:PFV pursue:INF Israelite:EN
  'Then he blew the battle horn, (and) his people pursued Israel no longer.' (2 Sam 2,28)

In the Adamawa Fula Communis data, expressions with the clause-final adverb *fahin* code NO LONGER concepts irrespective of different state-of-affairs types, (21a)–(21g). (However, I do not exclude the possibility that the (auxiliary) verbs *meeɗ-* 'to have done once before' or *acc-* 'to leave' occur in expressions that come close to NO LONGER meaning.) As can be seen from the examples in (21), the NO LONGER paradigm makes a distinction between perfective and imperfective and has thus one-to-one correspondences to the paradigm of standard negation in Adamawa Fula Communis.

(21) NO LONGER expressions with *fahin* in Adamawa Fula Communis (Quest 1-05a-c; 2-05a-c; traductions 4a, 13)
 a. *Aliyu Walaa haa Garua **fahin***
  A. COP.NEG PREP G. again
  'Aliyu is no longer in Garua.'
 b. *Aliyu won-aay (no) haa Garua **Fahin***
  A. be-NEG.PFV (PAST) PREP G. Again
  'Aliyu was no longer in Garua.'

c. *Aliyu won-ataa haa Garua **fahin***
   A. be-NEG.IFV PREP G. again
   'Aliyu will be no longer in Garua.'
d. *Aliyu huuw-ataa (kuugal) **fahin***
   A. work-NEG.IFV (work) again
   'Aliyu doesn't work/is not working/won't work anymore.'
e. *Aliyu huuw-aay (kuugal) **fahin***
   A. work-NEG.PFV (work) again
   'Aliyu hasn't worked anymore.'
f. Q: *haa Jonta yiite nge ɗon huɓɓi na?*
      PREP Now light:NGE DEM.13 LOC turn.on:PFV Q
   A: *a'aa, Yiite huɓɓaaki **fahin***
      no light:NGE turn.on:PFV.NEG.PAS again
   'Is the light still switched on?' – 'No, the light is no longer switched on.'
g. *Mi Nyaamata **fahin***
   1SG eat:IFV.NEG again
   'I don't eat anymore'

To sum up, we have seen that in both Fula varieties, the adverb *fahin* whose central function is repetitive ('again') in affirmative constructions has received an additional NO LONGER meaning component under negation. Or, to put it a different way, negative constructions with the clause-final adverb *fahin* may still signal repetition ('not V again'), but more likely they refer to a NO LONGER scenario. This specialization of a repetitive item under negation into a NO LONGER marker is rather common in the languages of the world (cf. Van Baar 1997: 50,104; Heine/Kuteva 2002: 260). Nonetheless, Adamawa Fula Communis and Standardized Adamawa Fula differ in that clause-final *fahin* is the main means for coding NO LONGER in negative constructions and is used in all negative paradigms in Adamawa Fula Communis, whereas in Standardized Adamawa Fula, the strategies for expressing NO LONGER scenarios (i.e. constructions involving *fahin, meeɗ-, acc-*) are sensitive to both lexical and grammatical aspect.

4 Summary and discussion

After having examined expressions to signal phasal polarity concepts in Cameroon-ian Fula, I can now state two different coding strategy systems. One system is based on data of the bible corpus for the Standardized Adamawa Fula variety, the other one is derived from fieldwork data for the Adamawa Fula

Communis variety (though it has to be kept in mind that the system stated for Adamawa Fula Communis is just one variant of a phasal polarity paradigm variable). To illustrate the Standardized Adamawa Fula and Adamawa Fula Communis systems, I have organized the phasal polarity items/constructions and their occurrence constraints in unrelated Löbnerian duality squares (Figures 2 and 3). Here, the Löbnerian squares do not indicate semantic or categorical relationships between the phasal polarity expressions but are merely used for a structured overview of frequently occurring expression strategies and their conditions in different Cameroonian Fula varieties.

ALREADY	
neutral	V_{PFV}
counterfactual	V_{PFV} + timmi

NO LONGER	+ dyn	− dyn
PFV	acci	fahin
IFV	meetataa	

NOT YET	
PFV/IFV	tawon
IFV	siwa

STILL
various [?tawon]

Figure 2: Phasal polarity expression strategy system of Standardized Adamawa Fula based on a corpus of bible texts (1995 [1983]; 2017).

ALREADY (counterfactual)
timmi/jinni

NO LONGER
fahin

NOT YET
tawon (siwa/a)

STILL (counterfactual)
(?fahin) taw(on)

Figure 3: Phasal polarity expression strategy system of Adamawa Fula Communis based on a corpus of field work data.

Figure 2 shows phasal polarity expression strategies in Standardized Adamawa Fula. Specialized phasal polarity expressions are auxiliary constructions with *siwa* (NOT YET) and *meetataa/jinni* (NO LONGER) + V_{INF}, clauses with the adverb *tawon* in final position (STILL, NOT YET), negative constructions with the clause-final adverb *fahin* (NO LONGER), and perfective constructions with *timmi* (ALREADY), which is (depending on one's (re)analysis) a clause-final adverb or a succeeding clause. One item only (*tawon*) is involved in the expression of two phasal polarity concepts (NOT YET and STILL), a formal relation that might display a semantic link of internal negation between the concepts (Löbner 1989). This coverage pattern determines the phasal polarity system of Standardized Adamawa Fula as flexible (cf. Kramer, this volume). Van Baar (1997: 165) labels this COVERAGE type with different items involved in ALREADY and NO LONGER expressions and a STILL item also covering the NOT YET slot *Type 3AL*, and shows it as most common among the languages of his sample. Although all four phasal polarity concepts may be expressed by specialized constructions (cf. EXPRESSIBILITY parameter), the system displays a rather large constructional diversity, which is conditioned by the interaction of the relevant expressions with other categories, namely pragmatic status, and grammatical/lexical aspect. The construction with *timmi* is restricted to the expression of counter-factual ALREADY scenarios, but the other phasal polarity expressions are not sensitive to PRAGMATICITY. Still more important here is the intrinsic interaction with grammatical aspect (NO LONGER: *acci* + V PFV vs. *meetataa* + V IFV; NOT YET: *siwa* + V IFV vs. *tawon* PFV/IFV) and with lexical aspect/*Aktionsart* (*acci/meetataa* + V ⁺dyn vs. NEG *fahin* ⁻dyn). Owing not least to the interaction of phasal polarity expressions with aspect, the Standardized Adamawa Fula system does not show one-to-one-correspondences between its members and members of the corresponding affirmative/negative paradigms, nor does it constitute a grammatical paradigm. Thus, according to the PARADIGMATICITY paradigm, it can be described as asymmetric, both internally and externally.

Figure 3 gives an overview of phasal polarity expression strategies in Adamawa Fula Communis. The Adamawa Fula Communis variety has dedicated clause-final adverbs dedicated for all four phasal polarity concepts. It should be noted that specialized expressions of positive phasal polarity concepts (ALREADY and STILL) are restricted to counterfactual scenarios and that the system is thus partly sensitive to PRAGMATICITY. The ALREADY items *timmi/jinni* are derived from perfective verb forms that are synchronically still used. Nonetheless, they qualify as 'adverbs' here because their possible occurrence in all affirmative verbal paradigms leads to the conclusion that the one-word-clause *timmi/jinni* 'it is finished', which exclusively follows a perfective sentence in Standardized Adamawa Fula, was reanalyzed as a fixed clause-final particle (or 'adverb') in Adamawa Fula Communis. Like in Standardized Adamawa Fula, the item *tawon* covers the STILL area, but also the NOT YET area and hence we can again state a flexible *Type 3AL* system showing a relationship of internal negation. If the occurrence of *fahin* as a STILL item in the Adamawa Fula Communis data is not biased by the language used for elicitation (i.e. French where *encore* signals STILL but also repetitive meaning 'again'), we have to state a second coexisting phasal polarity system. The item *fahin* then relates the concepts STILL and NO LONGER via external negation. According to Van Baar's (1997: 165) COVERAGE classification, such a system with separate expressions for ALREADY and NOT YET and one item covering STILL and NO LONGER areas is classified as *Type 3AY* and is rarely found in the languages of the world. Some Adamawa Fula Communis speakers accept the unrestricted appearance of clause-final phasal polarity items in the respective affirmative and negative verbal paradigms, while others do not. At least at the outer edge of the Adamawa Fula Communis continuum, the phasal polarity system shows a very high degree of PARADIGMATICITY.

The most obvious difference between the phasal polarity systems of Stan-dardized Adamawa Fula and Adamawa Fula Communis concerns their particular status of paradigmaticity. In discourse where phasal polarity scenarios are expressed by specific constructions and not periphrases nor context-induced interpretations, the Standardized Adamawa Fula system possesses various strategies that are subject to certain (partly interacting) restrictions. In contrast, the Adamawa Fula Communis system shows a tendency toward entire paradigmaticity with phasal polarity items that share the same categorical status ('adverbs') and syntactic behavior (clause-final slot), and whose occurrence in the corresponding affirmative and negative paradigms is at least a paradigmatic variant in the Adamawa Fula Communis continuum.

According to Lehmann (1995), paradigmaticity is one main factor of grammaticalization. Paradigmaticity concerns the "cohesion of a sign with other signs in a paradigm" (Lehmann 1995: 123). Thus, with increasing grammaticalization, the size of the paradigm that a specific item belongs to is reduced, whereby the formal and functional homogeneity of the paradigm increases and differences with which the paradigm members were equipped originally are levelled out (Lehmann 1995: 132–135). With regard to the paradigmaticity parameter (in the sense of Lehmann 1995: 164), the phasal polarity system of Adamawa Fula Communis hence shows tendencies towards processes of increased grammaticalization.

In this paper, I cannot, at least yet, present a definitive answer regarding the reasons for these paradigmaticity tendencies in Adamawa Fula Communis. It is likely that the various L1/L2 backgrounds of speakers who use Adamawa Fula Communis as a vehicular language play an important role in this paradigmatization process. The question is whether the phasal polarity system's paradigmatization is due to a general tendency of L2 speakers to 'simplify' more intricate and non-paradigmatic expression strategies, or whether it is a result of contact-induced grammaticalization. At least some of the contact languages of the Adamawa Fula Communis area make use of clause-final items (particles) to signal phasal polarity concepts; e.g., Mundang ɓà STILL/NOT YET (Elders 2000), Tupuri ɗa STILL/NOT YET (Ruelland 1988; 2003), Moloko fa(n) ALREADY/NOT YET (Friesen et al. 2017), Fali bak STILL/NO LONGER (own field notes), and possibly also Mada vvad STILL/NO LONGER (own field notes; Barreteau/Brunet 2000), Ngaoundéré Mbum ɓay STILL/NOT YET (own field notes), and Dii ɓɛt STILL/NO LONGER (own field notes). The few phasal polarity data available for languages of the northern Cameroonian area may raise the question whether particles appearing in the clause-final slot (like other pragmatic markers such as negative and question particles) are major grammatical means for expressing phasal polarity, and whether these phasal polarity systems actually affect phasal polarity variants of Adamawa Fula Communis.

Abbreviations

(D)O, BE, NGEL . . .	noun form classes	LOC	locative
		MID	middle voice
1, 2, 3 . . .	agreement classes	NEG	negative
ANT	Anterior	OBJ	object pronoun
CNJ	Conjunction	PAS	passive voice
COP	Copula	PFV	perfective
DEM	demonstrative	PL	plural
EMPH	Emphatic	POS	possessive pronoun
EXCL	Exclusive	PREP	preposition
FOC	Focus	Q	question marker
IDEF	Indefinite	REV	reversive
IFV	imperfective	SG	singular
INCL	Inclusive	TOP	topic
INF	Infinitive		

Bibliographic references

Arnott, David W. 1970. *The nominal and verbal systems of Fula*. Oxford: Clarendon Press.
Barreteau, Daniel & André Brunet. 2000. *Dictionnaire Mada: Langue de la famille tchadique parlée dans l'Extrême-Nord du Cameroun*. (Sprache und Oralität in Afrika, 16.) Berlin: Reimer.

Bible Society of Cameroon. 2013. *Fulfulde bible (FB): Fulfulde (Adamawa)*. https://www.bible.com/de/versions/906-fb-fulfulde-bible (accessed 06 April 2019).

Boutché, Jean Pierre. Forth. Fula spoken in the City of Maroua (Northern Cameroon): A sociolinguistic insight into its use by non-ethnic speakers. (Beiträge zur Afrikaforschung; 85). Münster (et al.): LIT Verlag.

Boutché, Jean Pierre. Forth. The spread of Fula as lingua franca in Northern Cameroon: Social factors and linguistic outcomes, in Friederike Lüpke (ed.): Oxford guide to the world's languages: Atlantic. Oxford: Oxford University Press.

Elders, Stefan. 2000. *Grammaire Mundang*. Leiden: Research School of Asian, African, and Amerindian Studies, Leiden University.

Friesen, Dianne, Mana Djeme Isaac, Ali Gaston & Mana Samuel. 2017. *A grammar of Moloko*. (African Language Grammars and Dictionaries; 3). Berlin: Language Science Press.

Garrido, Joaquín. 1992. Expectations in Spanish and German adverbs of change. *Folia Linguistica* 26 (3–4). 357–402.

Gottschligg, Peter. 2006. Elaboration and simplification in Fula verbal morphology. In Bernard Caron & Petr Zima (eds.), *Sprachbund in the West African Sahel* (Collection Afrique et Langage; 11), 145–165. Louvain/Paris: Peeters.

Heine, Bernd & Tania Kuteva. 2002. *World lexicon of grammaticalization*. Cambridge (et al.): Cambridge University Press.

Heine, Bernd & Mechthild Reh. 1984. *Grammaticalization and reanalysis in African languages*. Hamburg: Buske.

Jungraithmayr, Hermann & Al-Amin Abu-Manga. 1989. *Einführung in die Ful-Sprache*. (Sprache und Oralität in Afrika; 1) Berlin: Reimer.

Kassühlke, Rudolf, Philippe Manikasset, Leslie H. Stennes & Alliance biblique du Cameroun. 1995 [1983]. *Deftere Allah: Alkawal 'Booymawal bee Alkawal Kesal*. New ed. Yaoundé: Alliance biblique du Cameroun.

Klingenheben, August. 1963. *Die Sprache der Ful (Dialekt von Adamaua): Grammatik, Texte und Wörterverzeichnis*. Hamburg: Augustin.

Kramer, Raija. 2017 [2012]. On canines, classes and concordances: Linguistic variation and norm development in Fulfulde varieties of Ngaoundéré (Adamawa region, Cameroon). In Klaus Beyer & Raija Kramer (eds.), *Language Change under Multilingual Conditions: Case studies from Africa* (Frankfurter afrikanistische Blätter; 24), 29–50. Cologne: Köppe.

Kramer, Raija. 2017. Position paper on Phasal Polarity expressions. Hamburg: University of Hamburg. https://www.aai.uni-hamburg.de/afrika/php2018/medien/position-paper-on-php.pdf (accessed 06 April 2019).

Kramer, Raija. 2018. The role of central actors in distribution processes of linguistic variants: A multiple group analysis of motorcycle garages in Ngaoundéré (Cameroon). Paper presented at the World Congress of African Linguistics (WOCAL) 9, Mohammed V University of Rabat, Morocco, 25 August. Unpublished.

Lehmann, Christian. 1995. *Thoughts on grammaticalization*. (LINCOM studies in theoretical linguistics; 01). Munich/Newcastle: LINCOM EUROPA.

Löbner, Sebastian. 1989. German *schon – erst – noch*: An integrated analysis, *Linguistics and Philosophy* 12/2: 167–212.

Mittoch, Anita. 1993. The relationship between schon/already and noch/still: A reply to Löbner. *Natural Language Semantics* 2. 71–82.

Mohamadou, Aliou. 1985. *La morphologie du constituant nominal en fulfulde: Parlers de l'Aadamaawa*. Paris: Université de la Sorbonne Nouvelle, INALCO dissertation.

Mous, Maarten. 2007. Language documentation as a challenge to description. Talk presented at Annual Conference on African Linguistics 38, Gainesville (Florida). http://home.planet.nl/~gongg010/veldwerk/Language%20documentation%20as%20a%20challenge_article.pdf (accessed 06 April 2019).
Mufwene, Salikoko S. 2001. *The ecology of language evolution.* Cambridge (et al.): Cambridge University Press.
Noye, Dominique. 1974. *Cours de foulfouldé: Dialecte peul du Diamaré, Nord-Cameroun, grammaire et exercises, textes, lexiques peul-français et français-peul.* Maroua [et al.]: Mission Catholique [et al.].
Pelletier, Corinne A. & A. Neil Skinner. 1979. *Adamawa Fulfulde: An introductory course.* Madison: Dept. of African Languages and Literature, University of Wisconsin-Madison.
Ruelland, Suzanne. 1988. *Dictionnaire Tupuri-français-anglais: Région de Mindaoré – Tchad.* (Langues et cultures africaines; 10). Paris: Peeters.
Ruelland, Suzanne. 2003. Verbes, auxiliaires et déplacements dans l'espace en tupuri. In Stéphane Robert (ed.), *Perspectives synchroniques sur la grammaticalisation: Polysémie, transcatégorialité et échelles syntaxiques,* 127–147. (Collection Afrique et langage; 5). Louvain: Peeters.
Hans-Jürgen Sasse (ed.): *Aspektsysteme.* (Arbeitspapiere; 14). Cologne: Institut für Sprachwissenschaft.
Sasse, Hans-Jürgen. 1991. *Aspektsysteme.* Arbeitspapier 14 (n.F.), Cologne.
Segerer, Guillaume & Konstantin Pozdniakov. Forth. Genealogical classification of Atlantic languages. In Friederike Lüpke (ed.): Oxford guide to the world's languages: Atlantic. Oxford: Oxford University Press.
Stennes, Leslie H. 1967. *A reference grammar of Adamawa Fulani.* [East Lansing:] African Studies Center, Michigan State University.
Taylor, Frank W. 1953. *A Grammar of the Adamawa dialect of the Fulani Language (Fulfulde).* 2nd ed. Oxford: Clarendon Press.
Theil, Rolf. 2008. *Fulfulde: Grammatik over dialekten i 'Aadamaawa.* 7th ed. Oslo: Unipub AS.
Van Baar, Theodorus Martinus. 1997. *Phasal polarity.* Amsterdam: IFOTT.
van der Auwera, Johan. 1993. 'Already' and 'still': Beyond duality. *Linguistics and Philosophy* 16 (6). 613–653.
van der Auwera, Johan. 1998. Phasal adverbials in the languages of Europe. In Johan van der Auwera & Dónall P.O. Baoill (eds.), *Adverbial constructions in the languages of Europe,* 25–145. Berlin/New York: Mouton de Gruyter.

Klaudia Dombrowsky-Hahn
Phasal polarity expressions in Bambara (Mande): Pragmatic distinctions and semantics

1 Introduction

This contribution is a case study on phasal polarity expressions in the West African Mande language Bambara or Bamanankan (Glottocode: bamb1269, ISO 639–3), more precisely in the standard variety of Bambara spoken in Mali.[1] According to Van Baar, "expressions of phasal polarity are structured means of expressing polarity in a sequential perspective" (Van Baar 1997: 40). The basis is thus the phasal order of events, and the expressions involve "reference points at two related phases implying situations which are contrasted as opposites with different polarity values" (Kramer 2017: 1).

The following sentence pairs contrasted by their polarity illustrate phasal polarity expressions in Bambara.

(1) à   nà-na   só   kàbán   wà?
    3SG come-PFV.ITR.AFF home already Q
    'Has s/he already come home?'

(2) àyi, à   má   nà   fɔ́lɔ.
    No 3SG PFV.NEG come yet
    'No, s/he has not come yet.'

---

1 I am indebted to the organizers of the International Conference on Phasal Polarity in Sub-Saharan African Languages, Raija Kramer and Roland Kießling for having invited me to participate in this stimulating event. Many thanks are due also to the organizer of a meeting of the Cercle Linguistique de Bamako, Ibrahima Cissé, who gave me the opportunity to present a different aspect of the topic before a Bambara-speaking audience in Bamako at the end of February 2018. I am grateful to the participants of both events for their questions and remarks. I am very grateful to Valentina Serreli, University of Bayreuth, and Francesco Zappa, Sapienza University, Rome, for their views about a possible Arabic origin of háli bì and hálisà. I would like to express my deepest gratitude to my consultants M. Traoré, Aïssé Touré and Salabary Doumbia for their time and patience. Many thanks to the two reviewers whose comments helped me to improve the paper. All shortcomings are my responsibility.

Klaudia Dombrowsky-Hahn, University of Bayreuth

https://doi.org/10.1515/9783110646290-011

(3) À bέ   só   **háli bì**   wà?
    3SG COPLOC home even today Q
    'Is s/he still at home?'

(4) àyi, à tέ   só **túgun**.
    No 3SG COP.NEG home no.longer
    'No, s/he is no longer at home.'

For each of the phasal polarity expressions, Bambara speakers have more than one item at their disposal, namely:
(a) *kàbán* and *kélèn*, specialized as ALREADY-expressions
(b) *fɔ́lɔ*, *bán*, specialized as NOT YET-expressions
(c) *túgun* and *bìlen*, specialized as NO LONGER-expressions
(d) *hálisà* (or *háli sà*) and *háli bì*, *túgun* and, rarely, *bìlen*, specialized as STILL-expressions.

All the phasal polarity elements occur in clause-final position; they may precede a particle such as the interrogative *wà* in an interrogative clause; *hálisà* and *háli bì* can be moved to the initial position in some types of clauses.

The variation for the respective phasal polarity expression can be considered as *allolexy*. The term allolexy was coined by van der Auwera (1998: 77) in analogy to "allophony" and "allomorphy" to give an account of synonyms of phasal polarity expressions that are not simply due to different phonological shapes of one underlying form. The allolexy of individual phasal polarity expressions in Bambara raises the question whether an explanation for this variation can be found. There are several possibilities. First, the different items may be originally geographical variants; second their use may be pragmatically determined; or, third, they may originate from different sources. The aim of the paper is therefore to study especially the two latter questions, the pragmaticity and the sources of the phasal polarity expressions. First, the question of pragmaticity will be examined. Based on van der Auwera's Double Alternative Hypothesis (van der Auwera 1993), Van Baar (1997) proposes studying phasal polarity expressions in different situational contexts, which he names the neutral and the counterfactual scenarios. The tools found across languages to mark phasal polarity in counterfactual scenarios are intonation, the use of the same items as in neutral scenarios, specialized items, the combination of items, or additional coding. I will discuss extracts from Bambara texts that represent neutral scenarios on the one hand and counterfactual scenarios on the other hand.

Next, the sources of the phasal polarity expressions in Bambara will be identified. Crosslinguistic studies have shown that phasal polarity expressions have either system-internal, system-external but language-internal, or language-external origins. Not all items found as phasal polarity expressions in Bambara are of Mande origin, for *hálisà* and *háli bì* show the borrowed element *háli*. Most items can be shown to have also other functions in the language, suggesting language-internal origin of the phasal polarity expressions. I posit that the formal resemblance between items used as phasal polarity expressions and similar words in the language arose from different sources as a result of different processes of grammaticalization. Therefore, the Bambara sources will be identified and subsequently discussed in the light of Van Baar's crosslinguistic findings on the sources of phasal polarity expressions. It will also be shown that some of the items originate in other expressions of the phasal polarity system.

The paper is structured as follows. I will start with some notes on the structure of Bambara (section 2). They may facilitate the understanding of the sections on phasal polarity proper for readers who are not familiar with the language. Section 3 is dedicated to the expression of pragmatic distinctions. In section 4 the sources of the Bambara phasal polarity expressions will be identified. The final section provides a summary of the findings.

The data used in the present paper come from different sources: grammars, dictionaries, published printed texts, the digital Bambara Reference Corpus Bamadaba (Bailleul et al. (2011–2018), and, last but not least, information gathered with two consultants from Bamako, M. Traoré and Aïssé Touré. The sources of sentences originating from the Bambara Reference Corpus are indicated in the form of a html-address; sentences lacking an indication of a source were elicited in working sessions with the language consultants.

2 The Bambara language

In this section, I discuss typological aspects of Bambara insofar as they are needed for the understanding of the principal part of this article.

Bambara is a variety of the so-called Manding dialect continuum, spoken mainly in Mali. Next to several L1 varieties, a standardized variety plays a leading role as lingua franca all over the country. Bambara shows S(O)V(X) word order, in which the OV sequence is very strict. X refers to obliques and more peripheral elements. Morphemes that follow the subject NP, generally called predicate markers in Mande language studies, constitute the TMA-system of the language. This system distinguishes basically a perfective, an imperfective and a progressive aspect and two future tenses. However, the observation of a strong interaction between aspect and tense has been interpreted as the ongoing evolution from an aspectual to a temporal system (Idiatov 2000). In independent clauses, predicate markers or verbal suffixes are obligatory constituents. They are portmanteau morphemes that cumulate a TMA value and polarity. Table 1 summarizes the affirmative predicate markers and the single existing suffix and the corresponding negative morphemes appearing in clauses with a verbal predicate.

Table 1: Affirmative and negative predicate markers in clauses with a verbal predicate.

TAM	affirmative	gloss	neg.	gloss
transit. perfective	ye	PFV.TR.AFF	ma	PFV.NEG
intransit. perfective	-ra~-la~-na	PFV.ITR.AFF	ma	PFV.NEG
imperfective	bɛ	IPFV.AFF	tɛ	IPFV.NEG
future (intentional[2])	bénà	FUT.AFF	ténà	FUT.NEG
future (assertive)	na	FUT.ASS.AFF	ténà	FUT.NEG
subjunctive	ka	SBJV.AFF	kànâ	SBJV.NEG

In transitive clauses, predicate markers are inserted between the subject and the object NPs (5)–(6). In intransitive clauses, all TMA values but the perfective affirmative are marked by predicate markers that follow the unique obligatory nominal term (7)–(8); the perfective affirmative is replaced by a suffix -ra (or one of its allomorphs -la, -na) (9).

(5) cὲ-` ye mùso-` wéle.
 man-ART PFV.TR.AFF woman-ART call
 'The man has called the woman.'

(6) mùso-` ye cὲ-` wéle.
 woman-ART PFV.TR.AFF man-ART call
 'The woman has called the man.'

(7) dén-` kàna kàsi.
 child-ART SBJV.NEG cry
 'The child shouldn't cry ~ May the child not cry.'

---

[2] Idiatov (2000) calls this value also 'deontic or prospective'

(8) dén-` má kàsi (só-` kɔ́nɔ).
    child-ART PFV.NEG cry house-ART PP
    'The child didn't cry (in the house).'

(9) dén-` kàsi-ra (só-` kɔ́nɔ).
    child-ART cry- PFV.ITR.AFF house-ART PP
    'The child cried (in the house).'

As demonstrated by examples (5)–(6), grammatical relations are indicated by word order alone; there is no case marking, nor is there any indexation of the subject or the object on the verb. Oblique arguments (10) and more peripheral terms indicated in parentheses in (8) and (9) are marked by means of postpositions; there are also some prepositions used to introduce more peripheral terms.

(10) à màga-ra ń bólo-` lá.
     3SG touch-PFV.ITR.AFF 1SG arm-ART PP
     'It touched my arm.'

Next to clauses with verbal predicates, Bambara has several types of clauses with nonverbal predicates. Possible predicates in such clauses are nouns or NPs, adjectives (Dumestre (2003: 171), called "quality verbs" by Vydrin (2019) and "state verbs" by Creissels (1985)), and locative phrases. In these clauses, distinct copulae connect the subject to the predicate. They are listed in Table 2 together with their negative counterparts and illustrated in (11)–(14). The presentative clauses with dòn (neg. té) are more specifically thetic clauses lacking the bipartition into subject and predicate (11).

Table 2: Copulae in clauses with nonverbal predicates.

clause type	affirmative	gloss	negative	gloss
presentative	dòn	COPID	té	COP.NEG
equational	yé	COPEQU	té	COP.NEG
locative	bɛ́	COPLOC	té	COP.NEG
qualifying	ká	QUAL.AFF	mán	QUAL.NEG

(11) Presentative clause
    a. *fàli-`*   *dòn.*   b. *fàli*   *té.*
       donkey-ART COPID   Donkey   COP.NEG
       'This is a donkey.'   'This is not a donkey.'

(12) Equational clause
    a. *ń*   *dénkɛ-`*   *yé*   *kàlanden yé.*
       1SG son-ART COPEQU student   PP
       'My son is a student.'
    b. *Ń*   *dénkɛ-`*   *té*   *kàlanden yé.*
       1SG son-ART COP.NEG student   PP
       'My son is not a student.'

(13) Locative / existential clause
    a. *wáraba-`*     *bé*      *kúngo-`*   *lá.*
       lion-ART   COPLOC   wilderness- ART   PP
       'The lion is in the wilderness. ~ There is a lion in the wilderness.'
    b. *wáraba-`*   *té*      *kúngo-`*   *lá.*
       lion-ART   COP.NEG wilderness- ART PP
       'The lion is not in the wilderness.'
    c. *wáraba té*   *kúngo-`*   *lá*
       lion   COP.NEG wilderness- ART PP
       'There is no lion in the wilderness.'

(14) Qualifying clause
    a. *fòronto-`*   *ka*      *fárin.*   b. *fòronto-`*   *mán*   *fárin.*
       chili-ART QUAL.AFF hot   chili-ART QUAL.NEG hot
       'The chili is hot.'   'The chili is not hot.'

The locative type of clause is the source concept of several other, more abstract concepts, such as predicative possession (15) and physical (16) or mental experience constructions (17).

(15) *wári-`*   *bé*   *ń*   *bólo.*
     money-ART COPLOC 1SG PP
     'I have money.'

(16) *kɔ́ngɔ-`*   *b'*   *ù*   *lá.*
     hunger-ART COPLOC 3PL PP
     'They are hungry.'

(17) à tɔ́gɔ-` tɛ́ ń kɔ́nɔ bìlen.
    3SG name-ART COP.NEG 1SG PP no.longer
    'I have forgotten her name (lit. her name is not inside me anymore).'

Clauses with nonverbal predicates have present time reference, unless they are marked by the inactuality operator *tùn* or, especially in narrative texts, when an introductory sentence is marked by *tùn* locating the entire situation in a context in past time. *tùn* can also appear in verbal clauses. In independent clauses, it produces past meaning; in the subordinated clauses of complex sentences, it creates a pluperfect reading.

The presentative/existential, the locative copulae and the deictic identifier (*filɛ*, derived from the homonymous verb 'observe, watch' and which does not have a negative counterpart) are used together with the perfective participle[3] *V-len* to form resultative or perfect aspect.

(18) fɔ́lɔ-` jà-len bɛ́, jí fóyi tɛ́ à lá
    first-ART dry-PTCP COPLOC 1SG not.any COP.NEG 3SG PP
    [The child saw three wells]. The first was dry, there was no water at all in it. (04dinye_yaalala.dis.html)

Further aspectual values such as the progressive, continuative, iterative, prospective, and modal values such as the deontic and obligative are obtained by means of periphrases based on the basic clause types listed above[4] or by the use of auxiliaries grammaticalized to varying degrees (cp. Dumestre 1999; Idiatov 2000: 39–44).

The infinitive, which corresponds to the citation form of a verb, bears the infinitive morpheme *kà* (*k'* before a pronoun with initial vowel). In the citation form of intransitive verbs, the verb immediately follows the infinitive morpheme; transitive verbs are preceded by a pronoun replacing a possible object argument, and reflexive verbs by the pronoun of the second person singular standing for a pronoun coreferential with the subject referent.

kà síran   kà à bùgɔ [k'à: bùgɔ]   kà í sìgi
'be afraid' 'hit him/her/it'   'sit down'
(Dumestre 1987: 419)

---

[3] "Resultative" participle in Vydrin's terms (Vydrin 2019)
[4] For details, see Idiatov (2000).

The infinitive takes part in a series of constructions, among others, consecutive constructions. In the latter, only the first clause is complete, bearing a subject and a predicate marker or verbal suffix (Dumestre 1987: 421–444), while the consecutive clause is introduced by the infinitive morpheme (19).

(19) í   b'   ò   bɔ́   k'   ò   fili
     2SG IPFV.AFF AN take.out INF AN throw.away
     'You take it outside and throw it away'

3 Pragmatic distinctions in the expression of phasal polarity

According to Van Baar's definition of phasal polarity, only structured means that express polarity in a sequential perspective can be considered to be expressions of phasal polarity (Van Baar 1997: 40–41). As shown in the affirmative/negative pairs of Bambara sentences (1)–(4) in the introduction, a "small paradigm" is available to Bambara speakers to express phasal polarity. The polarity is expressed in sequential perspective, doing justice to the essential second and third features of the definition. Thus, a positive situation related to the negative preceding situation is marked by means of *kàbán*, an ALREADY-expression. For a positive situation related to the negative subsequent situation, one of the following items is used in an affirmative clause: *hálisà*, *háli bì*, *túgun* or *bìlen*; they can be considered to be STILL-expressions. On the negative side there are *bán* and *fɔ́lɔ* as NOT YET-expressions which relate a negative situation to a positive subsequent situation and *túguni* and *bìlen* as NO LONGER-expressions which relate a negative situation to a preceding positive situation. The phasal polarity is organized in a symmetric way, where all four phases "carry equal weight, i.e. STILL and NOT YET are conceptualized as unbound stretches of positive or negative situations at reference time, whereas ALREADY and NO LONGER are conceptualized as stretches of positive or negative situations bound to their beginning" (Kramer 2017: 10).

Bambara not only possesses phasal polarity expressions; there also exist several items for each phasal polarity expression. Next to dialectal variation this suggests the existence of a pragmatically determined difference between a neutral and a counterfactual scenario (Van Baar (1997), Kramer (2017)). Van Baar illustrates pragmatic differences by outlining diverse scenarios according to the temporal localization of the relevant situation. Thus, the Speaker who uses a phasal polarity expression relates a situation either to "the opposite situation *at an earlier/later stage*, or to an opposite situation *at the same time* which has somehow been evoked in the discourse", or which is present in the Speaker's or the Addressee's mind as an alternative to the factual situation (Van Baar 1997: 41, emphasis mine). According to Van Baar (1997: 30) the distinction between a neutral and a counterfactual scenario can be decided upon only by the determination of the correct context. The reason is that languages do not obligatorily mark formally the distinction between the two scenarios. Van Baar (1997: 134) identifies four ways of expressing the second scenario: A) a basic phasal polarity item is used as a copy of the first, the neutral scenario; B) there is a basic phasal polarity item different from the one used in the neutral scenario; it is unique to the second, the simultaneously counterfactual scenario; C) first scenario basic phasal polarity items are combined to form a unique association; D) additional coding is used to mark the second scenario. Additionally, a particular sentence intonation can be used to mark the distinction between the neutral and the counterfactual scenario. Thus, the intonation in the second scenario can signal surprise, while there is no surprise in a neutral scenario (Van Baar 1997: 30).

In the following, I will examine the Bambara mechanisms for each of the expressions of phasal polarity involving temporal-sequentially related phases on the one hand and simultaneous phases on the other hand. I have mainly identified two means by which Bambara speakers signal pragmatically different phasal polarity scenarios. The first one is the use of distinct items for the neutral and the counterfactual phasal polarity expressions; it concerns the two ALREADY-scenarios. The second mechanism is the accumulation of items used in neutral scenarios to signal more marked scenarios. I adopt van Baar's numbering 1, for the neutral, and 2, for the counterfactual expressions respectively, thus ALREADY1, ALREADY2, NOT YET1, NOT YET2, etc., and adapt his semantic representations to the Bambara examples.

3.1 Neutral and counterfactual scenarios of ALREADY

Neutral scenario of ALREADY (ALREADY1)

In a neutral scenario, the speaker uses an ALREADY element to express a situation that holds at the moment of reference implying its non-occurrence at a preceding phase. This is illustrated with sentence (20), extracted from the presentation of the writer's family, including its members who still live in the compound and those who left. Figure 1 visualizes this neutral ALREADY scenario.

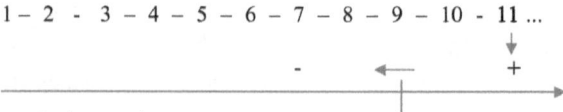

Figure 1: The neutral scenario of ALREADY.

(20) ń kɔ̀rɔmuso sàba bɛ́ɛ fúru-la kàbán,
1SG elder.sister three all be.married-PFV.ITR.AFF already
'All my three elder sisters are already married,
òlu tɛ́ ń fà-` ká dú-` kɔ́nɔ bìlen.
3PL.EMPH COP.NEG 1SG father-ART GEN compound-ART PP no.longer
they are no longer in my father's house.'
(Touré 1999: 76)

In the first clause 'all my three sisters are already married', the final *kàbán* (*kà bán*) contrasts the positive situation with the preceding time sequence at which the situation did not hold, i.e the sisters were not married (and were still living in the same compoud as the speaker). The numbers 1-2-3- . . . . represent a hypothetical time scale. The vertical dash signals the passage from one phase (the negative one) to another (the positive one). The positive polarity is indicated by (+), while the arrow pointing to the (-) reflects reference to the opposite, negative situation. In the concrete scenario, the current situation (the sisters being married) corresponds to the time marked as 11 on the scale, and the horizontal arrow signals reference to a previous time, here earlier than at point 9, which stands for the sisters' marriage as the transition from the negative (not being married) to the positive state (being married).

The item *kàkɔrɔ* is frequently translated by 'already', as well. However, it is not often likely to replace *kàbán* (nor *kélèn*). It is restricted to certain contexts, such as with the verb *dɔ́n* 'know' used in the imperfective aspect, and it maintains the idea of the source from which it derived, i.e. the verb *kɔ̀rɔ* 'be old' or 'date from a long time ago', so that a more appropriate translation is 'for a long time'. Therefore, the status of *kàkɔrɔ* as a phasal polarity item is questionable.

(21) án b' à dɔ́n fána kó
1PL IPFV.AFF 3SG know too That
sìginiden dɔ́-w núnnafɔ-len dòn kàkɔrɔ
letter some-PL nasalize-PTCP COPID already
'We know already that some letters (i.e. sounds) are nasalized.'
(776297 kibaru543_05konta-kalankene_nunnafoli.dis.html)

Another item, the verb *dèli kà V*, frequently translated by 'have already verbed' can definitely be excluded from the phasal polarity domain. When it combines with the suffix of the perfective, it is an auxiliary verb of the experiential perfect. However, it lacks the reference to a preceding opposite phase where the situation did not hold.

Counterfactual scenario of ALREADY (Already2)

For situations that are unexpectedly early when compared to the usual or original background situations, Bambara speakers use the word *kélèn*, hence a term that differs from the ALREADY1 item. (22) is uttered as a saying in a text by Oumar Diarra. A very young buffalo girl, still lacking in bodily strength because of her young age, provokes the strong evil buffalo Sìgidankelen to avenge her mother who had been hit and chased away by him into a dark forest. Sìgidankelen replies with this metaphorical warning saying that only just born, she must be tired of her life, since engaging in an argument with him equals her death. This saying is possible in situations in which a premature activity is being criticized.[5]

(22) ê   má   wólo   fɔ́lɔ,   dúnuya   nège-bɔ-ra
     2SG.EMPH   PFV.NEG   be.born   not.yet   world   desire-get.out-PFV.ITR.AFF
     ê   lá   kélèn   wà ?
     2SG.EMPH   PP   already   Q
     'You have not yet been born, but you have already got tired of the world?'
     (#127213 diarra-sigidankelen_ka_labanko.dis.html)

In order to visualise this counterfactual scenario, two lines are confronted with each other (see Figure 2). The dashed line reflects the presupposed scenario, the uninterrupted line the factual situation. The square represents a person's limited span on earth. According to experience, some humans get tired of their lives (*dúnuya*, lit. 'world') at a certain age, usually a long time after birth. This

---

5 Many thanks to Salabary Doumbia, who explained the context of the story to me and found a German equivalent to this saying: *keine Zähne im Maul aber La Paloma pfeiffen* '(you have) no teeth in the mouth but (want to) whistle La Paloma (a sailors' song)'. In spite of their resemblence, only the Bambara saying contains the phasal polarity expressions *fɔ́lɔ* and *kélèn*, stressing the simultaneous counterfactuality. In contrast, the German example expresses counterfactuality without a sequential perspective.

is signaled by the (+) somewhere within the square on the dashed line, i.e. the presupposed view.

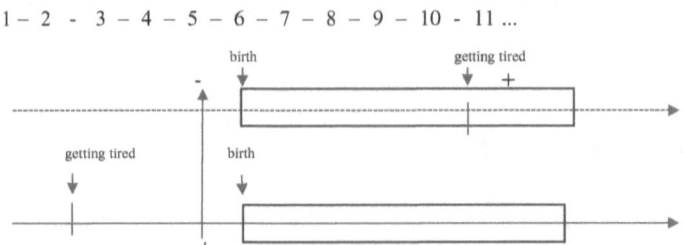

Figure 2: The counterfactual scenario of ALREADY.

In the factual situation, represented by the uninterrupted line, however, the tiredness occurs already before the person's birth, i.e. unexpectedly early when compared to the general life experience illustrated by the dashed line. The factual situation reflects a polarity opposition to the presupposed, i.e. counterfactual situation at moment 5 of the time-line.

The saying in (22) is an exaggerated way to point to a prematurely occurring situation. However, *kélèn* is not reserved to similar overstatements. It is heard in everyday conversations; frequently in contexts where a guest or visitor has to leave prematurely with regard to the host's expectation. An illustration is (23).

(23) A: í ká jèli-w y' ù sàra k' ù bɛ táa dɛ́
    2SG GEN griot-PL PFV.TR.AFF 3PL inform that 3PL IPFV.AFF go PRT
A: 'Your griots have announced that they are going to leave.'
B: ee, bàa, jèli-w k' ù bɛ táa kélèn?
    INTJ father griot-PL say 3PL IPFV.AFF go already
B: 'Oh, Dad, so the griots want to leave already?'
(#981587,sisoko-lamidu_soma.dis.html)

3.2 Neutral and counterfactual scenarios of STILL

The neutral scenario of STILL describes a situation that holds at the time of reference contrasted with a subsequent phase at which it does not hold. In the counterfactual scenario of STILL, the situation also implies the opposition to its non-occurrence; however, the opposed state-of-affairs is not situated at a later moment; it is rather contrasted with the opposite simultaneous presupposed or backgrounded situation.

Neutral scenario of STILL (STILL 1)

(24) àle   yé   dényɛrɛnin dè   yé. [. . .]
     3SG.EMPH COPEQU baby   FOC PP
     'It is a baby. [. . .]
     à   bɛ́   sín-`   ná háli bì.
     3SG COPLOC breast   PP even today
     'It is still being breastfed'.
     (Touré 1999: 76)

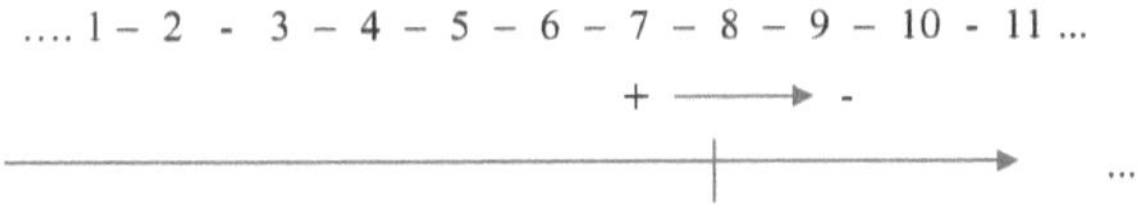

.... 1 – 2 - 3 – 4 – 5 – 6 – 7 – 8 – 9 – 10 - 11 ...
                         + ⟶ -
_____
                 | ⟶   ...

Figure 3: The neutral scenario of STILL.

In (24) *háli bì* is used in a neutral scenario. The speaker utters the sentence *à bɛ́ sín ná háli bì* 'it is still being breastfed' in order to stress the young age of his elder brother's last child. The situation of being breastfed (visualized by the vertical dash in Figure 3) is opposed to a later chain of events when the child will be grown older and will not be breastfed anymore (represented by the arrow pointing to the negative situation in Figure 3), and, in consequence, will not be considered a baby anymore.

Next to *háli bì*, *hálisà*, *túgun* and *bìlen* were found in the texts as phasal polarity expressions for the STILL1 value (STILL in neutral contexts). *túgunni* has the free alternants *túguni*, *túgun* and *tún*. The latter is represented in (25). *bìlen* or its free alternant *blɛ̀n* in positive clauses seems to be restricted to the Bambara variety spoken in Segu, and an example such as (26) was rejected as a STILL expression by the speakers from Bamako I asked, confirming the estimate that it is very little used in the variety spoken in Bamako (Masiuk 1994: 5). However, it is generally accepted as a NO LONGER item appearing in negative clauses (see section 3.4).

(25) nkà   ń   t'   à   dɔ́n   k'   à   fɔ́   à   bɛ́   bálo lá tún.
     but 1SG IPFV.NEG 3SG know INF 3SG say 3SG COPLOC life PP still
     '[. . .] but I don't know if she is still alive.'
     (banbera-faamanje_ni_faantanje.dis.html)

(26) ń   bɛ́   ò   báara   lá   bìlen,   ń   bɛ́   ò   báara   lá.
    1SG COPLOC DEM work   PP   still   1SG COPLOC DEM work   PP
    [My aunt taught me to do the painting with mud. Since that time I have not been able to abandon this work.] 'I am still doing it, I am doing it (lit. I am still at this work).' (basiya.dis.html)

tún (*túgun*) and *hálisà* are found in almost identical sentences (25) and (27), suggesting that they are free alternants. *hálisà* and *háli bì* tend to be used more frequently than the other two STILL-expressions.

(27) à   bálo-len   bɛ́   hálisà   wà ?
    3SG live-PTCP   COPLOC still   Q
    'Is she still alive?'

Counterfactual scenario of STILL (STILL2)

In a counterfactual scenario of STILL, the factual situation differs from the presupposed background situation as follows. The factual situation is late with respect to the expected view, evolving to a polarity opposition between the actual and the expected situation at the moment of reference. The illustration of a counterfactual scenario of STILL comes from the Bambara saying (28). It follows the statement that a slow horse has reached six villages. It is common sense that you do not continue to strain a weak animal if you want to keep it alive. The "common sense" or presupposed scenario reflected by the dashed line in Figure 4 includes a change of situation at moment 6 of the time line, representing for instance the arrival in the 6th village and at the same time the point at which the rider loses the snaffle and stops. The subsequent moments are characterized by the non-occurrence of the situation. Hence, tightening the snaffle beyond this moment in the factual situation (reflected ca. at time point 7) is late in the sense that loosening it and stopping was due to have occurred at time point 6. The vertical arrow reflects the polarity opposition of the actual situation in regard to the presupposed scenario.

(28) háli   bì   ê   kó   í   bɛ   nùgurɛjuru-ˋ   gɛ̀lɛya   bìlen !
    even   today 2SG.EMPH   say   2SG IFPV.AFF   snaffle-ART   tighten   still
    [A slow horse has already reached six villages]. 'But you still want to tighten the snaffle!'
    (Bailleul 2005: 289, proverb n°2905)

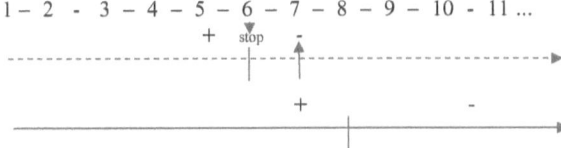

Figure 4: The counterfactual scenario of STILL.

An alternative to *háli bì . . . bìlen* in the counterfactual scenarios of STILL is simply *háli bì*, the phrase used in neutral scenarios, as well. As for the extended exponent *háli bì . . . bìlen*, I hypothesize *háli bì* to be the main exponent and *bìlen* the subsidiary one.[6] However, this hypothesis has to be examined for the variety spoken in Segu. Since *bìlen* is accepted there in neutral STILL scenarios, it is possible that speakers of this variety accept it as the only exponent of STILL in counterfactual scenarios, too.

3.3 Neutral and counterfactual scenarios of NOT YET

The two scenarios of NOT YET "are similar to those of STILL, with an inversion of the positive and negative values" (Van Baar 1997: 34). Their equivalents in Bambara will be illustrated in the two following sections.

Neutral scenario of NOT YET (NOT YET1)

NOT YET expressions used in a neutral scenario mark the non-occurrence of a situation at the reference point implying the opposite, i.e. its occurrence, at a later stage. The NOT YET expressions found in neutral scenarios in Bambara are *bán* and *fɔ́lɔ*. The answer in (29), meaning 'he has not come yet', bears the NOT YET item *fɔ́lɔ*, which can however be replaced by *bán*. The first speaker (A) asks a yes/no question signaling that they do not have a specific presupposition about Ntolofoori's presence. In the second speaker's (B) answer, the absence of Ntolofoori's coming, marked as the (–) in Figure 5 is referred to his arriving at a later phase, marked by the (+) in the figure.

---

6 According to Matthews, "in most instances of extended exponence it is possible to identify one formative as the main exponent" (Matthews 1991: 181). The other one can be considered as a subsidiary exponent.

(29) A: *Ntólofoori bɛ́   yàn dɛ́ ?* B: *àyi, à   má   nà   fɔ́lɔ.*
    Ntolofori COPLOC here PRT   no 3SG PFV.NEG come yet
    A: 'Is N. here?' B: 'No, he has not come yet.'
    (dukure-ni_san_cyenna.dis.html)

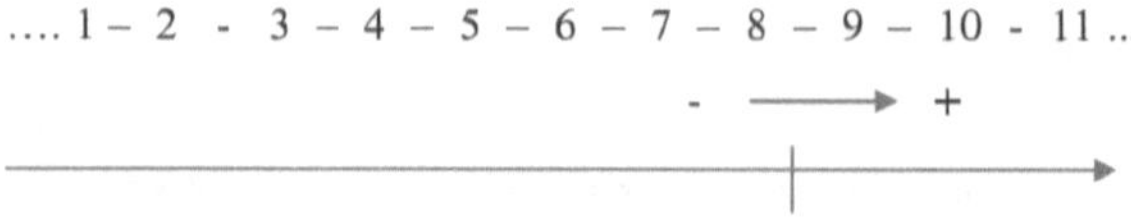

.... 1 – 2 - 3 – 4 – 5 – 6 – 7 – 8 – 9 – 10 - 11 ...
                         - ⟶ +

Figure 5: The neutral scenario of NOT YET.

Counterfactual scenario of NOT YET (NOT YET2)

In a NOT YET2 scenario, a negative situation is referred to a simultaneous opposite, positive situation. Sentence (30) illustrates a NOT YET2 scenario, using the extended exponent *háli bì . . . bán*. Like in NOT YET1 contexts, *bán* and *fɔ́lɔ* are interchangeable in NOT YET2 contexts, too.

(30) *nìn yé   kálo   sà-len   tlè mùgan dè yé*
     DEM COPEQU month die-PTCP day twenty FOC PP
     'The end of the month is 20 days ago,

     nkà   háli bì   án   ká   sàra-w   má   dí   bán.
     but   even today 1PL GEN wage-PL PFV.NEG give not.yet
     but we still have not got our wages (lit. our wages were not given).'
     (dukure-fatoya_ni_jigiya.dis.html)

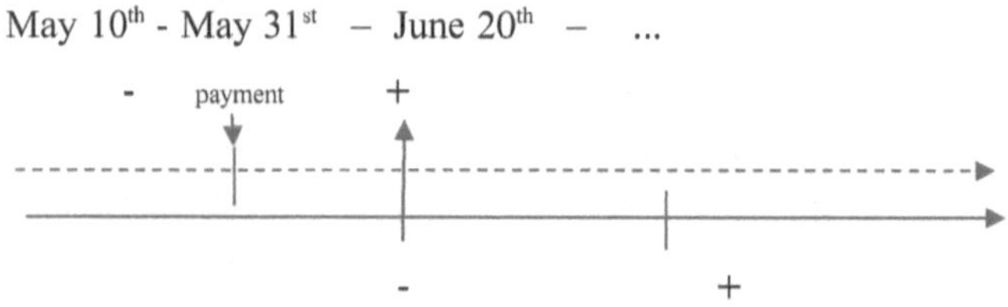

May 10th - May 31st – June 20th – ...
              - payment +
                         -         +

Figure 6: The counterfactual scenario of NOT YET.

The sentence is an explanation why the speaker, who is a worker, does not have any money. The dashed line in Figure 6 represents the generally expected situation: workers' wages are due at the end of a month, let's say May 31st. The factual situation mentioned in the text is the long overdue nature of the workers' wages, for the preceding month finished 20 days ago. Thus, the situation on June 20th (the wages were not paid) is opposed to what was expected for this time (the wages paid since May 31st). The vertical arrow connecting the (–) to the (+) signals the opposition between the presupposed and the factual situations at reference time (June 20th).

3.4 The expression of NO LONGER

Neutral scenario of NO LONGER

By using a NO LONGER expression (*túgun* or *bìlen* in Bambara), a speaker relates the absence of a situation to its occurrence at an earlier stage. An example is (31) saying that a woman stops giving birth at the age between 40 and 50, because she no longer undergoes (lit. 'sees') menstruation. The last clause is visualized in Figure 7, where the numbers above the time arrow represent a woman's age in years. At a point between 40 and 50 the menopause appears as a change of situation between the repeated occurrence of menstruation and its non-occurrence. The horizontal arrow relates the situation of the non-occurrence of the menstruation to the earlier stage in the course of life when menstruation still occurred.

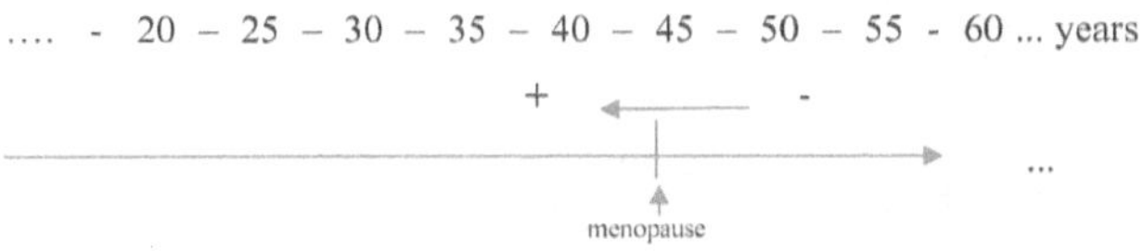

.... - 20 – 25 – 30 – 35 – 40 – 45 – 50 – 55 - 60 ... years

Figure 7: The neutral scenario of NO LONGER.

(31) [. . .] báwò   à   t'   à   ká   làada   yé   túguni
          because 3SG IPFV.NEG 3SG GEN menstruation see no.longer
    '[A woman stops giving birth at the age between 40 and 50],
    because she no longer undergoes menstruation.'
    (#584011,kibaru467_3konta-ce_san_bi_duuru.dis.html)

While the use of *bìlen* in affirmative clauses with the meaning of STILL is marginal and not accepted by the speakers I consulted, they agree with its use in negative sentences such as (32), meaning NO LONGER, even if they do not use it actively.

(32) bágan-w　kɔ̀ni　té　　à　　tá　yé　bìlen
　　　cattle　　TOP　COP.NEG　3SG　POSS　PP　no.longer
　　　'The cattle no longer belong to him. (lit.: are no longer his).'
　　　(217232 dumestre-manigances_2003_01.dis.html)

I have not found markedness distinctions in the expression of NO LONGER, therefore, only one scenario is considered here.

3.5 Summary: the Bambara phasal polarity system including pragmatic distinctions

Pragmatic distinctions are made by employing two mechanisms. The first one is the use of different elements for the neutral and the counterfactual scenarios; the second the cumulation of elements appearing in neutral phasal polarity-terms to mark counterfactual scenarios. The PhP system is summarized in Figure 8.

ALREADY 1	kàbán (kàkɔrɔ)
ALREADY 2	kélèn

NO LONGER 1	bìlen túgun
NO LONGER 2	

NOT YET 1	bán fɔ́lɔ
NOT YET 2 (‚still not')	háli bì ... bán háli bì ... fɔ́lɔ

STILL 1	háli bì, hálisà túgun (bìlen)
STILL 2	háli bì ...bìlen

Figure 8: The phasal polarity system including pragmatic distinctions.

The variation of items is determined pragmatically only in case of the ALREADY expressions. Thus, *kélèn* occurs for the ALREADY2 expression which differs from the ALREADY1 expressions *kàbán* and *kàkɔrɔ*, whereby the latter has only restricted usage. In the other cases the pragmatically more marked version consists of the cumulation of an item occurring for the respective unmarked expression and another one, which belongs to the phasal polarity system, too. Thus, *bán* and *fɔ́lɔ* occur in final position as NOT YET1 expressions; combined to the STILL item *háli bì* which in this case stands obligatorily in clause-initial position; they form NOT YET2, the more marked versions of NOT YET. While *bán* and *fɔ́lɔ* mark a negative situation that is referred to its opposite at a subsequent point, *háli bì* adds the notion of continuation and inclusion of the present moment. Similarly, *háli bì* is added to *bìlen* in an affirmative clause to yield the marked STILL2 expression. It is comparable to German *immer* added to *noch nicht* 'not yet' which yields the NOT YET2 expression *immer noch nicht*, and added to *noch*, the STILL2 expression *immer noch*, with the difference that *immer* is not part of the basic phasal polarity system in German. In contrast, counterfactual phasal polarity expressions in Bambara draw from the neutral phasal polarity-items, i.e. from the system itself.

4 The source concepts of the phasal polarity expressions in Bambara

The aim of this section is to discuss the origin of the Bambara phasal polarity expressions. Van Baar (1997: 80) establishes three possible kinds of origin: phasal polarity system-internal origin, phasal polarity system-external but language-internal origin, and language-external origin. According to van Baar (1997: 82) "relationships where a specific phasal polarity-item X re-appears in either or both of its polarity antagonists" are said to be phasal polarity-internal relationships. Items that have another language-internal origin are derived from non-phasal polarity expressions (van Baar 1997: 86). Phasal polarity expressions can also have language-external origin, this means they entered the language through borrowing.

Except for the words or phrases comprising *háli* as a constitutive element, the items of the phasal polarity-set arose from other words in the Bambara language, or even from the phasal polarity system itself. Because of the restricted space, I will identify them, without however discussing the difficult and controversial question of their assignment to word classes, a topic which will be dealt with in another paper.

We owe to Van Baar (1997) a list of sources of phasal polarity expressions, based on the results of his typological study. By identifying the sources of phasal polarity expressions in Bambara it is possible to state whether the language uses conceptualizations existing elsewhere, or whether it has developed its own new ways of expressing phasal polarity.

4.1 ALREADY

kàbán and *kàkɔrɔ*, the items expressing the positive polarity value ALREADY1, go back to van Baar's completion source. The author explains the plausibility of this source as follows. The ALREADY concept refers to a positive area with respect to a preceding negative one. Both areas are separated by a transition point. The use of the completion source imparts the information that the negative phase is finished or over (van Baar 1997: 87). The idea of finishing is manifest in *kàbán*. This item developed from the verb *bán* 'finish, terminate' which has maintained the infinitive morpheme *kà*. This element *kà* is discernible evidence that the form is based on the verb's occurrence as non-initial verb in a consecutive construction (cp. section 2). In a consecutive construction, an initial complete clause is followed by a non-finite consecutive clause, introduced by the infinitive morpheme *kà*. The consecutive clause itself lacks a subject and a predicate marker or verbal suffix. In some clauses containing *kà bán*, its status is ambiguous; it can be interpreted as a consecutive construction for instance in (33), and as phasal polarity expression 'already' in (34), distinguished only in the orthography by its spelling as two words or as one word. Its use in nonverbal clauses expressing states (35) and that are not generally combined with consecutive clauses[7] and with the verb *bán* itself (36) show that *kàbán* is not a verb anymore.

(33) *báara-ˋ   ké-ra   kà   bán.*
     work-ART   do- IPFV.AFF INF   terminate
     'The work has been done and has been terminated.'

(34) *báara-ˋ   ké-ra   kàbán*
     work-ART   do-IPFV.AFF   already
     'The work has already been done.'

(35) *móbili -ˋ   bé   Musa fɛ̀   kàbán*
     car-ART   COPLOC   Musa PP   already
     'Musa has a car already.'

(36) *filimu-ˋ   bán-na   kàbán*
     car-ART   COPLOC   already
     The film is already finished (*The film finished and finished).

As noted earlier, the status of *kàkɔrɔ* is not clear. It is added only to a few verbs, hence it is not (yet) specialized but possibly developing into a phasal polarity marker. *kàkɔrɔ* is based on the verb *kɔ̀rɔ* 'be old', indicating that the polarity

---

[7] There are exceptions, though. Dumestre (2003: 400–402) lists clause types with nonverbal predicates that allow being followed by an infinitive.

switch point is located a long time before the reference point. This lexical source in not unique crosslinguistically. In West Africa it is attested for instance in Ewe, where the adverb *xóxó* 'already' is related to the adjective *xóxó* 'old' and the noun *xó* 'ancient history' (van Baar 1997: 88).

The origin of the ALREADY2-expression *kélèn* is supposed to be the numeral 'one', *kélen*. The numeral 'one' has not been observed by Van Baar as a source of ALREADY-expressions. Actually, *kélen* 'one', meaning in other contexts 'same', is puzzling as the origin of the counterfactual *kélèn* 'already', all the more as 'one' appears in some languages as the source of STILL-expressions.[8] The explanation is that 'one' conveys the idea that the situation remains the same, is not changing, for STILL is used in "positive situations that have already been positive for a certain amount of time" (Van Baar 1997: 91). While it is easily perceivable why 'one' occurs as a source for STILL-expressions in the languages where this is the case, an explanation of the relation between 'one' and the ALREADY-concept is not available yet.

4.2 STILL

Crosslinguistically, van Baar (1997: 90–95) identifies several sources of STILL-expressions all of which are based on the concept of consistency or consistent extension. Some of them can also be identified in Bambara. One of the ways to express consistency is "to stress the continuation up to and including a specific point" (Van Baar 1997: 93). Such a point can be 'now' or another deictic element, for instance a proximate demonstrative 'this'. In Bambara, *háli bì* and *hálisà* (or *háli sà*) are elements expressing consistency including the present moment, where *háli* 'until' or 'even' expresses continuation and inclusion and *bì* and *sá* the temporal point 'today' and 'now'.

háli bì and *hálisà* are blendings: *háli* is borrowed from Arabic;[9] *bì* and *sá* are of Mande origin. The notion of continuation-and-inclusion originates from

---

8 The author cites Finnish *yhä* as an example, which is an old case-form of *yksi* 'one' (Van Baar 1997: 91).

9 The Arabic source of *háli* is unclear. According to Francesco Zappa (p.c.), a possible candidate is the word *ḥāl*, which has many meanings and is frequently used in Arabic. Its basic meaning is 'state, condition, case'. It does not have temporal sense, but can refer to a present situation. For instance, the adjective *ḥālī* derived from it is translated by 'current, present'. According to Wehr (1979: 216) *ḥāl* seems also to be used as a noun meaning 'present (as opposed to future)'. Although the origin of a word meaning 'state', stressing the consistency of a situation makes sense for Bambara *háli bì* and *hálisà*, it is difficult to imagine it as origin of *háli* 'even'. The Arabic equivalent of 'even' is *ḥatta* (Francesco Zappa, p.c.). Whether *ḥatta*

an Arabic item that is found in many other languages. Thus, a probable cognate of *háli* is not only attested in the West African language Hausa as *har yànzu* 'until now; still' (van Baar 1997: 93), but also in languages spoken outside the African continent, for instance the Nakh-Daghestanian language Lezgian *hele*, which borrowed it from Turkish *hâlâ~halen*, which itself borrowed it from Arabic (van der Auwera 1993: 631).

Next to continuation to a certain point, reiteration is another source of STILL-expressions, illustrated in Bambara by *túgun* and *bìlen*. In (37), *túgun* marks an iterative situation, i.e. the copy of an earlier situation, expressed by a dynamic verb in the perfective.

(37) à nà-na túgun.
    3SG come-PFV.ITR.AFF again
    'He came again (=he returned).'

In clauses encoding states, for instance (25), or marked for imperfective aspect (26), *túgun* and *bìlen* function as STILL-expressions.

4.3 NO LONGER

The NO LONGER-expressions are identical to the STILL-expressions *túgun* 'again, also' and *bìlen~blèn*. Crosslinguistically, repetitive / additive constructions are common sources for these two values. We can hypothesize that the NO LONGER-expression developed from the STILL-expression. In other words, this is an instance of system-internal origin.

4.4 NOT YET

Although *bán* 'not yet' lacks the infinitive morpheme *kà* of *kàbán* 'already', it is possible to hypothesize that it developed from the latter.[10] This development

---

should be considered the source of *háli* rather than *ḥāl* cannot be resolved here, for Bambara has certainly not borrowed the respective item(s) directly from Arabic. It is unknown through which language it passed before entering the Bambara vocabulary. In other, nonrelated languages in the region the equivalents of *háli* are Tamasheq *al*, *ar*, Songai *hala*, *har*, Fula *haa* (Vydrine 1999: 252).

10 See also Dumestre (2003: 328).

may have taken place in an early phase of the grammaticalization process, where *kà bán* was still conceived of as a consecutive clause. Consecutive constructions are common after an introductory affirmative clause; after an introductory negative clause, the infinitive *kà* is much less frequent, which may be the reason for *kà bán* to have been reduced to *bán*. The passage from a consecutive clause *kà bán* to the phasal polarity expression *kàbán* being fluid, I consider *bán* to have a phasal polarity system-internal origin.

The multivalent *fɔ́lɔ* can have the following meanings depending on the word class it represents: 'former times, in the past, previously; start with/by; first, for the moment being, at present'. As a phasal polarity expression it appears in a negative clause in final position. Occurring in the same position in affirmative clauses, this item means 'first, for the time being, at present, from now on'.

(38) Ø nà yàn fɔ́lɔ.
    IMP.AFF.SG. come here first
    'Come for the moment being ~ come first.' (Dumestre 2011: 339)

(39) án ná à tɔ̀ ké dògo lá fɔ́lɔ.
    2PL FUT.ASS.AFF 3SG rest do hiding PP first
    'We will do it (lit. its rest) secretely from now on.'[11] (Dumestre 2011: 339)

It is the expression of 'first, from now on' that is likely to be the origin of *fɔ́lɔ* 'not yet'. The phasal polarity is thus conceptualized as the opposition of a situation that is to occur/to begin in the future. The functioning of *fɔ́lɔ* is very similar to Hausa *tùkùna* 'first', which "only qualifies as a phasal polarity expression in negative contexts, whereas those expressions of *tùkùna* that occur in positive contexts fall outside the phasal polarity-domain" (Van Baar 1997: 53; Jaggar 2009: 65–66).

It is striking that the two allolexemes expressing NOT YET arise from lexemes that are opposite to each other: on the one hand, *bán*, whose direct source *kàbán* is grammaticalized from the verb *bán* 'finish', representing the completion source; on the other hand, *fɔ́lɔ* which, as a member of other word classes means, among others 'first, from now on, start with'. An explanation could be that these items focus on the two sides of the transition point between the

---

[11] Dumestre translates *fɔ́lɔ* in this sentence as 'désormais', 'from now on', one of my consultants as 'for the time being'.

negative phase representing the absence of the situation and the positive phase representing the situation that takes place in the future and which is the reference point for NOT YET. *bán* signals the absence of the completed transition from the negative to the positive situation referred to, *fɔ́lɔ* the absence of the future situation that is to come.

4.5 Summary: the origin of phasal polarity expressions in Bambara

The items that function as phasal polarity expressions in Bambara can be attributed to all three kinds of origin established by Van Baar (1997: 80). The ALREADY-expression *kàbán* and the NOT YET-expressions *bán*, and the STILL and NO LONGER-expressions *túgun* and *bìlen* are in a phasal polarity system-internal relationship of the NOT (X) shape to each other. *bán* 'not yet' is assumed to have developed from *kàbán* 'already' losing the infinitive morpheme *kà* of the consecutive construction it originates from and which is restricted to affirmative contexts.

The ALREADY1 expression *kàbán*, the ALREADY2 expression *kélèn*, the STILL-expressions *túgun* and *bìlen* and the NOT YET expression *fɔ́lɔ* have language-internal origin. The completion-concept (*kàbán*) is a well-known source for ALREADY-expressions, the repetitive (*túgun* and *bìlen*) is a well-known source for STILL expressions, and the item 'first' also appears in other West African languages for NOT YET-expressions. However, the 'one' origin for the counterfactual ALREADY seems to be an idiosyncratic element of Bambara up to now.

The STILL items *háli bì* and *hálisà* are not entirely borrowed; they are blended expressions, of which the continuation-and-inclusion part *háli* is borrowed, and the deictic elements *bì* 'today' and *sá* 'now' are items in the language itself.

5 Concluding remarks

I have shown that the allolexy of phasal polarity expressions in Bambara is due to their derivation from different sources. An exception is constituted by the items *túgun* and *bìlen*, meaning 'still' in affirmative and 'no longer' in negative clauses. Both developed from the term 'again'. They come originally from different dialects, and in the standard variety *bìlen* is well accepted as the negative expression NO LONGER but rejected as a STILL expression. The language-internal sources are resumed in Table 3, the phasal polarity system-internal sources in Table 4. Because of their mixed origin (Arabic and Mande), *háli bì* and *hálisà* figure in Table 3.

Table 3: Language-internal sources of phasal polarity-items in Bambara.

phasal polarity expression	concept		phasal polarity item	other elements in Bambara
ALREADY1	completion	end of negative phase	kàbán	bán 'terminate'
		past character of negative phase	kàkɔrɔ	kɔ̀rɔ 'be/get old'
ALEARDY2	oneness		kélèn	kélen 'one'
STILL	consistent extension	continuation-and-inclusion	háli bì	háli 'even' bì 'today'
			hálisà	háli 'even' sá 'now'
	repetition		túgun	túgun 'again'
			bìlen	bìlen 'again'
NOT YET	absence of future occurrence of the situation		fɔ́lɔ	fɔ́lɔ 'first, at present

Table 4: System-internal sources of phasal polarity-items in Bambara.

phasal polarity expression and item		source within phasal polarity system	
NOT YET	NEG + bán	AFF + kàbán	ALREADY
NO LONGER	NEG + túgun	AFF + túgun	STILL
NO LONGER	NEG + bìlen	AFF + bìlen	STILL

Pragmatic distinctions explain the allolexy only for *kàbán* (*kàkɔrɔ*) and *kélèn*, the ALREADY1 and ALREADY2 expressions. For STILL and NOT YET, Bambara speakers use rather the cumulation of items occurring for other expressions within the phasal polarity-domain.

Abbreviations

1, 2, 3	1st, 2nd, 3rd person	IMP	imperative affirmative singular
AFF	affirmative		
AN	anaphoric pronoun	INF	infinitive
ART	tonal article	INTJ	interjection
ASS	assertive	IPFV	imperfective
COP	copula	ITR	intransitive
COPEQU	copula in affirmative equational clause	NEG	negative
		PFV	perfective
COPID	copula in affirmative presentative clause	PL	plural
		POSS	possessum pronoun
COPLOC	copula in affirmative locative clause	PP	postposition
		PRT	particle
DEM	demonstrative	PTCP	participle
EMPH	emphatic	Q	interrogative particle
FOC	focus particle	QUAL	copula in qualifying clause
FUT	future	SG	singular
GEN	particle connecting possessee and possessed in genitive construction	SBJV	subjunctive
		TOP	topicalization particle
		TR	transitive

Bibliographic references

Bailleul, Charles. 2005. *Sagesse bambara. Proverbes et sentences*. Bamako: Donniya.

Bailleul, Charles, Artem Davydov, Anna Erman, Kirill Maslinsky, Jean Jacques Méric & Valentin Vydrin. 2011–2018. Bamadaba: Dictionnaire électronique bambara-français, avec un index français-bambara. http://cormand.huma-num.fr (accessed 04 January 2020).

Creissels, Denis. 1985. Les verbes statifs dans les parlers manding. *Mandenkan* 10. 1–32.

Dumestre, Gérard. 1987. *Le bambara du Mali: essais de description linguistique*. Paris: Université Paris III & INALCO dissertation.

Dumestre, Gérard. 1999. Des auxiliaires en bambara. *Mandenkan* 35. 1–16.

Dumestre, Gérard. 2003. *Grammaire fondamentale du bambara*. Paris: Karthala.

Dumestre, Gérard. 2011. *Dictionnaire bambara – français suivi d'un index abrégé français – bambara*. Paris: Karthala.

Idiatov, Dmitry. 2000. Le sémantisme des marqueurs aspecto-temporels du bambara: une tentative d'analyse. *Mandenkan* 36. 1–59.

Jaggar, Philip J. 2009. Quantification and polarity. Negative adverbial intensifiers ('never ever', 'not at all') in Hausa. In Norbert Cyffer, Erwin Ebermann & Georg Ziegelmeyer (eds.), *Negation patterns in West African Languages and Beyond*, 57–70. Amsterdam: John Benjamins.

Kramer, Raija. 2017. Position paper on Phasal Polarity expressions. Hamburg: University of Hamburg. https://www.aai.uni-hamburg.de/afrika/php2018/medien/position-paper-on-php.pdf (accessed 06 April 2019).

Masiuk, Nadine 1994. L'emploi des particules, des formes pronominales fortes, et de l'extraposition en bambara - parler de Bamako. *Mandenkan* 27. 1–110.
Matthews, Peter H. 1991. *Morphology*. Second edition. Cambridge: Cambridge University Press.
Touré, Mohamed 1999. *Bambara Lesebuch. Originaltexte mit deutscher und französischer Übersetzung. Livre de lecture Bambara. Textes originaux Bambara avec traductions allemandes et françaises* (Afrikawissenschaftliche Lehrbücher 11). Mit Zeichnungen von / avec illustrations de Melanie Leucht. Cologne: Köppe.
Van Baar, Tim. 1997. *Phasal polarity*. Amsterdam: IFOTT.
van der Auwera, Johan. 1993. 'Already' and 'still': beyond duality. *Linguistics and Philosophy* 16 (6). 613–653.
van der Auwera, Johan. 1998. Phasal adverbials in the languages of Europe. In Johan van der Auwera & Dónall P. Ó Baoill (eds.), *Adverbial constructions in the languages of Europe* (EUROTYP 3), 25–145. Berlin & New York: Mouton de Gruyter.
Vydrin, Valentin. 2019. *Cours de grammaire bambara*. Paris: Presses de l'Inalco.
Vydrin, Valentin. 1999. *Manding-English Dictionary (Maninka, Bamana)*. St. Petersburg: Dimitry Bulanin Publishing House.
Wehr, Hans 1979. *A dictionary of modern written Arabic (Arabic – English)*. Edited by J. Milton Cowan. Wiesbaden: Harrassowitz.

Georg Ziegelmeyer
What about phasal polarity expressions in Hausa – Are there any?

1 Introduction

This study examines a category of expressions in Hausa akin to *not yet*, *already*, *still*, and *no longer* and which henceforth will be referred to as phasal polarity. In her position paper Kramer (2017) argues that this category is well described in a bulk of European languages such as English, German, Dutch, French, or Russian, but so far in non-European languages, e.g. in most sub-Saharan African languages, this category has not received much attention. The questions which arise here in the first instance are: why is this so? Did former scholars of African languages simply neglect this category? Did they overlook it, or could it be the case that the category of phasal polarity simply does not exist in the bulk of African languages? While I could only speculate about African languages by and large, I will, nevertheless, argue that phasal polarity does not play a crucial role in Hausa.

Based on former studies, especially van der Auwera (1998), and Van Baar (1997), Kramer (2017) defines expressions like *not yet*, *already*, *still*, and *no longer* as phasal:

> [. . .] as they involve reference points at two related phases implying situations which are contrasted as opposites with different polarity values, i.e. one of the two situations in question holds (+) whereas the other does not (-). In other words, the expressions *already* and *still* in [. . .] signal that the state included in the proposition [. . .] is the case at reference time implying a further reference point at a prior (*already*) or subsequent (*still*) phase where this state is not the case [. . .]. Accordingly, the negative expressions *no longer* and *not yet* [. . .] mark the non-occurrence of the state [. . .] at reference time while implying a reference point at a prior (*no longer*) or subsequent (*not yet*) phase where this state holds [. . .]. Thus, Van Baar (1997:40) defines phasal polarity expressions as "structured means of expressing polarity in a sequential perspective". (Kramer 2017: 1)

While we find constructions in Hausa which have been translated by various linguists with our key expressions *not yet*, *already*, *still*, and *no longer*, it is, nevertheless, questionable whether the majority of these constructions really fall into the domain of phasal polarity.

Georg Ziegelmeyer, Universität Wien

https://doi.org/10.1515/9783110646290-012

Following typological approaches our methodology has been to look at various grammars, texts, and dictionaries of Hausa, and for comparative reasons also some grammars and dictionaries of other Chadic languages from different branches.[1] Not unsurprisingly, the first scrutiny revealed that phasal polarity is not a category which is treated separately in any of these grammars. In a second step we, therefore, looked at English (also German and French) translations containing one of the key words, i.e. *already, (not) yet, still*, and *no longer*. Our second scrutiny showed that there seems to be some bias within Chadic data with respect to the occurrence or non-occurrence of these key words. On the one hand, in Hausa studies[2] we do find the one or other notion of *already, (not) yet, still*, and *no longer*, however, in most cases these phasal polarity key words are used in rather free translations and do not necessarily always reflect the literal meanings of the constructions. On the other hand, the occurrence of our key words in studies on Chadic languages (except Hausa) are so minor that, at the stage where we are, it would be impossible to come up with a tentative hypothesis of the conceptualization of phasal polarity expressions in Chadic as a whole.

As already mentioned above, no major Hausa grammar[3] devotes special attention to the category of expressions which are referred to here as phasal polarity. This means, in order to deduce information, we had to search for key words in English translations in the respective grammars, dictionaries, and texts.[4] While tokens of our key words, of course, were found in grammars and dictionaries, it was quite surprising that they hardly appear in our text sample, i.e. in total three occurrences of 'already' (Hausa *rìgā* 'precede, have already done'), and not a single occurrence of 'still', '(not) yet', or 'no longer', respectively. Note that the text translations tend to be rather literal and do not intend to give carefully worded English sentences.

---

[1] According to Newman (1990) Chadic languages consist of four coordinate branches, viz. West, Biu-Mandara (=Central), East, and Masa (=Southern).

[2] Hausa is probably one of the best documented and analysed languages of sub-Saharan Africa.

[3] I consider the following grammars as the major Hausa grammars, which all appeared during the last 30 years: Jaggar (2001), Newman (2000), Wolff (1993).

[4] I looked at all translation files of Hausar Baka Volume 1–5, Bature & Schuh (2008). Hausar Baka is a set of 5 videotapes comprising about 5 hours of natural interaction in Hausa. Filmed in and around Kano, Nigeria, the more than 90 individual video segments show a broad range of cultural milieus, from domestic interaction in families through a tour of Daura, the site where, according to legend, the seven Hausa states originated. The segments are arranged in groups, beginning with greetings and simple question-answer dialogs, advancing through more complex interaction and narrative. Over fifty different individuals – men and women, children and adults – appear in the videos, representing a broad range of speaking styles.

Our observations leave us with the following question: do expressions of phasal polarity simply not exist in Hausa, and if so, how do Hausa speakers achieve similar semantic effects to what is expressed by specialized phasal polarity expressions in English, German, etc.? Trying to arrive at a possible and sound answer to this question presented in our conclusions (section 6), we first have to analyse the various Hausa constructions which were translated into English with one of our key words 'not yet' (section 2), 'already' (section 3), 'still' (section 4), and 'no longer' (section 5).

2 NOT YET in Hausa

The English phrasal adverbial construction *not yet* describes a situation that has not come into existence. In Hausa we primarily find the adverbial *tùkùn(n)a* = *tùkùn* 'first; (not) yet',[5] which most probably is a borrowing from neighbouring Kanuri *dùwô/dùwonyì* (old forms: *dùgô/dùgonyì*) 'first, before, though, although, (not) yet, etc.' (Cyffer & Hutchison 1990). This was first proposed in Hutchison (1975). The hypothesis is corroborated by the fact that many languages of the Wider Lake Chad Area (e.g. Chadic languages of Nigerian Borno and Yobe states, Shuwa Arabic) also use cognate forms to express FIRST; (NOT) YET.[6] That borrowed forms of *dùwô/dùwonyì* often retain the more original voiceless and voiced velars /k/ and /g/ shows that the borrowing process must have taken place during a period when consonant weakening in Kanuri was not yet active.[7] This probably was during a period when the Kanem-Borno Empire exercised its greatest power (i.e. 16th till 19th century).

In addition to this, syntactic properties outlined in Hutchison (1975) point out the fact that Kanuri's neighbouring languages not only borrowed forms of the adverbial *dùwô/dùwonyì*, but also copied the syntactic behaviour with its

---

[5] Transcription: *ā, ē, ī*, etc. = long vowel; *a, i*, etc. = short vowel; *ə* = high central vowel; *à* = low tone; *â* = falling tone; high tone is unmarked; ɓ, ɗ = laryngeal implosives; 'y = glottalized palatal glide; tl and jl = lateral fricatives, ř = apical tap/roll, c and j = palato-alveolar affricates.
[6] E.g.: Gashua Bade (*dùgo* 'still, first, (not) yet'), Western Bade (*dùwon(i)* 'but, still, first (not) yet'), Buduma (*dùgo* 'after'), Karekare (*dìgo* 'first'), Ngizim (*dəgo* = *dùgo* 'first, to start with, still, (not) yet'), Shuwa Arabic (*dugo* 'first, then'), and possibly Bole (*dòngo* 'first, to start with, (not) yet'), and Ngamo (*dòngô/dòngo* 'not yet').
[7] Thanks to the early Kanuri grammar of Koelle (1854) we are able to say that the weakening processes started to affect the language during the first half of the 19th century.

strictly clause-final syntax.[8] For instance, in Hausa adverbials usually have to be placed before the second discontinuous negation marker *ba*. Although there are some temporal adverbs that may occur either before, or after the second negation marker, it is quite remarkable that *tùkùna* practically is the sole adverb in Hausa which for many speakers has its position exclusively after the second negation marker.

Example 1 illustrates the prototypical use of Hausa *tùkùna* in sentence-final position, preceded by a negated statement. Note that *tùkùna* does not appear in our text sample, and therefore examples are taken from Newman (2000, 2007).

(1)   *bà*   *sù*   *dāwō*   *ba*   **tùkùna**
      NEG   3PL.PERF   return   NEG   first
      'They have**n't** returned **yet**.'
      (Newman 2007: 211)

What is a little surprising is that the adverbial *tùkùna* = *tùkùn* can be used alone, e.g. as a response to a question, meaning simply 'not yet' without any negating element being involved. This is shown in example (2).

(2)   Q: *yā*   *tàfi?*
            3M.PERF   go
      A: **tùkùna**
            first
      'Did he go? – **Not yet**'
      (Newman 2007: 211)

In Hausa, like in Kanuri and several other neighbouring languages which borrowed this adverb, *tùkùna* also functions as an expression of the notion 'first' in affirmative sentences (example 3).

(3)   *Bàri*   *mù*   *dūbằ*   **tùkùna**
      Let   1PL.SUB   look   first
      'Let's look **first** (and then do such and such).'
      (Newman 2007: 211)

---

8 Note that the Kanuri adverbial *dùwô/dùwonyì* has been subject to linguistic discussion for a long time. For other summary discussions see e.g. Hutchison (1975), or Ziegelmeyer (1999, 2008).

Newman (2000: 358) also points out that "the word *tùkùna* 'not yet' has variant forms, which for some speakers are syntactically limited to final position after *ba*", e.g. *tùkùn* or *tùkùnna*. This can be seen in examples 4 and 5.

(4) *Lādì   bà   tà   zaunà̄   ba   **tùkùn(na)***
    Ladi   NEG 3F.PERF sit.down NEG   first
    'Ladi has not sat down yet.' (lit. 'Ladi has not sat down first.')
    (Newman 2000: 358)

(5) **Lādì   bà   tà   zaunà̄   **tùkùn(na)** ba*
    Ladi   NEG 3F.PERF sit.down   first   NEG

Overall it appears to be difficult to classify *tùkùna* as a true phasal polarity expression, as it is not clear what inherent phasal or polarity values should be involved. As seen above the negation value is sometimes inherently involved, as in example (2), but most frequently it is not. In addition to this, its primary function most probably lies in a rather deictic temporal adverbial meaning 'first', but which (especially in Kanuri) has been extended into a variety of temporal, concessive, etc. domains. Last but not least, even if we imputed phasal polarity values to *tùkùna* constructions, we would be faced with hypothesis that they are borrowings from Kanuri and did not exist in Hausa at prior stages of language development.

According to Raija Kramer in her handout distributed during the Afrikanistentag in 2016[9] NOT YET-constructions in Hausa may also employ the preposition/conjunction *hař* 'until, up to, including' in combination with the temporal adverb *yànzu* 'now'. This is illustrated in examples 6 and 7. Note that here the phrase *hař yànzu* 'up to including now' is used with negative sentences to render 'not yet', while used in affirmative sentences it may render English 'still' (compare below examples (13) and (14)).

(6) *wutā   bā   tà̄   kùnne   **hař yànzu***
    light NEG 3F.IMPERF turn.on.ADV.STAT till now
    'The light is **not yet** switched on.'
    (lit. 'She didn't switch on the light up to now.')
    (Kramer handout)

---

[9] The 22nd Afrikanistentag took place in Berlin form 17th to 19th June, 2016.

(7) Fātimà bā tằ   Kanò **hař yànzu**
    Fatima NEG 3F.IMPERF Kano till now
    Fatima is **not yet** in Kano
    (lit. Fatima is not in Kano until now)
    (Kramer handout)

What becomes apparent again is that according to our definition the phrase *hař yànzu* is not a phasal polarity expression. Rather it specifies a single reference point until which an action/event did or did not take place. In our conception constructions with *hař yànzu* do not involve reference points at two related phases. Moreover, there seems to be no implication that the situations which are contrasted are opposites with different polarity values. E.g. the statement in 7 does not necessarily imply that the proposition (Fatima's being in Kano) will hold in a subsequent phase.

3 ALREADY in Hausa

English phasal adverbials include *already*, which indicates in a neutral reading that a situation has come into existence. In Hausa three different strategies were found which may be translated into English with 'already'.

For instance, the first strategy resorts to the verb *r̀gā* (= *rigā* = *r̀gāyằ*) 'precede' rendering in a specific construction also the meaning 'have already done something'. In this case the verb *r̀gā* co-occurs paratactically only with a following coordinate clause and with a matching Perfective TAM. When the verb *rig-* is used in a conjoined sentence to indicate 'have already done' it appears either as *rigā* with H-H tone or more often as *r̀gā* with L-H tone. This is shown in example 8.

(8) sun   **r̀gā**   sun   ga   sābon   watằ
    3PL.PERF   precede   3PL.PERF   see   new   moon
    'They have **already** seen the new moon.'
    (lit. 'They have already done, they have already seen the new moon.')
    (Jaggar 2001: 550)

Note that the verb *rigā* when it appears as a grade0 verb with H-H tone (example (9)) still can be used as a full verb meaning 'precede'.

(9) yā   **rigā**   mù
     3M.PERF precede DO.1PL
     'He preceded us.'
     (Newman 2000: 140)

In our text sample all equivalents of English 'already' (three tokens in total) use this verbal strategy. The verb *rig-* probably is the only real phasal polarity expression which can be found in Hausa. It becomes obvious that a grammaticalization process from 'precede' to 'have already done' has taken place, although a loss of the original meaning cannot yet be attested. What is interesting in a Chadic perspective is that some other West Chadic languages show similar grammaticalization processes, i.e. a verb with the primary meaning 'precede' is extended to also mean 'have already done'. Examples are provided in Table 1.

Table 1: The verb 'precede, have already done' in some West Chadic languages.

Language	Form	Gloss
Hausa	rìgā	'precede, have already done'
Gashua Bade	sàlau	'precede, arrive before, already'
Western Bade	sàru	'precede, be earlier than, already'
Bole	kàyā	'do before, precede in doing, be first to do, have already done'
Ngizim	wàrmu	'precede, have already done'
Goemai	riga < rigā	'precede, have already done'

A second translational equivalent of English 'already' has been found in various Hausa grammars. In these constructions the polyfunctional preposition/conjunction *hař*[10] 'as far as, up to; until; even, including; even though, even with; so much so that, etc.' is used to introduce a sentence in the perfective TAM, following a topicalized noun phrase. Note that examples 10 and 11 are yes-no questions where the addressees have been fronted. In the remainder of the sentences the impersonal form[11] of the perfective TAM is used.

---

[10] The preposition/conjunction *hař* is derived from *hàttā* which in turn is a borrowing from Arabic.

[11] Following Jaggar (2001), we label impersonal forms the *4th person plural* (4pl). These forms express impersonal subjects 'one, they' with arbitrary, often human reference. Note also that examples 3 and 4 are very special constructions insofar as the impersonal forms are usually used in sentences without subjects. In our examples, however, we do have underlying subjects and therefore would expect a third person subject pronoun. Newman (2000: 271) calls such

(10) *Mūsā* **har̃** *an kammàlà aikìn?*
　　 Musa　even[12]　4PL.PERF　finish　work.PRM
　　 'Musa, have you finished the work **already**?'
　　 (lit. 'As for Musa, even that one has finished work.')
　　 (Jaggar 2001: 210)

(11) *Audù* **har̃** *an ci àbincîn?*
　　 Audu　even　4PL.PERF　eat　food.PRM
　　 'Audu, did you eat **already**?'
　　 (lit. 'As for Audu, even that one has eaten the food.')
　　 (Newman 2000: 271)

Newman (2000: 466) describes *har̃* as a very common basic Hausa preposition which also functions as a conjunction, and which connotes action moving forward toward something, or some time, or some place. For a more detailed discussion of the preposition/conjunction *har̃* see e.g. Meyers (1974), Ziegelmeyer (2008). However, overall we may state that it is quite unclear what phasal polarity values should be depicted in the *har̃* examples (10) and (11). Despite the fact that Jaggar (2001) and Newman (2000) chose a translation with 'already', we nevertheless come to the conclusion that phasal polarity values are missing and other translations could be appropriate as well.

Last but not least, we find translational equivalents of English 'already' where the adverb *dâ* 'formerly, in former times; already' is employed. Often *dâ* is followed by the high-frequency modal particle[13] *mā* 'too, also, even, still'. The expression *dâ mā* typically is located in the topic slot at the left periphery of a statement and often translates as 'originally, beforehand, already, even in former times, etc.', as can be seen in example (12).

---

constructions 'oblique impersonal constructions' which serve to avoid direct reference to someone out of politeness or deference or for other stylistic purposes.
12 Note that in this example Jaggar (2001: 210) glosses *har̃* with 'already', while the example taken from Newman (2000: 271) is unglossed.
13 In Hausa linguistics the term *modal particle* (MP) encompasses a small, closed set of intensifying, specifying, restricting, focusing, or connecting particles which serve to express a personal attitude, state of mind, emphasis or contrast, corrective, conversational flow, or other pragmatic or discourse functions.

(12) **dâ**   **mā** Mūsā dà   Shēhù   àbòkan   gàske nḕ
      formerly   MP Musa and Shehu friends.of truly STAB
      'Musa and Shehu were **already** true friends.'
      (lit. 'Even formerly, Musa and Shehu are true friends.')
      (Newman 2000: 160)

However, what we can see here again is that our construction under investigation simply refers to a contextual reference point rather than depicting inherently phasal polarity values. Although translations with 'already' would be fitting in the one or other context, several other translations would be equally or even more suitable. For instance, in example (12) the translation 'even in former times Musa and Shehu were friends' would also be fine.

4 STILL in Hausa

Hausa has various constructions which are rendered as 'still' in English translations. They refer to situations that persist, and in many cases the adverbial *yànzu* 'now' is used as a temporal reference point at which the action, event, situation, etc. is still going on. Probably the clearest expression of continuative 'still' is done by the phrase *hař yànzu* 'until now, up to now' plus a verbal complex in the imperfective TAM. Note that Hausa imperfective TAM per se expresses continuative, ongoing situations. Thus, if a given situation is continuously happening up to including a reference point at the present, it is, of course still going on. This can be seen in examples (13) and (14). As already mentioned above, we consider the phrase *hař yànzu* to be deictic rather than depicting true phasal polarity values.

(13) **Hař   yànzu** kinā̀   jirànsà?
      until now   2F.IMPERF   wait.VN.POSS.3M
      'You are **still** waiting for him?'
      (lit. 'Up to now you are waiting for him.')
      (Jaggar 2001: 662)

(14) yanā̀   cikin   aikī̀   **hař   yànzu**
      3M.IMPERF inside.of work   until now
      'He is **still** busy.'
      (lit. 'He is inside work up to now.')
      (Newman 1997: 265)

Some rather special constructions rendering a translation with English 'still' are given in examples (15) and (16). Here the so called modal particles (see footnote 12) *mā* 'too, also, even, still', and *kùwa* 'particle used to affirm or contrast something' (similar to 'indeed' or 'however') are used. In example (15), *mā* 'too, also, even, still' topicalizes the reference point *yànzu* 'now', whereas in example (16), the modal particle *kùwa* co-occurs with a statement in the imperfective TAM. Although Newman (2000) translates these examples with 'still', several other translations might be even more suitable and virtually no values of phase and/or polarity seem to be involved. Note that it is extremely difficult to capture the exact meanings and functions of Hausa modal particles. Although they are essential in the Hausa language, or as Newman (2000: 326) puts it: "Their pragmatic significance in sprucing up a sentence is reflected in the Hausa term for these words, namely *gishirin Hausa*, lit. 'salt of the language'", they are nevertheless often untranslatable, their linguistic contribution being expressed in English by stress, intonation, or nonverbal gestures. For a treatment of Hausa modal particles see e.g. Schmaling (1991).

(15) yànzu **mā** anā̀ yî
Now also 4PL.IMPERF do.VN
'It is **still** being done.'
(lit. 'Also now one does it.')
(Newman 2000: 327)

(16) inā̀ **kùwa** dà râi
1SG.IMPERF indeed with life
'I am **still** alive.'
(lit. 'I am indeed with life.')
(Newman 2000: 331)

Note also the following constructions which are rendered with 'still' in English translations. In examples (17) and (18), the locative adverb *nan* 'there (near you); here in existence' is used to express that someone is here (still) in existence with a certain quality. Aspectually both sentences use an imperfective TAM signalling that the given quality is continuing. Example (18) additionally embeds the presentational phrase *gā̀ ta nan* 'look at her there being in existence'. The adverb *nan* is typical of the locative deictic domain, which may be extended into the temporal domain. However, what becomes apparent is that constructions shown throughout examples (15)–(20) do not really exhibit phasal polarity values, although in rather free English translations the phasal polarity item 'still' may be employed.

(17) kàkātā   tanằ   **nan** dà   rântà
    grandma.POSS.1SG 3F.IMPERF there with life.POSS.3F
    'My grandmother is **still** alive and kicking.'
    (lit. 'My grandma is here with her life.')
    (Newman 2000: 37)

(18) tsōhuwâř dà (takè)   gằ   ta   **nan** râi gà Allàh
    elder.PRM RM (3F.FOC_IMPERF) here.is DO.3F there life with God
    'The old woman who is **still** here (but) really old.'
    (lit. 'The old woman who, look at her there, life is with God.')
    (Newman 2000: 182)

In example (19), an adverbial clause with imperfective TAM signals that the event of the matrix clause took place during a period when the event of the adverbial clause was going on. Again, in the Hausa example there is no clear notion of a phasal value, as the English translation by Newman might suggest in the first instance.

(19) **tun** tanằ   kàramā akà   yi   matà aurē
    while 3F.IMPERF small 4PL.FOC_PERF do IO.3F marriage
    'She married while she was **still** very young.'
    (lit. 'While she was small, one did marriage to her.')
    (Newman 2000: 560)

Newman (1997), in her English-Hausa dictionary, lists under the entry 'still' also the adversative construction *àmma duk dà hakà* 'but despite all of that'. Here a certain quality, i.e. being my friend, holds against all expectations, as shown in example (20). This is another instance of English translations which, in the first instance, imply the presence of phasal polarity values, but where this simply does not hold for what is actually expressed in the Hausa structure.

(20) kīlằ   abîn   dà ya   yi   bằ daidai ba
    maybe thing.PRM RM 3M.FOC_PERF do NEG correct NEG
    àmma duk   dà   hakà shī àbōkīnā   nề
    but   all   with thus   3M   friend.POSS.1SG STAB
    'Perhaps what he did was wrong but **still** he is my friend.'
    (Newman 1997: 265)

5 NO LONGER in Hausa

The phasal polarity expression NO LONGER indicates that a situation has ceased to exist. Therefore, it is not surprising that Hausa uses the verbs *dainà* 'cease, quit doing', or *barī̀ (barř* before object) 'leave, stop doing, cease'. Note that in Hausa the respective phasal polarity notion is not directly expressed as in English, but it is rather inferred that a certain situation which has ceased to exist is no longer valid. This is shown in examples (21) and (22).

(21) lìttàttàfan Làřabcī sun **dainà** sằmuwā à Los Angeles
books.of Arabic 3PL.PERF cease findable.VN at Los Angeles
'Arabic books can **no longer** be found in L.A.'
(lit. 'Arabic books ceased to be findable in L.A.')
(Newman 2000: 67)

(22) nā **bař** shân tābà̄
1SG.PERF cease drink.VN.of tobacco
'I don't smoke **any longer**.'
(lit. 'I stopped the drinking of tobacco.')
(Kramer handout)

Another verbal construction can use the phrase *ci gàba* 'go forward (lit. eat forward)' in the scope of negation, as illustrated in example (23). Again, the notion of 'no longer' is inferred rather than effectively expressed on the surface.

(23) bà zân **ci gàba** dà jirā̀ ba
NEG FUT.1SG eat forward with wait.VN NEG
'I won't wait **any longer**.'
(lit. 'I will not go ahead with waiting.')
(Newman 2000: 504)

In a similar manner the phrase *dàgà yâu* 'from today (onwards)' in the scope of negation may be rendered with 'no longer' in English translations. This is illustrated in example (24). Here two negative existential clauses *bâ X bâ Y* 'there is not X, there is not Y' are used to indicate a serious incompatibility between people and things.

(24) Bâ   nī   bâ   cîn   ɗan-wāke   **dàgà**   **yâu**
     NEG   1SG   NEG   eat.VN.of   bean.dumpling   from   today
'As of today, I shall **no longer** eat small dumplings made of bean flour (i.e. I have learned my lesson).'
(lit. 'There is not me, there is not eating of bean dumplings from today.')
(Newman 2000: 181)

6 Conclusions

In the above sections, several Hausa constructions which were rendered in the various sources with English translations belonging to the set of phasal adverbials such as '(not) yet', 'already', 'still', and 'no longer' were illustrated. However, what we may conclude is that most of these constructions may appear to look like phasal polarity notions initially, but on closer examination it turns out that most of them either lack phasal, and/or polarity values which both are essential to the expression of phasal polarity as defined in this volume.

Therefore, we are tempted to say that the concept of phasal polarity does not play an essential role in Hausa, and probably at earlier stages of language development did not play a role at all. We have shown above that most often key words like 'already', '(not) yet', 'still', and 'no longer' may be found in carefully worded, but rather free translations into English, but when it comes to rather literal translation the key words are missing. Further analysis of these constructions often shows that values of phase and polarity are missing. For instance, Hausa speakers may say something like *nā bař shân tābầ* 'I stopped smoking' which in the real world has a similar effect like saying in English 'I don't smoke any longer', but the Hausa construction does not in fact entail any phasal polarity value. Likewise, Hausa speakers may say *hař yànzu Aishà tanầ Landàn* 'up to including now Aisha is in London' which might have a similar semantic effect like saying 'Aisha is still in London', but not necessarily so. This is to say that the Hausa sentence does not automatically imply that the proposition, i.e. Aisha's being in London, will not be the case in a subsequent phase.

In conclusion we may say that the concept of phasal polarity does not play a crucial role in Hausa, and probably in former stages of language development did not play a role at all. In present-day Hausa the verb *rig-* 'precede' which has been grammaticalized to 'have already done', seems to be the only expression depicting phasal polarity values.

Abbreviations

ADV.STAT	stative adverbial	PERF	Perfective
DEP_FUT	dependent future	PHASAL POLARITY	phasal polarity
DO	direct object	PL	Plural
F	feminine	POSS	possessive
FOC_IMPERF	focus imperfective	PRM	previous reference marker
FOC_PERF	focus perfective	RM	relative clause marker
FUT	future	SG	Singular
IMPERF	imperfective	STAB	Stabilizer
IO	indirect object	SUB	Subjunctive
M	masculine	VN	verbal noun
MP	modal particle	1, 2, 3, 4	1st, 2nd, 3rd, 4th person
NEG	negation		

Bibliographic references

Bature, Abdullahi & Russell G. Schuh. 2008. *Hausar Baka. "Gani Ya Kori Ji"*. Elementary and intermediate lessons in Hausa language and culture. Vol. 1–5. Windsor, CA: World of Languages.

Cyffer, Norbert & John P. Hutchison. 1990. *Dictionary of the Kanuri Language*. Dordrecht & Providence: Foris.

Hutchison, John P. 1975. Syntactic similarities across language families. A case from Hausa and Kanuri. *Harsunan Nijeriya* 5. 55–71.

Hutchison, John P. 1981. *A Reference Grammar of the Kanuri Language*. Madison: University of Wisconsin.

Jaggar, Philip J. 2001. *Hausa*. Amsterdam & Philadelphia: Benjamins.

Koelle, Sigismund W. 1854. *Grammar of the Bornu or Kanuri Language*. London: Church Missionary Society.

Kramer, Raija. 2017. Position paper on Phasal Polarity expressions. Hamburg: University of Hamburg. https://www.aai.uni-hamburg.de/afrika/php2018/medien/position-paper-on-php.pdf (accessed 06 April 2019).

Meyers, Laura F. 1974. The particles sai and har: Only, even and until in Hausa. In Erhard Voeltz (ed.), *Third Annual Conference on African Linguistics*, 213–221. Bloomington: Indiana University.

Newman, Paul. 1990. *Nominal and Verbal Plurality in Chadic*. Dordrecht & Providence: Foris.

Newman, Paul. 2000. *The Hausa Language. An Encyclopedic Reference Grammar*. New Haven & London: Yale University Press.

Newman, Paul. 2007. *A Hausa-English Dictionary*. New Haven & London: Yale University Press.

Newman, Roxana Ma. 1997. *An English-Hausa Dictionary*. Lagos: Longman Nigeria.

Schmaling, Constanze. 1991. Modalpartikeln im Hausa: 'Gishirin Hausa'. Hamburg: University of Hamburg MA thesis.

Van Baar, Theodorus M. 1997. *Phasal Polarity*. Amsterdam: IFOTT.

van der Auwera, Johan. 1998. Phasal adverbials in the languages of Europe. In Johan van der Auwera & Dónall P.O. Baoill (eds.), *Adverbial Constructions in the Languages of Europe*, 25–145. Berlin & New York: Mouton de Gruyter.
Wolff, H. Ekkehard. 1993. *Referenzgrammatik des Hausa*: *Zur Begleitung des Fremdsprachenunterrichts und zur Einführung in das Selbststudium*. (Hamburger Beiträge zur Afrikanistik, 2.) Münster: LIT.
Ziegelmeyer, Georg. 1999. *Areale Mermale in der weiteren Tschadseeregion. Die Partikeln sai/ sey und tùkùna/tawon/dùwô im Hausa, Fulfulde und Kanuri*. Vienna: University of Vienna MA thesis.
Ziegelmeyer, Georg. 2008. *Aspekte adverbialer Subordination im Hausa, Fulfulde und Kanuri*. Cologne: Rüdiger Köppe.

Yvonne Treis
The expression of phasal polarity in Kambaata (Cushitic)

1 Introduction

Kambaata[1] is a Highland East Cushitic language of Ethiopia which does not seem to have dedicated grammatical or lexical means to express phasal polarity. This first impression, which will undergo careful scrutiny in §4 of this chapter, is gained from a cursory review of parallel texts in which the phasal polarity adverbs *already*, *not yet*, *still*, *no longer* of the English translation usually have no apparent translational equivalents in Kambaata. In (1), it is seen that English *has not yet come* corresponds to Kambaata *has not come*, which conveys neither that the time will come later nor the speaker's judgement that this change will be later than expected (or hoped for). Similarly, in (2), English *are already white* is not reflected in the Kambaata translation, which is literally translatable as 'is gray/has become gray'. The Kambaata translation presupposes a preceding change (see the use of the inchoative-stative ideophone *búll=ih-* 'become gray'), but does not convey that the speaker considers the change to be earlier than expected.[2]

(1) *Yesúus-u<n>ku*   "*Mánch-o* (. . .)   *j-éechch-u-*'
     Jesus-mNOM<N>   person.SG-fOBL   time-SG-fNOM-1sPOSS
     iill-it-im-bá'a"   *y-ée-se.*
     arrive-3f-NIPV-NEG1   say-3mPFV-3fO
     'Jesus said to her: "Woman, (. . .) my hour (lit. time) has **not yet** come (lit. has not come).'" (John 2:4)[3]

---

[1] I am grateful to Deginet Wotango Doyiso for our discussions of the data and the analyses presented in this chapter.
[2] I have segmented, glossed and translated all Kambaata examples from locally published sources, and stress marks have been added.
[3] Here, and for all other examples from the Kambaata Bible, the English translation provided is the New King James Version (NKJV).

Yvonne Treis, COMUE Sorbonne Paris Cité, INALCO CNRS UMR 8135 LLACAN Langage, langues et cultures d'Afrique

(2) (. . .) *Ill-í-'nne xóqq=at-téen wíx-at*
       eye-fACC-2pPOSS lift.IDEO=do-2pPCO grain-fNOM
búll=ik-kóo=g-a   xuujj-iyyé!
gray.IDEO=become-3fPFV.REL=G-mACC   see-2pIMP
'(. . .) lift up your eyes and look at the fields, for they are **already** white for harvest (lit. lift up your eyes and see that the grain is gray/has become gray)!' (John 4:35)

Phasal polarity items express that two situations that are temporally related phases have contrasting polarity values. They also often convey the speaker's attitude towards the situation described, namely that a change is earlier (ALREADY) or later (NOT YET) than expected or that a situation persists longer (STILL) or ended earlier (NO LONGER) than anticipated. Based on a corpus of translated texts and a corpus of spontaneous and elicited fieldwork data, this chapter investigates how phasal polarity is expressed in Kambaata, in view of the apparent lack of dedicated means. I describe how phasal polarity is expressed periphrastically and which adverbials adopt a phasal polarity reading in certain contexts. The necessary background for the study is provided in §2, which introduces the sociolinguistic and typological profile of the language, and §3, which summarizes how negative polarity is marked. Section 4, the core of the chapter, shows that Kambaata has several "workarounds" to express ALREADY (§4.1), NOT YET (§4.2), STILL (§4.3) and NO LONGER (§4.4). Section 5 analyses the experiential perfect construction 'have (n)ever V-ed', which may sometimes adopt a phasal polarity reading. §6 concludes the discussion. To the best of my knowledge, the expression of phasal polarity has so far not been investigated for any Cushitic language or indeed any language of the Ethiopian Linguistic Area. Therefore, I am unable to say, at the present moment, whether Kambaata is a typical or untypical language within its family or area in this respect.

2 Sociolinguistic and typological profile

Kambaata is spoken by more than 600,000 speakers (Central Statistical Agency 2007: 74) in the Kambaata-Xambaaro Zone in the Southern Region of Ethiopia. The immediate neighbors are speakers of other Highland East Cushitic languages (Hadiyya and Alaaba) and Ometo languages of the Omotic family (Wolaitta and Dawro). The most widespread second language of Kambaata speakers is the Ethiopian lingua franca Amharic. Kambaata is used as a medium of instruction in public primary schools and is taught as a subject up to grade 12. In 2018,

Wachamo University started a Kambaata language BA program on its Duuraame campus. The official Kambaata orthography is based on the Roman script (Treis 2008: 73–80, Alemu 2016) and follows the spelling conventions of the Oromo Qubee orthography. The official Kambaata orthography is adopted in this contribution with one important adaptation: phonemic stress is marked by an acute accent. The following Kambaata graphemes are not in accordance with IPA conventions: <ph> /p'/, <x> /t'/, <q> /k'/, <j> /dʒ/, <c> /tʃ'/, <ch> /tʃ/, <sh> /ʃ/, <y> /j/ and <'> /ʔ/. Geminate consonants and long vowels are marked by doubling, e.g. <shsh> /ʃː/ and <ee> /eː/.

Kambaata is agglutinating-fusional and strictly suffixing. Its constituent order is consistently head-final; hence all modifiers precede the noun in the noun phrase, and all dependent clauses precede independent main clauses. The last constituent in a sentence is usually a fully finite main verb or a copula. The following open word classes are defined on morphosyntactic grounds: nouns, adjectives, verbs, ideophones and interjections.

Kambaata is a nominative-accusative language; the nominative is the subject case – see *jéechchu'* 'my time' in (1); the accusative marks direct objects – see *illí'nne* 'your (p) eyes' in (2) – and certain adverbial constituents, it also serves as the citation form of nouns and adjectives. Nouns are marked for gender (masculine vs. feminine); the assignment of grammatical gender is mostly arbitrary, with the exception of nouns referring to human beings and higher animals, where it is sex-based. Nouns distinguish nine case forms (nominative, accusative, genitive, dative, ablative, instrumental-comitative-perlative, locative, oblique, predicative), all of which are marked by a segmental suffix and a specific stress pattern. Attributive adjectives agree with their head noun in case and gender. The case system of attributive adjectives is reduced to three forms, namely nominative, accusative and oblique, with the oblique form marking agreement with non-nominative/non-accusative head nouns.

The word class of adverbs is negligibly small. So far I have only been able to determine a handful of morphologically invariant lexemes expressing adverbial relations, e.g. *léelan* 'carefully, slowly', *dángo* 'suddenly, unexpectedly'. In place of adverbs, Kambaata uses converbs or adjectives and nouns that are marked for adverbial cases (e.g. accusative, oblique, instrumental-comitative-perlative). Hence temporal adverbials are case-marked nouns in Kambaata, e.g. *ga'-áata* (fACC) 'tomorrow' and *kabár* 'today (mOBL)'.

Kambaata distinguishes between fully finite main clause verbs and various types of dependent clause verbs, which are reduced in finiteness, i.e. relative verbs, converbs, purposive verbs and (non-finite) verbal nouns. On affirmative main verbs, seven discontinuous subject indexes, which reflect the person, number, gender and honorificity of the subject, are distinguished. Main verbs are further marked for four aspectual categories (imperfective, perfective, perfect, progressive) and four modal categories (declarative, imperative, jussive/benedictive, apprehensive). Derivational morphology (e.g. passive, causative, middle) is found between the root and the inflection (Figure 1). The use of pronominal object suffixes is partly pragmatically determined and depends on the referential prominence of the object. If the verb is marked for past tense, the marker *íkke* is the last element of the verbal complex.

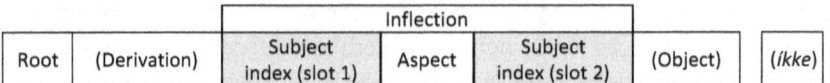

Figure 1: Structure of an affirmative declarative main verb.

The inflectional potential of dependent clause verbs is less rich than that of main verb forms: certain person/gender and aspectual distinctions are neutralized, they cannot be marked for mood, and only some of them allow for object suffixes.

3 Negation

The morphology of negative (as opposed to affirmative) verb forms has been described in detail in earlier publications – see Treis (2012a) on negative verb forms in Kambaata and related Highland East Cushitic languages, Treis (2012b: 86–90) on negative converbs and Treis (2012c) on negative participles – and is therefore only summarized briefly here. As in many languages in the world, the affirmative and negative verb forms and paradigms do not neatly match each other in a one-to-one relation; rather, paradigmatic and constructional asymmetries (Miestamo 2008) can be observed: Not all affirmative paradigms have dedicated negative counterparts, and negation may trigger changes in the morphological makeup of the verb form. Kambaata has five inflectional negation morphemes (Table 1). Negative morphemes are always located after the subject indexes and aspectual morphology, and before tense marking; their position relative to mood and object marking depends on the type of verb they combine with.

The standard negator *-ba('a)* (NEG1) is used for the negation of declarative main verbs (3), the existential verb *yoo-* (glossed: COP1) 'exist, be (located)' and non-verbal predicates (4).

Table 1: Inflectional negation morphemes.

-ba('a)	NEG1	Negator of declarative main verbs, existential verb yoo-, non-verbal predicates
´-oot	NEG2	Negator of imperatives
´-ka	NEG3	Negator of jussives
-ú'nna	NEG4	Negator of converbs
-umb	NEG5	Negator of relative verbs

(3) (...) dikk-ú-s   zahh-íteent   ikkí-i
          market-fACC-DEF wander-2fPRF   IRR.COND-ADD
     kank-á   xe'-anó   burtukaan-á
     EQ1_A_DEM-mACC become_sweet-3mIPV.REL orange-mACC
     dag-gáanti-**ba'a**.
     find-2sIPV-**NEG1**
     '(...) even if you trawled the market, you would not find oranges this sweet.' (Field notes 2014)

(4) (...) hittíin   íi-taa   lúus-a(-**ba'a**).
          P_DEM2.fNOM 1sGEN-fCOP2   fault-fPRED(-**NEG1**)
     'This is (not) my fault.' (Saint-Exupéry 2018: 12)

The four aspectual categories of main verbs, i.e. imperfective, perfective, perfect and progressive, are reduced to two, i.e. imperfective (3) vs. non-imperfective (NIPFV: (1)), under negation. In the imperfective aspect, the affirmative and negative paradigms are totally symmetrical. In contrast, the non-imperfective negative verbs lack the second subject slot of their affirmative counterparts and distinguish only five (not seven) subject indexes. The negator -ba('a) precedes the object morpheme in the non-imperfective (5a)[4] and follows it in the imperfective (5b).[5]

(5) (a) xuud-een-im-bá-nne
          see-3hon-NIPV-NEG1-1pO
          'S/he (honorific) didn't see us'
     (b) xuud-éenno-nne-ba'a
          see-3honIPV-1sO-NEG1
          'S/he (honorific) doesn't see us'

---

4 See also (18) and (25).
5 It also follows the object morpheme on the existential verb (26).

The morpheme ʹ-*oot* (NEG2) negates imperatives; it is located after the subject index but before the imperative marker and object suffixes (6).[6] The morpheme ʹ-*ka* (NEG3) is the negator of jussive verbs, i.e. directive verbs of the first and third persons; it follows the jussive morpheme -*un* and precedes the object suffix (7).[7]

(6) Kánne   hagág=y-ít-**oot**-i!
    P_DEM1.mOBL   linger.IDEO=say-2s-**NEG2**-2sIMP
    'Don't linger here!' (Saint-Exupéry 2018: 36)

(7) Lankaann-í   híil-u,   land-í   kotím-u
    paternal_uncle-mGEN bad-mNOM   leather_dress-mGEN   short-mNOM
    Laadd-í   gíd-u   gambá=y-ún-**ka**-he!
    PN-mGEN   cold-mNOM   encounter.IDEO=say-[3m]JUS-**NEG3**-2sO
    (Blessing:) 'May a bad uncle, a too short leather dress and the cold of Laadda (= windy place) not catch up with you!' (Alamu & Alamaayyo 2017: 101)

Kambaata makes a distinction between imperfective and perfective converbs, which are obligatorily marked for switch-reference (DS)[8] if the subject changes between the converb and the superordinate clause. Converbs are negated with the dedicated converb negator -*ú'nna* ~ -*u'nnáachch* (8) ~ -*u'nnáan* (19) (NEG4), whose three allomorphs are in free variation and express 'without V-ing, before V-ing'. Object morphemes are either infixes (8) or suffixes to the converb negator. In the negative converb paradigm, the distinction between the imperfective and perfective forms is neutralized; negative converbs are not sensitive to switch-reference. Negative converbs are further discussed in §4.2.

(8) Éjj   xuud-een-**u'nna**<'ée>**chch** hattig-óon
    before.mOBL   see-3hon-**NEG4**<1sO>   how-fICP
    dag-een-o<'é>ta   dand-éemma-la?
    know-3hon-PURP.SS<1sO>   be_able-3honPFV-MIT
    'How could he (honorific) recognize me without having seen me before?' (Saint-Exupéry 2018: 36)

---

[6] See also (19).
[7] Subject indexes that are realized as Ø are glossed in [square brackets] in the examples.
[8] See (34).

The negator *-umb* (NEG5) negates relative verbs and all relative-based verb forms in subordinate clauses (e.g. in temporal, reason, and conditional clauses). Negative relative verbs are almost perfect verb-adjective hybrids due to their combination of verbal and adjectival morphology (Treis 2012c). They index the person, gender, number and honorificity of their subject, and agree in case and gender with their head noun; in (9), *ut-á* 'thorn' is both the 3m subject and the masculine accusative head noun of the preceding negative relative verb.[9] While affirmative relative verbs distinguish four aspectual values (imperfective, perfective, perfect, progressive), these are completely neutralized under negation. The relative negator is found between the subject morphology (which is Ø for 3m in (9)) and the case/gender morphology.

(9) (. . .) *fiit-it   hoolam-á   haww-it-án*
          flower-fNOM   much-mACC   trouble-3f-ICO
     [*mexx-u=rr-á-a   kaa'll-**umb**-o-ssá*]Relative clause modifier
     single-mACC=NMZ4-mACC-ADD   help-[3m]NEG5-mACC-3pO.REL
     ut-á   kank-á   dooll-á   le'-icc-it-án
     thorn-mACC EQ1_A_DEM-mACC time-mACC grow-CAUS1.MID-3f-ICO
     eger-too'í-i   m-íiha-ati-ndo (. . .)?
     stay-3fPFV.REL-NMZ1.mNOM   what-mDAT-COP3-Q
     '(. . .) why (do) flowers go to so much trouble, from time immemorial, to grow thorns which are of no use to them (. . .)?' (Saint-Exupéry 2018: 29)

The apprehensive, a paradigm of main verb forms expressing dangers and threats, and the purposive, a paradigm of dependent verb forms used in purpose and certain complement clauses, have no corresponding negative paradigms and thus need to be negated periphrastically (Treis 2010: 22, Treis 2018).

4 Expression of phasal polarity

In this section I first look for translational equivalents of phasal polarity items in published parallel texts that are available in English, French and Kambaata, i.e. *Le Petit Prince* by Antoine de Saint-Exupéry (2018) and the Gospel of John

---

9 See also (33), in which a negative relative verb is indexed for a 1s subject and displays agreement with a feminine nominative head noun which is not coreferential with the subject.

(Kambaata and Hadiyya Translation Project 2005), which were translated by different Kambaata native speakers.[10] The second step will be to check the use of the constructions and lexical items that were obtained in this way against elicited and spontaneously produced data in my field notes, in order to determine whether these constructions and lexemes are dedicated phasal polarity items or whether they have another core meaning, with phasal polarity readings being restricted to certain contexts.

4.1 Already

The English version[11] of *Le Petit Prince* (Saint-Exupéry 1943) contains ten instances of *already*. However, in nine out of the ten cases, we do not find any translational equivalent in the Kambaata version (10).

(10) [English version] No. This sheep is **already** very sickly. Make me another.
Ti   hóol-ch-ut   abb-ís-s
A_DEM1.fNOM   sheep-SG-fNOM   become_big-CAUS1-3fPCO
moos-áan-ch-u-ta.
become_sick-AG-SG-fPRED-fCOP2
Wol-ú   misil-á   ke'-ís-e-'e!
other-mACC   picture-mACC   get_up-CAUS1-2sIMP-1sO
Lit. 'This sheep is very sick. Draw another picture for me!' (Saint-Exupéry 2018: 14)

In one case, English *already* is translated by *wón-a-n* (11).

(11) [English version] "Forget what?" inquired the little prince, who **already** was sorry for him.
*Kánn   dimb-aan-ch-íi   **wón-a-n***
A_DEM1.mOBL get_drunk-AG-SG-mDAT first-OBL[12]-N

---

10 Note that the Kambaata version of *Le Petit Prince* is a translation from English, checked against the French original. It is unknown to me from which language the Gospel of John was translated.
11 In the French original of the *Petit Prince* (Saint-Exupéry 1946), we find twelve instances of *déjà* 'already', two of which were left untranslated by the translator of the English version.
12 Usually, all lexemes with nominal, pronominal and adjectival morphology receive a gloss for case and gender. However, as the paradigms of many temporal nouns are defective, I am

kichché'-ee-si   qakkíchch-u láah-u
feel_sorry-3mPRF-3mO.REL   little-mNOM prince-mNOM
"(. . .)"   y-î=ké'   xa'mm-ée-s.
              say-[3m]PCO=SEQ   ask-3mPFV-3mO

'The little prince, who was **already** (?) sorry for the drunkard, asked him: "(. . .)".' (Saint-Exupéry 2018: 44)

Wónan is also attested as the translational equivalent of 'already' in the translation of John 9:27 ('I told you already, and you did not listen'); elsewhere in the same text, 'already' is left untranslated. Furthermore, *wónan* is found in sentence 31 of Dahl's perfect questionnaire (2000), which I elicited in 2005 and which is reproduced in (12).

(12) [The baby wakes up one hour earlier than expected and starts screaming. Mother (in another room):] Oh no! He WAKE UP already.
Wón-a-n   báqq=y-ée'u.
first-OBL-N   wake_up.IDEO=say-3mPRF
'He has **already** (?) woken up.' (Field notes, elicited)

In the above examples, the translation 'already' is followed by a question mark because I suspect it to be influenced by the English source or meta-language. *Wón-a-n* is a temporal adverbial and formally the oblique case form of the ordinal numeral 'first', *won-á*, combined with the pragmatically determined emphasis marker *-n*. *Wón-a-n* seems most appropriately translated as 'at first, firstly, before, at an earlier time'.[13] The corpus of recorded spontaneous data shows that *wón-a* and the emphatic form *wón-a-n* usually express that something happens first, in the beginning of a sequence of events (13), or that something happened at an earlier point in time (14). There is no indication that *wón-a-n* has the conventionalized implication that something is happening/has happened earlier than expected or that it establishes a contrast between a reference point where the situation holds and one where it does not.

---

sometimes unable to determine their gender. The ending ´-*a* could be the oblique case form of a masculine or feminine noun.

13 See Kramer (this volume) and Ziegelmeyer (this volume) for the use of Fula *tawon* 'first' and Hausa *tùkùna* 'first' as phasal polarity items.

(13) (...) *nuggúss-at wón-a-n xeem-íine-et*
circumcision-fNOM first-OBL-N laxative-mICP-COP3
jammar-taa'í-ihu.
begin-3fIPV.REL-NMZ1-mNOM
(Speaker describes the steps of a ceremony) '(...) the circumcision ceremony begins **first** with the (administration of the) *xeemu*-laxative.' (AN2016-02-19_001)

(14) (...) **wón-a-n** *atakaan-ú-s shol-een-óta*
first-OBL-N type_of_food-mACC-DEF cook-3hon-PURP.SS
qixx-an-s-eemmá xag-aakk-áta wor-éen (...).
get_ready-PASS-CAUS1-3honPFV.REL spice-PL2-fACC add-3honPCO
(Speaker describes the preparation of the *atakaanu*-dish) '(...) then one adds the different types of spices that one has prepared **earlier** to cook the *atakaanu*-dish (...).' (TH2003-06-26_atakaanu)

In Alemu's Kambaata-Amharic-English dictionary (2016: 276), *éjj-i-n* is translated as 'already'. Structurally similar to *wón-a-n* 'at first', *éjj-i-n* is the emphatic form of the oblique case adverbial *éjj*[-*i*] 'before, formerly, previously, in the past, in the old days' (15); see also (8). As my fieldwork database shows, it is likely to be a temporal but not a dedicated phasal adverbial.

(15) *Ku mín-u éjj-i-n bíishsh-a-a-ndo?*
A_DEM1.mNOM house-mNOM before-OBL-N red-mPRED-mCOP2-Q
(Speaker asking about the colour of a house that was recently painted) 'Was this house red **before**?' (Field notes 2004)

In interrogative clauses, the experiential perfect construction (§5) may also sometimes be translated as 'have already V-ed'. The discussion in §5 shows, however, that the construction does not qualify as a dedicated phasal polarity construction either.

4.2 Not yet

For the negative counterpart of ALREADY, i.e. NOT YET, we find various translational equivalents in the Kambaata texts. Of these, two constructions are recurrent.

In the English version of *Le Petit Prince* there are four instances of *not yet*, two of which are left untranslated, while the remaining two are translated by the temporal adverbial phrase *tadáa iillán=qaxee* 'until/up to now, so far' and a negated superordinate verb (16). The complex marker *iillán=qaxee*, which originated in an imperfective converb form of *iill-* 'reach' plus a dative form of the noun *qax-á* (m) 'extent', is the regular translation for spatial and temporal 'up to, until'; it is preceded by an accusative-marked spatial or temporal noun, or by an accusative-marked headless relative clause.

(16) [English version] "Ah," I said to the little prince, "these memories of yours are very charming; but I have **not yet** succeeded in repairing my plane[.]"
(. . .) *Ikkodáa* **tad-áa** **iill-án=qax-ee**
but now-ACC reach-[3m]ICO=extent-mDAT
án ka ba'-o-'é horophphill-á
1sNOM A_DEM1.mACC break-3mPFV-1sO.REL plane-mACC
*makk-icc-óta dand-im-**bá'a**.*
become_good-CAUS1.MID-[1s]PURP.SS be_able-[1s]NIPV-NEG1
'(. . .) But I have not yet succeeded (lit. **up to now** I have **not** succeeded) in repairing the plane that broke down to my disadvantage.' (Saint-Exupéry 2018: 76)

A spontaneous example from my corpus that illustrates the use of the same temporal phrase with an affirmative superordinate clause is given in (17).

(17) **Tad-áa iill-án=qax-ee** *isí=g-a*
now-ACC reach-[3m]ICO=extent-mDAT 3mGEN=G-mOBL/ACC
shool-ú fooq-á mínn-ee'i-i
four-mACC floor-mACC build-3mPRF.REL-NMZ1.mNOM
áy-i yóo?
who-mNOM COP1.3
'Who has **so far** built (a house with) four floors like he (has done)? (Message: Nobody has built such a house yet.)' (Field notes 2015)

In many verses where *not yet* is attested in the English translation of the Gospel of John, no direct Kambaata match can be determined – recall (1). However, in some examples from the same text, the translators have opted for a periphrastic verb form consisting of a negative converb ('without V-ing, before V-ing'; cf. §3) followed by the existential verb *yoo-* (COP1), as shown in (18)-(19). The converb and the existential verb are indexed for the same subject, i.e. the third person (feminine) of the noun 'time' in (18) and first person singular in (19).

(18) [English version] (. . .) and no man laid hands on him, for his hour had **not yet** come.
*Ikkodáa   j-éechch-u-s   **iill-it-u'nnáachch   yóo**=tannée*
but   time-SG-fNOM-3mPOSS   arrive-3f-NEG4   COP1.3.REL=REAS1
ay-í-i   af-im-bá-s.
who-mNOM-ADD   seize-[3m]NIPV-NEG1-3mO
'But no one seized him, because his time had not yet come (lit. his time was before/without arriving).' (John 8:20)

(19) [English version] Do not cling to me, for I have **not yet** ascended to my Father.
*Ann-i-'í=b-a   **ful-u'nnáan***
father-mGEN-1sPOSS=PLC-mACC   ascend-[1s]NEG4
yoommí=tannée   *áf-f-oot-e-'e.*
COP1.1s.REL=REAS1   seize-2s-NEG2-2sIMP-1sO
'Do not seize me, because I have not yet ascended (lit. I am before/without ascending) to my Father.' (John 20:17)

In a draft Kambaata translation of the Old Testament book of Deuteronomy to which I had access, the three examples of the construction {negative converb + existential copula} correspond to *not yet* in the English version. The same construction is also attested in my own field notes collected from various speakers at various times, e.g. (20). All registered examples were – independently of each other – translated as 'not yet'.

(20) *Tí   qáar-it   já'l-a-ta.*
     A_DEM1.fNOM   type_of_pepper-fNOM   weak-fPRED-fCOP2
     ***Laal-t-u'nnáan   yóo**-taa.*
     become_ripe-3f-NEG4   COP1.3.REL-fCOP2
     'This *qaarita*-pepper pod is weak. (Speaker gives a periphrasis of the first sentence:) It is not yet ripe.' (Field notes 2007)

As confirmed in discussions with a native speaker, the construction {negative converb + existential copula} contrasts two situations of opposing polarity, namely the actual situation in which a state does not hold and the expected subsequent situation in which it does. However, this construction does not seem to convey the speaker's attitude (surprise, disappointment) that the anticipated change is later than expected or hoped for. So the construction qualifies at best as a neutral 'not yet'-construction in the sense of Van Baar (1997: 34). A thorough semantic analysis of this construction is required to confirm this hypothesis.

As discussed below, the negative experiential perfect construction (§5) may sometimes also have a 'not yet' reading; I show, however, that the construction does not qualify as a dedicated phasal polarity construction. Furthermore, I demonstrate in §4.3 that the temporal adverbial *tees-ú-u* 'and/even now; still; again' acquires the reading 'still not' in negative sentences.

4.3 Still

English *still* opposes a situation in which a state holds, to one where it does not. In the Kambaata translation of *Le Petit Prince*, five out of 15 instances of English *still* can be matched with the adverbial *tees-ú-u* (21)-(22).

(21) **Tees-ú-u** híkku qakkíchch-u láah-u
now-mOBL-ADD A_DEM2.mNOM little-mNOM prince-mNOM
mat-ú bar-í Uull-áta fanqáll waal-áno
one-mACC day-mACC Earth-fACC return.[3m]PCO come-3mIPV
y-í=ké' horophphill-í búrr=a'-áan-ch-u tass-áa
say-[3m]PCO=SEQ plane-mGEN fly=do-AG-SG-mNOM hope-mACC
ass-áno.
do-3mIPV
'The pilot (lit. plane flyer) **still** hopes that the little prince will return to Earth one day.' (Translation of summary of Saint-Exupéry 2018, unpublished)

(22) (. . .) **tees-ú-u** áaz-u-s muddam-áyyoo íkke.
now-mOBL-ADD interior-mNOM-3mPOSS suffer-3mPROG PST
'(. . .) he was **still** worrying (lit. his interior was still suffering).' (Saint-Exupéry 2018: 88)

Tees-ú-u is the additive form of *tées-u* 'now'; thus its basic meaning is 'and now, even now' (23).

(23) **Tees-ú-u**   tosgoob-é   goob-á   barg-ít=ke'éechch
     now-mOBL-ADD   giraffe-fGEN   neck-mACC   add-3fPCO=SEQ
     wo<'>rr-itóo' (. . .).
     put_on<MID>-3fPFV
     (Speaker narrates which body parts the chameleon adopted from other animals: She[14] took body part 1 from Animal A, then took part 2 from B, then took part 3 from C . . .) '**And now** she added the neck of a giraffe and put it on herself (because she wished to see into the distance).' (TD2016-02-11_001)

Apart from the additive (or coordinative) meaning, the adverbial *tees-ú-u* can have a persistive or a repetitive meaning, as numerous elicited and spontaneously produced examples in my corpus illustrate. Alemu (2016: 988) also mentions these three meanings of *tees-ú-u* in his dictionary. The persistive meaning 'still' arises in combination with stative predicates such as 'hope' and 'suffer' (21)-(22). The repetitive meaning 'again' is triggered in the context of dynamic predicates (24).

(24) *Hikkanníi,*   *ám-i,*   **tees-ú-u**   *hafaaffá'-i.*
     P_DEM2.mDAT   come_once-2sIMP now-mOBL-ADD yawn-2sIMP
     (The king orders the little prince:) 'So, come on, yawn **again**!' (Saint-Exupéry 2018: 37)

In negative contexts *teesúu* invites the translation 'still not'.[15] In (25), the speaker expected the chameleon to be satisfied with all the useful and beautiful body parts that she had adopted from other animals.

(25) *Hikkáan*   *ík-k=ke'éechch*   **tees-ú-u**
     P_DEM2.mACC become-3fPCO=SEQ now-OBL-ACC
     hikkuuní-i   *duuss-im-bá-se.*
     P_DEM2.mNOM-ADD   become_satisfied.CAUS1-[3m]NIPV-NEG1-3fO
     'When she had become this (i.e. an animal with wings), this **still** did**n't** satisfy her.' (TD2016-02-11_001)

---

[14] The chameleon is grammatically feminine in Kambaata.
[15] According to Deginet Wotango Doyiso (p.c. 8 May 2019), *teesúu* is not used as 'again' in negative sentences. If the command in (24) were negated, the form *lankíi hafaaffá'oot* 'Don't yawn again, lit. a second (time)!' would be used rather than **teesúu hafaaffá'oot*, intended meaning: 'Don't yawn again, lit. and/even now!'.

Another option to express 'still' is given in Alemu's (2016) dictionary. He translates the phrase *tad-á-a iill-án=qax-ée* (lit.) 'up to now' (in affirmative sentences) as 'still' (2016: 978). Above in §4.2, we have seen this same phrase being used as a translational equivalent of 'not yet' in negative sentences, but I have dismissed the hypothesis that it is a dedicated phasal polarity item.

4.4 No longer

In the available parallel texts no translational equivalent for 'no longer' is found. For instance, the four instances of 'no longer' in the English translation of *Le Petit Prince* are all left untranslated in the Kambaata version (26).

(26) [English translation] The planet now makes a complete turn every minute, and I **no longer** have a single second for repose.
(. . .)   *esáa*   *méxx-u*   *fooloocc-uhú-u*   *yóo-'e-ba'a.*
          1sDAT   single-mNOM   rest-mNOM-ADD   COP1.3-1sO-NEG1
Lit. '(. . .) I don't have a single (moment to) rest.' (Saint-Exupéry 2018: 50)

Alemu's (2016) dictionary contains no Kambaata entry for 'no longer' but gives the following translations for *lankíi*, the adverbial (dative-marked) form of the ordinal numeral *lankí* 'second': 1. 'again', 2. 'never again', 3. 'any more'. Though not mentioned explicitly, translations 2 and 3 are likely to arise in combination with negative verbs, as data in my corpus confirms. The only text in which I ever used 'no longer' in the English translation of Kambaata data was in a folktale from a school textbook. The text tells the story of a heartless farmer who chases away his old horse. The farmer no longer wants to feed the horse, because it can no longer work for him. In (27), I chose to translate *kanníichch zakkíin* 'after this' (+ negation) as 'no longer'. Uninfluenced by Alemu (2016), which was published after (28) had been translated, I interpreted *lankíi* 'a second time, again' (+ negation) as 'no longer'.

(27) (. . .) **kanníichch**   **zakk-íin**   *kées*   *ze'-o<he>táa*
             P_DEM1.mABL   after-mICP   2sACC   graze-[1s]PURP.SS<2sO>
     íkko   *he'-is-o<he>táa*   *has-áam-ba'a.*
     or   live-CAUS1-[1s]PURP.SS<2sO>   want-1sIPV-NEG1
(Farmer:) '(. . .) I don't want to graze and keep you **any longer** (lit. after this).'
(Kambaatissata 1989: 6.123)

(28) (...) *"lankíi   ze'-áan-ke-ba'a"   y-í*
             second.DAT graze-1sIPV-2sO-NEG1 say-[3m]PCO
sharr-ée-'e.
chase_away-3mPFV-1sO
(Horse speaking about the master:) 'He said: "I won't graze you **any longer** (lit. a second time, again)! and chased me away."' (Kambaatissata 1989: 6.124)

4.5 Interim conclusion

As we have seen in the preceding sections, the phasal polarity effects of the adverbials as translational equivalents of 'already', 'not yet', 'still' and 'no longer' are contextual; none of these adverbials by themselves expresses phasal polarity:

- *wónan* 'at first, firstly, before, at an earlier time' may translate as 'already' (§4.1)
- *tadáa iillán=qaxee* 'until/up to now, so far' may translate in negative sentences as 'not yet' (§4.2) and in affirmative sentences as 'still' (§4.3)
- *teesúu* 'even now' may translate in affirmative sentences as 'still' (§4.3) and in negative sentences as 'still not' (§4.3)
- *lankíi* 'a second time' may translate in negative sentences as 'no longer' (§4.4)

If we assume that the {negative converb + existential}-construction for the expression of 'not yet' (§4.2) is the only potential candidate for a dedicated phasal polarity item (which would still need to be confirmed by more data and a more detailed semantic analysis), an evaluation of Kambaata phasal polarity items according to the six parameters proposed by Kramer (2017) is difficult. The Kambaata 'not yet'-construction has rigid COVERAGE and seems to be neutral with regard to Kramer's parameter of "pragmaticity", as the situations that are implicitly contrasted are temporally subsequent (a present situation where a state does not hold and an expected subsequent situation where it does). The expected change is in the future, therefore the 'not yet'-construction qualifies as non-telic (parameter: TELICITY). As regards the parameter "wordhood", the Kambaata 'not yet' expression represents a case that is not covered in Kramer (2017), as it is neither an independent word nor a bound morpheme but a periphrastic verb form consisting of two inflecting components that can also be used independently elsewhere. As to "expressibility", Kambaata has at least three "gaps" in the phasal polarity "system", because only one phasal polarity concept is expressed by a (potentially) dedicated item. It goes without saying that a single dedicated item cannot form a paradigm and that the parameter "paradigmaticity" is not relevant for Kambaata. There is no evidence of borrowed phasal polarity items in my corpus.

5 The experiential perfect construction

The Kambaata experiential perfect construction expressing 'have (n)ever (once) V-ed' (29) could be mistakenly interpreted as expressing phasal polarity, because it may invite the translation 'have already/not yet V-ed'. After a discussion of the morphological and syntactic properties of the experiential perfect construction and the word class status of the central '(n)ever'-morpheme, I argue that the experiential perfect should not be considered a phasal polarity construction.

(29) A: *Kám-i waayy-áno!*
    hold_back-2sIMP probably_not-3mIPV
    Át Duuball-í min-í már-t kása-ndo?
    2sNOM PN-mGEN house-mACC go-2sPCO ever-Q
    A: 'Come on, I doubt that! Have you **ever** (~ already?) been (lit. gone) to Duuballa's house?'
    B: ***Márr kása-ba'a gagás. Ikkodáa ...***
        go.[1s]PCO ever-NEG1 in_fact but
    B: 'I have **never** (~ not yet?) been (lit. gone) (there), in fact. But ...'
    (Field notes 2014)

5.1 Morphology and syntax of the experiential perfect construction

The experiential perfect construction consists of a perfective converb plus a phonologically independent, non-inflecting element *kása*, which together constitute a periphrastic verb form. The subject is marked on the converb; see *már-t* 2sPCO (= 3fPCO) and *márr* [1s]PCO (= [3m]PCO) in (29).[16] A pronominal object can be attached to *kása* (30)-(31). The independent past tense marker *íkke* is placed at the end of the complex verb form (31).

---

16 Certain subject index distinctions are neutralized in the converb paradigm (Table 2).

(30) *Aní-i   kées   xall-í   su'mm-íine-et   bagáan*
1sNOM-ADD 2sACC only-mGEN name-mICP-COP3 CNTR
daqq-ámm   xúujj   kása-he-ba'a.
find.MID-PASS.[1s]PCO   see.[1s]PCO   ever-2sO-NEG1
'I also know you only by name, but I have **never** met (or: not yet met) you.' (Kambaatissata 1989: 9.21)

(31) *Mexx-e-níi   daqq-ámm   kása-si-ba'a   íkke.*
single-MULT-ADD meet.MID-PASS.[1s]PCO ever-3mO-NEG1 PST
(Context: Did you know my father who died last year?) 'I **never** once met him (before he died).' (Elicitation, 2004, Dahl's (1985) TMA questionnaire: #50)

The perfective converb is a subordinate (non-final) verb form reduced in finiteness; it distinguishes five person indexes. If the perfective converb is the head of its own clause (and not part of a periphrastic verb form), the semantic relation between this clause and the superordinate clause is vague and may be interpreted as expressing anteriority, simultaneity, causality, purpose, conditionality or manner; the converb and its superordinate verb can also express two facets of one event. The perfective converb is one of three converb types; the imperfective and the negative, however, cannot form a complex verb form with *kása* 'ever'. Table 2 presents the perfective converb morphology; the marking consists of a segmental morpheme – the subject index – and a distinctive stress pattern. Only in certain 1s/3m forms can a segmental perfective converb marker *í* be isolated.

Table 2: Perfective converb inflection.

1s = 3m	(after C) ´(GEM/PAL)-Ø;
	(after CC) -Ø-í
2s = 3f = 3p	´-t
3hon	-éen
1p	´-n
2p = 2hon	-téen

The word class status of *kása* is not immediately apparent. However, there is little evidence that *kása* is nominal or adjectival in nature, even though the final *a* could be interpreted as a case/gender marker and its stress pattern as that of predicative nouns and adjectives (e.g. *dás-a* slow-mPRED '(it is) slow'). The use of the standard negator *-ba('a)* with *kása* neither proves nor disproves a nominal or adjectival origin, because NEG1 is used with nominal and adjectival predicates and declarative main verbs (§3). However, unlike nouns and adjectives, *kása* is never combined with a copula. Many aspects of *kása* speak in favor of a verbal origin. The pronominal suffixes on *kása* are from the set of object pronouns (on verbs) and not possessive pronouns (on nouns). A distinction between these two types of dependent pronouns is generally only made in the first and second person singular; in (30) a form of the object pronoun set, *-he* 2sO, is used. In two examples of the written corpus, a verbal variant of the 'ever'-morpheme is used as the main verb in questions. In both examples, *kas*- inflects for 3m imperfective (32).

(32) Kíi   hegeeg-óon   mánn-u   yáa'
     2sGEN   area-mLOC   people-mNOM   hold_a_meeting.[3m]PCO
     kas-áno?
     (do_)ever-3mIPV
     'Have the people in your area **ever** held a meeting?' (Kambaatissata 1989: 3.41)

The verbal origin of *kása* is further corroborated by its behavior in relative clauses. In (33), the head noun *láagat* 'voice' is preceded by the adjective *kohíchchut* 'strange' and a relative clause. The relative clause ends in the 'ever'-morpheme, which is combined with the negator *-umb* of relative verbs (§3).

(33) (. . .) [[*mexx-e-níi*   *maccoocc-í*   **kas-úmb-ut**]Relative Clause
             single-MULT-ADD   hear-[1s]PCO   (do_)ever-[1s]NEG5-fNOM
     [*kohíchch-ut*]Adjectival Modifier   [*láag-at*]Head Noun]Subject NP   *gisan-áachch*
     strange-fNOM   voice-fNOM   sleep-fABL
     báqq=át-t   *ke'-is-soo-'é*   *j-áata* (. . .).
     wake.IDEO=do-3fPCO   get_up-CAUS1-3fPFV-1sO   time-fACC
     '(. . .) when I was woken up from (my) sleep by a strange voice that I had **never** heard.' (Saint-Exupéry 2018: 11)

In (33), the negative relative form of *kas-* is glossed as 1s. The subject indexes of 1s and 3m are both Ø in the paradigm of negative relative verbs, but the reason clause in (34) proves that the verbal 'ever' does in fact inflect for person overtly. Reason clauses are relative clauses that are followed by an enclitic reason clause marker of nominal origin. In (34), the perfective converb (here: *xúudd*) and the verbal element *kas-* of the experiential construction are both indexed for a 3f subject.[17]

(34) [*Fénd-u-u   Ludág-u-u   ám-a-ssa*
     PN-fNOM-ADD   PN-mNOM-ADD   mother-fNOM-3pPOSS
     hittig-úta   ík-ki-yan   xúud-d
     SIM_P_DEM-fACC   become-3fPCO-DS   see-3fPCO
     kas-s-úmb-o]_{Relative Clause}=*bikkíi   hiliq-qóo'u.*
     (do_)ever-3f-NEG5-mOBL=REAS2   shock-3fPFV
     'Fendo and Ludago were shocked because they had **never** seen their mother (being) like this.' (Nibaabi Jaalae: 5)

The preceding examples have shown that the 'ever'-morpheme is verbal in nature and is synchronically analyzable as an auxiliary. It is morphologically defective and used in the invariant form *kása* in declarative clauses (30). In interrogative clauses, we mostly find the invariant form, too; in two exceptional examples, a verbal form is attested (32). In relative clauses, an inflecting verbal representation of the 'ever'-morpheme is required (33)-(34). There is a strong correlation between sentence type and polarity: The affirmative experiential perfect construction is used in questions ('Has X ever (once) V-ed?'),[18] the negative construction in declarative clauses ('X has never (once) V-ed').

Synchronically, the morpheme *kas-* is not used outside of the experiential perfect construction. Unlike other Ethiopian languages, e.g. Amharic (Leslau 1995: 141), no etymological link can be established between the experiential perfect marker and a Kambaata or Highland East Cushitic verb 'know', and the lexical origin of *kas-* remains opaque.

5.2 Semantics of the experiential perfect construction

Could the *kása*-construction be analyzed as a phasal polarity construction? A study of the contexts in which experiential constructions are used reveals that the translation 'not yet V-ed' is sometimes appropriate. In (30), which is

---

17 The 3f subject index is *-t*, which totally assimilates to preceding simplex obstruents. Therefore, it is realized as *d* after *xuud-* 'see' and *s* after *kas-* '(do) ever'.
18 According to a discussion that I had with native speakers in February 2018, the affirmative construction is possible in declarative clauses when a speaker is not sure about their experience. See *án márr kása* /1sNOM go.[1s]PCO ever/ 'I went (there) once, I think'.

repeated below as (30)', the speaker expresses that he has never seen the addressee; the wider context of the example makes clear that he wishes and expects this to change soon.

(30)' *Aní-i   kées   xall-í   su'mm-íine-et   bagáan*
       1sNOM-ADD 2sACC   only-mGEN name-mICP-COP3 CNTR
       *daqq-ámm   xúujj   **kása**-he-ba'a.*
       find.MID-PASS.[1s]PCO   see.[1s]PCO   ever-2sO-NEG1
       'I also know you only by name, but I have **never** met you (or: not yet met) you.' (Kambaatissata 1989: 9.21)

The experiential perfect construction lends itself to being translated as 'not yet' when it is clear from the context that the speaker considers an event to be realized in the near future and when this realization is considered to be late. However, native speakers did not confirm such an implication for most experiential examples in the corpus. The central semantic component of the experiential perfect construction is that an event has never happened to the subject in their lifetime. In most contexts in which the use of *not yet* would be natural in English – e.g. (mother speaking about daughter) *She has not yet arrived home; she must have missed the train* – the experiential perfect construction is considered inappropriate, because *min-í iill-ít kása-ba'a* /house-mACC arrive-3fPCO ever-NEG1/ would necessarily mean that the daughter has never come home before. Note also that the experiential construction is often reinforced by the adverbial *mexxenii* 'not even a single time' (33) or the synonymous *hináten*.

6 Conclusion

In this chapter we have seen that – with the possible exception of the NOT YET-construction discussed in §4.2 – Kambaata does not have dedicated grammatical or lexical means to express phasal polarity. It does, of course, have ways to express that a situation holds already, not yet, still or no longer, but the phasal interpretation of the temporal adverbials that are then employed is exclusively contextual. Furthermore, the means that were identified in the previous sections do not form a natural set in the language, i.e. they do not represent "structured means" in the sense of Van Baar (1997: 40f), and cannot be distinguished from other temporal adverbials in the language. It is the semasiological (function-to-form) approach adopted in this chapter that led me to discuss together grammatical means that are actually formally heterogeneous. The onomasiological (form-to-function) approach that is usually employed in the description of little-known languages would probably not have revealed any links between them.

Abbreviations

A	adjective	N	pragmatically determined morpheme (function as yet unclear)
ABL	ablative	NEG1	standard negator
ACC	accusative	NEG2	imperative negator
ADD	additive ('also', 'and')	NEG3	jussive negator
AG	agentive	NEG4	converb negator
C	consonant	NEG5	relative negator
CAUS1	simple causative	NIPV	non-imperfective
CNTR	contrast	NMZ1	nominalizer marked by a copy vowel
COND	conditional	NMZ4	nominalizer =r
COP1	existential verb *yoo-*	NOM	nominative
COP2	*-(h)a(a)/-ta(a)*-copula	O	object
COP3	*-Vt*-copula	OBL	oblique
DAT	dative	p	plural
DEF	definite	P_	pronoun
DEM	demonstrative	PAL	palatalization
DEM1	proximal demonstrative	PASS	passive
DEM2	medial demonstrative	PCO	perfective converb
DS	different subject	PFV	perfective
EQ1	equative (*kank-*)	PL2	plurative *–aakk*
f	feminine	PLC	place nominalizer
G	manner nominalizer =*g*	PN	proper noun
GEM	gemination	POSS	possessive
GEN	genitive	PRED	predicative
hon	honorific, impersonal	PRF	perfect
ICO	imperfective converb	PROG	progressive
ICP	instrumental-comitative-perlative	PST	past, hypotheticality
IDEO	ideophone	PURP	purposive
IMP	imperative	Q	question
IPV	imperfective	REAS1	reason clause with =*tannée*
IRR	irrealis	REAS2	reason clause with =*bikkíi*
JUS	jussive	REL	relative
LOC	locative	s	singular
m	masculine	SEQ	sequential
MID	middle	SIM	similative
MIT	mitigator	SG	singulative
MULT	multiplicative	SS	same subject

Bibliographic references

Alamu Banta & Alamaayyo G/Xiyoon. 2017. *Hambarrichcho Yaanata. Kambaatissa-Amaarsa Hayyo'ooma Yannaakkata* [Spices of Mount Hambarrichcho: Kambaata-Amharic Proverbs]. Addis Ababa: Addis Ababa University.

Alemu Banta Atara [= Alamu Banta]. 2016 [2009 E.C.]. *Kookaata*: *Kambaatissa-Amaarsa-Ingiliizissa Laaga Doonnuta* [Kambaata-Amharic-English Dictionary]. Addis Ababa: Berhanena Selam Printing.

Central Statistical Agency. 2007. *Ethiopia: Population and Housing Census of 2007*. http://catalog.ihsn.org/index.php/catalog/3583 (accessed 21 August 2018).

Dahl, Östen. 1985. The TMA questionnaire. In Östen Dahl (ed.), *Tense and Aspect Systems*, 198–206. Oxford: Blackwell.

Dahl, Östen. 2000. The perfect questionnaire. In Östen Dahl (ed.), *Tense and Aspect in the Languages of Europe*, 800–809. Berlin: Mouton de Gruyter.

Kambaatissata. Rosaanchi Maxaafa. [Kambaata Language. School Book.] 1989 E.C. Grade 1-8. Southern Nations, Nationalities, and Peoples Regional State: Education Bureau.

Kambaata and Hadiyya Translation Project-Hosaina. 2005. *Qarichcho Yesuus Kiristoositannee. Yohaannis Xaaffo Mishiraachchi Maxaafa / Latin Version of the Gospel of John in Kambaata Language*. Addis Ababa: The Bible Society of Ethiopia.

Kramer, Raija. 2017. Position paper on Phasal Polarity expressions. Hamburg: University of Hamburg. https://www.aai.uni-hamburg.de/afrika/php2018/medien/position-paper-on-php.pdf (accessed 6 April 2019).

Leslau, Wolf. 1995. *A Reference Grammar of Amharic*. Wiesbaden: Harrassowitz.

Miestamo, Matti. 2008. [Chapter 113] Symmetric and asymmetric standard negation. In Martin Haspelmath, Matthew S. Dryer, David Gil & Bernhard Comrie (eds.), *The World Atlas of Language Structures Online*. Munich: Max Planck Digital Library. http://wals.info/feature/113 (accessed 30 October 2018).

Nibaabi Jaalae 2014. Vol. 1–5. Addis Ababa: Spotlight.

Saint-Exupéry, Antoine de. 1943. *The Little Prince*. English translation by Katherine Woods. New York: Reynal & Hitchcock.

Saint-Exupéry, Antoine de. 1946. *Le Petit Prince*. Paris: Gallimard.

Saint-Exupéry, Antoine de. 2018. *Qakkichchu Laaha* [Le Petit Prince]. Kambaata translation by Deginet Wotango Doyiso & Yvonne Treis. Neckarsteinach: Tintenfaß.

Treis, Yvonne. 2008. *A Grammar of Kambaata*. Part 1: *Phonology, Morphology, and Non-verbal Predication*. Cologne: Köppe.

Treis, Yvonne. 2010. Purpose-encoding strategies in Kambaata. *Afrika und Übersee* 91. 1–38.

Treis, Yvonne. 2012a. Negation in Highland East Cushitic. In Ghil'ad Zuckermann (ed.), *Burning Issues in Afro-Asiatic Linguistics*, 20–61. Newcastle-on-Tyne: Cambridge Scholars Publishing.

Treis, Yvonne. 2012b. Switch-reference and Omotic-Cushitic language contact in Southwest Ethiopia. *Journal of Language Contact* 5. 80–116.

Treis, Yvonne. 2012c. Categorial hybrids in Kambaata. *Journal of African Languages and Linguistics* 33 (2). 215–254.
Treis, Yvonne. 2018. The apprehensive paradigm of Kambaata. Paper presented at the 51st Annual Meeting of the Societas Linguistica Europaea, 29 August – 1 September, Tallinn. https://hal.archives-ouvertes.fr/hal-01866064 (accessed 30 October 2018).
Van Baar, Theodorus M. 1997. *Phasal polarity*. Amsterdam: IFOTT.

Axel Fanego
Phasal Polarity in Amazigh varieties

1 Polarity shifts and stages of negation in Amazigh

Any language possesses mechanisms to express positive, affirmative statements, and their negation: *she is building a house* as opposed to *she is not building a house*. This is a simple polarity difference. Simple polarity contrasts by way of negating affirmative propositions have received a fair amount of attention with regard to varieties of Amazigh.[1] Among the issues discussed is a considerable degree of micro-variation among these varieties, concerning the use of various particles expressing negative polarity, sometimes on their own, sometimes in combination with one another and/or specialised negative verb stems (Galand 1994). A volume edited by Chaker & Caubet (1996) presents significant contributions on individual varieties (e.g. Lafkioui 1996 for Rif varieties) but also contrastive accounts such as Boumalk (1996) for Moroccan varieties, and Mettouchi (1996) comparing even more widely negation across Berber and Arabic varieties in the Maghreb. The possible interplay between aspect and negation is addressed by Mettouchi (1998) with regard to semantic/functional aspects, and from a more formal-comparative angle by Kossmann (1989). The discussion of negation in Berber/Amazigh has since been continued from within different theoretical perspectives. In a series of contributions, Brugnatelli compares across a wide range of Berber varieties, discussing the diachrony of the formally rather complex situation with regard to the grammaticalisation of negative particles and their syntactic placement (1987, 2006, 2014; see also Ouali 2004, for a formal syntactic account of these phenomena). Brugnatelli (2014) also provides a synopsis of earlier work on negation in

---

[1] I adhere to the use of Amazigh (in a wide sense) for those linguistic varieties that have traditionally been labelled as "Berber". The designation "Amazigh" appears to be preferred by the speakers from different regions that I have worked with. It also complies with the official practice in Morocco. It should thus be borne in mind that "Amazigh" does not refer specifically to the varieties of the Middle Atlas, as has been the case in a narrower use of that name. (In fact, nothing will be said at all about these particular varieties in the current paper.) The term "Berber" will be used occasionally, for instance when citing or discussing work by other scholars that use that label in their own work.

Axel Fanego, Goethe-Universität Frankfurt

https://doi.org/10.1515/9783110646290-014

Berber and may serve as a good starting point for readers interested in (simple) negation. What is mentioned only in passing or appears in examples but is not specifically and systematically addressed in earlier work is phasal polarity including polarity shifts. To my knowledge, the only exception is the unpublished work by Christian Rapold presented at the Phasal Polarity workshop in Hamburg (ms., 2018). I draw on Rapold's presentation on two significant occasions in this paper, but for the most part, the paper presents original data from two Amazigh varieties specifically addressing their phasal polarity constructions. What is phasal polarity?

In contrast to simple polarity, phasal polarity expresses an additional notion – a shift in polarity (NO LONGER, ALREADY), or the absence of an expected shift of polarity (STILL, NOT YET). It is actually easiest to explain this by simply illustrating it with four examples of phasal polarity expressions:

(1) Four core notions of phasal polarity (after Löbner 1985, Van Baar 1997, Kramer 2017)
 a. *She is still building a house*
 b. *She is not yet building a house*
 c. *She is already building a house*
 d. *She is no longer building a house*

The expressions *still*, *not yet*, *no longer* and *already* indicate polarity, so they indicate whether something takes place or not. But in addition to that, they also indicate how this relates to a second temporal phase. When I say *she is not working here any longer* this implies that she used to work here: the situation held in the past but does not do so now. *She is not yet working here* also expresses a negative situation in the present, but also an expected change to an affirmative situation in the future. We know – or, at least, we strongly assume – that she will eventually work here.

The choice of Amazigh varieties for this paper has to do with some of their fundamental typological properties. Grammatical aspect, rather than tense, is a central category in the verb system of these varieties. Since the cognitive domain of phasal polarity touches on aspectual notions, the interplay of the morphological exponents of phasal polarity and those of grammatical aspect can be expected to be interesting.

Moreover, the Amazigh varieties are interesting with regard to their clausal packaging mechanisms. Just how much image-schematic information can hinge on one finite verb appears to follow rules, constraints and preferences that may be significant also with regard to phasal complexity. For instance, with regard to motion events, Amazigh varieties are difficult to categorise in terms of Talmy's verb- versus satellite-framing distinction. Complex trajectories ("to move out of A through B into C") are usually broken up into sequences of shorter clauses each with its own inflected verb ("walk out A, move through B, and enter C"). Could it be the case that a similar tendency to avoid complexity within one clause applies in the domain of phasal polarity?

The objectives of this paper are to provide an overview of how phasal polarity is formally expressed in Amazigh varieties by grammatical means. These varieties are characterised by a great degree of similarity despite the fact that they are used across a geographically vast area and have evolved over an impressive length of time. At the same time, there is a very significant degree of micro-variation. Therefore, two varieties are contrasted in this paper that are used in geographically distant regions: Tarifit in northern Morocco (Ibeqquyen, Al Hoceima) and varieties used in southern regions of Morocco (Agadir and Guelmim).

This paper is about how to express ALREADY, NOT YET, STILL, and NO LONGER in Amazigh varieties, and what this may entail for the typological discussion of such terms under the label of "phasal polarity expressions". A number of suggestions are made here with regard to the wider discussion of phasal polarity. While phasal polarity can be argued to be a relevant domain showing systematic interplay of its formal exponents in Amazigh varieties, the concept ALREADY appears not to be conceptually closely related to the other three notions. In addition to the question of how meaning and functions are formally expressed, another question comes into play touching on the pragmatics of phasal polarity in Amazigh. Ideally, one would want to investigate this on the basis of larger natural speech corpora, but the in-depth interviews that provided the data for this paper allow at least some cautious reflections on possible pragmatic parameters, and these lead the way to the considerations concerning clauses and complexity towards the end of the paper.

A brief note on methodology: Authoring this text despite the fact that I am not a speaker, but at best a very deficient language user of Amazigh, is not without its challenges, but there is a benefit, too. Elicitation strategies were developed to test for specific notions, but the outcome – the understanding of the Amazigh-speaking interlocutors – would not necessarily conform to any of the expected categories. Rather than treating such dissonances as shortcomings of the specific tests, they are regarded here as significant pointers to mismatches in the phasal polarity construal across different systems.

Several different languages have been used in elicitation and in conversations about phasal polarity: French, Spanish, and English. Since they show significant differences in their ways of expressing phasal polarity, this is a significant point. Speakers have at times deliberately switched between languages, if they felt this helped them bring across semantic nuances that they would not have been able to express otherwise. In these regards, the current paper also deliberates the methodological challenges of capturing phasal polarity notions. More broadly it is also then an illustration of why I believe language typology should always follow anthropological linguistic avenues and practices.

In order to begin addressing these questions, the paper proceeds along the following steps. In section 2, theoretical notions that are directly relevant to this chapter are introduced. In section 3, the formal expression of phasal polarity in the two varieties under study is presented: in 3.1, for Tashelhiyt, in 3.2 for Tarifit. Section 4 briefly introduces the double alternative hypothesis in 4.1, which offers an alternative account of how especially the phasal polarity concept ALREADY could be treated, illustrated for Amazigh in 4.2. Section 5 deals with considerations around the pragmatics of phasal polarity constructions, paving the way to a short discussion of clause-packaging in section 6. Questions, challenges and opportunities in the course of the data elicitation and interviewing are addressed throughout the paper, where they apply. Together with a general outlook on where to take things from here, they will be taken up again especially in the concluding remarks of section 7.

2 Theoretical notions and earlier accounts of phasal polarity

A widely discussed proposal that sought to account for four core phasal polarity notions in formal semantic terms is that of Löbner (1989). He observes that ALREADY and STILL are logically linked by "dual negativity". Some languages derive a negative phasal polarity construction like NO LONGER from the notion of ALREADY having scope over a negated predicate ("already [not VERB]"). Spanish does exactly this. An affirmative sentence with *ya*, commonly, but not quite adequately, translated into English as 'already' (2a), contrasts with the sequence *ya* + [NEG + VERB] in (2b). The same applies to the continuative (or persistive) term *todavía* 'still' in Spanish (2c). When it applies to a negative predicate over which it has scope ("still [not VERB]"), it expresses what is rendered in English as 'not yet' (2d).

(2) Spanish (own knowledge)
    a. *ya   está   en Rabat*
       already 3SG.PRS.be in Rabat
       'S/he is already in Rabat.'
    b. *ya   no trabaja   aquí*
       already NEG 3SG.PRS.work here
       'S/he is no longer working here.'
    c. *todavía trabaja   aquí*
       still   3SG.PRS.work here
       'S/he is still working here.'
    d. *todavía No está   en Rabat*
       still   NEG 3SG.PRS.be in Rabat
       'S/he is not yet in Rabat.'

Table 1 illustrates these relations in both horizontal lines.

Table 1: Phasal polarity concepts in Spanish.

	Internal negation	
ya 'already'	→	*ya no* 'no longer'
todavía no 'not yet'	←	*todavía* 'still'

The formal markers in Spanish reflect the logical relation between the phasal polarity concepts arranged here horizontally through internal negation. Phasal polarity concepts can be logically related to each other also by external negation. This is the case for instance in isiZulu (Niger-Congo, Bantu; South Africa), where a persistive marker *sa-* 'still' that precedes the verb root expresses that something is still happening (3). The use of negation markers *a-* and *-i*, which occur at the periphery of the verb, together with persistive *sa-* expresses that something is no longer happening (more literally paraphrased: "not still happening") as shown in (4).

(3) isiZulu
    ngi-sa-fund-a   e-Primary   school
    1SG-still-study-FV LOC-Primary_ School
    'I am still attending Primary school.'
    (example from Instagram, 25 Feb 2018, https://www.instagram.com/p/BfnwSsyDM97/?tagged=olundi)

(4) a-ngi-sa-fund-i ngi-ya-sebenz-a e-Spar
NEG-1SG-still-study-NEG 1SG-DJ-work-FV LOC-Spar
'I am not studying any longer, I work at (the) Spar (supermarket).'
(isiZulu, example from facebook, 31 May 2016, https://www.facebook.com/IzigigabaZabaseshi/posts/622765387872657)

In some tense-aspect forms the first element of the discontinuous negative morpheme does not occur at the very beginning of the verb but occurs closer to the verb root within the morphologically complex verb form. Even in such cases, it is still true that negation markers are external to the persistive plus verb root sequence. This is illustrated by the contrast in (5) involving past continuous forms with the persistive (5a) and additionally the negative marker *nga-* and the final vowel *-i* as the verb ending (5b).

(5) isiZulu
 a. *Ngabe ngisakhuluma (~ngangisakhuluma).*
 nga-be ngi-sa-khuluma-a
 1SG.PST-be 1SG-still-speak-FV
 'I was still speaking.'
 (Poulos & Msimang 1998: 341; 343)
 b. *Izingane zazingasafundi.*
 izingane za-zi-nga-sa-fund-i
 10.children 10.PST-10-NEG-still-study-NEG
 'The children were no longer attending school.'

The affirmative sentences (3; 5a) entail an expected, but not effected, shift from positive to negative polarity at the respective reference time. In other words, that (5a) emphasises the continuation of the subject speaking at the (past) reference implies another situation (either later or counterfactually imagined) during which the subject would not speak any longer, but this change from speaking to not speaking has not occurred at the reference time. The utterance in (5b) entails the opposite: The children must have been attending school at some time prior to the situation expressed by the verb.

Using the same table configuration as in Table 1, the external negation would then appear as a significant operator between the vertically aligned upper and lower cells in Table 2, representing a conceptual link between STILL and NO LONGER (< "not [still VERB]"). The analogous examples for ALREADY and NOT YET (< "not [already VERB]") do not occur in isiZulu, but are known from other languages, see Kramer (2017).

Table 2: External negation linking the phasal polarity concepts 'still' and 'no longer' in isiZulu.

NEG + -sá- 'no longer'	
↑	External negation
-sá- 'still'	

3 Some common phasal polarity expressions in Amazigh

3.1 Tashelhiyt

In the southern Moroccan varieties from Agadir and further south, the basic array of formal devices to mark the four core notions of phasal polarity are as shown in Table 3. The English glosses are followed by French translation equivalents in brackets, because I relied on French to a significant extent in the conversations that produced the data for these varieties.

Table 3: Phasal polarity contrasts in Tashelhiyt.

yad	'already' [déjà]	ur sul	'no longer' [ne . . . plus]
ur ta (sul)	'not yet' [ne . . . pas encore]	sul	'still' [encore]

In accordance with the duality proposal made by Löbner, the externally negated *sul* 'still' expresses the notion NO LONGER, in a very similar way to what has been illustrated above for isiZulu. For 'already' and 'not yet' there are different, formally unrelated particles: *yad* and *ta*, the latter preceded by the negative marker *ur*. The combination of *ur ta* 'not yet' with *sul*, indicated in brackets in (6b), must be kept apart carefully from the construction *ur sul* 'no more' in the upper right cell of the table. Despite its position following the negation-phasal polarity complex *ur ta* 'not yet' and preceding the inflected verb *fḍaɣ* 'I ate lunch', the optional particle *sul* 'still' is not under the scope of the negation. When it is used, it expresses a notion of lateness (as in French *je n'ai toujours pas mangé*).

Word order and constituency in the clause seem somewhat problematic. The position of *sul* immediately preceding the verb may seem surprising, since it should be expected to be external to the scope of negation. In fact, it should be noted that *sul* has also been attested in clause-final position (see (22a) below, including a more in-depth discussion of these matters) and can be used as a confirming one-item fragment in reaction to a negative question (literal paraphrase: 'Have you not eaten yet?' – 'Still!', meaning '(still) not yet') as shown in (6b').

(6) Tashelhiyt (Guelmim variety, August 2018)
    a. *tššit   yad   lfḍur-nnek?*
       2SG.eat.PFV already lunch-yours?
       'Did you eat lunch already?'
    b. *uhu, ur   ta   (sul)   fḍary*
       no,   NEG yet (still) eat_lunch.PFV.1SG
       'No, I have (still) not eaten lunch yet.'
    b'. *sul*
       still
       'Not yet (lit.: still)'

The following example illustrates a common mechanism to express that something is no longer the case:

(7) Tashelhiyt (Guelmim variety, August 2018)
    nttni ur   sul   zdiyn   y=Ugadir;
    they   NEG still live.NEG.PFV.3PL.M in=Agadir
    ddan   s=Casa
    leave.PFV.3PL.M to=Casablanca
    'They do not live in Agadir any longer; they left for Casablanca.'

The example in (7) contains the negation marker *ur* immediately followed by *sul* which translates as 'still'. This term, *sul* 'still' is also used affirmatively, expressing the fourth core phasal polarity notion, illustrated in (8). What this example also shows is that *sul* 'still' applies in scalar contexts (see van der Auwera 1993: 616), not only in plain temporal phases.

(8) Tashelhiyt (Guelmim variety, August 2018)
    a. *llant   sul   dar-s   sddis n-tfunays,*
       be.PFV.3PL.F still at-him six   of-cow
       ur   ižli   ḥtta   yat
       NEG 3SG.M.lose.NEG.PFV even one
       'He still has six cows; he didn't lose any.'

b. *llan   sul   dar-s   sddis   n-lktub;*
   be.PFV.3PL.M still at-him six   of-book
   ur   ta yufi   ḥtta yan
   NEG   yet 3SG.M.find.NEG.PFV even one
   'He still has six books (only); he didn't get any others.'

In (8a), 'he still has six cows (not fewer)' is in a context in which, at that point, he might have easily lost some; so 'still' is understood against an expected decrease. In (8b) it is the opposite: he was supposed to have more already, but he still has (only) six. In scales, it does not make a difference whether the polarity point is expected to be reached through an increase or a decrease.

In the Tashelhiyt varieties of the south, a formal mechanism corresponding to each core phasal polarity notion is found. The negative phasal polarity expressions both contain *ur*, the common Amazigh negation marker. The term *yad* expressing 'already' does not occur with negative polarity, but *sul* 'still' can be externally negated. The only direct link between two phasal polarity notions is therefore the one between STILL and NO LONGER (< "not still").

With this in mind, we turn to Tarifit in the following, where both the formal markers and the conceptual connection between phasal polarity notions differ from what we have seen in the southern varieties.

3.2 Tarifit

Data for Tarifit were collected with speakers who are from Al Hoceima and identify as part of the Ibeqquyen section but have been residents in Catalonia for several decades. The language from which and into which examples have been translated is Spanish, which apart from Tarifit and Arabic is the language speakers felt most at ease with, and which was the most suitable common denominator in which I could operate in elicitation. In this northern variety from Al Hoceima, the basic array of formal devices to mark the core notions of phasal polarity are as shown in the following table. A noteworthy gap is the apparent lack of a term expressing the phasal polarity concept ALREADY.

Table 4 indicates *qa* as, arguably, a specialised ALREADY-term. Tilmatine et al. (1998: 134) list the term as such, i.e. with the respective translation equivalents *ja* in Catalan as well as French *déjà*. The term is placed in brackets in

Table 4: Phasal polarity contrasts in Tarifit.

(qa	'already' [Spanish *ya*])	ur ɛad	'no longer'	[Spanish *ya no*]
ɛad ur	'not yet' [Spanish *todavía no*]	ɛad	'still'	[Spanish *todavía, aún*]

Table 4, because it was not produced at all in elicitation, and nothing further can be said about it at this point in the current text.[2]

There is a much more commonly used specialised marker for the other positive phasal polarity concept, namely the term ɛad 'still', which is also used in Arabic and illustrated here in (9a). Things seem to follow Löbner's account with regard to the internal versus external negation of the positive phasal polarity expression ɛad 'still'. Based on this positive phasal polarity term expressing continuation or a persisting situation, the variant illustrated in (9b) with internal negation expresses the phasal polarity concept NOT YET. The externally negated ɛad 'still' in (9c) expresses the concept NO LONGER.

(9) Tarifit (Al Hoceima variety, August 2018)
    a. šek ɛad aqqa=k   gi=Barseluna?
        you still COP=2SG.M in=Barcelona
        'Are you still in Barcelona?'
    b. ɛad ur=d   tusi=ši   Yolanda?
        still NEG=PROX 3SG.F.come.NEG.PFV=NEG Yolanda
        'Has Yolanda not come yet?'
    c. ur ɛad zeddyeɣ   gi=Rubí
        NEG still live.NEG.IPFV.1SG in=Rubí
        'I am no longer living in Rubí.'

In contrast to other elements pertaining to the verb phrase, such as the progressive or negation clitics, Tarifit ɛad 'still' is not fully integrated into the verb phrase. Just like *sul* 'still' in Tashelhiyt, it can occur in different positions in the sentence. Given its greater syntactic autonomy, it is viewed here as a particle, which on occasions can serve as a sentence adverbial. It can even be

---

[2] One slightly unclear instance with a possible phasal polarity implication was an example overheard in natural speech in a spontaneous context. At the house of my host, someone entered the room asking whether to bring some water for me. My host reacted by answering that I had already been given water, the answer containing the element *qa*. In this (counterexpectional) context, English 'already' as a translation for *qa* is possible due to the respective functional polysemy of the English phasal polarity term, but obscures the fact that the function of *qa* in Tarifit is probably closer to that of expressing (counter)assertive verb focus.

used as a one-word answer to a question (with negative answer expectation) 'Do they not work in Terrassa (yet)?' where ɛad comes to mean 'not yet' (without any formally separate explicit negation marker).

(10) Tarifit (Al Hoceima variety, August 2018)
 war xeddm-en gi=Terrassa?
 NEG work.IPFV-3PL.M in=Terrassa?
 'Aren't they working in Terrassa?'
 ɛad!
 still
 'Not yet! (Lit.: Still!)'

As mentioned in 3.1 for the southern varieties, in principle the phasal polarity terms available do apply to both temporal and scalar understandings of phasality. The latter appeared to be more difficult to elicit from speakers of Tarifit than from speakers of southern varieties. Scenarios such as 'she still has three goats' (with both interpretations, 'only three goats so far' as opposed to 'only three goats left') were experienced as more cumbersome, or handled less straightforwardly, by Tarifit speakers in translation requests or when applying other elicitation techniques. This may point to possible restrictions or preferences in terms of phasal complexity and clausal packaging.

It would therefore be interesting to consider these observations within a broader range of possibly related phenomena, all pertaining to the packaging and distribution of information across clauses within and beyond sentences. This alludes to the seminal work by Talmy (1985, 2000) and Slobin (1996), and relates to central concepts in Bohnemeyer et al. (2007). Talmy's verb- v. satellite-framing distinction relies on the question by which means the concept PATH, which is central to motion events, is expressed: Is it part of the lexical information of the verb, or is it expressed through a satellite, e.g. a prepositional phrase? Bohnemeyer et al. (2007) build on these ideas and address the question of complex macro-events and the "limits" of just how much information may be coded in a clause (with one lexical verb at its core). Polar phasal notions are inherently complex, and it would be interesting to scrutinise correlations between degrees of complexity allowed in these various domains.

With regard to complexity in motion events, a preference to limit certain scenarios in single clause constructions has been described for Amazigh varieties (Fleisch 2011). Similarly, the Tarifit data, or rather the experience in eliciting relevant data from speakers of that variety, possibly reflect a conceptual preference to limit phasal polarity in notionally more complex events (here in terms of decrease versus increase 'still remaining' at the point of owning three goats). In fact, speakers often resorted to re-packaging their answers into clauses based on verbs that lexicalise the scalar notion (e.g. 'three goats remain' to express that someone has only three goats left), thereby disambiguating the trigger phrase. The prevalent use of Spanish as the main interlanguage with Tarifit speakers may have added to this effect, given that the verb-framing character of Spanish enhances lexicalisation of PATH-related notions, including arguably decrease and increase along a scale. In reply to a question *¿Cuántas cabras tiene Fátima ahora?* 'How many goats does Fátima have now?', in a contextually understood decrease scenario, (11a) is a grammatically acceptable answer, but (11b) sounds significantly more natural. (There is an additional semantic nuance in that (11a) implies a more transitory state, making it sound more likely that the subject will continue losing goats.)

(11) Castilian Spanish
 a. *todavía tiene tres cabra-s*
    still have.PRS.3SG three goat-PL
    'She still has three goats.' (=For now, she has three goats.)
 b. *le queda-n tres cabra-s*
    3SG.IO remain.PRS-3PL three goat-PL
    'She has three goats left.' (=Further expected loss is neither implied, nor ruled out.)

In summary, what we see is that Löbner's account based on the semantic polarity relations between the four basic phasal polarity concepts is supported to some extent by the Amazigh evidence. From the phasal polarity concept STILL, i.e. *sul* and *ɛad* in Tashelhiyt and Tarifit respectively, formal means of expressing related concepts are derived through formal negation. In Tashelhiyt this applies only through the relation of external negation. Therefore, only the right column under Tashelhiyt in Table 5 shows formal markers, here *ur sul* and *sul*. In Tarifit, in addition to the externally negated relation represented by the upper and lower cell of the right column, the lower row of the table represents the internal negation with *ɛad* and the negative marker *ur* in Table 5. The bar indicates that the position of both elements does not necessarily reflect the scope of internal negation on the surface order in the utterance.

Table 5: Relations between phasal polarity markers in Amazigh.

Tashelhiyt		Tarifit	
ur sul 'no longer'			*ur ɛad* 'no longer'
sul 'still' [encore]		*ɛad | ur* 'still not'	*ɛad* 'still'

In Tarifit then, NO LONGER is the external negation of STILL. The internal negation *εad ur* in Tarifit does not simply mean 'not yet', but emphasises a notion of counterexpectation (as in French *il n'est toujours pas . . .* ; not just *pas encore*)

As an alternative to the four-way matrix, a simple continuative account of subsequent stages from negative to positive to negative, together with the two polarity shifts marking the transition has been proposed (van der Auwera 1993: 627; Van Baar 1997: 35). If, as is the case in at least some Amazigh varieties, the phasal polarity terms other than ALREADY show formal links, it is plausible to assume that their similarity is based on the polar relations paraphrased as STILL NOT – STILL – NOT STILL. Using the actual English words, not the conceptual paraphrases, Figure (1) illustrates the conceptual link among the phasal polarity notions based on the continuative STILL concept.

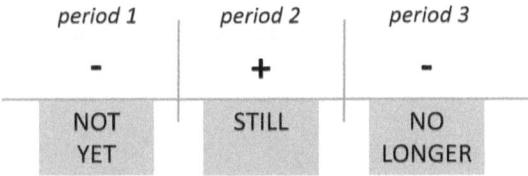

Figure 1: (Source: van der Auwera 1993).

Van Baar (1997: 35) characterizes van der Auwera's model as based on the view that "the phasal polarity-paradigm is essentially continuative". This continuative account (van der Auwera 1993; see also Van Baar 1997: 31–47) is based on phasal sequence, but it also captures the relevant polarity changes at the root of Löbner's dual negative matrix for the respective categories. For a language variety like Tarifit, the formal exponents of these three notions comprise the continuative phasal polarity concept *εad*. External negation derives the NO LONGER notion. Internal negation derives the NOT YET notion. The southern Tashelhiyt varieties have the specialised item *ur ta* for the latter, although at closer inspection we shall see that also there, the same system applies at least to a subset of verbs (see section 6).

But what about the discontinuative concept ALREADY in Amazigh varieties? What evidence do we find in support of, or against, its inclusion in a four-way matrix constituted by the polarity relations identified in Löbner's work based mostly on German and neighbouring or related languages? Tarifit does not seem to have a dedicated phasal polarity marker for the concept ALREADY. The formal device *qa* (see Table 4 and Footnote 2 above) is sometimes given as a corresponding term (Tilmatine et al. 1998: 134). It has partial functional overlap with ALREADY terms of other languages. Since its function appears to be closer to assertive verb focus than phasal polarity, it is questionable whether it should be included in this category at all.[3] It was not possible to produce phasal polarity-relevant systematic contrasts with *qa* through elicitation and its use is infrequent. In the next section, we therefore turn to the Tashelhiyt varieties and their ALREADY term *yad*. It is not formally related to other phasal polarity expressions in these varieties, so it does not point to the underlying functional logic hypothesised by Löbner (1989). The following section, which looks into ALREADY notions in Amazigh, is an attempt at applying the continuative model with its subsequent stages, because it promises to capture certain relevant properties better than the dual negation account.

4 Re-modelling phasal polarity notions: ALREADY in Amazigh varieties

4.1 The Double Alternative Hypothesis

Typological findings suggest that ALREADY terms are often missing from languages, or formally unrelated to other phasal polarity words (van der Auwera 1998: 28–29).[4] With this in mind, van der Auwera proposes a model that differs from Löbner's account in how it assesses ALREADY within the general system of phasal polarity. For Löbner it is a member of the four-way categorization based on dual negation strategies, a shift in polarity from negative to positive, applying to situations exemplified by the paraphrase "he did not DO earlier; now, he IS DOING". Van der Auwera (1993: 623) points out that, if the core meaning of *already* was "negative earlier state shifts to later positive", there is no good way of semantically telling apart *she has already built* from *she has finally built*.

---

[3] An anonymous reviewer whom I particularly thank for her/his insightful comments confirmed that an overall very similar situation holds in Tarifit varieties used to the east of the Rif variety (Ibeqquyen) relied on here.
[4] Van Baar relies on a sample of languages that is relatively small, but less biased toward European languages than earlier work on phasal polarity notions. Based on this sample, he relativizes van der Auwera's suggestions, pointing out that NO LONGER terms appear at least equally, if not more likely to be missing when he discusses expressibility and coverage types (Van Baar 1997: 118; 202–212).

Both clauses express a shift from negative to positive polarity, associated with an earlier and a later stage in the sequence of events.

Crucially, in addition to the specific polarity shift from negative to positive, English 'already' expresses a notion of earliness of completion: some situation applies earlier than expected. This may be the case for many, but by no means all languages. The Spanish phasal polarity word *ya* is commonly, but not fully adequately, translated into English as 'already'. In contrast to English, it makes no assumption about earliness. Nothing is semantically odd about the sentence in (12) which references a situation that holds later than expected (*por fin* 'finally') and contains *ya* indicating phasal shift from negative to positive polarity.

(12) Spanish (constructed example, cross-checked with native speaker)
 por fin, ya pod-emos pintar la pared
 by end already can-PRS.1PL paint the wall
 'Finally, we can [already] paint the wall'

Van der Auwera (1993, 1998) captures the difference between both languages by suggesting a cognitive model containing a first tier for the sequencing of (factual) temporal phases and a second tier in which non-factual, but expected sequences are aligned with the factual, real-time occurrences. This affords the possibility to add "expectedness" as a significant component in the meaning of these constructions. Figure 2 is an image-schematic representation of this model. It contains the idea of phasal sequencing as a necessary component: for ALREADY, a shift from negative to positive polarity. It provides two tiers onto which this phasal sequence is mapped: one for the situation as it unfolds in factual time, the other for a counterfactual domain associated with how the situation is assumed or expected to unfold.

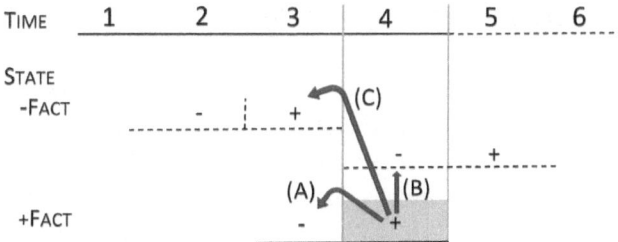

Figure 2: The double alternative hypothesis (van der Auwera 1998: 49).

The phasal polarity notion illustrated here is that of the Spanish ALREADY-term *ya*. The three arrows stand for different possible senses of ALREADY. English allows only for two of the three scenarios indicated by the arrows in Figure 2. One of them, (A), does not invoke any counterfactual notion (e.g.: "He moved from Rome to Nagasaki three years before I did. So, he was already living in Japan when I moved there."); this is represented by the left-bound arrow within the + FACT tier. The other scenario is that the negative-to-positive shift factually happened earlier than expected. In other words, the + FACT tier is dislocated to the left (an earlier time) compared to the counterfactual tier (e.g. someone was supposed to leave at 8 pm, but against expectation had already left one hour earlier). The small upward arrow (B) corresponds to this scenario. The third arrow, which is not part of the English range of 'already' also assumes a mismatch between the factual and counterfactual sequence of events, only this time, the factual situation occurs later than expected. As van der Auwera points out, in languages like Spanish this third interpretation of a shift from negative to positive polarity later than expected is possible for the respective ALREADY-word. In this case, the equivalent terms for 'already' and 'finally' can be combined in the same clause as in (12) without rendering it semantically odd.

The explanations provided here for the semantic range of English 'already' and Spanish *ya*, respectively, refer to the counterfactual tier: a mismatch between real world situation and expectation at least for some of the senses. This is not a universal property of ALREADY words. Possibly, ALREADY constructions of other languages may simply indicate a plain shift from negative to positive polarity without presupposing any mismatch between actual events and counterfactual expectation. The following section tackles the relevant construction type in Tashelhiyt and tries to shed more light on the question whether *yad* should be considered part of an integrated conceptual system of phasal polarity expressions in Berber varieties.

4.2 A closer look at ALREADY in the Tashelhiyt varieties

Spanish, as seen above, derives the phasal polarity notion NO LONGER from the positive phasal polarity concept ALREADY by way of the internal negation strategy. Hence, its phasal polarity paradigm is symmetrical (as initially shown in Table 1). For languages whose formal exponent for the phasal polarity concept ALREADY is different from and unrelated to any of the other three core phasal polarity notions, its inclusion in a systematic phasal polarity paradigm may simply not be warranted on logical grounds.

On formal grounds the phasal polarity concept ALREADY is not related to the other core phasal polarity concepts in Amazigh. But what evidence is there that may help us establish whether there are conceptual, semantic and pragmatic links that might still motivate us to speak of the phasal polarity system as an integrated paradigm in Amazigh? In Tarifit, there is very little to go by, since there is no unequivocal phasal polarity marker for ALREADY. We need to look at the southern varieties, then, in order to scrutinize some relevant aspects.

In Tashelhiyt, there is *yad*, and it seems natural to translate it into English as 'already'. The case of Spanish *ya* above has already shown that translation equivalence does not necessarily imply a semantic equivalence. The following paragraphs present evidence that Amazigh *yad* functions simply as a marker indicating a polarity shift from negative to positive. The idea of something happening earlier than expected seems not to play a role. At the same time *yad* situates the event in the here-and-now (of the utterance time). Overall then, its range of use is more restricted than in other languages mentioned earlier.

Christian Rapold presented a text count of *yad* in his contribution at the phasal polarity workshop in Hamburg in February 2018. It is based on a corpus of original Tashelhiyt narratives drawing on published text editions that include the collections of various early Berber scholars, compiled and edited by Harry Stroomer in several volumes in the Berber studies series (e.g. Stroomer 2002, 2003). What Rapold observes is a striking difference in frequency between Tashelhiyt *yad* and English 'already' in the translations that accompany the text collections. In the many texts that he considers, *yad* is only attested twice in total. Both occurrences are translated into English as 'already'. In addition to this, there are 37 further occurrences of 'already' in the translations, not based on actual phasal polarity expressions in the original texts. As Rapold points out, the translations apparently called for the use of an English phasal polarity marker in order to produce natural-sounding translations in many instances where the original text shows no such pragmatic tendency.

The argument presented by Rapold is corroborated by observations of natural speech and in interview situations. When prompting speakers to translate into Tashelhiyt, the answer rather often contained borrowed phasal polarity terms. Such loans are frequent in recorded data. Even when working with Berber-speaking migrants in Finland, where elicitation relied mostly on English and some Finnish, but no French at all, speakers would at times use the French loan *déjà* in order to render the phasal polarity notion ALREADY, probably due to a perceived need to render the notion of earliness which *yad* would not convey.

(13) Tashelhiyt (Agadir variety, August 2017)
    a. *tušk=id*   *déjà*   *s=dar=sn*
        3SG.F.PFV.come= PROX already to=at=theirs
    b. *tušk=id*   *s=dar=sn*   *déjà*
        3SG.F.PFV.come=PROX to=at=theirs already
        'She has already come to them.'

As the difference between (13a) and (13b) shows, there is some degree of syntactic freedom for *déjà*. The same is true for *yad*, which can also stand as a one-word answer to a question implying the expectation that something was going to happen: Has he done this (expecting an affirmative answer).

(14) Tashelhiyt (Agadir variety, August 2017)
     is   *tušk=id?*
     Q   3SG.F.PFV.come=PROX
     yad!   –
     already
     'Has she come here? – Yes!'

At the same time, *yad* seems to carry a much clearer "here-and-now" connotation, rooted in actual deixis. In past contexts (*he had already eaten, before we arrived*), its use appears at least pragmatically or semantically odd – if not strictly ruled out on grammatical grounds. Also, an experiential interpretation (*has she ever lived here?*) does not apply here easily. The implication of current relevance is fairly strong, possibly further enhanced by the fact that there is so little content material in the clause that might help to construe interpretations more permissive towards an experiential interpretation.

These semantic nuances are difficult to establish, since elicitation as a technique is pushed to its limits, maybe beyond them. The contexts construed are easily perceived as contrived, the conversations around the examples show that the actual construal of sense rests on much more than the simple selection of one form over another. Yet, what these conversations may lack in naturalness, they contribute in conveying general views and concepts of what it is significant to express.

In sum, *yad* can be characterised as a neutral ALREADY word marking a plain polarity shift. While it lacks any implication of earliness, Amazigh *yad* does imply the additional semantic notion of current relevance. It has not been attested when speakers refer to situations in the past.[5] In addition to a shift towards positive polarity, the term *then* expresses current relevance in the here-and-now of the speech situation. All available evidence from elicited data and spontaneous occurrences in uncontrolled situations points in this direction. Ideally, this point should be independently corroborated through the analysis of natural speech data – an investigation that has not been conducted at this point. It is important to note that the corpus would have to be very large, since the term *yad* is overall so rarely used. Which brings us back to the significance of pragmatics.

5 Semantic function or pragmatic potential: conventional phasal polarity usage patterns

Above, we saw how the Amazigh phasal polarity concept ALREADY differed in terms of pragmatics from English when comparing frequency of occurrence in translation as observed by Christian Rapold. Pragmatic preferences and frequency effects are part of a larger story of how the construal and expression of specific meanings is conventionalised in a given linguistic variety. It is therefore important to address what can be said about conventionalised semantic functions as opposed to malleable usage patterns determined by pragmatic preferences and needs, although with a cautious disclaimer concerning our methods.

It is, of course, very challenging to incorporate pragmatics into a kind of data collection and analysis that relies on elicitation. It would appear preferable to rely on natural language, for instance a corpus of recorded monologues, dialogues and conversations instead. Corpus analysis is not without its problems either. Rapold scrutinized tales and stories that constitute a specific genre. How a narrator of such texts expresses his intentions differs from the mechanics of pragmatics in spoken dialogues or in conversations. (In addition to that, we cannot be sure about how the collection techniques (dictation?)

---

[5] It is tempting to suggest that this is a typological correlate of aspect dominance. When aspect rather than temporality/tense is obligatorily marked on the verb, the use of a phasal polarity marker for negative to positive polarity (as is ALREADY) might establish a very strong preference for present relevance (=continued positive situation). Whether such a hypothesis holds true would need to be scrutinized in systematic typological comparison across a larger sample of relevant languages.

and preparation for printing may have affected the texts that are now available in written form.)

Elicitation has the advantage that examples can be replicated, tried out in slightly modified versions and re-tested with several speakers. I followed a two-pronged logic in elicitation. On several occasions when interviewing, I would give as little context and triggers as possible in order to learn which answers would come spontaneously; on other occasions, I would constrain the contexts as much as I could in order to trigger an expected outcome, pushing for an approach that tests for specific diagnostics, as is commonly done in linguistic elicitation.

In the latter case, my elicitation prompts often yielded replies without any phasal polarity term, even where one might have expected their use.[6] With regard to the finer nuances in meanings of *yad* 'already' we saw above that speakers would often circumscribe rather than use phasal polarity terms to describe most scenarios tested for. The following series of examples was developed to provide a richer background scenario, hoping that certain systematic differences would come to the fore more clearly. The language consultants were asked to imagine the following situation: Yesterday, speaker A saw speaker B waiting in front of his house. Speaker A knew that a certain Karim, a friend of speaker B, was expected to pay a visit. Today when speakers A and B meet, speaker A asks speaker B the question in (15):

(15) Tashelhiyt (Guelmim variety, August 2018)
 Iḍgam kudlli ẓriy-k tama n-tigmmi-nun ḥaqqan ar tqqalt s-Karim?
 iḍgam   kudlli   ẓriy=k   tama
 yesterday when   1SG.see.PFV=2SG.M.DO   side
 n=tigmmi=nun
 of=house=your.PL.M
 ḥaqqan   ar   tqqalt   s=Karim?
 actually IPFV   2SG.wait.IPFV   for=Karim
 'Yesterday, when I saw you at your house, were you (actually) waiting for Karim?'

Consultants were asked to imagine a negative scenario ('no, not any more') in response to the question. They overwhelmingly provided an answer without

---

[6] Especially given that the language consultants were at some point obviously aware of what I was interested in, it appeared logical to expect over-generation rather than omission of phasal polarity terms. Yet, this is not what happened.

any phasal polarity term. The long version in (16) does not sound most natural perhaps but was sometimes provided in elicitation situations as an explicit answer to the prompt.

(16) Tashelhiyt (Guelmim variety, August 2018)
 Uhu, ura sr=s tqqaly; yušk=id zik ṣbaḥ.
 uhu, ura   sr=s   tqqaly;   yušk=id
 no NEG.IPFV for=him wait.IPFV.1SG   3SG.come.PFV=PROX
 zik   ṣbaḥ
 early morning
 'No, I was not waiting for him; he (had) arrived early in the morning.'

The absence of phasal polarity terms here might simply be due to the fact that the phasal-temporal scenario is stated explicitly. Yet, even in a shorter version of an answer to the same prompt, usually no phasal polarity term appears.

(17) Tashelhiyt (Guelmim variety, August 2018)
 Uhu. Yušk-id zik ṣbaḥ.
 uhu, yušk=id   zik   ṣbaḥ
 no   3SG.M.come.PFV=PROX early morning
 'No. He (had) arrived in the morning.'

When suggesting to add *yad* 'already' to the example in (17), consultants indicated that the co-occurrence of *yad* and the temporal adverbial *zik ṣbaḥ* 'early in the morning' made the sentence sound unnatural to them. Even if not strictly mutually exclusive, speakers' statements attest to a tendency not to "overburden" the sentence with too much phasal-temporal information and therefore to avoid co-occurrence. In terms of word status, *yad* behaves like a full adverbial here.

An even shorter version of the answer would be *yušk-id yad* 'he came already; he has already come'. Speakers judged the phrase grammatically acceptable but were hesitant to accept it in the current context. It is not easy to tell whether this is for semantic or pragmatic reasons. This shorter phrase *yušk-id yad* refers to a polarity shift from negative to positive, but it also implies current relevance ('he arrived already [and is now here]'), rather than allowing for the expected polarity shift to be prior to a past reference moment (=his arrival already earlier than my seeing you at your house).

A comparable argument can be drawn from the first part of the answer, in its long version including the part stating 'I was not waiting for him (anymore)'. When such a longer answer was provided (instead of a simple negative *uhu* 'no' without repetition of the full predication), the use of *sul* (inside negation scope, adding the phasal information of a polarity shift from positive to negative) was not deemed ungrammatical, but semantically or pragmatically odd. Speakers tended not to include it in their answers.

(18) Tashelhiyt (Guelmim variety, August 2018)
Uhu, ura (sul) sr-s tqqaly
uhu, ura (sul) sr=s tqqaly
no NEG:IPFV (still) for=him wait.IPFV.1SG
'No, I wasn't waiting for him (any longer).'

This is true both when the stimulus question contained *sul*, and when it did not. Both stimulus questions, with and without *sul*, were tried in order to monitor for "echo" or "mirror" effects whereby in question-answer pairs, it could be the case that either there is a tendency to maintain the phasal polarity attention (a question containing *sul* would then make an echo answer *ur sul* more likely), or where perhaps the contrary might be the case: It could be sufficient to mark phasal polarity in the conversation once. (Note how in English a natural answer to anything like *Were you still doing this or that . . . ?* is *No, I wasn't.*" rather than *No, I wasn't any longer.*)

This is not just something that follows a universal Gricean efficiency maxim of not saying more than necessary, because it does not operate the same way across languages. With regard to the question how much and which material is or can be repeated in a question-answer pair between two speakers, it is challenging to ascertain what follows "proper constraints", and what is individual preference and just an instance of different degrees of emphasis or rather sparse ways of communicating. Yet, in the following examples, the conventional character comes to the fore quite clearly. Christian Rapold in his analysis of Tashelhiyt texts (and their English translations) points to the following phenomenon: Where Tashelhiyt uses a structure paraphrased as 'Do you VERB, or not yet?' the English translation has what sounds more natural in English, namely 'Do you already VERB, or not?'

(19) Tashelhiyt (Rapold 2018, drawing on a corpus of published Tashelhiyt texts)
Agg^w=id sr=sn, is nn ffuɣn nydd ur ta
look=PROX to=3PL.M whether DIST go.out.PFV.3PL.M or NEG yet
'The hedgehog said to the man: Come and look whether they have already gone out, or not.'

The behaviour of contrastive tags, and the question where the phasal polarity information is expressed, is intriguing also in elicited data from Tarifit.

(20) Tarifit (Al Hoceima variety, August 2018)
ur ssiney ma ixeddem ma ɛad
NEG know.NEG.PFV.1SG whether 3SG.M.work.IPFV whether still
'I don't know whether he is already working or not.'

As in Rapold's analysis, there is no indication of a polarity shift in the first complement clause (*ma ixeddem* 'whether he is working'). In the second part, a repeated complement clause, that contrastive notion (on-going negative situation) is expressed solely by the term *ɛad* 'still'. No negation marker is used in either the complement clause or the elliptical tag *ma ɛad*. This suggests that the construal of phasal notions and in fact negation can be extended over several clauses or clause-like utterance portions, and each clause or clausal chunk expresses a more nuclear notion of polarity or phasal continuation.

In this section, we have seen how triggering the use of phasal polarity particles or adverbs has been more difficult than one might have expected, given that there are dedicated formal devices for their expression in the various Amazigh varieties. This has been true for different phasal polarity notions, such as ALREADY and STILL. Elicitation was helpful, though, when it went beyond what is mainly a questionnaire-based translation exercise. In our case, the significance of clausal complexity came to the fore. What has not been systematically tested so far is the significance of aspect marking. The fact that the verb in the complement clause in (20) is in the imperfective may have an impact on the construal of phasal polarity across chains of smaller clausal chunks.

6 Phasal polarity, clausal complexity and aspect construal: towards a solution

The previous section deals with the distribution of phasal polarity information within and across sentences and looks at how this follows certain systematic patterns in both Tashelhiyt and Tarifit. It has also been suggested that the use of phasal polarity terms depends, among other things, on the aspectual properties of the situation conveyed in discourse. It is therefore plausible to assume interdependence and co-variation with grammatical aspect. In fact, for Bantu languages, a number of grammatical forms that are associated with phasal polarity semantics have been discussed in particular in connection with the general tense-aspect system of the respective languages (see e.g. Schadeberg 1990) rather than as part of a separate and cohesive phasal polarity system. It is noteworthy that Nichols (2010) analyses what he calls alterative constructions in siSwati in terms of tense and aspect more than as markers of a neutral polarity shift. (For more examples concerning Bantu and the interaction of the usually complex tense-aspect systems in those languages with phasal polarity, see also Nassenstein and Pasch, this volume.)

One of the motivations to investigate phasal polarity in Amazigh has been that these languages are aspect-dominant, with usually a fairly systematic binary distinction between perfective and imperfective, as well as possibly additional aspectual verb stems (for an accessible overview of aspect categories across Berber, see Belkadi 2013). This, in connection with certain syntactic alternations, will be discussed in the following based on a series of additional sets of elicited examples from the southern varieties.

(21) Tashelhiyt (Guelmim, August 2018)
    a. *ur   n-kmml*
       NEG   1PL-finish.PFV
       'We have not finished.'
    b. *ur   ta   n-kmml*
       NEG   yet 1PL-finish.PFV
       'We've not finished yet [but we are about to; shouldn't take long].'
    b' *ur   ta   y-kmml   tiyri=ns*
       NEG   yet 3SG.M-finish.PFV   task.PL=his
       'He's not finished his tasks yet' [but will!].'
       (ex. from El Mountassir 2003: 110)
    c. *ur   ta   sul   n-kmml*
       NEG   yet still 1PL-finish.PFV
       'We've still not finished' [although we were supposed to be done by now].'

The examples above illustrate the formal expression of a simple negative (21a), the addition of the phasal polarity expressing term *ta* 'yet' in the elicited example (21b) and a near identical example from the literature in (21b'), and the same construction extended by *sul*, conveying a sense of delay or lateness concerning the situation in (21c).

The utterance in (22a) was overheard in a spontaneous context.

(22) Tashelhiyt (Agadir, December 2018)
   a. *le filme   ur   ta   i-kmml   sul*
      the film   NEG yet 3SG.M-finish.PFV still
      'The film has not finished yet.'
   b. *le filme   ur   ta   sul   i-kmml*
      the film   NEG yet still 3SG.M-finish.PFV
      'The film has not finished yet.'
   c. *le filme   ur   ta   žžu   i-kmml*
      the movie NEG yet still 3SG.M-finish.PFV
      'The film has still not finished.'

The utterance-final position of *sul* 'still' in (22a) contrasts with (21c). In elicitation, (22b) was deemed acceptable and semantically equivalent to (22a). Apparently, when used together with *ur ta*, the syntactic position of *sul* is not strict. As an alternative to *sul*, the term *žžu* was used on occasions placing more emphasis on the fact that the situation was viewed as delayed (22c).[7]

All of these examples contain the element *ta* which expresses the phasal polarity notion NOT YET in combination with the negation marker *ur*. It is possible to construct sentences expressing the same phasal polarity notion NOT YET without *ta*.

(23) Tashelhiyt (Agadir variety, December 2018)
   a. *ur   sul   i-kmml*
      NEG still 3SG.M.finish.PFV
      'It has not finished yet.'
   b. *ur   i-kmml   sul*
      NEG 3SG.M.finish.PFV   still
      'It has not finished yet.'

This is unexpected insofar as (23a) appears to suggest external negation of the phasal polarity marker as opposed to (23b) with *sul* standing in utterance-final position. If semantics was closely mirrored by syntax, one would expect (23a) to be paraphrased as "it is NOT the case that it STILL finished", whereas (23b) could be understood as "it is STILL the case that it has NOT finished". Only the latter corresponds in a straightforward way to Löbner's account of negation with regard to phasal polarity terms. Following him, (23a) with a verb plus

---

[7] Boumalk (1996: 43) glosses the term *žžu* with Fr. *jamais* 'never', but the semantics of in (22c) suggest a different translation here.

persistive *sul* being externally negated would have been expected to yield a NO LONGER meaning (see e.g. Löbner 1989). It is easy to see that the combination of a perfective verb with persistive marking might create a semantic conflict. Yet, (23a) is well-formed and the persistive *sul* 'still' behaves as if it were outside the scope of the negation marker.

The following examples suggest, though, that there is another significant notion coming into play. Actionality and aspectual notions are not simply a matter of perfective versus imperfective grammatical aspect. A look at a dynamic verb of extended duration, *yr* 'read, study', appears to behave differently in combination with phasal polarity terms and negation markers.

(24) Tashelhiyt (Agadir, December 2018)
    a. *ur   ta   iɣra   sul*
       NEG yet 1SG.study.PFV still
       'He has not studied yet (=so far, he has not studied ever).'
    b. *ur   ta   sul   iɣra*
       NEG yet still 1PL.study.PFV
       'He has not studied yet (=he has still not begun to study).'

The difference in semantic nuance is subtle. In (24a), the context was that of an 8-year old boy who had never attended school (even though at his age, he was supposed to), and it is not clear that he actually ever will go to school. Example (24b) was deemed more suitable in a situation where someone was about to take his books and dedicate some time to reading/studying, but has not (yet) done so. A comparable difference could not be identified with regard to the sentences in (22a) and (22b).

A second piece of evidence that actionality and verb meaning may come into play comes from the following examples.

(25) Tashelhiyt (Agadir variety, December 2018)
    a. *ura   yaqqra   sul*
       NEG.PROG 3SG.M.study.IPFV still
       'He is not yet studying'
    b. *ura   sul   yaqqra*
       NEG.PROG still 3SG.M.study.IPFV
       'He is not studying any longer (=he quit school).'

Contrary to what we have seen in examples (23) and (24) above, the imperfective form of the durative verb in (25) shows the contrast between NOT YET and NO

LONGER being constructed solely by the position of the negation marker *ur* vis-à-vis the phasal polarity term *sul* 'still'.

A short summary of these observations then directs us to the main insights so far that concern the possible interaction between phasal polarity marking, the grammatical perfective-imperfective distinction and lexical aspect. The phasal polarity construction *ur ta* is used with perfective, but not imperfective verbs. If this is indeed a fairly strict constraint in the Tashelhiyt phasal polarity grammar, it may fall out from a logical semantic consideration. It is generally true that phasal polarity expressions do not abound in natural speech and texts in Amazigh varieties. This is even more true for the combination of negated imperfective verbs in connection with the phasal polarity notion NOT YET, since the latter highlights a polarity shift, i.e. an instantaneous change which may simply not invite the combination with situations conceived as durative and marked by imperfective aspect.

Imperfective verbs appear to build their range of phasal polarity options in Tashelhiyt departing from the general continuative (or persistive) marker *sul*. Scope of negation comes into play as suggested in the account by Löbner: [NEG [still VERB]] expresses 'no longer', [still [NEG VERB]] 'not yet'. In this, Tashelhiyt resembles what has been outlined as the core phasal polarity system for Tarifit in section 3.2, based on a different phasal adverb, *ɛad*, in Tarifit. This contrasts with the functions of *sul* 'still' accompanying perfective verbs in Tashelhiyt. In this case, with negative predicates it is interpreted as 'not yet' irrespective of the position of *sul* in the sentence. With perfective verbs there is a range of additional constructions, all referring to the overall phasal polarity notion NOT YET: *ur ta* 'not yet', *ur ta sul* '[still] not yet', *ur sul* 'not yet', *ur ta žžu* 'not yet; not ever, so far') On the basis of elicited material, it seems impossible to "tease out" distinctive semantic nuances. The tentative translations given here are vague pointers to these evasive differences. Again, corpus-based work should be relied on in future work.

7 Concluding remarks

The main question at the outset of this investigation into phasal polarity in Amazigh has been whether data from Amazigh varieties would provide support for the assumption that phasal polarity is best analysed as a unified conceptual domain. The description including the contrast between two different areas, the Rif and the southern regions including Agadir and Guelmim, has shown the concept ALREADY to be conceptually unrelated to the other three phasal polarity notions. There is either no term for 'already', or if there is, it appears to be unrelated to other phasal polarity notions. Negation of predicates with Tashelhiyt *yad* 'already' is not possible.

Alongside the form of phasal polarity markers and their semantic function, pragmatic evidence casts doubt on a strong view of phasal polarity as a domain whose component parts are best explained as derived from one another by logical operation. Neither the northern variety of Tarifit nor the southern Tashelhiyt varieties have a symmetrical system. Overall, it would appear more fruitful to interpret Amazigh phasal polarity in terms of a continuative(/discontinuative) account rather than in terms of Löbner's dual negation hypothesis. Explanations based on continuation and sequencing of phases relate to aspectuality/actionality, both lexical and grammatical, which has been shown to affect the use of phasal polarity terms in Amazigh.

At this point, we do not know for sure whether lexical verbs differ systematically with regard to phasal polarity marking. Evidence from grammatical aspect distribution, i.e. the restrictive use of certain phasal polarity terms with imperfectives, seems to suggest that also event-type could matter with regard to phasal polarity. Whether this implies a systematic difference between durative verbs and non-durative change-of-state verbs is a pertinent question for future investigation.

Abbreviations

1PL	1st person plural	IPFV	imperfective
1SG	1st person singular	LOC	locative
2SG	2nd person singular	M	masculine
3PL	3rd person plural	NEG	negative
3SG	3rd person singular	PRS	present
COP	copula	PST	past
DO	direct object	PFV	perfective
F	feminine	PROX	proximal(~ventive)
FV	final (default) vowel	Q	interrogative
IO	indirect object		

Bibliographic references

Belkadi, Aicha. 2013. Aspect and mood in Berber and the aorist issue. *SOAS Working Papers in Linguistics* 16. 127–150.
Bohnemeyer, Jürgen, Nicholas J. Enfield, James Essegbey, Iraide Ibarretxe-Antuñano, Sotaro Kita & Friederike Lüpke. 2007. Principles of event segmentation in language: The case of motion events. *Language* 83 (3). 495–532.
Boumalk, Abdallah. 1996. La négation en berbère marocain. In Salem Chaker & Dominique Caubet (eds.), *La négation en berbère et en arabe maghrébin*, 35–48. Paris: L'Harmattan.
Brugnatelli, Vermondo. 1987. La negazione discontinua in berbero e in arabo-magrebino. In Giuliano Bernini & Vermondo Brugnatelli (eds.), *Atti della 4. Giornata di Studi Camito-semitici e Indeuropei, Bergamo 28 November 1985*, 53–62. Milano: Unicopli.
Brugnatelli, Vermondo. 2006. La négation berbère dans le contexte chamito-sémitique. In Antoine Lonnet & Amina Mettouchi (eds.), *Les langues chamito-sémitiques (afro-asiatiques)*, vol. 2, 65–72. Paris: Ophrys.
Brugnatelli, Vermondo. 2014. Berber negation in diachrony. In Maj-Britt Mosegaard Hansen and Jacqueline Visconti (eds.), *The Diachrony of Negation*, 167–184. Amsterdam: John Benjamins.
Chaker, Salem & Dominique Caubet (eds.). 1996. *La négation en berbère et en arabe maghrébin*. Paris: L'Harmattan.
El Mountassir, Abdallah. 2003. *Dictionnaire des verbes Tachelhit-Français (parler berbère du sud du Maroc)*. Paris: L'Harmattan.
Fleisch, Axel. 2011. Construing motion in Berber. In Amina Mettouchi (ed.), *«Parcours berbères». Mélanges offerts à Paulette Galand-Pernet et Lionel Galand pour leur 90e anniversaire*, 485–503. Cologne: Köppe.
Galand, Lionel. 1994. La négation en berbère. *Matériaux Arabes et Sudarabiques* 6. 169–181.
Kossmann, Maarten. 1989. L'inaccompli négatif en berbère. *Études et documents berbères* 6. 19–29.
Kramer, Raija L. 2017. Position paper on Phasal Polarity expressions. Hamburg: University of Hamburg. https://www.aai.uni-hamburg.de/afrika/php2018/medien/position-paper-on-php.pdf (accessed 06 April 2019).
Lafkioui, Mena. 1996. La négation en tarifit. In Salem Chaker & Dominique Caubet (eds.), *La négation en berbère et en arabe maghrébin*, 49–77. Paris: L'Harmattan.
Löbner, Sebastian. 1985. Natursprachliche Quantoren. Zur Verallgemeinerung des Begriffs der Quantifikation. *Studium Linguistik* 17/18. 79–113.
Löbner, Sebastian. 1989. 'Schon – erst – noch': An integrated analysis. *Linguistics and Philosophy* 12 (2). 167–212.
Mettouchi, Amina. 1996. La négation dans les langues du Maghreb: Synthèse. In Salem Chaker & Dominique Caubet (eds.), *La négation en berbère et en arabe maghrébin*, 177–195. Paris: L'Harmattan.
Mettouchi, Amina. 1998. Aspect et negation. Remarques sur l'inaccompli et la negation en anglais et en berbère (kabyle). In Adree Borillo, Carl Vetters and Marcel Vuillaume (eds.), 191–205. *Regards sur l'aspect*, Amsterdam & Atlanta: Rodopi.
Nichols, Peter. 2010. *A Morpho-Semantic Analysis of Aspectuality in Siswati. A cognitive approach to the analysis of the Alterative, Persistive and Inceptive aspects in siSwati*. London: SOAS dissertation.

Ouali, Hamid 2004. Negation and Negative Polarity Items in Berber. *Berkeley Linguistics Society* 30. 330–340. http://dx.doi.org/10.3765/bls.v30i1.951 (accessed 06 April 2019).

Rapold, Christian J. 2018. Phasal Polarity expressions in Tashlhiyt. Paper presented at the International Conference on the Expression of Phasal Polarity in sub-Saharan African languages, University of Hamburg, 3–4 February.

Schadeberg, Thilo. 1990. Schon – noch – nicht – mehr: Das Unerwartete als grammatische Kategorie im Kiswahili. *Frankfurter Afrikanistische Blätter* 2. 1–15.

Slobin, Daniel I. 1996. Two ways to travel. Motions verbs in English and Spanish. In Masayoshi Shibatani & Sandra A. Thompson, *Grammatical Constructions: Their form and meaning*, 195–217. Oxford: Oxford University Press.

Stroomer, Harry. 2002. *Tashelhiyt Berber Folktales from Tazerwalt (South Morocco). A Linguistic Reanalysis of Hans Stumme's Tazerwalt Texts with an English Translation.* Cologne: Rüdiger Köppe.

Stroomer, Harry. 2003. *Tashelhiyt Berber Texts from the Ayt Brayyim, Lakhsas and Guedmioua Region (South Morocco). A Linguistic Reanalysis of "Récits, contes et légendes berbères en Tachelhiyt" by Arsène Roux with a Translation in English.* Cologne: Rüdiger Köppe.

Talmy, Leonard. 1985. Lexicalization patterns: semantic structure in lexical forms. In Timothy Shopen (ed.), *Language Typology and Syntactic Description. Vol. 3: Grammatical categories and the lexicon*, 36–149. Cambridge: Cambridge University Press.

Talmy, Leonard. 2000. *Toward a Cognitive Semantics*. [2 volumes.] Cambridge, Massachusetts: MIT Press.

Tilmatine, Mohamed, Abddelghani El Molghy, Carles Castellanos & Hassan Banhakeia 1998. *La llengua rifenya. Tutlayt tarifit.* Bellaterra: Universitat Autònoma de Barcelona.

Van Baar, Theodorus M. 1997. *Phasal polarity.* Amsterdam : IFOTT.

van der Auwera, Johan. 1993. 'Already' and 'still': Beyond duality. *Linguistics and Philosophy* 16 (6). 613–653.

van der Auwera, Johan. 1998. Phasal adverbials in the languages of Europe. In Johan van der Auwera & Dónall P.Ó. Baoill (eds.), *Adverbial constructions in the languages of Europe*, 25–145. Berlin & New York: Mouton de Gruyter.

Bernhard Köhler
Phasal polarity expressions in Ometo languages (Ethiopia)

1 The Ometo languages

1.1 Nomenclature, demographic notes, internal and external classification

The concept "Ometo" comprises a group of approximately thirteen languages spoken in southwest Ethiopia, that is, in the wider area of the Omo river after which the group is named. It is not fully clear who coined this name or what is meant by the suffix with -*t*-, but Cerulli (1925: 598) divides the so-called "Sidāmā" languages into four parts, one of which is called "Sidāmā dell'Omō" also known as "Omêti". Later on, it is Moreno (1938) who uses the modern term "Ometo", though he still considers the group as a single language. All in all, the Ometo languages have far more than 3 million speakers, with Wolaitta alone accounting for more than 1.5 million of these; see Hudson (2012: 215–217) for the most recent census figures from the year 2007.

Although structural and lexical features strongly suggest that the Ometo languages constitute a single language family (see also §1.2 for some characteristics), their genetic relations to each other are still partly controversial. First and foremost, there is – even post mortem – an open debate between Fleming (1974: 93), who distinguishes West, South, Central and East Ometo subgroups and considers C'ara as a separate branch of Omotic, and Bender (1987: 30), who has North and South Ometo which, together with C'ara, form Macro-Ometo. Therefore, it is not clear whether Fleming's four (five?) or Bender's two / three divisions within the Ometo family is more correct. Other authors have opted for one of the two approaches, both of which are based mainly on lexical data from word lists, but an in-depth revision of these internal classifications of Ometo languages has not yet been conducted. For the mere fact that Bender's later (2000) monograph is the only comparative Omotic study so far that relies on deeper morphological evidence, the present paper will adopt his subgrouping of Ometo as outlined in Figure 1. Some language names were changed in accordance with more modern spellings.

Bernhard Köhler, Goethe-Universität Frankfurt

https://doi.org/10.1515/9783110646290-015

Macro-Ometo	Ometo	Northwest	Wolaitta-Gamo-Gofa-Dauro-Dorze, Malo, Oyda, Baskeet, Maale
		Southeast	Koorete, Zayse, Haro
	C'ara		C'ara

Figure 1: Internal classification of the Ometo language family (Bender 2000: 2, 7, 46).

It is fortunate that, contrary to Bender's first (1987) attempt, North Ometo and South Ometo are represented as Northwest Ometo and Southeast Ometo in Bender's (2000) monograph, so there is no risk of confusion with Fleming's four subgroups as indicated above. Regardless of this terminological remark, the issue of the so-called Wolaitta cluster including the five varieties tied together with hyphens in Figure 1 remains unclear even today. On the one hand, Fleming (1974: 93) conceives of Central Ometo as a dialect cluster comprising more than 40 varieties such as Wolaitta, Gamo, Gofa, Dauro, Zala, Malo and possibly Oyda. On the other hand, Wondimu (2010: 7) claims that Gamo alone has "about 42 dialect varieties", which makes it rather unlikely that it should be merged with yet other varieties as a single language. Regarding Dorze, which is subsumed under Gamo also by, for example, Wondimu (2010: 182), field recordings made by the present author in November 2017 have shown that this variety has some idiosyncratic grammatical features. In the present paper, Dorze is considered a separate language and the same goes for Wolaitta, Gamo, Gofa and Dauro. Therefore, it is tentatively assumed that the Ometo family consists of thirteen languages: nine in the Northwest group, three in the Southeast group and also C'ara, until the latter's position is known more exactly. Ongoing studies on the comparative verbal morphology of Ometo languages, which were initiated by the present author in March 2016 with a financial grant by the "DFG" (German Research Foundation), will shed more light on the genetic relations within the Ometo family.

In spite of a number of interesting differences which remain to be investigated, also in view of areal phenomena, the Ometo languages are relatively similar to each other, both from a grammatical and from a lexical perspective. However, the unity of the Omotic language group to which the Ometo family belongs is still a controversial matter. Considering the morphologically-based findings on Omotic classification by Bender (2000: 202), it is quite safe to say that the Ta/Ne group with Macro-Ometo, Gimira, Yem and Kefoid constitutes a language family, while Dizoid may be more distantly related. Especially Mao and Aroid are sometimes excluded from what is called

Omotic, most obviously by Zaborski (2004), who assigns both groups to the Nilo-Saharan phylum and maintains the concept of West Cushitic for the remainder of the Omotic languages. The current investigations of the verbal morphology of Ometo languages are also open to comparisons with further Omotic varieties and C'ara may certainly be regarded as a kind of link between Ometo and non-Ometo.

The present paper will discuss some findings on phasal polarity in Ometo languages, that is, on linguistic items expressing the equivalents of English 'still', 'already', 'not yet' and 'no longer'. These items will be exemplified in §2, relying on published or unpublished materials from other authors as well as field recordings made by the present author, and it will be shown which conclusions can be drawn from the data at hand. The final §3 will summarise the most salient facts and point to open questions for further research. First of all, however, §1.2 will present some structural features shared by Ometo languages.

1.2 Some structural characteristics

One salient feature of Ometo as a whole, but also Omotic and many other Ethiopian languages, is their basic clause structure subject-object-verb, which is true for simple declarative sentences in virtually all Omotic languages (Azeb 2012: 488). Evidence of this word order in several languages is seen in examples throughout the present paper. More precisely, Ometo syntax, if pragmatic criteria are excluded, can be described as strictly verb-final and more or less strictly subject-initial, with most other constituents entering between the subject and the verb. Hence, if Ometo languages express phasal polarity items such as 'still' and 'already' in the form of adverbial phrases, then these are expected to take this "embedded" position and occur beside objects and other additional phrases. In practice, however, it is not rarely observed that adverbs come at the beginning of the sentence in front of the subject, although they more frequently occupy positions behind the subject. Moreover, phasal polarity concepts are not necessarily expressed by adverbs; there may be other means as well, as will be discussed in §2.

Not only the basic word order subject-object-verb, but also long and complex sentences are typical of Ometo languages: many different events and pieces of information are combined to form a single sentence. This syntactic complexity is accompanied by elaborate morphological systems, which contribute to the emergence of long words displaying a great variety of grammatical markers. In actual fact, canonical nominal and verbal roots in Ometo are monosyllabic and have the general shape CV(V)C(C)-, where the nucleus can consist in a short vowel or a long vowel or a diphthong and the second consonantal slot can be filled by a short consonant or a long consonant or a cluster. In Ometo languages, most simple nouns are formed from nominal roots by adding a so-called "terminal vowel" (Hayward 1987, 2001) without an obvious grammatical function. Various suffixes for definiteness, number, gender and especially case, including contexts with multiple case marking (Azeb 2012: 453–454), may need to be appended to a given noun or sometimes pronoun.

Regarding verbs, their – mostly suffixing – morphology is even more complex than that of nominal categories. It is common to all Ometo languages that an intriguing wealth of functions from areas such as tense, aspect, mood, modality, subject, polarity and derivation are formally indicated on the verb. Sections on typologically rare verb forms such as the mirative or the veridical in Maale, N. W. Ometo (Azeb 2001: 150–151), make their way into grammars of single languages. Depending on the language, some of these functions occur combined with each other in "portmanteau" morphemes so that there may be, among others, full-fledged negative or interrogative paradigms (Bender 2000: 4). In spite of such combinations, verbal suffixes tend to be quite long and finite verbs with three, four or even five syllables are by no means rare. Two sentential examples from different Ometo languages are given in (1) and (2).

(1) Koorete, S. E. Ometo
ʔis-i **hant-o-nni-ko**
she-NOM work-PST-3.SG.F-ASS.FOC.DECL
'She worked.'
(Binyam 2010: 119)

(2) Wolaitta, N. W. Ometo
ne taa-ną **maadd-idaa-kko**, ta nee-ssi̱ mat'aafa
you I-ACC help-REL.PFV-COND I you-DAT book

ʔimm-anaa-ga-ʃinị
give-SBJV.FUT-CONJ-CONJ
'If you had helped me, I would have given you a book.'
(Lamberti & Sottile 1997: 238)

These two sentences with multiple verbal suffixes, part of which mark more than one function, can be said to show morphological structures that are typical of Ometo languages. The example in (1) is especially intriguing since the verb root for 'work' is followed by the simple past tense suffix '-ed' in English, but by the sequence *-o-nni-ko* triggering seven different grammatical glosses in Koorete. The Wolaitta sentence in (2) includes two verb forms – also indicated in bold – which mark protasis and apodosis, respectively, of an unreal condition. However, it must be kept in mind that especially the sentence in (1) is not typical of Ometo discourse insofar as it only consists of a pronoun and a verb, while it is perfectly possible and not even uncommon to form much longer sentences spanning over several lines: compare, for instance, examples of half a page in narratives from Maale, N. W. Ometo (Azeb 2001: 279–281), or from Gofa, N. W. Ometo (Sellassie 2015: 259–261). To simplify matters and concentrate on the expression of phasal polarity, the present paper will mainly discuss rather short sentences, most of which were probably attained through elicitation. It is beyond doubt that all of them are grammatical in the languages where they come from and that, therefore, they can show which elements pertain to the given topic.

2 The expression of phasal polarity in Ometo languages

Examples (1) and (2) in §1.2 are meant to adduce some meagre evidence of the fact that Ometo languages are very rich in verbal morphemes and there is a wide variety of grammatical functions indicated by such morphemes. Bender (2000: 4) also states for Omotic as a whole that negation can be marked on the verb and it sometimes combines with categories like person and aspect to form separate verbal paradigms. The term "phasal polarity" itself merges two variables which may be expressed in verb phrases in Ometo languages: the phase of an event, which can, for example, be translated by a complex construction involving verbs such as *ħaas-* 'finish' in Oyda, N. W. Ometo (own field notes); and the polarity of an event, which relates to the dichotomy of affirmative versus negative. Given all this, one may expect that phasal polarity, which concerns the trueness or falseness of an event as opposed to its falseness or trueness at an earlier or a later point in time, is expressed by verbal morphemes in Ometo languages. On the other hand, adverbs occurring as separate words are readily available for a wide variety of meanings: compare, for example, adverbials signifying 'here', 'there', 'recently', 'today', 'quickly', 'really', 'well', 'slightly' etc. in Wolaitta, N. W. Ometo (Lamberti & Sottile 1997: 125–127). Some of these are nominals marked for certain cases or compounds, but most importantly, they can be inserted in typical positions of the sentence or even in the initial position in front of the subject, so they are syntactically independent of the verb. Therefore, it is far from certain that phasal polarity is expressed by verbal morphemes in Ometo languages. After all, in spite of all differences between the languages, English phasal polarity items like *still, already, not yet* and *no longer* are also basically adverbials without any formal connection to the verb.

It goes without saying that only the following discussions of concrete examples from Ometo can show which formal devices are used to express the desired meanings. However, examples relevant to the given topic are rather rare and it is not quite clear whether phasal polarity may be regarded as a grammatical or semantic category established in Ometo languages. At any rate, literal interpretations of the expressions at hand will be given and the forms and primary functions of elements marking phasal polarity will be identified. The consideration of "primary" functions is important because it will also be investigated whether the items under discussion are dedicated phasal polarity markers used exclusively for this purpose or they have other, more salient meanings in the languages. In line with the reflections above, a distinction will be made between §2.1 for expression by verbal morphemes and §2.2 for expression by separate adverbials. This primarily formal kind of distinction is deemed more practical than any semantic one because it will turn out that the equivalents of the four basic expressions *still, already, not yet* and *no longer* are not equally described for Ometo languages. At least in §2.2, a semantic order will be followed on a lower level. The examples will be discussed one after another.

2.1 Expression by verbal morphemes

In Wolaitta, N. W. Ometo, 'already' can occasionally be understood as a semantic side effect of two different verbal suffixes which, depending on person, number and gender of the subject, surface as *-aittʃ-* / *-iittʃ-* and as *-arg-* / *-irg-* (Wakasa 2008: 959–960). The variant with *-a-* occurs in the 1.SG, the 2.SG and the 3.SG.F, while the variant with *-i-* is used in the 3.SG.M as well as all plural forms. This alternation between /a/ and /i/ according to the subject is common in Ometo languages (Hayward 1991) and independent of any additional function or meaning, so it is not related to phasal polarity marking as such. The main function of the suffixes *-aittʃ-* / *-iittʃ-* and *-arg-* / *-irg-* is described as "completive", that is, an event is completed, and an ensuing event can take place. The three following examples from the relevant section (Wakasa 2008: 959–968) include the idea of 'already'.

(3) Wolaitta, N. W. Ometo
    ʔi   gákk-iyo   d-é   táanî b-**âittʃ**-aas
    he reach-REL.IPFV.NSBJ time-ABS I   go-**completely**-PFV.1.SG
    'I had **already** gone when he arrived.'
    (in the source: 'I had **already** gone when he reached.')
    (Wakasa 2008: 963)

(4) Wolaitta, N. W. Ometo
    néenî y-îyo   wod-é   táanî k'úm-aa
    you   come-REL.IPFV.NSBJ time-ABS I   food-ABS.SG.M

    m-**árg**-aas
    eat-**completely**-PFV.1.SG
    'When you came, I had **already** taken a meal.'
    (Wakasa 2008: 963)

(5) Wolaitta, N. W. Ometo
    ʔi   giy-âa   b-aan-á-u   har-îya
    he market-ABS.SG.M go-INF-OBL.SG.M-to donkey-ABS.SG.M

    tʃ'aan-**îittʃ**-iis
    load-**completely**-PFV.3.SG.M
    'He has **already** loaded (the things) onto the donkey [to go to the market].'
    (Wakasa 2008: 966–967)

Concerning (5), the embedded phrase meaning 'to go to the market' is omitted in Wakasa's translation for unknown reasons. Apart from this, on the one hand, it is obvious that the semantics of 'already' is triggered by the presence of the completive marker, which is generally glossed as a full-fledged adverb 'completely' by Wakasa. On the other hand, the three sentences in (3)–(5) contrast with about ten examples (Wakasa 2008: 961–968), and there are more throughout the thesis, that also include a completive morpheme, but do not explicitly refer to the semantics of 'already'. Here, it becomes clear that the two markers *-aittʃ-* / *-iittʃ-* and *-arg-* / *-irg-*, though invariably glossed as 'completely', can mean various things. There is even an interesting counterpart to the example in (5), namely the one shown in (6).

(6) Wolaitta, N. W. Ometo
ʔi   giy-âa   b-aan-á-u   har-îya
he   market-ABS.SG.M   go-INF.OBL.SG.M-to   donkey-ABS.SG.M

tʃaan-îrg-iis
load-completely-PFV.3.SG.M
'He has loaded (all the things) onto the donkey [to go to the market].'
(Wakasa 2008: 967)

Beside the phrase 'to go to the market' which is missing again in Wakasa's translation, in (6) there is also a lack of 'already' so that this example seems to have nothing to do with phasal polarity. While the presence of 'already' in (5) points to the completeness of the action of loading, its absence combined with the remark 'all the things' in (6) hints towards the completeness of the objects loaded. To be sure, both interpretations have the same implication: all things have 'already' been loaded onto the donkey and the person in question is ready to bring them to the market. However, the adverb 'already' seems to fit one interpretation only, although there is a completive verbal morpheme in both sentences. As shown in (3)–(5), the idea of 'already' can in fact, depending on the examples, be associated with both completive markers, that is, with *-aittʃ-* / *-iittʃ-* and with *-arg-* / *-irg-*. Therefore, the semantics in these sentences is that a completed action is 'already' accomplished.

Regarding verbal markers as indicators of phasal polarity in Ometo languages, the evidence seen in Wolaitta is not really strong: there are two completive morphemes which are obviously capable of transmitting the idea of 'already', but more often than not, these two morphemes seem to lack an explicit reference to this idea. Furthermore, although a number of Ometo languages use phrases including verbs to express phasal polarity as seen in §2.2, no other example of a verbal morpheme as a sufficient marker of this category could be found. This means that inserted adverbials or adverbial phrases of various kinds seem to be the most salient candidates for phasal polarity expressions in Ometo.

2.2 Expression by adverbials

For reasons of semantic structures of the expressions at hand, the equivalents of 'still' and 'not yet' will be discussed together, followed by the equivalents of 'already'. No information at all could be found on 'no longer' in any Ometo language, while clear phrases meaning 'already' were exclusively identified in the present author's field recordings, mostly in translations of sentences by Bouquiaux & Thomas (1992: 267).

2.2.1 The items 'still' and 'not yet'

This paragraph again starts with the best-described Ometo language Wolaitta, N. W. Ometo, where 'still' is translated by the adverbial *haʔʔi-kká* with *haʔʔi* meaning 'now' and *-kká* meaning 'too' (Wakasa 2008: 767). As the present paragraph will show, the adverb for 'now' is crucial for phasal polarity expressions in Ometo, but there is generally an additional element modifying this semantics. The formation with 'too' in Wolaitta is rather simple and a full-text search of *-kká*, also occurring as *-kka* without high tone, in Wakasa's voluminous thesis (2008) indicates that this suffix can be attached to numerous kinds of nominals as well as pronouns or verb forms. Given the wealth of examples including 'too', it is regrettable that *haʔʔi-kká* occurs only twice and only the sentence in (7) assigns a clear idea of 'still' to this adverbial.

(7) Wolaitta, N. W. Ometo
siik'-îdî   ?ó   ?ekk-îdî   **haʔʔi-kká**
love-CVB.3.SG.M   her   take-CVB.3.SG.M   **now-too**

sîik'-uwa-ni   ?iss-î-ppé   d-êes
love-OBL.SG.M-in   one-OBL-ABL   exist-IPFV.3.SG.M
'He loved and married her, and **still now** he lives together (with her) loving her.'
(Wakasa 2008: 767)

Here in (7), non-high-toned *siik'-* 'love' is a verb root, while high-toned *sîik'-* 'love' is the corresponding noun root. The other example containing *haʔʔi-kká* is translated as 'The children do the practice repeatedly, and knew. Now they passed the examination' (Wakasa 2008: 767) and may probably allow an interpretation in terms of 'still', though this needs further consideration. At any rate, the expression *haʔʔi-kká* for 'still' can be regarded as straightforward: a fact which was true in the past and is true 'now, too', is 'still' true.

The negative phasal polarity item 'not yet' in Wolaitta, N. W. Ometo, is expressed by the adverbial *haʔʔi-nné* together with a negative verb form (Wakasa 2008: 715, 778). While *haʔʔi* again means 'now', the morpheme *-nné* represents the general connector 'and'. As before with *-kká* 'too', this connector and its non-high-toned counterpart *-nne* are extremely versatile in the language and examples of it in Wakasa's work (2008) also include regular uses at the end of suffix chains and in numerals beyond 'ten'. Two occurrences of *haʔʔi-nné* are found in the whole of the thesis and both of them, combined with negative verb forms, can be said to refer to 'not yet'.

(8) Wolaitta, N. W. Ometo
haʔʔi-nné ʔer-ékkéfii
now-and know-NEG.INT.IPFV.2.PL
'do you **still not** know?' (Mark 8:17)
(in the source: 'do**n't** you know **still**?')
(Wakasa 2008: 715)

(9) Wolaitta, N. W. Ometo
haʔʔi-nné ʔakeek-ibeʔékkéfii
now-and become.aware-NEG.INT.PFV.2.PL
'do you **still not** understand?' (Mark 8:21)
(Wakasa 2008: 778)

It is interesting and possibly relevant to note that, first, both sentences in (8) and (9) contain literal 'not still' or 'still not' in their translations, and second, both represent questions. These coincidences may be due to the fact that these examples are taken from one and the same passage in the translation of the Gospel of Mark and they might therefore be phrased similarly. Nevertheless, (8) and (9) should be seen as independent instances of the expression of 'not yet' by 'and now' plus a negative verb form and it is beyond doubt that the literal 'still not' is semantically very near, if not identical to 'not yet'. Last, but not least, negative marking within the verb form is highly typical of Omotic languages (Bender 2000: 4; Azeb 2012: 468) so that the English adverbial 'not yet' is expected to be split into 'still' indicated by an adverbial and 'not' indicated by a verbal morpheme. The meaning 'and now' is related to 'still' because a fact which is true in the past 'and now' can be considered as 'still' true. The open question is why the affirmative form in (7) has *haʔʔi-kká* 'now, too', while the negative forms in (8) and (9) have *haʔʔi-nné* 'and now'. Given the small number of examples found in the literature, this may even be an accidental pattern, so further research is needed to confirm the phasal polarity meanings found for both expressions.

In Maale, N. W. Ometo, the expression of 'still' is also based on the adverb 'now', but the additional element leading to the desired semantics is not just a suffix. The complete phrase is *hátsì hèll-áʔʔò*, where *hátsì* means 'now', *hèll-* is the verb root for 'reach' and -á??ò is a converb marker (Azeb 2001: 144). More precisely, this converb marker implies that the event takes place immediately before the main event with the same subject (Azeb 2001: 191). Therefore, the sequence hátsĩ hèll-á??ò has the literal meaning 'having reached now', but its potential to express the phasal polarity item 'still' is seen in (10).

(10) Maale, N. W. Ometo
ʔiinî **hátsĩ hèll-á??ò** ʔá-á-nè
he.NOM **now reach-CVB** exist-IPFV-AFF.DECL
'He is **still** alive.'
(Azeb 2001: 144)

In accordance with the fact that the English simple adverb 'still' is rendered by a subordinate verb plus adverb in Maale, a more literal version of the sentence in (10) is 'he, having reached now, exists'. Here, the converb phrase hátsĩ hèll-á??ò implies that a fact was true in the past and its being true has 'reached now', that is, the fact is 'still' true. Unfortunately, there seems to be no other affirmative example of this phrase in the whole monograph by Azeb (2001), although three more sentences with a similar idea of 'still' in their English translations were found. One of them (Azeb 2001: 263) needs special attention: it is translated as 'oh! Will you still go up to your home to sleep?' and the Maale original includes an interesting word hàgî, which, however, is glossed ambiguously as 'yet' so that its exact contribution is not quite certain. The two other sentences occur in a narrative (Azeb 2001: 291–292), but both seem to lack an explicit expression of 'still'.

At least the negative counterpart of 'still', that is 'not yet', can be exemplified from Maale, N. W. Ometo. Its expression follows the principle seen in Wolaitta in (8) and (9): a phrase meaning 'still' is combined with a negative verb form, as would be expected in the context of the Omotic languages. In Maale, however, it is precisely the same phrase hátsĩ hèll-á??ò 'having reached now', composed of an adverb, a verb root and a converb suffix, that occurs in affirmative sentences for 'still' and in negative sentences for 'not yet' (Azeb 2001: 191). The latter meaning is shown in (11).

(11) Maale, N. W. Ometo
ʔiinî **hátsĩ hèll-á??ò** mùkk-ĩbá-sè
he.NOM **now reach-CVB** come-**NEG**.PFV-**NEG**.DECL
'He did **not** come **yet**.'
(Azeb 2001: 191)

It is noteworthy that the verb form in (11) indicates negation both in the aspect and in the sentence type marker, the affirmative counterpart to *mùkk-ībá-sè* being *mùkk-é-nè* (Azeb 2001: 130). This double marking underlines the fact that, from a logical point of view, the phrase *hátsĭ hèll-áʔʔò* alone means 'still' again and it is negated for the sake of 'not yet' in a second step. In other words, although this may sound paradoxical, it is his not-coming that has 'reached now' in (11) and is 'still' the case, so his coming is 'not yet' true.

The next language to be discussed is Oyda, N. W. Ometo, which is appropriate at this point because it combines the strategies witnessed in Wolaitta and Maale. In other words, there are two ways of expressing 'still' by an adverbial: either *ɦaátt-en* or *ɦannó ɦeell-i* can be used (own field notes). Regarding the former, its elements are not different from those of Wolaitta *haʔʔi-nné* in (8) and (9) in that *ɦaátt* means 'now' in Oyda and the suffix -*en* with the characteristic nasal is the connector 'and'. Therefore, in addition to Wolaitta, there is evidence from Oyda that 'and now' can represent 'still' in an affirmative context. The semantic analysis of *ɦannó ɦeell-i*, on the other hand, is somewhat tricky. It is beyond doubt that the root *ɦann-* is the proximal demonstrative 'this', but -*ó* suffixed to this root regularly marks the feminine accusative in opposition to -*á* for the feminine nominative. However, there exists a local adverb *ɦanné* 'here' suggesting spatial proximity to the speaker and it could well be the case that *ɦannó* in *ɦannó ɦeell-i* denotes 'now' and suggests temporal proximity. For *ɦeell-i*, it is tempting to assume a verb root *ɦeell-* 'reach', see *hèll-* from Maale in (10) and (11), and a suffixed converb marker -*i*. Unfortunately, the proper Oyda forms are *yell-* as a verb root for 'reach / arrive' and -*î* as a converb marker for a previous event with the same subject so that the exact equivalent of the Maale expression would be *ɦannó yell-î* 'having reached now' instead of *ɦannó ɦeell-i*. To simplify matters, it is tentatively proposed here that the actual form *ɦannó ɦeell-i* is a fixed variant of *ɦannó* plus *yell-î* with a modified pronunciation in the context of 'still'. At any rate, further research is needed to clarify this issue. Two examples illustrating the semantic equivalence of *ɦaátt-en* and *ɦannó ɦeell-i* in Oyda can be cited as follows.

(12) Oyda, N. W. Ometo
ʔé **ɦaátt-en** múune
he **now-and** eat.IPFV.PRS
'He is **still** eating.'
(personal field notes)

(13) Oyda, N. W. Ometo
 ʔé **hannó heell-i** haarg-zé giʃo ...
 he **now** **reach-CVB** be.ill-M.NOM because.of ...
 '... because he is **still** ill.'
 (personal field notes)

Although the sequence in (13) is not a full-fledged clause but rather a postpositional phrase headed by the postposition *gîʃo* 'because of / about', it clearly shows that *hannó heell-i* can be understood as 'still'. Further recorded Oyda examples include 'it is still raining' with *haátt-en* and 'I am still very well' with *hannó heell-i*, so it seems that both expressions are quite well-established in the language. In addition, their assumed semantics 'and now' and 'having reached now' support the Wolaitta and Maale evidence presented above.

For the negative phasal polarity item 'not yet', Oyda, N. W. Ometo, has the same strategy as Wolaitta and Maale: it uses the affirmative expression for 'still' and combines it with a negative verb form (personal field notes). In this case, it was even possible to find one sentence which can be formed either with *haátt-en* 'and now' or with *hannó heell-i* 'having reached now' for exactly the same meaning. That is to say that both expressions signify 'still', but it is not certain whether both may always be used in the same environments. At least, the following pair of sentences demonstrates that they are interchangeable in the given context.

(14) Oyda, N. W. Ometo
 ʔé **haátt-en** yeʔ-îkáay
 he **now-and** come-**NEG**.PFV.PST
 'He has **not** come **yet**.'
 (personal field notes)

(15) Oyda, N. W. Ometo
 ʔé **hannó heell-i** yeʔ-îkáay
 he **now** **reach-CVB** come-**NEG**.PFV.PST
 'He has **not** come **yet**.'
 (personal field notes)

Apart from the sentences in (14) and (15), there are instances of 'he has not eaten the fish yet' with *haátt-en* and of 'he has not eaten yet' with *hannó heell-i* in the data, with both sentences having negative verb forms as expected. All in all, the Oyda evidence shown in (12)–(15) further reinforces the Wolaitta and

Maale strategies discussed before and especially the importance of the simple adverb meaning 'now' in phasal polarity expressions of Ometo languages.

Also in Gofa, N. W. Ometo, the simple adverb for 'now' plays a great role in the expression of 'still', but it is joined by another kind of verb form. The phrase is *haʔʔi gás-ó* (personal field notes) where *haʔʔi* clearly signifies 'now'. Regarding *gás-ó*, it is rather *gákk-* which was recorded as a verb root for 'reach / arrive', also by Sellassie (2015: 362) who has, in addition, evidence of a causative form *gatt-* 'make reach' (Sellassie 2015: 284, 355). However, he also gives textual examples of *gats-* for the meanings 'arrive' (Sellassie 2015: 271), 'make arrive' (Sellassie 2015: 272–273) and 'reach' (Sellassie 2015: 318) so that *gás-* is here assumed to be the verb root for 'reach / arrive'. For suffixed *-o* with or without high tone, there are manifold data in Sellassie's thesis (2015) to show that it may be either a terminal vowel without a clear function (Sellassie 2015: 79–80) or a feminine accusative marker (Sellassie 2015: 115). Both solutions, however, would imply that *gás-* is a nominal or at least nominalised root, which is not quite plausible in the given context. Fortunately, both Sellassie (2015: 178) and the present author have recorded a verbal suffix which is quite rare, but invariably high-toned: namely *-ó* for the jussive. Sellassie restricts this suffix to the third person singular masculine and the present author's field recordings made in November 2017 also show some differences according to the subject. The use of *haʔʔi gás-ó* for 'still' is illustrated in (16) and (17).

(16) Gofa, N. W. Ometo
    haʔʔi gás-ó   *m-iʃin*   *dees*
    now reach-JUS.3.SG.M eat-PROG.3.SG.M be.IPFV.3.SG.M
    'He is **still** eating.'
    (personal field notes)

(17) Gofa, N. W. Ometo
    haʔʔi gás-ó   *sákk-ise*
    now reach-JUS.3.SG.M be.ill-PFV.3.SG.M
    'He is **still** ill.'
    (personal field notes)

The same phrase *haʔʔi gás-ó* for 'still' was recorded in the translation of 'it is still raining'. In Maale and Oyda as discussed above, 'still' can be expressed by phrases meaning exactly 'having reached now'. Here in (16) and (17) from Gofa, the two lexemes for 'reach' and 'now' are also present, but the verb form is a jussive instead of a converb. Unfortunately, it is not quite clear whether the third person singular masculine in the suffix *-ó* is a personal or an impersonal one: Sellassie (2015: 178) explicitly mentions forms for third persons only and he also glosses jussives in second persons (Sellassie 2015: 345–351), but these are formally identical to and translated as imperatives (Sellassie 2015: 177). Therefore, the jussive paradigm seems to be incomplete in a way to be further investigated and it may be plausible to assume that person is not marked by the *-ó* in *haʔʔi gás-ó*. As a result, (16), for example, would mean 'he is eating let it reach now', that is, 'it' refers to the event of eating itself which lasts until now and not to 'he' who is eating. Another example in the field recordings has *hagá gás-ó* instead of *haʔʔi gás-ó* for 'still' and it occurs in a non-verbal sentence and is followed by *dáro lóʔʔo* 'very well': 'I am still very well'. This might further support the impersonal nature of the suffix *-ó*, but Sellassie (2015: 351) even gives one example of *-o* – tone is not marked here – for a first person singular jussive in a text. Regarding *hagá* in Gofa, the present author has recorded the adverbial *ɦaátt ɦagá* 'just now' with *ɦaátt* 'now' in Oyda and there is the above-mentioned occurrence of *hàgî* glossed as 'yet' in Maale (Azeb 2001: 263). Although these data do not point to the exact meaning of *hagá* in Gofa, it is safe to say that the semantic difference between *haʔʔi gás-ó* and *hagá gás-ó* is very small, if at all present, and the structure is the same: adverb plus verb form.

The grammar and lexicon of Gamo, N. W. Ometo, is described in the voluminous monograph by Hayward & Eshetu (2014), yet it was not possible so far to find more than one obvious example of overtly expressed phasal polarity. The concept under discussion is 'not yet' and it corresponds to the phrase *haʔi gakk-ana-u*, which is again combined with a negative verb form (Hayward & Eshetu 2014: 526). Thus, it would be expected to mean 'still' in the affirmative, but evidence is lacking. In this phrase, *haʔi* signifies nothing else than 'now' and *gakk-* is glossed as a verb root for 'extend to', with the primary meaning 'reach / arrive' (Hayward & Eshetu 2014: 485–487) which will be used here by analogy with the expressions from other Ometo languages. The attached sequence *-ana-u* indicates neither a converb nor a jussive, but the glosses of *-ana-* point to a relative irrealis form which is nominalised so that it can carry an oblique function and attach the so-called "postposition" *-u* for 'in order to' (Hayward & Eshetu 2014: 162). Before the overall meaning of *haʔi gakk-ana-u* is further discussed, the illustrative sentence is presented in (18).

(18) Gamo, N. W. Ometo
 ta ʔaawa yeek-o **haʔi**
 my father mourn-NMLS **now**

gakk-ana-u   *kess-abiikke*
reach-REL.IRR.NMLS.OBL-in.order.to   go.out-NEG.PFV.1.SG
'I have **not** got (myself) out of mourning for my father **yet**.'
(Hayward & Eshetu 2014: 526)

In fact, Hayward & Eshetu (2014) generally omit tone marks in their sentential examples. However, their glosses are very detailed and also in (18) it is not easy to reconcile the phasal polarity meaning 'not yet' or probably 'still' with the grammatical functions assigned to the phrase *haʔi gakk-ana-u*. A literal translation of this phrase into English seems to be impossible because a neat English clause can hardly start with both 'in order to' and a relative element. Moreover, the meaning 'in order to' by itself does not fit a nominalised antecedent, but, as mentioned above, it is the only reasonable gloss that can be given for the postposition *-u*. Therefore, the phrase *haʔi gakk-ana-u* is assumed to correspond to an elliptical expression in English and to literally mean something like 'which (is done) in order to reach now', with the relative 'which' referring to the event. The connection between 'reach now' and 'not yet' or 'still' is not far-fetched and it is also seen in other Ometo languages above. Apart from this phasal polarity expression, Hayward & Eshetu's dictionary part (2014: 416) lists a very interesting word *bró*, which they translate as an adverb 'yet' and present in two sentences: 'if God were to grant us time, we should see yet more' and 'what have you seen yet?' meaning 'you have not seen anything yet!'. Thus, its semantics is not very clear, and its initial consonant cluster even violates canonical syllable structures of Ometo languages. The authors therefore suggest onomatopoeia as a possible explanation of the shape of *bró* (Hayward & Eshetu 2014: 36), which fact alone would merit further attention in the context of phasal polarity.

 The variety of Dorze, N. W. Ometo, is by far less well-known than the Gamo language to which it is sometimes assigned as a dialect (see §1.1). Although Dorze is here assumed to be a separate language – and the following examples will contain some expressions which would be different in Gamo –, it is not feasible to justify this view in the present discussion. At least, the new field recordings made with comparative Ometo studies in mind include equivalents of the two phrases seen in (16) and (17) from Gofa as well as (18) from Gamo. The actual Dorze forms are *haisá gáts-o* and *haisá gáss-ana-u*, both being used to express 'still' in affirmative contexts (personal field notes). The word *haisá* shared by both phrases poses a problem because, from a formal perspective, it is somehow more than the adverb *haʔʔi* '(just) now' occurring in the new field recordings and less than the adverb *haisán* 'here' listed by Haile (1981: 64). However, the deictic character of *haisá* becomes obvious and also comparative data such as Gamo *háissa* 'this (one)' (Hayward & Eshetu 2014: 522) suggest that it is plausible to assume the meaning 'now' again for this word in Dorze. Regarding the verb forms *gáts-o* and *gáss-ana-u*, clear parallels to Gofa *gás-ó* in (16) and (17) and Gamo *gakk-ana-u* in (18) are visible. There should be no objection to identifying *gáts-* or *gáss-* with a common Ometo verb root for 'reach', though the basic form is *gákk-* also in Dorze and it is not certain whether the affricate or fricative is due to a causative marker. Unless a causative derivative of this root is found in any source, it is assumed that the phrases under discussion include the simple root 'reach'. For the final, non-high-toned *-o* in *gáts-o*, the most appropriate solution is an analysis in terms of an infinitive marker 'to' or rather 'in order to' because this function is amply illustrated in Haile's data (1981: 66). As in Gofa above, see (16) and (17), the third person singular jussive suffix in Dorze is recorded as a high-toned *-ó* both by the present author and by Haile (1981: 26) in his form *gid-ó* 'let it be', so this does not fit the suffix in *gáts-o*. Against this background, it is even probable that the *-o* in *gáts-o* and the *-u* in *gáss-ana-u* are one and the same marker: Ometo languages generally do not have the diphthong /ao/, but the diphthong /au/, and a change from *gáss-ana-o* to *gáss-ana-u* may simply have occurred. Other than in (18) from Gamo above, the *-ana* in Dorze *gáss-ana-u* is taken provisionally as a mere future marker, as this is its most salient function in the language and some other Ometo languages like Wolaitta (Lamberti & Sottile 1997: 157). Therefore, examples with both expressions *haisá gáts-o* and *haisá gáss-ana-u* for 'still' in Dorze present themselves as follows.

(19) Dorze, N. W. Ometo
ʔizî **haisá gáts-o** múusa galais
he **now** reach-in.order.to eat.NMLS AUX.PROG.3.SG.M
'He is **still** eating.'
(personal field notes)

(20) Dorze, N. W. Ometo
ʔizî **haisá gáss-ana-u** harg-is
he **now** reach-FUT-in.order.to be.ill-IPFV.3.SG.M
'He is **still** ill.'
(personal field notes)

The verbal complex *múusa galais* in (19) with a kind of verbal noun followed by an auxiliary seems to represent the more usual strategy to express the progressive in Dorze, while shorter progressive forms consisting of only a verbal suffix were also found in the recorded data. This auxiliary could not yet be split into smaller parts – the suspicious 'say' verb root regularly has the shape *ga?-* in Dorze –, but it should not be related to phasal polarity. Coming back to the item 'still', the field recordings include two further examples with *haisá gáts-o*, one of these having a copula instead of a full verb, and one further example with *haisá gáss-ana-u*. If the analyses proposed here are correct, then both phrases literally mean 'in order to reach now', with one of them showing an explicit future marker and the other one lacking it, but it is clear that the 'now' point is later than the beginning of the event that 'still' endures. At any rate, the semantic patterns of the two expressions of 'still' in Dorze with 'reach' and 'now' further enrich the Ometo picture outlined before.

2.2.2 The item 'already'

In Gofa, N. W. Ometo, there is a rather simple way to express the phasal polarity concept of 'already', namely by means of the word *sintsá* (personal field notes). For Gamo, Hayward & Eshetu (2014: 88) mention a so-called "relational noun" *sintsá* for anteriority, which is said to be connected to the independent noun *sintsé* 'face / front / future'. The question of "relational nouns" versus "postpositions" notwithstanding, Gamo examples have *sintsá* translated as 'in front of' or 'facing' (Hayward & Eshetu 2014: 89–90) and *sintsé* simply as 'before' (Hayward & Eshetu 2014: 739). Also Gofa texts provided by Sellassie (2015) contain two sentences with *sintse* glossed as 'before' (Sellassie 2015: 271–272, 316) and one sentence with *sintsa-n* glossed as 'in front' plus locative suffix (Sellassie 2015: 309), where all three instances seem to follow nominals governed by them. Regarding *sintsá* as 'already' in Gofa, however, the phasal polarity meaning is obviously achieved without a preceding noun which could be governed by 'before'. That is, *sintsá* here appears as a proper adverb and modifies the verb representing the event that 'already' occurs. This strategy is illustrated in (21).

(21) Gofa, N. W. Ometo
 ʔeyî **sintsá** ʔoots-íʃin dees
 he **before** work-PROG.3.SG.M be.IPFV.3.SG.M
 'He is **already** working.'
 (personal field notes)

The field data include two further sentences with *sintsá* for 'already', in which only the verb root is different: 'he is already eating' and 'he is already coming'.

If 'already' implies that something happens earlier than expected, then the use of 'before' in this position is very plausible. On this reading, *sintsá* can be analysed either as an adverb in terms of 'before' or as a postposition / relational noun involving ellipsis in terms of 'before (the time expected)', with the sentence in (21) literally meaning 'he is working before' or 'he is working before (the time expected)'.

The same adverb 'already' has *sinó-rá* as its equivalent in Dorze, N. W. Ometo (personal field notes). Here, the word root *sin-* may be considered the same as in *sintsá* from Gofa above, but the formation is a bit different, as is shown by the fact that *sinó-rá* includes an obvious suffix. This *-rá* is a clear instance of an instrumental or comitative marker in Dorze and also in most other Northwest Ometo varieties (Bender 2000: 24) and, as a consequence, it requires *sinó* to be a noun. Comparative evidence of this word is given by Lamberti & Sottile (1997: 496–497), who mention *sino* with the semantics of 'forehead' in Malo and Zayse and similar forms with semantics like 'face' or 'front' in other Omotic languages, and *sinó* as 'forehead' in Oyda can be added from the present author's field notes. Since it is not clear whether this rather special meaning is attested for *sinó* in Dorze, the more metaphorical meaning 'front' is assumed here. The sentence in (22) demonstrates the possibility to express 'already' by *sinó-rá*, literally 'with the front' or 'by means of the front'.

(22) Dorze, N. W. Ometo
 ʔizî **sinó-rá**   yúusa   galais
 he   **front-INS** come.NMLS   AUX.PROG.3.SG.M
 'He is **already** coming.'
 (personal field notes)

Further evidence of *sinó-rá* translating 'already' is found in the examples 'he is already working' and 'he is already eating' recorded in the field. Although Dorze in (22) uses the same word root for 'already' as Gofa in (21), the suffixed noun in (22) is not as easy to interpret. However, it is not uncommon in Ometo languages to express adverbial meanings by a noun with an instrumental suffix: compare, for instance, *sohuwa-ra* 'suddenly' from *sohuwą* 'place' in Wolaitta (Lamberti & Sottile 1997: 491) or, with final vowel deletion, *ʔawá-r* 'at noon' from *ʔawá* 'sun' in Oyda (own field notes). Therefore, the sentence in (22) can literally be understood as 'he is coming in front', which again implies that he is coming before the time expected like in the Gofa example above.

From a formal point of view, Dauro, N. W. Ometo, has an even more complex strategy to render the concept of 'already' than Gofa in (21) or Dorze in (22), though the semantics is not so different. The word requiring an explanation is *kas-ett-îiddî* (personal field notes), which is related without doubt to the word *kase* meaning 'before' or 'then' in Wolaitta and 'past' in Gamo and Gofa (Lamberti & Sottile 1997: 416). The Dauro texts presented by Dawit (2016) also include a number of exact tokens of *kase*, glossed as 'before' or 'earlier / early' or even 'late' (Dawit 2016: 57, 65, 110, 158, 164). The interesting fact about *kas-ett-îiddî*, however, is that the final suffix *-îiddî* is a converb marker for an anterior event and thus needs to attach to a verb stem. The morpheme *-ett-* in turn is normally a passive marker in Dauro, but in wider Northwest Ometo the same morpheme may, depending on language and / or context, also indicate reflexive, reciprocal or intransitive functions (Bender 2000: 43). In the case of *kas-ett-îiddî* in Dauro, there seems to be no evidence of *kase* 'before / . . . ' being able by itself to appear as a verb root *kas-* in any Ometo language. Therefore, it is here assumed that *-ett-* acts as a kind of verbaliser, even if a causative marker, in Dauro *-iss-*, might be more suitable for such a derivation than a passive marker. An illustrative example of *kas-ett-îiddî* for 'already', literally meaning something like 'having been before', is given in (23).

(23) Dauro, N. W. Ometo
    ʔi   **kas-ett-îiddî**   *m-îididi*
    he **before-VBLS-CVB.3.SG.M** eat-PROG.3.SG.M
    'He is **already** eating.'
    (personal field notes)

The double occurrence of /d/ in the main verb suffix *-îididi* is not hard to explain. In actual fact, the basic form to be expected in (23) would be *m-îidi deʔ-ee* with *m-* 'eat' inflected in the progressive and *deʔ-* 'be' inflected in the imperfective. This form *m-îidi deʔ-ee* is no more and no less than the exact equivalent of Gofa *m-iʃin dees* 'is eating' as seen in (16) in §2.2.1. In (23) from Dauro, however, the full phrase *m-îidi deʔ-ee* is shortened to *m-îididi* in fast speech – and there would even be a third option *m-îididee* which is intermediate between the two others. Regarding the phasal polarity expression *kas-ett-îiddî* 'already', it is also present in another sentence from the field recordings: 'he is already coming'. Its literal meaning 'having been before' even includes two indications of the premature occurrence of an event which is crucial for the idea of 'already', once in the adverbial 'before' and once in the converb of anteriority translated as 'having been'.

3 Summary and conclusion

Now that a number of relevant phasal polarity expressions in Ometo languages were discussed in §2, it has become clear that these expressions show some interesting structural patterns. Although, from a morphological point of view, the items are generally more complex than the English adverbials 'still', 'not yet' and 'already', they are also based on relatively simple word stems. The results of the present study will be summarised according to the three different meanings observed – it needs to be remembered that evidence of 'no longer' in Ometo was not found.

The expression of the concept of STILL is obviously related to the simple adverb for 'now', though this adverb never occurs alone with this phasal polarity meaning – it is always accompanied by an additional element. The results from §2.2.1 are summarised in the table below.

Table 1: Expressions of 'still' in Ometo languages.

Language	Expression	Literal translation	Example(s)
Wolaitta	haʔʔi-kká	'now, too'	(7)
Maale	hátsī hèll-áʔʔò	'having reached now'	(10)
Oyda	ɦaátt-en	'and now'	(12)
Oyda	ɦannó ɦeell-i	'having reached now'	(13)
Gofa	haʔʔi gás-ó	'let it reach now'	(16), (17)
Dorze	haisá gáts-o	'in order to reach now'	(19)
Dorze	haisá gáss-ana-u	'in order to reach now'	(20)

The entries in Table 1 can be further classified into those consisting only of 'now' plus a suffix: Wolaitta haʔʔi-kká and Oyda ɦaátt-en, and those consisting of 'now' plus a separate word which is a verb form of 'reach': the five others. The two former expressions are adverbs in a strict sense, while the five latter are verb phrases in which 'now' can be regarded as a kind of temporal complement fitting the semantics of 'reach'. All seven expressions in their entirety, however, are separate phrases insofar as they may be added to a sentence as free-standing constructions – in Ometo languages normally between subject and verb – and need not be attached to any other word or constituent. Furthermore, from a semantic point of view, they all act as adverbials in that they emphasise that an event which was true formerly is true 'now' as well, so its trueness has 'reached' the present time and it is 'still' true.

Concerning the concept of NOT YET, its expressions in Ometo languages are very closely related to the expressions of STILL seen above, the main difference being that a negative verb form is used instead of an affirmative one. Therefore, the data in Table 2, taken from §2.2.1, can be compared closely to the data in Table 1.

Table 2: Expressions of 'not yet' in Ometo languages.

Language	Expression	Literal translation	Example(s)
Wolaitta	haʔʔi-nné + NEG	'and now' + NEG	(8), (9)
Maale	hátsî hèll-áʔʔò + NEG	'having reached now' + NEG	(11)
Oyda	haátt-en + NEG	'and now' + NEG	(14)
Oyda	hannó heell-i + NEG	'having reached now' + NEG	(15)
Gamo	haʔi gakk-ana-u + NEG	'which (is done) in order to reach now' + NEG	(18)

Apart from the fact that it was not possible to find evidence of both STILL and NOT YET in some languages, only in Wolaitta is there a difference between the phrases in Tables 1 and 2: 'now, too' versus 'and now'. This difference needs further research and it is not at all clear whether it is significant or accidental. In general, however, the five entries in Table 2 show the same dichotomy between 'now' plus suffix in Wolaitta haʔʔi-nné and Oyda haátt-en and 'now' followed by a verb form of 'reach' in the other expressions as the seven entries in Table 1. What really matters is the negative verb form in sentences including NOT YET, as indicated by the addition "+ NEG" in Table 2, compared to an affirmative verb form in sentences including STILL. This division of NOT YET into a separate phrase meaning 'still' and a negative marker on the verb is in full accordance with the morphological structure of Ometo and more or less all Omotic languages, which are well-known for the fact that negation is generally marked by verbal suffixes (Bender 2000: 4). At the same time, this Ometo principle of expression is a neat empirical proof of the logical assumption that NOT YET is the negative counterpart of STILL.

The concept of ALREADY is expressed in a more diversified manner than the concepts of STILL and NOT YET, both from a formal and from a semantic perspective. This is even shown by the fact that the information summarised in Table 3 comes from two different paragraphs, namely §2.1 and §2.2.2.

Table 3: Expressions of 'already' in Ometo languages.

Language	Expression	Literal translation	Example(s)
Wolaitta	-aittʃ- / -iittʃ-	'completely'	(3), (5)
Wolaitta	-arg- / -irg-	'completely'	(4)
Gofa	sintsá	'before'	(21)
Dorze	sinó-rá	'in front'	(22)
Dauro	kas-ett-ʔiddî	'having been before'	(23)

In fact, the five expressions of ALREADY in Table 3 display four different structural patterns, that is, exactly one per language. While Wolaitta -aittʃ- / -iittʃ- and -arg- / -irg- are verbal suffixes, the three other expressions share the characteristic of being free-standing words, but Gofa sintsá is a simple adverb, Dorze sinó-rá is a noun with a peripheral case marker and Dauro kas-ett-ʔiddî is a derived verb with a converb suffix. Furthermore, the semantics of these constructions are also different to a certain extent. The Wolaitta morphemes indicate a completive verb form, which is probably related to the perfective aspect – examples (3)–(5) have perfective markers –, and the English translations show present or past perfect forms. The three other expressions are similar to each other in a metaphorical sense because both 'before' and 'front' point to the fact that something is earlier than something else: in the case of 'already', the real starting point of an event is earlier than the expected starting point. Although this being before can in principle be interpreted either temporally or spatially, it is clear in the context of phasal polarity that a temporal interpretation is required. Compared to this, also the completive function in the two Wolaitta expressions is temporal by nature in that it says an event is completed 'before' a certain time referred to. Therefore, the semantics of the five entries in Table 3 may be considered as loosely related to each other, but they do not share any formal element.

All in all, the present paper has presented and discussed seventeen different phasal polarity expressions from seven different Ometo languages: Wolaitta, Gamo, Gofa, Dauro, Dorze, Oyda and Maale. It is especially noteworthy that two adverbial concepts recur in most of the relevant constructions – 'now' in the case of STILL and NOT YET, 'before' in the case of ALREADY. Both of these clearly are canonical lexemes for the expression of temporal relations, and thus they are very suitable for the field of phasal polarity. However, the present paper also has some gaps in the data which should be filled in the course of future research, and there can be no doubt that further field work on phasal polarity is necessary. Given that thirteen languages are assumed to belong to the Ometo family altogether as indicated in Figure 1 in §1.1, seventeen expressions for four concepts are not that much. Six languages, that is Malo, Baskeet and all representatives beyond Northwest Ometo: Koorete, Zayse, Haro and C'ara, could not be included at all due to the lack of data. The problem here is, on the one hand, that not all Ometo languages are well-described, though there are, for example, relatively recent monographs on Koorete (Binyam 2010) and on Zayse (Yeshimebet 2017). On the other hand, even some extant grammars seem to lack clear information on phasal polarity, as is true, for instance, of the "classical" book by Lamberti & Sottile (1997) on Wolaitta. At this point, it is admitted and at the same time regretted that the present author has made an unsuccessful attempt to collect information on the expression of 'still' in Dauro, N. W. Ometo: five sentences with this English phasal polarity item are found in the data, but all of the translations include lengthy constructions which are obviously used for this purpose and no two of these are the same. This leads to the assumption that Dauro does not have a fixed phrase for 'still' – unless any can be identified in other sources or future research.

Here, the general question arises in how far phasal polarity is standardised in Ometo languages: is this category of expressions less important in discourse than in, for example, some European languages such as English or German or is it simply the case that researchers have so far neglected it? Of course, standard constructions, also for NO LONGER which was not found at all, can only be specified when the amount of available data is sufficiently extensive and widespread patterns become visible. It might be an option for further research to investigate phasal polarity expressions in Bible texts in Ometo languages, some of which are available on special sites on the internet. These texts are extensive and they surely contain a wealth of relevant sentences, but the researcher must keep in mind that they are written translations and thus do not well represent the languages.

Concerning phasal polarity in Ometo languages in general, what remains for the time being is the pool of data in Tables 1–3. Fortunately, expressions of three of the four canonical concepts – STILL, NOT YET and ALREADY – could be found in a number of languages. It is also helpful to see that there are indeed recurrent structural patterns, namely the use of 'now' for STILL and NOT YET and the use of 'before' for ALREADY, which suggest that phasal polarity expressions are not totally spontaneous creations in Ometo languages, but there is a deeper foundation. However, only future research in the field or with texts can show how common these expressions are in the single languages and whether the patterns have equivalents in yet other languages. In the long run, the present study may also contribute to wider comparisons within the Omotic language group and even beyond.

Abbreviations

1	first person	INT	interrogative
2	second person	IPFV	imperfective
3	third person	IRR	irrealis
ABL	ablative	JUS	jussive
ABS	absolutive	M	masculine
ACC	accusative	NEG	negative
AFF	affirmative	NMLS	nominaliser
ASS	assertive	NOM	nominative
AUX	auxiliary	NSBJ	non-subject-oriented
C	consonant	OBL	oblique
COND	conditional	PFV	perfective
CONJ	conjunction	PL	plural
CVB	converb	PROG	progressive
DAT	dative	PRS	present
DECL	declarative	PST	past
F	feminine	REL	relative
FOC	focus	SBJV	subjunctive
FUT	future	SG	singular
INF	infinitive	V	vowel
INS	instrumental	VBLS	verbaliser

Bibliographic references

Azeb Amha. 2001. *The Maale language*. Leiden: Research School of Asian, African, and Amerindian Studies (Universiteit Leiden).

Azeb Amha. 2012. Omotic / Notes. In Zygmunt Frajzyngier & Erin Shay (eds.), *The Afroasiatic languages*, 423–504, 626. Cambridge: Cambridge University Press.

Bender, M. Lionel. 1987. First steps toward proto-Omotic. In David A. Odden (ed.), *Current approaches to African linguistics (vol. 4)*, 21–35. Dordrecht & Providence: Foris.

Bender, M. Lionel. 2000. *Comparative morphology of the Omotic languages*. Munich: LINCOM EUROPA.

Binyam Sisay Mendisu. 2010. *Aspects of Koorete verb morphology*. Cologne: Köppe.

Bouquiaux, Luc & Jacqueline M. C. Thomas. 1992. *Studying and describing unwritten languages*. Dallas: Summer Institute of Linguistics.

Cerulli, Enrico. 1925. Note su alcune popolazioni Sidama dell'Abissinia meridionale. *Rivista degli Studi Orientali* 10 (2–4). 597–692.

Dawit Bekele GebreGiorgis. 2016. *Language documentation based lexical study of the earlier Dawuro kingdom. Appendices*. Addis Ababa: Addis Ababa University dissertation.

Fleming, Harold C. 1974. Omotic as an Afroasiatic family. In William R. Leben (ed.), *Studies in African Linguistics. Supplement 5: Papers from the fifth Annual Conference on African Linguistics*, 81–94. Los Angeles: Department of Linguistics & African Studies Center (University of California).

Haile Eyesus Engdashet. 1981. *A phonetic and phonemic study of Dorze*. Addis Ababa: Addis Ababa University Senior essay.

Hayward, Richard J. 1987. Terminal vowels in Ometo nominals. In Herrmann R. Jungraithmayr & Walter W. Müller (eds.), *Proceedings of the fourth international Hamito-Semitic congress. Marburg, 20–22 September, 1983*, 215–231. Amsterdam & Philadelphia: Benjamins.

Hayward, Richard J. 1991. Concerning a vocalic alternation in North Omotic verb paradigms. *Bulletin of the School of Oriental and African Studies* 54 (3). 535–553.

Hayward, Richard J. 2001. A further consideration of terminal vowels in Ometo. In Andrzej Zaborski (ed.), *New data and new methods in Afroasiatic linguistics. Robert Hetzron in memoriam*, 53–63. Wiesbaden: Harrassowitz.

Hayward, Richard J. & Eshetu Chabo. 2014. *Gamo-English-Amharic dictionary. With an introductory grammar of Gamo*. Wiesbaden: Harrassowitz.

Hudson, Grover M. 2012. Ethnic group and mother tongue in the Ethiopian censuses of 1994 and 2007. *Aethiopica* 15. 204–218.

Lamberti, Marcello & Roberto Sottile. 1997. *The Wolaytta language*. Cologne: Köppe.

Moreno, Martino M. 1938. *Introduzione alla lingua Ometo*. Unknown place: A. Mondadori.

Sellassie Cheru Hirboro. 2015. *Documentation and grammatical description of Gofa*. Addis Ababa: Addis Ababa University dissertation.

Wakasa, Motomichi. 2008. *A descriptive study of the modern Wolaytta language*. Tokyo: The University of Tokyo dissertation.

Wondimu Gaga Gashe. 2010. *Sociolinguistic facts about the Gamo area. South Ethiopia*. Addis Ababa: ARCCIKCL.

Yeshimebet Bogale. 2017. *Documentation and grammatical description of Zaysete*. Addis Ababa: Addis Ababa University dissertation.

Zaborski, Andrzej. 2004. West Cushitic – a genetic reality. *Lingua Posnaniensis* 46. 173–186.

Anne-Maria Fehn
Phasal polarity in Khwe and Ts'ixa (Kalahari Khoe)

1 Introduction

Khwe and Ts'ixa are two related languages belonging to the southern African language family Khoe-Kwadi which forms part of the typological unit Khoisan[1] (Güldemann 2014). Although their affiliation to the Kalahari Khoe subgroup of Khoe (Vossen 1997) is undisputed, it is not entirely clear whether Ts'ixa is a peripheral dialect of Khwe (Westphal 1971; Fehn 2016; Fehn 2018; Fehn 2019) or a member of the geographically adjacent Shua dialect cluster (Köhler 1971; Vossen 1997) (Figure 1).[2]

Khwe is a dialect cluster consisting of at least two distinct varieties, Khwe proper and ǁAni (Brenzinger 1998; Fehn 2019), and is spoken by 7,000–8,000 speakers (Brenzinger 2013) in southeastern Angola, along the Namibian Caprivi Strip and around the Okavango Delta in Botswana. Ts'ixa is spoken by less than 300 individuals, all of whom reside in the village Mababe in northern

---

[1] Following Güldemann (2014), the term "Khoisan" is used to refer to the non-Bantu, non-Cushitic click languages of southern and eastern Africa. It does not denote a genealogical unit as postulated by Greenberg (1966).
[2] The Khwe data discussed in this paper was assembled within the frame of the project 'Die Welt der Kxoé-Buschleute – Wissenschaftliche Bearbeitung des Materials zur Khwe-Kultur im Nachlass des Afrikanisten Oswin Köhler' [The world of the Kxoé Bushmen – scientific edition of materials on Khwe culture in the legacy of the Africanist Oswin Köhler] funded by the Deutsche Forschungsgemeinschaft (DFG) and led by Rainer Vossen. Data on Ts'ixa was collected under a research permit issued by the Ministry of Youth, Sports and Culture of the Government of Botswana and funded by the a.r.t.e.s. Graduate School of the University of Cologne, the German Academic Exchange Service (Deutscher Akademischer Austauschdienst) DAAD, the project "The Kalahari Basin area: a 'Sprachbund' on the verge of extinction" within the European Science Foundation EUROCORES programme EUROBABEL led by Tom Güldemann, and by the Humboldt University of Berlin. The author is currently funded through contract CEECIND/02765/2017 financed by the Foundation for Science and Technology (FCT, Portugal); part of the work for this paper was carried out within the project PTDC/BIA-GEN /29273/2017, led by Jorge Rocha and funded by FCT.

I would like to thank Tom Güldemann for drawing my attention to the similarity of Ts'ixa xáwèè 'still' to Khoekhoe xàwè~xàwé~xabe 'but', and two anonymous reviewers for valuable comments on an earlier version of this paper.

Anne-Maria Fehn, Universidade do Porto

https://doi.org/10.1515/9783110646290-016

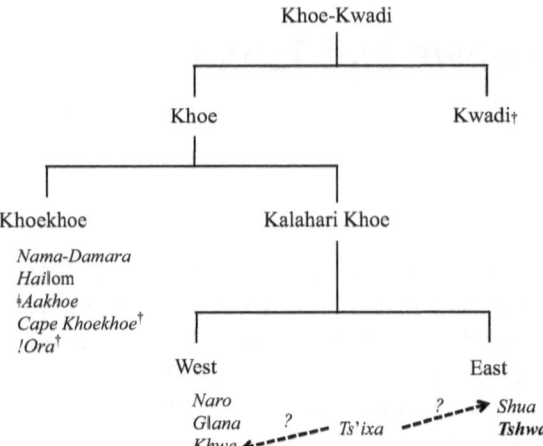

Figure 1: The Khoe-Kwadi language family (Güldemann, 2014; Vossen, 1997); the position of Ts'ixa is debated.

Botswana (Fehn 2016). The geographical distribution of Khwe and Ts'ixa is outlined in Figure 2. The Khwe data presented in this article is restricted to Khwe proper and was collected by Köhler (1981, 1989, 2018), who carried out most of his fieldwork in the western part of the Namibian Caprivi Strip and around the mission at Andara, and by Kilian-Hatz (2003, 2008), whose work focused on the settlement Mǔtc'iku, close to Divundu. The Ts'ixa data was collected by the present author at Mababe (Fehn 2016).

At present, information on phasal polarity systems in Khoe-Kwadi languages is sparse, and no dedicated research on the topic has been published. However, Khwe and Ts'ixa have been described within the frame of language documentation projects (see, e.g., Fehn 2016; Kilian-Hatz 2008; Köhler 1981), and corpora of elicited data as well as texts are available for both languages.[3] The present study therefore constitutes a preliminary attempt at creating an overview of phasal polarity systems, items and coding strategies in Khwe and Ts'ixa without intending to be exhaustive.

---

[3] To facilitate comparison, the Ts'ixa data has been transliterated to match the practical working orthography for Khwe (Schladt 2000). In addition to the Khwe sound inventory, Ts'ixa has non-affricated ejective clusters that are represented by <|k', ||k', ǂk'>. Deviating from Schladt (2000), word-initial glottal stops are marked by <'>. <′> and <`> mark high and low tone on vowels and nasals, no marking indicates mid tone. The tone marking on the Ts'ixa data partly deviates from Fehn (2016), as the author has since revised her tonal analysis.

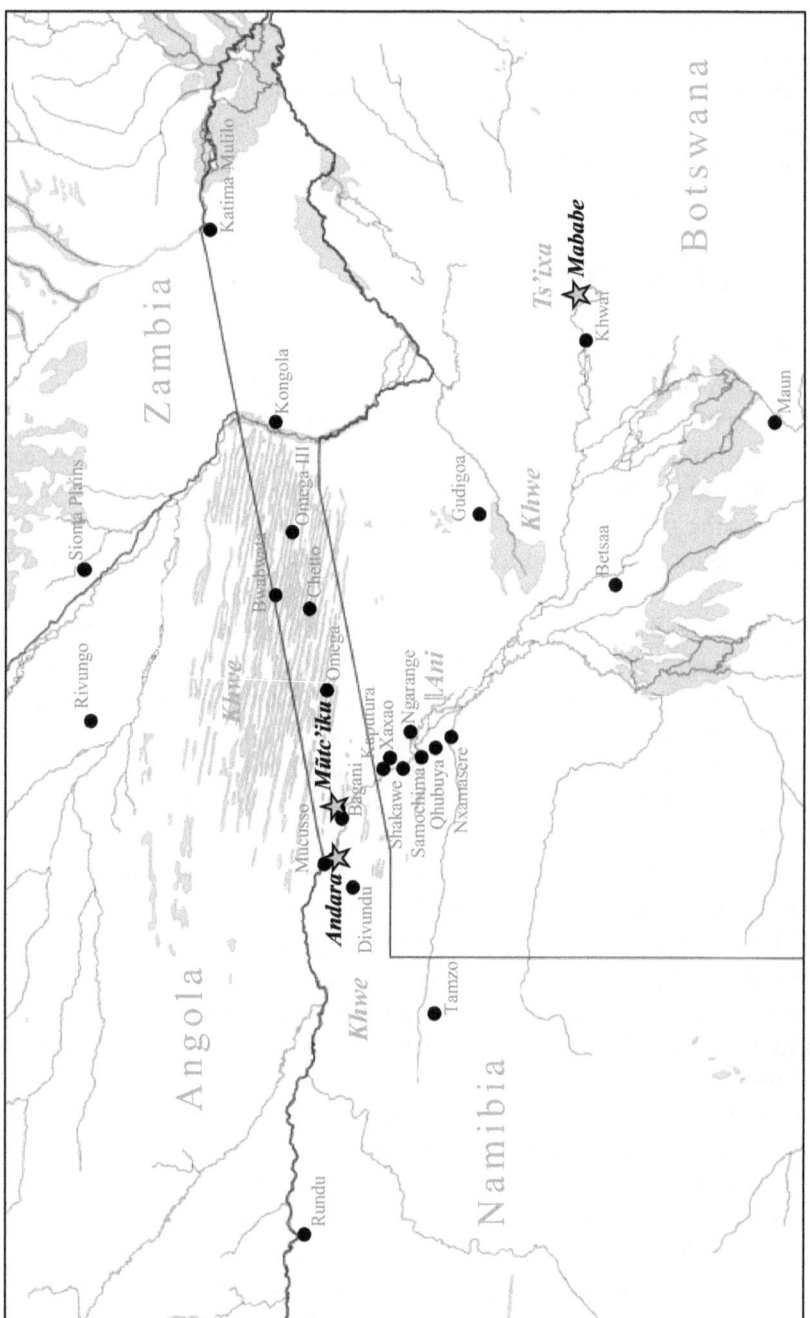

Figure 2: Geographical distribution of Khwe and Ts'ixa along the northern Kalahari Basin fringe; the star symbol indicates locations where the data presented in this article was collected.

In §1, I provide a structural overview of Khwe and Ts'ixa, supplemented by more specific information on negation templates and tense-aspect marking. §2 presents their phasal polarity systems and discusses coverage and semantics of individual items, and §3 looks at the data from a comparative perspective, taking into account other members of the Khoe language family.

2 Structural features

Khwe and Ts'ixa are typologically close members of the Khoe-Kwadi language family. The basic word order of both languages is SOV, but pragmatic considerations allow for both SVO and OSV. The basic constituent order in the noun phrase is head-final. In Ts'ixa, pragmatic considerations may trigger inversion. Nouns in Khwe and Ts'ixa are optionally marked by portmanteau morphemes encoding person, gender and number (PGN). These clitics serve the function of specific articles and attach to about 75% of the languages' noun phrases. Like other Khoe languages, Khwe and Ts'ixa have a rich suffixing morphology: Derivational suffixes attach to both verbs and nouns, and a subset of the languages' tense-aspect morphemes is linked to the verb stem via a so-called juncture morpheme. While Ts'ixa, like other Kalahari Khoe languages, has only one juncture morpheme (glossed as 'J'), Khwe distinguishes between two juncture morphemes triggering different morpho-tonological processes (Köhler 1981; Kilian-Hatz 2008), one for NON-PAST ('I') and one for PAST ('II').

In Ts'ixa, subject and direct object are optionally case-marked by means of the above-mentioned PGN clitics, which (in singular and plural, but not in dual) display a nominative-accusative distinction. In both languages, the direct object may optionally be marked by the postposition 'à, which interacts with the argument's information-structural properties. Oblique (peripheral) participants are obligatorily marked by a set of semantically specified postpositions.

Ts'ixa and Khwe distinguish between three syntactic verb classes, according to the number of core participants they may take: intransitives, transitives and S/O-ambitransitives. Ditransitives in the sense of Kittilä (Kittilä 2006), i.e., with two objects treated like the single object of a transitive predication, are only attested in Khwe.

Predicates may be simple or complex. Complex predicates display semantic features similar to serial verb constructions and involve two or more verbs, which are connected by the juncture morpheme (Fehn 2016; Kilian-Hatz 2006).

2.1 Negation

Due to their structural and formal differences, the negation patterns of Khwe (§1.1.1) and Ts'ixa (§1.1.2) are described separately.

2.1.1 Negation in Khwe

Khwe has a default negation marker *vé*, which negates both verbal (1a) and non-verbal predicates (1b).

(1) a. *tc'ípa-t'í   pá   -à -llòè, dìnì-à-t'í pá   -à -llò vé.*
       tc'ipa.bee sting -I -HAB dini.bee sting -I -HAB NEG
       'The tc'ipa-bee stings, the dini-bee does not sting.'
       (Kilian-Hatz 2008: 256)
    b. *xà   -má   Góává   -mà   vé.*
       DEM -3sg.M Mbukushu -3sg.M NEG
       'He is not a Mbukushu.'
       (Kilian-Hatz 2008: 253)

The notions of 'never' or 'not at all' are either expressed by *vé*, or by an emphatic form derived from *vé* (2a). They may be accompanied by emphatic adverbials (2b).

(2) a. *pákò, tí   kṵ̋ṵ̋ -à -tè   vé   -tè.*
       never 1sg go -I -PRES NEG -EMPH
       'Never, I don't go / I never go / I don't go at all.'
       (Kilian-Hatz 2008: 257)
    b. *lx'ṵ̋ vé   córò   -m̀   tama -xa.*
       kill NEG rock.monitor -3sg.M even -GER
       'He can't even kill a rock monitor.'
       (Kilian-Hatz 2008: 257)

In the above examples, *vé* is best analysed as a particle. However, it may appear as a suffix with adjectives and adverbials derived with the gerund suffix *-xa* (3a–b).

(3) a. *mṵ̋ṵ̋ -ve -re -xa*
       see   -NEG -II -GER
       'blind, ignorant (lit. not seeing)'
       (Kilian-Hatz 2008: 167)

b. 'ó   -ávà   -ve -re -xa tέ -έ -hĩ   ǁgὲɛ-khòè -hὲ.
   PRIV   -give.birth -NEG -II -GER be -II -PST5 woman   -3sg.F
   'virgin (lit. woman that was never pregnant)'
   (Kilian-Hatz 2008: 167)

Apart from the clausal negation marker *vé*, Khwe has a verbal negation suffix *-ŋya* which forms part of the verbal stem (4a–b) (Kilian-Hatz 2008: 165f).

(4) a. nà-tíú tcá   tí   'à   kx'úí-tcao -ŋya -à -tè?
       why   2sg.M 1sg   O   answer   -NEG -I PRES
       'Why don't you answer me?'
       (Kilian-Hatz 2008: 165)
    b. tí   ki   yaá   -ŋya -à -ǁòè xó   -hè   nǎű   rè?
       1sg LOC come -NEG -I -HAB thing   -3sg.F which Q
       'Why do you never come to me?'
       (Kilian-Hatz 2008: 257)

In addition, Khwe has a copula verb *hámbe* 'be absent' which is used as a negative existential marker (5a–b). *hámbe* is a contraction of the verb *hãã* 'be there' and the general negation particle *vé* (Kilian-Hatz 2008: 138):

(5) a. kyǎĩ   'à   hámbe.
       peace   FOC   be.absent
       'There is no peace.'
       (Kilian-Hatz 2008: 138)
    b. 'ú   ǁé   hámbe   -e -gòè.
       tomorrow 1pl.M be.absent -I -FUT
       'Tomorrow we will not be there.'
       (Kilian-Hatz 2008: 138)

2.1.2 Negation in Ts'ixa

Ts'ixa has a general negation particle *'íté* which appears in non-verbal (6a) and verbal clauses (6b–d). *'íté* combines with all tense-aspect markers, except the imperfective *kò* and the sequential *nǀgè~nè*:

(6) a. ǁgaa   -kyxóa   'íté, k'áò -kyxóa   'è.
       female -elephant   NEG   male -elephant   it.is
       'It is not a female elephant, it is a male elephant.'

b. *ǁʼáа̰ -kù -m̀ íḭ́ -m̀ gérè khudí ʼíté.*
   fight -REC -3sg.M DEM.ref -3sg.M FUT end NEG
   'This fight will not end.'
c. *tí tè kúm̀ ʼíté.*
   1sg PST1 hear NEG
   'I do not understand.' (lit. I did not hear.)
d. *ǀxúú-khòè -m̀ ǁám -a -ta ʼíté.*
   fortune.teller -3sg.M perceive -J -PST2 NEG
   'The fortune teller did not understand (the future).'

Adjectives derived with *-xa* are also negated by *ʼíté* (7).

(7) *sugírí -xà ʼíté tíí tí kò kʼáà.*
   sugar -ADJ NEG tea 1sg IPFV drink
   'I drink tea without sugar.' ('I drink non -sugar-y tea.')

The imperfective particle *kò* has a negative counterpart, the suffix *-ta̰* (8a–b).

(8) a. *sáò ʼà túú -ta̰.*
      winter OBL rain -IPFV.NEG
      'It does not rain in winter.'
    b. *tí ǁʼum̀ -ta̰.*
      1sg sleep -IPFV.NEG
      'I am not sleeping / I do not sleep.'

The sequential *ǀgè~nè* is negated by means of the suffix *-té* (9).

(9) *ǁṵ̋ṵ̋ -xa -dzì ǀgè mṵ̋ṵ̋ -a ʼáа̰ -té lúú -sì*
   parent -ASSOC -3pl.F SEQ see -J know -NEG one.of -3sg.F
   lṵ̋а̰́ kà tè káu tà.
   child ATTR PST1 stay.behind COMP
   'The (zebra) mothers (and their associates) did not notice one of the young ones had stayed behind.'

Like Khwe, Tsʼixa has a specialized marker expressing negated existential, the copula verb *haáté* (10). *haáté* is probably a contraction of the verb *hа̰́а̰́* 'to exist' and the negation particle *ʼíté*.

(10) n-tshéè haáté   túú -mà.
     today be.absent rain -3sg.M
     'Today there is no rain.'

2.2 Tense and aspect marking

The verbal morphology of Khwe and Ts'ixa encompasses both suffixes and particles, many of which are portmanteau morphemes combining temporal and aspectual notions (Fehn 2016: 142; Kilian-Hatz 2008: 106). While Ts'ixa displays a preference for particles in the domain of non-past, Khwe almost exclusively relies on suffixes. Both languages display a considerable degree of overlap in the past tense morphology, but their tense-aspect systems are sufficiently differentiated to be described separately.

2.2.1 Tense and aspect in Khwe

Khwe has nine suffixes marking tense-aspect, four in the domain of non-past, and five past-tense markers. All suffixes likely grammaticalized from full verbs and are linked to the bare verb by means of the juncture morpheme; there are different junctures for non-past ('I') and past ('II').

The domain of non-past is constituted by *-tè* (present/imperfective) (11a), *-llòè* (habitual) (11b), *-nǂùè* (progressive) (11c) and *-gòè* (future) (11d).

(11) a. tcá   nǎű xú   -m̀   'à nlé-kà kyá   -á -tè   mà?
        2sg.M what thing -3sg.M O here   search -I -PRES Q
        'What are you looking for here?'
        (Köhler 2018)
     b. kx'á-khòè -m̀   à   ǁgèε-khòè -hè xù   -á -tè
        husband -3sg.M O   woman   -3sg.F leave -I -PRES
        nò   híí   -ì   -llòè   kx'éí 'à.
        when do   -IMPS -HAB   how
        'What happens to a woman who leaves her husband'
        (Köhler 2018)
     c. tí yà   -á -hã   yà ǂ'óa -a -nǂùè.
        1sg come -II -PST1 MOV ask -I -PROG
        'I have come and am now asking...'
        (Köhler 2018)

d. *tímà   xàvánaxa tcá   ū̀ū   -a -gòè vé.*
   therefore again   2sg.M marry -I -FUT NEG
   'Therefore you will not marry (her) again.'
   (Köhler 2018)

Khwe has five past tense suffixes marking different stages of anteriority. Among them, the immediate past *-hã* ('PST1') (12a) also functions as a marker of current relevance or perfect (12b).

(12) a. *tí   kóḿ -á -hã, tákò tí dò   -á -tè.*
        1sg hear -II -PST1 then 1sg admit -I -PRES
        'I have heard (what the man just said), and I admit it.'
        (Köhler 2018)
     b. *ngyáve -lõã líní   -na -hã*
        giraffe -DIM become.thin -II -PST1
        'A young giraffe is thin'
        (Köhler 2018)

The remaining four suffixes denote hodiernal past (*-ta* 'PST2') (13a), yesterday's past (*-ǁ'om* 'PST3') (13b), a moderately remote past (*-tĩ* 'PST4') (13c), and a very remote past (*-hĩ* 'PST5') (13d).

(13) a. *tcá   mū̌ū̌ -è -tè   vé tí ǁx'áa -can -ka -ra -ta?*
        2sg.M see -I -PRES NEG 1sg wash -REFL -CAU -II -PST2
        'Don't you see that I have washed myself (earlier today)?'
        (Kilian-Hatz 2008: 103)
     b. *tcá   'à tí mū́ū -a -ǁ'òm̀.*
        2sg.M O 1sg see -II -PST3
        'I saw you yesterday.'
        (Kilian-Hatz 2008: 103)
     c. *té   'á -m̀   'à ǁháó 'à mā̌ā   -na -tĩ vé.*
        1pl.C DEM -3sg.M O hoe O give.as.gift -II -PST4 NEG
        'We did not present him with a hoe (some time ago).'
        (Köhler 2018)
     d. *tá   ǂaḿ-kuri   hĩ́ĩ -t -a   -hĩ   khóá-xa*
        thus in.the.old.days do -HAB -II -PST5 as
        nlé-kyaó   tamaxa hĩ́ĩ -è -ǁòè.
        nowadays also do -I -HAB
        'As it was done in the old days, we still do it today.'
        (Köhler 2018)

Among the numerous derivational suffixes of Khwe (Kilian-Hatz 2008: 140ff), the habitual suffix -t(i)[4] (14a–b) and the completive/telic suffix -xu (14c–d) are frequently used in combination with other tense-aspect markers:

(14) a. tí   'à djàò -ró -mà -ŋya -can -t   -a -tè.
       1sg O work -II -BEN -NEG -REFL -HAB -I -PRES
       '(Your daughter) does not work for me.'
       (Köhler 2018)
    b. 'ávuru -m̀   'à guúrú -t   -a -hĩ.
       goods -3sg.M O lay.out -HAB -II -PST5
       '(They) would (customarily) lay out the goods . . .'
       (Köhler 2018)
    c. lú-l'e-no   tó   Ix'û̂ -ku -a -xu   -a -gòè.
       some.day 2pl.C kill -REC -II -COMPL -I -FUT
       'Some day you will kill each other.'
       (Köhler 2018)
    d. 'á   -m̀   m̀   tc'ấã̂ -hè
       DEM   -3sg.M   POSS   theft -3sg.F
       khùrĩ́   -na   -xu   -a   -ll'òm̀.
       be.finished -II   -COMPL -II   -PST3
       'His theft is settled (lit. is finished).'
       (Köhler 2018)

Finally, Khwe has an aspect-marking particle, the continuous té (König 2007) which precedes the finite verb phrase (15a–b).

(15) a. tíú   xà   -ná   'éí -á -xu   -a -kò
       then DEM -3pl.C stay -II -COMPL -II -CONV
       gómbò   -m̀   ki   té
       abandoned.house   -3sg.M LOC CONT
       kx'ốấ   -ấ̂ -hĩ.
       wait.for   -II -PST5
       'While staying behind at the abandoned homestead, they kept waiting.'
       (Köhler 2018)

---

4 Kilian-Hatz (2008) analyzes this suffix as frequentative.

(15) b. *tí   djéxò   kx'á-khòè -à   ki   tí   tɛ́   ǁgèù   -á -gòè vé.*
     1sg be.bad man   -GEN LOC   1sg   CONT suffer -I -FUT NEG
     'I will not stay with a bad man and keep suffering.'
     (Köhler 2018)

2.2.2 Tense and aspect in Ts'ixa

Ts'ixa has ten primary tense-aspect markers, six of which are pre-verbal particles. The remaining four are suffixes, three of which are linked to the verb stem by means of the juncture morpheme ('J'). Tense marking in Ts'ixa is always relative, i.e., future and past markers express temporal deixis to a reference point which does not necessarily coincide with the time of speech.

Unlike Khwe, Ts'ixa has a generic imperfective marker *kò* which covers the semantic domains of present, habitual and progressive (16a). In addition, a dedicated progressive, *kùè*, exists (16b).

(16) a. *tí   kò   bala -sè   Bilí   -ḿ   kyã̌ã̌ -na -ha.*
        1sg IPFV   read -ADV personal.name -3sg.M enter -J   -PST3
        'While I was reading, Bill came in.'
     b. *tí   kùè   bala*
        1sg PROG   read
        'I am reading.'

Ts'ixa distinguishes between two future (or posterior) categories, the near future *nà* (17a), and the generic future *gérè* (17b).

(17) a. *tí   nà   Mãú̌ 'ò   kṹṵ̌.*
        1sg NEAR.FUT Maun LOC   go
        'I am about to go to Maun (now).'
     b. *tí   gérè Mãú̌ 'ò   kṹṵ̌.*
        1sg FUT   Maun LOC   go
        'I will go to Maun (at some unspecified point in the future).'

Ts'ixa distinguishes four stages of anteriority: an immediate past *tè* ('PST1') (18a), a hodiernal past *-ta* ('PST2') (18b), yesterday's past *-'o* ('PST3') (18c), and a remote past *-ha~hã* ('PST4') (18d). While all past tense markers may take on the function of a current relevance marker or perfect, this particular aspectual function is most prominent with the suffix *-hã~ha* (18e), which is also used as a generic past tense marker.

(18) a. ná -llù tè llóé -xò kyxóa -mà 'à.
DEM.ref -3pl.M PST1 lie.down -CAU elephant -3sg.M O
'They (m.) just brought the elephant down.'
b. gúà -sì biyé -lũã -sà 'à k'oó -tá.
hyena -3sg.F zebra -DIM -3sg.F O eat.meat:J -PST2
'The hyena ate the zebra filly (today).'
c. Khwáí 'ò Maxwell -m̀ gllái -na -'o.
Khwai LOC personal.name -3sg.M run -J -PST3
'Maxwell ran to Khwai (yesterday).'
d. tsé kũ̀ũ -a kyúu -a -ha qáré -dzà 'à.
1pl go -II gather -II -PST4 sweet -3pl.F O
'(In the past,) we went (there) to gather sweet things.'
e. tí 'aná -hã̌.
1sg know:J -PST4
'I know (lit. 'I got to know and now I know).'

In addition to these, Ts'ixa has a suffix -nà, which does not require the juncture morpheme and denotes stative and current relevance. In most instances, -nà may be replaced by -hã~-ha without an apparent change in meaning (19).

(19) ti 'ã̌ã̌ -nà.
1sg know -STAT
'I know.'

The particle n/gè ~nè marks sequential perfective and is mostly found in stories where it encodes events on the main narrative line (20a–b).

(20) a. hii -lũ̌ã̌ hakáà -sè thà nlgè kũ̀ũ -a llk'ám̀ góè -sà 'à.
stick -DIM bring -ADV and.then SEQ go -J beat cattle -3sg.F O
'Bringing a small stick, (the girl) went and beat the cow with it.'
b. thà góè -sì nlgè tan
and.then cattle -3sg.F SEQ stand.up
'Then the cow stood up.'

Like Khwe, Ts'ixa also has a set of derivative suffixes which combine with other tense-aspect morphology: the frequentative/habitual -ti (21a), the durative -'íí-sì (21b) and the completive/telic marker -xu (21c). Verbs derived with -xu can never be used with the imperfective kò (Fehn 2016: 170).

(21) a. *llxáá   'à   'é.m̀   sĩ́ĩ   -ti   -na -ha.*
       morning OBL 3sg.M work -FREQ -J -PST4
       'He often works in the morning.'
   b. *guni.khò -llù   kò   lláró   -'íí.sì*
       hunter   -3pl.M IPFV shoot:J -DUR
       'The hunters keep shooting.'
   c. *gllaa.khóè -sì   Pitá -mà   'à   llk'ám̀ -na -ha   thí.'à   llxarò*
       woman   -3sg.F Peter -3sg.M O   hit   -J   -PST4 and.then chase
       -na -xu.
       -J -COMPL
       'The woman hit Peter and chased him away.'

3 The expression of phasal polarity

As a dedicated study on phasal polarity (phasal polarity) expressions in Khwe and Ts'ixa is still lacking, the data presented in the following sections was taken from elicitations and texts available from published sources (Kilian-Hatz 2003; Kilian-Hatz 2008; Fehn 2016), the author's own field notes, and the Oswin Köhler Archive at the University of Frankfurt (Köhler 2018). Nevertheless, it is hoped that it will provide a first overview and serve as a starting point for future research.

The phasal polarity systems of Khwe and Ts'ixa are provided in Table 1 below:

Table 1: The expression of phasal polarity concepts in Khwe and Ts'ixa.

phasal polarity concept	KHWE	TS'IXA
ALREADY	*-xu* 'COMPL' (< *xùú 'leave behind') ?*kx'éí-á-xa* (< *kx'éí* 'first, front')	*tű̃ũ*[5]
STILL	*góáná-ò(-m̀)-xa* (< *góáná-ò* 'soon, later') *tamaxa* 'also, even'	*xáwèè* (?< *xa 'DEM', *úè* 'also')
NO LONGER	*vé* 'NEG'	*'íté* 'NEG'
NOT YET	*vé* 'NEG'	*xáwèè + -tã* 'IPFV.NEG'

---

[5] erroneously given as <thũũ̀> in Fehn (2016)

The phasal polarity systems of Khwe and Ts'ixa are characterized by a limited number of specialized phasal polarity items, and no language displays a rigid system, i.e. a system covering the entire spectrum with one dedicated phasal polarity item per concept (Kramer 2017). While both languages appear to have specialized items to cover STILL, *góáná-ò(-m̀)-xa* (Khwe) and *xáwèè* (Ts'ixa) are probably derived from more general adverbial expressions and therefore not restricted to phasal polarity contexts. Ts'ixa *xáwèè* is also involved in the expression of NOT YET, suggesting a system at least partly characterized by internal negation (Löbner 1989). The only item fully dedicated to the expression of a specific phasal polarity expression found in the corpus is Ts'ixa *tű̃ű̃* 'already'.

3.1 Already

3.1.1 Khwe

In Köhler's extensive Khwe corpus, the most widespread strategy to express ALREADY involves the completive suffix *-xu* which emphasizes the telicity of the state of affairs described by the verb. *-xu* goes back to a verb *xùú 'leave behind, abandon' acting as V2 in a multiverb construction and therefore requires use of the juncture morpheme. This particular grammaticalization is attested throughout Kalahari Khoe and the suffix can thus be reconstructed as *-xu for this sub-branch of the Khoe family (Vossen 1997: 354, there called "Terminativ-Itiv").

Since in Khwe, usage of *-xu* is not restricted to contexts carrying the implicit notion of ALREADY (cf. §1.2.1 above), the suffix cannot be analysed as a specialized phasal polarity item. In the examples found in the corpus (22a-d), *-xu* was only found conveying ALREADY in combination with past tense suffixes.

(22) a. ǁáò   kyá   -à -tè   -m̀   ǀóã́   -m̀
       2pl.M search -II -PRES -3sg.M child -3sg.M
       'à ǁé   ǀx'ű̃ -á   -xu   -a   -ǁ'òm̀.
       O   1pl.M kill -II -COMPL -II -PST3
       'We have (already) killed the boy you are looking for.'
       (Köhler 2018)
    b. 'ű̃ű̃   -a -xu   -a   -hĩ   nò kx'á-khòè -m̀   ǀxòà ǁóé -t
       marry -II -COMPL -II -PST5 if husband   -3sg.M COM lie -HAB
       -a -hĩ.
       -II -PST5
       'If she was (already) married, she would then lie with the husband.'
       (Köhler 2018)

c. *laává   -na -xu   -a -hĩ   wòcáń -hɛ̀ laává   -m̀ tcóò*
   be.of.age -II -COMPL -II -PST5 friend -3sg.F maturity -3sg.M medicine
   'ú   -/xòà -à -//òè.
   gather   -COM -I -HAB
   '[. . .] a friend who has (already) come of age gathers maturity medicine with her.'
   (Köhler 2018)

d. *nlé-lam énò   lú   -mà //'ó -ó -xu   -a -hã̀.*
   today   perhaps someone -3sg.M die -II -COMPL -II -PST1
   'Maybe today someone has (already) died.'
   (Köhler 2018)

Sometimes the reading ALREADY has to be solely deduced from context, without overt marking of any kind. Contrary to the examples quoted in (22) above, the verb in (23) below is in the present tense, suggesting that use of telic *-xu* would have been incompatible:

(23) *ǂ'ú   -m̀   'à ǂ'ú -à -tè   nò ǂ'ú   -m̀   kà kx'ṹĩ -è -//òè.*
     food -3sg.M O eat -I -PRES if food -3sg.M OBL live -I -HAB
     'If (the child) is (already) eating food, it lives off the food.' (Köhler 2018)

The Khwe dictionary (Kilian-Hatz 2003: 73, 231) gives 'already' as one of the various adverbial meanings of *kx'éí-á-xa*, a form presumably derived from *kx'éí* 'face, first, front'. However, no example is provided, and no evidence for use of *kx'éí-á-xa* in phasal polarity contexts could be obtained from a dedicated search in Köhler's (2018) text corpus. Whether the form *kx'éí-á-xa* may actually be used to express ALREADY therefore remains a topic of future research.

3.1.2 Ts'ixa

In Ts'ixa, ALREADY is expressed by the specialized adverbial *tṹũ*. Following pragmatic rules, the unmarked position of *tṹũ* is after the subject, but before the verb (24a–b). *tṹũ* can be focused by occupying the slot before the subject (24d–e). Although more evidence is needed, it may be speculated that unmarked *tṹũ* preferentially appears in neutral statements, while focusing of *tṹũ* may indicate a counterfactual statement. In the corpus, *tṹũ* is only attested with verbs marked for past tense.

(24) a. haà   'é.dzì kónò tṹũ   gúà   -sì   k'oró
       come   3pl.F when already hyena -3sg.F eat.meat:J
       khudí   -na   -ta   lṹã́   -sà   'à.
       end   -J   -PST1 child -3sg.F   O
       'When they came, the hyena had already finished eating the young (zebra).'
   b. tsá   tṹũ   'yṹṹ -á -ta   rè kana tsá   kò   síí   -à 'yṹṹ?
       2sg.M already   eat -J -PST1 Q or   2sg.M IPFV arrive -J eat
       'Have you already eaten or are you going to eat?'
   c. tṹũ   'é.mà   'à garo   -ta.
       already 3sg.M O   look:J -PST2
       '[They] have already looked at it.'
   d. subárà -dzà   tṹũ   tí   sámbà -na -ta.
       clothes -3pl.F already 1sg   wash   -J -PST2
       'I have already washed the clothes.'
   e. tsóò   -mà   tṹũ   tí   k'áa   -ta.
       medicine -3sg.M already 1sg   drink:J -PST2
       'I already drank my medicine.'

3.2 Still

Both Khwe and Ts'ixa have specialized, albeit unrelated items to express STILL.

3.2.1 Khwe

Khwe expresses STILL by means of the adverbial *góáná-ò(-m̀)-xa*. The adverbializing suffix *-xa* indicates the item's derived status, whereas the PGN suffix *-m̀* (3sg.M), which appears in some examples (25d), suggests a nominal origin. However, a form *góáná(-ò)* is only attested as an adverbial meaning 'soon, shortly, at once, later'.

In the Khwe corpus, *góáná-ò(-m̀)-xa* is attested in non-verbal clauses (25a–b), and in present tense and habitual contexts (25c–d). One example, a conditional clause, featured the adverbial in combination with a past tense suffix (25e).

(25) a. laává   -khòè   -hè   'á   góáná-ò-xa ngú -m̀   'ó-ki   tı̃̀
       be.of.age   -person -3sg.F DEM still   hut -3sg.M inside be
       yá   -xa
       while -GER

ǂ'ű -m̀ 'à ǂ'ű -à -tè nò tc'áó-ǂ'ũ -m̀ ǀxòà
food -3sg.M O eat -I -PRES when bushfood -3sg.M COM
cǟ-ǂũ -m̀.
crop -3sg.M
'If the girl who has come of age eats food while she is still inside the hut, a bird eats all the bushfood and the crops.'
(Köhler 2018)

b. *"Pheru"* góáná-ò-xa lőǎ́ 'àm̀ -ì -llòè vé.
personal.name still child greet -IMPS -HAB NEG
'Pheru is still a child, he is not greeted.'
(Köhler 2018)

c. *Havo -m̀* 'òkà góáná-ò-xa tǐ -à -kó hǐǐ -è -tè.
Havo -3sg.M LOC still be -II -CONV do -I -PRES
'In Havo, there are still women who do it.'
(Köhler 2018)

d. *nǀé-kyaó khóé -nà* góáná-ò-m̀-xa tǐ -à -kó Mũũ-tc'i-ku
nowadays person -3pl.C still live -II -CONV Mũtc'iku
kà tcóo-ǀxɛ -ku -a -llòè.
LOC poison -REC -I -HAB
'Nowadays the people living in Mũtc'iku still poison each other.'
(Köhler 2018)

e. *'á díxa -llgɛ̀ɛ-khòè -mà à* góáná-ò-xa
DEM owner -woman -3sg.M O still
nǀám -a -hĩ́ tínò kx'éí -á -xa
love -II -PAST5 then first -II -GER
llàè-khóé -mà díxa -llgɛ̀ɛ-khòè -m̀ 'à ǂ'óa nò:
arbiter -3sg.M owner -woman -3sg.M O ask and
'If the husband of the woman still loved her, then the arbiter would first ask the husband of the woman'
(Köhler 2018)

Although a specialized item exists, STILL is frequently expressed by the adverbial *tamaxa* 'also, even' which also appears outside of phasal polarity contexts. While all examples in the corpus referred to present habitual contexts (26a–c), this might be coincidence due to a bias in Köhler's (2018) text collection.

(26) a. ǃǵé-kyaó   kúrí   tamaxa   tá-khòè   -ǁù   ǀúí   -ǁùà   kx'ó   -á
       nowadays   time   also   elder   -3pl.M   only   -3pl.M eat.meat -I
       -ǁòè.
       -HAB
       'In modern times, still only elders eat it.'
       (Köhler 2018)

  b. nǃé-kyaó   tamaxa   nǁàtá   -xa   hĩ́   -è   -ǁòè.
       nowadays   also   like.that -GER   do   -I   -HAB
       'Nowadays they still do it like that.'
       (Köhler 2018)

  c. 'úì   tamaxa   kx'óa   -ra   -tà   nò   ǁ'áǹ   -a   -xu   -a
       evening also   be.raw   -II   -PAST2 if   be.ripe -II -COMPL   -II
       -kò
       -CONV
       kx'áà   -ì   -ǁòè.
       drink   -IMPS   -HAB
       'If it is still raw in the evening, one drinks it when it is done.'
       (Köhler 2018)

Finally, the notion of STILL may also be implicit to a context without displaying overt marking (27a–c). Again, habitual and present tense marking dominate, suggesting a clear link between non-telic aspect and non-telic phasal polarity contexts in Khwe.

(27) a. ndéku   -lõã   'à   lóḿ   -á   -tè
       small.child -DIM O   suck   -I   -PRES
       nò   ǁúũ   -hè   'àvà   -na   -kò
       when   parent -3sg.F carry.child   -II   -CONV
       'ṹ   -ǀxòà   -à   -ǁòè.
       gather -COM   -I   -HAB
       'When a small child is (still) breastfeeding, the mother takes it in a garment and goes gathering with it.'
       (Köhler 2018)

  b. kx'éí-tá-khòè -nà   hĩ̀   -é   -hĩ̀   khóá-xa   nǃé-kyaó   Khwe   -nà
       forefather   -3pl.C do   -II -PST5 as   nowadays   Khwe   -3pl.C
       ǀhɛé   -ku   -a   -ǁòè.
       chip.teeth -REC   -I   -HAB
       'Like the forefathers, the Khwe nowadays (still) chip each other's teeth.'
       (Köhler 2018)

c. *Ndumba   -m̀   lúí-xa -m̀   ki   tṹṹ.*
   personal.name -3sg.M only   -3sg.M LOC   exist
   'Only at Ndumba's, it (still) exists.'
   (Köhler 2018)

3.2.2 Ts'ixa

In Ts'ixa, STILL is expressed by the specialized adverbial *xáwèè*. *xáwèè* behaves similarly to *tṹũ* 'already' in that its neutral position is after the subject and before the verb, while its appearance in the pre-subject slot indicates focus and possibly encodes counterfactual statements. *xáwèè* preferably occurs in imperfective contexts (28a–c), but also occurs with the current relevance suffix *-ha* ~ *-hã* (28d).

(28) a. *'abá -mà   tṹũ   'é.ǹ   garo -ta   rè   kana xàwèè kò   'é.mà*
        dog   -3sg.M already 3pl.C   look:J -PST2 Q   or   still IPFV 3sg.M
        'à   gáò?
        O   look
        'Have they already looked at the dog or are they still looking?'

   b. *xàwèè 'é.sì   kò   'yṹṹ   rè   ǁxám.gyírà.kàà -dzà   'à   kana 'yṹṹ*
      still 3sg.F IPFV eat   Q   bean   -3pl.F O   or   eat
      -á   -ta?
      -J   -PST2
      'Is she still eating the beans or has [she] eaten [them already]?'

   c. *xáwèè kò   'yṹṹ.*
      still IPFV eat
      '(She is) still eating.'

   d. *tí   kò   tan   nò   ǁxáà   'à   tí   xáwèè tsxãã   -ha*
      1sg   IPFV get.up   when   morning   OBL   1sg   still be.tired:J -PST4
      -sè   'è.
      -ADV   it.is
      'When I got up in the morning, I was still tired.'

   e. *khoe   -m̀   ǁ'óó -na   k'òsò xáwèè k'ṹĩ́   'è*
      person -3sg.M die   -STAT   but   still be.alive   it.is
      'The man was in a dying state, but he is still alive.'

The phasal polarity adverbial *xáwèè* 'still' does not follow the phonotactic structure of genuine Ts'ixa lexical roots (Fehn 2018). As no donor for a possible borrowing could be identified, one may speculate that the form is a contraction of /xa/, a demonstrative base not present in modern Ts'ixa but attested in other Khoe languages, and an element /ue/ which is possibly identical with the adverbial úè~'úè 'also' (29a–b). The range of meanings covered by úè~'úè resembles Khwe *tamaxa* (26a–c above), which is also used to express the notion of STILL.

(29) a. thà   nè   xũĩ̀   góè   -sà,   khoe   -sì
and.then   SEQ   get.pregnant   cattle   -3sg.F   person   -3sg.F
nè   úè   xũĩ̀.
SEQ   also   get.pregnant
'And then, [it] got pregnant, the cow, and the woman also got pregnant.'
b. kárí   'íté   xúù   kaxórè   'é.m̀   úè   tí   ǁũ̀ũ̀   'è
be.hard   NEG   thing   because   3sg.M   also   1sg   parent   it.is
'It is not a problem [a hard thing] because he is also my father.'

3.3 No longer

Neither Khwe nor Ts'ixa has a specialized phasal polarity item to express NO LONGER. Since both languages simply use their general negation markers *vé* (Khwe) (30a–b) and *'íté* (Ts'ixa) (31a–b), the phasal polarity meaning has to be deduced from context. The available data is sparse and does not allow for generalizations on tense-aspect markers in NO LONGER phrases.

Khwe:
(30) a. nlé-kyaó   ǁgɛ̀ɛ-khòè   -djì   tc'áó   -m̀   'à   ṹ   -à   -ǁòè   vé.
nowadays   woman   -3pl.F   bush   -3sg.M   O   gather   -I   -HAB   NEG
'Nowadays women no longer gather in the bush.'
(Köhler 2018)
b. lὲ-xá   tcóo   -ku   -a   -ǁòè   vé.
now   treat   -REC   -I   -HAB   NEG
'Now people no longer treat each other with medicine.'
(Köhler 2018)

Ts'ixa:
(31) a. tsá   tí   tṹã   'íté.
2sg.M   1sg   friend   NEG
'You are no longer my friend / You are not my friend.'

b. *thuú 'à kṹũ -a -ta kónò llé kámà -tã̀ kaxórè*
Night OBL go:J -J -PST2 when 1pl.M track -IPFV.NEG because
llé gérè síí -à hítera 'íté tà 'aná -há 'yòò.
1pl.M FUT arrive -J find NEG COMP know:J -PST4 because
'When [the animals] passed at night, we do not track [them], because we know that we can no longer find them.'

3.4 Not yet

While Khwe has no specialized phasal polarity item for the notion of NOT YET, the limited data available for Ts'ixa suggests a combination of the adverbial *xáwèè* 'still' with the negated imperfective suffix *-tã*. It therefore seems that in the terms of Löbner's "Duality Hypothesis" (Löbner 1989), the phasal polarity paradigm of Ts'ixa is at least partly coded on the basis of internal negations.

3.4.1 Khwe

Khwe does not have a specialized phasal polarity item to express NOT YET. Like in the case of NO LONGER, the implicit meaning has to be deduced from context (32a-c).

(32) a. *kx'éí llóé -lxòà -ve -re -xa kṍã́ -ã́ -xu nò llóé -lxòà -à*
    first sleep -with -NEG -II -GER pay -II -COMPL if sleep -COM -I
    -llòè.
    -HAB
    'If they have not yet slept (with a man), they sleep with him after he has paid.'
    (Köhler 2018)
b. *llṹũ -ǹ lxòà tí kóḿ -ku -a -tà vé.*
    parent -3pl.C with 1sg hear -REC -II -PST2 NEG
    'I have not (yet) reached an understanding with (her) parents.'
    (Köhler 2018)

c. *ndéku   -m̀   ki   lx'ón   -mà   hámbe   nò   "ndéku*
small.child -3sg.M for name -3sg.M be.absent if small.child
-m̀"   tà   nlláà   -ku   -i   -llòè.
-3sg.M COMP talk -REC -IMPS -HAB
'If a child does not have a name (yet), one talks about him as "ndeku-m".'
(Köhler 2018)

3.4.2 Ts'ixa

The data for Ts'ixa NOT YET is limited and remains restricted to contexts corresponding to the temporal notion of BEFORE (33a–c). It is therefore not possible to say whether the combination of *xáwèè* 'still' and the negated imperfective suffix *-tã̀* is the default expression for NOT YET, or whether it constitutes a feature restricted to subordinate clauses.

(33) a. *lám-tsã̋ã̋   -sì   xáwèè   ky'oá   -tã̀   -sè   tsé   kṹũ   -a   -ta.*
sun -3sg.F still go.out -IPFV.NEG -ADV 1pl.C go -J -PST2
'When the sun had not risen yet, we went out. (We went out before sunrise.)'
b. *t'ṹĩ   -na   -ha   xáwèè   'é.sì   kyìì   -tã̀   -sè.*
be.beautiful -J -PST4 still 3sg.F be.sick -IPFV.NEG -ADV
'She was beautiful when she was not sick, yet. ([She] was beautiful before she got sick.)'
c. *kṹũ   -ì   'è   ll'áé   -ḿ   'ò   xáwèè   ngyĩ̀.káò*
go IMPS ?IMPS homestead -3sg.M:I DIR still be.dark
-tã̀   -sè.
-IPFV.NEG -ADV
'One has to go home when it is not yet dark. (One has to go home before darkness falls.)'

4 Discussion

Previous studies on various linguistic domains, including phoneme inventories (Fehn 2018) and morphosyntax (Fehn 2016), have shown Khwe and Ts'ixa to be closely related. At first glance, it therefore seems surprising that their respective phasal polarity systems display little similarity with each other. However, if the limited data available from other Khoe languages is considered as well, it becomes apparent that the entire family is characterized by considerable variation in the way in which phasal polarity concepts are expressed. Table 2 below provides an overview of the available data on various Khoe languages which could be gathered from dictionaries and grammatical descriptions:

Table 2: Expression of phasal polarity concepts in various Khoe languages; if available, additional meanings and lexical sources are provided in brackets.

	Source	ALREADY	STILL	NO LONGER	NOT YET
ǁAni	(Heine 1999)	?	-tsà (< Bantu)	?	?
Shua	(McGregor 2017)	?	xobe	?	?
Naro	(Visser 2001)	kx'áí-xà ('regularly, usually, always')	!ane	?	!ane-xa + NEG
Gǀui	(Nakagawa 2014)	cūū(-kʰá), ǂʔàā ('early in the morning'), qx'áí-à (< 'far')	koo-kʰá	?	?
Gǁana ("Kua")	(Collins & Chebanne 2016)	ká ('PRF')	kuo	?	?
Nama	(Haacke & Eiseb 2002)	nǀàí ('long/some time ago')	gànúpḗ, gŏrósè, noxoba (< Afrikaans)	?	gànúpḗ + NEG, gŏrósè + NEG

Despite the considerable variation and data gaps, some preliminary conclusions may be drawn from the available material: (1) the phasal polarity concept most likely to be expressed by a specialized item is STILL; (2) ALREADY is commonly expressed by an adverbial which may or may not be specialized; (3) dedicated expressions for NO LONGER are either rare or do not exist at all; (4) if a dedicated expression for NOT YET exists, it involves STILL and a negation marker. Like Ts'ixa, Khoe languages in general therefore display a tendency for phasal polarity systems structured on the basis of internal negations (Löbner 1989).

Based on my preliminary survey, no phasal polarity item featured in the data can be reconstructed for Proto-Khoe. One item, the adverbial tūū 'already' may merit a reconstruction for Proto-Kalahari Khoe, as reflexes are found in Ts'ixa (*tv́ṽ*) and the geographically distant language Gǀui (*kyṽṽ* [cṽṽ]). A probably related form *tṽṽ̀-xàrè* is also found in Naro (Visser 2001: 97), albeit with meanings not immediately related to any phasal polarity context: 'perhaps, again, but, in addition, in fact, besides, moreover, more than that, however, just so, although, anyway, at least'. Tonally, the three forms display regular correspondences (cf. Elderkin 2008; Fehn 2019) of a low-toned proto-form *tṽ̀ṽ̀. However, *tṽ̀ṽ̀* may not be an inherited Khoe item, but a borrowing from a Kx'a language: Juǀ'hoan (Dickens 1994: 272) has a verb *tòàn* ([tṽ̀ã̀]) 'be finished, come to an end' which might have been borrowed into proto Kalahari Khoe or even independently into Gǀui and Ts'ixa to derive the meaning ALREADY. While grammaticalization from a verb 'to finish' into a phasal polarity item 'already' is cross-linguistically common (Heine & Kuteva 2002), it should be kept in mind that such a process would not only have involved borrowing of *tṽ̀ã̀*, but also vowel assimilation and a change in meaning not found in Juǀ'hoan itself. For the time being, the status and origin of *tṽṽ* have to be considered unresolved.

A second phasal polarity item possibly meriting reconstruction on a narrower scale is the adverbial *koo* 'still' which is found in the closely related languages Gǀui and Gǁana and might therefore form part of a shared proto-language. However, a reconstruction with the meaning 'still' should be treated with caution, as Gǀui has a homonymous verb *koo* 'to refuse', leaving at least the possibility of a cross-linguistically rare grammaticalization path.

Apart from these two potentially specialized items with a distribution encompassing more than one language, a form involving *qx'áí, kx'áí or kx'éí* is attested in Naro, Gǀui and possibly also Khwe to express the concept ALREADY. Although Nakagawa (2014) suggests an adjective *qx'áí* 'far' as immediate source, the cross-linguistic distribution of the item makes it more likely that the origin is the form *k(x)'áí, which can be reconstructed for Proto-Khoe and is attested with both nominal ('face, front') and adjectival/adverbial ('first, since, before') meanings. The semantic extension of these meanings to cover ALREADY seems plausible and might even have occurred independently within individual languages, rather than in a shared proto-language.

The Ts'ixa form *xáwèè* expressing STILL has already been identified as a likely contraction of an element /xa/, possibly a demonstrative, and the additive marker *úè~'úè* 'also'. T. Güldemann (p.c.) notes the similarity of the item to Khoekhoe *xàwè~xǎwé~xabe* 'but' (Haacke & Eiseb 2002: 460) and considers the possibility of a relationship between the two. In this scenario, the Ts'ixa form would constitute a poorly grammaticalised stage which still preserves the three morae of the original contraction, while the Khoekhoe form would have been reduced to fit the default two-moraic pattern of Khoe lexical roots. In addition, one would have to assume a semantic shift from an additive marker ('also') to an adversative conjunction ('but'), which seems more difficult to account for than the shift from additive to STILL observed in Ts'ixa. Hence, I alternatively suggest that the Khoekhoe form may be a contraction of an element /xa/ and a negation particle *be which is still preserved in its original function in Khwe (as vé), rather than an element historically linked to xâwèè. However, more research will be needed to arrive at a more conclusive hypothesis on the origin of both the Ts'ixa and the Khoekhoe forms.

Apart from the above-mentioned case of tũũ 'already', the data contains at least two more borrowings, both of which concern the concept of ALREADY: The Khwe dialect ǁAni has a suffix -tsà 'already', which, according to Heine (1999), is a borrowing from Setswana.[6] Following the summary provided by Löfgren (2018), Tswana has sà or sántse, Kgalagadi has sha and Kalanga has tja, suggesting that the source for the ǁAni item is indeed an eastern Bantu language. Nama noxoba, according to (Haacke & Eiseb 2002), is a borrowing from Afrikaans <nog> or German <noch> plus a suffix. Following cross-linguistic studies on phasal polarity (Van Baar, 1997: 126–129; van der Auwera, 1993: 628–629), borrowing of phasal polarity expressions is frequent and most often involves items conveying the notion of ALREADY. This is confirmed by my observations on Khoe.

Apart from the form and origin of existing phasal polarity items, the absence of specialized items for NOT YET and NO LONGER needs to be addressed. While instances of NOT YET suggest a cross-Khoe tendency for phasal polarity coding on the basis of internal negations, evidence for NO LONGER is sparse and might suggest a complete absence of a dedicated expression throughout the family. This would be in line with cross-linguistic tendencies observed by Van Baar (1997: 118) who states that gaps in the paradigm most often concern ALREADY and NO LONGER. However, more data will be required to draw a final conclusion on the subject.

Further research should also take into account the tendency of some Khoe languages, including Khwe and Ts'ixa, to have tense-aspect systems with a specialized morphology for different stages of anteriority. The ability to specify distance to a time of reference might impact the expression of phasal polarity concepts, including the presence or absence of specialized items as well as possible constraints on the co-occurrence of phasal polarity items and tense-aspect markers.

---

6 An anonymous reviewer points out that a suffix -tsà denoting ALREADY in ǁAni (Heine 1999) appears to be absent in other doculects of the same language, such as Vossen (2000). Irrespective of its origin, the formative may therefore constitute an idiolectal feature, rather than a widely used phasal polarity expression.

Abbreviations

I	juncture Non-Past (Khwe)	IPFV	imperfective
II	juncture Past (Khwe)	IMPS	impersonal
1	1st person	J	juncture (Ts'ixa)
2	2nd person	LOC	locative
3	3rd person	M	masculine
ADJ	adjectivizer	MOV	movement (itive & ventive)
ADV	adverbializer	NEG	negation
ASSOC	associative	O	object
ATTR	attributor	OBL	oblique
BEN	benefactive	PGN	person-gender-number
C	common gender	pl	plural
CAU	causative	POSS	possessive
COM	comitative	PRES	present
COMP	complementizer	PRIV	privative
COMPL	completive	PROG	progressive
CONT	continuous	PST1	near past
CONV	converb	PST2	hodiernal past
DEM	demonstrative	PST3	yesterday's past
DIM	diminuitive	PST4	moderately remote past
DUR	durative	PST5	very remote past
EMPH	emphatic	Q	interrogative
F	feminine	REC	reciprocal
FOC	focus	ref	referential
FREQ	frequentative	REFL	reflexive
FUT	future	SEQ	sequential
GEN	genitive	sg	singular
GER	gerund	STAT	stative
HAB	habitual		

Bibliographic references

Brenzinger, Matthias. 1998. Moving to survive: Kxoe communities in arid lands. In Mathias Schladt (ed.), *Language, identity, and conceptualization among the Khoisan*, 321–357. Cologne: Köppe.

Brenzinger, Matthias. 2013. The twelve modern Khoisan languages. In Alena Witzlack-Makarevich & Martina Ernszt (eds.), *Khoisan languages and linguistics. Proceedings of the 3rd international symposium, July 6- 10,2008, Riezlern/Kleinwalsertal*, 5–31. Cologne: Köppe.

Collins, Chris & Andy Chebanne. 2016. *A Grammatical Sketch of Kuasi*. Unpublished Manuscript.

Dickens, Patrick J. 1994. *English – Ju|'hoan Ju|'hoan – English Dictionary*. Cologne: Köppe.

Elderkin, Edward D. 2008. Proto-Khoe tones in Western Kalahari. In Sonja Ermisch (ed.), *Khoisan Languages and Linguistics: Proceedings of the 2nd international symposium, January 8 –12,2006, Riezlern/Kleinwalsertal*, 87–136. Cologne: Köppe.
Fehn, Anne-Maria. 2016. *A grammar of Ts'ixa (Kalahari Khoe)*. Cologne: University of Cologne dissertation.
Fehn, Anne-Maria. 2018. New data on northeastern Kalahari Khoe phoneme inventories. A comparative survey. *Africana Linguistica* 24. 5–29.
Fehn, Anne-Maria. 2019. Phonological and Lexical Variation in the Khwe Dialect Cluster. *Zeitschrift der Deutschen Morgenländischen Gesellschaft* 169 (1). 9–39.
Greenberg, Joseph H. 1966. *The languages of Africa*. 2nd ed. wi. Bloomington: Indiana University Press.
Güldemann, Tom. 2014. "Khoisan" Linguistic Classification Today. In Tom Güldemann & Anne-Maria Fehn (eds.), *Beyond "Khoisan": Historical relations in the Kalahari Basin*, 1–41. Amsterdam & Philadelphia: John Benjamins.
Haacke, Wilfrid H. G. & Eliphas Eiseb. 2002. *A Khoekhoegowab dictionary with an English-Khoekhoegowab index*. Windhoek: Gamsberg Macmillan.
Heine, Bernd. 1999. *The //Ani: Grammatical notes and texts* (Khoisan Forum, Working Papers, 11). Cologne: University of Cologne.
Heine, Bernd & Tania Kuteva. 2002. *World Lexicon of Grammaticalization*. Cambridge: Cambridge University Press. doi:10.1017/CBO9780511613463.
Kilian-Hatz, Christa. 2003. *Khwe Dictionary with a supplement on Khwe place-names of West Caprivi by Matthias Brenzinger (Namibian African Studies, 7)*. Cologne: Köppe.
Kilian-Hatz, Christa. 2006. Serial Verb Constructions in Khwe (Central Khoisan). In Alexandra Yurievna Aikhenvald & Robert M. W. Dixon (eds.), *Serial verb constructions: a cross-linguistic typology*, 108–123. Oxford: Oxford University Press.
Kilian-Hatz, Christa. 2008. *A grammar of modern Khwe (Central Khoisan) (Research in Khoisan Studies, 23)*. Cologne: Köppe.
Kittilä, Seppo. 2006. The anomaly of the verb "give" explained by its high (formal and semantic) transitivity. *Linguistics* 44 (3). 569–612.
Köhler, Oswin. 1971. Die Khoe-Sprachigen Buschmänner der Kalahari: Ihre Verbreitung und Gliederung. *Forschungen zur allgemeinen und regionalen Geographie (Festschrift Kurt Kayser)*, 373–411. Wiesbaden: Franz Steiner.
Köhler, Oswin. 1981. La langue kxoe. In Jean Perrot (ed.), *Les langues dans le monde ancien et moderne, première partie: Les langues de l'afrique subsaharienne*, 483–555. Paris: Centre National de la Recherche Scientifique.
Köhler, Oswin. 1989. *Die Welt der Kxoé-Buschleute im südlichen Afrika: Eine Sebstdarstellung in ihrer eigenen Sprache. Vol. I: Die Kxoé-Buschleute und ihre ethnische Umgebung*. Berlin: Dietrich Reimer.
Köhler, Oswin. 2018. *Khwe Lexicon*. Toolbox Archive, edited by Anne-Maria Fehn with the assistance of G. Boden and T. Chedau. Unpublished database, Oswin Köhler Archive, Goethe University, Frankfurt.
König, Christa. 2007. The interaction between tense, aspect and modality in Khwe. *Annual Publications in African Linguistics* 4. 109–125.
Kramer, Raija. 2017. Position paper on Phasal Polarity expressions. Working paper, University of Hamburg. https://www.aai.uni-hamburg.de/afrika /php2018/medien/position-paper-on-php.pdf (accessed: 31 July 2019).

Löbner, Sebastian. 1989. "Schon-Erst-Noch": An integrated analysis. *Linguistics and Philosophy* 12 (2). 167–212.

Löfgren, Althea. 2018. Phasal Polarity Systems in East Bantu. Stockholm: University of Stockholm BA thesis.

McGregor, William B. 2017. Unusual manner constructions in Shua (Khoe-Kwadi, Botswana). *Linguistics* 55 (4). 857–897. doi:10.1515/ling-2017-0013.

Nakagawa, Hiroshi. 2014. *Glui Dictionary*. Unpublished Manuscript.

Schladt, Mathias. 2000. A Multi-Purpose Orthography for Kxoe: Development and challenges. In Herman M. Batibo & Joseph Tsonope (eds.), *The State of Khoesan Languages in Botswana*, 125–139. Gaborone: Tasalls.

van der Auwera, Johan. 1993. "Already" and "still": Beyond duality. *Linguistics and Philosophy* 16 (6). 613–653. doi:10.1007/BF00985436.

Van Baar, Theodorus M. 1997. *Phasal Polarity*. Amsterdam: IFOTT.

Visser, Hessel. 2001. *Naro dictionary: Naro-English, English-Naro*. D'Kar, Botswana: Naro Language Project / SIL International.

Vossen, Rainer. 1997. *Die Khoe-Sprachen: Ein Beitrag zur Erforschung der Sprachgeschichte Afrikas (Research in Khoisan* Studies, *12)*. Vol. 12. Cologne: Köppe.

Vossen, Rainer. 2000. Khoisan languages with a grammatical sketch of llAni (Khoe). In Petr Zima (ed.), *Areal and Genetic Factors in Language* Classification *and* Description: *Africa South of the Sahara*, 129–145. Munich. Lincom.

Westphal, Ernst O. J. 1971. The click languages of southern and eastern Africa. In Thomas A. Sebeok (ed.), *Linguistics in Sub-Saharan Africa*, 367–420. The Hague: Mouton.

Alice Mitchell
Phasal polarity in Barabaiga and Gisamjanga Datooga (Nilotic): Interactions with tense, aspect, and participant expectation

1 Introduction

"Phasal polarity" has to do with reference to a temporal phase of an event or state, where an adjoining phase with the opposite polarity value is entailed.[1] A straightforward example of a phasal polarity expression is the English adverb *no longer*, which indicates that a given state-of-affairs is in a negative phase but has been preceded by a positive phase. For example, *my leg no longer hurts* means that during some period of time previous to the time of speaking it was true that the speaker's leg was hurting and that utterance time intersects with a second phase in which, in contrast to the earlier period, the leg does not hurt. While one could similarly use the lexical item *stop* to encode a change in the polarity of a situation across time intervals, e.g., *my leg has stopped hurting*, this utterance does not refer to the negative phase of the state-of-affairs, but rather to the termination of the positive phase. Since the negative phase is only implied, *stop* is not considered a phasal polarity expression (Van Baar 1997).

The phasal polarity concepts STILL, NO LONGER, NOT YET, and ALREADY have been treated as a coherent group by formal semanticists such as Löbner (1989) because of their semantic equivalences under conditions of negation. Whether such a typological grouping is justified in other languages is one question that this volume addresses (cf Kramer's [2017] PARADIGMATICITY parameter). This paper takes these four concepts as its starting point, looking for their equivalents in two dialects of Datooga, a Southern Nilotic language spoken in Tanzania. Section 3 discusses each concept in turn, showing that (a) Datooga does not encode NOT YET; (b) there are two possible equivalents of ALREADY, a

---

[1] Thanks to my Datooga consultants and host families for helping me collect the data on which this paper is based. Special thanks to Herman Malleyeck and Mama Happy for in-depth discussion of some of the linguistic items discussed here. I also thank Raija Kramer for inviting me to the phasal polarity Conference in Hamburg and for her helpful suggestions on this paper. Any misinterpretations of the data are of course my own responsibility.

Alice Mitchell, University of Cologne

https://doi.org/10.1515/9783110646290-017

rarely-used auxiliary and a verb meaning 'be early'; and (c) the meanings STILL and NO LONGER can be expressed by the continuative prefix *údú-* in combination with the affirmative or negative polarity prefix, respectively. Though phasal polarity meanings can arise with these items in particular discourse contexts, the only "true" phasal polarity expression – semantically encoding a polar contrast between two phases of an event – appears to be the infrequent 'already' auxiliary. The remainder of the paper focuses on the semantics and pragmatics of the much more common continuative prefix and its range of meanings in combination with different tense, aspect, and polarity values.

In some cases, phasal polarity involves two phases that occur not in temporal sequence but simultaneously, where a state-of-affairs is imagined to obtain during the same period that it in fact does not obtain (or vice versa). These two possibilities are captured in Hansen's (2008: 86) definition of phasal adverbs in European languages as involving "*actual* or *potential* transition between different phases of a state-of-affairs" (my emphasis). Kramer's (2017) PRAGMATICITY parameter invokes this distinction, with its two values of NEUTRAL – the polarity value of two phases alternates in temporal sequence – and COUNTERFACTUAL – two alternative polarity values of a state-of-affairs occur simultaneously. For example, the English sentence *she has already left* can have a neutral or counterfactual reading:

a) Neutral: the transition from the not leaving phase to the leaving phase happened prior to utterance time, with nothing unexpected about the transition point.
b) Counterfactual: the transition from not leaving to leaving happened prior to utterance time, but the transition point was expected to occur later.

In the latter case, *already* points to a contrast between the possible and the actual polarity value of a state-of-affairs at a given time. Kramer (2017: 9) notes that counterfactual meanings, i.e. the role of possible alternative states-of-affairs, may be more or less central to the expression of phasal polarity in a given language. In Datooga, imagined alternatives to actual states-of-affairs are essential for interpreting the continuative prefix in one particular linguistic context, namely, when it occurs in negated, nonfuture verbal complexes with telic predicates. In other semantic configurations, both neutral and counterfactual readings are possible.

Methodologically, most of the research on phasal polarity has relied on intuition and semantic judgements of elicited sentences. Data in this paper are mostly drawn from a corpus of recordings of Datooga conversation (approximately 133,000 words) in order to see how phasal polarity operates in interactional contexts. In section 5, I take a closer look at three uses of continuative *údú-* in context and consider what an interactional perspective on this grammatical item can tell us about its meaning, especially with respect to the significance of participants' expectations about how events might temporally unfold. Data drawn from elicitation contexts is indicated as such.

2 The Datooga language

Datooga is a Southern Nilotic language spoken in Tanzania, primarily in northern regions of the country but also increasingly further south as families seek out more productive areas for cattle herding. According to Muzale & Rugemalira (2008), there are around 140,000 speakers of Datooga, though a further 20,000 individuals are listed as speakers of 'Taturu', another name for the same language. Datooga is both an ethnonym and the name of a dialect cluster. Rottland (1982) divides this cluster into East Datooga, comprising the dialects of Bajuuta, Gisamjanga, Barabaiga, and Isimjeega, and West Datooga, comprising the dialects of Rootigeenga, Bureadiga, Biyeanjiida (my spellings, based on Barabaiga pronunciation). The data presented in this paper come from speakers of Barabaiga and Gisamjanga Datooga and may not be representative of the other dialects. For the sake of brevity I will often use the label 'Datooga' where I mean Barabaiga and Gisamjanga Datooga.

Barabaiga and Gisamjanga Datooga are mutually intelligible dialects with synthetic morphology, grammatical tone, and relatively flexible word order, though the basic order is VSO. Grammatical sketches of the Datooga dialects can be found in Rottland (1982) and article-length treatments of various aspects of Gisamjanga grammar are presented in Kießling (1998, 2000a, 2000b, 2007a, 2007b). Since I will be discussing the verbal formative *údú-* and its interaction with tense and aspect, I will briefly sketch the Datooga verb and the TAM system, though I emphasise that much work remains to be done on analysing TAM in Datooga.

A simplified representation of the Datooga verbal complex for main verbs is given in (1):

(1) Datooga verbal complex
 a) POLARITY–(FUTURE)–SUBJECT–ROOT–(DERIVATIONAL SUFFIXES)–(OBJECT)
 b) PERFECT-SUBJECT- ROOT–(DERIVATIONAL SUFFIXES)–(OBJECT)

Verbal prefixes include polarity, TAM, and subject prefixes; suffixal material includes a wide range of derivational suffixes (see Kießling [2007b: 124] for an overview) and object suffixes. Morphological tense marking on the Datooga verb includes the future prefix *ày-* and the perfect prefix *n-* (*s-* in first person plural).[2] Unlike the future prefix, the perfect does not combine with the polarity prefixes, hence the adjusted verbal complex indicated in (1b).[3] Verb forms without future or perfect morphology are effectively tenseless, or "nonfuture", through implicature, also called "aorist" by Kießling (2000a). Time reference can be indicated with time adverbials such as *héeta* 'yesterday' or *qáy* 'in the past'. Other aspects of the TAM system include a sequential prefix *ag-* (see Rottland 1982: 176) and the continuative prefix *údú-* that will be discussed here. Tonal distinctions may also play a role in the TAM system; further work is required on this front.

3 Encoding phasal polarity concepts in Barabaiga and Gisamjanga Datooga

In this section I briefly characterize how each of the four phasal polarity expressions NOT YET, ALREADY, STILL, and NO LONGER is realized in Datooga. As we shall see, only the second of these has dedicated encoding and this is a low frequency item.

3.1 'Not yet'

The concept NOT YET has no dedicated encoding. The idea that a scenario does not obtain at a particular time interval but will do subsequently would usually be translated by means of the negative perfect. Extract 1 provides illustration. In line 1, Majirjir asks her sister whether Shamqee has arrived, which, assuming the maxim of relevance, implies that she knows that Shamqee is due to arrive at some point. Her sister replies by referring to the negative phase of the arrival event. Nothing in line 2 encodes that the positive phase of this state-of-affairs is

---

[2] The perfect is a tense inasmuch as it locates an event prior to topic time. It also has aspectual qualities, though, as it can indicate that a resulting state continues to hold at topic time, as in line 2 of Extract 1.
[3] The affirmative perfect is not coded for polarity; the negative perfect is formed by combining the negative copula *míi* and the dependent form of the subject prefixes, as in line 2 of Extract 1.

anticipated (even though this might be inferred from Majirjir's question) – and thus there is no equivalent to *not yet* in this (or indeed any other) example.[4]

Extract 1

1	Majirjir	*Shámqée nìhídú?*	
		Shámqée	*n-ì-hídú*
		PSN	PRF-3-come.CP
		'Has Shamqee arrived?'	
2	Deaqweeda	*mìi qwáhídù*	
		mìi	*qwá-hídù*
		NEG.COP	3.SBJV-come.CP
		'He hasn't arrived.'	

3.2 'Already'

The concept ALREADY can be expressed by means of an auxiliary-like form *góolá* combined with a dependent verb (i.e. a verb bearing a subjunctive subject prefix), as shown in the elicited example in (1):

(1) *góolá dàwa*
    góolá   dà-wa
    AUX   1SG.SBJV-go
    'I've already gone.' [elicited]

Góolá is so far only attested in utterances referring to completed events. In (1), it signals that the completed action of 'going' is in its positive phase at utterance time, and implies a prior, negative phase during which the speaker had not gone. This construction is infrequent in my corpus, appearing only ten times. Since it only occurs in the speech of Gisamjanga-Datooga, it may be restricted to the Gisamjanga dialect.

In English, *already* denotes that "the state included in the proposition [. . .] is the case at reference time[,] implying a further reference point at a prior [. . .] phase where this state is not the case" (Kramer 2017: 1). Many

---

4 The Datooga orthography used here is adopted from the Datooga Bible Translation Project, with two differences: the uvular stop is transcribed here as <q> rather than <gh> and I also transcribe surface tone (é = high tone; è = low tone; ê = falling tone). Characters that differ from the IPA are as follows: <j>= [ɟ], <ng'>= [ŋ], <ny>= [ɲ], <y>= [j], <r>= [ɾ], <sh>= [ʃ], <ch>= [c], <ea>= [ɛː], <oa>= [ɔː]. Double vowels represent long vowels, e.g. <ee>= [eː].

scholars have also emphasised the 'earliness' meaning implied by *already* (see discussion and citations in Vander Klok and Matthewson 2015: 294), i.e. that the transition point of an event occurs earlier than expected. This is a counterfactual meaning which relies on two possible alternative time frames. Earliness can feature in the interpretation of *góolá*, as Extract 2 demonstrates. In line 1, Majirjir asks Ng'araajaan whether a splint tied to a goat's broken leg has come undone. She uses the negative perfect construction, implying that the situation has recently occurred relative to utterance time. Ng'araajaan responds that the splint *already* came undone some time ago, thus specifying the actual time as earlier than the time presupposed by Majirjir's question. (See section 5 for discussion of the implications of negative polar questions.)

Extract 2

1 Majirjir *mìi góotínéadá gìda?*
   mìi   góo-tín-éadá   gìda
   NEG.COP   3.SBJV-untie-ALM.CF.IS   thing
   'Hasn't the thing [splint on goat's leg] come undone?'

2 Ng'araajaan *góolá góotìnéadà gáràÿ*
   góolá   góo-tìn-éadà   gáràÿ
   AUX   3.SBJV-untie-ALM.CF.IS   while
   'It already came undone a while ago.'

Akin to Krifka's (2000) analysis of German *schon*, we can say that *góolá* restricts the utterance to the earliest option among a set of alternative propositions and is thus sensitive to pragmatic considerations. Nonetheless, neutral interpretations are possible, too: example (1) could mean that the speaker left at the intended time, not early, but simply prior to the time of utterance.

The notion of earliness is also encoded in Datooga by the verb form *bay* which combines with a dependent verb phrase to convey that an event happened early relative to some normative timeframe, e.g.:

(2) *báy hínní!*
     báy   hínní
     be.early.IMP 2SG.SBJV.come.CP
     'Come early!' [elicited]

(3) ùnqáqájéeg gábày qwáak múwàash
 ùnqáq-ájée-ga g-á-bày   qwá-ag   múwàash
 chicken-PS-MR AFF-3-be.early 3.SBJV-eat thirst
 'The chickens are thirsty early.'

This construction is sometimes translated with 'quickly', e.g. *jéekka gábày qwányìit* 'the bucket filled quickly'. The 'quickly' reading is possible with verbs denoting accomplishments, which have internal duration: here, *bay* means that the time it took to reach the end state is shorter than possible alternative durations. This is an evaluation of the internal dynamics of the event, whereas the earliness reading takes an external viewpoint, specifying that the event completion occurred prior to possible alternatives. In some cases, 'already' is a possible translation of *gábày* constructions, e.g. (3) could equally be translated as 'The chickens are already thirsty', meaning the change of state from not thirsty to thirsty happened earlier than normal. Since *bay* encodes a change of state from a negative to a positive state-of-affairs that is evaluated as occurring early, we can classify it as an "*already* inchoative" according to van der Auwera's (1998: 50) typology, though it is not a true phasal polarity expression as it refers to the relative timing of the transition point rather than two contrastive phases. The verb *bay* appears to be restricted to counterfactual use, since it always involves an evaluation relative to a more usual alternative.

3.3 'Still' and 'no longer'

The concepts STILL and NO LONGER can be encoded by means of the continuative prefix *údú-*, preceded by the affirmative or negative prefixes, *g-* and *m-*, respectively. This aspectual prefix adds the meaning of continuation, or, in negation contexts, termination, to the state-of-affairs denoted by the verb stem, as illustrated in (4) and (5):

(4) *gúttágáwìischì*
 g-údú-dá-gáw-ìi-s-chì
 AFF-CONT-1SG.SBJV-milk-PLUR-TERM-AP
 'I'm still milking.'

(5) *múdúgwálìl*
 m-údú-gwá-lìl
 NEG-CONT-3.SBJV-sleep
 'S/he is no longer sleeping.'

By default, *údú-* points to the temporal boundaries of an event, locating the endpoint beyond reference time (in the affirmative), or prior to reference time (in the negative). While *údú-* involves phasal semantics – relating to the duration of events – it does not directly encode phasal polarity. The example in (5) does not refer to a non-sleeping phase, but rather to the endpoint of the sleeping phase (though this of course implies a non-sleeping phase). This is a phasal polarity-like meaning, and other pragmatically-derived phasal polarity meanings arise in particular discourse contexts, as we will see below. Depending on the lexical aspect of the verbal complex, the continuative prefix can contribute a range of meanings other than an ongoing or finished state-of-affairs, as discussed in Section 4.2, where I also consider the appropriateness of the label "continuative".[5]

An uncommon variant of *g-údú-* is *dúu-*, shown in example (6). The verb form *dúugwánda* appears five times in my corpus, while the variant *gúdúgwánda* appears 38 times. The prefix *dúu-* does not combine with the polarity prefixes and appears to be used only in the affirmative. It is also only attested in the third person in my data, but appears with other person categories in the Datooga Bible translation.[6] Two speakers had the intuition that the *dúu-* form and *gúdú-* form differ in meaning but discussion of multiple examples did not reveal any clear semantic distinction. It may be that *dúu-* is an archaic or dialectal variant of *g-údu-*.[7]

(6) *dúugwánda*
     dúu-gwá-nda
     CONT-3.SBJV-be.at
     'S/he's still alive' or 'S/he/it's still there.'

Returning to Kramer's (2017) paradigmaticity parameter, Datooga clearly does not have a four-part system of phasal polarity expressions. The concept NOT YET is not formally coded. The concept ALREADY has two equivalents: an (infrequent) auxiliary form *góolá* and a verb *báy* that expresses earliness of an event, and which is restricted to the counterfactual sense of 'already' – only *góolá* appears to be a true

---

[5] In Rottland's (1982: 177, 1983: 226) work on Datooga, he labels *údú-* a *Perstitiv*/perstitive morpheme. The terms 'persistive', 'durative', and 'continuative' are all found in the literature on different languages, but I prefer 'continuative' because its counterpart verb, 'continue', is an everyday, high-frequency word, more likely to be familiar to non-native speakers.

[6] For instance, "As long as I am in the world" (John 9:5) is translated as *hiji duu dandeewa jeeda ng'eanyiidean*.

[7] The continuative *dúu-* is homophonous with adjective *dúu* meaning 'black', which may constitute a possible (but highly speculative) lexical source for *údú-* as well. The form *dúu* is incorporated into the temporal expression *íidùu* 'later', so there is some precedent for grammaticalization.

phasal polarity expression. Concepts akin to STILL and NO LONGER are coded by means of the continuative prefix *údú-*, which is associated with phasal polarity through discourse-pragmatic processes rather than semantics. We now turn to a more in-depth analysis of the distribution and function of the morpheme *údú-*.

4 The continuative prefix *údú-*

This section describes the form and meaning of *údú-*. I look first at how this prefix combines with other TAM morphology (4.1) and then I characterise the various semantic facets of *údú-* when used with predicates belonging to different Vendlerian *Aktionsart* categories (Vendler 1957) (4.2). While *údú-* can combine with both telic and atelic verbs, the resulting meanings are not predictable.

4.1 Combination of *údú-* with TAM markers

Here I will be concerned with how *údú-* combines with basic aspects of TAM morphology. See Section 2 for a brief overview of the Datooga verb and the TAM system. As shown in examples (7–9), *údú-* is compatible with future tense and with verbs modified by past time adverbials; *údú-* in nonfuture tense is evidenced in (4–5). When future and continuative prefixes co-occur, they are arranged as follows: polarity prefix {*g-* / *m-*}; future prefix (*ay-* ~ *aj-*); affirmative polarity prefix (*g-*); continuative (*údú-*); and then subjunctive subject prefix, verb root, and any derivational suffixes. The polarity value of the verb is specified by the initial polarity prefix, while the prefix immediately preceding *údú-* is always in its affirmative form.

(7) gàygúdúgwásín ánágádìi?
    g-ày-g-údú-gwá-sín   áná-gádìi?
    AFF-FUT-AFF-CONT-3.SBJV-do which-work
    'What work will she still be doing?'

(8) màygútqwáawál gwéargwèeda
    m-ày-g-údú-qwáa-wál   gwéargw-èe-da
    NEG-FUT-AFF-CONT-3.SBJV-fear old.man-PS-UR
    'She will no longer fear her father-in-law.'

(9) *qáy gútgwándà gíirgwêagéedá Màléeyeéka àbà–*

qáy	g-údú-gwá-ndà	gíi-rgwêag-ée-dá	Màléeyeéka	àbà
PST	AFF-CONT-3.SBJV-be.at	NMLZ-hold.council-PS-UR	clan.name	LOC

'There were still Malleyeck clan meetings at–'

The continuative does not co-occur with perfect tense prefixes. This can be explained in terms of semantic incompatibility: since one function of the perfect is to indicate the completed state of some process, a continuative meaning cannot be applied. For instance, if someone uses the perfect form *nìláng'úudí*, 'you (sg.) have become full', it means that their state of fullness from having eaten is complete and cannot continue.[8]

Several pieces of evidence point to a verbal origin for *údú-*: that it triggers the subjunctive form of the verb; that it retains a polarity prefix when combined with the future tense prefix; and its position before the main verb stem. In this scenario, *ú-* would be a subject prefix that assimilated with the vowel of the lexical stem **dú(u)-*, the meaning of which is unknown.

4.2 The semantics of *údú-*

In the broadest terms, the prefix *údú-* conveys aspectual meaning. So far I have described its semantics as continuative: *údú-* denotes that the state-of-affairs referred to by the verb continues (or does not continue). However, the meaning that *údú-* contributes to the verbal complex in fact depends on the telicity of the predicate. All examples of *údú-* given so far have involved states and activities, where this prefix indicates continuation or termination of that state or activity. The use of *údú-* contributes different meanings with achievement and accomplishment predicates, though, which are telic (i.e. have an inherent endpoint). With these predicates, the meaning of *údú-* also depends on the polarity and tense of the verb. Table 1 summarises the range of meanings of *údú* and the following paragraphs discuss these meanings in greater detail.

With achievement and accomplishment predicates in the future tense, *údú-* indicates that an event will or will not occur again. The concept of iteration is related to that of continuation: with atelic events (states and activities), *údú-* refers to continuation or termination of the state-of-affairs from an internal viewpoint, as we have seen; with telic events, *údú-* refers to continuation or termination of the state-of-affairs as a whole, from an external viewpoint. Phasal adverbs in European languages, such as French *encore* and German *noch*, can also have both continuative

---

[8] Thanks to an anonymous reviewer for providing this analysis.

Table 1: Meanings of *údú-* in combination with tense, polarity, and lexical aspect.

Lexical aspect	Tense	Polarity	
		Aff	Neg
activities; states (atelic)	Future	'*p* will continue'	'*p* will stop'
	Nonfuture	'*p* continues'	'*p* stops'
achievements; accomplishments (telic)	Future	'*p* will repeat'	'*p* will not repeat'
	Nonfuture	'*p* just occurred'	'*p* did not actually occur'

and iterative meanings (Hansen 2008: 155–6). In (10), the combination of *údú-*, future tense, and the accomplishment predicate *gwears-* 'light a fire' indicates that there will be a repeated instance of a prior fire-lighting event (as opposed to a continuation of a current fire-lighting event, which would only be possible if the fire was not yet lit). The form *gìchá* 'again' supports this reading. Example (11) illustrates a negated iterative reading, i.e. '*p* will not repeat/occur again'.

(10) *gàygúdêegwèarsíina gìchá?*
  g-ày-g-úd-êe-gwèar-síin-a   *gìchá*
  AFF-FUT-AFF-CONT-1PL.SBJV-light.fire–TERM-IS again
  'Shall we light the fire again?'

(11) *màygúdúgábíigu*
  m-ày-g-údú-gá-bíigu
  NEG-FUT-AFF-CONT-3.SBJV-return.CP
  'They [things of the past] won't return again.'

In combination with the prohibitive mood, *údú-* specifies that some prior action should not be repeated. It often occurs in the context of scolding, such as (12), which is taken from a recording in which a man scolds a girl for bringing the cattle home so late that she was followed by a hyena.

(12) *ádá gùttáyíi (.) ádá gùdóobíiktí (.) ádá gùdóosínyì níi* [unclear] *nìhít*
  ádá   *g-ùdú-dá-yíi*   *ádá*   *g-ùdú-óo-bíig-dí*
  PROH AFF-CONT-1SG.SBJV-hear PROH AFF-CONT-2PL.SBJV-return-CF.IS

>   ádá   g-ùdú-óo-sín-yì   níi   n-ì-hít
>   PROH AFF-CONT-2PL.SBJV-do-IS DEM.PROX PRF-3-come.CF
>   'Don't let me hear this again; don't repeat this again; don't do this again; it's done.'[9]

More unusually, when *údú-* occurs with achievements and accomplishments in combination with affirmative, nonfuture morphology, we get an immediate past reading, equivalent to English 'just V-ed'. For example, in (13) and (14), the continuative prefix indicates that the transition point of the event of arriving, or dying, respectively, is very close to the time of speaking:

(13) *gúttáhídù*
     g-údú-dá-hídù
     AFF-CONT-1SG.SBJV-arrive.CP
     'I've just arrived.' [elicited]

(14) *gúdúqàm(i)*
     g-údú-qà-m(i)
     AFF-CONT-3.SBJV-die
     'He's just died.' [elicited]

The two verbs in (13) and (14) describe an event that has no internal duration. In English, use of the adverb 'still' with progressive aspect makes possible a continuative reading of achievements by suspending the end point, e.g. 'He is still dying'. In Datooga, the continuative prefix does not seem to be able to alter the telicity of the predicate, and instead we get an immediacy reading, in which the transition to the resulting state happens close to topic time. With activity verbs that may also have a telic interpretation, e.g. 'eat' (where the implication is that one ate *something*), both continuative and recent past readings are possible, e.g.:

(15) *gúttéaágìischì*
     g-údú-déa-ág-ìi-s-chì
     AFF-CONT-1SG.SBJV-eat-PLUR-TERM-AP
     'I've just eaten' or 'I'm still eating.' [elicited]

---

[9] It is not clear what accounts for the tonal changes on *údú-* in combination with the prohibitive particle.

What relates the continuative and immediate past meanings associated with *údú-*? The limited examples of the immediate past usage preclude a satisfactory analysis, but I would suggest that these meanings may be linked by the concept of posteriority on a context-dependent timeframe. With telic predicates, the change from the negative to positive state is nearly contiguous with time of speaking, and thus posterior on a time frame that extends back into the past; with atelic predicates, the transition from positive back to negative – i.e. the end point – is projected beyond the time of speaking, and thus posterior relative to utterance time. The relevance of a posteriority interpretation is suggested by the following example:

(16) gábày èa míi dáyíi hà gúttàyíi qámnà
    g-á-bày   èa   míi   dá-yíi   hà   g-údú-dà-yíi
    AFF-3-be.early CONJ NEG.COP 1SG.SBJV-hear DSC AFF-CONT-1SG.SBJV-hear
    qámnà
    now
    'I've never heard this; I've just heard it now.'

In (16), the speaker states that she had not previously heard something (a tongue-twister that has just been uttered). She uses the construction '*gábày èa* + negative verb form', which can be translated with 'never', though it literally involves the concept of earliness, i.e. 'earlier/prior to this point I have not . . .'. By juxtaposing 'never hearing' with 'just now hearing', she makes relevant the time scale of her whole life up to this point, a scale on which the transition point from not hearing to hearing can be evaluated as posterior (or 'late') on such a timescale.

Negative nonfuture achievement and accomplishment predicates with *údú-* do not denote a negation of an immediate past event, as we might expect based on their affirmative counterparts. Rather, when these types of predicate occur in the negative nonfuture, *údú-* indicates that an event that was anticipated to happen did not in fact occur. Consider the examples in (17)–(19):

(17) [nì]néekíid àbà híji áa múdúqwáahìidu
    [n-ì]-néek-íid   àbà   híji   áa   m-údú-qwáa-hìidu
    PRF-3-close-INCH LOC here CONJ NEG-CONT-3.SBJV-arrive.CAUS.CP
    'He approached here but he didn't bring it.'

(18) àa mútqwáalá hêayda hà
    àa   m-údú-qwáa-lá   hêay-da   hà
    CONJ NEG-CONT-3.SBJV-tread.on   OX-UR   DSC
    'But it didn't actually drive into the ox.'

(19) múdúqàm
    m-údú-qà-m
    NEG-CONT-3.SBJV-die
    'S/he didn't actually die' [elicited]

In terms of phasal polarity, *údú-* here indicates that the transition from the negative to positive phase of all the states-of-affairs referred to in these examples – bringing something, driving into something, and dying – did not occur. More specifically, though, *údú-* tells us that the change in state was *expected* to occur: the polarity contrast is between the situation expected to obtain and the situation that obtained in actuality. In this particular linguistic configuration (negative + nonfuture + telic semantics), *údú-* is restricted to a counterfactual interpretation while also indexing "counter-expectation" (Plungian 1999: 318). There is a strong modal character to this use of *údú-*, in the "possible worlds" sense of modal (Michaelis 1998: 87), which the English equivalent 'no longer' can also bear in certain contexts, e.g. *she's no longer coming to the party*.

This use of *údú-* is reminiscent of the category of avertive, defined by Kuteva (2004: 78) as meaning "was on the verge of V-ing but did not V". Kuteva (2004: 84) identifies three essential characteristics of the avertive, namely, imminence, pastness, and counterfactuality. This use of *údú-* is necessarily counterfactual: no neutral (or purely temporal) reading is possible here, since there was no actual transition point, as indicated through negation. All examples necessarily refer to events in the past, otherwise one could not rule out the event actually happening. However, it is not clear that Kuteva's first criterion of 'imminence' is always relevant in the Datooga case: example (18), for instance, does not necessarily entail that the referent was extremely close to death, but only that death was the expected outcome.

As we've seen, the meaning expressed by *údú-* varies depending on a combination of factors that we can order as follows: first, whether the predicate is telic or atelic; second, for atelic predicates, whether the tense is future or nonfuture; and third, for nonfuture, whether the polarity is negative or affirmative. Figure 1 represents this information in a kind of decision tree format and shows the four distinctive meanings associated with *údú-*. The question arises whether *údú-* should be considered polysemous, or whether these different facets of meaning can be accounted for by the particular configurations of tense, lexical aspect, and polarity. As I discussed above, the iterative meaning that arises with telic predicates in future tense is not far removed from a continuative meaning. With telic predicates, the concept of continuation applies not to the internal dynamics of the event but from an external, and in this case, prospective, viewpoint, giving an iteration of the whole event. Why the iterative reading is only available in the future tense is less clear, however. As for a possible relation between the immediate past and continuative meanings, above I speculated that it may have to do with the concept of relative lateness or posteriority on a time frame: with atelic predicates, in counterfactual scenarios, a state-of-affairs holds until later than assumed; with telic verbs, a state-of-affairs is located late in time, just previous to utterance time. The final meaning, 'p did not actually happen', can logically obtain only in negative past contexts, and the relevance of a continuative meaning obtains only on the level of an expected course of events – a possibility that was entertained earlier now no longer holds. Given the pragmatic richness of phasal polarity, and the frequent availability of counterfactual interpretations, I think it probable that there are pragmatic pathways between these four meanings, which a more in-depth study could elaborate on. 'Continuative' is thus an appropriate basic label for the form údú-, though its meaning extends beyond this in semantic configurations with telic predicates.

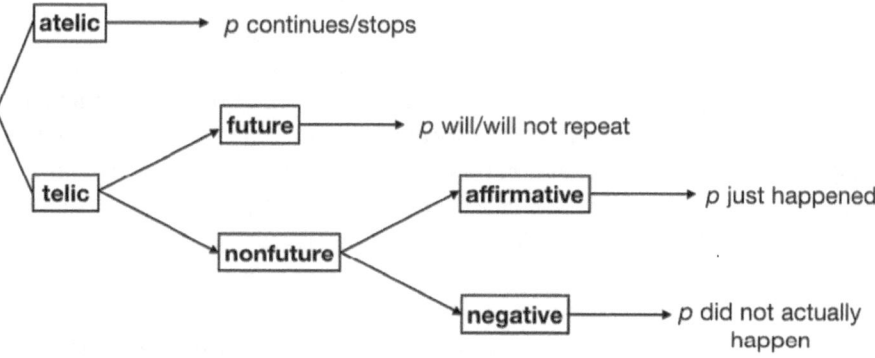

Figure 1: Meanings of údú- as determined by lexical aspect, tense, and polarity.

5 Interactional perspectives on phasal polarity

As mentioned above, the majority of research on phasal polarity has relied on intuition and elicited data. In this section I analyse the meaning of three tokens of *údú-* taken from everyday conversation and consider what an interactional perspective can tell us about the semantics and pragmatics of this morpheme. Research in discourse-pragmatic and interactional linguistics explores the relationship between grammatical resources and speakers' interactional goals. Taking this perspective here, I try to unpack in each case what speakers use *údú-* for. How does *údú-* help speakers to converge on shared understandings of a sequence of events?

One area of debate in the phasal polarity literature is the extent to which phasal polarity expressions encode neutral, counterfactual, and/or counter-expectational meaning, or, particularly in the latter case, whether such meanings arise purely through pragmatic inference (see discussion in Hansen 2008: 119–121). Löbner (1989: 176) cites an analysis which includes the speaker's expectations in the truth conditions of phasal polarity expressions; he challenges this approach with a counterexample. Van Baar (1997) characterises unexpectedness as a secondary, or more peripheral, meaning of phasal polarity expressions. Krifka (2000: 405) writes that a typical interpretation of *schon* and *erst* in German is that "they express a deviation from expected values in a particular direction", and that the alternative values are implicatures accountable for by the common ground. In the following paragraphs, I consider to what extent counterfactual and counter-expectational meaning is relevant to understanding specific instances of *údú-*. I restrict my examples to affirmative contexts with verbs denoting activities or states. In line with work in conversation analysis, I look at those aspects of participants' expectations that are publicly observable to others, as opposed to speculating on participants' private understandings of the world.

Extract 3 illustrates a situation in which a purely neutral reading of *údú-* obtains, where neither counterfactual nor counter-expectational scenarios are relevant to its use. This extract also shows how a speaker's use of *údú-* depends, in this case, on a timeframe established just previously by another speaker, and thus how phasal meanings are intersubjectively achieved.[10]

Extract 3

1 Deaqweeda *gìbày ríttá sàktêaydà qée síidà gìtínéada (màydáah)*
                         g-ì-bày   *ríd-dá*   *sàktêay-dà*   *qée*
                         AFF-2SG-be.early 2SG.SBJV.go.out-CF.IS morning-UR house

---

[10] Bracketed words indicate that the sound was unclear and that this was a native speaker's best guess of what was said.

		síi-dà gì-tín-éada (m-ày-dáah)

      síi-dà   gì-tín-éada   (m-ày-dáah)
      person-UR DRV-open-ALM.CF.IS NEG-FUT-see
      'If you leave early in the morning, (you won't see) an open compound.'
2 Majirjir gúdúgwálìlà búunèeda
      g-údú-gwá-lìlà   búun-èe-da
      AFF-CONT-3.SBJV-sleep.IS people-PS-UR
      'The people are still asleep.'

Deaqweeda and Majirjir are talking about what time people typically get up nowadays in comparison to the past. Deaqweeda asserts that if you leave your house early, you won't see any compounds with their gates open yet.[11] The timeline she sets up here is a generalised one of the prototypical *sàktéayda* 'morning', and what constitutes 'early' is culturally determined – probably the hours around dawn, before 7am. Majirjir elaborates on Deaqweeda's description by offering an explanation for the closed compounds: the people are still sleeping. In using *údú-* here, Majirjir orients to the time point of leaving that Deaqweeda established in the previous turn, indicating that this point is located prior to the transition from sleeping to waking. There is no inference that the transition point from sleeping to waking occurs later than expected. The punctual event of leaving the house simply bisects the positive sleeping phase, and *údú-* indicates that the sleeping event is ongoing at that point. This scenario is diagrammed in Figure 2, which we interpret as neutral since only one scenario is present in the common ground.[12] By contrast, Figure 3 represents two scenarios (one real, one counterfactual), as I now explain.

  In Extract 4, Damung'aan returns to her compound and calls over to her daughter-in-law, Majirjir, to ask whether she has finished milking, an activity she was engaged in when Damung'aan left.

---

11 In rural areas, the openings to Datooga compounds are closed off by means of several large, thorny branches, some pulled in from the outside and others placed alongside them from the inside. In the village in which this recording was made, some compounds had metal gates.
12 In this particular example, the state-of-affairs described is a generic one and the endpoint of the sleeping phase is therefore known, based on cultural knowledge of typical sleeping patterns: this is indicated with a solid line. In Figure 3, by contrast, the endpoint of the milking phase is unknown, and its continuation is therefore indicated with a dotted line.

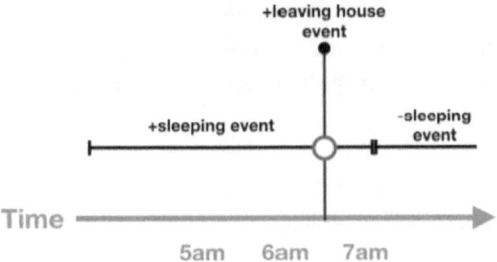

Figure 2: Diagram of single scenario relevant to use of údú- in Extract 3.

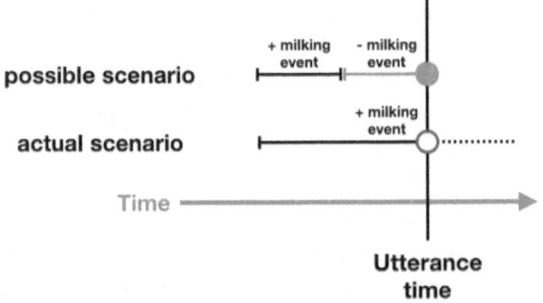

Figure 3: Diagram of the two scenarios relevant to use of údú- in Extract 4.

Extract 4

1 Damung'aan géaléabu qwêenga íiyá níihíidí gáwíischòoda?
g-éa-léabu   qwêen-ga   íiyá   n-íi-híidí
AFF-1SG-step.CP firewood-MR mother PRF-2SG-arrive.CAUS.IS
gáw-íi-s-ch-òo-da
milk-PLUR-TERM-AP-PS-UR
'I'm back from firewood, dear; have you finished milking?'

2 Majirjir   gúttágáwìischì
g-úd-dá-gáw-ìi-s-chì
AFF-CONT-1SG.SBJV-milk-PLUR-TERM-AP
'I'm still milking.'

In line 1, Damung'aan makes relevant a scenario in which the milking is finished at utterance time. She does not commit to the truth value of this proposition, since it is formatted as a question, but she does introduce the proposition as a possibility into the common ground (Farkas and Bruce 2010). In line 2, her daughter-in-law orients to this proposition but alters it by using the continuative to indicate that the milking is not in fact finished but ongoing. The use of *údú-* here is motivated by the contrasting entailments of the two scenarios. I diagram these scenarios in Figure 3. The verb form *gúttágáwìischì* describes the state-of-affairs at the white circle *relative* to the counterfactual scenario at the grey circle. The grey circle is located within the negative/completed phase; the white circle is located within the (simultaneous) positive/ongoing phase. The disjuncture that *údú-* highlights here is thus between a real and a counterfactual scenario.

Though counterfactual, the scenario is not necessarily counter-expectational. Moreover, what the participants do or do not expect is not especially relevant here: we can account for the occurrence of *údú-* simply in terms of the disjuncture between possible and actual scenarios. The 'possible' scenario – that the milking is finished – *might* be an expectation on the part of the mother-in-law, but in interactional terms, the polar question is a default request for information, uncommitted to whether or not the proposition is true.

In Extract 5, we have a polar question in which the speaker does make an epistemic commitment to one state-of-affairs, such that *údú-* in a later turn bears counter-expectational force. Extract 5 is taken from a recording during which two women are eating. Just prior to this extract, a third woman, their host, offers to top up the butter they're dipping their *ugali* into. A fourth woman, Sagealan, who's sitting next to the host, then asks (line 1) if the butter (or 'side dish') is finished, to which one of the women eating, Deaqweeda, replies 'no'. After a short period of laughter, Sagealaan asks whether there is still some side dish left, to which the reply is yes:[13]

Extract 5

1   Sagealan   *nèa (.) nèa mìi góoshá gíchchéa ámúksîindà?*
              nèa   nèa   mìi   góo-shá   gídá   jéa
              CONJ CONJ NEG.COP 3.SBJV-finish thing   REL.FUT
              á-múksîindà
              3-eat.TERM.CF.IS
              'Isn't the side dish ('thing to eat it with') finished?'

2   Deaqweeda *mánda íiyá*
              no   mother
              'No, dear.'

---

[13] The cause of the laughter is unclear to me. It's possible that it's occasioned by the informal way in which the woman refers to the butter – *gíchchéa ámúksîindà*, which involves the verb stem *muks-* 'eat (of dogs)'.

3		(one unclear utterance during four seconds of laughter)
4	Sageolan	gùtgwándá gíchchéa ámúksîin[dá?
		g-údú-gwá-ndá gídá jéa á-múksîindà
		AFF-CONT-3.SBJV-be.at thing REL.FUT 3-eat.TERM.CF.IS
		'There's still something to eat it with?'
5	Deaqweeda	[éa: héasôy
		'Yes'.

Similarly to Extract 4, in line 1 Sageolan uses a polar question to ask whether something is finished. However, unlike Extract 4, the polar question is formulated negatively rather than affirmatively. In Datooga, as has been suggested for English, negative polar questions imply that the speaker is epistemically committed to the "proposition in the scope of the negative operator" (Farkas & Bruce 2010: 96), i.e. Sageolan believes that the side dish is indeed finished. While bringing the proposition 'the side dish is finished' into the common ground, the speaker also orients to the truth value of that proposition. The other woman negates this proposition by saying 'no'. Sageolan then utters a second polar question, this time formatted affirmatively, about the continued existence of the side dish. Her use of *údú-* here serves to contrast the possible state-of-affairs that she made relevant in line 1 (-food) with its inverse (+food). (The latter is then confirmed as the actual state-of-affairs in line 5 with the affirmative token *éa*.) If we were to diagram this example, it would look very similar to Figure 3, and indeed we have a counterfactual use of *údú-* here. What's different in this example is that *údú-* is also associated with a counter-expectational meaning: the speaker is emphasising that the possible state-of-affairs described in her utterance is the polar opposite of the state-of-affairs she oriented to as true in line 1. As analysts, we can only retrieve this counter-expectational meaning from the broader interactional context, which tells us that it is an entirely pragmatically motivated interpretation.

These three examples have demonstrated how the meaning of *údú-* is context-specific, and how interpretations regarding neutral, counterfactual, or counter-expectational scenarios are built up over the course of several utterances. Atelic verbs with *údú-* locate a polarity change on some time frame, and that time frame is projected from elsewhere in the interaction. Since the meaning of *údú-* always draws on other aspects of the common ground – such as the habitual time frame of morning (as in Extract 3), or the speaker's prior commitment to an alternative state-of-affairs (as in Extract 5) – there is rich pragmatic work going on in its interpretation. Counter-expectational meanings are triggered by the context, not by the form *údú-* itself. With respect to neutral vs counterfactual meanings, it does not seem especially useful to designate one of these as semantically primary, since the semantics of *údú-* change according to different configurations of the verb. Nonetheless, a larger scale study might look at how frequently *údú-* is used in neutral and counterfactual contexts and to what extent its appearance is sensitive to participants' epistemic commitments.

6 Summary

This paper began by identifying one dedicated phasal polarity expression in Gisamjanga and Barabaiga Datooga – the auxiliary-like form *góolá* 'already', which appears infrequently in my corpus data – and one item associated with phasal polarity meanings – the verbal prefix *údú-*, a continuative marker. There is no attested equivalent form for English 'not yet'. I also discussed the form *gábày (èa)*, which locates events as early with respect to some established time frame, and which can sometimes be translated with 'already' in its counterfactual sense. The rest of the paper focused on *údú-* and the range of meanings it contributes in different semantic configurations: continuative, iterative, immediate past, and avertive-like. I began to explore the semantic and pragmatic relatedness of these different facets of meaning, though a detailed explanation of the pragmatic pathways between each use of this prefix remains outstanding for future research. Using conversation data, I explored some real-life examples of how *údú-* is used, and showed that in different interactional contexts, neutral, counterfactual, and counter-expectational interpretations of utterances with *údú-* are all possible. However, the interactional analysis supports the view espoused in the literature (e.g. Krifka 2000) that participants' expectations are relevant only at the level of pragmatic inference; counter-expectation is not directly encoded in the form *údú-*. On the other hand, we cannot assign counterfactual meanings of *údú-* to pragmatics: counterfactual scenarios are frequently invoked by utterances containing this form, and in one particular semantic configuration (negative non-future with telic verbs), only counterfactual interpretations are possible. Diachronic and cross-dialectal work may help determine any directionality in the neutral and counterfactual uses of the continuative prefix.

Abbreviations

1	first person	IS	inflectional suffix
2	second person	LOC	locative
3	third person	MR	multiple reference
AFF	affirmative	NEG	negative
ALM	associated locomotion	NMLZ	nominalizer
AP	antipassive	PRF	perfect
AUX	auxiliary-like form	PL	plural
CAUS	causative	PLUR	pluractional
CF	centrifugal	PROH	prohibitive
CP	centripetal	PROX	proximal
CONJ	conjunction	PS	primary suffix
CONT	continuative	PSN	personal name
COP	copular	PST	past
DEM	demonstrative	REL	relative
DSC	discourse marker	SBJV	subjunctive
DRV	derivational suffix	SG	singular
FUT	future	TERM	terminal
IMP	imperative	UR	unit reference
INCH	inchoative		

Transcription conventions are as follows: ? indicates a question, signalled by rising intonation; (.) indicates a pause; [marks a point of overlapping speech. Participant names are pseudonyms.

Bibliographic references

Farkas, Donka F. & Kim B. Bruce. 2010. On reacting to assertions and polar questions. *Journal of Semantics* 27 (1). 81–118.

Hansen, Maj-Britt Mosegaard. 2008. *Particles at the semantics/pragmatics interface: Synchronic and diachronic Issues: A study with special reference to the French phasal adverbs*. Amsterdam: Elsevier.

Kießling, Roland. 1998. Der Pluraktionalis im Datooga. In Ines Fiedler, Catherine Griefenow-Mewis & Brigitte Reineke (eds.), *Afrikanische Sprachen im Brennpunkt der Forschung*, 179–196. Cologne: Rüdiger Köppe.

Kießling, Roland. 2000a. Verb classes in Nilotic: Evidence from Datooga (Southern Nilotic). In H. Ekkehard Wolff & Orin D. Gensler (eds.), *Proceedings of the 2nd World Congress of African Linguistics, Leipzig 1997*, 603–616. Cologne: Rüdiger Köppe.

Kießling, Roland. 2000b. Number marking in Datooga nouns. In Rainer Vossen, Angelika Mietzner & Antje Meissner (eds.), *Mehr als nur Worte. Afrikanistische Beiträge zum 65. Geburtstag von Franz Rottland*, 349–366. Cologne: Rüdiger Köppe.

Kießling, Roland. 2007a. The "marked nominative" in Datooga. *Journal of African Languages and Linguistics* 28. 149–191.

Kießling, Roland. 2007b. Space and reference in Datooga verbal morphosyntax. In Doris L. Payne & Mechthild Reh (eds.), *Advances in Nilo-Saharan Linguistics. Proceedings of the 8th Nilo-Saharan Linguistics Colloquium*, 123–142. Cologne: Rüdiger Köppe.

Kramer, Raija L. 2017. Position paper on Phasal Polarity expressions. Hamburg: University of Hamburg. https://www.aai.uni-hamburg.de/afrika/php2018/medien/position-paper-on-php.pdf (accessed 06 April 2019).

Krifka, Manfred. 2000. Alternatives for aspectual particles: Semantics of still and already. *Proceedings of the Twenty-Sixth Annual Meeting of the Berkeley Linguistics Society*, 401–412.

Kuteva, Tania. 2004. *Auxiliation: An enquiry into the nature of grammaticalization*. Oxford: Oxford University Press.

Löbner, Sebastian. 1989. German Schon – Erst – Noch: An integrated analysis. *Linguistics and Philosophy* 12 (2). 167–212.

Michaelis, Laura A. 1998. Aspectual grammar and past-time reference. London: Routledge.

Muzale, Henry R. T. & Josephat M. Rugemalira. 2008. Researching and documenting the languages of Tanzania. *Language Documentation & Conservation* 2 (1). 68–108.

Plungian, Vladimir A. 1999. A typology of phasal meanings. In Werner Abraham & Vladimir P. Nedjalkov (eds.), *Tense-aspect, transitivity and causativity: Essays in honour of Vladimir Nedjalkov*, 311–322. Amsterdam: Benjamins.

Rottland, Franz. 1982. *Die südnilotischen Sprachen: Beschreibung, Vergleichung und Rekonstruktion*. Berlin: D. Reimer.

Rottland, Franz. 1983. Southern Nilotic (with an outline of Datooga). In M. Lionel Bender (ed.), *Nilo-Saharan Language Studies*, 208–238. East Lansing, Michigan: African Studies Center, Michigan State University.

Van Baar, Theodorus M. 1997. *Phasal polarity*. Amsterdam: IFOTT.

van der Auwera, Johan. 1998. Phasal adverbials in the languages of Europe. In Johan van der Auwera & P.O. Baoill Dónall (eds.), *Adverbial constructions in the languages of Europe*, 25–145. Berlin: Mouton de Gruyter.

Vander Klok, Jozina & Lisa Matthewson. 2015. Diagnostics for already vs. perfect aspect: A case study of Javanese *wis*. In Amber Camp, Yuko Otsuka, Claire Stabile & Nozomi Tanaka (eds.), *AFLA 21: The Proceedings of the 21st Meeting of the Austronesian Formal Linguistics Association*, 289–306. College of Asia and the Pacific, The Australian National University: Asia-Pacific Linguistics.

Vendler, Zeno. 1957. Verbs and times. *The Philosophical Review* 66 (2). 143–160.

III Grammaticalization processes and historical developments of phasal polarity expressions in African languages

Ljuba Veselinova, Maud Devos
NOT YET expressions as a lexico-grammatical category in Bantu languages

1 Introduction

The focus of this work is the distribution of one phasal polarity marker, specifically NOT YET in Bantu languages, cf. (1) below for an introductory illustration. The reasons for choosing this phasal polarity term are as follows.[1] (i) Bantu languages are typically cited as the family where NOT YET expressions are often part of the grammatical system rather than adverbs. However, there is still no comparative study which offers a thorough survey of this feature in the family, cf. for instance Nurse and Philippson (2003) as well as Nurse (2008). Our work is intended to fill this gap. (ii) The current data indicate that among all phasal polarity markers, NOT YET is the one most commonly expressed in Bantu, cf. Löfgren (2019). (iii) From a wider-cross-linguistic point of view, NOT YET expressions rank among the most common special expressions of negation, cf. Veselinova (2013).

Our study is both synchronically and diachronically oriented. On the synchronic level, we strive to achieve a detailed description of the structural encoding and the lexico-grammatical status of NOT YET expressions together with a description of their uses in individual languages. One of our main goals is to propose a semantic map for these expressions. We also use the collected material to formulate informed hypotheses about the evolution of NOT YET markers.

This article proceeds as follows. In section 2, we give a brief overview of previous studies on this topic. Our methodology, including the definition of a comparative concept for the identification of NOT YET expressions is presented in section 3. Sections 4 and 5 are devoted to the results of the synchronic part of this work. In section 4 we discuss the structural characteristics and the

---

[1] We would like to thank Johan van der Auwera, Rasmus Bernander, Sebastian Dom, Hilde Gunnik, Steve Nicolle, Malin Petzell and the participants in the workshop *The semantics of verbal morphology in under-described languages*, June 2–3, Gothenburg, Sweden and the participants in the Conference on Phasal Polarity in African Languages, University of Hamburg, Germany, for their help and encouragement and finally Raija Kramer för her infinite patience during the editing process. Ljuba Veselinova gratefully acknowledges the financial support of the Swedish Research Council, grant number 2016–01045.

Ljuba Veselinova, Stockholm University, Sweden
Maud Devos, Royal Museum for Central Africa and University of Ghent, Belgium

https://doi.org/10.1515/9783110646290-018

degree of grammaticalization of NOT YET markers. In section 5, we discuss the uses of NOT YET markers. The focus of section 6 is the diachronic development of NOT YET expressions. A summary together with a general discussion concludes the article in section 7.

2 Previous studies

As mentioned above, Bantu languages are typically used to illustrate the distinction between plain negation and the encoding of both the non-realization of a situation, and the expectations of the speaker for its future realization. This is shown in (1) below by data from Digo, a Bantu language from Kenya and Tanzania.

(1) Digo [dig][2]
    a. *u-ka-rim-a*
       SBJ.2SG-ANT-farm-FV
       'You have farmed/you farmed.'
       (Nicolle 2013: 150)
    b. *ta-m-ka-fwih-a*
       NEG-SBJ.2PL-ANT-dance-FV
       'You have not danced.'
       (Nicolle 2013: 150)
    c. *ta-ri-dzangbwe-dung-a*
       NEG-SBJ.5-INC-pierce-FV
       'It has not yet pierced.'
       (Nicolle 2013: 157)

In Digo negation is expressed by the prefix *ta-* for a number of tenses, including the anterior, cf. (1b) The form *–dzangbwe-* is glossed 'INC(EPTIVE)'; it is a bound item observed only in the context of negation or in questions. That is, it is an example of a *negative polarity item*, hereafter NPI.

    The prefix *–dzangbwe-* indicates "that an event has not occurred prior to and including the reference time" (Nicolle 2013: 157). This author goes on to state that this form typically also implies that the non-realized event may occur at some point after the reference time. The form *–dzangbwe-* appears in the same position as other tense-aspect markers in Digo; thus it can be seen to be

---

[2] All languages are introduced with their ISO 639-6 codes in order to facilitate their identification.

in opposition with them. It is considered a grammatical rather than a lexical item based on the following features (i) it is a bound, rather than a free form; (ii) it has a fixed position within verb forms, (iii) it is restricted to specific contexts, e.g. negation and questions, and (iv) it has an abstract rather than specific meaning. Following the practice suggested by Bybee, Perkins and Pagliuca (1994: 2), grammatical markers are also referred to as gram-types in this article.

The distinction between a negated anterior as in (1b) and a NOT YET form in (1c) is a very important one in Bantu languages. However, Nurse (2008: 200) points out that "since most analysts of [Bantu languages] are speakers of European languages where this distinction is made by adverbs, [. . .] not yet verb forms are not considered of much importance". The distinction between a plain negative and a negative inceptive, to borrow Nicolle's term for right now, is observed in many languages outside Bantu, cf. Veselinova (2017) for an overview.

In addition to the works cited above, other key references on this topic include Comrie (1985), Contini-Morava (1989) Kozinskij (1988), Heine, Claudi, and Hünnemeyer (1991), van der Auwera (1998), Van Baar (1997), Schadeberg (2000), Plungian (1999; 2000; 2011) Nurse & Philipson (2003), Nurse (2008) as well as Kramer (2018).

NOT YET grams have received different interpretations. Comrie and Schadeberg treat them as temporal or aspectual markers restricted to the negative domain; Kozinskij (1988: 522–523) sees them as one of several semantic types of *antiresultatives*. These are expressions which encode the non-realization of a state in different ways. In his view, they are 'not yet', 'not at all', 'not sufficiently', 'no longer'. Kozinskij notes that only 'not yet' expressions are known to be encoded by special grammatical means in the languages of the world. Van der Auwera (1998), Van Baar (1997), as well as Plungian (1999, 2000, 2011) are all scholars who treat NOT YET expressions as part of a larger semantic domain that covers the different phases of an event or a state. In many descriptive works, NOT YET expressions are seen as special negators, typically used to negate the perfect or related categories.

Since this volume is inspired by the recent work of Kramer (2018), we allot special attention to the six parameters she outlines for the study of phasal meanings. They are *coverage, pragmaticity, telicity, wordhood, expressivity* and *paradigmaticity*.

Coverage refers to the range of phasal polarity concepts covered by specific phasal polarity terms. Kramer distinguishes between two kinds of systems for this parameter, *rigid* and *flexible*. In rigid systems one phasal polarity term covers one phasal polarity concept; in flexible systems, a single phasal polarity term may cover several phasal polarity concepts. We assume that coverage is to be understood in synchronic terms. If a diachronic perspective is adopted, it is possible to show that a system may change from being flexible to rigid in the course of time.

Pragmaticity has to do with the polarity values of the different situations in a phasal polarity concept. For instance, for a concept such as NO LONGER, there are two phases; one that is in the past and has a positive polarity value; the other is current and has a negative polarity value. Thus NO LONGER involves two polarity values that are temporarily related and sequential. In Kramer's terms, the concept NO LONGER is pragmatically neutral. Other phasal polarity terms may involve simultaneous phases or an actual and an expected one; for instance, STILL and NOT YET cover such phases. They can be defined as counterfactual. Kramer points out that many phasal polarity terms may fluctuate between the pragmatically neutral and the counterfactual scenario and this is language specific. It has to be pointed out that phasal polarity terms do not always involve two points in time. For instance, a sentence like the one in (2) is fully legitimate; yet, it is clear that there is no previous point in time t_i that can possibly exist. Two points in time would be relevant for an expression such as *still not* as in (3)[3] (Östen Dahl, p.c.).

(2) *When a child is born, she has not yet experienced anything.*

(3) *She still does not know if she loves me or not.*

Telicity refers to the presence or absence of polarity change. Telic phasal polarities involve a point of polarity change. In Kramer's view such phasal polarity include ALREADY and NO LONGER. Conversely, STILL and NOT YET are atelic, because, according to Kramer, their moment of polarity change lies in the future.

The parameter wordhood refers to the word class status of phasal polarity markers. We cover it for NOT YET in section 4.

Expressibility is about whether or not all four concepts of a phasal polarity system are expressed in a language. Since our focus is on the encoding of NOT YET, our data on the encoding of the other phasal polarity concepts are still preliminary. Löfgren (2019) offers a detailed overview of the phasal polarity systems in a stratified sample of 50 East Bantu languages. She shows that the most

---

[3] A detailed discussion on preference of specific tenses with these adverbial phrases cannot be offered here. For now, suffice it to observe that in English the perfect is preferred with *not yet* while the simple present is preferred with *still not*. However, the perfect in Swedish can co-occur with both *inte än* 'not yet' and *fortfarande inte* 'still not'.

frequently expressed concept is NOT YET, followed by ALREADY, STILL and finally NO LONGER.

Paradigmaticity is about the oppositions that phasal polarity terms enter into. The oppositions can be internal, e.g. within the phasal polarity system, or external, that is, within the more general grammatical system in their language. Kramer distinguishes between symmetric and asymmetric phasal polarity terms. Symmetric are those which have a corresponding alternative and asymmetric are those which do not. We discuss the polysemy pattern of NOT YET expressions with other phasal markers in section 5.2. However, since our focus is on NOT YET rather than the whole phasal system, we do not claim to be exhaustive on this issue.

3 Methodology

3.1 Sampling and data collection procedure

For this study, our main data sources have been grammars and other equivalent descriptions. As stated above, we strive to achieve an overview of the occurrence and functions of NOT YET expressions in the Bantu family. To this end we assembled a geographically stratified sample of 141 languages, cf. https://arcg.is/1e0iqz. It has to be said that the sample is bibliographically biased since our language selection has also been guided by the availability of sources and also by their quality. That is, we included all languages with descriptions of acceptable quality; this means that languages with poor descriptions were excluded from this study.

3.2 Identifying and labeling NOT YET expressions

NOT YET expressions are identified based on a functional definition. Specifically, when a construction is used for the encoding of non-realized expectations for either actions or states as in (1) from Digo above or as in Sukuma (4) and Teke-Fuumu (5) below, we dubbed it a NOT YET expression or a NONDUM.

The following can be said with regard to providing a term for NOT YET expressions. There is a great deal of variation in referring to them, cf. *not yet tense* (Comrie 1985: 54), *tardative* (Schadeberg 2000: 12), *cunctative*, from the Latin verb *cunctari* 'hesitate, delay' (Plungian 1999: 319), *negative contituative* (van der Auwera 1998), *imminent negation* (Chappell and Peyraube

2016: 487). The term NONDUM we suggest here is based on the Latin word *nondum* 'not yet'. It can be suitable to use a Latin-based term to match *iamitive*, from Latin *iam* 'already', which is currently making its way as a denomination for a distinct perfect category in the affirmative, cf. Olsson (2013) as well as Dahl & Wälchli (2016). However, since it is not clear whether introducing yet another label in addition to the ones already suggested, will really be useful, we will use the terms NOT YET and NONDUM interchangeably in this text.

A couple of examples where NONDUM is expressed by a bound form or by an adverb follow in (4) and (5) below.

(4) Sukuma (F.20), [suk]
    a. *batiízilę́*
       bá-tá-iz-ilę́
       SBJ.3PL-NEG-come-PFV
       'They did not/have not come.'
    b. *batenaámala*
       bá-těna.a-mal-a
       SBJ.3PL-NOND-finish-FV
       'They haven't finished yet.'
       (Batibo 1985: 279, 284–285)

(5) Teke-Fuumu (B.77b), [ifm]
    a. *Bàà̀rù ká bá-yìnì wó*
       2.men NEG SBJ.3PL-go.PFV NEG
       'The men did not/have not gone.'
    b. *Kíní á-yì (wó)*
       not_yet SBJ.3SG-arrive.PFV NEG
       'He has not yet arrived.'
       (Makouta-Mboukou 1977: 454, 476)

The structural characteristics of NONDUMS are discussed in section 4 below together with their integration into the systems of individual languages, that is, whether they appear to be lexical or grammatical elements.

3.3 Morphological analysis: synchrony versus diachrony

The morphological analysis of the Bantu data is done on purely synchronic criteria. That is, morphemes are identified as such based on their functions in the modern languages, not based on what is known about their origin. Data from Kagulu in (6) are used for this discussion.

(6) Kagulu (G.10) [kki]
    a. *Ni-ng'hali*   *ku-lim-a*
       SBJ.1SG-NOT YET INF-cultivate-FV
       'I have not yet cultivated'
    b. *Ni-ng'hati*   *ni-lim-e*
       SBJ.1SG-NOT YET SBJ.1SG-cultivate-FV
       'I have not yet cultivated'
       (Petzell 2008: 146)

The form *ng'hali* in (6a) can be identified as an univerbation that resulted from the fusion of a reconstructed persistive marker -*(n)ka* and the copula -*di*, cf. Güldemann (1996: § 4.1.1.2) and Güldemann (1998: § 2.2.2). However, in modern Kagulu, the form –*ng'hali*- as well as allomorphs such as -*ng'hati*- from (6b) function as single meaningful units with the sense 'not yet', cf. more data in (13). There is no justification for positing any further morpheme boundaries for these forms and for a synchronic analysis that would be misguided. Information about the origin of specific forms, when available, is relevant for the discussion of their evolution and is brought up in the discussion on diachrony.

4 General characteristics of identified nondums

The concept NOT YET is encoded by a variety of constructions in Bantu languages. For the purposes of data summary and classification we found the following parameters to be most relevant: (i) whether NOT YET is encoded by a free or bound form, cf. 4.1.; in this sub-section, we also discuss the degree of grammaticalization of various NONDUMS. Further characteristics of the different kinds of constructions encoding NONDUMs are offered in sections 4.1.1, 4.1.2 and 4.1.3. (ii) whether there is a negation marker in the NOT YET construction, cf. 4.2. These parameters have a bearing both on the synchronic and on the diachronic description of NONDUM constructions.

Before we proceed with the analysis along the lines listed above, we consider it necessary to present the Bantu verb in a general manner since we will be discussing many different verb forms in this article. The morphological structure of Bantu verbs is typically described in terms of a template, cf. (7).

(7) Bantu verbal template, adapted from Güldemann (1999: 546) 7

SLOT	pre-initial	initial	post-initial	pre-radical	radical	pre-final
FUNCTION	TAM/polarity	subject	TAM/polarity	object	verbal root	derivation/TAM

SLOT	final	post-final				
FUNCTION	TAM/polarity	clause type/object/polarity				

NONDUM markers, when bound forms, occur predominantly in post-initial position. As shown in Table 1 below, there are 63 languages where NONDUMS appear as bound forms; out of them 53 appear in post-initial position.[4] Thus, it appears safe to say that bound NONDUMS are clearly associated with a very specific position in the Bantu verbal template.

4.1 Free or bound form

Bantu languages are cited as an example of a rather uniform language family, with agglutinative morphology. Tone is used for both grammatical and lexical distinctions. We have to caution that tone is not always clearly indicated in grammars. Since they are our main data source, we have not been able to include tone as a structural feature for NONDUMS.

It is also a tricky issue to distinguish between free or bound forms. We use the following criteria to distinguish between the two: (i) position in the construction; (ii) morphological marking; (iii) mobility of the NOT YET form.

Generally, a form is considered to be bound if it always appears in the same position; the construction where it is observed can be described as a single morphological form, with a single marker of finiteness. Thus the forms –*dzangbwe*- in (1) from Digo as well as the discontinuous marker -*těna.a*-VERB-*a* in (4b). represent examples of bound forms. Bound forms can be dedicated to the NOT YET sense; there are also cases where a specific

---

[4] We have only one example of a language with a nondum in pre-initial position: Kande [kbs]. There are also cases of nondums in post-initial position that are more accurately described as discontinuous markers involving both a post-initial and a final marker. Examples of such are Lika [lik], Mongo-Nkundu [lol] and Poke [pof]. In our current dataset, there are five examples of NONDUMS occurring after the verbal root: one, in Kumu [kmw], is in final position, and in 4 languages, Kaamba [xku], Koongo [kng], Budza [bja] and Herero [her], the nondum marker is in post-final position.

tense-aspect category under negation is used to express it. We discuss this in detail in section 4.1.1.

A periphrastic construction tends to have at least one of the following characteristics (i) a finite and a non-finite form in the same construction, cf. (11) and (13d) below; (ii) multiple finite forms in the same construction cf. (13c); (13e) and (13f) illustrate this as well. Examples and a discussion of periphrastic constructions are offered in section 4.1.2.

A free form is one that does not carry any morphological marking, cf. (5) from Teke-Fuumu above. We classify as adverbs invariable elements that are clearly not part of a morphological construction. The data in grammars are often too limited to allow for further specification of the mobility of adverbs in their function of adverbials within the clause; nor is there sufficient information about their compatibility with different tense-aspect categories.

The quantitative distribution of NONDUM markers based on their morphological status is presented in Table 1 below. The counts in the table reflect the number of constructions of various kinds rather than the number of languages. There are 11 languages where multiple expressions for the sense NOT YET are observed.

Table 1: Quantitative distribution of NONDUM markers with regard to their morphological status.

TYPE OF MARKER	NUMBER OF CONSTRUCTIONS	% OF TOTAL
Bound morpheme	63	39.87%
Bound or auxiliary (status is ambiguous)	6	3.80%
Auxiliary construction	47	29.75%
Adverb	25	15.82%
No information in source	17	10.76%
	Total: 158	100%

Examples of all structural types of NONDUMs listed in Table 1 can be found in the Appendix. As demonstrated by the figures above, a solid proportion, some 40% of NONDUMs are expressed by bound forms. About one-third of the identified NONDUMS are encoded by auxiliary constructions. There are also languages where NONDUMS appear to be encoded either as bound forms or as auxiliaries; Digo is a case in point, cf. data in (8).

(8) Digo [dig]
   a. *ta-ri-dzangbwe-dung-a*
      NEG-SBJ.5-INC-pierce-FV
      'It has not yet pierced.'
   b. *Kala si-dzangbwe   ku-tayarish-a   ma-somo*
      PST   NEG.SBJ.1SG-NOND INF-prepare-FV   6-lesson
      'I had not yet prepared the lessons.'
      (Nicolle 2013: 150, 157)

The NOT YET sense is expressed by adverbs in 16% of the constructions under study. The geographic distribution of these different kinds of markers is not random, cf. data on our map server, https://arcg.is/1e0iqz. Bound NONDUMS are observed all over the Bantu area except for the South-Western parts. Auxiliary constructions appear especially frequent in the Central-East and also South-Central parts of the Bantu territory. Adverbs are used for the expression of NONDUM in the South-West. Finally, several grammars of languages spoken in the North-West (Forest Bantu) do not contain any information about NOT YET expressions. We take this as an indicator that such expressions are not lexicalized/grammaticalized in these languages to the same extent as they are in rest of the Bantu family. The general distribution of NONDUMS, especially the clear path of auxiliary constructions from the Central-East to the South falls in very well with the suggested pathways for Bantu migration and spread, cf. Grollemund (2015). This together with the obvious areal patterns of the structural types of NONDUMS also leads us to hypothesize that the development of these lexico-grammatical expressions is a contact-driven innovation rather than an inherited feature of the Bantu family.

The analysis of NONDUM forms in terms of their degree of morphological bondedness can also be used for a discussion of their status as grammatical or lexical items. Specifically, we can interpret the data presented in Table 1 as a grammaticalization cline. Thus, the forms which are clearly integrated into the morphological structure of the verb can be seen as the most grammaticalized ones while the adverbs can be seen closest to the lexical scale. Periphrastic constructions can be considered to represent an intermediate stage in the grammaticalization process. Of course, one should not forget that the fact that an element is bound does not necessarily mean that it is part of the grammatical system, cf. (Mithun 1988) on lexical affixes and also (Wälchli 2016). However, as already pointed out, a substantive part of bound NONDUM markers occur in one and the same position in the Bantu verb, usually a slot devoted to tense or polarity/negation marking. Therefore, we consider these markers as part of the grammatical rather than the lexical system in the languages where they are observed.

4.1.1 Dedicated vs. non-dedicated nondum markers

As indicated by the counts in Table 1., there are 63 NONDUMS encoded by a bound form. Out of them we find that 50 are dedicated to the sense 'not yet'. There are, however, 11 constructions which are actually the negated variant of a specific tense-aspect category. They are illustrated by data from Chichewa in (9) below.

(9) Chichewa (N.31) [nya]
    a. *Si-ndi-na-kuman-e*   *na-ye*
       NEG-SBJ.1SG-RECPST-meet-SBJV COM-him
       'I haven't met him.'
    b. context 'The king is expected to arrive'
       Mfumu   *si-i-na-fik-e*
       3.king   NEG-SBJ.4-RECPST-arrive-SBJV
       'The king hasn't arrived yet.'
       (Kiso 2012: 156)

As shown above, the prefix *si-* appears in pre-initial position to negate the recent past tense, cf. (9a).[5] The same construction, that is, the negated recent past, when used in an appropriate context as in (9b), may come to mean 'not yet VERB'. Kiso (2012, *ibid.*) comments that the construction *si-..-na-* . . . *-e* [NEG- . . . -RECPST- . . . -SBJV] is used in a broad variety of contexts; it often indicates simply the non-occurrence of a situation in the past and sometimes 'not [VERB] in the past but maybe in the future'. This author goes on to state that the distinction between the plain negation of a situation and negation with expectation for its future realization can be made explicit by including the persistive marker *–be* in the construction, cf. (10) below.

(10) Chichewa (N.31) [nya]
    Context 'The king is expected to arrive'
    Mfumu si-i-na-fik-e-be
    3.king   NEG-SBJ.4-RECPST-arrive-SBJV-PER
    'The king hasn't arrived yet.'
    (Kiso 2012: 157)

---

5 As noted by an anonymous reviewer, the recent past meaning might well have developed out of a perfect meaning. Kiso (2012: 97–130) describes a complicated system of perfect and past tense markers in Chichewa with partly overlapping meanings. She also notes, in accordance with Nurse (2008), that the distinction between perfect and recent past is notoriously hard to make (Kiso 2012: 56–57).

Thus, we can say that that the NOT YET sense is expressed by grammatical means in Chichewa. However, it does not have a dedicated encoding, clearly integrated into its grammatical system, as the ones observed in, say, Digo (1) or Sukuma in (4).

As mentioned above, about one-fifth (11/63) of the constructions with bound NONDUM markers show encoding similar to the one presented for Chichewa above. At this stage of our research, it is not clear that these languages form a coherent group. The tense aspect categories which are negated and also used to express the sense 'not yet VERB' show a wide range: perfect/anterior, recent past, progressive, habitual. It has to be said, however, that there is some geographical coherence to this group since 6 out these 11 languages are located in the North-East, cf. data on https://arcg.is/1e0iqz. It is currently not clear whether this fact has any implications for the spread or grammaticalization of this construction or if it is merely a coincidence.

4.1.2 Nondums expressed by periphrastic constructions

Periphrastic constructions include an auxiliary and a lexical verb. Three variables are relevant for the analysis of these constructions: (i) subject indexation of the elements involved; (ii) negation marking; and finally, (iii) the kinds of verbs used as auxiliaries.

Variation in the subject indexation of both the auxiliary and the lexical verb is possible. First, the auxiliary may be indexed for subject and the lexical verb appears in the infinitive as in (11).

(11) Manda (N.11) ISO-693 [mgs] (Bernander 2017:263)
    Ákóna   kulèmba
    a-kona   ku-lemb-a
    SBJ.3SG-still/yet INF-write-FV
    'She hasn't written yet.'

The combination auxiliary followed by infinitive is observed in 28 out of 43 periphrastic constructions, that is, in 65% of them. Thus, it appears to be the dominant option. In the remaining 35%, subject indexation appears on both the auxiliary and the lexical verb as in (12) or there is variation as in (13).

(12) Nilamba (F. 31) [nim] (Johnson 1925:181)
    U-kali   u-let-e
    SBJ.2SG-NOND   SBJ.2SG-bring-SBJV
    'You have not yet brought.'

In Kagulu, the auxiliary is always indexed for subject but the lexical verb may appear as either a finite or an as non-finite form, cf. (13c), e, f vs. (13d) below.

(13) Kagulu (G.10) [kki]
    a. *Dibwa   disabilima*[6]
       di-bwa   di-si-a-bilim-a
       5-dog   SBJ.5-NEG-PST-run-FV
       'The dog did not run.'
    b. *Dibwa   sidyabilime*
       di-bwa   si-dy-a-bilim-e
       5-dog   NEG-SBJ.5-PST-run-FV
       'The dog did not run.'
    c. *Ni-ng'hati   ni-lim-e*
       SBJ.1SG-NOND   SBJ.1SG-cultivate-FV
       'I have not yet cultivated.'
    d. *Ni-ng'hali   ku-lim-a*
       SBJ.1SG-NOND   INF-cultivate-FV
       'I have not yet cultivated.'
    e. *Si-ng'hati   ni-lim-e*
       NEG.SBJ.1SG-NOND   1SG-cultivate-FV
       'I have not yet cultivated.'
    f. *Si-naki   ni-lim-e*
       NEG.SBJ.1SG-NOND   SBJ.1SG-cultivate-FV
       'I have not yet cultivated.'
       (Petzell 2008:111, 128, 146)

The following can be said about negation marking in periphrastic constructions. Although the constructions cited in (11) and (12) do not contain a negation marker, the majority of periphrastic constructions do, cf. 4.2 for further discussion of this issue. There are also languages like Kagulu in (13) where constructions with or without negation are in free variation. The Kagulu data also demonstrate that a language may have several different forms of nondums and these can be, again, in free variation. We will come back to these facts during the discussion on the evolution of NONDUM expressions, see section 6.1.2.

---

[6] Author's emphasis.

As regards the types of auxiliaries, our current dataset allows us to distinguish five kinds of verbs: verbs/auxiliaries dedicated to the 'not yet' sense, copulas, quotative verbs, lexical verbs which show polysemy, that is they are used both with their lexical sense and as NONDUM auxiliaries, and finally auxiliaries that belong to the phasal domain such as 'still' and 'already'. The frequency of occurrence of the different kinds of verbs used in periphrastic constructions is presented in Table 2.

Table 2: Types of verbs observed in periphrastic constructions.

TYPES OF VERB	NUMBER OF CONSTRUCTIONS	%
Auxiliaries dedicated to the 'not yet' sense	18	33.96%
Copulas	9	16.98%
Quotative verbs	9	16.98%
Lexical verbs	6	11.32%
'still'	8	15.09%
'already'	3	5.66%
Total	53	100%

As demonstrated above, the predominant group is that which includes verbs dedicated to the 'not yet' sense; such verbs are exemplified by data from Kagulu in (13) above. The next in frequency are copulas and quotative verbs. It has to be said that copulas commonly appear together with a persistive prefix and sometimes in combination with negation when expressing the 'not yet' sense, see (14) from Fwe below for an illustration. We will return to this issue during the discussion on diachrony.

(14) Fwe (K.402) [fwe]
 Ka-ndi-shi-ní   *ku-shésh-iw-a*
 NEG-SBJ.1SG-PER-COP INF-marry-PASS-FV
 'I am not yet married.'
 (Gunnink 2018: 504)

The so called *quotative verbs* are reflexes of **ti* '(be/do) thus, like this/that' (Güldemann 2012: 68) and **gàmb* 'speak, answer' Bastin et al. (2002) and they are frequently used as quotative markers in Bantu languages, i.e. they figure in constructions introducing (direct) reported discourse and related constructions (Güldemann 2002, 2008, 2012). However, and independent of the quotative function, they are also sometimes known to be used as light verbs/dummy auxiliaries in what Güldemann (2008: § 7.1) refers to as 'foregrounding constructions'. Periphrastic nondum constructions are among them. Shona is an example of a language where the quotative verb *-ti* is used to introduce reported discourse (15a) and also figures in the periphrastic nondum construction (15b).

(15) Shona (S.10) [sna]
 a. *Nda-ti   uya   neni*
    SBJ.1SG.PRF-QUOT come.IMP COM.1SG
    'I said: Come with me!'
    (Güldemann 2012: 69)
 b. *Ha-u-sa-ti   wa-ndi-on-a   ndi-chi-rw-a*
    NEG-SBJ.2SG-NEG.PRF-QUOT SBJ.2SG.ANT-OBJ.1SG-see-FV SBJ.1SG-SIM-fight-FV
    asi   nhasi   u-cha-ndi-on-a
    but   today   SBJ.2SG-FUT-OBJ.1SG-see-FV
    'You have not yet seen me fighting, but today you will.'
    (Güldemann 2008: 490)

In Shangaji, however, the verb *-tthi* figuring in the periphrastic nondum construction in (48), is not used as a quotative marker. Instead, the quotative verb *-ira* is used (Devos & Bostoen 2012).

(16) Shangaji P.312 [nte]
    kaw-ír-í   ni-laáw'   ó-muú-ti
    SBJ.1SG-PST-QUOT SBJ.1PL-leave-SBJV 17-3-town
    'I said: Let's go home.'
    (Devos & Bostoen 2012: 99)

So, the quotative use is not a necessary prerequisite to the use in nondum constructions, rather, it singles out a trait these verbs have in common crosslinguistically.

Lexical verbs as well as auxiliaries with phasal meanings such as 'still' and 'already' represent the smaller groups among the NONDUM auxiliaries. Auxiliaries that are also used as main lexical verbs such as, for instance, 'start' or 'know' are illustrated by data from Hunde in (17).

(17) Hunde (JD.51) [hke]
Tu-t-eci tw-á-bírang-ir-a mu-ndu
SBJ.2PL-NEG-know SBJ.2PL-COND-call-APPL-FV 1-person
'We have not yet called someone.'
(Mateene 1992: 35)

Finally, the constructions where the auxiliary means 'still' are shown by Manda in (11) above or 'already' as in Ndebele, in (18) below.

(18) Ndebele (S.44) [nbl]
Ú-bíyó áá-wát-I kú-swáphel-a
SBJ.3SG-already/not_yet NEG.SBJ.3SG-know-NEG.PRS INF-close-FV
sí-báya s-áákhe
7-kraal 7-POSS.3SG
'He does not yet know how to close up his kraal.'
(Ziervogel 1959: 153)

Shifts between these kinds of auxiliary constructions and from auxiliaries to bound NONDUMS are discussed in section 6 below.

4.1.3 not yet adverbs

Our main criterion for considering a NOT YET marker as an adverb is the absence of morphological marking. The data in grammatical descriptions are often too limited to allow us to determine whether the position of adverbs in the utterance is free or fixed. For example, a number of West-Central Bantu languages have cognate NOT YET adverbs. In the available Lobala example (19) the adverb figures before the verb, whereas in examples from Eboi [mdw], Loi [biz] and Ndoobo (20) it comes after the verb.

(19) Lobala (C.16) [loq]
Naíno si-w-e
still/yet[7] NEG.SBJ.1SG-die-PRF
'I am not yet dead.'
(Motingea 1990: 104)

---

[7] The form *naíno* is translated 'still' by Motingea. However, it is only found in examples with negation and rendered as 'not yet' in the idiomatic translations.

(20) Ndobo (C.312) [ndw]
　　 Bíyo tó-i-yéb-a　　　　　　naíno　　si-kambo sînâ　ká
　　 we　SBJ.2PL-NEG-know-FV　still/yet　7-case　　7.DEM　NEG
　　 'We do not yet know that case.'
　　 (Motingea 1990: 272)

Whether this variation is suggestive of synchronic variability of the position of the adverb or language change (from pre-verbal to post-verbal or the other way around) is, as yet, unclear. A similar case is attested in Comorian languages. Whereas the NOT YET adverb appears in pre-verbal position in the available examples from Ngazija (21) and Maore (22), the same adverb, *raha*, appears after the verb in Nzuani [wni], as shown in (23).

(21) Ngazija (G.44a) [zdj]
　　 Raha　ka-ri-ja-hul-a
　　 yet　　NEG-SBJ.2PL-NEG.PST-buy-FV
　　 'We haven't yet bought.'
　　 (Nurse & Hinnebusch 1993:710)

(22) Maore (G.44D) [swb]
　　 Rasa　ka-ra-nunu-a　　　ṯovi
　　 yet　　NEG-SBJ.1PL-buy-FV　10.banana
　　 'We haven't yet bought bananas.'
　　 (Rombi 1983:152)

(23) Nzuani (G.44b) [wni]
　　 Ka-wá-j-a　　　　　　rahá
　　 NEG-SBJ.3PL-come-FV　yet
　　 'They have not yet arrived.'
　　 (Ahmed-Chamanga 1992:182)

The data as found in grammars do not give a clear picture of the compatibility of NOT YET adverbs with different tense-aspect categories. Sometimes multiple examples demonstrate that there are no co-occurrence restrictions. This is clearly the case for the NOT YET adverb in Olunyaneka [nyk]. The adverb *nkhere* can combine with verbs in the perfect (24a), future (24b), imperative/subjunctive (24c), etc.

(24) Olunyaneka (R.13) [nyk]
　　 a. Nkhere　sa-ring-ile
　　　　Yet　　　NEG.PRF.SBJ.1SG-do-PRF
　　　　'I haven't done yet.'

b. *Nkhere hi-ma-ri*
   yet   NEG.SBJ.1SG-FUT-eat
   'I will not yet eat.'
c. *Nkhere u-ha-fet-e*
   yet   SBJ.2SG-NEG-pay-SBJV
   'Do not yet pay!'
   (Anonymous 1908: 26–27)

However, in some grammars, co-occurrence restrictions are clearly stated. In Luvale, for example, the pre-verbal adverb can only co-occur with a subjunctive.

(25) Luvale (K.14) [lue] (Horton 1949:162)
  Kanda va-manyis-e   ku-ly-a
  not_yet SBJ.3PL-finish-SBJV INF-eat-FV
  'They have not yet finished eating.'

One could argue that such a form is actually not free but rather bound, given this clear restriction to a specific context. We have chosen to include these and otherwise restricted forms in the group of adverbs (free forms) because of their invariable nature.

NOT YET adverbs may or may not co-occur with negative marking in the clause. When negative marking is present, the adverbs are very often not dedicated to the sense of 'not yet' but occur in affirmative contexts with meanings ranging from 'still' (26) to 'already' in (27) and 'first' in (28).

(26) Swahili (G.42) [swh]
  a. *Ni-po   bado hapa*
     SBJ.1SG-LOC.COP Still 16.DEM
     'I am still here.'
  b. *Bado   ha-ja-j-a*
     still/yet NEG.SBJ.3SG-PRF-come-FV
     'He has not yet come.'
     (Sacleux 1939: 85)

(27) Ruund (L.53) [rnd]
  a. *Na-yi-lej-in   kal*
     SBJ.1SG.PST-OBJ.3PL-tell-RECPST already
     'I've (already) told them.'

b. *Ù-lond-in-àp*   *kal*   *côm*
SBJ.2SG-speak-RECPST-NEG   already/yet   7.thing
'You haven't yet said a thing.'
(Nash 1992:759)

(28) Lega-Shabunda (D.25) [lea] (Botne 1994:31, Botne p.c.)
    a. *Boból-á*   *menkombo*   *rănga*
        soak-IMP   6.elephant_skin   First
        'Soak the elephant skins first.'
    b. *Nt-ú-ly-έ*   *rănga*
        NEG-SBJ.2SG-eat-SBJV   first/yet
        'Don't eat yet.'

NOT YET adverbs that do not co-occur with negation may or may not be dedicated to the expression of 'not yet'. As can be seen in (29), Swahili *bado* 'still' can be used in combination with an (affirmative) infinitive to express 'not yet'. In Holo (30), the pre-verbal adverb *kaanzi* appears to be dedicated to the expression of 'not yet'.

(29) Swahili (G.42) [swh]
     Bado   *ku-ju-a*
     still/yet   INF-know-FV
     'One does not yet know.'
     (Sacleux 1939: 85)

(30) Holo (L.12b) [hol] (Daeleman 2003:67) 30
     Kaanzi   *túu-dy-a*
     not_yet   SBJ.2PL-eat-FV
     'We have not eaten yet'

4.2 The occurrence of a negation marker in the NONDUM construction

This parameter is further specified along the following lines: (i) the presence or absence of a negator in the NONDUM construction; (ii) the position of the negator in the construction. In Table 3 below we present a summary of the issue about the presence or absence of a negation marker.

Table 3: Negation markers in NONDUM constructions.

	Number of constructions	%
Negation marker present and obligatory	116	73.42%
Negation marker present but optional	4	2.56%
No negation marker	18	11.39%
Unclear data	3	1.90%
No nondum	17	10.76%
Total	158	100%

As indicated in Table 3 above, most NONDUM constructions contain a negation marker, see, for instance, an example of such a construction where NONDUM is expressed by a bound element in (1) above, from Digo. In periphrastic constructions that contain an auxiliary and a lexical verb, the negator may appear on the auxiliary as in (31) from Yeyi or on the lexical verb as in Chingoni in (32).

(31) Yeyi (R.41) [yey]
Ba-pundi ka-ba-tjire ku-ly-a zu-luwa za-wo
2-children NEG-SBJ.3PL-(not_)yet_done.FANT INF-eat-FV 8-food 8-their
'The children have not yet eaten their food.'
(Seidel 2008: 439)

(32) Chingoni (N.12) [ngo]
Wa-kona na-ku-geg-a chi-lengu
SBJ.2SG-still NEG.INF-INF-carry-FV 7-basket
'You have not yet carried the basket.'
(Ngonyani 2003: 87)

There are also NONDUM constructions where the negation marker is optional. In our dataset, they are only 4, illustrated by data from Kagulu in (13) above. However, languages like Kagulu will be important for one of the diachronic hypotheses we suggest.

Finally, there are NONDUM constructions without any negation markers: 18 constructions. As indicated on the map, they are observed in languages mostly to the West and NONDUM is expressed by a free adverbial in 9 of them, that is, half of the constructions in this group (cf. (33) below for an example). There are also 6 periphrastic constructions that express NONDUM with no negator in the construction, illustrated by (11) from Manda. Finally, there are 3 constructions where NONDUM is a bound element and there is no negator as in (34) from Chopi. Note that *-sanga-* might be an erstwhile univerbation of a negative marker *-nga-* and another element but the data are inconclusive. Synchronically, *-sanga-* is a single morpheme.

(33) Luchazi (K.13) [lch] (Fleisch 2000: 344)
Mbati   likeye tele kandá   a-a-hét-a,   Ø-na-sal-a
Tortoise 3SG   still not_yet SBJ.3SG-PFV-reach-FV SBJ.3SG-ANT-stay-FV
ku-nima
17-back
'The tortoise, however, had not arrived yet. She remained behind on the way.'

(34) Chopi (S.61) [cce] (Smyth and Matthews 1902: 39)
ni-sanga-vona
1SG-NOND-see
'I have not yet seen.'

The discussion of the presence or absence of a negative marker in a NONDUM is important for understanding the structure of NONDUM constructions. However, it is also relevant for the formulation of hypotheses for their development. Specifically, the scope/kind of negation used in a periphrastic constructions appears especially important for formulating hypotheses for the evolution of NONDUM markers, cf. Table 7 below for relevant counts.

5 Functions/Semantics

5.1 Discussion of uses as observed in grammars and parallel texts

As stated in section 3.2, for a marker to be considered a NONDUM marker, it has to be used for the expression of the sense "not yet *situation*" where "situation" is typically expressed by some kind of predicate, be it verbal or non-verbal. Thus the NOT YET use is a defining and central one for these markers. In this section we discuss this sense in greater detail, with a special focus on speaker's or addressee's expectations for the realization of the predicated situation. We will also list other uses of NONDUM markers observed in grammars and in biblical texts.

The issue of whether expectations are part of the sense of NONDUM markers has been a point of disagreement in the literature so far. Comrie (1985: 54–55) sees any expectation about the future realization of the event as an implicature dependent on context and not as part of the sense of the not yet gram. Thus, in his treatment, NOT YET is a purely temporal category that relates a past and a current situation. Unlike Comrie, Schadeberg (2000) describes a NOT YET gram in terms of aspectual parameters and sees the possibility for the realization of the situation in the future as part of its meaning; this author also claims that the form denies the expectations of the addressee, not of the speaker. This latter view is, however, questioned by Nurse (2008: 166), who states that addressee's expectations may be part of certain contexts, though far from all, so they are to be viewed as an implicature, at best. The data in grammars that we examine typically consist of a few example sentences and are consequently highly insufficient to determine semantic and pragmatic details of NONDUM markers. Generally, information about this is better obtained from a questionnaire or texts. However, having a questionnaire filled out for a large amount of languages is practically impossible for a large-scale comparative study. We have a questionnaire filled out for a handful of languages. We also use data from parallel texts (translations of the New Testament) to highlight the issue of speaker's expectation in NONDUM markers.

Olsson (2013) introduces an important distinction for the analysis of expectations. Specifically, this author suggests to set apart expectations that stem from specific circumstances, *situational expectations*, and expectations which are based on broad, shared knowledge, often even unspoken assumptions that characterize a culture/society; the latter are dubbed *general expectations*.[8] Examples of general expectations include things such as: if you are at a certain age, you are supposed to be married; if you have been married for a while, the expectation is that you will have children. Both situational and general expectations are encountered with NONDUM markers in the New Testament texts. Apart from them, there are a number of other uses: (i) use of NONDUM in narrative to indicate the narrator who knows what lies ahead and chooses what to disclose. This is labeled here "omniscient knowledge"; (ii) temporal subordination or the sense 'before'; (iii) (near) future; (iv) surprise or counter-expectations; (v) 'never, ever' or emphatic negation; (vi) general negation marker. Due to space restrictions all senses listed for NONDUM markers are illustrated in the Appendix.

---

8 Another way to analyze general expectations is found in the work of Dahl & Wälchli (2016) who introduce the notion *natural development predicates* for situations/predications which clearly belong to a naturally occurring sequence.

Senses that are listed in grammars only include 'first', and 'just'. The Biblical text and grammars present somewhat different pictures of the semantic span of NONDUM markers. Senses that recur in both sources are those of 'before' and 'temporal subordination', 'never'/'ever' and 'general negation', examples can be found in the Appendix.

NONDUM markers also show polysemy with two other phasal polarity markers, STILL and ALREADY. Since this issue is important both for the semantic analysis of NONDUM markers and for the phasal polarity domain as a whole, it is allotted a separate section, cf. 5.2.

The uses identified here are also arranged on a semantic map, cf. 5.3.

5.2 Relation/polysemy with other phasal polarity markers, specifically STILL and ALREADY

In our data set there are 33 NONDUM constructions that show an identifiable relation to the construction meaning STILL (SITUATION); NONDUM constructions related to ALREADY observed in 16 constructions. Thus constructions related to STILL are clearly dominant. If we see this in terms of the semantic parameter of *coverage*, as suggested by Kramer (2018), then one and the same term is more often used to cover STILL and NOT YET; next in frequency come terms covering ALREADY and NOT YET. It is probably no surprise that we find no occurrences of the same term covering NOT YET and NO LONGER.

We can also observe different degrees of grammaticalization within constructions related to STILL and constructions related to ALREADY. We use correlations with the structural kinds of NONDUMS to gauge their degree of grammaticalization. Pertinent data are presented in Tables 4 and 5.

As the data in Tables 4 and 5 demonstrate, NONDUMS related to STILL are for the most part expressed by auxiliary constructions; conversely, NONDUMS related

Table 4: NONDUM constructions related to STILL.

STRUCTURAL TYPE	NUMBER OF CONSTRUCTIONS	%
Adverb	10	30.30%
Auxiliary	19	57.58%
Bound	4	12.12%
Total	33	100%

Table 5: NONDUM constructions related to ALREADY.

STRUCTURAL TYPE	NUMBER OF CONSTRUCTIONS	%
Adverb	4	25.00%
Auxiliary	4	25.00%
Auxiliary/Bound	1	6.25%
Bound	7	43.75%
Total	16	100%

to ALREADY appear to be mostly expressed by bound forms. This suggest that historically the forms related to ALREADY must be older, with greater degree of grammatical maturation.

A comparison with regard to negation in the NONDUM constructions reveals the following. NONDUMS related to STILL show (i) internal negation, that is STILL + NEG-VERB; (ii) conventionalization of negative inference STILL + VERB-ing > NOT YET VERB (iii) external negation, that is STILL-NOT (NEG STILL) VERB. In our current data set the three scenarios just outlined show very similar proportions: So it is impossible to determine whether any of them is dominant/preferred. However, if all periphrastic constructions are taken into account, external negation is the dominant option; internal or no negation are observed with constructions marked 'persistive', cf. section 6.1.2 below.

As regards NONDUMS related to ALREADY, in all instances where they are encoded by an auxiliary, we observe cases of external negation, that is, NEG ALREADY + VERB. Since most constructions related to ALREADY are cases of bound forms, the negator obviously applies to the entire form and its scope can be only discussed in diachronic terms.

5.3 Towards a semantic map of NONDUM markers

The sense for NONDUM markers as identified in grammars and in parallel texts can be arranged in semantic space, cf. Figure 1. Before we embark on the discussion of the semantic map suggested here, some general remarks are in order. There are different kinds of semantic maps. Van der Auwera (2013) makes a distinction between *connectedness maps* and *proximity maps*. On connectedness maps explicit links are shown between different senses and the adjacency of different senses is significant. Specifically, if a marker is used for two functions, then any function that comes in between them on the map has to be observed among its

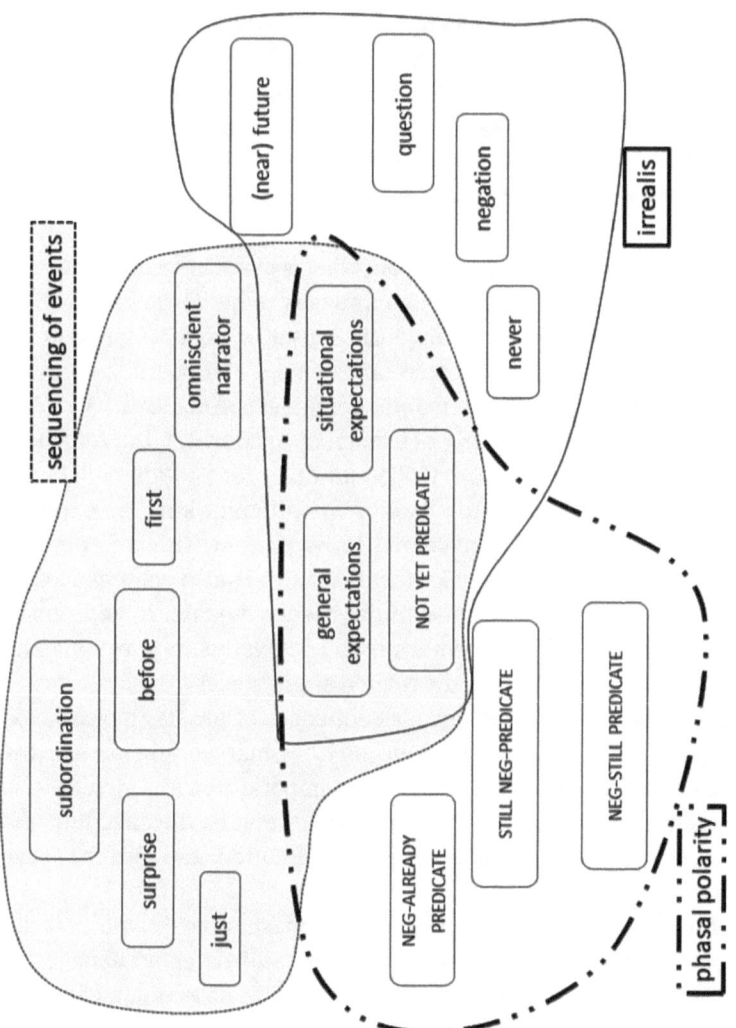

Figure 1: Semantic map for NONDUM markers.

possible uses as well. The links between different senses can also be given a diachronic interpretation when tracing the directionality of semantic change. Proximity maps, on the other hand, do not make explicit indications of connectedness between different senses or diachronic development. The semantic map presented for Bantu NONDUMS is a proximity map.

As indicated in Figure 1, NOT YET markers may have a variety of functions; all of them are exemplified in the Appendix. The functions listed on the map above are more numerous than is typically seen on other semantic maps, cf. for instance the semantic map of indefinite pronouns suggested by Haspelmath (1997).

In the map above, we strive to arrange the senses of NONDUM markers according to semantic cohesion. As indicated on the map, it is possible to group the different senses into three broad semantic domains: irrealis, cf. section 1 in the Appendix for examples, sequencing of events, cf. section 2 in the Appendix for examples and phasal polarity, cf. (11), (19) and (29) for NONDUMS related to STILL and (18) for a NONDUM related to already. The different kinds of expectations mentioned in 5.1 above are considered to be present with the 'not yet' sense in one way or another. The sense '(near) future' is also seen as closely related to speaker's expectations but also to the irrealis domain. In addition to '(near) future', the irrealis domain includes uses of NONDUMS in questions and also for various kinds of negation and the related sense 'never'.

NONDUMS are commonly used to encode sequences of events, typically expressed in complex clause structures where NONDUM markers are part of the subordinating construction. Uses related to the temporal domain include also the recent occurrence of a situation or 'just situation', that is, the encoding of a the very recent occurrence of an event, or 'surprise situation' and also the sense of 'omniscient narrator' as outlined above.

Finally, NONDUMS are clearly connected to the phasal domain, via both internal and external negation to the continuative STILL and via external negation to ALREADY, cf. also the discussion in section 5.2 above. This observation allows us to address the parameter of paradigmaticity, cf. Kramer (2018) above. Specifically, we can describe NONDUMS as being paradigmatically related to either STILL or ALREADY; this relation is language specific.

6 Diachronic hypotheses

In this section we present several possible paths of change involving two main processes (i) conventionalization of a negative inference and (ii) reanalysis of periphrastic constructions or lexical items with several different outcomes.

6.1 Conventionalization of a negative inference

Two kinds of sources take part in this path of change. First, specific negated tense-aspect categories can have 'not yet' as an inferential reading. Conventionalization of this inference gives rise to a NONDUM. Next, persistent periphrastic constructions of the type 'I am still writing this article' may lead to the negative inference 'I have not yet written the article'; a subsequent conventionalization of this negative inference leads to the evolution of a NONDUM sense.

6.1.1 Negation of tense-aspect categories

The recurring bound NONDUMS *-na-*, *-ka-*, *-la(a)-* and *-nga-* seem to be cognate with TA markers which are widespread in the Bantu domain. Some of them have even been (tentatively) reconstructed for Proto-Bantu (Nurse 2008). However, 'not yet' is in most cases not listed as a primary sense of these TA markers. Nurse (2008) cites the following senses for some of these markers on a synchronic level, cf. (35).

(35) Senses for some recurring bound NONDUMS (Nurse 2008: 240, 250–253)
    a. *-na-*:   'narrative, progressive/imperfective, *not yet*, future, past';
    b. *-ka-*:   'itive, narrative, (far) future, (far) past';
    c. *-la(a)-*: 'future, disjunctive, past, *not yet*';
    d. *-nga-*: 'conditional, potential, irrealis, may, would, could if/when, past, hortative, negative, future'.

It is our hypothesis that the NONDUM markers cognate with the morphemes listed above acquired the 'not yet' sense through conventionalization of a negative inference. Changes in the TA paradigm may even give lead to a dedicated NONDUM category without a correlative in the affirmative domain.

In our current dataset the bound NONDUM marker *-na-* is typically dedicated to the 'not yet' sense. It is encountered in no less than 19 bound constructions, so it is motivated to describe it as fairly frequent. It occurs almost exclusively in Eastern Bantu languages where *-na-* is known to express either imperfective/non-past or perfect/past (positive or negative) meanings, the latter meaning being prevalent in interior Eastern Bantu languages (Wald 1981, Nurse & Hinnebusch 1993: 408–409). Wald (1981: 144) argues that in many of these languages the use of *-na-* has "further deteriorated (through replacement by other markers) so that it is restricted to the negative perfect", a label he uses to refer to 'not yet/before' (Wald 1981: 143).

What follows is an outline of some of the comparative data relevant here. In languages like Chichewa (9a) above and Kamba (36a), -*na*- occurs in affirmative contexts expressing a perfect/recent past meaning. In combination with standard negative marking a negative perfect/recent past is expressed. Depending on context, that negated perfect/recent past may be interpreted as 'not yet VERB', as seen in (9b) for Chichewa, and in (36b) for Kamba. In Chichewa addition of the enclitic -*be* 'persistive' is needed to unambiguously express 'not yet' as in (10).

(36) Kamba (E.55) [kam]
    a. *nĩ-nĩ-naa-koot-ie*
       FOC-SBJ.1SG-PRF-pull-PFV
       'I pulled yesterday'
    b. *Tʊ-i-naa-siisy-a   valʊa*
       SBJ.2PL-NEG-PRF-look-FV 9.letter
       'We have not (yet) looked at the letter.'
       (Whiteley & Muli 1962: 51)

Thus, in languages like Chichewa and Kamba, the marker –*na*- is used in both the affirmative and in the negative domain but its senses are not always symmetric between the two domains. In fact, it should be pointed out that with the occurrence of the 'not yet' sense, an asymmetry starts to evolve. This asymmetry appears to be fully established in languages such as Zaramo and Matuumbi. In Zaramo, -*na* - also appears to be ambiguous between a perfect and a 'not yet' reading but the negative tense does not (any longer) correlate with an affirmative perfect.

(37) Zaramo (G.33) [zaj] (Nurse 2007)
    ha-tu-na-gul-a
    NEG-SBJ.2PL-ANT-buy-FV
    'We have not bought (yet).'

For Matuumbi, Odden (1996: 66) notes that in "Kimatuumbi negation is mostly accomplished syntactically by addition of the post-verbal element *lị* or *lịilị*. Still, the language has one tense employed in main clauses, the negative persistive (Meeussen 1967),[9] which has no positive counterpart."

---

9 The reference to Meeussen (1967) is present in the original text.

(38) Matuumbi (P.13) [mgw]
 nị-ná-kalaang-a   lị
 SBJ.1SG-NOND-fry-FV   NEG
 'I haven't yet fried.'
 (Odden 1996: 66)

In languages like Matuumbi (38) then, the NOT YET sense has been conventionalized giving rise to a dedicated bound NONDUM marker without any correlation in the affirmative domain. In Table 6 we summarize the hypothesized path of change.

Table 6: From negative inference to a NONDUM tense/marker.

	POSITIVE	NEGATIVE
Chichewa, Kamba	perfect/recent past	perfect/recent past (+ persistive), not yet
Zalamo	–	perfect, not yet
Matuumbi	–	not yet

Space restrictions do not allow us to discuss all bound markers in detail. However, similar developments can be shown for many of them. That is, we observe cases where one and the same morpheme appears with slightly different content in different languages. For instance, the post-initial prefix *-raa-*, cognate of *–la(a)-* in (35c), is associated with the 'not yet' sense in several languages. In Kuria, (39), *-raa-* in combination with negation expresses a negative anterior which in appropriate contexts can come to mean 'not yet VERB'. That is, in this language, the 'not yet' reading is inferred rather than being part of the sense of the gram. In Ha, (40), *-raa-* is a dedicated NONDUM marker. Again, conventionalization of a negative inference appears to have given rise to a new gram type.

(39) Kuria (E.43) [kuj] (Cammenga 2004: 288)
 te-ßa-raa-søm-a   hai
 NEG-SBJ.3PL-ANT-read-FV   NEG
 'They have not (yet) read (up to now)' / 'They have not read (just now)'
 (Cammenga 2004: 288)

(40) Ha (JD.66) [haq]
 nti-ba-ráa-ronk-a
 NEG-SBJ.3PL-NOND-receive-FV
 'They have not yet received.'
 (Harjula 2004: 103)

6.1.2 From persistive to 'not yet'

Our current dataset contains a number of periphrastic NONDUM constructions which include a persistive marker. This marker can be either an auxiliary which in affirmative contexts means 'still', as in Manda in (11) above, or it can be a copula marked with a persistive TA prefix, as in Bungu in (41) below.

(41) Bungu (F.25) [wun]
 To-ce-le *to-ta-kal-a*
 SBJ.2PL-PER-COP SBJ.2PL-NEG-buy-FV
 'We have not bought yet'
 (Nurse 2007)

Negation in this type of constructions is either external as in (42), internal as in (41) or absent as in (11).

(42) Fwe (K.402) [fwe]
 Ka-tu-shi-ní *ku-rí-bon-a*
 NEG-SBJ.2PL-PER-COP INF-REFL-marry-FV
 'We have not yet seen each other.'
 (Gunnink 2017: 504)

As was noted in Section 5.2 the three possibilities show similar proportions when the auxiliary in the periphrastic construction also means 'still'. However, if we look at all periphrastic constructions, not just those which involve 'still', it becomes clear that external negation is the dominant option in them, cf. Table 7.

Table 7: Negation in periphrastic constructions.

TYPE OF NEGATION	NUMBER OF CONSTRUCTIONS	%
External [NEG-AUX VERB]	35	66.04%
Internal [AUX NEG-VERB]	7	13.21%
No negation [AUX VERB]	7	13.21%
Varying [(NEG)-AUX (NEG)-VERB]	4	7.55%
Total	53	100%

As the counts in Table 7 demonstrate, the constructions with internal or no negation appear to form much smaller groups; together they amount to 14 constructions. However, it has to be pointed out that the greater part of them (13/14), are marked by a persistive marker as for instance, Ndali in (45) below. Persistive marking is as good as absent in the periphrastic constructions with external negation.[10] Thus, absence of negation or internal negation are closely associated with persistive marking in the construction. This is significant for the diachronic development we outline below.

We first consider constructions without negation like Manda in (11) above. They typically involve a non-finite main verb.[11] A plausible hypothesis proceeds as follows: the affirmative persistive construction expressing 'be still to do X' leads to a negative inference 'to not yet have done X'. The NONDUM meaning is the result of conventionalization of this negative inference, cf. also Güldemann 1996: 129–130, Güldemann 1998: 163 and Nurse 2008:148 for a very similar reasoning. In an analogous way the adverb *bado* 'still' can be used to express 'not yet' without additional negative marking, as seen in (26) from Swahili and (43) from Makwe.

(43) Makwe (P.231) [ymk] (Devos 2008:410)
 Méedi   ya-ni-púngúuk-a   akiíni báado   ku-púngúk-íiy-a
 6.water SBJ.6-PFV-decrease-FV but   still/yet INF-decrease-EXCE-FV
 'The tide has gone out but it has not gone out completely yet.'

One could further hypothesize that as the NONDUM sense becomes established, the construction becomes associated with negation and a negative marker may be introduced. This would explain the optionality of the negative marker in Kagulu (13) and the obligatory presence of a negative marker in an otherwise very similar construction in Fwe (42). Of course, and in line with the non-deterministic nature of grammaticalization processes, addition of negative marking is not a necessary byproduct of the conventionalization of the negative reading. Data from Bemba show morphologization of an erstwhile persistive

---

10 Fwe in (36) is the only language where NONDUM is encoded by a periphrastic construction with external negation and a persistive marking is present.
11 The only examples figuring a finite main verbs come from Nilamba [nim] and Kagulu. In Nilamba the copula with the persistive prefix is followed by a subjunctive main verb. In Kagulu the main verb is either finite (subjunctive) or non-finite (infinitive).

auxiliary (44a) into a bound nondum marker (44b) in the absence of a separate negative marker.

(44) Bemba (M.42) [bem] (Güldemann 1996:132, Güldemann 1998:164 taken form Givón 1969: 175)
    a. *n-ci-li   mbomb-a   sana*
       SBJ.1SG-PER-COP SBJ.1SG.work-PRS very
      'I still work a lot.'
    b. *ba-cilii-bomb-a*
       SBJ2-NOND-work-FV
      'They're not yet working, they're (still) about to work.'

We then turn to constructions with internal negation marked on either a finite verb form as shown in (41) from Bungu or on a non-finite main verb, cf. (32) from Chingoni. An additional example comes from Ndali in (45).

(45) Ndali (M.301) [ndh] (Botne 2008:119)
    liingá a-kaa-lí   a-t-oog-íte
    if   SBJ.3SG-PER-COP SBJ.3SG-NEG-wash-PFV
    'If she has not washed yet.'

The NONDUM sense may have evolved from a negative persistive construction referring to the persistent non-occurrence of an event: 'she [is] still she has not washed' which implies 'she has not washed yet'. Again, conventionalization of the negative implicature gives rise to the NONDUM meaning. Interestingly, Nyakyusa, a language closely related to Ndali and spoken some 50 kilometers East of it, has both types of constructions. Consider the data in (46).

(46) Nyakyusa (M.30) [nyy]
    Context
    A: How old is your child now?
    B: She is 2 years old.
    A: Is she talking?
    B: No, she NOT TALK [sentence translated by the consultant]
    a. *Himma, umwene a-kali   pa-ku-job-a*
       No   3SG   SBJ.3SG-PERS 16-INF-talk-FV
      'No, she does not talk yet.'

b. *Himma, umwene a-kali   a-ti-ku-job-a*
   No   3SG   SBJ.3SG-PERS SBJ.3SG-NEG-PRS-talk-FV[12]
   'No, she does not talk yet.'
   (Jeffy Mwakalinga, native speaker, Questionnaire data)

In (46a) the persistive auxiliary is followed by an infinitive with locative marking and the construction is without negation. In (46b), on the other hand, we observe internal negation as the persistive auxiliary is followed by a finite verb in the negative present perfective. Persohn (this volume) argues that the construction with internal negation 'still have not' is strongly preferred in counterfactual scenarios.

It should be noted that NONDUM auxiliaries show different degrees of transparency or lack thereof. This can be taken as a gauge for their maturation as gram types. For instance, the ones in Bemba (44), Ndali (45), and Nyakyusa (46) are fairly transparent univerbations between a persistive marker and a copula. However, the Kagulu data in (13) show complete loss of transparency and can consequently be regarded as more mature and more grammaticalized markers of the NOT YET sense.

6.2 Reanalysis of various periphrastic constructions

6.2.1 Foregrounding constructions and cyclical change

In this section we take a closer look at a particular periphrastic construction found in a number of Eastern Bantu languages. It consists of an auxiliary followed by the main verb, mostly an infinitive, sometimes a finite verb form. The auxiliary is marked for negation and can, at least on historical/comparative grounds, be analyzed as consisting of a bound tense marker and a dummy/quotative auxiliary, typically a reflex of *ti or *gàmb (Bastin *et al* 2002, Güldemann 2002, 2008, 2012). The bound marker is known as a dedicated NONDUM marker in the same language or, as is more often the case, in other Eastern Bantu languages. Data from Shangaji illustrate the first case: -*na*- can be used on the main verb (47) or on the auxiliary -*tthi* (48) to express 'not yet'.

---

[12] The example is reproduced exactly the consultant wrote it. We are aware of the fact that the form –*kali* is transcribed with a long /a/ in Persohn (2017, this volume); likewise, the vowels shown as /i/ /u/ by here are said to be of a more central quality by Persohn (2017), that is /ɪ/ and /ʊ/.

(47) Shangaji [nte] (P.312) [nte]
Si-náá-c-e   nkaása   ki-c-i   ńgíisi
NEG.SBJ.1SG-NOND-eat-FV 9.tortoise SBJ.1SG-eat-PFV 9.squid
'I have not eaten tortoise yet, I have eaten squid.'
(Devos *field notes*)

(48) Shangaji (P.312) [nte]
Si-ná-tthí   o-cuúw-a   wiírá mwanáanga
NEG.SBJ.1SG-NOND-QUOT INF-know-FV that child.POSS1SG
oo-khól-á   khaázi
SBJ.3SG.PST.IPFV-seize-FV 9.work
'I did not yet know that my child was working.'
(Devos *field notes*)

In line with Güldemann (2008: 479–508) we believe that the auxiliary *-tthi* in the periphrastic NONDUM construction in (48) has a 'foregrounding function': 'not yet' perfects are inherently focused and this pragmatic value is carried by the dummy auxiliary.

Interestingly, these foregrounding constructions apparently can instigate cyclical change (from bound prefix to auxiliary construction to bound prefix again) along the following lines. First, 'not yet' is expressed by a bound verb prefix. This stage is seen in (47) from Shangaji. An additional example is found in Kikae (49) where the bound NONDUM marker is derived from *-yìj-* 'come' (Nurse & Hinnebusch 1993, and cf. Section 6.2.2).

(49) Kikae [swh] G43c
basi   ha-li-ja-fik-a
5.bus NEG-SBJ5-NOND-arrive-FV
'The bus hasn't arrived yet.'
(Racine-Issa 2002: 121)

Yet another example comes from Mwani, where – at least following older descriptions of the language (cf. (54) below) – 'not yet' can be expressed through *-na-* in combination with standard negation, just as in Shangaji.

(50) Mwani (G.403) [wmw]
si-ná-mw-on-a
NEG.SBJ.1SG-NOND-OBJ.3SG-see-FV
'I haven't seen him yet.'
(Nurse & Hinnebusch 1993: 440)

Next, the 'not yet' sense is reinforced through the use of a foregrounding auxiliary, i.e. a dummy/quotative verb. Example (48) illustrates this for Shangaji. Another example is found in Sena, where the bound marker -*dza*-, cognate with -*ja*- in the Kikae example in (49), is used with the dummy/quotative auxiliary -*ti* (51). Note that, as far as Sena goes, we cannot ascertain whether -*dza*- was ever used as a NONDUM marker on its own. It is used in affirmative constructions to express 'already', as seen in (52). As soon as it co-occurs with the dummy/quotative auxiliary -*ti*, it expresses 'not yet' and, as shown in (53), negation can even be omitted.

(51) Sena (N.44) [seh]
anthu   nkha-dza-ti   ku-dz-a
2.person NEG.2SBJ-ALREADY/NOND-AUX INF-come-FV
'The people have not arrived yet.'
(Albano Alves 1939)

(52) Sena (S.44) [seh]
nd-a-dza-dy-a
SBJ.1SG-PST-ALREADY/NOND-eat-FV
'I have already eaten.'
(Nurse 2007)

(53) Sena (S.44) [seh]
(Ha-)nd-a-dza-ti   ku-dy-a
(NEG-)SBJ.1SG-PST-ALREADY/NOND-QUOT 15-eat-FV
'I have already eaten.'
(Nurse 2007)

More recent data from Mwani show that nowadays the expression of 'not yet' always involves a periphrastic construction in which the bound marker -*na*- has merged with -*amba*, a reflex of *gàmb*.

(54) Mwani (G.403) [wmw] (Devos *field notes*)
A-wa-náamba   ku-fik-a
NEG-SBJ.3PL-NOND   INF-arrive-FV
'They have not yet arrived.'

Finally, univerbation of the verb prefix and the dummy auxiliary followed by morphologization of the auxiliary construction may give rise to a 'new' bound verb prefix (cf. the first stage). This is exactly what appears to have happened in Digo. We suggest that the bound NONDUM -*dzangbwe*-, which we used to open the article in (1) above, results from the morphologization of a periphrastic construction. The periphrastic construction is still used in Digo and in closely related Mijikenda languages like Giryama, as evidenced in (55) and (56), respectively.

(55) Digo (E.73) [dig]
Kala si-dzangbwe ku-tayarish-a ma-somo
PST NEG.SBJ.1SG-NOND INF-prepare-FV 6-lesson
'I had not yet prepared the lessons.'
(Nicolle 2013: 157)

(56) Giryama (E.72a) [nyf]
Kha-dzangwe ku-hend-a
NEG.SBJ.3SG-NOND INF-do-FV
'He hasn't done yet.'
(Nurse & Hinnebusch 1993: 715)

It is very plausible, considering the data in (47) to (54), that the auxiliary is the result of merger between the bound marker -*dza*- and the dummy/quotative -*angbwe* (related to **gàmb*, Nurse & Hinnebusch 1993: 715).[13]

6.2.2 Reanalysis of periphrastic constructions with various other auxiliaries

As already outlined above, auxiliary constructions are a common source of bound TA prefixes in Bantu languages. Some of our less recurrent bound NONDUM

---

[13] The quotative apparently includes a passive suffix -*w*- (reflex of **-ʊ-/-ibʊ*- Schadeberg 2003:78). The same combination of quotative + passive extension is found in Mijikenda languages (cf. the Giryama example in 56) and in Swahili dialects like Vumba (G.42H) and Chifundi. We cannot, at present, explain the presence of the passive suffix.

Chifundi (G.42F)
muri kha-u-jambwa ku-gw-a
3.tree NEG-SBJ.3-NOND INF-fall-FV
'The tree has not yet fallen'
(Lambert 1958: 47)

markers clearly have an origin in an auxiliary verb. Such is the case for *-ja-* and related markers (*~-ya-~-dza-~-za-*), which all derive from the verb **-yìj-* 'come' and are typically dedicated to the sense of 'not yet' (Nurse & Hinnebusch 1993: 418). In the example from Pemba (57) the bound NONDUM marker *-ja-* combines with the lexical verb *-ja* 'come'.

(57) Pemba (G.43a)
Wa-geni wa-na-j-a?   **ha-wa-ja-j-a**   *ela*
2-guest SBJ.3PL-RECPST-come-FV NEG-SBJ.3PL-NOND-come-FV but
wa-ta-j-a
SBJ.3PL-FUT-come-FV
'Have the guests come? They have not yet come, but they will come.'
(Whiteley 1956: 16)

Note that initially post-initial *-ja-* might not have been a dedicated NONDUM marker. In Ngazija it marks a past negative tense. Addition of the adverb *raha* is needed to unambiguously refer to 'not yet' (21).[14]

(58) Ngazija (G.44a) [zdj]
ka-ri-ja-hul-a
NEG-SBJ.2PL-NEG.PST-buy-FV
'We didn't buy / We haven't bought.'
(Nurse & Hinnebusch 1993:710)

See also data from Kikae, Sena, Digo and Giryama in Section 6.2.1 above for cognates of Pemba and Ngazija *-ja-* and their development.

6.2.3 From auxiliary to adverb/particle?

In this section we tentatively suggest that some adverbs/particles in our current dataset are the outcome of reanalysis of an auxiliary construction. For instance, the adverb/particle *kíni* 'still/not yet' attested in the West Western Bantu languages Fumu (59) and also in Iyaa could have derived from an auxiliary. A similar form, *kírì* is attested in the West Western language Beembe, (60). In the

---

[14] The same might be true for Standard Swahili, where addition of the adverb *bado* is, at least for some speakers, necessary to unambiguously refer to 'not yet'(10b) (Bernander, p.c.).

latter language it is inflected for both subject and TA which leads us to hypothesize loss of inflectional marking In Fumu and Iyaa.[15]

(59) Fumu (B.72a) [ifm]
    Kíni   *á-y-ì*
    not_yet   SBJ.3SG-arrive-PFV
    'He hasn't arrived yet.'
    (Makouta-Mbuuku 1977: 476)

(60) Beembe (H.11) [beq]
    Bùtòtò *w-à kírì*   *kù-bút-à*   *pè*
    Butoto SBJ.3SG-PFV NOND INF-give.birth-FV NEG
    'Butoto has not yet given birth.'
    (Nsayi 1984: 155)

The dedicated adverb *kand* (or *kaanzi*) presents a similar puzzle. It is recurrent in South-Western Bantu languages. Horton (1949: 66) suggests that the phasal adverb *kánda* is derived from the verb *-kánda* 'forbid' which is also used to express negative commands. Although we are not certain about this particular etymology, which is not confirmed by data from closely related languages (except maybe for Lunda), we do think the adverb might ultimately derive from an auxiliary. One element pointing in this direction is the fact that *kanda* sometimes combines with the adverb expressing 'already' (61b) which normally always follows the inflected verb (61c), as shown by the examples from Holo.

(61) Holo (L.12b) [hol] (Daeleman 2003:45, 67)
    a. *kaanzi*   *túu-dy-a*
       not_yet   SBJ.2PL-eat-FV
       'We have not yet eaten.'
    b. *kaanzi* *Káadi*   *eez-a*
       not_yet Already SBJ.3SG.come-FV
       'He has not yet arrived.'
    c. *wáá-dy-á*   *káadi*
       SBJ.3SG.RECPST-eat-FV already
       'He has already eaten.'

---

[15] Although *-kíri* and *kíni* cannot be considered cognates on the basis of regular sound changes, we do consider them to be related seeing that similar variation between /r/ and /n/ is attested in other Bantu languages (Gunnink p.c.).

Another indication is that the Kaonde grammar by Broughall Woods (1924: 23) mentions two defective verbs involved in the expression of 'not yet': *-change* and *-kanda*. Both are inflected for subject and are followed by an infinitive. Unfortunately only examples with *-change* are given (62).

(62) Kaonde (L.41) [kqn]
 U-change kw-iy-a
 SBJ3SG-NOND INF-come-FV
 'He has not yet come.'
 (Broughall Woods 1924: 23)

The *kanda* forms in the other South-Western Bantu languages might thus have lost subject marking.[16] Such developments are probably best described as re-lexification, cf. Güldemann (2012) for a discussion of the notion and similar developments in other African languages. More examples of particles recruited from different parts of speech can be found in Güldemann (2003: 188–190).

6.3 Reanalysis and morphologization of lexical items

A remarkable change from adverb to bound NONDUM marker has been suggested for some Northern Swahili varieties. In Tikuu/Bajuni (63) and Mtang'ata (64) the expression of 'not yet' involves the bound post-initial markers *-yatasa-* and *-tasa-* which, following Sacleux (1941: 873), ultimately derive from merger and subsequent erosion of an auxiliary construction involving the verb *-dya* 'come' followed by the adverbial expression *hatta sasa* 'until now'.

(63) Tikuu/Bajuni (G.41)
 ha-ču-yaṯasa-mvon-a
 NEG-SBJ.2PL-NOND-OBJ.3SG-see-FV
 'We haven't seen him yet.'
 (Nurse & Hinnebusch 1993: 694)

---

[16] Note that some particles are also known to 'gain' subject marking and become a (defective) auxiliary in Bantu languages (cf. Güldemann 2002, 2008 & 2012 on the evolution of the manner deictic **ti* in Bantu languages). An evolution from adverb to (defective) verb thus also remains a possibility.

(64) Mtang'ata (G.42c)
 Ka-na-fik-a?　　　　　　kha-tasa-fik-a　　　　　　bado
 SBJ.3SG-RECPST-arrive-FV　NEG.SBJ3SG-NOND-arrive-FV　still
 'Has he arrived? Not yet!'
 (Whiteley 1956: 29)

The auxiliary in (65) from older Swahili poetry would be an example of an intermediary stage where the verb 'come' (-ya) has merged with an eroded form of the adverbial expression (tasa).

(65) Swahili (G.42) (Miehe 1979: 253)
 na-ye　u-kali　bikira　ha-yatasa　ku-olew-a
 and-she　SBJ1-still　1a.lady　NEG.SBJ1-NOND　INF-be.married-FV
 'She is still a young lady, she has not yet been married.'
 Kiamu, then, shows the same construction be it without the auxiliary -ya- (through erosion?).

(66) Kiamu (G.42a) (Sacleux 1941:873)
 Čakula　ha-ki-tasa　ku-w-a　tayari
 7.food　NEG-SBJ.7-NOND　INF-be-FV　ready
 'The food is not yet ready.'

7 Summary and concluding discussion

As stated in the beginning one of the main goals of this article has been to offer a thorough survey of NOT YET expressions as a lexico-grammatical feature in Bantu languages. We also used the collected data to formulate informed hypotheses about the evolution of this feature.

The following can be said about the synchronic distribution of NOT YET expressions.
- They are observed all over the Bantu area except for the North-Western parts (Forest Bantu).
- NOT YET expressions are encoded by a variety of means: bound markers, periphrastic/auxiliary constructions or adverbs.
- The distribution of these different encodings appears to be geographically conditioned. Bound nondums are very common in Bantu languages from Gabon and all across the continent to Kenya; likewise, bound nondums are also common in parts of Mozambique. Periphrastic NONDUMS are very common

in Eastern and Southern parts of Tanzania, and further across the Central and Southern parts of the Bantu area all the way to South Africa. Adverbs are common in the South-West and also on the Comoro Islands.
- The different encodings of NOT YET expressions were further analyzed with regard to (i) whether they are dedicated to the 'not yet' sense; (ii) whether there is a negation marker in the expression. The greater part of NONDUMS, bound, periphrastic or free are dedicated to the 'not yet' sense. About one-fifth of the bound NONDUMS are actually negated forms of specific tense-aspect categories, that is they are not dedicated to the not yet sense. However, these turn out to be important for at least one diachronic development, cf. 6.1.1 above and also our discussion below. A negation marker is present in about 70% of the identified NONDUM constructions.
- The parameters which turned out to be most relevant for periphrastic constructions are (i) the kind of verb which figures in the construction; (ii) the presence of a negation marker; (iii) the position/scope of the negation marker in the construction, e.g. whether negation is external or internal.
    - Five kinds of verbs are observed in periphrastic NOT YET constructions: auxiliaries dedicated to the not yet sense, copulas, quotative verbs and finally auxiliaries with phasal meanings such as 'still' and 'already'.
    - Most periphrastic constructions contain a negation marker. In the greater part of them, it is on the auxiliary, that is, we observe external negation. Internal negation or absence of negation are observed in about 30% of the periphrastic constructions, cf. Table 7 above. However, all of these constructions contain a persistive marker. Conversely, the externally negated periphrastic constructions do not contain a persistive marker. As we discussed in 6.1.2 above, when cast in a diachronic perspective, this turns out to be significant.
    - A number of NOT YET auxiliaries show polysemy or a clear diachronic connection with other phasal markers such as STILL and ALREADY. The ones related to STILL clearly outnumber those related to ALREADY. So in terms of Kramer's parameter of *coverage*, we can say that one and the same term is more often used to cover STILL and NOT YET than ALREADY and NOT YET, cf. also Van Baar (1997) for similar observations. Likewise, STILL and NOT YET are paradigmatically related more often than ALREADY and NOT YET.
- Semantically, NOT YET expressions are used to indicate a non-realized situation with possible expectations for its future realization. However, they also show a number of other uses which can be broadly grouped in the following semantic domains: (i) irrealis, which covers uses to indicate (near)

future, emphatic or plain negation and finally questions; (ii) temporal subordination which includes uses such as 'before', 'general temporal subordinator', 'first'; (iii) other uses that have to do with temporality, though not necessarily subordination include narration and selective unfolding of events, labeled above OMNISCIENT NARRATOR as well as 'just', 'surprise/counterexpectation' and finally (iv) the already discussed uses in the phasal domain.

Diachronically, NOT YET expressions appear to evolve via several different pathways. The main mechanisms involve (i) conventionalization of negative inference or (ii) reanalysis of various constructions. Similarly to the evolution of many other (lexico-)grammatical categories in Bantu languages, auxiliary constructions are, in many cases, the source for NONDUMS.

Conventionalization of negative inference is observed with two kinds of sources. First, negated tense-aspect categories can have 'not yet' as an inferential reading. Conventionalization of this inference gives rise to a NONDUM. Second, persistive periphrastic constructions of the type 'I am still writing this article' may lead to the negative inference 'I have not yet written the article'; a subsequent conventionalization of this negative inference leads to the evolution of a NONDUM sense. This pathway appears to include the creation of a phasal marker 'still' and further the attraction of a negative marker to the construction, first as an optional internal negation, that is, 'I STILL NOT-write article'. As the negative inference 'NOT YET write article' is conventionalized and becomes a sense, the negative marking becomes obligatory and we observe a change from a continuing activity to negated completive with expectations for the future realization of the negated situation.

Reanalysis of periphrastic constructions and their further morphologization is another pathway whereby NOT YET markers evolve. A particularly common source in this pathway appear to be periphrastic constructions that involve a quotative verb and a lexical element which has been/is reanalyzed as a phasal marker. In many cases the quotative verb and the lexical element merge into a single auxiliary, dedicated to the 'not yet' sense. Further morphologization/univerbation of the construction leads to a new bound NONDUM marker. Thus with such developments we also observe a cyclical change in the sense that an extant function continues to exist but is rendered by a new encoding. NOT YET markers can be also created via reanalysis and re-lexification of periphrastic constructions. Finally, reanalysis and morphologization of specific lexical items also lead to the creation of NOT YET expressions.

To address some of the concerns raised in previous studies: The following can be said with regard to NONDUMS relating to different phases of specific situations or being regarded more as temporal markers. NOT YET expressions are clearly related diachronically and in many cases, also synchronically, to the phasal domain. However, the more they mature as single, independent morphemes, the more they dissociate from the phasal domain and when fully established as units dedicated to the 'not yet' sense, they appear to end up in the temporal domain. As demonstrated above, bound NONDUMS are clearly associated with the post-initial position in the Bantu verbs, which is typically occupied by tense-aspect or negation markers.

As regards the issue of expectations being an implicature or part of the sense of NONDUMS: a diachronic perspective/analysis demonstrates quite clearly that conventionalization of a negative inference is the driving force for the emergences of many NOT YET expressions. It has to be said that in many cases, it is impossible to determine whether we are dealing with an implicature (the speaker's intentions) or an inference (what the addressee chooses to understand/hear). However, it is clear that the statement about the unrealization/non-completion of an action/situation also implies expectations about its future realization. So there is no doubt that implicature/inference are the original point of departure for the creation of NOT YET expressions. As they become consolidated as units of meaning, the expectations for the future realization of a non-realized situation become part of their sense.

The evolution of NONDUM markers as a lexico-grammatical category highlights the importance of inference for the creation of grammar in a very direct way. Thus, the creation of this category is pragmatically motivated and probably one of the best instantiations of the way the unsaid contributes to the evolution of grammatical structure. Given the clear areal patterns associated with the different structural expressions of NOT YET, e,g. bound forms everywhere except in the South-West, where adverbs are common and auxiliary constructions in the central parts, it is also fully possible that we are also dealing with contact-driven development.

Abbreviations

ANT	anterior	NEG	negation
APPL	applicative	NOND	nondum, not yet
COM	comitative	OBJ	object
COND	conditional	PER	persistive
COP	copula	PFV	perfective
DEM	demonstrative	PL	plural

EXCE	excessive	POSS	possessive
FANT	fossilized anterior	PRF	perfect
FOC	focus	PRS	present
FUT	future	PST	past
FV	final vowel	QUOT	quotative
IMP	imperative	RECPST	recent past
INC	inceptive	REFL	reflexive
INF	infinitive	SBJ	subject
IPFV	imperfective	SBJV	subjunctive
LOC	locative	SG	singular
NCL	noun classifier		

Appendix: Additional data

Unless otherwise indicated, the data presented below come from the parallel Bible corpus. We present the English version first and the translation to Digo [dig] after it. The digit introducing the verse indicates the specific part (Gospel) of the New Testament, then the chapter number and the number of the verse in that chapter. Only the text in bold has been glossed.

1 Uses of nondum markers in the domain of irrealis

1.1 General expectations

They are typically based on broad cultural knowledge, shared background. In the verse cited below the English version contains the notion 'unmarried man', which in Digo is rendered as a 'man not-yet-married'. The latter is presumably based on the assumption/expectation that at some point in life, people get married.

(1) Digo [dig] Parallel Bible Corpus, glossing by Steve Nicolle
46007032
My desire is to have you free from all anxiety and distressing care. **The unmarried man** is anxious about the things of the Lord – how he may please the Lord;
Enehu, nataka msikale na wasi-wasi. **Mutu ambaye kadzangbwelóla** nkudzishugulisha na kazi ya Bwana, yani jinsi ambavyo nkumhamira.

Mutu ambaye ka-dzangbwe-lóla
Man   rel   neg-not.yet-marry

1.2 Situational expectations

Expectations tied to specific circumstances. In this case, Jesus is disappointed that his disciples have not yet understood his message.

(2) Digo [dig] Parallel Bible Corpus, glossing by Steve Nicolle
46008007
Therefore **they have not yet understood** that (an) idol is nothing (lit. is. not thing), so they (habitually) see themselves (as) doing sin
Lakini si atu osi amanyao ukpweli huno. Anjina kala akabara kuvoya sanamu kama milungu yao. Hata achirya chakurya cholaviwa sadaka kpwa sanamu, anaona kala chakurya hicho chikalavirwa milungu. Kpwa vira **taadzangbwe** elewa kala sanamu si chitu, phahi nkudziona anahenda dambi.

ta-a-dzangbwe elewa
NEG-3PL-not.yet understand

1.3 (Near) future

(3) Digo [dig] Parallel Bible Corpus, glossing by Ljuba Veselinova
44018014
But when Paul was about to open his mouth to reply [. . .]
Kabla Paulo **kadzangbwegomba**, Galio wagomba achiamba, "Mwi Ayahudi, kama che mnalavya mashitaka kuhusu mahendo mai mai ama kosa iyi sana, ingekalato kukusikizani.

Ka-dzangbwe-gomb-a
NEG-NOND-answer-FV

1.4 General negation marker

(4) Digo [dig] Parallel Bible Corpus, glossing by Ljuba Veselinova
66003002
[...] I have not found a thing you have done [...]
Hebu lamukani ! Gafufuleni higo gosala ambago ga phephi na kufwa. Mana mahendo genu **tagadzangbwefikira** vira Mlungu wangu alondavyo.

ta-ga-dzangbwe-fikir-a
NEG-OBJ-NOND-find-FV

1.5 Never/emphatic negation

(5) Digo [dig] Parallel Bible Corpus, glossing by Ljuba Veselinova
51002001
for all who [like yourselves] have never seen or known me personally
Nalonda mmanye kukala nahenda bidii iwezekanavyo kukuteryani mwimwi afuasi a mudzi wa Kolosai, na hinyo ario mudzi wa Laodikia, na hata afuasi anjina osi ambao **sidzangbwekutana** nao

si-dzangbwe-kutana
NEG.1PL-NOND-get

1.6 Question

(6) Digo [dig] Parallel Bible Corpus, glossing by Ljuba Veselinova
58001013
Besides, to which of the angels has He ever said, Sit at My right hand [associated with Me in My royal dignity] till I make your enemies a stool for your feet?
Mlungu **kadzangbwemuambira** malaika yeyesi, "Sagala mkpwono wangu wa kulume, phatu pha ishima kulu sana, hadi nihende maaduigo gakugbwerere maguluni."

Ka-dzangbwe-mu-amb-ir-a
NEG-NOT YET-OBJ-say-?-FV

2 Uses of nondums in the domain of sequencing of events

2.1 Omniscient narrator

The narrator with omniscient knowledge, the one who knows what lies ahead and chooses how to dislose it to the readers/listerners.

(7) Digo [dig] Parallel Bible Corpus, glossing by Steve Nicolle
53002006
As you(pl) know that which prevents him that evil person right now **is that his time it has not yet arrived**. But his time when it comes you(pl) will know it clearly.

Kama mmanyavyo chimzuwiyacho yuya mui hipha sambi **ni vira waka- tiwe taudzangbwefika**. Ela wakatiwe uchifika andamanyikana wazi.

wakati-we ta-u-dzangbwe-fika
11.time-11.3SG.POSS NEG-11-not.yet-arrive

2.2 'before' and/or temporal subordination

(8) Digo [dig] Parallel Bible Corpus, glossing by Steve Nicolle
51002013
Before you (pl) had not yet believed in Jesus, you had died spiritually because of sin, and you were ruled by your human natures. But after trusting in him, God gave you(pl) new life. And he (also) forgave you all your sins

Hipho kala tamdzangbwemkuluphira Jesu, kala mkafwa chiroho kpwa sababu ya dambi, na kala mnatawalwa ni asili zenu za chibinadamu. Lakini bada ya kumkuluphira, Mlungu wakuphani maisha maphya. Naye wahusamehe dambi zehu zosi.

Hipho kala ta-m-dzangbwe-m-kuluphira Jesu,
COMP PAST.NEG-2PL-not.yet-3SG-trust.in

2.3 Surprise/counter-expectation

(9) Digo [dig] Parallel Bible Corpus, glossing by Steve Nicolle
41002012
And he arose at once and picked up the sleeping pad or mat and went out before them all, so that they were all amazed and recognized and praised and thanked God, saying, **We have never seen anything like this before**!
Saa iyo-iyo achiunuka, achihala chitandache na achiuka kuno atu osi anamlola. Na osi aangalala na achimtogola Mlungu, achiamba, "Mambo higa ! **Tahudzangbwegaona** bii."

Ta-hu dzangbwe-ga-on-a
NEG-1PL-NOT.YET-OBJ-see-FV

2.4 First

(10) Lega-Shabunda [lea] (Robert Botne, p.c.)
    a. *nt-ú-ly-ɛ́*   *rănga.*
       NEG-2S-eat-IMP yet
       'Don't eat yet.'
    b. *bɔbɔ́l-á*   *me-nkombo* *rănga*
       soak-FV 4-skin   first
       'Soak the elephant skins first.'

2.5 Just

(11) Luba-Kasai [lua] (Morrison 1906: 62)
    a. Wa-ku-anza ku-lua
       3SG-?-begin   INF-come
       'He has just come.'
    b. kena mu-anze   ku-lua
       ?   3SG.NEG-begin INF-come
       'He has not yet come.'

References

Ahmed-Chamanga, Mohamed. 1992. *Lexique comorien (shindzuani) français*. Paris: L'Harmattan.
Alves, Albano. 1939. *Gramática e dicionário da lèngua chisena*. Braga: Tipografia das Missões Franciscanas.
Anonymous. 1908. *Guia de conversação olunyaneka*. Huilla: Missões do distrito da Huilla.
Bastin, Yvonne, André Coupez, Evariste Mumba & Thilo C. Schadeberg. 2002. Bantu lexical reconstructions 3/Recontructions lexicales bantoues 3. Tervuren: Royal Museum for Central Africa.
Batibo, Herman. 1985. *Le Kesukuma (Langue Bantu de Tanzanie): Phonologie, Morphologie*. Recherche sur les civilisations Cahier 17. Paris: Éditions Recherche sur les Civilisations.
Bernander, Rasmus. 2017. *Grammar and grammaticalization in Manda. An analysis of the wider TAM domain in a Tanzanian Bantu language*. Gothenburg: University of Gothenburg.
Botne, Robert. 1994. *A Lega and English Dictionary with an Index to Proto-Bantu Roots*. East African Languages and Dialects 5, 3. Cologne: Köppe.
Botne, Robert. 2008. *A grammatical sketch of Chindali (Malawian variety)*. Philadelphia: American Philosophical Society.

Broughall Woods, Robert E. 1924. *A short introductory dictionary of the Kaonde language, with English-Kaonde appendix*. London: The Religious Tract Society.

Bybee, Joan, Revere Perkins & William Pagliuca. 1994. *The Evolution of Grammar*. Chicago: The University of Chicago Press.

Cammenga, Jelle. 2004. *Igikuria phonology and morphology: a Bantu language of South-West Kenya and North-West Tanzania*. Cologne: Köppe.

Chappell, Hilary & Alain Peyraube. 2016. A Typological Study of Negation in Sinitic Languages: Synchronic and Diachronic Views. *New Horizons in the Study of Chinese: Dialectology, Grammar, and Philology*, 483–534. Hong Kong: The Chinese University of Hong Kong.

Comrie, Bernard. 1985. *Tense*. Cambridge: Cambridge University Press.

Contini-Morava, Ellen. 1989. *Discourse Pragmatics and Semantic Categorization: The Case of Negation and Tense-aspect with Special Reference to Swahili*. Berlin & New York: Mouton de Gruyter.

Daeleman, Jan. 2003. *Notes grammaticales et lexique du Kiholu*, Munich: Lincom.

Dahl, Östen.; and Bernhard Wälchli. 2016. Perfects and iamitives: Two gram types in one grammatical space. *Letras de Hoje* 51. 325–348. doi:10.15448/1984-7726.2016.3.25454.

Devos, Maud. 2008. *A grammar of Makwe*. Munich: Lincom Europe.

Devos, Maud & Koen Bostoen. 2012. Bantu DO/SAY polysemy and the origins of a quotative in Shangaci. *Africana Linguistica* 1. 97–132.

Fleisch, Axel. 2000. *Lucazi grammar: a morphosemantic analysis*. Vol. 15. Grammatische Analysen afrikanischer Sprachen. Cologne: Köppe.

Givón, Talmy. 1969. *Studies in Chibemba and Bantu grammar*. Studies in African Linguistics, Suppl. 3. Los Angeles: University of California.

Grollemund, Rebecca, Simon Branford, Koen Bostoen, Andrew Meade, Chris Venditti & Mark Pagel. 2015. Bantu expansion shows that habitat alters the route and pace of human dispersals. *Proceedings of the National Academy of Sciences of the United States of America* 112 (43). 13296–13301.

Güldemann, Tom. 1996. *Verbalmorphologie und Nebenprädikation im Bantu: Eine Studie zur funktional motivierten Genese eines konjugationalen Subsystems*. Bochum: Universitätsverlag Dr. N. Brockmeyer.

Güldemann, Tom. 1998. The relation between imperfective and simultaneous taxis in Bantu. Late stages of grammaticalization. In Ines Fiedler, Catherine Griefenwo-Mewis & Brigitte Reineke (eds.), *Afrikanische Sprachen in Brennpunkt der Forschung*, 157–177. Cologne: Köppe.

Güldemann, Tom. 1999. The Genesis of Verbal Negation in Bantu and Its Dependency on Functional Features of Clause Types. In Jean-Marie Hombert and Larry M. Hyman (eds.), *Bantu Historical Linguistics*, 545–587. Stanford, CA: Center Study Language & Information.

Güldemann, Tom. 2002. When 'say' is not say: The functional versatility of the Bantu quotative marker ti with special reference to Shona. In Tom Güldemann and Manfred von Roncador (eds.), *Reported Discourse: A meeting ground for different linguistic domains*, 253287. Amsterdam & Philadelphia: John Benjamins.

Güldemann, Tom. 2003. Grammaticalization. In Derek Nurse & Gérard Philippson (eds.), *The Bantu languages*, 182–194. London & New York: Routledge.

Güldemann, Tom. 2008. *Quotative indexes in African languages: A synchronic and diachronic survey*. Berlin & New York: Mouton de Gruyter.

Güldemann, Tom. 2012. Relexicalization within grammatical constructions. In Johan van der Auwera & Jan Nuyts (eds.), *Grammaticalization and (inter)-subjectification*, 65–80. Brussels: Koninklijke Vlaamse Academie van België voor Wetenschappen en Kunsten.
Gunnink, Hilde. 2018. A grammar of Fwe. Ghent: Ghent University dissertation.
Harjula, Lotta. 2004. *The Ha Language of Tanzania: Grammar, text and vocabulary* Cologne: Köppe.
Haspelmath, Martin. 1997. *Indefinite Pronouns*. Oxford: Oxford University Press.
Heine, Bernd, Ulrike Claudi & Frederike Hünnemeyer. 1991. *Grammaticalization. A Conceptual Framework*. Chicago: The University of Chicago Press.
Horton, Alonzo E. 1949. *A grammar of Luvale*. Johannesburg: Witwatersrand University Press.
Johnson, Frederick. 1925. Notes on Kiniramba. *Bantu Studies* II. 167–192, 233–263.
Kiso, Andrea. 2012. Tense and aspect in Chichewa, Citumbuka and Cisena: A description and comparison of the tense-aspect systems in three southeastern Bantu languages. Stockholm: Stockholm University dissertation.
Kozinskij, Isaak Š. 1988. Resultative: results and discussion. In Vladimir P. Nedjalkov (ed.), *Typology of resultative constructions*, 497–525. Amsterdam & Philadelphia: John Benjamins.
Kramer, Raija. 2018. Position paper on Phasal Polarity expressions. Hamburg: University of Hamburg. https://www.aai.unihamburg.de/afrika/php2018/medien/position-paper-on-php.pdf.
Lambert, Harold Ernest. 1958. *Chi- Jomvu and Ki- Ngare, sub- dialects of the Mombasa Area*. (Studies in Swahili Dialect—III). Kampala: East African Swahili Committee.
Löfgren, Althea. 2019. Phasal Polarity in Bantu Languages: A typological study. Stockholm: Stockholm University BA thesis.
Makouta-Mboukou, Jean-Pierre. 1977. *Étude descriptive du fumu, dialecte teke de Ngamaba, Brazzaville*. Paris: Université de la Sorbonne Nouvelle (Paris 3).
Mateene, Christophe. 1992. *Essai de Grammaire du Kihunde*. Munster: LIT.
Meeussen, Achiel E. 1967. Bantu grammatical reconstructions. *Africana Linguistica* 3: 80–122.
Miehe, Gudrun. 1979. *Die Sprache der ältern Swahili-Dichtung (Phonologie une Morphologie)*. Marburger Studien zur Afrika- und Asienkunde, Serie A: Afrika 18. Berlin: Reimer.
Mithun, Marianne. 1988. Lexical Categories and the Evolution of Verbal Number. In Michael Hammond & Michael Noonan (eds.), *Theoretical Morphology*, 211–233. SanDiego: Academic Press.
Motingea Mangulu, Andre. 1990. *Parlers Riverains de l'entre Ubangi-Zaire: éléments de structure grammaticale*. Etudes Aequatoria 8. Bamanya: Centre Aequatoria.
Nash, Jay. 1992. Aspects of Ruwund Grammar. Urbana-Champaign: University of Illinois dissertation.
Ngonyani, Deo. 2003. *A Grammar of Chingoni*. Munich: LINCOM Europa.
Nicolle, Steve. 2013. *A grammar of Digo: a Bantu language of Kenya and Tanzania*. Dallas, TX: SIL International Publications in Linguistics.
Nsayi, Bernard. 1984. Approche du kibeembe: première et deuxième articulations. Paris : Université René Descartes Paris V-Sorbonne dissertation.
Nurse, Derek & Thomas J. Hinnebusch. 1993. *Swahili and Sabaki: A linguistic history*. Berkeley & Los Angeles: University of California Press.
Nurse, Derek. 2007. Bantu tense and aspect systems. http://www.ucs.mun.ca/~dnurse/ta bantu.html
Nurse, Derek. 2008. *Tense and Aspect in Bantu*. Oxford, New York: Oxford University Press.

Nurse, Derek & Gérard Philippson. 2003. *The Bantu Languages*. London: Routledge.
Odden, David. 1996. *The phonology and morphology of Kimatuumbi*. New York: Clarendon Press.
Olsson, Bruno. 2013. *Iamitives: Perfects in Southeast Asia and beyond*. Stockholm: Stockholm University MA thesis.
Persohn, Bastian. 2017. *The Verb in Nyakyusa: A focus on tense, aspect, and modality*. Berlin: Language Science Press. doi:10.5281/zenodo.926408. http://langsci-press.org/catalog/book/141.
Petzell, Malin. 2008. *The Kagulu language of Tanzania: grammar, text and vocabulary*. Cologne: Köppe.
Plungian, Vladimir. 1999. A typology of phasal meanings. In Werner Abraham & Leonid Kulikov (eds.), *Tense-Aspect, Transitivity and Causativity: Essays in honour of Vladimir Nedjalkov*, 311–322. Amsterdam & Philadelphia: John Benjamins.
Plungian, Vladimir. 2000. *Общая морфология: Введение в проблематику/Obshtaja morfologija. Vvedenie v problematiku*. Moskva: Editorial URSS.
Plungian, Vladimir. 2011. *Введение в грамматическую семантику: грамматические значения и грамматические системы языков мира*. Moskva: Российский государственный гуманитарный университет/RGGU.
Racine-Issa, Odile. 2002. description du kikae: Parler swahili du sud de zanzibar : Suivie de cinq contes. Leuven : Peeters Publishers.
Rombi, Marie-Françoise. 1983. *Le shimaore (île de Mayotte. Comores). Première approche d'un parler de la langue comorienne*. Paris: SELAF.
Sacleux, Charles. 1939–1941. *Dictionnaire swahili-français*, 2 vol. Paris: Université de Paris, Travaux et Mémoires de l'Institut d'Ethnologie.
Schadeberg, Thilo C. 2000. Schon – noch – nicht – mehr: das Unerwartete als grammatische Kategorie im Swahili. *Frankfurter afrikanische Blätter* 2. 1–15. G42.
Schadeberg, Thilo C. 2003. Derivation. In Derek Nurse and Gérard Philippson (eds.), *The Bantu languages*, 71–89. London & New York: Routledge.
Seidel, Frank. 2008. *A Grammar of Yeyi: A Bantu Language of Southern Africa*. Grammatical Analyses of African Languages 33. Cologne: Köppe.
Smyth, William E. & John Matthews. 1902. *A vocabulary with a short grammar of Xilenge: the language of the people commonly called Chopi, spoken on the east coast of Africa between the Limpopo River and Inhambane*. London: Society for Promoting Christian Knowledge (SPCK).
Van Baar, Tim. 1997. *Phasal Polarity*. Amsterdam: IFOTT.
van der Auwera, Johan. 1998. Phasal adverbials in the languages of Europe. In Johan van der Auwera and Dónall P. Ó Baoill (eds.), *Adverbial Constructions in the Languages of Europe*, 25–145. Berlin & New York: Mouton de Gruyter.
van der Auwera, Johan. 2013. Semantic maps, for synchronic and diachronic typology. In Anna Giacalone Ramat, Caterina Mauri & Piera Molinelli (eds.), *Synchrony and diachrony: a dynamic interface*, 153–176. Amsterdam: John Benjamins.
Veselinova, Ljuba. 2013. Lexicalized negative senses: a cross-linguistic study. Paper presented at the 10th Annual meeting of the Association of Linguistic Typology, University of Leipzig, Leipzig, 15–18 August.
Veselinova, Ljuba. 2017. Expectations shaping grammar: searching for the link between tense-aspect and negation. Paper presented at the 12th Annual meeting of the Association of Linguistic Typology, Australian National University, Canberra, 11–15 December.

Wälchli, Bernhard. 2016. Typology of heavy and light again or the eternal return of the same. *Studies in Language* 30. 69–113.
Wald, Benji. 1981. On the evolution of tense marker na in Eastern Bantu (summary). Studies in African linguistics, supplement 8. 142–144.
Whiteley, Wilfred Howell & Matthew G. Muli. 1962. *Practical Introduction to Kamba*. London: Oxford University Press.
Whiteley, Wilfred Howell. 1956. *Ki-Mtang'ata: A Dialect of the Mrima Coast*. Kampala: East African Swahili Committee.
Whiteley, Wilfred Howell, 1958. *The Dialects and Verse of Pemba: An Introduction*. Kampala: East African Swahili Committee.
Woodward, Herbert W. 1902. *Collections for a handbook of the Zigula language*. Msalabani: Universities' Mission, Magila, Deutsch-Ostafrika.
Ziervogel, Dirk. 1959. *A Grammar of Northern Transvaal Ndebele*. Pretoria: J. L. van Schaik Ltd.

Dmitry Idiatov
The historical relation between clause-final negation markers and phasal polarity expressions in Sub-Saharan Africa

1 Introduction

Clause-final negation markers are elements that may be used in the right periphery of negative verbal predications with clause scope negation but that do not appear in the corresponding positive predications and whose position is determined with respect to the clause as a whole.[1,2] A clear example of a clause-final negation marker is provided by the Gbaya Kara [gya][3] marker *ná* in (1) which is the sole marker of negation placed at the very end of the utterance, also following the subordinate clause which is not negated itself.

Gbaya Kara
(1) *ʔám gbɛ́   sàdī   hã̌   kóò   kɔ́m   ɲɔ́ŋ   ná*
    1SG kill\IPFV animal so.that wife POSS.1SG eat\IPFV NEG
    'I did not kill game to feed my wife (lit.: so that my wife eats).'
    (Roulon-Doko 2012: 5).

As I show in Idiatov (2018), clause-final negation markers form a clear areal pattern within Sub-Saharan Africa and typologically represent the most striking property of negation marking in Sub-Saharan Africa. On a world-wide scale, clause-final negation markers are much more unusual than post-verbal negation markers and multiple negation exponence, the other two features of negation

---

[1] This work is part of the projects LC2 "Areal phenomena in Northern Sub-Saharan Africa" and GL7 "Reconstruction, genealogy, typology and grammatical description in the world's two biggest phyla: Niger-Congo and Austronesian" of the Labex EFL (program "Investissements d'Avenir" overseen by the French National Research Agency, reference: ANR-10-LABX-0083). I would like to thank Mark Van de Velde for his comments on an earlier version of this paper. Last but not least, I am grateful to the referees and the editor for their comments.
[2] See Idiatov (2018:122–133) for a discussion of various aspects of this definition.
[3] The three-letter codes between square brackets after the name of language are ISO 639-3 language codes.

Dmitry Idiatov, LLACAN (CNRS – USPC/INALCO)

https://doi.org/10.1515/9783110646290-019

marking that have been shown to be common in Sub-Saharan Africa and whose distribution has also been argued to show a certain areal skewing (cf. Beyer 2009, Dryer 2009, Devos & van der Auwera 2013). As I argued elsewhere (Idiatov 2012a), clause-final negation markers in Sub-Saharan Africa tend to be characterized by a number of peculiarities in their morphosyntax and diachronic development that set them apart from similar markers elsewhere in the world. Some of these differences are more a matter of degree, yet some do seem to be more fundamental. For instance, clause-final negation markers in African languages are often associated with the presence of multiple negation exponence within a clause, most commonly double but sometimes also triple and occasionally quadruple. Clause-final negation markers in Africa often happen to be morphosyntactically deficient as compared to more canonical grammatical markers in being optional or lacking in some types of clauses as conditioned by the TAM value of the predicate of the clause, the subordination status of the clause, the associated information structural and speech act type values or the discourse type that the clause belongs to (cf. Idiatov 2015). Diachronically, clause-final negation markers in the area tend to be rather unstable and appear to be relatively easily borrowable (cf. Idiatov 2012b; 2015), unlike negators in other parts of the world but more like discourse markers, focus particles and phasal polarity expressions (cf. Matras 2009).

In Sub-Saharan African languages, phasal polarity expressions tend to occupy the same clause-final constructional slot as clause-final negation markers, the slot they equally tend to share with markers of illocutionary force, epistemic stance and various other intersubjective operators (or "monitoring-and-directing operators" in terms of Matras 2009: 99). In a given language, this competition for the slot on the right periphery of a clause may be resolved in different ways (cf. Idiatov 2018: 127–129). For instance, in Dzuun [dnn] the clause-final phasal polarity expression ŋē 'yet, still', as in (2), when combined with negation would usually be used without the default clause-final negation marker wáā, as in (3), in which case ŋē functions as a semantically specific clause-final negation marker occupying the clause-final negation marker slot of the default clause-final negation marker wáā. However, the two markers can also be used together, in which case the phasal polarity expression precedes the clause-final negation marker, as in (4) (cf. Idiatov 2015:256). In Bena-Yungur [yun], the clause-final phasal polarity expression kālkāl 'yet, still', as in (5), when combined with negation follows the clause-final negation marker ré, as in (6).

(2) Dzuun
dzîn nīī kéréū shē, tà kó nīī dón nī
child REL born.PFV today DEM and REL belly COP
ē náà ɲàn **ŋē**, twēī ráá wár'là bèé min
REFL mother in yet DEM POSS money.DEF go.IPFV where
'[The tax, as its amount was not settled,] where did the money go of a child that has been born today or of a child that is yet in his mother's belly?'
(Solomiac 2007: 571)

(3) kàbī mún kéréū, mún **nā** kèīn nèē tsūrū jà **ŋē**
since 1SG born.PFV 1SG NEG bird DEM like see yet
'Since I was born, I have never seen a bird like that (yet).'
(Solomiac 2007: 250)

(4) tɔ̀ y'á tàrà wó **nā** kéré **ŋē wāā**
DEM SBJV.3SG find 2SG NEG born yet NEG
'[The old man should tell you that there has been this intelligence like this], while you were not yet born.' (Solomiac 2007:252)

(5) Bena-Yungur
áyà kə̄ɓ mbú kə́fā **kālkāl**
3SG.AN.COP.at eating thing eaten still
'He is still eating (food).'

(6) ā **sóm** á kə̄ɓ mbú kə́fā **rē kálkāl**
3SG.AN COP.NEG at eating thing eaten NEG yet
'He is not eating (food) yet.'

Given that clause-final negation markers tend to occupy the same constructional slot as phasal polarity expressions in Sub-Saharan African languages and that strong semantic and often also formal links are known to exist between phasal polarity expressions and negation (cf. various semantic and typological accounts of phasal polarity expressions, such as Löbner 1989; van der Auwera 1993; van der Auwera 1998; Van Baar 1997), clause-final negation markers may be expected to often develop out of phasal polarity expressions. Yet, this expectation is not borne out by the data available on the development of clause-final negation markers in the languages of Sub-Saharan Africa (cf. Idiatov 2012a; 2012b; 2015; Devos & van der Auwera 2013). In fact, it seems to be a broader cross-linguistic generalization that phasal polarity expressions rarely develop into default negation markers. Thus, in some cases of a Jespersen cycle type of emergence of negation markers (cf. van der Auwera 2009), phasal polarity expressions are known to have been competing for the status of the new default negation marker and to have lost this competition to expressions of other semantics. For instance, in the history of French it was the minimizer *pas* '(not) a step' which has become generalized as the default negation marker rather than a phasal polarity expression such as *plus* '(not) anymore'.

This paper discusses a number of cases from Mande languages where clause-final negation markers may be argued to be historically related to phasal polarity expressions. In line with the general rarity of the change from phasal polarity expressions to default clause-final negation markers, when evolving into negation markers phasal polarity expressions tend to maintain the phasal element of their semantics or become restricted to certain TAM constructions (Section 2). In the rare cases where phasal polarity expressions may be argued to have evolved into default clause-final negation markers, this evolution is not direct and necessarily proceeds through the addition and foregrounding of a free-choice indefinite semantic component (such as 'not yet' > 'not ever yet, not on any occasion yet') and the development of the implicature of an intersubjective operator processing hearer-sided expectations and presuppositions (such as 'not ever yet, not on any occasion yet' > 'not at all, really not') (Section 3). Finally, I highlight the fact that we need to pay careful attention to the source semantics of the element that has both phasal polarity expressions and default clause-final negation markers as reflexes, as the phasal polarity expression uses may not be the source of the clause-final negation marker uses (Section 3).

2 The historical relation between phasal polarity expressions and non-default clause-final negation markers

In this section, I illustrate that in their evolution to negation markers, phasal polarity expressions tend to maintain the phasal element of their semantics, such as the non-default clause-final negation marker *ŋē* '(not) yet' in Dzuun [dnn] (2.1) or the emergent negative polarity item *bĭlen* 'anymore' in Bamana [bam] (2.2), or become restricted to certain TAM constructions, such as the Negative Perfect clause-final negation marker *ɓé* 'not yet' in Tura [neb] (2.3). I particularly highlight the intricate historical relations between the phasal polarity and negation uses of these markers.

2.1 Dzuun ŋē '(not) yet'

As I discuss in more detail in Idiatov (2015; 2018:125–127), Dzuun [dnn], a Western Mande language spoken in Burkina Faso and described by Solomiac (2007), has a default clause-final negation marker *wāā*, as in (7), which may be omitted under certain conditions. In addition, Dzuun has a number of clause-final negation markers that are semantically narrower than the default clause-final negation marker *wāā*, such as *dē* 'anymore, no more', *kūrāā* '(n)ever; (not) at all' and *ŋē* '(not) yet'. In fact, some of the forms that function as non-default clause-final negation markers can also occur in positive constructions, as the clause-final phasal polarity expression *ŋē* 'yet, still' in (2). Although semantically specific clause-final negation markers, such as *ŋē*, can be combined with the default clause-final negation marker *wāā*, as in (4), in which case *ŋē* functions as a phasal polarity expression rather than a clause-final negation marker, usually semantically specific clause-final negation markers replace the default clause-final negation marker *wāā*, as in (3). It is precisely the fact that *ŋē* occupies the clause-final negation marker slot of the default clause-final negation marker *wāā* that makes us analyze it in (3) as a semantically specific clause-final negation marker rather than a phasal polarity expression. From a theoretical perspective, semantically specific clause-final negation markers, such as Dzuun *ŋē*, are particularly interesting for two reasons. First, they illustrate a possibility that a marker need not be a dedicated negation marker (be intrinsically negative in its meaning) to be a clause-final negation marker. Second, they showcase that a particular way of expressing negation within a negation construction, such as the clause-final negation marking, may be obligatory while the negation markers themselves may be optional to various degrees (since all clause-final negation markers can replace each other, albeit sometimes with a change in propositional meaning). The situation in Dzuun is a somewhat more complicated version of what one finds in French, where the new default (post-verbal) negation marker *pas* can be replaced by a number of more specific negation markers, such as *jamais* '(n)ever' or *nulle part* 'nowhere', some of which can also be used in positive constructions, such as *si jamais* 'if ever' and *pour jamais* 'forever'.

(7) Dzuun
 à **náà** wù è tsî **wāā**
 3SG NEG.PST good 3SG.SBJV save NEG
 'It was not good that he be saved.'
 (Solomiac 2007: 270)

2.2 Bamana bĩlen 'anymore'

The marker *bĩlen* (*bèlen*, *bĩle*) in Bamana [bam], a Western Mande language spoken in Mali without a default clause-final negation marker, can be used in a number of constructions, where it functions as a phasal polarity expression 'anymore', repetition marker 'again', discourse marker 'though, yet, however, but', interjection 'still?!, now?!' (with a nuance of surprise and reproach)' or a negative conditional clause marker (cf. Bailleul 1996; Dumestre 1990; 2003:311; Vydrin & Tomchina 1999).[4] The last three uses (discourse marker, interjection and negative conditional marker) are marginal. The most common usage of *bĩlen* is in negative clauses as a clause-final phasal polarity expression with the meaning 'not anymore, no longer', as in (8). The negation is expressed by the negative TAM auxiliary or copula in the immediately post-subject slot.

(8) Bamana
 né **tɛ́** fàama yé **bĩlen**
 1SG.EMPH COP.NEG king.ART as anymore
 'I am not the king anymore.'
 (Dumestre 2003: 311)

Although in verbal clauses with non-present semantics, such as (9) and (10), *bĩlen* may also sometimes be interpreted as the negation of 'again', it is not a repetition marker, as explicitly stated by Dumestre (2003: 311) who decomposes the meaning of *bĩlen* in such examples as 'from this point forward' (French *désormais*) plus negation.[5]

(9) Bamana
 é **tɛ́** dénmisɛn bùgɔ **bĩlen**
 2SG.EMPH IPFV.NEG child.ART beat anymore
 'You will not beat the children anymore.'
 (Dumestre 2003: 311)

---

[4] All these uses are historically related and ultimately go back to the verb which has also resulted in the Bamana verb *bàli* '(vt) prevent, stop (from doing something); (vi) fail, not succeed (with something, in doing something)'. Both *bĩlen* and *bàli* are reflexes of the Intransitive form of the Proto Mande verb *bàdáŋ* 'bump into, stumble into, unexpectedly come across an obstacle'. A discussion of the details of the reconstruction goes beyond the scope of this paper.

[5] Presumably, because similarly to the French non-default negation marker *plus*, it should not be possible to use it in contexts like 'Today, the bus did not come on time again'.

(10) à   **má**   nà   **bïlen**
      3SG PFV.NEG come anymore
      'He did not come anymore.'
      (Bailleul 1996)

The free-choice indefinite component inherently present in the semantics of the negative clause-final phasal polarity expression *bïlen* 'not anymore' may sometimes become foregrounded at the expense of the phasal polarity component, viz. 'not (on any occasion) from the reference point forward' > 'not on any occasion, not at all (from the reference point forward)' > 'not on any occasion, not at all', as in (11).

(11) Bamana
     ù   **má**   sɔ̀n   kà   dòn   sánsara   kɔ́nɔ   **bïlen**
     3PL PFV.NEG   agree INF enter cage.ART in   on.any.occasion
     'They did not agree to enter the cage on any occasion.'
     (Vydrin & Tomchina 1999)

Like Dzuun *ŋē* (2.1), *bïlen* can also be occasionally used in positive clauses, as in (12), where it has the meaning 'again'. In this rare positive use, *bïlen* can not only be used in the clause-final slot, like its negative counterpart, but also in the operator slot immediately after the subject and before the TAM and polarity auxiliary, as in (13), or before the verb in predicative constructions without an auxiliary, as in (14). This operator slot also hosts *bïlen* in its use as a discourse marker and as a negative conditional marker. Finally, as a negative conditional marker *bïlen* can also itself occupy the TAM and polarity auxiliary slot.

(12) Bamana
     î   bɛ́   yàn   **bïlen!**
     2SG COP here again
     'You are again here!'
     (Vydrin & Tomchina 1999)

(13) kɔ̀nɔba   **bïlen** y'à   fɔ́ ...
     big.bird.ART again   PFV.TR=3SG   say
     'The big bird said again ...'
     (Dumestre 2003: 311)

(14) à **bìlen** bòli-la kà n'à fɔ́ à bámuso yé
 3SG again run-PFV.IT INF come=3SG say 3SG mother.ART to
 'She ran again to tell her mother about it.'
 (Vydrin & Tomchina 1999)

As a clause-final phasal polarity expression, *bìlen* 'anymore' can be characterized as an emergent negative polarity item, since the clause needs to be negative for *bìlen* to have its phasal polarity expression meaning 'anymore' and *bìlen* has a different meaning, 'again', when it is used in the same clause-final position in a positive clause. Moreover, *bìlen* as 'again' in positive clauses can equally occupy a different slot in the clause structure, viz. the post-subject operator slot. From a Mande comparative perspective, the emergence of such a negative polarity item is noteworthy, since generally Mande languages have only few negative polarity items, such as the Bamana determiner *sî* 'none' and the clause-final marker *féwú* 'absolutely not, no way'. Another interesting point with respect to the clause-final phasal polarity expression *bìlen* as an emergent negative polarity item is that it illustrates how the foregrounding of the free-choice indefinite semantic component of a phasal polarity expression may lead to the development of the implicature of an intersubjective operator, such as 'not at all (contrary to what you may have expected)'. This kind of semantic evolution may eventually result in a clause-final negation marker. Thus, in a number of Southeastern Bamana dialects that have default clause-final negation markers, these markers have evolved through a similar semantic change from a frequency adverbial 'once, at one time, at a certain moment' (cf. Idiatov 2012b).

2.3 Tura ɓé 'not yet'

Tura [neb], a Southeastern Mande language spoken in Côte d'Ivoire and described by Bearth (1971), does not have a default clause-final negation marker but it has a non-default clause-final negation marker *ɓé* that is part of the Negative Perfect construction, as in (15–17).

(15) Tura
 ě lő=ó wó-ó, **ɔ̀ó** nṹ **ɓé**
 3SG.CONJ go=FOC do\PFV-PFV 3SG.PFV.NEG come yet
 'Since he left, he has not come back.'
 (Bearth 1971:283)

(16) ě   wàà=á   zě, à   ɓɔ̌ɔ́=ɔ́   ǒó   mɔ́ ɓê
     3SG.CONJ arrive\PFV-PFV here 3SG duration=FOC 3SG.PFV.NEG last yet
     'Since he arrived here, not much time has passed.'

(17) mɔ̌ɔ́   à̰ yé dó   ɓê
     1SG.PFV.NEG 3SG see once yet
     'I have never seen him.' (lit.: 'I have not seen him once')

Although ɓê can be glossed as 'not yet', I do not use 'yet' in the translation because ɓê is obligatory in the Negative Perfect construction. The presence of the clause-final negation marker ɓê is the only thing that distinguishes the Negative Perfect construction from the Negative Perfective construction, as in (18) that can be compared to (17).

(18) Tura
     mɔ̌ɔ́   à̰ yé
     1SG.PFV.NEG 3SG see
     'I did not see him.' (e.g., as an answer to the question 'Did you see him at the market?') (Negative Perfective)

Therefore, one might also wish to say that ɓê is a phasal polarity expression and at the same time a negative polarity item restricted to the Negative Perfective construction, where its presence just implies the negative perfect meaning. However, I prefer the analysis of ɓê as a clause-final negation marker of a dedicated Negative Perfect construction because in the positive polarity, the Perfect and the Perfective constructions are clearly two different constructions. Thus, the Positive Perfect construction, as in (19), differs from the Positive Perfective construction, as in (20), by the TAM auxiliary used (fused with pronominal subject indexes) and the absence of additional TAM marking on the verb itself.

(19) Tura
     ŋ́ nɛ̄=ḛ̌   lő bŏi̯
     1SG father=PRF go in.the.field
     'My father has gone to the field.' (Positive Perfect)

(20) ŋ́ nɛ̄ kḛ̌ ló-ó   bŏi̯
     1SG father COP go\PFV-PFV in.the.field
     'My father went to the field.' (Positive Perfective)

Outside of the Negative Perfect construction, ɓé is used as an adverbial with existential semantics, usually with the copula or the verb tő 'be(come)', as in (21–23).

(21) Tura
pónĕ kĕ **ɓé**
something COP EXIST
'There is something.'
(Bearth 1971: 205)

(22) pónĕ ằá **ɓé**
something 3SG.COP.NEG EXIST
'There is nothing.'
(Bearth 1971: 205)

(23) gbɛ̋ɛ́=ɛ̋ **ɓê**, ằ lè=ȅ gîé=é wó gwɛ̀ɛ̂ɪ lè gɔ̋
dog=COP EXIST 3SG FOC=IPFV.FOC pass=FOC do baboon FOC at
zà é
though this
'Here you are, it's the dog though who wins over the baboon.' (lit.: 'There is the dog, it is it who wins over the baboon, though, here you are.')
(Bearth 1971: 381)

This strongly suggests that, originally, ɓé is not a phasal polarity expression, but some kind of deictic adverbial. That is, ɓé did not become confined to the Negative Perfective construction as a phasal polarity expression with this combination being later conventionalized as the Negative Perfect construction. What is more likely to have happened is that ɓé first developed its phasal polarity semantics when used in the Negative Perfective construction with the verb tő 'be(come)', then its phasal polarity use became available for other verbs in the Negative Perfective construction and only after that the combination of ɓé and the Negative Perfective became conventionalized as the negative counterpart of the Positive Perfect construction.

3 The historical relation between phasal polarity expressions and default clause-final negation markers: intersubjective implicatures as the middleman and the importance of the source meanings

In this section, I consider the two Mande examples where earlier phasal polarity expressions can be argued to have resulted in default clause-final negation markers. Both examples come from Bobo and Samogo languages, two distantly related Western Mande groups spoken in the same general area in the west of Burkina Faso and the bordering regions of southeastern Mali. The first example (Section 3.1) is represented by the reflexes of the etymon *kè in a number of Samogo languages, viz. the clause-final negation markers of the Samogo languages Jo [jow] kĭ, Seen [sos] ŋè and presumably the Kpeen [cpo] nè or nĭ. The same etymon *kè also resulted in the Dzuun non-default clause-final negation marker and phasal polarity expression ŋē 'yet, still' already discussed in Section 2.1 (also see examples 2–4 in Section 1). The second example (Section 3.2) comprises a number of reflexes of the etymon *kútà-Cá,[6] viz. the default clause-final negation markers of Northern Bobo [bbo] kɔ́, Sya Southern Bobo [bwq] gā ~ gá, the optional clause-final negation marker kpá of Benge Southern Bobo [bwq], the default clause-final negation markers of the Samogo languages Dzuun [dnn] wāā, Ban [bxw] mā and Kpaan [dnn] ũ ~ w̃, and the Dzuun non-default clause-final negation marker kūrāā '(n)ever; (not) at all'. I discuss both cases in more detail in (Idiatov 2015), where I focus on the formal reconstruction of the two etymons and where I particularly highlight the complex history of parallel evolution and borrowing of these clause-final negation markers in Bobo and Samogo languages. Here, I will focus on the details of their semantic evolution, in particular on the details of the historical relations between their uses as phasal polarity expressions and their uses as clause-final negation markers. The main generalization is that the evolution from a phasal polarity expression to a default clause-final negation marker has proceeded through the addition and foregrounding of a free-choice indefinite semantic component. Furthermore, in the case of *kè its original meaning as an indefinite determiner 'some, a certain' suggests that it its

---

6 In Idiatov (2015), I reconstruct this etymon as *kƱDà(C)á. The revised reconstruction *kútà-Cá presented here does away with the underspecified first vowel and second consonant, introduces a morpheme boundary before the final syllable and confirms the presence of the third consonant, whose identity remains unknown.

evolution into a default clause-final negation marker need not have proceeded through a phasal polarity expression stage.

3.1 Reflexes of *kè

The default clause-final negation markers of the Samogo languages Jo [jow] *kǐ*, Seen [sos] *ŋè* and presumably Kpeen [cpo] *nè* or *nǐ* are all related to the Dzuun non-default clause-final negation marker and phasal polarity expression *ŋē* 'yet, still'. Example (3), reproduced here as (24), shows how a clause-final negation marker meaning 'yet' may acquire an additional overtone of universal quantification, as 'ever yet', 'never (yet)'.

(24) Dzuun
 kàbī́ mún kéréū, mún **nā** kȅin nèē̄ tsūrū jà **ŋē**
 since 1SG born.PFV 1SG NEG bird DEM like see yet
 'Since I was born, I have never seen a bird like that.' (lit.: 'Since I was born, I have not seen a bird like that yet.')
 (Solomiac 2007:250)

Example (24) contrasts with the Tura example (17) where the adverb *dó* 'once' (meaning 'not once' under negation) is used to add the same universal quantification meaning. From here, the temporal directionality inherent to the meaning 'yet, still' of *ŋē* may weaken, especially if the marker becomes confined to negative predications, to come to mean plainly 'never'. A further foregrounding of the free-choice indefinite component present in the semantics of 'never (yet)' at the expense of its temporal semantics to something like '(not) at all' is easy to conceive, viz. 'not (on any occasion) before the reference point' > 'not on any occasion, not at all (before the reference point)' > 'not on any occasion, not at all'. In this respect, recall the possibility of a similar foregrounding of the free-choice indefinite component in the semantics of the Bamana negative clause-final phasal polarity expression *bílen* 'not anymore' in (11). Also compare several other Dzuun non-default clause-final negation markers, such as *fyēū* '(n)ever; (not) at all' and *kūrāā* '(n)ever; (not) at all', that can equally express both meanings. In addition to the restriction of the marker in question to negative predications, this addition of a free-choice indefinite semantic component as a possible implicature and later foregrounding and conventionalization of the latter at the expense of the phasal polarity component are necessary steps for the evolution of this marker into a default clause-final negation marker.

Comparative Mande data show that the original meaning of the etymon *kè is an indefinite determiner 'some, a certain, any'. Thus, among its cognates across Mande we find the Tura [neb] determiner ké 'a certain, some; a little; another; again',[7] its adverbial derivate ké-wó 'again; (not) anymore', the Gban [ggu] determiner ké 'another, again', the Bokobaru [bus] determiner kē 'a certain; any; none, (not) any'. The semantic evolution starting with 'a certain, some' proceeding through 'another' to, as a verbal modifier, 'again', and subsequently to a phasal polarity expression 'still' is not particularly striking. No more striking is the subsequent shift within the domain of phasal polarity expressions from 'still' to 'not yet', through the mechanism of "internal negation" (viz. 'still (not P)' = 'not yet P'), and from 'still' to 'not anymore', through the mechanism of "external negation" (viz. 'not (still P)' = 'not anymore P') (cf. the Duality Hypothesis of Löbner 1989 describing the semantic relations between various phasal polarity expressions in terms of internal and external negation). However, the origin of *kè in an indefinite determiner 'some, a certain, any' also makes conceivable another path towards a default clause-final negation marker through a minimizer and without passing through the stage of a phasal polarity expression, viz. 'some, a certain' > 'a bit, a little' > '(not) a bit' > '(not) at all'. Both paths are equally plausible. Thus, the history of *kè highlights the fact that we need to pay careful attention to the source semantics of the element that has both phasal polarity expressions and default clause-final negation markers as reflexes, as the phasal polarity expression uses may not be the source of the clause-final negation marker uses.

3.2 Reflexes of *kútà-Cá

The default clause-final negation markers of Northern Bobo [bbo] kɔ̄, Sya Southern Bobo [bwq] gā ~ gá, the optional clause-final negation marker kpá of Benge Southern Bobo [bwq], the default clause-final negation markers of the Samogo languages Dzuun [dnn] wāā, Ban [bxw] mā and Kpaan [dnn] ũ ~ w̃, and the Dzuun [dnn] non-default clause-final negation marker kūrāā '(n)ever; (not) at all' can all be argued to be reflexes of the etymon *kútà-Cá. As I argue in (Idiatov 2015), the Dzuun non-default clause-final negation marker kūrāā '(n)ever; (not) at all' is the direct reflex of *kútà-Cá, while the default clause-final

---

[7] This determiner may have the meaning 'again' when it modifies a nominalized verb in a construction with a light verb wó 'do', viz. something like 'do another going' meaning 'go again'. In the same construction, this determiner may also have an indefinite quantifying meaning, viz. something like 'do some, a bit of going' meaning 'go a bit'.

negation markers of Dzuun, Kpaan and Ban are only indirect reflexes resulting from a lateral transfer of the Bobo clause-final negation marker, which expanded an already rich system of semantically more specific clause-final negation markers in these Samogo languages. The initial part *kútà is originally a modifier 'new, next, recent', in its adverbial use meaning 'anew, again'. Thus, among its cognates across Mande we find the Bamana adjective kúrá 'new, next, recent' (corresponding to Mandinka [mnk] kútá), also as part of the adverb kó-kúrá 'again' (lit. 'matter new'), the Bamana expressive adverb kúdáyî 'forever; definitely; (not) forever, never again', Susu [sus] kɔ̀rɛ́ 'henceforth, from now/then on; (not) anymore, never', and the Tige Bozo [boz] adverb or operator xua 'again; (not) again; (not) anymore'. The final part *-Cà must be an adverbial marker, most likely sourced from a postposition or a light verb.[8]

Given the original meaning 'new, next, recent', we can be much more sure than in the case of *kè discussed in 3.1 that the semantic evolution of this etymon to a default clause-final negation marker has proceeded through a phasal polarity expression stage. However, like in the case of the phasal polarity expression-scenario for the evolution of *kè into a default clause-final negation marker, the phasal polarity expression stage in the evolution of *kútà-Cá towards a default clause-final negation marker must also have proceeded through the addition of a free-choice indefinite semantic component as a possible implicature and later foregrounding and conventionalization of the latter at the expense of the phasal polarity component. This later evolution is exemplified by the Dzuun non-default clause-final negation marker kūrāā '(n)ever; (not) at all'. The proposed semantic development of *kútà-Cá can be summarized as follows (focusing on the use of this marker in negative predications): 'new, recent, next' > 'anew, again' > 'again; still' > (through the mechanism of "external negation" of 'still') '(not) anymore' > 'not (on any occasion) from the reference point forward' > 'not on any occasion, not at all (from the reference point forward)' > 'not on any occasion, not at all' > clause-final negation marker.

4 Conclusions

Although in Sub-Saharan African languages clause-final negation markers tend to occupy the same constructional slot as phasal polarity expressions and strong

---

8 Thus, compare Tura ké-wó 'again; (not) anymore', the adverbial derivate of the determiner ké 'a certain, some; a little; another; again' mentioned in Section 3.1, where the adverbial marker goes back to the light verb wó '(vt) do; (vi) happen'.

semantic and often also formal links are known to exist between phasal polarity expressions and negation, phasal polarity expressions rarely develop into default clause-final negation markers. As I have argued using the example of a number of Mande languages, in those rare cases when phasal polarity expressions do develop into default clause-final negation markers, this evolution necessarily proceeds through a number of intermediate steps (Section 3). It begins with the addition of a free-choice indefinite semantic component as a possible implicature. This implicature is later foregrounded and conventionalized at the expense of the phasal polarity component. For instance, a phasal polarity expression such as 'not yet, not before the reference point' by preference used in negative predications may be added a free-choice indefinite semantic component as a possible implicature to mean 'not (on any occasion) before the reference point' (i.e. 'never yet'). This implicature may later be foregrounded at the expense of the phasal polarity component resulting in 'not on any occasion, not at all (before the reference point)' and finally conventionalized as 'not on any occasion, not at all' with the loss of the phasal polarity component. On this last stage before being conventionalized as a default clause-final negation marker, i.e. when these markers are generally glossed as 'not at all', they effectively become integrated in the paradigm of clause-final intersubjective operators processing hearer-sided expectations and presuppositions ("monitoring-and-directing operators" in terms of Matras 2009: 99), particularly common in the languages of Sub-Saharan Africa, especially in its northern part. Most commonly, this integration is manifested by the competition for the clause-final slot between clause-final negation markers and various other intersubjective operators, as briefly illustrated in Section 1 (see also Idiatov 2015: 242–245 for an illustration of some less trivial manifestations of this integration in Dzuun). Finally, I draw attention to the fact that when considering an apparent relationship between a phasal polarity expression and a default clause-final negation marker in a given language, we need to pay careful attention to the source semantics of the element that has both phasal polarity expressions and default clause-final negation markers as reflexes, as the phasal polarity expression uses may not be the source of the clause-final negation marker uses (Section 3.1).

Another type of historical relations between phasal polarity expressions and clause-final negation markers that I illustrated in the paper with the help of Mande data is the possibility of an evolution of phasal polarity expressions into non-default clause-final negation markers (Section 2). The historical relations between the phasal polarity and negation uses of a given marker can be rather intricate, but the main generalization is that when evolving into negation markers phasal polarity expressions tend to maintain the phasal element of their semantics or become restricted to certain TAM constructions.

Abbreviations

AN	animate	NEG	negation
ART	article	PFV	perfective
COP	copula	POSS	possessive
CONJ	conjoined	PRF	perfect
DEM	demonstrative	PST	past
EMPH	emphatic	REFL	reflexive
EXIST	existential	REL	relative
FOC	focus	SG	singular
INF	infinitive	SBJV	subjunctive
IPFV	imperfective	TAM	tense-aspect-modality
IT	intransitive	TR	transitive

Bibliographic references

Bailleul, Charles. 1996. *Dictionnaire bambara-français*. Bamako: Éditions Donniya.

Bearth, Thomas. 1971. *L'énoncé toura (Côte d'Ivoire)*. Norman: Summer Institute of Linguistics, University of Oklahoma.

Beyer, Klaus. 2009. Double negation marking: A case of contact-induced grammaticalization in West-Africa? In Norbert Cyffer, Erwin Ebermann & Georg Ziegelmeyer (eds.), *Negation patterns in West African languages and beyond*, 205–222. Amsterdam: John Benjamins.

Devos, Maud & Johan van der Auwera. 2013. Jespersen Cycles in Bantu: double and triple negation. *Journal of African Languages and Linguistics* 34 (2). 205–274.

Dryer, Matthew S. 2009. Negation patterns in West African languages and beyond. In Norbert Cyffer, Erwin Ebermann & Georg Ziegelmeyer (eds.), *Verb-object-negative order in Central Africa*, 307–362. Amsterdam: John Benjamins.

Dumestre, Gérard. 1990. Notes sur le morphème de l'hypothétique *bilen* en bambara. *Mandenkan* 20. 41–46.

Dumestre, Gérard. 2003. *Grammaire fondamentale du bambara*. Paris: Karthala.

Idiatov, Dmitry. 2012a. On the history of clause-final negation in the Mande languages of the Bani – upper Mouhoun rivers area. Paper presented at the Workshop "The history of post-verbal negation in African languages" (7th World Congress of African Linguistics). http://idiatov.mardi.myds.me/WOCAL7_Negation/IDIATOV_2012_Presentation.pdf.

Idiatov, Dmitry. 2012b. Clause-final negative markers in southeastern Bamana dialects: a contact-induced evolution. *Africana Linguistica* 18. 169–192.

Idiatov, Dmitry. 2015. Clause-final negative markers in Bobo and Samogo: parallel evolution and contact. *Journal of Historical Linguistics* 5 (2). 235–266. DOI: 10.1075/jhl.5.2.02idi.

Idiatov, Dmitry. 2018. An areal typology of clause-final negation in Africa: language dynamics in space and time. In Daniël Van Olmen, Tanja Mortelmans & Frank Brisard (eds.), *Aspects of linguistic variation*, 115–163. Berlin: De Gruyter Mouton. DOI: 10.1515/9783110607963-005.

Löbner, Sebastian. 1989. German *schon – erst – noch*: An integrated analysis. *Linguistics and Philosophy* 12 (2). 167–212. DOI: 10.1007/BF00627659.

Matras, Yaron. 2009. *Language contact*. Cambridge: Cambridge University Press.

Roulon-Doko, Paulette. 2012. Le marqueur de négation *ná* en gbaya. Paper presented at the Workshop "The history of post-verbal negation in African languages" (7th World Congress of African Linguistics), Buea. http://idiatov.mardi.myds.me/WOCAL 7_Negation/ROULON-DOKO_2012_Presentation.pdf.

Solomiac, Paul. 2007. *Phonologie et morphosyntaxe du dzùùngoo de Samogohiri*. Lyon: Université Lumière Lyon 2 dissertation.

Van Baar, Tim. 1997. *Phasal polarity*. Amsterdam: IFOTT.

van der Auwera, Johan. 1993. "Already" and "still": Beyond duality. *Linguistics and Philosophy* 16 (6). 613–653. DOI: 10.1007/BF00985436.

van der Auwera, Johan. 1998. Phasal adverbials in the languages of Europe. In Johan van der Auwera & Dónall P.O. Baoill (eds.), *Adverbial constructions in the languages of Europe*, 25–145. Berlin & New York: Mouton de Gruyter.

van der Auwera, Johan. 2009. The Jespersen cycles. In Elly van Gelderen (ed.), *Cyclical change*, 35–71. Amsterdam: John Benjamins.

Vydrin, Valentin & Svetlana Tomchina. 1999. *Manding-English dictionary (Maninka, Bamana)*. Vol. 1 (A, B, D-DAD, supplemented by some entries from subsequent volumes). St. Petersburg: Bulanin.

Lijun Li, Peter Siemund
From phasal polarity expression to aspectual marker: Grammaticalization of *already* in Asian and African varieties of English

1 Introduction

Without any doubt, Singapore is a fascinating linguistic laboratory. We here find languages of diverse genetic affiliations, speakers of different ethnic identity – autochthonous and foreign, international immigration and migration, a highly dynamic pattern of language shift and change, and a strong government that places language policy issues fairly high on their political agenda.

Established as an independent city-state in 1965, the southernmost tip of the Malay peninsula that is now known as Singapore was placed on the international landscape in 1819 when Sir Stamford Raffles was quick to realize the strategic importance of the island for the British Empire as a military bulkhead and international trading post. The indigenous Malay population was very low in number at that time, but with the British arrival a process of international immigration was set into motion that is still in full swing today. The increasing demand for human labor was primarily satisfied by drawing on Chinese immigrants who had been in the greater area for a long time, perhaps as far back as 1000 A.D. (Siemund & Li 2020). These Chinese immigrants hailed from the southern provinces of China, especially Fujian, Guangdong, and Hainan, taking their respective Chinese languages and dialects with them, namely Cantonese, Hainanese, Hakka, Hokkien, and Teochew. Previous to Singapore, major Chinese settlements could be found in Penang and Malacca, often based on mixed relations between male Chinese settlers and local Malay women that gave rise to the distinct ethnic group of Peranakans (Khoo 1998). Besides these Chinese settlers, the British also augmented the local labor force by shipping in people from India, primarily Tamils from Southern India and what is today Sri Lanka.

An important outcome of these demographic developments is that the Chinese today represent the main ethnic group in Singapore, contributing about 75 per cent of the local population. The autochthonous Malays are the second

---

Lijun Li, Peter Siemund, University of Hamburg

https://doi.org/10.1515/9783110646290-020

strongest ethnic group, but range far behind the Chinese with a share of about 13 per cent of the Singaporean population. The Indian population hovers at around 9 per cent. Table 1 provides an overview of these developments since 2000.

Table 1: Demographic development in Singapore (Wong 2011, 2016, 2019).

%	2000	2005	2010	2015
Chinese	76.8	75.7	74.1	74.3
Malays	13.9	13.9	13.4	13.3
Indians	7.9	8.4	9.2	9.1
Others	1.4	2.0	3.3	3.2

The linguistic model strongly promoted by the Singaporean government is one of bilingualism between one of the so-called 'mother-tongues', i.e. Mandarin Chinese, Malay, and Tamil, as well as English as the language of education, politics, business, administration, and much of the public sphere. The mother tongues primarily serve as home languages and for intra-ethnic communication. They are considered the anchor to Asian civilization and heritage, whereas English is the language of globalization that connects Singapore to the world at large. As has often been observed, Singapore as of today is a multilingual city-state of primarily bilingual speakers. This has not always been the case. For example, in the 1960s, i.e. in the times when Singapore was founded as an independent state, English and Mandarin practically played no role, though there was great diversity of Chinese vernacular dialects, as these were the languages imported by the immigrants from Southern China (Cantonese, Hainanese, Hakka, Hokkien, and Teochew). These Chinese vernaculars are quite distinct from Mandarin Chinese, typically lacking mutual comprehensibility with the latter. Figure 1 documents these developments from 1957 to 2015 in regards to home language use. While home language use of Malay and Tamil remained stable, the usage of Chinese languages underwent important changes. Moreover, English too increasingly came to be used as a home language, and there is evidence to suggest that it is rising further.

Since nothing is left to chance in Singapore, the society being tightly monitored and given the orientation deemed correct by the Singaporean government, the developments shown in Figure 1 can be directly related to language policy measures instigated by the government, as, for example, a general bilingual policy of English and mother tongues, English as the language of instruction of the education system, and nation-wide movements such as the Speak Mandarin

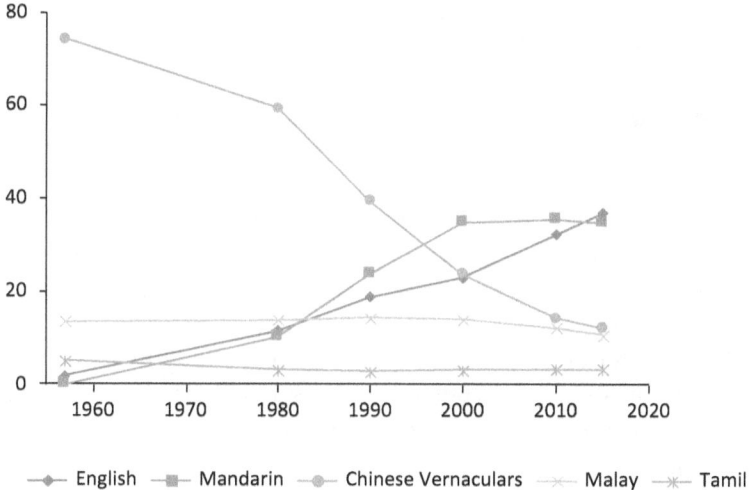

Figure 1: Home language use in Singapore in per cent (Cavallaro & Bee (2021) Wong 2011, 2016, 2019).

Campaign whose principal aim consists in the replacement of the Chinese vernaculars by Mandarin Chinese. Its success is plain to see, however much the concomitant loss of linguistic diversity is deplorable from a scientific point of view.

Another important governmental campaign targeted the purification of English. This Speak Good English Movement aims at reducing the very noticeable gap between Standard Singapore English, which is a variety that shows considerable overlap with Standard British English, and Colloquial Singapore English (Singlish), which can be viewed as a spectrum of varieties ranging from a basilectal vernacular to more acrolectal linguistic systems. Colloquial Singapore English, or CSE for short, is a contact vernacular that shows heavy influence from the Chinese substrate spoken in Singapore, but that also manifests influence from Malay, though less from Tamil. In one interpretation, basilectal Colloquial Singapore English is an English relexified Chinese vernacular with most of the grammatical system drawn from Chinese. The present contribution will be about highlighting one particular aspect of this grammatical system.

In another interpretation, Singapore is locked in a still ongoing language shift situation from Chinese to English, in which speakers strongly impose features of their Chinese substrate onto English. Since English and Chinese have coexisted for a long time and new immigrants from China keep pouring into the city-state, there are good arguments supporting a continued language contact situation based on imposition in the sense of Kusters (2003) and Winford

(2003). This process of imposition, or rather its outcome, is illustrated in (1) for the CSE perfective marker *already* that is directly calqued on Chinese *le* 了.[1]

(1) He take go **already**. [PROSE: 2]
 'He has taken it with him.'

The CSE perfective marker *already* is a central feature of the relevant grammatical system and represents our main interest here. Additional important features of Colloquial Singapore English are copula *be* deletion (2a) or non-standard agreement (2b) as well as the extensive use of discourse particles like *lah*, *ah*, *hah*, *meh*, and *lor* (3), all borrowed from Chinese, especially Cantonese, and Malay. Apart from that, there is of course also considerable lexical influence from all the languages spoken in the area, i.e. Malay, Hokkien (*ang moh* 'red hair'), Teochew, Cantonese, etc.

(2) a. *Now St Margaret's school, also a mission school now.* [OHI-000213-EQ]
 'St Margaret's school [is] also a mission school now.'
 b. *My father **do** the church works.* [OHI-000213-EQ]
 'My father do[es] the church works.'

(3) *Go to Chinatown **lah**.* [ICE-SG-S1A-007]
 'Let's go to Chinatown.' (assertive suggestion)

Interestingly enough, the Speak Good English movement introduced further above has not been particularly successful in eradicating these non-standard features of English, including several others. Apparently, for reasons of identity formation, Colloquial Singapore English has come to be accepted as a local solidarity code not only by the less affluent and less educated strata of society, but increasingly also by the educated middle and upper middle classes. Needless to say, there is great variation in the extent of the use of non-standard features, with educated Singaporeans largely restricting it to emblematic and symbolic uses. They nevertheless embrace Colloquial Singapore English and report

---

1 Example (1) is drawn from the archives of the PROSE project (Promotion of Standard English): Singlish Expressions and their Standard English Equivalents. Unless specified otherwise, the examples shown here are taken from the Oral History Interviews (OHI) and the International Corpus of English, the Singaporean component (ICE-SG).

very positive attitudes towards it (Siemund, Schulz & Schweinberger 2014; Leimgruber, Siemund & Terassa 2018).

Colloquial Singapore English has been widely researched synchronically (see among many Bao 2015; Lim, Pakir & Wee 2010; Leimgruber 2012; Ziegeler 2015), but we find hardly any publications that would probe into its history. This is primarily a data problem, as suitable data sources either do not exist or are difficult to develop. The principal aim of the present contribution consists in making a modest contribution to the diachronic reconstruction of Colloquial Singapore English based on one particular grammatical domain, namely the perfective marker *already*. As far as the data source is concerned, we will here make use of the Oral History Interviews held by the National Archives of Singapore (OHI-NAS). In comparison with the International Corpus of English – Singapore (ICE-SG), which represents the most widely used data source for the study of Colloquial Singapore English, the use of the Oral History Interviews allows a significant step back in time, as the speakers sampled there were born between approximately 1900 and 1950. Moreover, the Oral History Interviews contain substantial metadata that results in a fairly elaborate characterization of speaker backgrounds. The present study is one of the first contributions to make use of this data source. We here ask if and to what extent Colloquial Singapore English has been diachronically stable. For that purpose, the Oral History Interviews will also be placed in relation to ICE-SG.

Our contribution is organized as follows. In section 2, we will introduce different types of perfect constructions and their respective paths of grammaticalization. Section 3 assembles the descriptive generalizations concerning the differences between *already* as a phasal polarity expression in standard varieties of English and as an aspectual maker in Colloquial Singapore English. Section 4 outlines the data base to be used in the analysis of the grammaticalization of *already* that follows in section 5. In Section 6, we will examine similar linguistic phenomena in other Asian and African varieties of English followed by the summary and conclusion in section 7.

2 Typology of perfects and their grammaticalization

Perfect and perfective are very different, albeit overlapping grams. The label 'perfect' is typically used in relation to some specific morphosyntactic form, such as the English present perfect (Schwenter & Cacoullous 2008: 3). Semantically, perfects are relational, signaling a past situation that is related to (discourse) at speech time and is therefore currently relevant. In contrast, perfectives report an event "for its own sake" (Bybee et al. 1994: 54), and indicate that a situation is viewed as bounded (Bybee & Dahl 1989: 55). The change from perfect to perfective use involves a generalization of meaning, with loss of the component of current relevance (Bybee et al. 1994: 86–87).

Perfect constructions including their genesis are reasonably well understood grammatical phenomena. As is well known (Bybee & Dahl 1989; Dahl & Velupillai 2013), perfects grammaticalize from essentially three construction types and, accordingly, appear in different shapes cross-linguistically. Example (4) shows a perfect based on a resultative construction, i.e. a means of encoding the final state in the developmental trajectory of a situation.

(4) Finnish
   Juna   on   saapunut.
   train   is   arrive.supine
   'The train has arrived.'
   [world-atlas-Dahl & Velupillai 2013-chapter 68-example 1]

A second type of perfect construction involves a verb of possession (such as *have*), which, of course, presupposes the existence of such a verb. This type can be widely encountered in European languages and is illustrated in (5).

(5) German
   *Paul **hat** den Keks **gegessen**.*
   Paul has the cookie eaten
   'Paul has eaten the cookie.'

The third prominent construction type relies on phasal adverbs such as *already* or verbs describing the terminating phase of an event (*finish*). This perfect type is fairly widely attested in South-East Asia and also in equatorial Africa. Illustration is provided in (6).

(6) Yoruba
   *O **ti**   ka   iwe   na.*
   he PFV/already read book this
   'He has read this book.'
   [world-atlas-Dahl & Velupillai 2013-chapter 68-example 2]

Dahl & Velupillai (2013) explore perfect constructions in a sample of 222 languages and find that merely seven languages select the possessive construction, another 21 languages boast perfects based on 'finish' or 'already', whereas 80 languages rely on other construction types including resultatives. Interestingly enough, 114 languages in their sample lack the category of a perfect altogether, especially Australian languages. The different perfect types give rise to clear areal patterns, as specified above.

The aspectual particle of Chinese signaling completion and current relevance (了 *le*) was grammaticalized from the verb *liǎo* 'to finish', and this particle can be considered the origin of the corresponding use of *already* in Colloquial Singapore English. Here illustrated on the basis of Swahili, the step from example (7) to (8) illustrates the grammaticalization of 'finish' as a verb to an adverb meaning 'already' (Heine & Kuteva 2002: 134), even though the form of 'already' looks like an inflected auxiliary rather than an adverb. In a subsequent step, this adverb/inflected auxiliary can develop into a marker of completive aspect.

(7) Swahili
 i- me- (kw-) **isha**
 C9 PERF INF   finish
 'It is finished.'
 (Heine & Kuteva 2002: 134)

(8) Swahili
 i- me- (kw-) **isha** fika
 C9 PERF INF   finish   arrive
 'It is arrived already.'
 (Heine & Kuteva 2002: 134)

Above and beyond these well-known paths of grammaticalization, Heine & Kuteva (2002: 135) show that verbs meaning 'finish' can also develop into markers expressing consecutive relations and markers of perfective aspect.

3 Phasal polarity expressions and aspectual markers

As pointed out by van der Auwera (1993), phasal polarity *already* in Standard English is phasal as it involves two reference points situated before and after a phasal change. It expresses the occurrence of a change of state, typically enriched by connotations of unexpectedness, anteriority, and counterfactuality. English examples of phasal polarity *already* are depicted in (9).

(9) a. *When I finally arrived, John was **already** sleeping.* (BrE)
    b. *Even though I arrived early, John was **already** sleeping.* (BrE)

In (9a), the act of arriving happens in the post-time of the change of state from not sleeping to sleeping. It is expressed that the speaker arrives too late to meet John, though the actual change of state happens as expected. In (9b), the change of state occurs earlier than expected, and again, the speaker fails to meet John. This example describes a counterfactual situation, as the sleeping event began prior to expectation.

Following Löbner (1989), van der Auwera (1993: 619) holds that the following three points should be considered when describing the temporal uses of *already*. They sufficiently explain the intuitions behind the examples in (9).
i. the time axis;
ii. the obtainment of a positive state resulting from a change from a negative state; and
iii. an alternative to the envisaged positive state (ii) obtaining at a point of time on the axis (i). (van der Auwera 1993: 619)

This implies that, first of all, *already* involves a change of state from negative (with the state not holding at the reference point) to positive (the state holding at the reference point) in English. And second, as mentioned earlier, two reference points are required for the contrasting alternative. Moreover, any additional connotations have the status of implicatures and can be cancelled. Consider the pair of examples in (10), where (10a) expresses a sense of earliness that (10b) clearly lacks (adapted from van der Auwera 1993: 621).

(10) a. *I've met a girl who is only 13 years old but she is **already** married.*
     b. *Suppose you want to marry a certain woman. You propose and you find out that she is **already** married. There is nothing necessarily early about this marriage. You simply come too late to have a chance [. . .]*

3.1 Already as a completive aspectual marker in Colloquial Singapore English

Already as a completive (or perfective) aspectual marker in Colloquial Singapore English does not signal a change of state and the above mentioned *concomitant* connotations of unexpectedness, anteriority, and counterfactuality, but simply expresses the completion of an event. As a common greeting expression in

Colloquial Singapore English, the question "Have you eaten?" is usually responded to with the answer "Yes, I eat already", as shown in (11). What we can observe is a lack of inflectional marking on the verb and that *already* in Colloquial Singapore English assumes the function of a grammatical marker, typically rendering the completive aspect that is expressed with the past tense or the present perfect (*I ate* or *I have eaten*) in the standard varieties (Platt & Weber 1980). Here, *already* expresses that the eating event is over, i.e. fully occurred before the moment of utterance.

(11) A: *Have you eaten?*
 B: *Yes, I eat **already**.*
 'Yes, I have eaten.'

In example (12) below, the speaker informs the interlocutor that the ship has sunk and he is merely reporting the completion of the event. A similar situation obtains in (13). Judging from the context of example (13), the early immigrants in Singapore experienced tremendous hardship that outsiders could not have imagined, but the hard workers did not become millionaires prior to a certain reference point in a change of state schema.

(12) *Do you know that the ship has sunk **already**?* [OHI-000123-NB]
 'Do you know our ship has sunk?'

(13) *But they worked very hard. Some of them **already** became millionaires.* [OHI-000237-HCY]
 'But they worked very hard. Meanwhile, some of them have become millionaires.'

If CSE completive *already* occurs together with expressions describing a reference point in the past, interpretations equivalent to the Standard English past perfect arise, as examples (14) and (15) illustrate.

(14) *By that time, I think, Singapore fell **already**.* [OHI-000013-SEA]
 'By that time, I think, Singapore had fallen.'

(15) *I was sixteen years old. Then I **already** learned quite a lot. I become an Assistant Shipping Clerk.* [OHI-000057-LYC]
 'I was sixteen years old. By then I had learned quite a lot. After that I became an Assistant Shipping Clerk.'

In sentences with aspectual *already* in Colloquial Singapore English, explicit progressive marking is often lacking, though the relevant sentences do express ongoing situations, as shown in (16).

(16) *He went to the Royal College or something like that. He **already** studied there. But after sometime I went there, I can't find him.* [OHI-000057-LYC]
'He went to the Royal College. He was already studying there when I went there. But I couldn't find him.'

3.2 Inchoative use of *already* in Colloquial Singapore English

The second usage of *already* in CSE is referred to as "inchoative" because the relevant sentences describe the beginning of an action (see Bao 1995: 183–184). Two readings are possible with example (17). With the completive interpretation, sentence (17) is interpreted as "My son has left for school". However, the second reading is more frequent in which the sentence means "my son has started school".

(17) *My son go to school **already**.*
'My son has left for school.' (completive)
'My son has started school.'(inchoative)
(Bao 1995: 183)

The completive and inchoative uses of *already* are commonly considered to be modelled after the Chinese aspectual marker 了 *le*, which expresses precisely the corresponding meanings (Bao 1995; Platt & Weber 1980). We are aware that the relevant Chinese substrate in contact in the earlier history (pre-1800s to 1979) of Singapore are the southern Chinese varieties such as Hokkien, Cantonese, Teochew, etc. (see Gupta 1994; Li, Saravanan & Hoon 1997; Lim 2007; Platt & Weber 1980). However, given the typological similarities of these aspectual particles, as shown in (18) – (20), we consider it appropriate to use Mandarin Chinese for comparison with the CSE examples.

(18) Mandarin Chinese
我 儿子 上学 了。
wǒ érzi shàngxué le
my son go school ASP
'My son has started school.'

(19) Cantonese Chinese
 我　个仔　番学　　啦。
 ngo5　go3 zai2　faan1 hok6　laa1
 my　CLF son　go school　ASP
 'My son has started school.'

(20) Hokkien
 我　儿子　顶学　　啊.
 goa2　ji5chu2　teng2oh8　ah0
 my　son　go school　ASP
 'My son has started school.'

The inchoative use of *already*, however, is not an exclusive phenomenon of Colloquial Singapore English. Such use of *already* is treated in Olsson (2013) and Dahl & Wälchli (2016) under the label 'iamitive' (from Latin *iam* 'already'). Besides Mandarin, Indonesian/Malay *sudah*, Tai *lɛ́ɛw*, Vietnamese *đã* and *rồi* are considered as iamitive. *Iamitive* and *inchoative* are overlapping grams. For a detailed description of these, the interested reader is referred to Dahl & Wälchli (2016).

Inchoative *already* in Colloquial Singapore English only signals a change without another referent point. Example (21) is perhaps uttered by TCM (traditional Chinese Medicine) practitioners who can tell whether a patient is healthy or not by examining the color of the tongue. We can see that there is no second reference point in the example; *already* seems to signal the change itself. Inchoative *already* in Colloquial Singapore English does not require a contrasting alternative to the envisaged positive state obtaining at a point of time (van der Auwera 1993: 621). As illustrated by (21) and (22), the speaker does not assume that the hearer expects that *the tongue turned red* and that *the patient eats food*. Thus, there are no conflicting expectations.

(21) *The tongue red **already**, you see?*
 'The tongue has turned/turned red./*The tongue was red.'
 (Kwan-Terry 1989: 40, cited in Bao 2005: 239)

(22) *The patient eat food **already**.*
 'The patient has started to eat food.'
 (Bao 1995: 183)

The temporal schema proposed by Bao (2005: 240) captures inchoative *already* in Colloquial Singapore English quite accurately. This schema illustrates that the use of *already* marks the change from Not-P to P (it was not the case before, and it is the case now). What is more, sentences with *already* as an inchoative marker in Colloquial Singapore English are not ambiguous. There are two entailments in sentence (23), namely (i) that Mary did not live in Singapore in the past, and the other (ii) that she lives there now. Without the use of inchoative *already*, a similar sentence in Standard English, as in (24), is ambiguous because the interlocutor can conclude from the sentence that either Mary still lives in Singapore, or that she no longer lives there. It is noteworthy that inchoative *already* in Colloquial Singapore English usually occurs sentence-finally (see Bao & Hong 2006; Siemund & Li 2017).

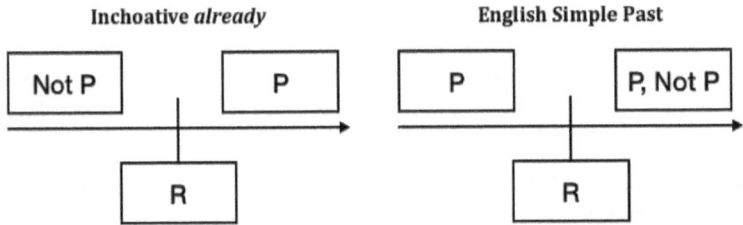

Figure 2: Inchoative *already* and the English simple past (Bao 2005: 240).

(23) Colloquial Singapore English
 *Mary live in Singapore **already**.*
 Means: 'Mary did not live in Singapore in the past.' and 'She lives there now'.
 (adapted from Bao 2005: 240)

(24) Standard English
 Mary lived in Singapore.
 Means: 'Marry still lives in Singapore.' or 'Marry no longer lives in Singapore.'
 (adapted from Bao 2005: 240)

4 Methodology and data base

The analysis of *already* in Colloquial Singapore English in the current study is based on data drawn from the Singaporean component of the International Corpus of English (ICE-SG) and the Oral History Interviews held by the National

Archives of Singapore. The ICE project was initiated in the early 1990s (Greenbaum 1991), and its informants were educated speakers of at least eighteen years of age at the time of data collection. ICE Singapore is a one-million-word corpus containing spoken and written material in roughly equal proportions. We here restrict the analysis to the spoken section of the Singaporean component of ICE to compare it with the Oral History Interviews, as the latter data source only includes spoken data. The Oral History Interviews represent speech by informants who were born between the 1890s and 1940s, and the recordings include detailed metadata. As the Oral History Interviews represent a type of CSE that was spoken and learned at least five decades before CSE was sampled in ICE-SG, a comparison between the two datasets can provide us with a glimpse on developments from past to present.

4.1 Previous findings

Siemund & Li (2017) explore the spoken sections of ICE-SG and ICE-GB (International Corpus of English – the British English component). As we can see in Table 2, the frequency differences of *already* between ICE-SG and ICE-GB are impressive. Here N represents the number of occurrences of *already* (*ptw* = per thousand words). Testing the absolute numbers of *already* against the overall number of words yields statistically highly significant differences: X-squared = 127.38, df = 1, p-value < 2.2e-16 (all tests done using R). It appears plausible to conclude that higher ratios of *already* are indicative of higher substrate influence.

Table 2: Frequencies of *already* in ICE-SG (from Siemund & Li 2017: 22).

	Words (N)	already (N)	already (ptw)
ICE-GB	630903	208	0.33
ICE-SG	601980	491	0.82

Tables 3 and 4 offer a closer look at the individual frequency differences of *already* between the ten speakers with the highest *already* ratio in ICE-SG and ICE-GB. We here only include speech contributions above one thousand words to avoid bias due to low numbers of words.

Table 3: The ten speakers with highest *already*-ratios in ICE-SG (Siemund & Li 2017: 22).

Text/speaker ID	Word count	already (sum)	already (ptw)
<icesg-s1a-007:1$b>	1200	12	10.000
<icesg-s1b-057:1$c>	1589	10	6.293
<icesg-s1a-051:1$b>	1136	7	6.162
<icesg-s1a-020:1$b>	1051	6	5.709
<icesg-s1a-042:1$b>	1527	8	5.239
<icesg-s1a-049:1$a>	1016	4	3.937
<icesg-s1b-034:1$a>	1342	5	3.726
<icesg-s1a-054:1$a>	1379	5	3.626
<icesg-s1a-091:1$a>	1140	4	3.509
<icesg-s1a-013:1$a>	1392	4	2.874

The highest ratio in this sample is 10 instances of *already* per thousand words; the lowest is approximately 2.9. These individual figures are considerably higher than the average figures shown in Table 2. In comparison with the data drawn from ICE-GB (see Table 4), we can see that the highest ratio is around 3.7 while the lowest is approximately 1.7, which are much lower than the corresponding values in ICE-SG.

The bottom line of the preceding discussion is that the per thousand words ratios of a prominent grammatical item differ markedly in the varieties of Singapore and Great Britain, the values in Colloquial Singapore English being generally higher. In the following section, we will introduce the data drawn from Oral History Interviews held by National Archives of Singapore and compare the two data sets.

Table 4: The ten speakers with highest *already*-ratios in ICE-GB (Siemund & Li 2017: 23).

Text/speaker ID	Word count	already (sum)	already (ptw)
<icegb-s2b-041:2$a>	1074	4	3.724
<icegb-s1b-001:1$a>	1893	5	2.641
<icegb-s1a-082:1$a>	1161	3	2.584
<icegb-s1b-004:1$a>	1648	4	2.427
<icegb-s2b-022:2$a>	1004	2	1.992
<icegb-s1b-061:1$b>	1022	2	1.957
<icegb-s1a-023:1$b>	1048	2	1,908

Table 4 (continued)

Text/speaker ID	Word count	already (sum)	already (ptw)
<icegb-s2b-034:1$a>	2205	4	1.814
<icegb-s1b-054:1$b>	1696	3	1.769
<icegb-s1a-066:1$b>	1155	2	1.732

4.2 The Oral History Interviews (OHI)

The Oral History Interviews project held by the National Archives of Singapore was initiated in 1979. The interviews contain rich metadata: biographical information, such as the age, gender, ethnicity, heritage language, educational background, and occupation of the speakers precedes the text data. A sample of the biographical information of the speakers is shown in Table 5.

The informants of the project come from all walks of life in Singapore, including governors, politicians, teachers, shop owners, medical professionals, artists, etc. Concerning ethnicity, there are speakers of various ethnic backgrounds, including Chinese, British, Malay, Indian, Iraqi, Tamil, etc. In total, 3992 interviews (in different languages) have been compiled in the OHI project. Based on a sample of 97 English interviews, the average length of interviews is 163.9 pages. The first content page of the interview 000001 TMK counts 316 words. The oldest speaker in the sample was born in 1899. Such data is of great value as the metadata is often either excluded or neglected in large scale linguistic corpora. The detailed metadata in the Oral History Interviews and the cross-corpora comparison (ICE-SG vs. Oral History Interviews) could bridge the diachronic gap in studying contact-induced grammaticalization of certain lexical items in Singapore English.

For the present study, we chose 13 interviews in the recordings of Oral History Interviews. The year of birth of the interviewees ranges from 1899 to 1948. The interviews were conducted from 1979 to 1999. The length of each interview varies from 40 to 276 pages.[2] Consider the overview in Table 6.

The interviews can be divided into three groups according to the ethnic background of the interviewees. Table 7 provides an overview of the three groups and their respective sample sizes. The first group consists of 8 interviewees with Chinese ethnic background whose heritage languages are Chinese, Hokkien,

---

[2] Before around 2015, it was possible to use the pdfs of the interviews to approximate the word tokens contained in them and thus their length. The National Archives of Singapore have meanwhile enforced a more restrictive access policy so that the length of the interviews now needs to be given in terms of their overall page number.

Table 5: Metadata of selected Oral History Interviews.

ACC ID	Initials	Year of birth	Place of birth	Sex	Ethnicity	Language	Level of English	Education	Inter-view
000001	TMK	1921	Malaysia	m	Chinese	Hokkien	mesolect	medium	1979
000013	SEA	1918	Singapore	m	Malay	Malay	acrolect	medium	1980
000021	CCS	1932	Singapore	m	Chinese		mesolect	high	1980
000057	LYC	1906	China	m	Chinese	Teochew	mesolect	medium	1981
000071	CKM	1922	Malaysia	m	Peranakan		acrolect	high	1981
000237	HCY	1905	China	f	Chinese		mesolect	medium	1982
000213	EQ	1899	Singapore	f	Chinese	Hokkien	basilect	low	1982
000237	HCY	1905	China	f	Chinese		mesolect	medium	1982
000265	LTS	1925	Singapore	m	Chinese		basilect	low	1983
000259	AJ	1915	UK	m	British	English	mesolect	low	1983
000404	RW	1948	UK	m	British	English	mesolect	medium	1984
001953	LAS	1940	Singapore	m	Chinese		basilect	low	1997
002206	MH	1937	Singapore	f	Chinese	Hakka, Cantonese	mesolect	low	1999

Table 6: Overview of year of birth and year of interviews conducted.

	Born in	Interview in	Length (pages)
min	1899	1979	40
max	1948	1999	276
average	1923	1984	147

Table 7: Three groups of interviewees according to ethnic background.

Ethnicity	Interviews	Length (pages)
Chinese	8	1216
British	2	317
Other	3	384
Total	13	1917

Hakka, Teochew, and Cantonese. The second group of 2 interviewees are of British ethnic background. The third group "Other" consists of 3 interviews with speakers of different ethnic backgrounds (Malay, Indian, and Peranakan).

Table 8 lists the summary of the metadata of the selected interviews. The majority of the participants were born in Singapore (6), followed by Malaysia (2), and China (2) as well as the UK (2). 10 out of the 13 of the interviewees are male. Education level ranges from low, medium, to high. Low refers to an interviewee who received up to primary (elementary) school education; medium accounts for participants with secondary (high school) education; and high means that the speaker finished college and/or further education. As far as heritage languages are concerned, not every interview reveals the interviewee's heritage language. As a result, 5 Chinese interviewees are noted with 5 unspecified Chinese languages.

The occurrences of *already* were annotated in each text of the Oral History Interviews. The frequency distribution of *already* in the Oral History Interviews was then compared with that in the ICE-SG data. In a next step, the meaning of *already* in each occurrence was determined, namely whether *already* appears as a phasal polarity expression or as an aspectual marker.

Table 8: Summary of metadata of the selected interviews.

Place of birth		Ethnicity	
Singapore	6	Chinese	8
UK	2	British	2
Malaysia	2	other	3
China	2		
India	1		
Heritage language[3]		**Education**	
Chinese unspecified	5	high	2
English	2	low	6
Malay	1	medium	5
Tamil	1		
Hokkien	2	**Gender**	
Teochew	1	Female	3
Cantonese	1	Male	10
Hakka	1		

4.3 eWAVE

Another research question that we would like to address is whether we can find similar grammaticalization process of *already* from an adverb marking phasal polarity to an aspectual marker in other varieties of English. For that question, we use eWAVE (the electronic World Atlas of Varieties of English; Kortmann & Lunkenheimer 2013) to explore whether the aspectual function of *already* is a shared feature of other Asian and African varieties of English.

5 Grammaticalization of *already*

As mentioned earlier, the data in the Oral History Interviews represent a type of Singapore English four to five decades older than the English sampled in the ICE corpus. The two interviewees with a British ethnic background in the Oral History Interviews were born in the UK but grew up in Singapore while the British component of the ICE corpus represents British English in the home country. Consider Figure 3. What we can observe is that British speakers produced

---

[3] The total number adds up to more than 13 because speaker MH considers both Hakka and Cantonese as her heritage languages.

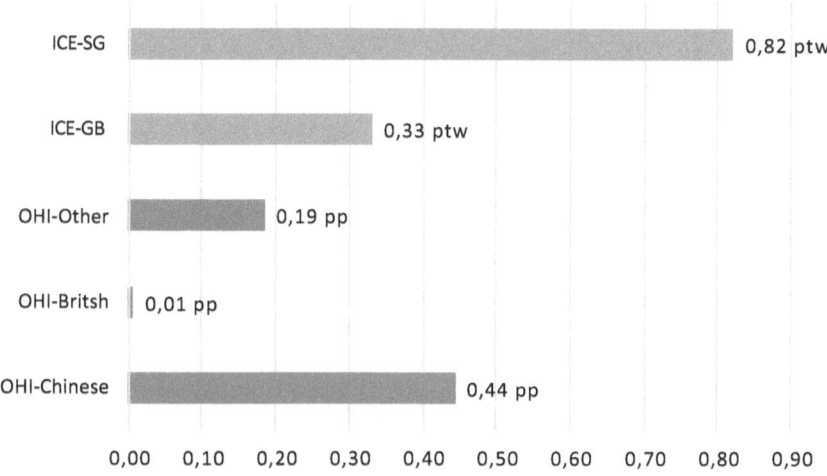

Figure 3: Frequencies of *already* ptw in ICE-SG and pp in the Oral History Interviews.

relatively low frequencies of *already*. At the same time, the average frequency of *already* in ICE-SG (0.82 ptw) seems to echo the average frequency produced by the interviewees with a Chinese (0.44 pp) or other ethnic background (0.19 pp) in that they are much higher than the British group. Judging from these figures, it is not possible to detect a decline in the usage of *already* or a shift towards the British norm. However, we can conclude that *already* has long been used as an aspectual maker in Singapore English and that there are no signs of Colloquial Singapore English being replaced by Standard English, at least not in the grammatical domain considered here.

Calculating the frequency of *already* across the entire corpora does not reveal any information about individual differences, but such information would be highly desirable. Figure 4 provides information on the frequencies of *already* in the Oral History Interviews produced by individual speakers who were born between 1899 and 1948. We here only focus on the Chinese group in an attempt to see whether there is a clear diachronic trend. As indicated by the wobbly line in Figure 4, there are substantial differences in the frequencies produced by individual speakers. The two speakers born in 1937 and 1940 produce higher frequencies of *already* than the other speakers. High frequencies of *already* generally point to the more basilectal speakers or stronger substrate influence. The results seem to suggest that CSE has remained stable over the past 50 years, with a slight increase among younger speakers. Evidently, there have always been substantial individual differences.

Figure 4: Frequencies of *already* pp of individual speakers born between 1899–1948 (OHI-Chinese).

Moreover, the group of speakers with a Chinese background manifests the greatest range of individual variation. This is shown in in Figure 5. This speaker group is very heterogeneous, probably due to a diverse range of social backgrounds.

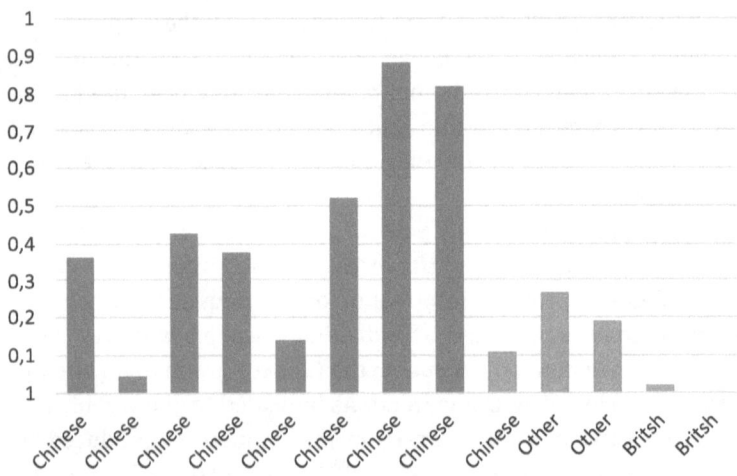

Figure 5: Frequency of *already* pp among speakers of different ethnic backgrounds.

The Chinese group attains the highest frequency of *already* in this data set, followed by the group "Other", while the British group manifests a very low ratio of *already* compared with the other groups. Moreover, *already* with substrate-influenced meanings can only be detected in the Chinese group and the mixed group, but rarely, if at all, in the British group. This once again confirms that *already* is more likely to be influenced by the Chinese substrate than other contact languages. The result is in line with the spoken section of ICE-SG, in which the frequency of *already* is significantly higher than that in ICE-GB.

In the qualitative part of the study, we analyzed 108 occurrences of *already* found in the last two reels (approximately one hour) of all the 13 interviews. 93 tokens can be analyzed as clear examples of substrate-influenced variants. As Figure 6 shows, most of the tokens function as aspectual markers, either completive/perfective markers or inchoative markers. The total number of substrate-influenced variants adds up to more than 93 as in some cases, *already* may have two substrate features (e.g. inchoative and in negative sentences). Again, there are no examples manifesting substrate-influenced meanings of *already* in the British group.

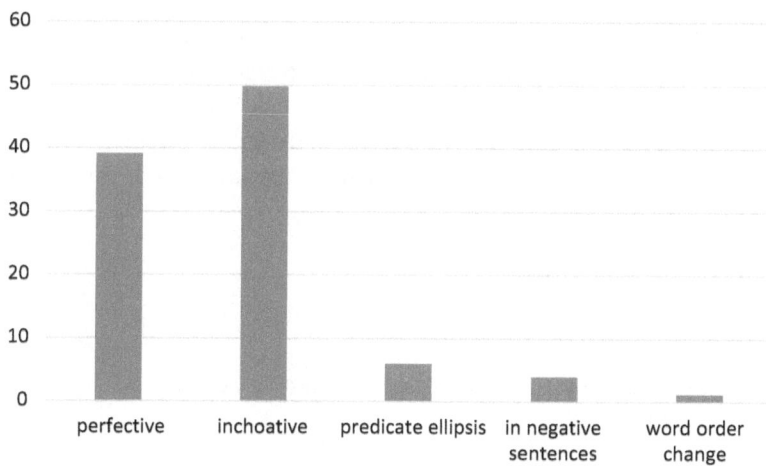

Figure 6: Categories of substrate-influenced uses of *already* (absolute figures).

Some of the examples of each category are listed below:

(25) As tense/aspectual marker:
 a. That time, once the fire start up **already**, all people said, "Wow, big fire." [OHI-001953-LAS]
 b. But the water was not very. Quite high. It is up to the chest **already**. [OHI-002206-MH]

c. So obviously there were smell? Ah, now, it's cleared **already**. Since that time they have cleared a lot. [OHI-001953-LAS]

We can notice that whenever *already* occurs, the predicate that it modifies remains in its bare, unmarked form. It seems that *already* triggers the deletion of inflectional markers and is used instead of an inflectional marker (the equivalent to English *-ed*). The usual associative presupposition of the hearer's prior knowledge of the event and a potential implicature of "earlier than expected" is missing in the above examples.

(26) Inchoative:
   A: We go and take the pineapple skin, the second layer, we eat with that.
   B: That was during the war years? After the war?
   A: After the war, it was quite comfortable **already**. [OHI-002206-MH]

From the above conversation, we can discern that during the war, the conditions of life were extremely harsh. This is reflected in the fact that people ate pineapple skin. The predicate combining with *already* is *was quite comfortable* and can be characterized, using Dahl & Wälchli's (2016: 328) term, as a "natural development predicate" that refers to "a predicate which becomes true sooner or later under normal circumstances." The answer of the interviewee underlines the change after the war by using inchoative *already*, marking the beginning of a new situation.

(27) Copula *be* ellipsis:
   a. The Government's requisition **already** one million over.
      [OHI-000057-LYC]
   b. Where got the energy? Even our mind, all blank **already**.
      [OHI-001953-LAS]

The above use of *already* is often found in cases where the copula *be* is absent. As shown in (27), the predicate combining with *already* usually involves a number or an adjective. It seems that besides functioning as an aspectual marker, *already* can also assume the function of the copula *be*.

   Already in CSE also occurs in a negative sentence. The translation of *not . . . already* can be seen as equivalent to *no longer*, which marks the "non-occurrence of the state [. . .] at reference time while implying a reference point at a prior (*no longer*) [. . .] phase where this state holds" (Kramer 2017: 1), i.e. the speaker being young in (28a) and practicing many hours in (28b).

(28) In the context of negation:
   a. I was not young *already*, *already* reaching the age of 27, 28. [OHI-000071-CKM]
   b. So I said, I would call it a day. At my age, I was not practicing that many hours *already*. [OHI-000838-SMK]

Although the default assumption is that there is only one occurrence of aspectual *already* per clause, actual usage shows that speakers may also produce two such occurrences in one and the same clause. This provides further evidence in favor of the grammaticalization of sentence-final *already* as an aspectual marker, as the other occurrence of *already* in sentence-medial position resembles canonical *already* in Standard English.

(29) Double use of *already*:
   a. They were *already* actually piling their arms *already*. [OHI-000001-TMK]
   b. After all this news going on, after the screening, the people were *already* living in fear *already*. [OHI-000265-LTS]

6 Perfective marker *already* in other Asian and African varieties of English

The grammaticalized use of *already* as an aspectual marker can also be observed in other Asian and African varieties of English. It turns out that aspectual marking via the adverb *already*, as in Colloquial Singapore English, is not at all typologically rare. A number of English varieties across the world exhibit cases of the adverb *already* functioning as an aspectual marker.

Out of the 76 varieties of English investigated so far by Kortmann and Lunkenheimer (2013) as part of the eWaves project, 24 varieties of English are documented as possessing aspectual *already*. Nine varieties of English are reported to have the aspectual marker *already* as a pervasive or obligatory feature, including Krio (Sierra Leone Creole), Cape Flats English, Hong Kong English, Colloquial Singapore English, and Malaysian English, to name a few.

Another ten varieties have the aspectual marker *already* as neither a pervasive nor extremely rare feature. These include Ghanaian Pidgin, Nigerian English, and Cameroon English. Interestingly, most of these varieties, except for Cape Flats English (McCormick 2004: 995) are found in equatorial areas. These observations correspond to the typology of perfects in the local substrate languages, which typically rely on phasal adverbs such as *already* or verbs such as *finish* to express the perfective aspect. It appears plausible to hypothesize that the grammaticalization of *already* as a phasal polarity expression to an aspectual marker is modelled on the local substrate languages. Example (30) illustrates these findings for Cape Flats English.

(30) Cape Flats English
   a. *We did move here a week **already**.*
      'We had moved here a week previously.'
   b. *Were you there **already**?*
      'Have you been there before?'
      (McCormick 2004: 994–995)

Cape Flats English is a spoken contact variety of English in Cape Town and its environs, which shows converging grammar features of English and Afrikaans (see Finn 2004; McCormick 2004). McCormick (2004) offers a detailed documentation of the tense-aspect systems of Cape Flats English, in which unstressed *did*, a stigmatized feature of Cape Flats English and one of the targets of corrective exercises in grammar lessons at school, is considered to give rise to the past tense meaning in (30a). However, the use of sentence-final *already* is neglected in this discussion, although it may also contribute to the perfective interpretation. As (30b) exemplifies, it is the combination of the past tense marker *were* and the use of *already* that serves as an alternative form for expressing the perfective meaning.

The substrate of Hong Kong English is Cantonese, and together with English, they serve as the most important spoken languages in Hong Kong, despite the fact that Mandarin Chinese is becoming increasingly important in post-colonial Hong Kong (see Li 1999). The example in (31) is very similar to the example of Colloquial Singapore English discussed earlier in (10). We can almost find a one by one direct translation in Cantonese, as in (32).

(31) Hong Kong English
   *I ate my lunch **already**.*
   'I have had my lunch.'
   [ewaves-atlas-Hong Kong English-example 287]

(32) Cantonese Chinese (personal knowledge)
   我   食咗   飯   啦
   ngo5   sik6 zo2   faan6   laa1
   I   eat.COMPL   rice   ASP
   'I have just had my lunch.'

In Cantonese, *zo2* following the verb marks the completion of the predicate, the sentence final aspectual marker *laa1* is close to what Li & Thompson ([1981]1989: 296) call the "current relevant state", or "the perfect of recent past" (Comrie 1976: 60), meaning that "the present relevance of the situation is simply one of the temporal closeness, i.e. the past situation is very recent". The whole sentence can be interpreted as "I have just had my lunch." In the Hong Kong English example, *already* seems to have taken on the functions of both aspectual markers from the substrate Cantonese, marking the completion of the action and that the completion of the action is very recent. Again, we can confirm that the grammaticalization of *already* is modelled on the substrate language.

Similar observations apply to the *already* perfect in Ghanaian Pidgin, where *already* specifies that the event happened in the past. Without *already*, the temporal interpretation of (33a) *ìn nem spɔil* is ambiguous and relies heavily on a given context: the phrase could mean that something (usually someone's name) was spoiled in the past, is being spoiled now, or will be spoiled in the future. If we replace *ɔlrɛdi* with the seemingly alternative form *finish*, as in *ìn nem spɔil, finish* (typically preceded by an intonational break), the sentence is still ambiguous: 'Its name had been/is spoiled' (i.e. the company was/will be over) (Bonnie p.c. 2018). Therefore, *ɔlrɛdi* 'already' contributes an unambiguous past interpretation to the utterance which is close to the "resultatives" (Dahl & Velupillai 2013) or "perfect of recent past" (Comrie 1976: 60) mentioned earlier. Again, one can find a parallel one by one translation in Twi, the most-widely spoken language in Ghana, the equivalent form to *already* being *dadaada* (see (33b)).

(33) a. Ghanaian Pidgin
      *ìn   nem   spɔil   **ɔlrɛdi.***
      Its   name   spoil   PFV/already
      'It has (come to have) a bad reputation.' (lit.: 'Its name has spoiled already.').
      [ewave-atlas-Ghanaian Pidgin-example 3716]
  b. Twi
      *zɛ   din   sɛe   **dadaada***
      3sg   name   spoil   PFV/already
      'His/her/its name (reputation) had been (spoiled) ruined.'
      (Bonnie 2018 p.c.)

An interesting example of aspectual *already* is found in Ugandan English, though this use of *already* is a rare feature in this variety. In example (34), *already* does not imply *that we finished the tasks* earlier than expected, but is used as a temporal adverb to indicate that the action of the subclause had been completed before that in the main clause.

(34) Uganda English
*He came when we finished **already**.*
'He came when we had finished.'
[ewave-atlas-Uganda English-example 1763]

7 Summary and conclusion

In this paper, we analyzed the contact-induced grammaticalization of *already* from a phasal polarity expression to an aspectual marker. We studied Colloquial Singapore English with an unused diachronic data source, namely the Oral History Interviews held by the National Archives of Singapore, comparing these to the Singaporean component of the International Corpus of English (ICE-SG), which represents the more commonly used corpus for Colloquial Singapore English. The grammaticalization of *already* is the result of dynamic and intensive language contact between English and the local substrate languages.

The substrate-influenced use of *already* has stabilized over the past five decades and has acquired properties of indexicality relating to age and ethnicity. As our results show, there are substantial differences between individual speakers and a slightly increasing popularity among the younger generation of Singaporeans. Also, the frequency of aspectual *already* differs among the ethnic groups distinguished here. These differences have remained relatively stable, too. We would like to submit that there is an ongoing grammaticalization process of *already* as an aspectual marker, especially in view of the resurgence in the prominence of Mandarin and the recent immigration of people from all parts of China.

In contrast to Standard English, which relies on verb inflection to mark perfectivity in its tense and aspect system, many Asian and African varieties of English express the relevant aspectual meaning with the adverb *already*. Besides expressing the completive and perfective aspect, *already* has taken on the function of marking the inchoative/iamitive aspect. This further supports our hypothesis that *already* represents a case of grammaticalization from a phasal polarity expression to an aspectual marker. The close affinity between *already* in the English varieties with corresponding expressions in the local substrate languages suggests that such grammaticalization first started as a contact-induced interference.

Abbreviations

ASP	aspectual marker	CLF	classifier
CSE	Colloquial Singapore English	N	number of occurrences
PFV	perfective	ptw	per thousand words
ICE	International Corpus of English	pp	per page

References

Bao, Zhiming. 1995. Already in Singapore English. *World Englishes* 14 (2). 181–188.
Bao, Zhiming. 2005. The aspectual system of Singapore English and the systemic substratist explanation. *Journal of Linguistics* 41 (2). 237–267.
Bao, Zhiming. 2015. *The making of vernacular Singapore English: System, transfer and filter* (Cambridge Approaches to Language Contact). Cambridge & New York: Cambridge University Press.
Bao, Zhiming & Huaqing Hong. 2006. Diglossia and register variation in Singapore English. *World Englishes* 25 (1). 106–114.
Bonnie, Richard. July 29, 2018. Personal communication.
Bybee, Joan L. & Östen Dahl. 1989. The creation of tense and aspect systems in the languages of the world. *Studies in Language* 13 (1). 51–103.
Bybee, Joan L., Revere Perkins & William Pagliuca. 1994. *The evolution of grammar: The grammaticalization of tense, aspect and modality in the languages of the world*. Chicago: University of Chicago Press.
Cavallaro, Francesco & Ng Bee Chin. 2021. Multilingualism and multiculturalism in Singapore. In Peter Siemund & Jakob Leimgruber (eds.) *Multilingual Global Cities: Singapore, Hong Kong, Dubai*. Singapore: Routledge. Multilingual Asia series.
Comrie, Bernard. 1976. *Aspect: An introduction to the study of verbal aspect and related problems* (Cambridge textbooks in linguistics). Cambridge & New York: Cambridge University Press.
Dahl, Östen & Viveka Velupillai. 2013. The Past tense. https://wals.info/chapter/66 (accessed 6 September 2018).
Dahl, Östen & Bernhard Wälchli. 2016. Perfects and iamitives: Two gram types in one grammatical space. *Letras de Hoje* 51 (3). 325–348.
Finn, Peter. 2004. Cape Flats English: phonology. In Bernd Kortmann, Burridge Kate, Mesthrie Rajend, Edgar W. Schneider & Upton Clive (eds.), *A handbook of varieties of English: Volume 2: Morphology and Syntzx*, 964–984. Berlin & New York: Mouton de Gruyter.
Greenbaum, Sidney. 1991. ICE: The International Corpus of English. *English Today* 7 (04). 3.

Gupta, Anthea F. 1994. *The Step-Tongue: Children's English in Singapore*. Clevedon: Multilingual Matters.
Heine, Bernd & Tania Kuteva. 2002. *World Lexicon of Grammaticalization*. Cambridge: Cambridge University Press.
Khoo, Joo E. 1998. *The Straits Chinese: A Cultural History*. Amsterdam: The Pepin Press.
Kortmann, Bernd & Kerstin Lunkenheimer (eds.). 2013. *The Electronic World Atlas of Varieties of English*. Leipzig. http://ewave-atlas.org (accessed 7 September 2018)
Kramer, Rajia. 2017. Position paper on phasal polarity expressions. https://www.aai.uni-hamburg.de/afrika/php2018/ medien/position-paper-on-php.pdf (accessed 06 April 2019).
Kusters, Wouter. 2003. *Linguistic complexity: the influence of social change on verbal inflection*. Utrecht: LOT Publications.
Kwan-Terry, Anna. 1989. The specification of stage by a child learning English and Cantonese simultaneously: a study of acquisition processes. In Hans-Wilhelm Dechert & Manfred Raupach (eds.), *Interlingual processes*, 33–48. Tübingen: Gunter Narr Verlag.
Leimgruber, Jakob R. E. 2012. Singapore English: An indexical approach. *World Englishes* 31 (1). 1–14.
Leimgruber, Jakob R. E., Peter Siemund & Laura Terassa. 2018. Singaporean students' language repertoires and attitudes revisited. *World Englishes* 37 (2). 282–306.
Li, Charles N. & Sandra A. Thompson. 1989 [1981]. *Mandarin Chinese: A functional reference grammar*. Berkeley, Cal.: University of California Press.
Li, David C. 1999. The Functions and Status of English in Hong Kong: A Post-1997 Update. *English World-Wide* 20 (1). 67–110.
Li, Wei, Vanithamani Saravanan & Julia N. L. Hoon. 1997. Language Shift in the Teochew Community in Singapore: A Family Domain Analysis. *Journal of Multilingual and Multicultural Development* 18 (5). 364–384.
Lim, Lisa. 2007. Mergers and acquisitions: On the ages and origins of Singapore English particles. *World Englishes* 27 (4). 446–473.
Lim, Lisa, Anne Pakir & Lionel Wee. 2010. *English in Singapore: Modernity and management*. Singapore: NUS Press.
Löbner, Sebastian. 1989. 'Schon – erst – noch': An integrated analysis. *Linguistics and Philosophy* 12 (2). 167–212.
McCormick, Kay. 2004. Cape Flats English: morphology and syntax. In Bernd Kortmann, Burridge Kate, Mesthrie Rajend, Edgar W. Schneider & Upton Clive (eds.), *A handbook of varieties of English: Volume 2: Morphology and Syntax*, 993–1005. Berlin & New York: Mouton de Gruyter.
Olsson, Bruno. 2013. *Iamitives: Perfects in Southeast Asia and beyond*. Stockholm: Stockholm University MA Thesis.
Platt, John T. & Heidi Weber. 1980. *English in Singapore and Malaysia*. Kuala Lumpur: OUP.
Schwenter, Scott A & Rena Torres Cacoullous. 2008. Defaults and indeterminacy in temporal grammaticalization: The 'perfect' road to perfective. *Language Variation and Change* 20 (2008). 1–39.
Siemund, Peter & Lijun Li. 2017. Towards a diachronic reconstruction of Colloquial Singapore English. In Debra Ziegeler & Zhiming Bao (eds.), *Negation and Contact: With Special Focus on Singapore English*, 11–32. Amsterdam: Benjamins.

Siemund, Peter & Lijun Li. 2020. Language Policy in Singapore. In Henning Klöter (ed.), *Language Diversity in the Sinophone World*. Abingdon, UK and New York: Routledge.

Siemund, Peter, Monika E. Schulz & Martin Schweinberger. 2014. Studying the linguistic ecology of Singapore: A comparison of college and university students 33 (3). 350–362.

van der Auwera, Johan. 1993. 'Already' and 'still': Beyond duality. *Linguistics and philosophy* 16 (6). 613–653.

Winford, Donald. 2003. *An Introduction to Contact Linguistics*. Oxford: Blackwell Publishing.

Wong, Wee Kim (ed.). 2011. Census of Population 2010. Statistical Release 1: Demographic, Characteristics, Education, Language and Religion. Singapore: Department of Statistics. http://www.singstat.gov.sg. (accessed 10 February 2020)

Wong, Wee Kim (ed.). 2016. *General Household Survey 2015*. Singapore: Department of Statistics, Ministry of Trade & Industry. http://www.singstat.gov.sg. (accessed 10 February 2020)

Wong, Wee Kim (ed.). 2019. Population Trends 2019. Singapore: Department of Statistics, Ministry of Trade and Industry, http://www.singstat.gov.sg. (accessed 10 February 2020)

Ziegeler, Debra. 2015. *Converging grammars: Constructions in Singapore English*. Boston: De Gruyter Mouton.

Index

a second time 325
adverb 453, 460, 481
again 48, 103, 120, 122, 153, 205, 251, 257,
    288, 325, 502
Aktionsart 262, 427
allolexy 268, 290
also 302, 403
Amazigh 335
Arabic 287
aspect 130, 357, 521, 537
at last 152
Atlantic-Congo 237
auxiliary 172, 184, 188, 453, 456, 464, 474

Bamana 502
Bambara 267
Bantu 41, 73, 96, 129, 162, 445
Barabaiga Datooga 421
be old 276
before 144, 149, 383
Berber 335
borrowed 124, 176
borrowing 204, 285, 297

calque 518
cease 306
Central Ring 210
clause-final negation marker 497
completive 371, 400
contact 95, 108, 125
continuative 420, 425
continue 113, 248
conventionalization of negative
    inference 468, 486
copulative 62
counter-expectation 54
counterexpectation 347
counterexpectational 32, 37, 169, 174
counterfactual 80, 138, 145–146, 420
counterfactuality 243, 250, 274, 277–278, 281
coverage 180, 194, 229, 241, 262, 467
current relevance 352
Cushitic 311
Cuwabo 163

Datooga 419
Dauro 384
discourse pragmatics 420
Dorze 366
Duality Hypothesis 26, 29, 95, 117, 341,
    411
Dzuun 498

earlier 202
early 424
etymology 62, 507
even 301
even now 248, 323
existential 506
experiential perfect 327
Expressibility 85, 155, 186, 241
extension 67
external negation 75, 205, 210, 339

finish 77, 86, 99, 110, 115, 244–245, 286
first 249, 297, 319, 405
first, from now on 289
focalised past tense 201
formerly 302
French 98, 109
from today 306
Fula 237
future 190

Gamo 366
generalization and specialization 5
Gisamjanga Datooga 421
go forward 306
Gofa 378
grammaticalisation 207
grammaticalization 47, 98, 110, 184,
    263, 301, 404, 414, 451, 467, 519,
    532
Grassfields Bantu 199, 215

Hausa 295
have done before 257
historical linguistics 500, 507
hybrid adverbial 200, 202, 205, 207

imperfective 135
in front of 382
in the past 85–86
inchoative 524
indeed 304
internal negation 95, 124, 254, 262, 346
interrogative sentence 219, 228, 231
intersubjectivity 507
Isu 199
iterative 429

Jespersen cycle 500

Kalahari Khoe 391
Kambaata 311
Kanuri 297
Khoe 391
Khwe 391

language contact 41
leave 171, 257, 306
leave behind 404
Lingala 93, 96

Maale 368
Manda 42
Mande 267, 500
Men 210
minimizer 509
mirativity 177

negation 314, 395, 497
negation marker 463
negative polarity item 500, 504
never ever 206
new/next/recent 510
Nguni 62
Nilotic 419
nondum 50, 67, 449
not at all 503, 508
now 65, 373, 376
Nyakyusa 129
Ŋgâmbà 215

Ometo 365
Omotic 365

one 287
only 165, 185
Oyda 369

paradigmaticity 8, 18, 49, 86, 156, 186, 241, 262
perfective 77, 86, 102, 130, 145, 174, 186, 242, 245, 519, 522, 537
periphrastic construction 456
persistive 50, 66, 75, 80, 87, 131, 133, 451, 472, 475
perspectivity 11, 15
polysemy 200
Portuguese 176
pragmaticity 80, 142, 182, 241, 268
pragmatics 231
precede 300

reach 375, 378, 385
readily 202
reanalysis of periphrastic constructions 480
reiteration 288
remain 114
restrictive 172, 185
right periphery 498
Ruuli 73

Sango 93, 108
scalar notions 342
semantic change 504
Singapore English 517
soon 406
source concept 285
standardization 238
start 244
substrate 524, 533

TAM 43, 56, 314, 421
Tarifit 343
Tashelhiyt 341
telicity 83, 155, 182
tense-aspect morphology 394
there 304
too, as well 178, 185
Ts'ixa 391
Tura 504

Ubangi 93
until now 168, 248, 303, 321

variation 337
verb serialisation 207

West Chadic 301
West Ring 208
while 305
without 321
Wolaitta 365
wordhood 183, 207, 229, 241

www.ingramcontent.com/pod-product-compliance
Lightning Source LLC
Chambersburg PA
CBHW031408230426
43668CB00007B/240